"Romantic love is an integral part of Western culture, yet researchers have been reluctant to take it on. In this age of 'serial monogamy,' Dr. Hemesath's book is long overdue. She examines the process of relationship dissolution weaving together theories, empirical research, and personal stories of the angst of breaking-up. This engaging and beautifully written book is a welcome addition to the field of family studies that will be of interest to anyone wishing to understand why love sometimes fades."

Dr. Susan D. Stewart, Professor of Sociology,
Iowa State University

"To love and be loved are among the most significant and fundamental human life experiences. Finding love can bring us immense joy; losing it can plunge us into the depths of despair. Here, in this well-written text, author Crystal Wilhite Hemesath has given us a book that invites, engages, and instructs both the next generation of scholars and those of us (all of us!) who have ever wondered about, sought, found, and lost love."

Dr. Pamela Regan, author of *The Mating Game and
Close Relationships*

"This is the definitive book on one of the most common and scary experiences in romantic relationships. The author comes across as a warm and approachable scholar and therapist, and the book has much to offer anyone interested in the phenomenon of falling out of love."

William J. Doherty, PhD, Professor and Director of the
Minnesota Couples on the Brink Project at the University of
Minnesota, and author of *Take Back Your Marriage: Sticking
Together in a World That Pulls Us Apart*

D1525130

Falling Out of Romantic Love

In this innovative and user-friendly guide, Crystal Wilhite Hemesath identifies the factors that lead to relationship breakdown and suggests key strategies for the prevention and treatment of falling out of romantic love (FORL).

Grounded in research and two decades of clinical experience, *Falling Out of Romantic Love* outlines strategies for preparing and maintaining healthy, enduring, romantic relationships as well as what to do when FORL becomes a threat. Applicable to daily life, and relevant to a wide range of scenarios, this book contains a plethora of information for individuals just beginning an intimate partner relationship, long-married couples, or for those simply curious about romantic relationships and the problems that may arise. Helpful tips are also provided for individuals trying to decide if they should remain in a relationship and for those experiencing the heartbreak on the receiving end of FORL.

Rich in real-life examples, this book arms professionals with a greater understanding of why people fall out of romantic love. It's an indispensable guide for marriage and family therapists, as well as other mental health professionals or clergy looking to incorporate additional tools and clinical interventions into their work.

Crystal Wilhite Hemesath is a Licensed Marriage and Family Therapist and Licensed Mental Health Counselor with over 20 years of clinical experience, having received her PhD from Iowa State University in 2016. She owns a mental health private practice where she is a practicing clinician. Dr. Hemesath is also clinical member of the American Association of Marriage and Family Therapy.

Falling Out of Romantic Love
A Therapeutic Guide for Individuals, Couples, and Professionals

Crystal Wilhite Hemesath

Routledge
Taylor & Francis Group

NEW YORK AND LONDON

First published 2020
by Routledge
52 Vanderbilt Avenue, New York, NY 10017

and by Routledge
2 Park Square, Milton Park, Abingdon, Oxon, OX14 4RN

Routledge is an imprint of the Taylor & Francis Group, an informa business

© 2020 Taylor & Francis

Library of Congress Cataloging-in-Publication Data
A catalog record for this title has been requested

ISBN: 978-1-138-32754-2 (hbk)
ISBN: 978-1-138-32755-9 (pbk)
ISBN: 978-0-429-44919-2 (ebk)

Typeset in New Century Schoolbook
by Swales & Willis, Exeter, Devon, UK

For my bright lights – Quinn, Ellie, and Ivy.
And
For all who struggle in love.

Contents

Preface

I know I'm opening a big ol' can of mushy, tangled-up worms. Falling out of romantic love (FORL) is not an easy topic and there are many different beliefs about love and intimate partner relationships. But something inside me says to keep going. As in therapy, talking helps sort things out. As I write, dialog runs constantly in my mind, and you are the "lucky" recipient of my muddled sorting through. I'm sure you are hopeful that by the end of this book, we will have figured out the cause and the cure for FORL. Unfortunately, today, I can't guarantee that. However, I promise to provide the most up-to-date, empirically based information possible, shored up with the knowledge gained from being in the trenches with amazing people like you. At the very least, I believe I can provide insight into many of the pressing questions about FORL.

As to my background, I earned a PhD in Human Development and Family Studies from Iowa State University. I own a mental health private practice in central Iowa, where I am also a practicing clinician. Professionally, I have been a Licensed Marriage and Family Therapist and a Licensed Mental Health Counselor for over 20 years. Throughout the course of my career, many clients have presented with the difficult issue of FORL. I have also witnessed the disheartening phenomenon among friends and family members who have experienced it. This combination of personal and professional experience has provided me with a well-rounded background, bringing practical experience and contextual knowledge to this topic.

I am grateful and honored for the time I have spent with every single client. It takes immense courage to share the most vulnerable and wounded parts of ourselves, especially with a stranger. However, I will admit: at times I feel tremendous guilt. FORL is like a python, wrapping around the neck of an unsuspecting victim. Desperate and choking, they come to me, the supposed snake charmer. Unfortunately, I haven't always been able to mesmerize the snake enough to release its victim.

I wish relationships and love were as simple as playing mystical music and waving a wand. However, therapy isn't magic – and relationships can be exceedingly complicated. Overall, I am very proud of what I have been able to offer clients in response to a variety of presenting issues and the subsequent healing that has transpired. The interventions and therapeutic strategies I employ in my daily work are research-based and have been proven effective. Yet, not every topic brought to therapy has been thoroughly studied, as in the case of FORL. Even as a seasoned clinician, I had little idea how to adequately assist clients desperate to address this matter. Despite this, I can assure you, I've walked beside each one, bringing all that I had.

Unfortunately, my situation is not unique. Other mental health providers I queried (see Hemesath, 2016; Hemesath & Hurt, 2016) also lack certainty regarding how to effectively address FORL, leaving many professionals with a sense of helplessness. After grappling with this conundrum throughout my career, I finally had my chance to attack this serpent. When recently pursuing my doctorate, one of the first tasks was to identify a dissertation topic. It was wisely suggested by faculty to study a subject of genuine interest, because perseverance is the key to accomplishing the grueling doctoral requirements. I knew immediately the choice would be FORL.

Even though my qualifications, education, and years of experience as a marriage and family therapist were valuable, I needed something backed by research, not simply opinion. Why does that matter? Because if you are reading this book, the words *I've fallen out of love* or *I don't know if I love you anymore* probably sound familiar, and a relationship of utmost importance could be on the line. I don't take that lightly. My goal is to provide a trusted source of information.

As a result, I devoted countless hours to researching, reading, questioning, learning, and contemplating how to provide the best care for clients struggling with FORL. As a precursor to writing this book, I administered focus groups and individual interviews with those who have experienced FORL, as well as clinical focus groups comprised of mental health providers and clergy (see Hemesath, 2016; Hemesath & Hurt, 2016, 2017). I worked hard to suspend any pre-conceived notions as I set forth investigating alternative points of view. Beyond my research, you will find many references to academic work conducted by exceptionally talented clinicians and scholars who have gone before me. Further, I note the insights gained from my personal correspondence with renowned relationship frontrunners. Together, this material formed the groundwork for the ideas presented in the coming chapters. What I acquired in the process has been invaluable to me, as a clinician, and undoubtedly helpful to my clients. Because I believe knowledge should be accessible to everyone, the idea for this book, based on my doctoral dissertation, was born.

I have written the contents for a wide audience, including general readers, students, mental health providers, couple's therapists, and others working in the context of relationships, as well as individuals struggling with FORL. Please be forewarned, this is not meant to be an exhaustive summary of all research on romantic love. I did my best to include what I felt was most relevant, but surely there will be something I miss, for which I apologize in advance. It should be mentioned that FORL can occur in marital and non-marital relationships alike. Although both contexts are attended to, depending on your personal circumstances some of the contents may not apply to you.

As you continue reading, I want you to think of this as a conversation among friends. Not the kind of friend who tries to look good, or, alternatively, tells you what you want to hear, but one that's real. One who will say it like it is. Because the reality is, romantic relationships are hard. And if you say they aren't, you're either lying, in denial, or just haven't experienced the difficulties yet. Unfortunately, sometimes relationships are not only painstaking, but one or both partners fall out of romantic love. My intention is not to be pessimistic about romantic relationships or marriage. To the contrary, they hold extraordinary meaning and importance in life and are often amazingly wonderful and fulfilling. My goal is to guide and educate individuals toward having the most successful and healthy romantic relationship possible, as well as to provide up-to-date information and strategies for relationship professionals. Ultimately, I hope the pages ahead provide a fresh view of the timely and extraordinary topic of FORL and that each of you comes away with something that speaks to you, inspiring your personal relationships or professional work.

References

Hemesath, C. W. (2016). *Falling out of romantic love: A phenomenological study of the meaning of love in marriage* (unpublished doctoral dissertation). Iowa State University, Ames, Iowa.

Hemesath, C. W. & Hurt, T. R. (2016). *Falling out of romantic love: A focus group study* (unpublished manuscript). Department of Human Development and Family Studies, Iowa State University, Ames, Iowa.

Hemesath, C. W. & Hurt, T. R. (2017). *Falling out of romantic love: An integrated theoretical framework* (unpublished manuscript). Department of Human Development and Family Studies, Iowa State University, Ames, Iowa.

Acknowledgments

Throughout this priceless endeavor, my gratitude list has grown by the day. First, I would like to thank my participants and clients for sharing your lives with me. Your stories and experiences will help many. I have been honored to sit beside each one of you on your journey. Every day, I am reminded that there is nothing I would rather be doing, for which I feel truly blessed.

Next, I would like to thank Tera Jordan, my major professor at Iowa State University. Your commitment to excellence made this project what it is today. I also want to express my gratitude to you for introducing me to Katrina McDonald, whose kindness was critical in making this book happen – allowing me the opportunity to share what I learned with the world. I also want to extend my appreciation to the folks at Routledge, including Dean Birkenkamp for placing my manuscript in the right hands and George Zimmar for seeing something special in my proposal. Finally, to my editor, Clare Ashworth, your calming presence and professionalism has been a joy. Thank you to all the other individuals behind the scenes that make the magic happen, including Dan Shutt, my copy-editor and Jess Bithrey for her project management.

And thank you to the many brilliant scholars and clinicians in the field of human development and family studies who contributed to my knowledge and research in critical ways by responding to emails or taking the time to meet in person: Andrew Cherlin, Paul Amato, Scott Stanley, Bianca Acevedo, Harvey Joanning, Barry McCarthy, William Allen, Ellen Berscheid, William Doherty, Pamela Regan, and Melissa Fritchle. I greatly admire all of you and your work. And to my dissertation committee members, Brenda Lohman, Wade Nathanial, Tricia Neppl, and Carolyn Cutrona-Russell – thank you for pushing me with tough questions. You made me stretch beyond what I thought was possible.

I also want to thank Cassandra Dorius, a trusted colleague and friend. Your confidence in me has provided the much-needed courage to keep going. Susan Stewart, thank you for your gracious guidance and support. And to my wonderful colleagues at 515 Therapy and Consulting, thank you for your unending patience. All the little things you do are so meaningful. Many of you took care of my clients when I was away writing, while others assisted with my research, read portions of my work, or brainstormed with me. Thank you to Christina Johnson, Haley Wedmore, Mollie Mertens, Kelcee Foss, Lynn Martin, Julie McClatchey, Liz Young, Rachel Klobassa, Angela Porath, Paula McManus, Erica Krolak, Kari Uhl, and Abby Wilson-Rector for the input, time, and support you have given to this endeavor. A special thank you to my colleague and dear friend, Ramona Wink, for "unsticking me" when I felt so stuck. You have true gifts! And to Molly Sexton – I threw you in at the deep end and you swam like a champ! To Bailey Wilson and Darien Bahe, thank you for your time and effort; it did not go unnoticed. And thank you to the folks at West Lakes Hy-Vee Market Grill for greeting me with a smile every morning at 6 AM!

Enormous admiration goes to my mom, Sue Wilhite, for teaching me perseverance. Thank you for your unending support. For my dad, Alan Wilhite, for keeping me on my toes about love and relationships. And to my sister, Virginia Kotarba, your participation on this journey is more important and special than you will ever know. Although the last to be thanked, the following come with an abundance of gratitude. Thank you to my endearing children, Quinn, Ellie, and Ivy. As I wrote this book, I realized how often you are on the receiving end of my bantering and anecdotes about love and life. Thank you for listening (or at least pretending to). I inundate you with these tidbits because I want your journey to be as successful and pain-free as possible. However, pain is a part of love – one doesn't exist without the other. And there I go again! And to my carefree, engineer husband. I truly admire your spirit. Thank you for supporting me in my marathon, while you were training for one of your own. I love you all!

About the Author

Crystal Wilhite Hemesath received a doctoral degree in Human Development and Family Studies from Iowa State University and a master's degree, specializing in marriage and family therapy, from Kansas State University. She is a Licensed Marriage and Family Therapist and a Licensed Mental Health Counselor with over two decades of experience treating couples, individuals, and families. Crystal is a clinical member of the American Association of Marriage and Family Therapy. She owns a private practice in West Des Moines, Iowa, where she resides with her husband and three children.

Introduction

It doesn't matter where you live, what your marital status, sexual orientation, socioeconomic status, or other demographic factors are – if you are curious about romantic love, the contents of this book will apply to you. More specifically, this book is for you if you are considering a romantic relationship, casually dating, seriously dating, cohabitating, contemplating marriage, have a great marriage, are unhappy in your marriage, are questioning love, are a relationship professional, an educator, religious leader, student ... And the list goes on!

A majority of people marry at some point in their lives (US Census Bureau, 2012). Because marriage is a substantial social institution, and represents significant public and political interest, I will spend ample time devoted to love in the context of marriage. However, this book is relevant to a wide variety of people and situations, including those in long-term dating and cohabitating relationships. After all, long-term relationships, of any type, are a big deal, and it's time we try to make sense of FORL. As a side note, long-term relationships are identified as lasting over 20 years in length for some researchers (see Bachand & Caron, 2001), although there is no specific number representing a cut-off. For many, a relationship of five years may constitute a long-term relationship.

Romantic love is considered essential for most marriages in Western culture (Acevedo & Aron, 2009; Dion & Dion, 1991) and is thought to be experienced by people around the world (Fisher et al., 2016; Sprecher, Sullivan, & Hatfield, 1994). The purpose of this book is to explore the phenomenon of falling out of romantic love (FORL), which can be a path to relationship dissatisfaction and divorce that, unfortunately, has received little scholarly attention (Hemesath & Hurt, 2016; Kayser, 1990, 1993; Sailor, 2013). Lack of sexual attraction/desire, emotional connectedness, and/or sense of relationship inevitability can be contributing factors to FORL (Berscheid, 2006). When one or more of these components are missing, the nature of romantic love changes and may be lost. Despite the broad ramifications of FORL, few researchers have studied this phenomenon. The minimal research and existing literature on FORL calls for new insights and understanding. Subsequently, graduates of training programs in marriage and family therapy, mental health counseling, psychology, social work, and the clergy are not adequately trained on this topic.

Although FORL looks different for everyone, the following example illustrates the experience of one individual. Michelle is a 41-year-old female who has been married ten years to her spouse, with whom she reports having fallen out of romantic love. Michelle met her husband when she was a single mom, living with her parents. She describes feeling very lucky to have such a nice guy love her and her young child. However, their interpersonal dynamics became difficult for her as the marriage progressed. She identified a polarization between them, which grew over time. Michelle describes herself as a go-getter who wanted to grow as a person (e.g., obtain an advanced degree, improve her health) while he was more laid-back. Michelle reports that her spouse seemed increasingly unmotivated and emotional, creating the sense that she had to be the strong one. She reports being no longer physically or emotionally attracted to him and states she has fallen out of love, although they continue to stay married. Maybe this story, or one similar, sounds like you or someone you know?

My goal is to provide insight and education about FORL, including recommendations for everyday people interested in relationships, as well as professionals. It's not enough to simply address what to do when things go wrong in a relationship, but to avoid going off-course in the first place! In the pages ahead, several topics will be covered that are essential to understanding how and why FORL occurs, such as types and definitions of love, relationship trends, and factors involved in FORL (i.e., family of origin, personality characteristics, attachment dynamics, mate selection, biological and sub-conscious factors, environmental influences, and the role of commitment). Common components experienced by those who have fallen out of romantic love will be identified and case examples will be used for illustration. (Note: all names and details have been changed to protect anonymity.) Recommendations for individuals contemplating a romantic relationship as well as those who may be on the path to FORL will be offered.

Additionally, I will arm professionals by informing therapist education and clinical treatment. To more effectively conceptualize FORL, theoretical underpinnings will be outlined, and a new integrated theoretical framework of FORL will be proposed. I will also offer several treatment recommendations for professionals. I'm hopeful this book will be a springboard to further research on this topic, and spur additional clinical techniques that are so desperately needed. Ultimately, it is essential for providers like myself to be more confident and competent in their work with FORL.

This book primarily addresses FORL in mainstream US culture, as much of the limited research to date attends to heterosexual relationships in the USA. It is believed the development of intimate partner relationships of lesbian, gay, bisexual, and transgender (LGBTQIA+) individuals hold similar processes and dynamics to heterosexual relationships by virtue of parallel processes across all close relationship formation (Herek, 2006; Kassin, Fein, & Markus, 2017; Kurdek, 2005; Peplau & Fingerhut, 2007). Thus, although far more research is needed, it could be cautiously suggested that FORL may hold similar patterns for LGBTQIA+ couples as it does for their heterosexual counterparts. The pronouns "he" and "she" will be used in this book, not out of disrespect for non-binary individuals, but based on the lack of available research. Additionally, romantic love and FORL have been found globally, therefore individuals from a variety of backgrounds and cultures may benefit from the information offered. Differences that have emerged throughout this investigation have been noted; however, ultimately, we are in the nascent phases of understanding the experience of FORL in diverse populations. Future scholarly investigation and analysis should attend to diversity to thoroughly identify cultural, gender, and sexual orientation differences in relation to FORL.

Background

To be sure, societal rules and expectations regarding family formation and marriage are changing; however, most Americans still marry at some point in their lives (Amato, 2010; Coontz, 2016; Martin & Bumpass, 1989; Nock, 2005; Regan, 2017). Scholars have outlined a plethora of benefits adults gain from marriage (Blackman et al., 2005; Hawkins & Booth, 2005; Nock, 2005). With that said, many marriages are not long-lasting. Although marriage and family values are still important to most people (Lamanna, Riedmann, & Stewart, 2018), marital instability has marked the last half of the twentieth century in America (Cherlin, 2010). Components contributing to marital instability include shifts toward individual happiness (Amato, 2004), personal freedom (Zaidi & Morgan, 2017), and higher expectations for marriage and love (Hurt, 2014; Kayser, 1993; Regan, 2017). Divorce rates rose sharply in the 1960s and 1970s (Kelly, 2006) and peaked in 1980 (Cherlin, 2017). Although many report rates have declined since then (Cherlin, 2017), marital instability continues to flourish (Zaidi & Morgan, 2017). During a person's lifetime, the probability of experiencing divorce is between 40 and 50 percent (Amato, 2010; Cherlin, 2010; DePaulo, 2017). Further, the probability for divorce is even higher for re-marriages than first marriages (Marquardt et al., 2012).

Divorce rates in the USA and many other high-divorce countries have been described as dropping or stabilizing in recent years (Cherlin, 2017). However, recent research suggests flawed data is responsible for this notion. As Kennedy and Ruggles (2014) describe, divorce is now far more common among those 40 and older but many of the divorce studies rely on statistics that exclude these couples, potentially skewing the divorce statistics. Despite this, formal divorce rates are expected to decline over time due to less societal pressure to marry, more acceptance of cohabitating, and better partner selection practices (Kennedy & Ruggles, 2014), keeping in mind the rise in cohabitation leads some to believe that overall union dissolution may be increasing even if divorce rates drop (Cherlin, 2017).

The landscape in the USA, and many other countries, is changing (Cherlin, 2017). Fewer individuals are choosing to marry and more are entering cohabitating unions instead of marriage. Having children out of wedlock is no longer taboo. Thus, the formal "divorce statistics" and measurements of the past may be too narrow to account for the dissolution of modern romantic unions, which differ in form and function than marriages of days gone by.

Assumptions and Contextual Foundation

My research, education, and experience as a licensed marriage and family therapist and licensed mental health counselor lend themselves to eight primary assumptions regarding romantic relationships and FORL. These assumptions comprise the contextual foundation of this book.

1. Romantic relationships are of great importance to most people, an assumption based on both my corroborating research and my experiences with clients who have reported symptoms such as depression, anxiety, and physical illness resulting from their

loss of romantic love (Hatfield & Rapson, 1993; Lebow, Chambers, Christensen, & Johnson, 2012; Mearns, 1991).

2. Many marriages and romantic unions end, with partners sometimes citing FORL as a reason for their relationship dissatisfaction. This assumption is supported by the 40–50-percent divorce rate in America, the observations and information I have gained as a licensed mental health provider, and previous literature (Kayser, 1990, 1993; Sailor, 2006, 2013).

3. Romantic love, including emotional connection and physical/sexual desire, is the most sought-after type of love in marital relationships (see Acevedo & Aron, 2009; Berscheid, 2006; Dion & Dion, 1991). This assumption is guided by my research on expectations of marital relationships in the USA as well as by the results of my treating individuals, couples, and families for many years. However, it's important to point out that not all relationships are built on or sustained by romantic love. As discussed in subsequent chapters, there are many kinds of love and no "right" type of love for marriage.

4. Satisfying long-term marriages are positive experiences for individuals, families, couples, and society, all of whom would benefit from better understanding the phenomenon of FORL. This assumption is guided by research results supporting the benefits of satisfying marriages on finances, emotional health, physical health, children, and society (Blackman et al., 2005).

5. Relationships are very complex and are best understood through the lens of General Systems Theory. General Systems Theory proposes that the whole is greater than the sum of its parts (Nichols & Schwartz, 1995; von Bertalanffy, 1968). In other words, something different is created from what each part contributes. As further postulated by this theory, a relationship is a system comprised of many moving parts, constantly influenced and affected by many other systems, people, and things.

6. Adults, scholars, and mental health providers often struggle to understand or define FORL, as well as how to address it. This assumption is borne out of my personal and professional experiences, research findings, and literature reviews, all of which highlight the significant lack of available information, education, and theory on this topic. Further, what little exists often contains conflicting and confusing terminology.

7. Common couples' problems such as infidelity, communication breakdown, and chronic conflict are not the same as FORL. For example, it is possible that a relationship will experience any one, or all three of those problems, but not experience FORL. It is certainly feasible that communication breakdown or chronic

conflict could be a factor contributing to FORL; however, FORL is a stand-alone construct representing an accumulation of various individual and relational circumstances and events, and associated thoughts, feelings, and behaviors (Hemesath, 2016; Hemesath & Hurt, 2016; Hemesath & Hurt, 2017).
8. There are numerous pathways leading to FORL. "Each pathway consists of multiple 'stepping stones' or contributing factors" (Hemesath & Hurt, 2017, p. 2). Thus, FORL rests on the principle of *equifinality*, meaning that any given outcome or endpoint can be reached by numerous pathways or set of conditions (Lerner, 2002). No two relationships are the same and the variables and factors leading up to FORL differ between partners and situations.

Your Journey

As you begin to process and apply the contents of this book to your personal relationships, please hold your thoughts and judgments lightly. When taking in new information, if you are like me, you might be thinking, "Wow, that sounds like me!" or "That isn't anything like me!" Either response may induce a sense of panic, or at the very least lead you to question what you thought you knew. Throughout the book, new information will be unpacked that may change the way you relate to earlier chapters, so grab your favorite warm beverage and snuggle in for this conversation among friends.

References

Acevedo, B. P. & Aron, A. (2009). Does a long-term relationship kill romantic love? *Review of General Psychology, 1*(13), 59–65.
Amato, P. R. (2004). Divorce in social and historical context: Changing scientific perspectives on children and marital dissolution. In M. Coleman & L. H. Ganong (eds), *Handbook of contemporary families: Considering the past, contemplating the future* (pp. 265–281). Thousand Oaks, CA: Sage.
Amato, P. R. (2010). Research on divorce: Continuing trends and new developments. *Journal of Marriage and Family, 72*(3), 650–666.
Bachand, L. L. & Caron, S. L. (2001). Ties that bind: A qualitative study of happy long-term marriages. *Contemporary Family Therapy, 23*(1), 105–121.
Berscheid, E. (2006). Searching for the meaning of love. In R. J. Sternberg & K. Weis (eds), *The new psychology of love* (pp. 171–183). New Haven, CT: Yale University Press.
Blackman, L., Clayton, O., Glenn, N., Malone-Colòn, L., & Roberts, A. (2005). *The consequences of marriage for African Americans:*

A comprehensive literature review. New York: The Institute for American Values.

Cherlin, A. (2010). Demographic trends in the United States: A review of research in the 2000s. *Journal of Marriage and the Family: Decade in Review, 72*(3), 403–419.

Cherlin, A. J. (2017). Introduction to the special collection on separation, divorce, repartnering, and remarriage around the world. *Demographic Research, 37*, 1275–1296.

Coontz, S. (2016). *The way we never were: American families and the nostalgia trap*. New York: Basic Books.

DePaulo, B. (2017, February 2). *What is the divorce rate, really?* Retrieved June 3, 2018 from www.psychologytoday.com/us/blog/living-single /201702/what-is-the-divorce-rate-really.

Dion, K. K. & Dion, K. L. (1991). Psychological individualism and romantic love. *Journal of Social Behavior & Personality, 6*, 17–33.

Fisher, H. E., Xu, X., Aron, A., & Brown, L. L. (2016). Intense, passionate, romantic love: A natural addiction? How the fields that investigate romance and substance abuse can inform each other. *Frontier in Psychology, 7*, 1–10.

Hatfield, E. & Rapson, R. L. (1993). *Love, sex, and intimacy: Their psychology, biology, and history*. New York: Harper Collins.

Hawkins, D. N. & Booth, A. (2005). Unhappily ever after: Effects of long-term, low-quality marriages on well-being. *Social Forces, 84*(1), 445–465.

Hemesath, C. W. (2016). *Falling out of romantic love: A phenomenological study of the meaning of love in marriage* (unpublished doctoral dissertation). Ames, Iowa: Iowa State University.

Hemesath, C. W. & Hurt, T. R. (2016). *Falling out of romantic love: A focus group study*. Manuscript in progress.

Hemesath, C. W. & Hurt, T. R. (2017). *Falling out of romantic love: An integrated theoretical framework* (unpublished manuscript). Ames, Iowa: Department of Human Development and Family Studies, Iowa State University.

Herek, G. M. (2006). Legal recognition of same-sex relationships in the United States: A social science perspective. *American Psychologist, 61*(6), 607–621.

Hurt, T. R. (2014). Black men and the decision to marry. *Marriage & Family Review, 50*(6), 447–479.

Kassin, S. M., Fein, S., & Markus, H. R. (2017). *Social Psychology*, 10th edn. Boston, MA: Cengage Learning.

Kayser, K. (1990). The process of marital disaffection: Interventions at various stages. *Family Relations, 39*(3), 257–265.

Kayser, K. (1993). *When love dies: The process of marital disaffection*. New York: Guilford Press.

Kelly, J. B. (2006). Children's living arrangements following separation and divorce: Insights from empirical and clinical research. *Family Process, 46*(1), 35–52.

Kennedy, S. & Ruggles, S. (2014). Breaking up is hard to count: The rise of divorce in the United States, 1980–2010. *Demography, 51*, 587–598.

Kurdek, L. A. (2005). What do we know about gay and lesbian couples? *Current Directions in Psychological Science, 14*(5), 251–254.

Lamanna, M. A., Riedmann, A., & Stewart, S. (2018). *Marriages, families, and relationships: Making choices in a diverse society.* Boston, MA: Centage Learning.

Lebow, J. L., Chambers, A. L., Christensen, A., & Johnson, S. M. (2012). Research on the treatment of couple distress. *Journal of Marital and Family Therapy, 38*(1), 145–168.

Lerner, R. M. (2002). *Concepts and theories of human development,* 3rd edn. Mahwah, NJ: Lawrence Erlbaum.

Marquardt, E., Blankenhorn, D., Lerman, R. I., Malone-Colón, L., & Wilcox, W. B. (2012). The President's marriage agenda for the forgotten sixty percent. The state of our unions. *Marriage in America,* 1–48.

Martin, T. C. & Bumpass, L. L. (1989). Recent trends in marital disruption. *Demography, 26*(1), 37–51.

Mearns, J. (1991). Coping with a breakup: Negative mood regulation expectancies and depression following the end of a romantic relationship. *Journal of Personality and Social Psychology, 60,* 327–334.

Nichols, M. P. & Schwartz, R. C. 1995. *Family therapy: Concepts and methods.* Needham Heights, MA: Allyn and Bacon.

Nock, S. L. (2005). Marriage as a public issue. *The Future of Children, 15*(2), 13–32.

Peplau, L. A. & Fingerhut, A. W. (2007). The close relationships of lesbians and gay men. *The Annual Review of Psychology, 58,* 405–424.

Regan, P. C. (2017). *The mating game: A primer on love, sex, and marriage,* 3rd edn. Thousand Oaks, CA: Sage.

Sailor, J. L. (2006). *A phenomenological study of falling out of romantic love as seen in married couples* (doctoral dissertation). Retrieved from ProQuest. (UMI Number, 3238277.)

Sailor, J. L. (2013). A phenomenological study of falling out of romantic love. *The Qualitative Report, 18*(19), 1–22.

Sprecher, S., Sullivan, Q., & Hatfield, E. (1994). Mate selection preferences: Gender differences examined in a national sample. *Journal of Personality and Social Psychology, 66*(6), 1074–1080.

US Census Bureau. (2012). *2012 American Community Survey. Table S1201. Marital status.* Retrieved April 20, 2018 from http://factfinder. census.gov/faces/tableservices/jsf/pages/productview.xhtml?src=bkmk.

von Bertalanffy, L. (1968). *General systems theory: Foundations, development, applications.* New York: George Braziller.

Zaidi, B. & Morgan, S. P. (2017). The second demographic transition theory: A review and appraisal. *Annual Review of Sociology, 43,* 473–492.

PART I

Romantic Love and Falling Out of It
The Lay of the Land

This Thing Called Love

How do I love thee? Let me count the ways.
I love thee to the depth and breadth and height
My soul can reach, when feeling out of sight
For the ends of being and ideal grace.
I love thee to the level of every day's
Most quiet need, by sun and candle-light.
I love thee freely, as men strive for right.
I love thee purely, as they turn from praise.
I love thee with the passion put to use
In my old griefs, and with my childhood's faith.
I love thee with a love I seemed to lose
With my lost saints. I love thee with the breath,
Smiles, tears, of all my life; and, if God choose,
I shall but love thee better after death.

Elizabeth Barrett Browning, Sonnet 43

If you are lucky, you have felt this way a time or two in your life, and hopefully still do! Most adults utter the magical words *I love you* to just a couple special partners throughout a lifetime – between one and three (Chalabi, 2015). Unfortunately, for some, the love experience fades, like summer vanishes into fall, then winter – which can be bleak and downright cold. Here in Iowa, we are no strangers to erratic, harsh seasons and wild weather. In fact, last spring we transitioned from an insanely frigid winter (the coldest on record) to 96 degrees (the warmest on record), with only a few days of spring in between! Like the seasons, love and loss of love can be unpredictable – sneaking up on us and leaving us to wonder where it came from. Sometimes it is slow and steady, other times it is jolting and erratic.

Regardless of the painful, confusing, and seemingly unmanageable aspects of falling out of romantic love (FORL), this book is intended to enlighten and infuse hope. I am a firm believer in the cliché, *knowledge is power*. In fact, those who know me well might say I'm persistently inquisitive. Not the annoying type that asks 20 questions during an already-long seminar, adding another at the end, just as everyone is trying to leave. I'm more of the thinking type. Sometimes I ponder things so much that I drive myself wild. In fact, I have always been intrigued with why and how things work. I remember, as a little girl, riding in the back of my family's maroon Chevy Caprice Classic, looking up at the bright white stars against the backdrop of midnight blue, wondering in awe how it was all possible. My questions didn't blossom during just one car ride; I thought about them every time I saw the stars, which was often, considering we lived in a rural farming community. The universe was (and still is) far too big for me to comprehend, yet I tried anyway.

Another example of my inquisitive nature comes from my high school days. Although somewhat embarrassed to admit, I played with a ouija board, which is a cheap "family board game" made of cardboard and plastic, said to summon spirits from the afterlife. I recall being equal parts intrigued and terrified – so much that it kept me up at night. All I knew was, that sucker worked! I asked my church youth group leader about the mysterious board game and the response was an unsatisfying: "stay away from it." I even questioned one of my teachers from school, who seemed to know the answer to just about anything. Unfortunately, he didn't know how it worked, either. Even more regrettable, the Internet didn't exist yet, so a simple Google search wasn't an option. Needless to say, I haven't played with a ouija board since! (More on the ouija board experience and how it relates to this discussion in Chapter 5.) I certainly don't have all the answers to the life questions that have arisen. But over the years I have been able to quiet many of my wonderings about the universe, except for one, which presented itself in 1993 in the European countryside and happens to be the topic of this book.

It's interesting how your mind captures certain moments with such clarity that years later you can recall the details like they happened yesterday. I remember being on a bus with my sister in England during our college study-abroad program. As we meandered through the British countryside, we chatted about one of our favorite subjects – boys. We were discussing how scary relationships are because they can be here one day and gone the next. Our vulnerabilities were showing through. At age 19 and 21 we were all too aware of the wonders and risks of love. We had both fallen in and out of love and, unfortunately, had had our fair share of heartbreaks by then. Not little bumps in the road, but huge, razor-sharp road spikes that rip your tires (and your heart), to shreds – you know ... the ones you think you won't survive. In that conversation, we discussed the sobering truth we both knew: nothing is a guarantee. No matter how wonderful the person is, the promises made, or how many times *I love you* is declared with conviction, things can change. At the end of that conversation, we made a pact that we would both earn degrees, so we could take care of ourselves. We kept good on our word. My sister went on to be an attorney and I earned a doctorate, practicing marriage and family therapy for the past two decades. My career, although very satisfying personally, did nothing to quell the inquisitive side of me – in fact, it made it stronger. The question of how and why two people's deep, intimate love can seemingly disappear, creating sadness at best and suicide at worst, remained a nagging blind spot. I desperately wanted to understand my clients' accounts of FORL and my own love experiences that led to that memorable bus conversation.

To begin this quest for knowledge, it seemed that gaining a better understanding of romantic love, as well as the formation and function of romantic relationships, would provide a foundation for being more confident about relationship success and preservation. To be sure, this isn't a simple equation. Relationships are incredibly complex because of the multiple factors involved. Pamela Regan (2011), a leading social psychologist and author in relationship science, does an excellent job of illustrating the three major influences on relationships, including personal, relational, and environmental factors (i.e., physical, social, cultural) (see Figure 1.1).

Examples of personal factors are past experiences, personality, religion, health, education, temperament, beliefs, attachment formation, and values. Relational factors are a blend of both partners' attributes and interactions resulting in chemistry, attraction, communication, and conflict resolution styles. Environmental factors include such influences as social and cultural norms, resources, financial status, social networks, and family history, to name a few. In Chapter 5 we will look at how evolutionary factors and our unconscious mind drive our relationship decisions.

Yes, it's true, unfortunately some romantic relationships end due to FORL and some continue, albeit unhappily. But, like the beautiful flower that resurrects after a seemingly unsurvivable Iowa winter, relationships can also live on, and even flourish, despite bouts of difficulty and changes in love. This is good news, because I don't know a long-term relationship that hasn't experienced hard times and change!

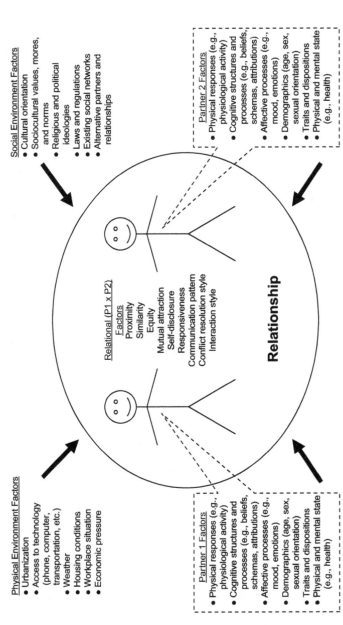

Social Environment Factors
- Cultural orientation
- Sociocultural values, mores, and norms
- Religious and political ideologies
- Laws and regulations
- Existing social networks
- Alternative partners and relationships

Partner 2 Factors
- Physical responses (e.g., physiological activity)
- Cognitive structures and processes (e.g., beliefs, schemas, attributions)
- Affective processes (e.g., mood, emotions)
- Demographics (age, sex, sexual orientation)
- Traits and dispositions
- Physical and mental state (e.g., health)

Relational (P1 x P2)
Factors
Proximity
Similarity
Equity
Mutual attraction
Self-disclosure
Responsiveness
Communication pattern
Conflict resolution style
Interaction style

Relationship

Physical Environment Factors
- Urbanization
- Access to technology (phone, computer, transportation, etc.)
- Weather
- Housing conditions
- Workplace situation
- Economic pressure

Partner 1 Factors
- Physical responses (e.g., physiological activity)
- Cognitive structures and processes (e.g., beliefs, schemas, attributions)
- Affective processes (e.g., mood, emotions)
- Demographics (age, sex, sexual orientation)
- Traits and dispositions
- Physical and mental state (e.g., health)

Figure 1.1 **Relationship phenomena are affected by a vast array of variables. In general, these variables can be grouped into three broad classes: (1) personal factors that are associated with the individual partners (Partner 1 and Partner 2), (2) relational (P1 X P2) factors that reflect the combination of the two partners' characteristics or that emerge from their interactions, and (3) environmental factors that are located in the physical and sociocultural environments surrounding the relationship.**

Source: Regan, P. C. (2011). *Close relationships*. New York: Routledge. Figure adapted with permission of Routledge.

Before we move further, let's break down what type of relationship is center stage in this discussion. At the risk of sounding elementary, I want to ensure we are on the same page regarding terminology. When someone states they have fallen out of love, they typically mean romantic love with a significant other, not platonic love with a friend or sibling. Romantic love is defined in greater detail soon; however, it traditionally combines physical and emotional intimacy. According to the Merriam-Webster dictionary, *intimacy* is marked by closeness, warmth, and privacy. For the purpose of this book, the terms *physical/sexual intimacy* will be used interchangeably and include sensual and sexual activities such as holding hands, hugging, and sexual intercourse, cultivating physical/sexual closeness. *Emotional intimacy* is marked by mutual warmth, trust, support, and a willingness to share thoughts, feelings, and vulnerabilities. The greatest capacity for emotional intimacy requires the ability to properly recognize, identify, and express emotions (Masters, 2013) – more to come in later chapters.

I have used the term romantic relationship, thus far, to describe the entities at risk of FORL. We will dive into love terminology soon, but first, let's identify what is meant by a relationship. A *relationship* must possess the required ingredient of *interaction*, leading to *interdependence* – meaning the two parties "mutually influence each other – how one partner behaves (i.e., acts, thinks, or feels) influences how the other partner behaves (i.e., acts, thinks, or feels), and vice versa" (Regan, 2011, p. 4). As further described by Regan (2011), the interaction must *not be a role-based* interaction, such as between a customer and a cashier – it must be unique to the dyad, whereby both parties hold a special mental representation about the other and the relationship. With that said, there are many kinds of relationships that share these ingredients, including those among friends, family, or lovers. For this discussion we are interested in love relationships, but not just any kind of love relationship. Parents love their children and many friends love each other, but FORL refers to a unique type of love – romantic love. Romantic relationships, as I use the term here, represent two people who identify themselves as intimate "partners" (see Lomas, 2018).

Throughout the book the term *romantic relationship* or alternatively *intimate partner relationship* will be used to identify the specific type of relationship most often associated with falling out of love. Because intimate relationships can refer to a variety of relationship types (including friendship), *partner* was added to the term, because it implies a special type of intimate relationship, usually of romantic origin. Thus, although the term *romantic relationship* is preferred, *intimate partner relationship* will substitute throughout this book when describing the dyadic union where FORL occurs.

Confusing Expressions and Terminology

This chapter opened with well-known *Sonnet 43*, by Elizabeth Barrett Browning, first published in 1850. *Sonnet 43* describes a very deep love. Although beautiful, the sonnet does not define what kind of love is being referenced. Part of the confusion is likely due to the time period in which it was written and what was considered appropriate for public discussion. One could assume it was written about a romantic lover, but without investigating, a person could reasonably deduce it was about a sibling, or a child. Actually, Browning wrote it for her fiancé, with whom she eloped due to her father's disapproval of the marriage and subsequent disowning of Browning (Spacey, 2017). When a friend, client, or someone we care about uses the expression *falling out of love* to describe their experience, you may find yourself uncertain about exactly what is meant. As you will see, you are not alone in this mystification.

Barriers to verbalizing and understanding love, including FORL, begin with confusing terminology in the literature, which varies and overlaps considerably. First, *love* is a generic term highly dependent on context. Today, for example, love is thrown around loosely in the teen population. "ILY" is commonly seen on social media posts between friends and acquaintances. Second, there are many *types of love*. In fact, Fehr and Russell (1991) identified 93 different types of love, the most common being maternal love, parental love, and friendship love. Third, each type has various names assigned to it throughout the literature. Historically, when considering adult intimate relationships (also known as mating, romantic, dating, and marital relationships; Regan, 2011), it has been unclear what is meant by love, because definitions are often inconsistent. The term *romantic love* has often been used, but in other literature, *love* or *passionate love* may appear. Additionally, *erotic love, addictive love, obsessional love, in love, infatuation*, and *lovesick* are terms used to denote love in intimate relationships (Berscheid, 2010; Sternberg & Weis, 2006). As you can see, there is a double whammy of confusion, considering the vast terminology encompassing both love and intimate relationships.

This leads us to consider how everyday people describe love in their romantic relationships. Interestingly, simple language rather than sophisticated terminology is generally used to describe love, despite its complexity (Hendrick & Hendrick, 1992). Phrases such as *I'm crazy about you* or *we are one*

(Hendrick & Hendrick, 1992) are often used. Similarly, language such as *I've fallen out of love, I'm just not into you*, or *I love you but I'm not in love with you* are used to describe the loss of love (Berscheid, 2006). When asked directly, individuals often have both a difficult time talking about love within their romantic relationships (Carter, 2013) and defining the terms they use. Essentially, the language of love is impoverished, and researchers have not made much progress toward a meaningful, common conceptual language for love (Berscheid & Meyers, 1996).

Categorizing Love

The study of love has an interesting history. Love has always been a fascination to humans (Berscheid & Meyers, 1996). However, researchers have only begun to seriously research love over the last few decades (Regan, 2011; Reis & Aron, 2008). One of the means researchers have used in understanding love is through taxonomies.

Taxonomies are important for understanding broad con-structs (Reis & Aron, 2008). Simply put, a *taxonomy* is a classification system that provides a means to analyze or dis-cuss a group of objects or concepts. For example, the taxonomy of food identifies five basic food groups. Certain foods, with specific criteria, belong to the dairy group and others to the grain group, and so on. Some taxonomies will include all aspects of a topic area, and others only address specific segments. Referring to the food group example, one taxonomy could address all foods and another taxonomy could organize information about only vegeta-bles. Conceptually, the food group taxonomy is beneficial because it assists us in understanding and discussing the vast area of nutrition. Taxonomies are not perfect and are sometimes chal-lenged and/or updated, yet useful because they provide the means of discussing a topic and can assist in early theory development.

So, what do taxonomies have to do with love? Similar to the example above, love taxonomies categorize the wide array of love types, helping us to organize them better. For example, renowned behavioral scientist Ellen Berscheid (2006) categorized *all* types of love (i.e., parent/child, friendship, marital) into four types, each meeting two criteria – being associated with *different behaviors* and being generated by *different causes*. The four types of love include: *attachment love, compassionate love, companionate love*, and *romantic love* (Berscheid, 2006). According to her taxonomy, attachment love is a form of automatic protection from harm by being in close proximity to a loving protector. Compassionate love (also called caregiving love) is a giving kind of love or altruism, where benefits to the self are not taken into account. Companionate love would be equal to pragmatic love or affection. Finally, romantic love includes sexual desire (Sternberg & Weis, 2006). Berscheid (2006) found these four types to be biologically based and inborn yet separate from each other. Alternatively, some taxonomies identify love specific to intimate partner relationships. For example, Sternberg's Triangular Theory of Love (1986) is a popular taxonomy that gave rise to eight types of love, useful in identifying and conceptualizing romantic love.

Sternberg's Triangular Theory of Love

Sternberg's Triangular Theory of Love (1986) incorporates both emotion and cognition. Typical of love's history, the terminology used by Sternberg can be confusing, but his ideas are well worth reviewing. Psychologist Robert Sternberg (1986) used a triangle to illustrate the three components of love in intimate partner relationships: *intimacy* (emotional connection), *passion* (physical attraction), and *commitment* (decision) (see Figure 1.2.). To clarify, intimacy as used by Sternberg refers to emotional connection, passion equates to physical attraction, and commitment is the decision to maintain a future together. Sternberg (1986) posited that intimate partner relationships/marriages could possess any combination of these three aspects, generating eight different relationship types:

- *non-love* (having none of the three; indifferent to the relationship)
- *friendship/liking* (having only emotional intimacy; this includes friendships and acquaintances)
- *infatuated love* (having only sexual passion; occurs early in a relationship and is often short term)
- *empty love* (having only commitment; a stronger love may deteriorate into empty love or an arranged marriage may start as empty love but develop into more)
- *romantic love* (having emotional intimacy and sexual passion, but no commitment; an example is an affair or dating relationship where no commitment has been made)
- *companionate love* (having emotional intimacy and commitment, but lacking sexual passion; often observed in long-term marriages, close friendships, or among close family members)
- *fatuous love* (having sexual passion and commitment, but no emotional intimacy; an example is a quick courtship and marriage)

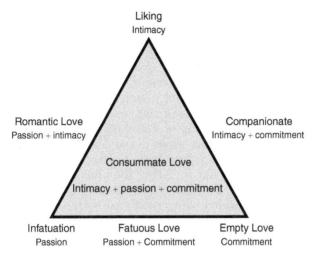

Figure 1.2 **Illustration of Sternberg's Triangular Theory of Love.**
Source: Wikimedia Commons.

- *consummate love* (having all three, emotional intimacy, sexual passion, and commitment, is considered ideal for long-term relationships/marriage; the "perfect couple"; may be more difficult to maintain than to achieve)

Even if all three aspects are present, there is no guarantee love will last; however, consummate love is considered the most complete love, according to Sternberg. Relationships that share just one component of the three are less likely to survive than those that share two or more. It is thought that more than one type of love may exist in a single relationship. (See more information in Chapter 5 about Sternberg's Triangular Theory of Love.)

To reiterate, Sternberg's Triangular Theory of Love identifies types of love in intimate partner relationships. His model has received empirical support and is helpful to our discussion of FORL because it provides a mental roadmap for further refining love specific to FORL. Although there are many more taxonomies of love than reviewed here, Sternberg's theory resonates best when taking into consideration our goal of conceptualizing and understanding FORL.

Key Terminology and Types of Love

Although there are numerous kinds of love, to better understand love in intimate partner relationships, the major forms most relevant to this discussion will be compared, including passionate love, romantic love, consummate love, and companionate love. You will recognize these from Sternberg's Triangular Theory of Love above. The order in which they are listed is not intended to imply that one type is superior, or that love has a pre-destined path. Some people never experience certain types of love in a given relationship. However, boundaries of love types are blurred and each type possesses many of the same characteristics of other types, with only one or two modifications. Further, it is helpful to understand that when asked about a specific type of love, most people have a rather loose quality to their conceptions (Reis & Aron, 2008). "That is, rather than having a formal definition with necessary and sufficient conditions, concepts of love may represent a set of graded categorizations, with some characteristics being more central than others" (Reis & Aron, 2008, p. 82).

Passionate Love

"Passionate love is as old as humankind ... [and] most anthropologists agree that passionate love is a cultural universal" (Sternberg & Weis, 2006, p. 276; see also Miller, 2012). It is important to note that some researchers use the terms passionate love and romantic love interchangeably (Fisher, Aron, & Brown, 2006), creating significant confusion. I will attempt to differentiate them as this chapter continues. *Passionate love* is the term most often used to describe powerful new-courtship love, with characteristics of obsession, intrusive thinking, extreme absorption, excitement, uncertainty, unrealistic idealization, and sexual desire for another (Aron, Fisher, & Strong, 2006; Crooks & Baur, 2014; Fisher, Aron, & Brown, 2006; Hatfield et al., 2008; Sternberg, 1987). Passionate love has a relatively short duration (weeks or months) (Berscheid & Regan, 2005; Crooks & Baur, 2014), and is involuntary and difficult to control (Fisher, Aron, & Brown, 2006); however, it is considered a healthy and important aspect of life, for both men and women. Passionate love is often considered to be unsustainable due to the energy required to maintain it at high levels (Fisher, 2006). "Our bodies simply are not equipped to sustain for long periods the physiological arousal associated with passionate love, desire, and other intense emotional experiences" (Regan, 2017, p. 215).

Because passionate love takes place early in relationships, when a loved one is not well known, it often results in idealization and dismissal of a person's faults (Fisher, Aron, & Brown, 2006). Once reality sets in and flaws are acknowledged, some choose to end a relationship while others may move into a more stable form of love with the same partner. Sometimes lovers become engaged or married during this period of passionate love, later to be disillusioned after realizing the full character or flaws of their partner (Crooks & Baur, 2014). Other terms that have been used for passionate love are in-love, limerence, and infatuation (Hatfield et al., 2008), as well as obsessive love, and lovesickness (Sternberg & Weis, 2006). Passionate love was considered to be both evil and shameful until the eighteenth century (Hatfield & Rapson, 1996), likely because it interfered with collective or community goals (see Sternberg, 2013). Additionally, some viewed passionate love as irrational and fleeting. All of these reasons are why various cultures de-emphasize love in marriage and focus on arranged marriages instead (Shah, 2009).

Passionate love has a biological and evolutionary purpose. Although passionate love "developed mainly to help us concentrate on winning the attention of a desired partner and is designed to last long enough for the relationships to bear offspring" (Sternberg, 2013), it has been postulated that, in marriage, passionate love is likely maladaptive due to the burdens and responsibilities of parenting, holding a job, and running a household (Acevedo & Aron, 2009). As passionate love wanes, attachment begins, which is said to "provide children with calmer and stabler conditions in which to grow up" (Sternberg, 2013). It is interesting to note that some researchers believe that passionate love can renew in older couples after children have been launched; as such, passionate love is less likely to exist when roles are routine in relationships (Knox, 1970). In this book, passionate love will be used to describe the obsessive love that is typically found in new courtship. *Falling in love* is often the phrase used to characterize this experience and is described next.

Falling in Love

The *onset* of a strong desire to be in a close, intimate relationship with a specific person is considered *falling in love* (Aron, Paris, & Aron, 1995). Falling in love is generally equivalent to the term passionate love, characterized by infatuation, intrusive thinking, uncertainty, mood swings, sexual desire, and unrealistic idealization. The term falling in love is limited to the early stages of a new courtship and is said to happen at least once in a lifetime for most Americans (Aron, Paris, & Aron, 1995). Some say, however, that not everyone has this experience (Tennov, 1979). As repeated elsewhere, the phase of *falling in love* is not to be confused with the more long-term state of *being in love* (Fromm,

1956; Grant, 1998). If all goes well in a relationship, falling in love progresses to being in love.

For clarification purposes, the following couple will be used as an example throughout this chapter to illustrate the various types of love. Joe noticed Andrea right away while playing against her team in a co-ed volleyball game. She was a beautiful brunette, with bright green eyes. Andrea noticed Joe, too. She loved his witty sense of humor. He seemed friendly and cracked funny jokes, which made everyone laugh. After the game, Joe made a point of talking to Andrea and asked her and their other teammates to meet for drinks. Andrea, who thought Joe was attractive, said yes to the suggestion, hoping to get to know him better. The night went well, and it wasn't long before both wanted to spend as much time as they could together, despite their busy schedules as college seniors. Andrea often daydreamed about when she would see Joe next. Joe loved the scent of Andrea's sweet perfume and made a point to text her throughout the day, often surprising her with little gifts or flowers. Andrea couldn't always spend as much time with Joe as she wanted, due to her demanding internship. Sometimes Joe would worry about how much Andrea really liked him or if she was attracted to other men. Joe didn't want to admit it, but he was a little jealous when she played volleyball with the guys on her team. He had no explanation to his worry, because Andrea gave him no reason to doubt her interest in him. Andrea frequently told Joe how much she missed him and wished she could be with him. Their phone messages were filled with hearts and kissy-face emojis. When they were apart, Joe often thought about Andrea, which made his heart race. Both described they hadn't felt this attracted to another person in a long time. Joe admitted he was "falling" for Andrea and Andrea responded that she felt the same. Joe and Andrea were *falling in love*, also known as passionate love. To recap, passionate love, also called infatuation, is high on sexual desire, uncertainty, and excitement but low on emotional intimacy and commitment. Passionate love is often found in new courtships. Most researchers report that this phase is time-limited and lasts weeks or months, at best.

Differentiating Love versus In-Love

Similar to passionate love and romantic love, many researchers use the terms *love* and *in-love* synonymously (Berscheid & Meyers, 1996); however, it has been found that people indeed report a distinction between the two (Meyers & Berscheid, 1997). In fact, when Meyers, Ridge, and Berscheid (1991) asked college students if there was a difference in the two terms, a whopping 82 percent agreed. Relationship expert Ellen Berscheid (2006) said it well:

> When another is liked (a friend) and sexually attractive, that person qualifies for membership in the "in love" category, but if a person is *only* liked or *only* sexually attractive, that individual is less likely to be in the "in love" category.
>
> (p. 180)

Additionally, in a study using a sample of over 200 undergraduate men and women who categorized their social contacts as love or in-love, on average the participants reported that one of their social contacts fit the in-love category, while nine of their social contacts fit the love category (Berscheid & Meyers, 1996). Thus, *in-love* is a specific type of love, while *love* is generic. The term *in-love* is generally equivalent to romantic love (Berscheid, 2006; Berscheid & Meyers, 1996; Meyers & Berscheid, 1997; Meyers, Ridge, & Berscheid, 1991), while *falling in love* denotes passionate love.

Romantic Love

Love is an essential factor for mate selection (Johnson, 2013). In Western culture, romantic love is considered highly important for marriages (Acevedo & Aron, 2009), and represents the underpinnings of marital unions (Dion & Dion, 1991). In many countries, romantic love is the *sine qua non* for marriage (Berscheid, 2006; Sprecher, Sullivan, & Hatfield, 1994), including most collectivist countries, where arranged marriages are still somewhat common (see Sternberg & Weis, 2006). There is a notable difference between passionate love, also termed *falling in love*, and the more stable, permanent state of *being in love*, considered romantic love (Fromm, 1956). *Romantic love* combines sexual desire, high emotional intimacy (Davis & Todd, 1982; Miller, 2012), intensity and engagement (Berscheid, 2006), but *not* the obsession or anxiety of passionate love (Sprecher & Regan, 1998). It is important to emphasize that *sexual desire*, an interest in sexual activity with one's partner, is a requirement for romantic love (Berscheid, 2010; Berscheid & Regan, 2005; Regan, 2000; Regan & Berscheid, 1999), as compared to other types of love (e.g., friendship love, companionate love) (Berscheid, 2006; Davis & Todd, 1982; Miller, 2012). Sexual desire is highly important for long-term relationship satisfaction and quality (see Muise et al., 2013). In fact, as noted by Regan (2000), high sexual desire decreases thoughts of leaving a relationship.

Now, let's refer back to Andrea and Joe. Six months after meeting they continue to spend as much time together as they reasonably can, but Joe no longer worries about Andrea being attracted to someone else, nor has doubts when they can't be together due to her work schedule. He is sure Andrea's feelings for him are strong and he feels the same way about her. They have grown to enjoy each other's friends and have learned more about each other over the last few months. One of their favorite things to do is snuggle up together watching Netflix. The couple benefits from an increasingly meaningful emotional relationship, often sharing feelings with one another. Both Joe and Andrea continue to find each other physically attractive and look forward to romantic moments together. They find comfort in each other and are a positive source of support. Joe and Andrea describe *being in-love*. The state of being in-love, akin to romantic love, is inclusive of emotional and physical interest and intimacy with the other.

Falling Out of Romantic Love

As discussed previously, romantic love is the type of love involved when individuals report the phenomenon of falling out of love (Acevedo & Aron, 2009; Berscheid, 2006; Dion & Dion, 1991). Based on the research, FORL includes a substantial decrease or loss in physical/sexual desire and/or loss of emotional connection to one's partner, along with related thoughts, feelings, and behaviors (see Chapter 7). It is imperative to recognize that fluctuations or declines in these components may not result in marital dissatisfaction or FORL and are often considered to be normal shifts in romantic relationships – alternatively, they may indicate problems in the relationship if one or both partners are troubled by aspects of the relationship (Regan, 2017).

Consummate Love

Consummate love was coined by Sternberg (1987), who postulated that Americans see it as the ideal type of love for long-term romantic relationships and marriage (see Sternberg's Triangular Theory of Love presented earlier in this chapter). *Consummate love* includes sexual desire, emotional intimacy, and *commitment*. It can be challenging to maintain over time due to the unstable and uncontrollable nature of sexual desire (Miller, 2012; Sternberg, 1987) and the difficulty of individuals to consistently express physical and emotional intimacy, as well as commitment to their partner, long-term (Sternberg, 1987).

Consummate love is equivalent to romantic love; however, it has the additional component of commitment (Sternberg, 1987). As used throughout this book, romantic love may or may not include commitment. For example, a long-term physical and emotional affair could be considered romantic love, but not consummate love, as an affair implies lack of commitment. A marriage, on the other hand, could be considered both romantic love and consummate love. Chapter 8 reviews the factor of commitment; however, in the context of FORL, consummate love and romantic love are both at risk of FORL because they include sexual and emotional intimacy, which could be lost. For example, an individual could fall out of romantic love with a partner in a romantic relationship lacking commitment (i.e., dating, affair) or high in commitment (i.e., marriage). On the other hand, an individual may fall out of romantic love but remain highly committed to their significant other (i.e., stay married).

Checking back in with Joe and Andrea ... A year has passed, and they recently settled into an apartment, together. They have both graduated and started their first jobs out of college. A week before moving into their new place, Joe popped the question. Andrea was elated and the couple are making wedding plans. Their relationship remains strong, with the addition of commitment, resulting in engagement and impending marriage. Joe and Andrea are experiencing consummate love.

Companionate Love

Companionate love is strong in commitment, friendship, respect, and common goals (Lamanna, Riedmann, & Stewart, 2018). In my undergraduate coursework the popular teaching was that romantic relationships often progress in a linear fashion from passionate love to companionate love (e.g., Cancian, 1987; Coleman, 1977; D'Emilio & Freedman, 1988; Berscheid & Walster, 1978; Safilios-Rothschild, 1977; Sternberg, 1988). I believe my professors were teaching Berscheid and Walster's (1978) *theory of passionate and companionate love* (see Sternberg & Weis, 2006), which encompasses the idea that passion dies, and is replaced by a more enduring, deep-friendship-type love – the traditional view of marital love. "First, there is the fire and passionate attraction that over time morphs into the quiet satisfaction of companionate love, if the relationship survives the initial stage of passionate love" (Sternberg & Weis, 2006, p. 163). The original theory proposed that both types of love could not exist simultaneously in the same relationship (Hendrick & Hendrick, 2003); however, over time that version was replaced by the idea that both could exist at the same time, but are difficult to maintain (Hatfield, 1988). There is now more research on love in marriage, including the emergence of romantic love (see Chapter 6).

As postulated by Berscheid and Hatfield (1969), companionate love is a more subdued and enduring form of love. It is friendship-based, and is defined as encompassing trust, commitment, familiarity, stability, and emotional closeness (Hatfield et al., 2008). But, it is generally not strong with respect to physical intimacy and can be void of sexual desire (Acevedo & Aron, 2009; Miller, 2012). It is possible in such a relationship to feel physical attraction, but it is less frequent or intense, and is not central to the tenets of companionate love (Sprecher & Regan, 1998). "With regard to human love, many scholars believe that one can equate attraction with passionate love and can equate attachment with companionate love" (Reis & Aron, 2008, p. 84). Companionate love is believed to be stable (Hatfield, Traupmann, & Sprecher, 1984) and durable (Berscheid & Regan, 2005), and thought by some to last a lifetime (Hatfield et al., 2008; Hatfield, Traupmann, & Sprecher, 1984; Huesmann, 1980; Safilios-Rothschild, 1977). Although, historically, it is regarded as the natural evolution of love after many years of marriage (Acevedo & Aron, 2009; Hatfield, Traupmann, & Sprecher, 1984) and some partners find companionate love satisfying, its potential lack of physical intimacy (Acevedo & Aron, 2009) can result in unhappiness or discontent.

It is important to point out that although companionate love is generally regarded as short on sexual intimacy, some researchers include physical aspects to some extent for companionate lovers (see Berscheid & Regan, 2005, p. 346). Based on this lack of consensus, *romantic love*, as defined earlier in this section, bridges the gap between passionate love and companionate love. Unlike passionate love, romantic love is not obsessive or anxious; however, sexual desire is a mainstay in romantic love to a greater extent than is typically recognized with companionate love.

Andrea and Joe have now been married 20 years. Their two children are the light of their lives. Their first child just left for college. They have been through a lot over the years with several moves, job changes, Joe's diabetes diagnosis, and the recent loss of Andrea's father. However, the couple have experienced many good times, as well. They have continued to communicate and share their feelings despite life challenges. Andrea has been away more, helping her mom and dad for the last couple of years, while Joe has been doing more around the house. Sometimes Andrea and Joe hold hands, but for the most part sexual desire and activity is low. Although they acknowledge wishing it were different at times, they are both content with the way things are. During her dad's illness,

Andrea was happy to have Joe's support with their girls. Through the loss of her dad, Andrea feels more appreciation for the emotional relationship with Joe because she saw how meaningful her parents' relationship was. Joe is also grateful that Andrea has been there for him over the years. Although the physical intimacy is not what it used to be, they both still enjoy snuggling in for a good movie and occasionally spending time together with friends. Joe hopes that once their youngest graduates from high school, Andrea and he can go on a nice trip together. Andrea and Joe are experiencing companionate love. They are supportive of each other, caring, and have a steady relationship. Companionate love can be wonderful. It is safe, secure, and familiar, encompassing shared experiences and common values over sexual intimacy. However, problems can arise if one or both members in the partnership have differing desires or expectations.

The *amount* of physical and emotional intimacy seems to matter. For example, depending on the person, *a little* intimacy may be enough; however, *no* intimacy could create dissatisfaction. Although not a hard-and-fast rule, age and length of time the couple have been together bring different values and priorities into play, which guide the type of love desired and formed. This makes sense, because all phases and stages of life are different. For example, when a couple transitions from engagement, to marriage, to having children, to launching children, to an empty nest, to retirement, values and priorities often change (as do our bodies).

Summary

The nature of love is exceedingly important, affecting both the formation and durability of relationships. The term *love* is used frequently to describe various feelings across a range of situations, thereby making it increasingly difficult to define exactly what love is. In fact, a sign of immaturity with respect to the science of love is evidenced by a lack of common vocabulary (Rubin, 1988). Although numerous definitions of love have been identified by researchers (Ackerman, 1994; Berscheid, 2006; Hendrick & Hendrick, 1992; Sprecher & Regan, 1998), there is no universally accepted term or definition of love for marriage and other intimate partner relationships or for FORL. Narrowing the relevant types of love and corresponding terminology was imperative to achieving a meaningful discussion and exploration of FORL in both marital and nonmarital relationships and has been the focus of this chapter.

A full review of existing literature and research, including classification systems called taxonomies, guided this process. Taxonomies assist with categorization and are useful for expanding knowledge and developing models of love. Although sometimes overlapping, and containing similar terminology, they can also be quite different from one another. The limitations of taxonomies include confusion with respect to commonly held beliefs about love, often because researchers are conceptualizing love using varied frameworks. However, the variety found in the models could be considered a benefit, because it allows us to compare multiple types and definitions of love. Finally, some taxonomies overlook essential factors or require more research in regard to specific elements (i.e., the influence of attachment on love). Thus, utilizing multiple taxonomies is beneficial to compensate for what may not be addressed in a single model. To date, Sternberg's Triangular Theory of Love, which breaks romantic relationship love down into eight types, based on varying amounts of intimacy, passion, and commitment, seems to be the best fit for conceptualizing love in romantic relationships.

As we consider the different types of love, it is important to point out that there is no one *right* way to love in romantic relationships. Ultimately, it depends on the needs and desires of the individuals involved. However, for clarification, *romantic love* will be used to identify the type of love most Westerners view as important in marriage and is the type of love referred to when one expresses they have *fallen out of love* with an intimate partner. *Romantic relationships* or *intimate partner relationships* will be used to define the relationships where FORL typically occurs. Although the preoccupation with love seems to be an American pastime, men and women across a variety of cultures (i.e., individualistic, collectivist, urban, rural, wealthy, and poor) appear to be just as romantic (Sternberg & Weis, 2006).

Exploration Questions

1   Relationships are complex because of the multitude of variables involved. Can you name the three main factors that influence relationships?

2   One of the greatest challenges in love research, today, is the lack of common vocabulary, which creates significant confusion. For example, passionate love is often used interchangeably with romantic love, yet they are very different conceptually. Can you explain the difference?

3   Ask three people (who have not read this book): "what does it mean to fall out of love with a significant other?" List the key elements included in each response. Then compare the three responses – how are they alike or

different from each other? What were the most common or uncommon elements mentioned? Why do you think some people included certain criteria, but others did not? What clarifying questions might you ask each respondent to get a better understanding of what they mean?

Key Concepts

being in-love	intimate partner relationship
companionate love	long-term relationship
consummate love	passion
commitment	physical/sexual intimacy
emotional intimacy	relationship
falling out of romantic love (FORL)	romantic relationship
interaction	Sternberg's Triangular Theory of Love
interdependence	taxonomy
intimacy	types of love

References

Acevedo, B. P. & Aron, A. (2009). Does a long-term relationship kill romantic love? *Review of General Psychology, 13*(1), 59–65.

Ackerman, D. (1994). *A natural history of love.* New York: Random House.

Aron, A., Fisher, H. E., & Strong, G. (2006). Romantic love. In A. Vangelisti & D. Perlman (eds), *The Cambridge handbook of personal relationships* (pp. 595–614). Cambridge; New York: Cambridge University Press.

Aron, A., Paris, M., & Aron, E. N. (1995). Falling in love: Prospective studies of self concept change. *Journal of Personality and Social Psychology, 69*(6), 1102–1112.

Barrett Browning, E. (1845). *Sonnet 43: How do I love thee?* Retrieved from www.poets.org/poetsorg/poem/how-do-i-love-thee-sonnet-43.

Berscheid, E. (2006). Searching for the meaning of love. In R. J. Sternberg & K. Weis (eds), *The new psychology of love* (pp. 171–183). New Haven, CT: Yale University Press.

Berscheid, E. (2010). Love in the fourth dimension. *Annual Review of Psychology*, *61*, 1–25.

Berscheid, E. & Hatfield, E. (1969). *Interpersonal attraction*. New York: Addison-Wesley.

Berscheid, E. & Meyers, S. A. (1996). A social categorical approach to a question about love. *Personal Relationships*, *3*(1), 19–43.

Berscheid, E. S. & Regan, P. C. (2005). *Psychology of interpersonal relationships*. Upper Saddle River, NJ: Pearson Education.

Berscheid, E. S. & Walster, E. (1978). *Interpersonal attraction*, 2nd edn. Reading, MA: Addison-Wesley.

Cancian, F. M. (1987). *Love in America: Gender and self-development*. New York: Cambridge University Press.

Carter, J. (2013). The curious absence of love stories in women's talk. *The Sociological Review*, *61*(4), 728–744.

Chalabi, M. (2015). I love you, you love me, we've probably never said that to more than three. Retrieved January 12, 2016 from https://fivethir tyeight.com/features/i-love-you-you-love-me-weve-probably-never-said-that-to-more-than-three/.

Coleman, S. B. (1977). A developmental stage hypothesis for non-marital dyadic relationships. *Journal of Marital and Family Therapy*, *3*(2), 71–76.

Crooks, R. & Baur, K. (2014). *Our sexuality*, 12th edn. Belmont, CA: Wadsworth.

D'Emilio, J. & Freedman, E. B. (1988). *Intimate matters: A history of sexuality in America*. New York: Harper & Row.

Davis, K. E. & Todd, M. J. (1982). Friendship and love relationships. *Advances in Descriptive Psychology*, *2*, 79–122.

Dion, K. K. & Dion, K. L. (1991). Psychological individualism and romantic love. *Journal of Social Behavior & Personality*, *6*, 17–33.

Fehr, B. & Russell, J. A. (1991). The concept of love viewed from a prototype perspective. *Journal of Personality and Social Psychology*, *60*(3), 425–438.

Fisher, H. (2006). The drive to love: The neural mechanism for mate selection. In R. J. Sternberg & K. Weis (eds), *The new psychology of love* (pp. 87–115). New Haven, CT: Yale University Press.

Fisher, H. E., Aron, A., & Brown, L. L. (2006). Romantic love: A mammalian brain system for mate choice. *Philosophical Transactions of the Royal Society of London B: Biological Sciences*, *361*(1476), 2173–2186.

Fromm, E. (1956). *The art of loving*. New York: Harper.

Grant, D. (1998). "Desolate and sick of an old passion": The psychodynamics of falling in and out of love. *Psychodynamic Counselling*, *4*(1), 71–92.

Hatfield, E. (1988). Passionate and companionate love. In R. J. Sternberg & M. L. Barnes (eds), *The Psychology of Love* (pp. 191–217). New Haven, CT: Yale University Press.

Hatfield, E. & Rapson, R. L. (1996). *Love and sex: Cross-cultural perspectives*. Boston, MA: Allyn & Bacon.

Hatfield, E., Traupmann, J., & Sprecher, S. (1984). Older women's perceptions of their intimate relationships. *Journal of Social and Clinical Psychology*, *2*(2), 108–124.

Hatfield, E. & Walster, G. W. (1978). *A new look at love*. Reading, MA: Addison-Wesley.

Hatfield, E. C., Pillemer, J. T., O'Brien, M. U., & Le, Y. C. L. (2008). The endurance of love: Passionate and companionate love in newlywed and long-term marriages. *Interpersona*, *2*(1), 35.

Hendrick, C. & Hendrick, S. S. (2003). Love. In J. J. Ponzetti Jr. et al. (eds), *International encyclopedia of marriage and family*, 2nd edn, vol. 3 (pp. 1059–1065). New York: Macmillan Reference USA.

Hendrick, S. S. & Hendrick, C. (1992). *Romantic love*. Newbury Park, CA: Sage.

Huesmann, L. (1980). Toward a predictive model of romantic behavior. In K. S. Pope (ed.), *On love and loving* (pp. 152–171). San Francisco, CA: Jossey-Bass.

Merriam-Webster online dictionary. (n.d.). Entry for "Intimate". Retrieved January 27, 2019 from www.merriam-webster.com/diction ary/intimate.

Johnson, S. (2013). *Love sense: The revolutionary new science of romantic relationships*. New York: Little Brown and Company.

Knox, D. H. (1970). Conceptions of love at three developmental levels. *Family Coordinator*, *19*(2), 151–157.

Lamanna, M. A., Riedmann, A., & Stewart, S. (2018). *Marriages, families, and relationships: Making choices in a diverse society*. Boston, MA: Centage Learning.

Lomas, T. (2018). The flavours of love: A cross-cultural lexical analysis. *Journal for the Theory of Social Behaviour*, *48*(1), 134–152.

Masters, R. A. (2013). *Emotional intimacy: A comprehensive guide for connecting with the power of your emotions*. Boulder, CO: Sounds True.

Meyers, S. & Berscheid, E. (1997). The language of love: The difference a preposition makes. *Personality and Social Psychology Bulletin*, *23*(4), 347–362.

Meyers, S. A., Ridge, R. D., & Berscheid, E. (1991). *"Love" vs. "in love"* (unpublished manuscript). University of Minnesota, Department of Psychology, Minneapolis.

Miller, R. S. (2012). *Intimate relationships*, 6th edn. New York: McGraw-Hill.

Muise, A., Impett, E. A., Kogan, A., & Desmarais, S. (2013). Keeping the spark alive: Being motivated to meet a partner's sexual needs sustains sexual desire in long-term romantic relationships. *Social Psychological and Personality Science*, *4*(3), 267–273.

Regan, P. C. (2000). The role of sexual desire and sexual activity in dating relationships. *Social Behavior and Personality*, *28*, 51–59.

Regan, P. C. (2011). *Close relationships*. New York: Routledge.

Regan, P. C. (2017). *The mating game: A primer on love, sex, and marriage*, 3rd edn. Thousand Oaks, CA: Sage.

Regan, P. C. & Berscheid, E. (1999). *Lust: What we know about human sexual desire*. Thousand Oaks, CA: Sage.

Reis, H. T. & Aron, A. (2008). What is it, why does it matter, and how does it operate? *Perspectives on Psychological Science*, *3*(1), 80–86.

Rubin, Z. (1988). Preface. In R. J. Sternberg & M. L. Barnes (eds), *The psychology of love* (pp. vii–xii). New Haven, CT: Yale University Press.

Safilios-Rothschild, C. (1977). *Love, sex, and sex roles*. Englewood Cliffs, NJ: Prentice Hall.

Shah, M. (2009). Falling out of love? *Berkeley Scientific Journal, 12*(2). Retrieved from https://escholarship.org/uc/item/58v0q3qr.

Spacey, A. (2017, February 5). *Analysis of poem "how do I love thee?" by Elizabeth Barrett Browing*. Retrieved August 5, 2018 from https://owlca tion.com/humanities/Analysis-of-Poem-How-Do-I-Love-Thee-by-Elizabeth-Barrett-Browning.

Sprecher, S. & Regan, P. C. (1998). Passionate and companionate love in courting and young married couples. *Sociological Inquiry, 68*(2), 163–185.

Sprecher, S., Sullivan, Q., & Hatfield, E. (1994). Mate selection preferences: Gender differences examined in a national sample. *Journal of Personality and Social Psychology, 66*(6), 1074–1080.

Sternberg, K. (2013). *Psychology of love 101*. New York: Springer Publishing Company.

Sternberg, R. J. (1986). A triangular theory of love. *Psychological Review, 93*(2), 119.

Sternberg, R. J. (1987). Liking versus loving: A comparative evaluation of theories. *Psychological Bulletin, 102*(3), 331–345.

Sternberg, R. J. (1988). Triangulating love. In R. J. Sternberg & M. L. Barnes (eds), *The psychology of love* (pp. 119–138). New Haven, CT: Yale University Press.

Sternberg, R. J. & Weis, K. (eds). (2006). *The new psychology of love*. New Haven, CT: Yale University Press.

Tennov, D. (1979). *Love and limerence: The experience of being in love*. New York: Stein and Day.

What Gives?
Why We Don't Know More about FORL

Loss of love is listed as a main cause for relationship dissatisfaction and divorce (Albrecht, Bahr, & Goodman, 1983; see Gigy & Kelly, 1993; see Huston, 2009), yet falling out of romantic love (FORL) has not been adequately researched and is curiously absent in existing clinical resources (i.e., literature, training programs). As poignantly stated by Berscheid and Regan (2005),

> Love, and the lack of it in a relationship expected to provide it, has been a 'forgotten variable' in marital therapy even though, as Roberts (1992) wrote, most couples marry because they have "fallen in love" and tend to divorce when they "fall out of love".
>
> (p. 429)

The goal of this chapter is to outline the reasons why FORL has not received more attention from scholars and practitioners and discuss how FORL is different from other commonly identified reasons for dissatisfaction and divorce.

Lack of Information on FORL

Some may wonder why FORL, seemingly known and accepted by many scholars and practitioners in the social sciences, as well as everyday citizens, would not have been more thoroughly investigated. An extensive review of the literature uncovered only two previous studies, prior to my work, that focused on FORL (Kayser, 1990, see 1993; Sailor, 2006, see 2013). Possibly the most significant difference unique to Kayser's (1990, 1993) study of FORL was its non-specificity to a type of love, whereas Hemesath (2016), Hemesath and Hurt (2016, 2017), and Sailor (2006, 2013) identified romantic love as the focal point of their studies, utilizing the phrase falling out of romantic love. Kayser's (1990, 1993) label for FORL was *marital disaffection*, which she defined as "the gradual loss of emotional attachment, including a decline in caring about the partner, an emotional estrangement, and an increasing sense of apathy and indifference toward one's spouse" (Kayser, 1993, p. 6). Of significance, Kayser's definition of *marital disaffection* did not include loss of sexual attraction; however, her end results did indicate its reduction or absence.

Unfortunately, there have been several obstacles to studying love and romantic relationships in general, which explains a good portion of the shortage of research on FORL. Quite surprisingly, love relationships have only been studied since the mid-1970s (Berscheid & Regan, 2005; Garza-Guerrero, 2000). To start, some believed the topic of love and marriage was unworthy of scientific study (Burgess & Wallin, 1953). Further, taboo societal views have traditionally discouraged the study of close relationships (Regan, 2011); "Widespread belief that relationships, especially close relationships, were not an appropriate subject for scientific study was evident far into the twentieth century" (Berscheid & Regan, 2005, p. 64). As such, there was difficulty recruiting research participants due to the overarching societal view that personal relationships should not be studied and should be kept private (Berscheid & Regan, 2005; Burgess & Wallin, 1953). Yet others worried that researching love relationships would take the mystery and enjoyment out of the experience (Berscheid & Regan, 2005; Regan, 2011).

Through the latter half of the twentieth century the few investigators who attempted to study love and relationships faced consequences such as employment termination (Berscheid & Regan, 2005). In fact, in 1975, William Proxmire, an influential US Senator, gave the first of several so-called *Golden Fleece Awards* to the National Science Foundation for awarding federal grant money to two prominent researchers, Ellen Berscheid and Elaine Hatfield (then Elaine Walster), for the study of attraction and romantic love, which Proxmire viewed as a misuse of tax dollars for something "better left to poets" (Reis & Aron, 2008, p. 81; see Regan, 2011; Sternberg, 2013).

Additionally, some psychologists and scientists believed that even if research was conducted on relationships, nothing useful could be gained because of their complex elements, which were thought to be inaccessible for scientific inquiry and analysis (see Regan, 2011). Indeed, relationships are in perpetual flux (Felmlee, 1995) as dynamic, ever-changing systems. As can be imagined, relationship prediction and intervention is difficult, at best; however, this is not unique to the behavioral sciences – it's also the case for any science that studies complex open systems (e.g., economics) (Berscheid & Regan, 2005).

Studying relationship phenomena requires enormous amounts of knowledge from many areas of expertise, including neurology, physiology, human development, social sciences, economics, anthropology, marriage and family therapy, and psychology – to add insult to injury, some of the knowledge relationship scientists need is not yet available in these very disciplines (Berscheid & Regan, 2005). Although researchers certainly struggled with the previously mentioned hardships, as well as methodological and analytic challenges of the unit of study (i.e., relationships), advancements in analytical techniques have allowed relationships to be researched adequately (Berscheid & Regan, 2005).

It's possible research on FORL has been avoided, not unlike other relationship topics, because of its complexity (see Tashiro, 2014) combined with historically negative views of love and relationship research. However, the conclusion that FORL has been sparsely researched because it is not worthy of study seems unlikely, based on the importance of close romantic relationships (Acevedo & Aron, 2009; Berscheid, 2006; Dion & Dion, 1991) and the long-standing value of marriage in America (Hawkins & Booth, 2005; Nock, 2005). Coinciding with the scarce scholarly research on FORL, there has been virtually no clinical technique information on lack of romantic love and sexual attraction (i.e., FORL) as presented in marriage therapy (Roberts, 1992) – likely the outcome of the limited research. Although these reasons are ample enough to explain why FORL has been overlooked, there are other possibilities.

FORL is Different from Other Standard Couple Problems and Phenomenon

Infrequently, falling out of love is mentioned in clinical literature; however, this is generally as a side note. For instance, some relationship professionals view an individual's claim of FORL as a *skewed perception*, or a distorted interpretation. For example, Weiner-Davis (1993), in her best-selling book *Divorce Busting*, speaks of the phenomenon in terms of *selective memory* and *faulty thinking* regarding the relationship magic being gone. In other words, a partner may highlight certain negative memories or misrepresent the past in a way that fits their current perception of the relationship. Although there is substantial research that supports Weiner-Davis's (1993) theory about relationship memory being influenced by current mood, personal views, and other factors, it is worth noting that the skew in memory could be in either a positive or negative direction (Berscheid & Regan,

2005). For example, Karney and Coombs (2000) found a memory bias among wives in a 20-year longitudinal study with a skewed *positive* perception that the relationship was *more satisfying* than it once was. The investigators deemed this finding as a mechanism to sustain the relationship long-term (more on this in Chapter 8). Further, several studies have found that partner idealization takes place in romantic love relationships, including those of long duration (see Murstein, 1976; Simpson, Gangestad, & Lerma, 1990). Additional research would be beneficial for understanding the influence of memory on relationships and love.

Further, FORL has been categorized the same as other standard couples' concerns. For example, well-known psychologist and author David Schnarch (1991) described falling out of love as no different than other typical issues, such as communication problems or irreconcilable differences. However, the presence of these typical obstacles does not always lead to FORL. Further, although offering much to the field of relationship science, neither Weiner-Davis (1993) nor Schnarch (1991) identified the definition of the phrase *falling out of love*. References to love are often generic and dependent on context, therefore a clear definition is critical for a useful discussion.

Additionally, some may consider FORL as *socially constructed*, instead of naturally occurring. In other words, a socially constructed phenomenon is created by a culture as a perceived reality, based on shared assumptions, though not naturally occurring or found outside of that society (Leeds-Hurwitz, 2009). An example of a social construction is football (i.e., American football). It can be played in a variety of ways, using any type of ball; however, rules have been developed by Americans that dictate all aspects of the American football game – which differ across the globe – notably, most countries do not participate in American football (see American Football – Participating Countries 2018). Ultimately, as researchers and practitioners, we are cautioned to avoid a reductionist conceptualization of FORL so that we can better understand the complex etiology and consequences of the phenomenon (W. Allen, personal communication, July 26, 2016).

In sum, FORL is no less real than other naturally occurring, universal, psychological or biological experiences. For example, consider passionate love, a natural, universal human experience found in many biological, anthropological, and psychological studies (Fisher, 2006). The experience may be slightly different among individuals, but overall, the essence of passionate love is recognizable from person to person (see Chapter 1 for more on passionate love). The same could be said for grief, which is also a universal experience (Mayo Clinic, 2018). The sentiment that falling out of love (FORL) is no less *real* and represents a universal phenomenon is shared by leaders in the field and major contributors to research on close relationships (W. Allen, personal communication, July 26, 2016; E. Berscheid, personal communication, August 10, 2016; P. Regan, personal communication, August 10, 2016; H. Joanning, personal communication, June 12, 2015). Further, the experience of FORL is not unique to the United States, as demonstrated by the Spanish terms *desenamorarse* and *dejar de querer* and the Russian word *razluibit*, depicting FORL.

Summary

Although the study of love and relationships is quite new to the field of psychology, it has sparked interest over the past few decades (Sternberg & Weis, 2006). Prior to this, however, most scholars believed these constructs were too difficult, complex, or elusive to study (Berscheid, 1988). Although it has been discovered that love and relationships can indeed be researched sufficiently, FORL has received little scholarly attention to date. This is unfortunate, considering the aim of relationship science is to identify causal conditions that can be used by relationship specialists to help distressed or unhappy couples (Berscheid & Regan, 2005).

Regrettably, there are limited empirically based resources available for those who have been affected by FORL. However, the field of marriage and family therapy is relatively young, and it is not uncommon for research to be ahead of practice (Berscheid & Regan, 2005). This likely substantiates why FORL does not often appear in clinical literature or training programs (i.e., if research is not yet available, it would follow that the clinical literature and training would also be missing). The hope is that additional research will lead to more substantial treatment recommendations and resources.

Further, we are cautioned to steer clear of a reductionistic view of FORL by simplifying this complex phenomenon (Hemesath & Hurt, 2016; Hemesath & Hurt; 2017). For example, the following reasons are listed for marital dissatisfaction in divorce literature: disconnection, communication problems, financial disagreements, drugs or alcohol, and sexual problems (Hawkins, Willoughby, & Doherty, 2012), however FORL is qualitatively different. As discussed in the Introduction, FORL is a unique construct representing an accumulation of various individual and relational circumstances and events, and associated thoughts, feelings, and behaviors (Hemesath & Hurt, 2016, 2017).

Exploration Questions

1 Researching any topic is both time consuming and presents many difficulties; yet, every year countless academic articles are published. After reading this chapter, what do you believe are the three biggest challenges associated with researching FORL?
2 FORL is an extremely broad topic. What smaller research topics do you predict could potentially come out when studying FORL that may be a new direction for future studies?
3 This chapter made note that FORL has been classified in the same category as common couple concerns, such as communication problems. Do you agree with this classification? Or do you think it is different – why or why not?

Key Concepts

skewed perception

selective memory

faulty thinking

socially constructed

References

Acevedo, B. P. & Aron, A. (2009). Does a long-term relationship kill romantic love? *Review of General Psychology*, *1*(13), 59–65.
Albrecht, S. L., Bahr, H. M., & Goodman, K. L. (1983). *Divorce and remarriage: Problems, adaptations, and adjustments*. Westport, CT: Greenwood Press.
American Football – Participating Countries (2018). Retrieved September 5, 2018 from www.tutorialspoint.com/american_football/american_football_participating_countries.htm.
Berscheid, E. (1988). Some comments on love's anatomy. In R. J. Sternberg & M. L. Barnes (eds), *The psychology of love* (pp. 359–374). New Haven, CT: Yale University Press.
Berscheid, E. (2006). Searching for the meaning of love. In R. J. Sternberg & K. Weis (eds), *The new psychology of love* (pp. 171–183). New Haven, CT: Yale University Press.

Berscheid, E. S. & Regan, P. C. (2005). *Psychology of interpersonal relationships*. Upper Saddle River, NJ: Pearson Education.

Burgess, E. W. & Wallin, P. (1953). *Courtship, engagement and marriage*. Philadelphia, PA: Lippincott.

Dion, K. K. & Dion, K. L. (1991). Psychological individualism and romantic love. *Journal of Social Behavior & Personality*, *6*, 17–33.

Felmlee, D. H. (1995). Fatal attractions: Affection and disaffection in intimate relationships. *Journal of Social and Personal Relationships*, *12*(2), 295–311.

Fisher, H. (2006). The drive to love: The neural mechanism for mate selection. In R. J. Sternberg & K. Weis (eds), *The new psychology of love* (pp. 87–115). New Haven, CT: Yale University Press.

Garza-Guerrero, C. (2000). Idealization and mourning in love relationships: Normal and pathological spectra. *The Psychoanalytic Quarterly*, *69*(1), 121–150.

Gigy, L. & Kelly, J. B. (1993). Reasons for divorce: Perspectives of divorcing men and women. *Journal of Divorce & Remarriage*, *18*(1–2), 169–188.

Hawkins, A. J., Willoughby, B. J., & Doherty, W. J. (2012). Reasons for divorce and openness to marital reconciliation. *Journal of Divorce & Remarriage*, *53*(6), 453–463.

Hawkins, D. N. & Booth, A. (2005). Unhappily ever after: Effects of long-term, low-quality marriages on well-being. *Social Forces*, *84*(1), 445–465.

Hemesath, C. W. (2016). *Falling out of romantic love: A phenomenological study of the meaning of love in marriage* (unpublished doctoral dissertation). Iowa State University, Ames, IA.

Hemesath, C. W. & Hurt, T. R. (2016). *Falling out of romantic love: A focus group study* (unpublished manuscript). Department of Human Development and Family Studies, Iowa State University, Ames, IA.

Hemesath, C. W. & Hurt, T. R. (2017). *Falling out of romantic love: An integrated theoretical framework* (unpublished manuscript). Department of Human Development and Family Studies, Iowa State University, Ames, IA.

Huston, T. L. (2009). What's love got to do with it? Why some marriages succeed and others fail. *Personal Relationships*, *16*(3), 301–327.

Karney, B. R. & Coombs, R. H. (2000). Memory bias in long-term close relationships: Consistency or improvement? *Personality and Social Psychology Bulletin*, *26*(8), 959–970.

Kayser, K. (1990). The process of marital disaffection: Interventions at various stages. *Family Relations*, *39*(3), 257–265.

Kayser, K. (1993). *When love dies: The process of marital disaffection*. New York: Guilford Press.

Leeds-Hurwitz, W. (2009). Social construction of reality. In S. Littlejohn & K. Foss (eds), *Encyclopedia of communication theory* (pp. 892–895). Thousand Oaks, CA: Sage.

Mayo Clinic (2018). What is grief? Retrieved September 10, 2018 from www.mayoclinic.org/patient-visitor-guide/support-groups/what-is-grief.

Murstein, B. I. (1976). *Who will marry whom? Theory and research in marital choice*. New York: Springer.

Nock, S. L. (2005). Marriage as a public issue. *The Future of Children,* *15*(2), 13–32.

Regan, P. C. (2011). *Close relationships.* New York: Routledge.

Reis, H. T. & Aron, A. (2008). Love: What is it, why does it matter, and how does it operate? *Perspectives on Psychological Science, 3*(1), 80–86.

Roberts, T. W. (1992). Sexual attraction and romantic love: Forgotten variables in marital therapy. *Journal of Marital and Family Therapy, 18*(4), 357–364.

Sailor, J. L. (2006). *A phenomenological study of falling out of romantic love as seen in married couples* (doctoral dissertation). Retrieved from ProQuest. (UMI Number, 3238277.)

Sailor, J. L. (2013). A phenomenological study of falling out of romantic love. *The Qualitative Report, 18*(19), 1–22.

Schnarch, D. M. (1991). *Constructing the sexual crucible: An integration of sexual and marital therapy.* New York: Norton.

Simpson, J. A., Gangestad, S. W., & Lerma, M. (1990). Perception of physical attractiveness: Mechanisms involved in the maintenance of romantic relationships. *Journal of Personality and Social Psychology, 59*(6), 1192–1201.

Sternberg, K. (2013). *Psychology of love 101.* New York: Springer Publishing Company.

Sternberg, R. J. & Weis, K. (eds). (2006). *The new psychology of love.* New Haven, CT: Yale University Press.

Tashiro, T. (2014). *The science of happily ever after: What really matters in the quest for enduring love.* Don Mills, ON: Harlequin.

Weiner-Davis, M. (1993). *Divorce busting: A step-by-step approach to making your marriage loving again.* New York: Fireside.

Why Does FORL Matter Anyway?

At the most fundamental level, FORL matters because it can lead to substantial grief and loss, as well as unwanted major life changes, for both parties in the relationship. However, FORL does not only impact the two partners. Regarding FORL in marriage, "the factors associated with the maintenance and stability of marital relationships have been of special concern to relationship scholars because of the importance of the marital relationship to the partners, to their children, and to society" (Berscheid & Regan, 2005, p. 192).

Unrequited Love

I have always believed that our relationships with others are what matter most in life. Even when I am not providing couples therapy, many of my individual clients are addressing issues in the context of relationships (i.e., coworkers, family, friends, neighbors). Ultimately, at the heart of our humanness is our need for genuine relationships. As described by Regan (2011), relationships play a significant role in important life outcomes, both positive and negative. Further, "People suffer when they are deprived of close contact with others, and at the core of our social nature is our need for intimate relationships" (Miller, 2012, p. 1).

It may be accurate that grief would not exist without love (Reis & Aron, 2008); however, I imagine joy wouldn't exist either. The true power of love does not exist in a vacuum – it lies between us. Love can make everything seem right with the world through amazing feelings of warmth, connection, happiness, and euphoria. In fact, most often, love's positive consequences are touted, yet "love is also capable of producing profound disorganization, including distress, uncertainty, and erratic behavior" (Baumeister, Wotman, & Stillwell, 1993, p. 390). Undoubtedly, it can bring the worst pain imaginable.

Loss of love can incite violence, jealousy, and conflict (Buss, 2006), as well as feelings of disappointment, depression, anxiety, despair, abandonment, and rejection (Fisher, 1992) – and has even been known to drive people to commit suicide (Westefeld & Furr, 1987) and homicide (see Fisher, 1992). As described by Ackerman (1994), "Love is the most important thing in our lives, a passion for which we would fight or die" (p. xix). For this reason, the end of a romantic relationship, especially when it is not wanted by one or both partners, is often considered to be distressing and traumatic (Boutwell, Barnes, & Beaver, 2015).

Unrequited love can be any kind of unreciprocated romantic attraction or love (see Baumeister, Wotman, & Stillwell, 1993) that induces yearning for more full and complete love (Bringle, Winnick, & Rydell, 2013). For example, a pair could have a platonic friendship, when one begins to desire the other romantically but the feelings are not returned. For the purpose of this book, unrequited love refers to a relationship that is already romantically coupled, but one party has rejected the other due to FORL. Although FORL is not to blame for all cases of unrequited love, surely it is a top contender. Research shows a significant majority of us are likely to have a powerful experience of unreciprocated love at some point in our lives (Aron, Aron, & Allen, 1998; Baumeister, Wotman, & Stillwell, 1993).

FORL with a partner can happen to one or both partners (W. Allen, personal communication, July 26, 2016). Although situations where both parties agree to end a relationship are not typical (Davis, Ace, & Andra, 2002), they appear to be less painful. As such, it would be ideal for rejected partners to fall out of romantic love in return, because when one partner ends a relationship, it is not in the best interest of the mate to continue to pine for that individual for years to come, which, sadly, is not uncommon (Fraley & Shaver, 2000; Hatfield & Rapson, 1993). A major frustration with FORL is that it can occur when a person does not want it to and may not happen when individuals want or need to move on from unrequited love.

"Unrequited love presents a case of emotional interdependence, insofar as one person's actions determine another person's emotions" (Baumeister, Wotman, & Stillwell, 1993, p. 378). Interestingly, according to Aron, Aron, and Allen (1998) the intensity of the emotional response to unreciprocated love is dependent on three factors: perceived value of having a relationship with the potential partner, perceived probability of having a relationship with the individual, and the appeal of being in love. Put another way, if you highly value or desire another person with whom you believe you have a chance (regardless of the reality), and the idea of being in love (with this person) makes you giddy, these factors will increase the pain of unrequited love. Further, it's likely that individual personality traits play a role in the response to unrequited love (see Chapter 7). Being rejected by a lover often involves a decrease in self-esteem, sadness, humiliation, and possibly despair (Baumeister, Wotman, & Stillwell, 1993). See Chapter 10 if you have experienced the end of a relationship and want recommendations for getting back on track. Unfortunately, although time is considered the only known cure to romantic rejection (Regan, 2017), what is done during that time matters. Although it's understandable to experience pain when on the receiving end of a partner's declaration of FORL, both parties may suffer. Possibly surprising to some, a consistent observation I have made of the rejecting partner is deep sadness – often wishing it were different, not only for their own sake, but for the sake of their partner, family, and friends. Emotional turmoil, inner conflict, second-guessing, and guilt are typically felt by the rejecting partner (Baumeister, Wotman, & Stillwell, 1993). Beyond the highly meaningful nature of relationships, and the potential pain when they end, there are additional reasons FORL matters.

Love and Human Existence

"Love has great evolutionary significance" (Sternberg, 2013) and virtually every facet of human development and behavior takes place within the context of our relationships with others (Regan, 2011). As noted by Reis and Aron (2008), in human beings, love is a highly adaptive and evolved regulatory system. From an *evolutionary perspective of love*, for our species to flourish, successful procreation is necessary, and children need to survive long enough to find a mate and bear their own offspring (Newman & Newman, 2007). Love solves the former part of this evolutionary dilemma through attraction, which leads to sex and relationship building behavior; love also manages the latter part of the task through attachment, trust, caring, and longevity in adult relationships (see Reis & Aron, 2008). Without love, it's likely humanity would not exist. Although many believe romantic love is a mystery, Sue Johnson (2013), reputable clinical psychologist and researcher, suggests, "romantic love is not the least bit illogical or random. It is the continuation of an ordered and wise recipe for our survival" (p. 20). Unfortunately, many of us don't seem to be skilled at keeping romantic love healthy and alive, or surviving the seeming torture of its absence.

Significance of Love Relationships on Health and Well-being

As we begin to understand the gravity of love on the human condition, we also realize the enormous impact love relationships have on our health and well-being (Reis & Aron, 2008). Both mental and physical health are negatively affected when adults experience intimate relationship difficulties (Berscheid & Regan, 2005); however, positive relationship bonds of all types are beneficial for health and well-being. Specific to marriage, there are many collective advantages. Some of these include higher levels of psychological, physical, and financial well-being (Blackman et al., 2005; Nock, 2005), a greater sense of meaning in life, the potential to participate in multiple roles, healthier lifestyles, affordance of better healthcare, and the opportunity to live in safer neighborhoods, to name only a few (Hawkins & Booth, 2005).

Regarding role specialization, persons who marry have an advantage (Nock, 2005). Partners generally have different skill sets that allow them to accomplish tasks together more efficiently and effectively. Additionally, married couples have the luxury of reaping the benefits of belonging to a social institution. Marriage carries legal and moral implications as well as better social treatment and higher self-esteem creating positive assumptions about the parties involved (Nock, 2005). Thus, addressing the issue of FORL could benefit adults by reducing mental health and physical health problems (Goldberg, 2010), as well as increasing efficiency in day-to-day life and benefitting from financial and social aspects.

Although it is possible that married individuals are naturally healthier, wealthier, and more often selected into marriage, Hawkins and Booth (2005) reported that, even if previously healthier and happier people are selected at a greater rate for marriage, "it is clear that marrying has at least some additional effect on improving psychological well-being" (p. 446). It is worth noting that the benefit of psychological well-being associated with being married is closely related to the quality of the relationship (Kiecolt-Glaser & Newton, 2001; Kim & McKenry, 2002). Not all marriages have a positive effect on well-being. Intense marital conflict and long-term marital dissatisfaction are examples of relationship components that may undermine the benefits of marriage (Kelly, 2012). Similar results have been found between physical illness and marital quality. For example, Wickrama et al. (1997) discovered that as marital quality decreases the chance of becoming physically ill increases.

Hawkins and Booth (2005) described the consequences of remaining in an unhappy marriage as causing "significantly lower levels of overall happiness, life satisfaction, self-esteem, and overall health along with elevated levels of psychological distress compared to remaining otherwise continuously married" (p. 451). This creates a conundrum as to staying in the relationship or leaving, as both options could have negative consequences. Not only could these outcomes be detrimental to the physical and emotional health of the adult partners, but also to children because of the potential for reduced parenting quality, witnessing negative exchanges or behavior between their parents, or experiencing a less positive relationship between child and parent(s).

Positive adjustment and outcomes for children are significantly impacted by both the relationship between the child and parent and the relationship between the parents (Lamb, 2012). Couples' relationship problems typically lead to stress or other mental health issues for parents, which can harm parenting quality and be disadvantageous for children (Lamanna & Riedmann, 2012). "Both harmony and conflict appear to affect children directly (by providing models of contentment and support, civil relationships and by fostering affective self-regulation) as well as indirectly (by affecting the parents' well-being and thus affecting their ability to function as effective, engaged, warm, and competent parents)" (Lamb, 2012, p. 101). Thus, understanding FORL, which can lead to an unsatisfying relationship or less-than-ideal parental functioning, would be beneficial for children. Furthermore, the benefits that adults might gain from satisfying marriages are also advantageous for children. For example, healthier lifestyles, safer neighborhoods, higher-quality healthcare (Hawkins & Booth, 2005), and greater financial well-being (Blackman et al., 2005; Nock, 2005) are positives for both married adults and their children. Ultimately,

> Children's or adolescents' adjustment depends overwhelmingly upon such qualities as the parents' affection, consistency, reliability, responsiveness, and emotional commitment, as well as on the quality and character of the relationships between the parents and their intimates, and on the availability of sufficient economic and social resources.
>
> (Lamb, 2012, p. 102)

The benefits of a satisfying union extend beyond the family, to society as a whole. Although questions regarding the true scope of the marital advantage have arisen when comparing marriage to other types of modern relationships (i.e., cohabitation), many scholars believe that societal gains accrue from the institution of marriage (Musick & Bumpass, 2012). Through the reduction of physical and mental health symptoms, described previously in this chapter, societal gains can include lower government and taxpayer healthcare costs, increased work performance, and reduced poverty, to name a few (Kelly, 2012; Ooms, 2002).

Importance of FORL for Mental Health Providers

Relationship struggles are the most common presenting problem of those entering psychotherapy (Pinsker et al., 1985), and long-standing, chronic relationship issues rather than acute problems are presented most commonly in couple's therapy (Doss, Simpson, & Christensen, 2004). Further, lack of love is the most difficult problem to treat in couple's therapy (Whisman, Dixon, & Johnson, 1997). Therefore, it isn't surprising FORL is often a topic of discussion in professional consultation due to absence of theoretical frameworks, education, and training with which to confidently and adequately address this phenomenon.

Marital therapy has been shown to be effective for 70 percent of couples seeking treatment (Lebow et al., 2012). However, based on the minimal literature and research to date on the topic of FORL, relationship professionals are not adequately trained to assess or treat FORL. Further, one of the main components of romantic love, sexual desire, has been rarely researched with respect to protecting and bolstering desire in established relationships (Muise et al., 2013). Even if there was evidence-based information available on FORL, certain relationship issues can be exceedingly difficult to treat. As described by Berscheid and Regan (2005) even if the problems responsible for relationship distress can be identified, some conditions cannot be changed (Berscheid & Regan, 2005) (i.e., one partner wants children and the other does not). Ultimately, providers need more tools in their clinical toolbelt to address FORL and the issues leading up to it.

Summary

Just as love matters significantly to humans, so does FORL. The impact is consequential and far-reaching for individual, child, marital, and family health and well-being, as well as for society at large. The ability to effectively address relationship dissatisfaction and mitigate FORL could reduce mental and physical health challenges such as loneliness, depression, anxiety, and high blood pressure (Fisher, 2004; Fraley & Shaver, 2000; Goldberg, 2010; Hatfield & Rapson, 1993; Lebow et al., 2012). Further, cultivating marital quality is important because *healthy* marriages offer considerable gains for spouses psychologically, physically, socially, and financially (Blackman et al., 2005; Hawkins & Booth, 2005; Kelly, 2012; Kim & McKenry, 2002; Nock, 2005; Ooms, 2002). These gains are also important for children. Moreover, adult relationship problems can undermine parenting quality and be disadvantageous for children (Kelly, 2012; Lamanna & Riedmann, 2012; Ooms, 2002). In fact, beyond parent relationships with each other and relationships with their children, economic and social resources greatly affect child well-being and adjustment (Lamb, 2012).

FORL is also a significant issue for both mental health providers and relationship professionals. For example, there is considerable overlap between individual mental health issues, such as depression or anxiety, and couple distress (Lebow et al., 2012; Mearns, 1991). Further, although romantic love is considered an essential ingredient in marriage (Berscheid, 2006; Dion & Dion, 1991; Johnson, 2013), the lack of loving feelings is the most difficult problem to treat in couples therapy (Whisman, Dixon, & Johnson, 1997). Yet, scholars and clinicians have little consensus about how to keep romantic love alive in long-term relationships. Finally, unrequited love experienced by the rejected partner is often fraught with emptiness and other painful feelings (Hatfield & Rapson, 1993). Gaining insight into FORL is important, because although it varies from situation to situation, there are many substantial reasons why FORL matters.

Exploratory Questions

1 FORL can affect an individual, their partner, children, and others close to them. How have some of the factors detailed impacted you personally, through friends, family members, or your own relationship?
2 Pick one or two sentences or facts from the chapter that resonate with you. Why did these stand out to you? Connect them to your own experience or what you have noticed in friends, family members, or partners.
3 Aron, Aron, and Allen (1998) identify three factors that determine the intensity of the emotional response to unreciprocated love. What are these three factors? Would you change or add any factors – if so, what?

Key Concepts

unrequited love

evolutionary perspective of love

References

Ackerman, D. (1994). *A natural history of love*. New York: Random House.
Aron, A., Aron, E., & Allen, J. (1998). Motivations for unreciprocated love. *Personality & Social Psychology Bulletin*, *24*(8), 787–796.
Baumeister, R. F., Wotman, S. R., & Stillwell, A. M. (1993). Unrequited love: On heartbreak, anger, guilt, scriptlessness, and humiliation. *Journal of Personality and Social Psychology*, *64*(3), 377–394.
Berscheid, E. (2006). Searching for the meaning of love. In R. J. Sternberg & K. Weis (eds), *The new psychology of love* (pp. 171–183). New Haven, CT: Yale University Press.
Berscheid, E. S. & Regan, P. C. (2005). *Psychology of interpersonal relationships*. Upper Saddle River, NJ: Pearson Education.
Blackman, L., Clayton, O., Glenn, N., Malone-Colòn, L., & Roberts, A. (2005). *The consequences of marriage for African Americans: A comprehensive literature review*. New York: The Institute for American Values.
Boutwell, B. B., Barnes, J. C., & Beaver, K. M. (2015). When love dies: Further elucidating the existence of a mate ejection module. *Review of General Psychology*, *19*(1), 30–38.
Bringle, R. G., Winnick, T., & Rydell, R. J. (2013). The prevalence and nature of unrequited love. *SAGE Open*, *3*(2), 1–15.
Buss, D. M. (2006). The evolution of love. In R. J. Sternberg & K. Weis (eds), *The new psychology of love* (pp. 65–86). New Haven, CT: Yale University Press.
Davis, K. E., Ace, A., & Andra, M. (2002). Stalking perpetrators and psychological maltreatment of partners: Anger-jealousy, attachment, insecurity, need for control, and break-up context. In K. E. Davis, I. H. Frieze, & R. D. Maiuro (eds), *Stalking: Perspective on victims and perpetrators* (pp. 407–425). New York: Springer.
Dion, K. K. & Dion, K. L. (1991). Psychological individualism and romantic love. *Journal of Social Behavior & Personality*, *6*, 17–33.
Doss, B. D., Simpson, L. E., & Christensen, A. (2004). Why do couples seek marital therapy? *Professional Psychology: Research and Practice*, *35*(6), 608–614.
Fisher, H. (1992). *Anatomy of love: A natural history of mating, marriage, and why we stray*. New York: Ballantine Books.
Fisher, H. (2004). *Why we love: The nature and chemistry of romantic love*. New York: Henry Holt.
Fraley, R. C. & Shaver, P. R. (2000). Adult romantic attachment: Theoretical developments, emerging controversies, and unanswered questions. *Review of General Psychology*, *4*(2), 132–154.

Goldberg, D. (2010). The detection and treatment of depression in the physically ill. *World Psychiatry*, *9*(1), 16–20.

Hatfield, E. & Rapson, R. L. (1993). *Love, sex, and intimacy: Their psychology, biology, and history*. New York: Harper Collins.

Hawkins, D. N. & Booth, A. (2005). Unhappily ever after: Effects of long-term, low-quality marriages on well-being. *Social Forces*, *84*(1), 445–465.

Johnson, S. (2013). *Love sense: The revolutionary new science of romantic relationships*. New York: Little Brown and Company.

Kelly, J. B. (2012). Risk and protective factors associated with child and adolescent adjustment following separation and divorce: Social science applications. In K. Kuehnle & L. Drozd (eds), *Parenting plan evaluations: Applied research for the family court* (pp. 49–84). New York: Oxford University Press.

Kiecolt-Glaser, J. K. & Newton, T. L. (2001). Marriage and health: His and hers. *Psychological Bulletin*, *127*(4), 472–503.

Kim, H. K. & McKenry, P. C. (2002). The relationship between marriage and psychological well-being: A longitudinal analysis. *Journal of Family Issues*, *23*(8), 885–911.

Lamanna, M. A. & Riedmann, A. (2012). *Marriages, families, and relationships: Making choices in a diverse society*, 11th edn. Belmont, CA: Cengage Learning.

Lamb, M. E. (2012). Mothers, fathers, families, and circumstances: Factors affecting children's adjustment. *Applied Developmental Science*, *16*(2), 98–111.

Lebow, J. L., Chambers, A. L., Christensen, A., & Johnson, S. M. (2012). Research on the treatment of couple distress. *Journal of Marital and Family Therapy*, *38*(1), 145–168.

Mearns, J. (1991). Coping with a breakup: Negative mood regulation expectancies and depression following the end of a romantic relationship. *Journal of Personality and Social Psychology*, *60*, 327–334.

Miller, R. S. (2012). *Intimate relationships*, 6th edn. New York: McGraw-Hill.

Muise, A., Impett, E. A., Kogan, A., & Desmarais, S. (2013). Keeping the spark alive: Being motivated to meet a partner's sexual needs sustains sexual desire in long-term romantic relationships. *Social Psychological and Personality Science*, *4*(3), 267–273.

Musick, K. & Bumpass, L. (2012). Reexamining the case for marriage: Union formation and changes in well-being. *Journal of Marriage and Family*, *74*(1), 1–18.

Newman, B. M. & Newman, P. R. (2007). *Theories of human development*. Mahwah, NJ: Lawrence Erlbaum Associates, Inc.

Nock, S. L. (2005). Marriage as a public issue. *The Future of Children*, *15*(2), 13–32.

Ooms, T. (2002, August). Marriage and government: Strange bedfellows? Center for Law and Social Policy, Couples and Marriage Series, Policy Brief No. 1, 1–7. Retrieved August 12, 2018 from www.clasp.org/resources-and-publications/archive/0102.pdf.

Pinsker, H., Nepps, P., Redfield, J., & Winston, A. (1985). Applicants for short-term dynamic psychotherapy. In A. Winston (ed.), *Clinical and research issues in short-term dynamic psychotherapy* (pp. 104–116). Washington, DC: American Psychiatric Association.

Regan, P. C. (2011). *Close relationships.* New York: Routledge.

Regan, P. C. (2017). *The mating game: A primer on love, sex and marriage,* 3rd edn. Los Angeles, CA: SAGE.

Reis, H. T. & Aron, A. (2008). Love: What is it, why does it matter, and how does it operate? *Perspectives on Psychological Science, 3*(1), 80–86.

Sternberg, K. (2013). *Psychology of love 101.* New York: Springer Publishing Company.

Westefeld, J. S. & Furr, S. R. (1987). Suicide and depression among college students. *Professional Psychology, Research and Practice, 18*(2), 119–123.

Whisman, M. A., Dixon, A. E., & Johnson, B. (1997). Therapists' perspectives of couple problems and treatment issues in couple therapy. *Journal of Family Psychology, 11*(3), 361–366.

Wickrama, K. A. S., Lorenz, F. O., Conger, R. D., & Elder, G. H. (1997). Marital quality and physical illness: A latent growth curve analysis. *Journal of Marriage and the Family, 59*(1), 143–155.

Family and Relationship Trends

Based on significant societal and cultural shifts, family form and function have morphed dramatically since the mid-twentieth century (Dorius, 2015). Yet, families are nonetheless meaningful to Americans (Coontz, 2016). Family and relationship trends are important to consider because the same factors that influence family change directly impact the function and expectation of modern-day marriages – including the meaning of love and FORL in marriage. The goal of this chapter is to shed light on the ways in which marriages and families have changed over time, highlighting the importance of love and FORL in today's marriage.

Families Past and Present

The family structure of preindustrial societies comprised extended family and whole kinship groups, including aunts, uncles, grandparents, and other relatives. However, in the 1950s the Progressive Era and Industrial Revolution began to give way to the *modern family*, which evolved through changes in religious beliefs, social attitudes, and laws – shrinking the family size to the *nuclear family*, consisting of parents and children (Lamanna, Riedmann, & Stewart, 2018). The iconic television sitcom *Leave it to Beaver* emulated the new American family ideal, inclusive of the wife as homemaker, husband as breadwinner, and their children (Coontz, 2016). As described by Finkel (2018), Americans do not spend nearly the amount of time with friends and relatives outside our marriages as we did in past decades. As discussed previously, we rely on just our spouse to provide all emotional and physical resources that were once provided by our larger social networks and extended family, including companionship, compassion, reassurance, sex, financial resources, child rearing, friendship, emotional support, physical care, etc. (Perel, 2007).

As social and legal definitions have become increasingly flexible, family is no longer only defined through blood, marriage, adoption, or limited to the nuclear family with the working dad and stay-at-home mom. In fact, mothers are the primary breadwinner in four of ten families, and there has been a sharp increase in stay-at-home dads compared to past years (Pew Research Center, 2015). Today, less than 10 percent of families fit the traditional two-parent married household (Coontz, 2016). Same-sex marriages, single parenting, blended families, and cohabitation are on the rise (Pew Research Center, 2015). As we take on more diversity, freedom of choice, and a multitude of various family structures, the *postmodern family* has come into existence (Stacey, 1990).

Despite these shifts, family has not lost its importance, even in contemporary times (Costa, 2013). The following three functions define American families, as well as highlight their importance, regardless of the form they take: 1) raising children responsibly; 2) providing members with economic and other practical support; 3) offering emotional security, affection, companionship, and intimacy (Lamanna, Riedmann, & Stewart, 2018).

Marital Trends

"People have always loved a love story. But for most of the past our ancestors did not try to live in one" (Coontz, 2005, pp. 9–10). Historically, the purpose of marriage was to secure property rights, wealth, and power, although changes in the mid-twentieth century led to marriage as a source of individual happiness and fulfillment, instead of communal gain (Herek, 2006). "Throughout the first 5,000 years of human history in all the world's cultures that we know of, people probably fell in love, but they weren't expected to do so with their spouses" (Lamanna, Riedmann, & Stewart, 2018, p. 172). The Scientific Revolution and the Industrial Revolution changed how the West viewed love through an increase in the importance of individualism, personal happiness, and reduction of emotional pain (Hatfield & Rapson, 1996). Today, love is used as the main criteria in the decision to marry (Johnson, 2013; Mathes & Wise, 1983; Miller, 2012) and is the building block of the crucial family unit (Johnson, 2013).

"Definitionally, *marriage* is a long-term mating arrangement that is socially sanctioned and that typically involves economic, social, and reproductive cooperation between the partners" (Regan, 2017). Marriage is also considered a key task of human development. For example, Erikson's sixth stage of psychosocial development, intimacy versus isolation, highlights long-term commitments to others, including marriage (Erikson & Erikson, 1998). In fact, approximately two-thirds of people in the United States marry at least once in their lifetime (US Census Bureau, 2012) and of those who have never married, almost two-thirds would like to marry (Cohn et al., 2011). Beyond marrying for love, Americans say the other important reasons to marry are for life-long commitment and companionship (Lamanna, Riedmann, & Stewart, 2018). Interestingly, the average age of first marriage in 1980 was 24.7 for men and 22 for women, but climbed to 29.8 for men and 27.8 for women in 2018 (US Census Bureau, 2018).

The rise in age at first marriage is primarily due to the increase of women's educational attainment and the narrowing of the gender gap in job earnings, as well as the advent of birth control, which, coupled with more accepting views of women having children out of wedlock, allowed women to have more control over their relationship status (Boxer, Noonan, & Whelan, 2015). Specifically, many women are waiting for marriage until they have finished their education and have begun a career.

Well-known psychotherapist and best-selling relationship author Esther Perel (2017) brings up an interesting question about today's marriage. Are we asking too much from a relationship of two? She notes that what an entire community was once responsible for (i.e., raising children, gathering water and food, support) is now expected to exist between two people alone. It's safe to say that expectations in all areas of marriage are far greater today (Kayser, 1993). As pointed out by Perel (2017), in more ancient times the privilege of happiness was thought to be unavailable, and couples could only escape marriage through death; later, people divorced because they were *unhappy*; now, modern-day couples divorce because they could be *happier*. Instead of marriage being an economic decision, it is now an *experience* of trust and connection, where happiness is *expected* (Perel, 2017). As you can see, there have been extraordinary shifts in expectations and views related to love and marriage, making the possibility of FORL even more impactful.

Divorce Trends

Many unhappy marriages end in divorce, including those affected by the phenomenon of FORL. It can be helpful to view the state of marriage today from two perspectives popular among family scholars: the marital decline perspective and the marital resilience perspective (Amato, 2004b). The *marital decline perspective* views marriage as weakening, posing negative consequences to society (i.e., increased poverty, decreased child well-being). As described by Amato (2004b), marriage is being threatened by individualistic pursuits and personal happiness, fueling less obligation and commitment to others. "As a result, people no longer are willing to remain married through the difficult times, for better or for worse" (Amato, 2004b, p. 960). Advocates of the marital decline perspective believe society should implement more programs, including education that strengthens marriage as an institution. However, there are some limitations to this viewpoint. Although we know there are benefits from marriage (see Chapter 3), low-quality unions undermine the positives (Kelly, 2012), often creating negative outcomes for adults (Hawkins & Booth, 2005) and their children (Lamanna & Riedmann, 2012; Lamb, 2012).

Alternatively, the proponents of *marital resilience perspective* acknowledge that marriage is changing, but not necessarily weakening, and all family types (including non-marital) should receive social support and programming. Supporters of this model suggest adults are both resilient and adaptable and able to succeed within a wide array of family structures. In fact, "Rather than view the rise in marital instability with alarm, advocates of this perspective suggest that divorce provides a second chance at happiness for adults and an escape from dysfunctional and aversive home environments for many children" (Amato, 2004b, p. 960). Furthermore, couples who stay together today are more likely to be in highly satisfying relationships if their emphasis is on happiness and fulfillment instead of commitment and security (Kayser, 1993). Some scholars argue that greater freedom of choice strengthens, not reduces, the quality of intimate relationships (Amato, 2004b). Furthermore, expectations for marriage are far greater than they were in the past (Kayser, 1993) and some couples may try harder to achieve what has been deemed possible (Acevedo & Aron, 2009).

Marital Instability

Divorce trends in America illustrate contemporary *marital instability*. During the 1960s and 1970s, the divorce rate in America rose sharply (Kelly, 2006; Lamanna, Riedmann, & Stewart, 2018) from 1.3 divorces per 1,000 population in 1933 to 5.3 per 1,000 population in 1979 (Glick & Lin, 1986). Divorce declined slightly in the 1990s under the influence of pro-marriage movements and government-enacted programs, along with a retreat from marriage and the rising occurrence of cohabitation (Sabatelli & Ripoll, 2004). Divorce rates then stabilized; however, Americans continued to experience high rates of divorce.

As reported by the Centers for Disease Control and Prevention (n. d.), divorce rates have declined slightly from a rate of 4.0 per 1,000 total population in 2000 to 3.2 per 1,000 total population in 2016. However, marriage rates have also declined, from 8.2 per 1,000 total population in 2000 to 6.9 per 1,000 total population in 2016. The number of people marrying is the lowest it has ever been and although "cohabitation was very rare in 1960 ... it is now ordinary" (Miller, 2012, p. 7). Some scholars contend it is too soon to tell if divorce is declining, due to the complexity of predicting divorce rates and trends (Schoen & Canudas-Romo, 2006; Teachman, Tedrow, & Hall, 2006). It is worth noting that erroneous perceptions regarding divorce rates result if certain factors are not considered (e.g., fewer marriages taking place, rise in cohabitation and singlehood, specific populations excluded in divorce research).

Current Divorce Statistics

The popular divorce statistic floating around is that approximately 50 percent of all marriages end in divorce. One thing to keep in mind is that divorce rates vary greatly by social class (i.e., education) and divorce rates are lower for those with college degrees (Aughinbaugh, Robles, & Sun, 2013; Cherlin, 2010; Regan, 2017). For example, Aughinbaugh, Robles, and Sun (2013) report that only 27 percent of college graduates ever experience divorce, but the rate almost doubles for those with just a high school degree or some college education. The current probability for divorce is estimated at between 40 and 50 percent (Cherlin, 2010). However, Amato (2010) describes that the estimate of one in two marriages ending in dissolution was most likely accurate when permanent separations are also taken into account. Although there is scholarly disagreement on the average divorce risk, the risk is substantial, nonetheless (Stanley, 2015).

"More than half of all divorces involve children under the age of 18" (Amato, 2000, p. 1269) and the median length of a first marriage that ends in divorce is approximately 12 years (Payne, 2014). Although divorce can happen at any time, many divorces take place early in a marriage (i.e., five years or less) (Paul, 2003), but very few divorces take place within weeks or months of saying "I do" (Lamanna, Riedmann, & Stewart, 2018). Long-term marriages are often protected by the longevity of the marital bond, as well as the strength of long-standing family and friend networks, and joint financial interests (Brown, Orbuch, & Maharaj, 2010); however, there have been recent spikes in divorce among older couples (i.e., baby-boomers), including those in long-term marriages. In fact, as found by Brown and Lin (2012), the baby boomers (born between 1946 and 1964) were the only age group where the divorce rate grew in 2010, making up 25 percent of all divorce. Researchers believe this spike is due to several factors, including baby-boomers being the largest generation on record, having a longer life expectancy in which to endure unhappy marriages, and many baby-boomers having multiple marriages by later life (Lamanna, Riedmann, & Stewart, 2018). We know that second and higher-order marriages have an even greater rate of divorce than first marriages (Brown & Booth, 1996). Interestingly, education does not have the same protective factors against divorce for older couples (Brown, Lin, & Payne, 2014). Although major differences are not expected between same-sex couples and their heterosexual counterparts, divorce in regard to same-sex marriages will require additional research because of the relatively recent legal rights to marry in the US (see Lamanna, Riedmann, & Stewart, 2018).

Who Initiates Divorce

In a longitudinal study from 2009 to 2015, composed of 2,262 heterosexual participants in the US, it was found that women initiate divorce more than twice as often as men (69 percent wife-initiated, versus 31 percent husband-initiated) (American Sociological Association, 2015; Rosenfeld, 2018). The researcher Rosenfeld (2018) noted that the trend of female-initiated divorce has been consistent since the 1940s. Interestingly, there was no significant difference in the percentage of male- and female-initiated breakups of heterosexual *non-marital* unions (i.e., cohabitations, long-term dating relationships). The research suggests that women are more dissatisfied with marital relationships than men, pointing to feelings of oppression and the idea that marriage is slow to catch up to modern-day gender expectations of equality (i.e., pressure to take surname, higher expectations for childcare and housework despite dual-earner families) with non-marital unions trending as more flexible (see American Sociological Association, 2015; see Cotton, Burton, & Rushing, 2003; Rosenfeld, 2018).

Reasons for Divorce

Although somewhat counterintuitive, the greatest reasons for marital breakdown and divorce are generally not *hard reasons* such as addiction or abuse issues, but instead *soft reasons* such as lack of communication or affection, and growing apart (De Graaf & Kalmijn, 2006; Hawkins, Willoughby, & Doherty, 2012;

Hetherington, Cox, & Cox, 1981). Hard reasons generally refer to destructive and more serious issues, whereas soft reasons are more interpersonal in nature, yet often nonetheless difficult. Worth nothing, loss of love is frequently cited as a reason for divorce. In fact, in a study of 500 divorced people conducted by Albrecht, Bahr, and Goodman (1983), the top two reasons cited for divorce were loss of love and infidelity. Growing apart and lowered levels of love or appreciation were found to be factors of divorce by Gigy and Kelly (1992). Finally, Huston (2009) maintained that reduced feelings of love, declining affectionate behavior, ambivalence toward the marriage, and spousal withdrawal are associated with divorce.

Why Do Some Marriages Last?

There are various views as to why some couples' marriages survive the threat of divorce. Many scholars adhere to the *emergent distress model* to explain lowered marital satisfaction and divorce, positing that all newlyweds are happy and in-love, whereas maladaptive coping with stressful events and conflict creates dissatisfaction and divorce. In contrast, Huston, Niehuis, and Smith (2001) reported on data from a 13-year, 168-couple longitudinal study designed to investigate long-term marital satisfaction and stability. Contrary to the popular emergent distress model, their study supported the *enduring dynamics model*, which proposed that not all newlyweds are happy and blissful to begin with and that early relationship patterns persisted into marriage. In other words, early relationship dynamics, even premarital dynamics, can predict future marital unhappiness and stability. Further, Huston, Niehuis, and Smith (2001) found that what happens in the first two years of marriage is predictive of later divorce. Even happy newlyweds were at more risk for divorce if in the first two years they showed greater-than-normal declines in love and affection. In fact, the couples most likely to divorce were those who had the biggest decline in happiness, even if they were happier than couples who did not divorce. Therefore, although high satisfaction matters, relationship stability and commitment are greatly associated with the fluctuation in satisfaction levels over time instead of high satisfaction alone (see Arriaga, 2001; Berscheid, 2010; Berscheid & Regan, 2005; Huston, Niehuis, & Smith, 2001).

  In regard to marital satisfaction, a number of longitudinal studies indicate satisfaction levels are reasonably high in early years, generally decreasing over time (Regan, 2011). However, some research suggests that many couples experience increased marital satisfaction after children are raised (Gorchoff, John, & Helson, 2008; Lupri & Frideres, 1981). It's important to note that even though there seems to be a general decline in satisfaction over the course of marriage, that does not mean couples are necessarily destined to be unhappy. In fact, according to Regan (2011) most spouses report a greater-than-average level of satisfaction over the course of marriage, even though it may be to a lesser degree than in the past. Marital satisfaction is supported by positive affect (i.e., smiling, showing interest, affection) between spouses during daily interaction (Gottman & Levenson, 2000), as well as offering understanding and compassion when difficulties or disagreements arise (Sullivan et al., 2010). This is important because relationship satisfaction is thought to play a role in FORL (see Kayser, 1993).

Marital Happiness: Past and Present

The rise in the divorce rates over the last several decades begs the question if marriages have become more dissatisfying. Interestingly, marriages of the past were likely no happier than those of today (Sabatelli & Ripoll, 2004). In fact, the *Leave it to Beaver*-style family of the 1950s represents what many refer to as the happiest time for couples in America (Coontz, 2016). Everyone had their role – husbands went to work and upon their return wives had dinner on the table, with the kids bathed, the homework done, and the house cleaned. However, there was significant and widespread marital unhappiness for many of those couples (Coontz, 2016), with less than one-third considering themselves happy in their marriage (see Komarovsky, 1962). Until the middle of the twentieth century, most marriages continued "till death do us part," often because individuals felt they had no other choice (Hatfield & Rapson, 1996). Families who veered from the traditional nuclear, two-parent family were considered deviant and detrimental to the well-being of children (Amato, 2004b). Amato (2004a, 2004b) cites not only stigma, but difficulty of obtaining a divorce, religious views, fear, and poverty as reasons many people did not divorce.

Summary

There has been a shift away from traditional, communal marriage to a more individualized view, based on love (Hurt, 2014; Kayser, 1993). Although families continue to be important, this fundamental shift, along with other social and cultural changes (i.e., sexual revolution, birth control, the feminist movement, shifts in women's roles), accounts for the increased divorce rate in the latter half of the twentieth century (see Cherlin, 2010; Kayser, 1993; Nock, 2005; Sabatelli & Ripoll, 2004). Some might say the rise in divorce is due not only to individualism, but to high and potentially unrealistic expectations of marriage (Kayser, 1993; Sabatelli & Ripoll, 2004). Understanding FORL would be of great benefit to the stability of marriage and other long-term, non-marital relationships that provide important family functions.

One might assume that skyrocketing divorce rates in the last 50 years confirm that contemporary marriages are *unhappier* than marriages of the past; however, researchers have found this to be untrue (Coontz, 2016; see Komarovsky, 1962; Sabatelli & Ripoll, 2004). Although divorce rates in America appear to be stabilizing, it would be inaccurate to suggest the state of marriage is secure. Some divorce measures do not account for fewer marriages taking place to begin with, or certain populations. In other words, divorce statistics may not tell the entire story.

There are many reasons couples divorce; however, some of the most common are loss of love (Albrecht, Bahr, & Goodman, 1983; Gigy & Kelly, 1992; Huston, 2009), infidelity (Albrecht, Bahr, & Goodman, 1983), and growing apart (Gigy & Kelly, 1992; Huston, 2009). Women tend to be the initiator of most divorces, based on evidence suggesting more women are dissatisfied in marriage than men (American Sociological Association, 2015; Rosenfeld, 2018). Interestingly, research suggests couples who have lower satisfaction at the start of the relationship and remain consistent over time have a higher likelihood of staying together than happier couples who experienced fluctuations in relationship satisfaction (Arriaga, 2001). Paradoxically, it is not always the unhappiest couples who divorce (Regan, 2017), which leads us to consider other factors, such as personality, commitment, and perceived rewards or consequences of remaining married versus divorcing – which will be discussed in later chapters.

Exploration Questions

1 In the United States, the average age of first marriage has increased from 24.7 for men and 22.0 for women in 1980, to 29.8 for men and 27.8 for women in 2018 (US Census Bureau, 2018). Is this the trend you see among those known to you who are marrying? How do you feel about the current average age of marriage for men and women (i.e., is it too young or too old? What are the pros and cons?)?

2 The *marital decline perspective* and the *marital resilience perspective* are two viewpoints regarding the current state of marriage. Can you explain how the perspectives differ? Which viewpoint do you most agree with and why?

3 This may be surprising; however, research shows marriages in the past were likely no happier than they are today. List the main reasons someone might assume modern-day marriages are less satisfying. Explain why relying on these factors may be inaccurate.

Key Concepts

enduring dynamics model

emergent distress model

marital decline perspective

marital instability

marital resilience perspective

modern family

nuclear family

postmodern family

References

Acevedo, B. P. & Aron, A. (2009). Does a long-term relationship kill romantic love? *Review of General Psychology*, *13*(1), 59–65.

Albrecht, S. L., Bahr, H. M., & Goodman, K. L. (1983). *Divorce and remarriage: Problems, adaptations, and adjustments.* Westport, CT: Greenwood Press.

Amato, P. R. (2000). The consequences of divorce for adults and children. *Journal of Marriage and the Family*, *62*, 1269–1287.

Amato, P. R. (2004a). Divorce in social and historical context: Changing scientific perspectives on children and marital dissolution. In M. Coleman & L. H. Ganong (eds), *Handbook of contemporary families: Considering the past, contemplating the future* (pp. 265–281). Thousand Oaks, CA: Sage.

Amato, P. R. (2004b). Tension between institutional and individual views of marriage. *Journal of Marriage and Family*, *66*(4), 959–965.

Amato, P. R. (2010). Research on divorce: Continuing trends and new developments. *Journal of Marriage and Family*, *72*(3), 650–666.

American Sociological Association (2015, August 22). Women more likely than men to initiate divorces, but not non-marital breakups. *ScienceDaily*. Retrieved September 3, 2018 from www.sciencedaily.com/releases/2015/08/150822154900.htm.

Arriaga, X. B. (2001). The ups and downs of dating: Fluctuations in satisfaction in newly formed romantic relationships. *Journal of Personality and Social Psychology*, *80*, 754–765.

Aughinbaugh, A., Robles, O., & Sun, H. (2013). Marriage and divorce: Patterns by gender, race and educational attainment. *Monthly Labor Review*, October 2013, 1–13. Retrieved July 25, 2018 from www.bls.gov /opub/mlr/2013/article/marriage-and-divorce-patterns-by-gender-race-and-educational-attainment.htm.

Berscheid, E. (2010). Love in the fourth dimension. *Annual Review of Psychology*, *61*, 1–25.

Berscheid, E. S. & Regan, P. C. (2005). *Psychology of interpersonal relationships*. Upper Saddle River, NJ: Pearson Education.

Boxer, C. F., Noonan, M. C., & Whelan, C. B. (2015). Measuring mate preferences: A replication and extension. *Journal of Family Issues*, *36*(2), 163–187.

Brown, E., Orbuch, T. L., & Maharaj, A. (2010). Social networks and marital stability among Black American and White American couples. In K. Sullivan & J. Davila (eds), *Support processes in intimate relationships* (pp. 319–334). New York: Oxford University Press.

Brown, S. L. & Booth, A. (1996). Cohabitation versus marriage: A comparison of relationship quality. *Journal of Marriage and the Family*, *58*, 668–678.

Brown, S. L. & Lin, I. F. (2012). The gray divorce revolution: Rising divorce among middle-aged and older adults, 1990–2010. *Journals of Gerontology Series B: Psychological Sciences and Social Sciences*, *67*(6), 731–741.

Brown, S. L., Lin, I. F., & Payne, K. K. (2014). *Age variation in the divorce rate, 1990–2010*. FP-14–16. Resource document. National Center for Family and Marriage Research. Retrieved September 15, 2018 from www.bgsu.edu/content/dam/BGSU/college-of-arts-and-sciences /NCFMR/documents/FP/FP-14-16-age-variation-divorce.pdf.

Centers for Disease Control and Prevention (n.d.). National marriage and divorce rates (2000–2016). Retrieved October 1, 2018 from www.cdc.gov /nchs/data/dvs/national_marriage_divorce_rates_00-16.pdf.

Cherlin, A. (2010). Demographic trends in the United States: A review of research in the 2000s. *Journal of Marriage and the Family: Decade in Review*, *72*(3), 403–419.

Cohn, D., Passel, J. S., Want, W., & Livingston, G. (2011). Barely half of U.S. adults are married: A record low. Retrieved July 31, 2018 from www .pewsocialtrends.org/2011/12/14/barely-half-of-u-s-adults-are-married -a-record-low/.

Coontz, S. (2005). *Marriage, a history: How love conquered marriage*. New York: Viking Penguin.

Coontz, S. (2016). *The way we never were: American families and the nostalgia trap*. New York: Basic Books.

Costa, R. P. (2013). Family rituals: Mapping the postmodern family through time, space and emotion: We are what we celebrate. Amitai Etzioni (2004). *Journal of Comparative Family Studies*, *44*(3), 269–289.

Cotton, S. R., Burton, R., & Rushing, B. (2003). The mediating effects of attachment to social structure and psychosocial resources on the relationship between marital quality and psychological distress. *Journal of Family Issues, 24*(4): 547–577.

De Graaf, P. M. & Kalmijn, M. (2006). Divorce motives in a period of rising divorce: Evidence from a Dutch life-history survey. *Journal of Family Issues, 27*(4), 483–505.

Dorius, C. (2015). Family instability. In C. L. Shehan (ed.), *The Wiley Blackwell encyclopedia of family studies* (pp. 775–779). Hoboken, NJ: Wiley-Blackwell.

Erikson, E. H. & Erikson, J. M. (1998). *The life cycle completed (extended version)*. New York: Norton.

Finkel, E. J. (2018). *The all-or-nothing marriage: How the best marriages work*. New York: Dutton.

Gigy, L. & Kelly, J. B. (1992). Reasons for divorce: Perspectives of divorcing men and women. *Journal of Divorce and Remarriage, 18*, 169–187.

Glick, P. C. & Lin, S. L. (1986). Recent changes in divorce and remarriage. *Journal of Marriage and the Family, 48*(4), 737–747.

Gorchoff, S. M., John, O. P., & Helson, R. (2008). Contextualizing change in marital satisfaction during middle age: An 18-year longitudinal study. *Psychological Science, 19*(11), 1194–1200.

Gottman, J. M. & Levenson, R. W. (2000). The timing of divorce: Predicting when a couple will divorce over a 14-year period. *Journal of Marriage and Family, 62*(3), 737–745.

Hatfield, E. & Rapson, R. L. (1996). *Love and sex: Cross-cultural perspectives*. Boston, MA: Allyn & Bacon.

Hawkins, A. J., Willoughby, B. J., & Doherty, W. J. (2012). Reasons for divorce and openness to marital reconciliation. *Journal of Divorce & Remarriage, 53*(6), 453–463.

Hawkins, D. N. & Booth, A. (2005). Unhappily ever after: Effects of long-term, low-quality marriages on well-being. *Social Forces, 84*(1), 445–465.

Herek, G. M. (2006). Legal recognition of same-sex relationships in the United States. *American Psychologist, 61*(6), 607–621.

Hetherington, E. M., Cox, M., & Cox, R. (1981). Effects of divorce on parents and children. In M. Lamb (ed.), *Nontraditional families* (pp. 233–288). Hillsdale, NJ: Erlbaum.

Hurt, T. R. (2014). Black men and the decision to marry. *Marriage & Family Review, 50*(6), 447–479.

Huston, T. L. (2009). What's love got to do with it? Why some marriages succeed and others fail. *Personal Relationships, 16*(3), 301–327.

Huston, T. L., Niehuis, S., & Smith, S. E. (2001). The early marital roots of conjugal distress and divorce. *Current Directions in Psychological Science, 10*(4), 116–119.

Johnson, S. (2013). *Love sense: The revolutionary new science of romantic relationships*. New York: Little Brown and Company.

Kayser, K. (1993). *When love dies: The process of marital disaffection*. New York: Guilford Press.

Kelly, J. B. (2006). Children's living arrangements following separation and divorce: Insights from empirical and clinical research. *Family Process, 46*(1), 35–52.

Kelly, J. B. (2012). Risk and protective factors associated with child and adolescent adjustment following separation and divorce: Social science applications. In K. Kuehnle & L. Drozd (eds), *Parenting plan evaluations: Applied research for the family court* (pp. 49–84). New York: Oxford University Press.

Komarovsky, M. (1962). *Blue-collar marriage*. New Haven, CT: Vintage.

Lamanna, M. A. & Riedmann, A. (2012). *Marriages, families, and relationships: Making choices in a diverse society*, 11th edn. Belmont, CA: Cengage Learning.

Lamanna, M. A., Riedmann, A., & Stewart, S. (2018). *Marriages, families, and relationships: Making choices in a diverse society*. Boston, MA: Centage Learning.

Lamb, M. E. (2012). Mothers, fathers, families, and circumstances: Factors affecting children's adjustment. *Applied Developmental Science, 16*(2), 98–111.

Lupri, E. & Frideres, J. (1981). The quality of marriage and the passage of time: Marital satisfaction over the family life cycle. *Canadian Journal of Sociology / Cahiers canadiens de sociologie*, 283–305.

Mathes, E. W. & Wise, P. S. (1983). Romantic love and the ravages of time. *Psychological Reports, 53*(3), 839–846.

Miller, R. S. (2012). *Intimate relationships*, 6th edn. New York: McGraw-Hill.

Nock, S. L. (2005). Marriage as a public issue. *The Future of Children, 15*(2), 13–32.

Paul, P. (2003). *The starter marriage and the future of matrimony*. New York: Random House Incorporated.

Payne, K. K. (2014). *Median duration of first marriage and the great recession* (FP-14–20). Retrieved August 1, 2018 from www.bgsu.edu /content/dam/BGSU/college-of-arts-and-sciences/NCFMR/documents/ FP/FP-14-20-median-duration-first-marriage.pdf.

Perel, E. (2007). *Mating in captivity: Unlocking erotic intelligence*. New York: Harper.

Perel, E. (2017, October 2). How to find the sweet spot between love and desire. Retrieved July 7, 2018 from www.youtube.com/watch?v=ier RipP-7JA.

Pew Research Center (2015, December 14). *In four-in-ten families, mom is the primary breadwinner*. Washington, DC. Retrieved July 18, 2018 from www.pewsocialtrends.org/2015/12/17/parenting-in-america /st_2015-12-17_parenting-20/.

Regan, P. C. (2011). *Close relationships*. New York: Routledge.

Regan, P. C. (2017). *The mating game: A primer on love, sex, and marriage*, 3rd edn. Thousand Oaks, CA: Sage.

Rosenfeld, M. J. (2018). Who wants the breakup? Gender and breakup in heterosexual couples. In D. F. Alwin, D. H. Felmlee, & D. A. Kreager (eds), *Social networks and the life course: Integrating the development of human lives and social relational networks* (pp. 221–243). Cham: Springer International Publishing.

Sabatelli, R. M. & Ripoll, K. (2004). Variations in marriage over time: An ecological/exchange perspective. In M. Coleman & L. H. Ganong (eds), *Handbook of contemporary family: Considering the past, contemplating the future* (pp. 79–94). Thousand Oaks, CA: Sage.

Schoen, R. & Canudas-Romo, V. (2006). Timing effects on divorce: 20th century experience in the United States. *Journal of Marriage and Family, 68*(3), 749–758.

Stacey, J. (1990). *Brave new families: Stories of domestic upheaval in late twentieth century America*. New York: Basic Books.

Stanley, S. (2015). Seven ways to make yourself divorce-proof. Retrieved October 14, 2018 from www.psychologytoday.com/us/blog/sliding-vs-deciding/201503/7-ways-make-yourself-divorce-proof.

Sullivan, K. T., Pasch, L. A., Johnson, M. D., & Bradbury, T. N. (2010). Social support, problem solving, and the longitudinal course of newlywed marriage. *Journal of Personality and Social Psychology*, *98*(4), 631–644.

Teachman, J., Tedrow, L., & Hall, M. (2006). The demographic future of divorce and dissolution. In M. Fine & J. Harvey (eds), *Handbook of divorce and relationship dissolution* (pp. 59–82). New York: Routledge.

US Census Bureau (2012). *2012 American community survey. Table S1201. Marital status*. Retrieved June 18, 2018 from http://factfinder.census.gov/faces/tableservices/jsf/pages/productview.xhtml?src=bkmk.

US Census Bureau (2018, November). *Estimated median age at first marriage, by sex: 1890 to the present* (Table MS-2). Retrieved January 8, 2019 from www.census.gov/content/dam/Census/library/visualizations/timeseries/demo/families-and-households/ms-2.pdf.

A New View

In previous chapters, key terms and vocabulary related to love and relationships were clarified and defined through comparing the existing literature and classification systems. The few research studies done on FORL were also reviewed. Beyond these important elements, theory is also essential for understanding FORL. Many people shudder at theory, the "T" word – I've been there! If you are tempted to skip to the next chapter, take a peek at Figure 5.1 first. It quickly highlights the main components of the Megatheory of FORL and their usefulness in conceptualizing love in the context of intimate partner relationships.

So why does theory matter? The short answer is that theory helps us understand the world around us. *Theory* guides researchers in identifying and organizing relationships between various phenomena, providing insight into how things work (Garner, Wagner, & Kawulich, 2016). Human development theories, for example, are important because they help us understand complex human behavior and functioning (Newman & Newman, 2007). Theory also affords clues to solutions, key interventions, and treatment planning. In a nutshell, theory leads to research and research leads to theory. When new or conflicting information is discovered, the theory is updated or changed, and the cycle of theory and research continues. This process brings us closer to understanding various phenomenon – including FORL. Although there are countless theories addressing an endless array of topics, there has been no specific theory pertaining to FORL, until now. The goal of this chapter is to introduce you to a means of conceptualizing and understanding FORL through a new theoretical framework that I coined the Megatheory of FORL: Romantic Relationship Formation, Maintenance, and Outcomes.

Love and Tornadoes

As I watched television with my daughter Ivy one hot and muggy July afternoon, the sky began to darken. Local weatherman Ed

Wilson broke in to announce the "MegaDoppler" radar had indicated rotation and possible tornadic activity in central Iowa. Heavy rain began to pound on the windows as the TV screen exploded with bright green, blue, red, orange, yellow, and fuchsia – and then it struck me. Romantic relationships are like tornadoes!

As far as meteorology is concerned, when the atmosphere is stable, the weather is calm. Tornadoes, on the other hand, erupt in unstable conditions. Under the right set of circumstances, a tornado forms and begins to rotate, gaining energy – eventually morphing into a magical, monster vortex of spinning wind and debris, picking up anything and everything in its path. But there's something that makes tornadoes even more interesting and potentially dangerous – they are unpredictable. For example, a truck might be tossed through the air like a toy, yet the motorcycle parked next to it is untouched. A tornado has a mind of its own, changing direction on a whim. Twisters eventually fall apart, fading away into nothingness and the calm returns as quickly as it left.

Overall, tornadoes are a near-perfect metaphor for love in intimate partner relationships. Humans crave stability because it brings a sense of calm and predictability; yet, as with weather, instability in love makes things interesting. After all, most romantic relationships start with passionate love, which is anything but calm and stable. Further, certain elements and conditions are required for love's formation (see Chapter 7). It can be powerful and strong or weak and fleeting. There is constant interaction between variables within and outside both the individual and the relationship, causing perpetual change. This exciting, new love often creates an atmosphere ripe for building momentum, drawing us in to its spinning vortex. Like a tornado, the stronger the energy, the more powerful the experience and the greater the risk.

It's important to point out that most tornados are feared, and rightly so! However, they are not entirely bad. Like love, mesmerizing beauty exists within this weather wonder. These experiences are so alluring that we often take our chances with the possibility of poor outcomes and pain. Ask the tornado chasers around the Midwest and tornado alley! It's starting to make sense why people chase tornadoes, as well as love!

The tornado metaphor influenced my view of intimate partner relationship formation, maintenance, and outcomes (including FORL) by reminding me of the complexity and constant change inherent to open systems, as well as their powerful, captivating, often unpredictable nature. This is depicted in the theoretical framework by "Mega" in the model name, and its spiral-like, twister shape.

The Megatheory of FORL: Romantic Relationship Formation, Maintenance, and Outcomes

This new theoretical framework is comprised of six pre-existing theories or models, which when uniquely combined are extraordinarily useful in conceptualizing and understanding love in the context of intimate partner relationship formation, maintenance, and outcomes – including FORL. Important to this model is the form it takes – a spiral-like twister exemplifying the unique, powerful, unpredictable nature of romantic relationships (see Figure 5.1). The Megatheory of FORL incorporates 1) general systems theory, 2) biopsychosocial approach, 3) biological/evolutionary theory of love, 4) social exchange theory, 5) attachment theory, and 6) Sternberg's Triangular Theory of Love (see Box 5.1).

Box 5.1 Components Comprising the Megatheory of FORL: Romantic Relationship Formation, Maintenance, and Outcomes

General Systems Theory

- An interdisciplinary means of explaining complex systems (Ludwig von Bertalanffy, 1968).
- The whole is greater than the sum of the parts.
- All parts inside and outside a system affect other parts.
- Change is inevitable.
- Relationships are complex.

Biopsychosocial Theory

- Interdisciplinary model based on General Systems Theory principles (Engel, 1977).
- Originated for understanding health and disease – now used across many disciplines, including mental health.
- Biological, social, and psychological factors interact to explain various phenomena.

Biological Factors

Genetics	Behavior	Personality
Sex drive	Needs	Temperament
Attachment	Brain activity	Health
Attraction	Hormones	Non-conscious processes

Psychological Factors

Non-conscious processes	Attitudes	Spirituality
Cognitions, thoughts	Self-esteem	Personality
Social skills	Behavior	Life experiences
Mood, emotions, feelings	Coping skills	Values
Expectations	Mental health	Personal goals
Beliefs, schemas, attributions	Familiarity	

Societal Factors

Gender norms	Demographic factors	Behavior
Economic factors	Family-of-origin dynamics	Religion
External stressors	Environment	Education
Previous relationships	Peers	Lifestyle
In-laws and extended family	Cultural values, expectations	Proximity

Biological/Evolutionary Theory of Love

- Love develops instinctively based on biological evolution promoting survival and reproduction (Sternberg & Weis, 2006).
- Different types of love develop to meet various human needs (i.e., affiliation: friendship, protection: parent/child, mating: intimate romantic partners) (Kenrick, 2006).

- Biological mating drives include motivational systems of attachment, attraction, and sex drive (Fisher, 2006).
- Brain chemistry and hormones play a role in love (Fisher, 2006).
- Non-conscious processes influence our thoughts, feelings, actions, and decisions, including those involving romantic relationships (Bargh, 2017).

Social Exchange Theory

- Originally an economic theory applied to businesses and work settings; however, it has also been applied widely to relationships (Homans, 1958; Thibaut & Kelley, 1959).
- Social behavior, including mate selection and retention, is based on maximizing rewards and minimizing consequences, as well as comparing available alternatives.

Attachment Theory

- A psychological theory rooted in biology, affected by societal/family/primary caregiver experiences (Bowlby, 1980).
- Children have an innate drive to create emotional bonds, through specific attachment behaviors intended to elicit responses from caregivers that meet their needs for survival.
- Caregivers respond to child attachment behaviors in various ways (i.e., consistent, inconsistent).
- Children develop one of three main attachment styles based on experience with primary caregivers: secure, anxious, or avoidant (Ainsworth et al., 1978).
- Caregiver experiences teach children what to expect from others and tend to be replicated in their adult relationships.

Sternberg's Triangular Theory of Love

- A triangle depicts the three components of love in intimate partner relationships: intimacy (emotional), passion (physical), and commitment (decision) (Sternberg, 1987).
- Through different combinations of the three components, eight types of love can be generated: non-love, friendship/

liking, infatuated love, empty love, companionate love, fatuous love, romantic love, and consummate love.
- Consummate love contains all three components, and is considered the most ideal for long-term relationships, although may be difficult to maintain long-term.
- Relationships are in flux and may move between categories.

General Systems Theory

As we discuss the theoretical foundation of the Megatheory, it is important to acknowledge the contribution of General Systems Theory, which was noted in the Introduction of this book as a main assumption underlying my understanding of FORL. *General Systems Theory* was founded by Ludwig von Bertalanffy (1968), who believed many disciplines could benefit by utilizing the same set of laws and principles that apply to all systems. In fact, General Systems Theory has been applied to a wide range of research areas including biology, nursing, sociology, psychology, human development, mathematics, and many more. Not only does General Systems Theory assist in understanding FORL, it is a basic building block to our understanding of all complex systems, including human relationships. Not surprisingly, General Systems Theory is at the crux of most marriage and family therapy graduate training programs and the basis of relationship conceptualization and treatment planning.

General Systems Theory rests on the concept of *holism*, proposing "the whole is greater than the sum of its parts" – in other words, something different is created from what each part contributes (Morgan, 2009; Nichols & Schwartz, 1995; von Bertalanffy, 1968). Consider the following examples, "a watch is more than a pile of machine parts or a piece of music is more than a cluster of notes" (Nichols & Schwartz, 1995). In the context of relationships, a family, couple, or friendship is more than its members. This is an important concept, because it explains how individual parts come together to create something entirely new and unique – keeping in mind that watches and music are not complex living organisms.

Human beings are an example of an *open system*, meaning they exchange elements with the environment and each impacts the other (von Bertalanffy, 1968). The concept of the open system comes from natural science. Among many other things, we exchange oxygen and carbon dioxide with the environment and

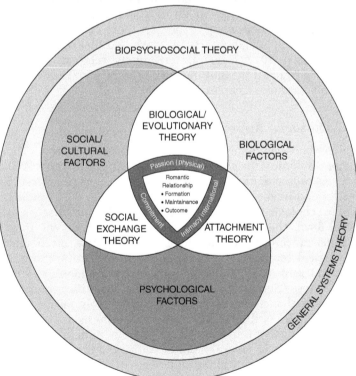

Figure 5.1 The Megatheory of FORL: Romantic Relationship Formation, Maintenance, and Outcomes

both systems are affected in the process. In relationships, not only is there interaction between the two individuals involved, but there is interaction between each individual and the environment (other systems and people), and the dyad to the environment. Thus, a relationship is composed of many moving parts, constantly influenced and affected by many other organisms, people, and things. To cope with these influences and maintain balance and functioning, "systems, are by their very nature, always in the process of change" (Newman & Newman, 2007, p. 276). General Systems Theory illustrates why relationships can be so confusing and complicated. What each of us brings to a relationship, including our family history, experiences, personality, attachment formations, values, beliefs, education, health, and so on, affects how we interact and relate to our partner, and the same is true for what our partner brings to the relationship. Figure 1.1 in Chapter 1 gives a nice illustration of how General Systems Theory works. The web of interactions between our partner, our environment, and other systems is ever-changing, complex, and often not expected, acknowledged, or understood by even those in the relationship. "People in love relationships, just as in all relationships, are not distinct entities, acting independently; they are part of a dynamic dyad, within which each person's actions spark and fuel reactions in the other" (Johnson, 2013, p. 17). Unfortunately, relationships are not like a puzzle where if the missing piece is found it solves everything, for they are far more complex.

Biopsychosocial Approach

The biopsychosocial approach is based on General Systems Theory, including holistic aspects and the complexity of linked variables. The *biopsychosocial approach* was founded by George Engel (1977), an acclaimed medical internist and psychiatrist who studied the role of psychological and social factors in health and disease. In its original form, the biopsychosocial model recognized the inextricable importance of biological factors (i.e., genetics, biochemistry), psychological factors (i.e., values, personality traits, mood), and societal factors (i.e., cultural norms, environment, peers) to human illness (Santrock, 2007). This was a significant shift from the traditional biomedical approach, which only focused on the biological causes of illness. The biopsychosocial model is now seen as a comprehensive scientific framework for understanding complex phenomenon in several fields of study, and in recent years has been suggested as a unifying approach in the multi-framework world of mental health conceptualization and treatment (see Melchert, 2011). Biological, psychological, and social factors play a role in love (Sternberg, 2014). These same factors appeared time and again throughout the investigation of FORL, earning biopsychosocial theory a place in the Megatheory of FORL.

Biological/Evolutionary Theories of Love

Several biological theories of love are based on Charles Darwin's (1859) evolution and natural selection work, proposing that human traits and features that promote survival and reproduction are retained and continue to develop over time (Sternberg, 2014). "If love had not evolved as a binding force between mother and child, and between men and women, we would not have endured" (Ackerman, 1994, p. 146). Couples would not form a pair and bond. Parents would not care for their children. Evolution selected love as a biological imperative for humans because of love's significant survival value (Ackerman, 1994). Further, in the brains of participants who are in-love, biological researchers have consistently revealed elevated activity in areas of the brain rich in the neurotransmitters dopamine and norepinephrine and lowered activity of serotonin – suggesting biological processes with strong reward properties, as well as obsessive tendencies associated with infatuation (Bartels & Zeki, 2000, 2004, 2005; Fisher et al., 2003). All are intended to encourage love!

Two popular biological theories of love, the Dynamical Evolutionary View of Love (Kenrick, 2006) and the Drive to Love (Fisher, 2006), will be outlined briefly with specific attention to their usefulness in understanding the processes of love. Biology, reproduction, and advancement of the species is central to *biological/evolutionary theories of love.*

The Dynamical Evolutionary View of Love

The *Dynamical Evolutionary View of Love* (Kenrick, 2006) proposes that love comes in many forms, including love for intimate partners, friends, and family members. This theory also includes the idea that love develops differently based on instinctive parts of human nature. For example, the love one feels for their partner will differ from the love one feels for children (Sternberg & Weis, 2006). It can be noted that each form of love is meant to address common social problems regularly faced by humans, such as affiliation, status, self-protection, mate-seeking, mate-retention, and parental care.

Evolutionary decisions, outside our mental awareness, called *decision biases*, are central to this theory and are thought to be a factor in loving (Kenrick, 2006). Decisions are made based on human inclination (innate bias) to pay attention to some aspects of our environment over others. "They [decision biases] filter through information overwhelm, they help make sense of the world, they allow us to make quick decisions in a fast-paced world" (Comaford, 2017, para. 9). The concept of decision biases represents the underpinnings of love, ultimately designed to promote survival and reproduction.

Decision biases can be complex, differing somewhat based on gender, and are specific to the problems faced over the course of human history. An example of decision bias, for males, is to be more attentive to attractive women of childbearing age and for women to be attentive to men of status, with the goal of each gender being to gain desirable reproductive partners and to maximize procreation success (Regan, 2017). As described by Christine Comaford (2017), we each create our own "subjective reality" from our personal decision biases. These biases are likely responsible for decision making that doesn't seem rational or doesn't have logic to back it up – maybe it's a gut feeling, or we know we like or don't like something or someone but don't know exactly why. While there are some cultural variations in decision biases, they are thought to be minimal due to decision biases forming based on basic, early human life difficulties applicable to all humans (Sternberg, 2014).

It is difficult to know why love ends without examining why it begins, therefore, understanding the purpose of love is an important part of uncovering the factors involved in FORL. Finally, this theory highlights the role of decision bias and the unconscious mind in decision making, which will be discussed in more depth later in this chapter. The Dynamical Evolutionary View of Love contributes to this discussion because it explains why human beings love in many unique ways (i.e., love of children, love of romantic partner).

The Drive to Love

Another prominent and useful biological theory is the *Drive to Love* (Fisher, 1998, 2006). This theory is different from the Dynamical Evolutionary Theory of Love because instead of addressing all relationship types, it homes in on *mating drives* that facilitate reproduction, by outlining three core motivational systems: attachment, attraction, and sex drive (Fisher, 2006). Fisher (2006) explained that intimate partner love can start with any of these three experiences. Specifically, the sex drive motivates us to have sexual unions with others, attachment creates sustained connections, and attraction encourages preference for a particular mating partner (Yovell, 2008). Each has interactional effects on the other two systems, including the risks that may come with love rejection (Fisher, 2014). When a relationship ends, attempts to reconnect with the lover so as to not lose reproductive advantage are tied to reproductive drives. Further, there are often frantic efforts by the rejected party to reunite with the loved one in an effort to keep the euphoric feeling alive, as well as to preserve feelings of safety and security. As discussed in Chapter 3, the loss of romantic love can incite hopelessness, depression, resignation, and despair, sometimes culminating in suicide (Fisher, 2004, 2006), jealousy, conflict, and violence (Buss, 2006).

The Drive to Love is relevant to this discussion because it assists in both outlining the important role of romantic love as well as explaining the negative emotional effects of FORL. Fisher, Aron, and Brown (2006) describe this theory as having cross-cultural applicability, due to romantic love's broad effect on the universal goal of reproduction.

The Unconscious Mind

The role of biology and the unconscious mind are woven throughout the literature regarding love and relationships. We have learned how biology plays a significant role in love, which evolved for procreation and survival of our species (Sternberg, 2014). However, to exclude *non-conscious* processes, which occur outside our awareness, from the discussion on FORL would be remiss.

Remember my intriguing yet unsettling ouija board experience I mentioned in Chapter 1? Although some would say my friend and I were moving the game "planchette" ourselves, others would believe it was the spirit world communicating from the afterlife. Research suggests the ouija board works through the power of non-conscious processes and implicit memories of the players (see Gauchou, Rensink, & Fels, 2012). Implicit memories are memories or knowledge acquired unconsciously, said to affect thoughts and behaviors, without awareness (Schacter, 1987). As it turns out, nonconscious processes appear to be responsible for that mysterious board game, and much more!

Legendary father of psychoanalysis Sigmund Freud (1895) used the analogy of an iceberg to describe the structure and function of the mind, believing that most of our thoughts exist beneath the waterline and outside conscious perception (see Figure 5.2). Compared to the mental processes we are aware of, the unconscious mind is a storehouse of memories, urges, thoughts, and feelings that exist outside our awareness, yet powerfully influence our everyday judgments, behavior, and experiences in ways our conscious mind cannot recognize, much less explain (Westen, 1999; Wilson, 2004).

Figure 5.2 Illustration of the conscious and unconscious mind through the analogy of an iceberg. The unconscious exists below the waterline, while the conscious resides above.

Source: Wikimedia Commons.

Over the years, cognitive psychologists have faced the seemingly insurmountable task of understanding the human mind. Like the study of love, research on the unconscious aspects of our mind had a slow beginning due to belief that it could not be researched adequately (Bargh, 2017). This challenge isn't surprising considering "most mental activities not only are not accessible to other people – they are not accessible to the very person whose mind it is" (Berscheid & Regan, 2005, p. 228). Researchers cannot simply ask introspective questions about someone's thinking, such as why individuals immediately knew they were drawn to certain people, because chances are they do not really know the answer (Berscheid & Regan, 2005). However, science is slowly making progress in understanding these hidden yet important and fascinating workings of the brain – not only in our daily lives, but in love and relationships. Evidence suggests Freud may have been right about certain aspects of the unconscious mind, including the idea that not everything we do is a product of our conscious choice. Although there is far more to learn, there appear to be significant biological and evolutionary processes happening outside our awareness that influence our thoughts, actions, and decisions (Bargh, 2017), including relationship decisions. Specifically, it has been determined that mating behavior and mate selection are strongly influenced by factors that operate outside conscious awareness (Hazan & Diamond, 2000; Regan, 2011). For example, as humans, we need to know if a potential mate is trustworthy and is someone who will help, not harm, us; therefore, we make split-second, non-conscious judgments evaluating these properties (Berscheid & Regan, 2005; see Bargh et al., 1996). From a biological perspective, people are most likely to enhance our well-being when they share the same or a similar background. Non-conscious properties such as proximity (people who live close in distance) and familiarity (often a by-product of living close) distinguish friend from foe (Regan, 2011). Selecting a partner who lives in our city or state or attends the same college is an example of choosing based on proximity, which also cultivates familiarity.

Another example of evolutionary unconscious mate selection includes preferences for specific physical characteristics such as facial symmetry and scent (see Perilloux, Webster, & Gaulin, 2010; Thornhill et al., 2003). Yet, when you ask someone what attracted them to their partner, most people do not reply with "because their face was symmetrical." According to Fugère (2016), like physical traits, we may not be accurate about which personality traits are most important to us in mate selection. In a study by Eastwick et al. (2011), it was found that the traits people reportedly wanted in a mate had no impact on their actually liking the individual upon a favorable in-person interaction.

Further, unconscious mind is thought to be a primary source of human behavior (Freud, 1915). For example, individual goals and values are not static and often change over the course of a person's life, causing individuals to shift their attention to other areas (Lamanna, Riedmann, & Stewart, 2018, p. 24). As illustrated below, a change in goals may explain variance in an individual's behavior or views that do not seem typical for them and may even surprise themselves.

What we want and what we need strongly determine what we like and don't like. For example, one notable experiment showed that when women are prompted to think about finding a mate to settle down with, their disapproval of tanning salons and diet pills (ostensible ways to strengthen attraction) decrease. Why? Because we unconsciously see the world through goal-colored glasses. The tanning salons and diet pills are suddenly a good thing when our mind is unconsciously focused on becoming more attractive in order to find a mate.

(Bargh, 2017, p. 10)

Many clients who present with FORL desperately want to feel differently and do not understand why, despite repeated attempts and a strong desire to experience romantic love for their spouse, they still cannot seem to renew their lost love. Attention to the non-conscious processes are important to understanding FORL because what we are mentally unaware of may hold the answer to why some individuals who experience FORL are confused and/ or frustrated by the occurrence.

Attachment Theory

Attachment theory was formulated in the 1950s by John Bowlby, a British psychologist and psychoanalyst, and developed with the help of his colleague, Mary Ainsworth. Attachment theory is primarily a psychological model, but contains other influences (i.e., evolutionary, social). It is viewed by researchers as useful in predicting relationship behaviors (Berscheid & Regan, 2005). Attachment theory suggests that children come into the world predisposed to create strong emotional bonds with their primary caregivers, through innate attachment behaviors (i.e., crying, smiling, clinging) that illicit responses in their attachment figures necessary for the child's survival (Regan, 2011). As a result of caregiver responsiveness, children go on to develop one of three main styles of attachment: *secure attachment, anxious attachment*, or *avoidant attachment* (see Ainsworth et al., 1978). Anxious attachment and avoidant attachment are considered *insecure attachment* types. Between one-third and one-half of individuals of all ages are believed to have an insecure attachment type (Ein-Dor et al., 2010).

As you can imagine, not all caregivers respond the same way to the attachment needs of children – some are readily available and consistently responsive, and others are either inconsistent or unavailable almost entirely. Because young children cannot leave their caregivers in response to inconsistent or unavailable caregiving, they must somehow learn to manage their situation.

Ainsworth and colleagues researched attachment using a procedure called the Strange Situation, which included exposing a young child (usually 12–18 months of age) to an unfamiliar situation where the primary caregiver left the child with a stranger then returned. The responses of the child were used to assess the attachment style of the child to the primary caregiver. As the name implies, securely attached children see their caregiver as a secure base in which to explore the world, who is responsive and provides safety and protection. When the caregiver leaves, the child is not unreasonably upset and expects his/ her return. Anxiously attached children tend to stay close to the caregiver, are distraught if the caregiver leaves, and are angry upon their return, not wanting to accept attempts of comfort from the caregiver. Finally, children with avoidant attachment generally interact with the caregiver as though they are a stranger, neither being upset upon their leaving or seeing them when they return.

It is important to understand that attachment is not synonymous with love and affection (Prior & Glaser, 2006), in that a child can be attached to someone and not receive much affection or love. Additionally, in adult relationships, attachment does not ensure that sex, attraction, and love will exist. It is possible for these entities to be split among many different people or relationships.

> Men and women can express deep attachment for a long-term spouse or mate, *while* they express attraction for someone else, *while* they feel the sex drive in response to visual, verbal, or mental stimuli unrelated to either partner. And men and women can copulate with individuals with whom they are not "in love"; they can be "in love" with someone with whom they have had no sexual contact; and they can feel deeply attached to a mate for whom they feel no sexual desire or romantic passion.
> (Fisher et al., 2002, p. 414)

Ultimately, we can feel love, attachment, attraction, and sex drive for one or more than one person.

Although our attachments are strongest in childhood, attachment in adult relationships, specifically romantic love relationships, often parallel our childhood attachment to our parents or primary caregivers (Ackerman, 1994; Hatfield & Rapson, 1996; Tashiro, 2014). Children's interactions with primary caregivers promote enduring working models of close relationships, which Regan (2011) explains nicely,

> from that first relationship the child comes to develop a set of internalized expectations and beliefs about what other people

are like (e.g., trustworthy, responsive, available, supportive) as
well as internalized views of himself or herself as valued and
self-reliant or unworthy and incompetent. These *internal
working models*, in turn, influence the child's interpersonal
expectations and behaviors and, therefore, his or her
subsequent relationship outcomes.

(p. 46)

"A growing body of research links the quality of early attachments
with a person's orientation to and capacity for social relationships
within the context of friendships, intimate relationships, and parent-
child relations" (Newman & Newman, 2007, p. 36). The notion of
childhood attachment influencing adult attachment is based on the
assumption that the same motivational system that creates a close
bond between parents and children is also responsible for the bond in
emotionally intimate relationships in adulthood (Fraley & Shaver,
2000). Adult relationships will serve the same basic functions of the
childhood attachment relationship, such as feelings of safety and
security (Davila & Bradbury, 2001). Through experiments, John
Bowlby (1980) solidified that attachment styles (i.e., secure, anxious,
or avoidant) formulated in childhood will be sought in adult relationships based on familiarity and internal working models.

However, although our early attachment experiences shape our
adult relationships, this does not automatically mean adults will
have the same attachment style they did with their parents (Breatherton & Munholland, 1999). Beyond the individual's childhood
attachment style, attachment styles in adult romantic relationships
are based on many interacting factors, such as the context of the
relationship, the partner's attachment style, and current circumstances (Berscheid & Regan, 2005). The attachment style of any one
individual may vary across adult relationships. For example, some
researchers believe that each partner's attachment styles can influence the others attachment style, thus magnifying or lessening the
effects (Lamanna & Riedmann, 2012).

The goal for adult attachment is to have a sense of stability
and security. Those with secure attachments in adult relationships
may not have unilaterally smooth love relationships, because love
is difficult for everyone (Hatfield & Rapson, 1996). However, in
romantic relationships a secure attachment style is associated with
greater commitment, trust, and satisfaction, as well as more frequent positive emotions and less frequent negative emotions than
anxious or avoidant attachment styles (Lamanna & Riedmann,
2012; Simpson, 1990).

Alternatively, not having an early secure attachment could
result in marital problems and difficulties with trust and intimacy

(Ackerman, 1994). Although the quality of romantic relationships is influenced by attachment orientation, relationship stability is a mixed bag (Berscheid & Regan, 2005). For example, individuals with insecure attachment (i.e., anxious attachment or avoidant attachment) have higher rates of relationship dissolution (Hazan & Shaver, 1987). However attachment styles also influence commitment in couple relationships (Stanley, Rhoades, & Whitton, 2010). When there is low attachment to a spouse (in terms of abandonment fear and love worthiness), marriages may be unhappy yet endure through fears (Davila & Bradbury, 2001). This is more attributable to insecurity than satisfaction. Individuals with anxious attachment can become frightened by closeness and push back in anger or push away due to fear that the loved one will leave (Stanley, Rhoades, & Whitton, 2010; Tashiro, 2014). "Once the loved one begins, understandably, to distance himself or herself, the anxious adult clings once again, and so begins a long cycle of push and pull interactions" (Tashiro, 2014, p. 196). Alternatively, when adult closeness begins for an avoidant-attached individual, it is not uncommon for that person to leave or shut down emotionally because of the anticipation of not being cared for and a desire to eliminate further pain (Tashiro, 2014), often limiting their ability to become close to others (Atkinson, 2005, 2014). For some individuals, being alone is easier than having unmet expectations. In fact, avoidant attachment may not lead to falling in love or a relationship commitment because individuals may be guarded and fearful (Stanley, Rhoades, & Whitton, 2010). Ultimately, the type of attachment bonds in adult romantic relationships contribute to the overall health and satisfaction of a marriage (Stanley, Rhoades, & Whitton, 2010) or other long-term intimate partner relationship.

It is also important to consider how attachment might affect self-esteem and thereby impact love. As indicated by Acevedo and Aron (2009), individuals with secure attachment experience tend to have higher self-esteem, leading to greater confidence in themselves and in their partner, resulting in mutual support and development. This yields an increase in security related to the adult love relationship. The opposite is true of anxiously attached individuals, who may have a greater chance of experiencing obsessive or anxious love (Acevedo & Aron, 2009), or the avoidant-attached individual who may not fully engage in love to begin with.

In sum, attachment is innate in humans, but the style is learned through our experiences. Attachment is viewed by some as the first and most important instinct of humans – a requirement for care, connection, and survival that doesn't end in childhood, but continues in our adult relationships and throughout our lives (Johnson, 2013). The attachment experienced by each individual can provide clues to the stability and quality of that particular relationship. Ultimately, FORL can be understood, at least in part, by examining attachment styles and exploring how they promote or undermine romantic relationship satisfaction. A limitation of attachment theory is that it does not specifically address FORL. However, as found by Aron, Aron, and Allen (1998) those experiencing the highest rates of unreciprocated love were individuals with an anxious attachment style. Although this is helpful information, most individuals are unaware of their personal attachment style or that of their partner and, more broadly, are not well-informed regarding attachment and relationship outcomes. For a useful web questionnaire designed to measure attachment style across a variety of close relationships (mother, father, romantic partner and friend) go to: www.yourpersonality.net/relstructures/ (Fraley, n.d.a). For attachment style specific to a romantic partner go to: www.web-research-design.net/cgi-bin/crq/crq.pl   (Fraley,   n.d.b). These questionnaires were designed by psychologist Chris Fraley, based off the Experiences in Close Relationships-Relationships Structures Questionnaire (ECR-RS) (Fraley et al., 2011) and the Experiences in Close Relationships-Revised Questionnaire (ECR-R) (Fraley, Waller, & Brennan, 2000).

Social Exchange Theory

In the late 1950s, *social exchange theory*, which views social behavior as an exchange of goods, was introduced by sociologist George Homans (1958). Around the same time, social psychologists Thibaut and Kelley (1959) were developing a similar framework. Although originally based on an economic model, the theory was first applied to marriages by Levinger (1965). The tenets of social exchange theory, including maximizing rewards and minimizing consequences, are useful in understanding relationships and the phenomenon of FORL.

Social exchange theory asserts that all human relationships are formed and maintained by a subjective cost/benefit analysis and a comparison of alternatives. A relationship thus may only develop if both parties believe the rewards and costs are balanced more sufficiently than for competing alternatives such as singlehood, or a different partner (Sabatelli & Ripoll, 2004).

Some scholars question the applicability of social exchange theory, which is based on rational, sensible consideration of costs and rewards, to intimate partner relationships (see Cutrona, 2004), which are often consumed by the illogical nature of passionate love. However, I propose social exchange theory *can* be applied to intimate partner relationships and FORL. If an individual has FORL with a partner, it can be assumed that passionate love has dissolved; therefore, the individual would not be disillusioned by illogical beliefs of early love, giving way to a more realistic assessment of their partner and the situation and a potentially more logical assessment of costs and benefits.

The rewards or consequences perceived by individuals in relationships span a wide range of considerations (e.g., finances, housing, insurance benefits, children, emotional connection, sexual attraction), none of which are of greater or lesser value. The perception of what constitutes a benefit or liability varies from person to person. For example, sexual attraction may be the most important reward to one individual while financial security may be most important to another. Usually, many reward mechanisms are simultaneously at play in any given relationship. Due to the complex nature of relationships, even the most straightforward costs and benefits can get entangled in subtle nuances, which can lead to periods of confusion and ambivalence.

"Ultimately, relationships characterized by low levels of attraction, a small number of barriers, and attractive alternatives are likely to end in dissolution, according to proponents of the social exchange theory" (Rodrigues, Hall, & Fincham, 2006, p. 85). In other words, if an individual perceives the costs of a relationship to be greater than its benefits, they may choose to leave. Alternatively, the individual may choose to continue the relationship, unsatisfied, if he or she believes that the exit is compromised because of finances, religious views, obligations to children, or other conflicts. It is useful to acknowledge that relationship satisfaction and standards are based on a comparison level that is influenced by an individual's personal experiences and expectations related to what one feels is deserved (Hurt, 2014). A final important concept in social exchange theory is the *principle of least interest*, which asserts that the partner who is the least dependent, has the least emotional involvement, and is the least committed also has the most power in the relationship (Lamanna, Riedmann, & Stewart, 2018).

As summed up nicely by West, Turner, and Zhao (2010), social exchange theory asserts three primary assumptions about human nature: 1) people seek rewards and avoid punishments; 2) people are rational beings; 3) the criteria used to evaluate rewards and costs varies over time and from person to person. In conclusion, social exchange theory in its simplest form can help explain FORL, through the cost/benefit analysis of relationships, despite its historical underpinnings as an economic model.

Sternberg's Triangular Theory of Love

Sternberg's Triangular Theory of Love (Sternberg, 1986) was introduced in Chapter 1, but will be described in greater detail due to its significance in understanding FORL. Sternberg uses a triangle to depict three main components of intimate partner love: intimacy (emotional connection), passion (physical desire), and commitment (decision). He posited that a love relationship could have any combination of these three, creating eight different types of love relationships: non-love, friendship/liking, infatuated love, empty love, companionate love, fatuous love, romantic love, and consummate love. For example, a relationship containing none of the three aspects would create *non-love*. With non-love, there is no commitment, as well as no connection emotionally or physically – it is likely this type of relationship will end. If an individual has only emotional intimacy, but no physical attraction (passion) for another, the result would be *liking* or *friendship*. Alternatively, *infatuated love* only includes physical attraction. *Empty love* contends there is only commitment (i.e., an arranged marriage, or a more complete love that has dissipated). A combination of emotional intimacy and commitment results in *companionate love* – the commitment factor makes it a stronger bond than friendship. Having both intimacy (emotional connection) and passion (physical attraction) creates *romantic love*, which may be a more serious relationship, such as a long-term dating couple, or not as serious (i.e., a one-night stand). Finally, having all three produces *consummate love* – the ideal situation for most long-term love relationships. As a reminder, in Sternberg's view, the difference between consummate and romantic love is the added factor of commitment for consummate love. Commitment reflects a decision to stay together long-term but is not essential to romantic love. An example would be a dating or cohabitating couple who may be very romantically in love but have not yet committed to marriage. For the purpose of this conversation, however, Sternberg's categories of consummate love and romantic love are interchangeable and are equivalent to the state of being romantically in-love, and at risk of FORL.

Sternberg (1986) provided an important distinction to the three components of love with respect to intimacy, passion, and commitment:

> the emotional and other involvement of the intimacy component and the cognitive commitment of the decision/commitment component seem to be relatively stable in close relationships,

whereas the motivational and other arousal of the passion component tends to be relatively unstable and to come and go on a somewhat unpredictable basis.

(p. 120)

Sternberg went on to say that emotional intimacy and commitment are generally within some degree of conscious control, but there is very little control over sexual desire or physical attraction to another. Additionally, although they are separate components, the three interact: "For example, greater intimacy may lead to greater passion or commitment, just as greater commitment may lead to greater intimacy or, with lesser likelihood, greater passion" (Sternberg & Weis, 2006, p. 186).

Sternberg asserted that it may be easier to arrive at consummate love (or romantic love) than to maintain it, due to the difficulty of expressing the three components of love over time (Sternberg, 1987). Feelings of intimacy, passion, or commitment are expressed by action, and action in turn reinforces feelings; however, if actions or feelings cease to exist and love is not expressed in any one area, consummate love may die (Sternberg, 1987). While Sternberg's Triangular Theory of Love (1986) has been a useful resource in identifying and conceptualizing the type of love in any love relationship, it does, however, pose a limitation in that it does not address how to deal with FORL once it has taken place.

In conclusion, Sternberg's Triangular Theory of Love identifies three components of love (intimacy, passion, and commitment), each of which is strongly associated with relationship happiness and satisfaction, and in different combinations forms eight types of love (i.e., non-love, friendship, infatuated love, empty love, romantic love, companionate love, fatuous love, and consummate love) in intimate partner relationships (Sternberg & Weis, 2006). This theory provides a framework for understanding FORL, which could occur if any of the components were lost, or if there had never been one or more of the components in the relationship to start. It is worth noting that relationships are generally categorically in flux, even if only slightly, due to individual changes in the level of each component, and it is unlikely that any couple fits purely into one category, because of subtle differences in the amount of each component that may exist in any relationship (Sternberg & Weis, 2006).

Summary

Theory is important for providing understanding of human complexities. FORL has not been adequately researched, leaving many couples, mental health providers, and relationship professionals at a loss, demonstrating the need for a comprehensive theoretical framework. When in combination, six theories, chosen for their individual aspects, assist in our conceptualization of FORL. General Systems Theory, biopsychosocial model, biological/evolutionary theory of love (including non-conscious processes), attachment theory, social exchange theory, and Sternberg's Triangular Theory of Love comprise the Megatheory of FORL: Romantic Relationship Formation, Maintenance, and Outcomes. The six components comprising the theory have a twister-like structure, taking the form of a tornado, which highlights the complex dynamics and numerous variables involved in romantic relationships and FORL.

General Systems Theory (GST) provides the foundational roots of complex systems and is considered the bedrock for the Megatheory. The defining features of General Systems Theory are that all parts, both inside and outside of a system, interact to make something new yet are in constant change and flux (von Bertalanffy, 1968). GST applies to FORL because of the enormous complexity and interaction of variables.

Next, biopsychosocial approach, built on the tenets of General Systems Theory, considers the interplay of biological, psychological, and sociocultural factors for understanding complex phenomena including human relationships. The biopsychosocial approach is applicable to the discussion of FORL because biological, psychological, and sociocultural factors contribute to relationship formation, maintenance, and outcomes, including FORL.

Third, biological/evolutionary theories of love postulate that love is biologically innate in all human beings for the continuance of the human race. Physical and psychological features and traits are fine-tuned throughout the course of human history, specifically to ensure life and reproduction. Further, unconscious processes combine with conscious decisions to assist with survival (Kenrick, 2006). Love and relationships can seem confusing and illogical, based on hidden yet innate biological drives and processes (see Bargh, 2017). Biological/evolutionary theories of love are included in the Megatheory of FORL because confusion and frustration have also been found in the experience FORL, suggesting similar processes may be at play. It was also included because understanding how and why love begins is likely useful in understanding its end.

Fourth, attachment theory is based on the evolutionary, inborn motivational system of children to illicit nurturing from caregivers, which extends to adult relationships. People generally form significant attachments to a small number of people at every phase of life, producing strong affectional bonds, which are thought to be innate and biologically driven for the advancement of the species (Bowlby, 1979). Attachment theory is useful for conceptualizing FORL because individual attachment styles are an important contribution to understanding adult romantic relationships, including their success or failure.

Fifth, social exchange theory suggests romantic relationships are based on a comparison of rewards and costs, as well as available alternatives (Homans, 1958). Relationships will only form and sustain if partners believe that the rewards of being romantically involved outweigh the costs and other alternatives (e.g., singlehood) are not as attractive (Sabatelli & Ripoll, 2004). For this reason, social exchange theory is useful in conceptualization of FORL.

Finally, Sternberg's Triangular Theory of Love (Sternberg, 1986; Sternberg, 2006), comprised of passion (physical connection), intimacy (emotional connection), and commitment (decision), classifies eight different types of love specific to intimate partner relationships. Sternberg asserts that consummate love, comprising passion, intimacy, and commitment, is ideal for marriage, yet may be difficult to maintain. As used throughout this book, consummate love is equivalent to romantic love. Intimacy, passion, and commitment are strongly linked to relationship happiness and satisfaction (Sternberg, 2006), thus, these dimensions are significant to consider in the study of FORL.

Theory is meant to be tested and built upon. It is believed this new integrated theoretical framework will provide a starting point for a more complete understanding of FORL, as well as other love outcomes, in the context of intimate partner relationships. Greater availability of evidence-based literature and informed treatment recommendations would be of enormous benefit to practitioners and those affected by the experience of FORL.

Exploration Questions

1 Explain your personal experience and general feelings associated with "theory." List three reasons why theory can be important or useful.
2 How might insecure attachments (i.e., anxious attachment, avoidant attachment) in childhood impact adult love relationships?
3 Non-conscious processes apply to love and relationships and are weaved throughout this chapter (i.e., biological/ evolutionary theory, attachment theory). How do you

think unconscious processes may have guided your personal romantic relationships?

Key Concepts

anxious attachment	holism
avoidant attachment	the Megatheory of FORL
biopsychosocial approach	the principle of least interest
the biological/evolutionary theories of love	social exchange theory
the Drive to Love	secure attachment
decision biases	the Dynamical Evolutionary View of Love theory
General Systems Theory	open system
secure attachment	

References

Acevedo, B. P. & Aron, A. (2009). Does a long-term relationship kill romantic love? *Review of General Psychology*, *13*(1), 59–65.

Ackerman, D. (1994). *A natural history of love*. New York: Random House.

Ainsworth, M. D. S., Blehar, M., Waters, E., & Wall, S. (1978). *Patterns of attachment: A psychological study of the strange situation*. Hillsdale, NJ: Lawrence Erlbaum Associates Inc.

Aron, A., Aron, E., & Allen, J. (1998). Motivations for unreciprocated love. *Personality & Social Psychology Bulletin*, *24*(8), 787–796.

Atkinson, B. (2005). *Emotional intelligence*. New York: Norton.

Atkinson, B. (2014, January/February). The great deception: We're less in control than we think. *Psychotherapy Networker*. Retrieved July 9, 2018 from www.psychotherapynetworker.org/magazine/article/142/the-greatdeception.

Bargh, J. A. (2017). *Before you know it: The unconscious reasons we do what we do*. New York: Simon & Schuster, Inc.

Bargh, J. A., Chaiken, S., Raymond, P., & Hymes, C. (1996). The automatic evaluation effect: Unconditional automatic attitude activation with a pronunciation task. *Journal of Experimental Social Psychology, 32*(1), 104–128.

Bartels, A. & Zeki, S. (2000). The neural basis of romantic love. *Neurore-port*, *11*(17), 3829–3834.

Bartels, A. & Zeki, S. (2004). The neural correlates of maternal and romantic love. *Neuroimage*, *21*(3), 1155–1166.

Berscheid, E. S. & Regan, P. C. (2005). *Psychology of interpersonal relationships*. Upper Saddle River, NJ: Pearson Education.

Bowlby, J. (1979). *The making and breaking of affectional bonds*. London: Tavistock.

Bowlby, J. (1980). *Attachment and loss: Loss, sadness and depression* (Vol. 3). New York: Basic Books.

Breatherton, I. & Munholland, K. A. (1999). Internal working models in attachment relationships: A construct revisited. In J. Cassidy & S. Pr (eds), *Handbook of attachment: Theory, research and clinical applications* (pp. 89–114). New York: Guilford Press.

Buss, D. M. (2006). The evolution of love. In R. J. Sternberg & K. Weis (eds), *The new psychology of love* (pp. 65–86). New Haven, CT: Yale University Press.

Comaford, C. (2017). *Why smart people make stupid decisions*. Retrieved September 10, 2018 from www.forbes.com/sites/christinecomaford/2017/03/11/why-smart-people-make-stupid-decisions/#4f83385f5405.

Cutrona, C. E. (2004). A psychological perspective: Marriage and the social provisions of relationships. *Journal of Marriage and Family*, *66*(4), 992–999.

Darwin, C. (1859). *On the origin of species by means of natural selection, or preservation of favoured races in the struggle for life*. London: John Murray.

Davila, J. & Bradbury, T. N. (2001). Attachment insecurity and the distinction between unhappy spouses who do and do not divorce. *Journal of Family Psychology*, *15*(3), 371–393.

Eastwick, P. W., Eagly, A. H., Finkel, E. J., & Johnson, S. E. (2011). Implicit and explicit preferences for physical attractiveness in a romantic partner: A double dissociation in predictive validity. *Journal of Personality and Social Psychology*, *101*(5), 993–1011.

Ein-Dor, T., Mikulincer, M., Doron, G., & Shaver, P. R. (2010). The attachment paradox how can so many of us (the insecure ones) have no adaptive advantages? *Perspectives on Psychological Science*, *5*(2), 123–141.

Engel, G. L. (1977). The need for a new medical model: A challenge for biomedicine. *Science*, *196*(4286), 129–136.

Fisher, H. (1998). Lust, attraction, and attachment in mammalian reproduction. *Human Nature*, *9*(1), 23–52.

Fisher, H. (2004). *Why we love: The nature and chemistry of romantic love*. New York: Henry Holt.

Fisher, H. (2006). The drive to love: The neural mechanism for mate selection. In R. J. Sternberg & K. Weis (eds), *The new psychology of love* (pp. 87–115). New Haven, CT: Yale University Press.

Fisher, H. (2014). Broken hearts: The nature and risks of romantic rejection. In A. C. Crouter & A. Booth (eds), *Romance and sex in adolescence and emerging adulthood: Risks and opportunities* (pp. 3–22). New York: Psychology Press.

Fisher, H., Aron, A., Mashek, D., Strong, G., Li., H., & Brown, L. L. (2003). Early-stage intense romantic love activates cortical-basal-ganglia reward/motivation, emotion and attention systems: An fMRI study of a dynamic network that varies with relationship length, passion intensity and gender. *Society for Neuroscience Abstracts, 725,* 27.

Fisher, H. E., Aron, A., & Brown, L. L. (2006). Romantic love: A mammalian brain system for mate choice. *Philosophical Transactions of the Royal Society B: Biological Sciences, 361*(1476), 2173–2186.

Fisher, H. E., Aron, A., Mashek, D., Li, H., & Brown, L. L. (2002). Defining the brain systems of lust, romantic attraction, and attachment. *Archives of Sexual Behavior, 31*(5), 413–419.

Fraley, R. C. (n.d.a). Relationship structures-attachment styles across relationships. Retrieved August 12, 2018 from www.yourpersonality.net /relstructures/.

Fraley, R. C. (n.d.b). Attachment styles and close relationships. Retrieved August 12, 2018 from www.webresearch-design.net/cgi-bin /crq/crq.pl.

Fraley, R. C., Heffernan, M. E., Vicary, A. M., & Brumbaugh, C. C. (2011). The experiences in close relationships – Relationship Structures Questionnaire: A method for assessing attachment orientations across relationships. *Psychological Assessment, 23*(3), 615–625.

Fraley, R. C. & Shaver, P. R. (2000). Adult romantic attachment: Theoretical developments, emerging controversies, and unanswered questions. *Review of General Psychology, 4*(2), 132–154.

Fraley, R. C., Waller, N. G., & Brennan, K. A. (2000). An item response theory analysis of self-report measures of adult attachment. *Journal of Personality and Social Psychology, 78*(2), 350–365.

Freud, S. (1895 [1954]). The project of a scientific psychology. In M. Bonaparte et al. (eds), *The origins of psychoanalysis.* New York: Basic Books.

Freud, S. (1915). The unconscious. The standard edition of the complete psychological works of Sigmund Freud, Volume XIV (1914–1916): On the history of the psycho-analytic movement, papers on metapsychology and other works. London: The Hagarth Press.

Fugère, M. A. (2016, August 2). *Why your perfect partner doesn't need to be ideal.* Retrieved September 19, 2018 from www.psychologytoday.com/us/ blog/dating-and-mating/201608/why-your-perfect-partner-doesnt-need-be-ideal?amp.

Garner, M., Wagner, C., & Kawulich, B. (Eds.). (2016). *Teaching research methods in the social sciences.* New York: Routledge.

Gauchou, H. L., Rensink, R. A., & Fels, S. (2012). Expression of nonconscious knowledge via ideomotor actions. *Consciousness and Cognition, 21*(2), 976–982.

Hatfield, E. & Rapson, R. L. (1996). *Love and sex: Cross-cultural perspectives.* Boston, MA: Allyn & Bacon.

Hazan, C. & Diamond, L. M. (2000). The place of attachment in human mating. *Review of General Psychology, 4*(2), 186.

Hazan, C. & Shaver, P. (1987). Romantic love conceptualized as an attachment process. *Journal of Personality and Social Psychology, 52*(3), 511–524.

Homans, G. C. (1958). Social behavior as exchange. *American Journal of Sociology, 63*(6), 597–606.

Hurt, T. R. (2014). Black men and the decision to marry. *Marriage & Family Review, 50*(6), 447–479.

Johnson, S. (2013). *Love sense: The revolutionary new science of romantic relationships*. New York: Little Brown and Company.

Kenrick, D. T. (2006). A dynamical evolutionary view of love. In R. J. Sternberg & K. Weis (eds), *The new psychology of vove* (pp. 15–34). New Haven, CT: Yale University Press.

Lamanna, M. A. & Riedmann, A. (2012). *Marriages, families, and relationships: Making choices in a diverse society*, 11th edn. Belmont, CA: Cengage Learning.

Lamanna, M. A., Riedmann, A., & Stewart, S. (2018). *Marriages, families, and relationships: Making choices in a diverse society*. Boston, MA: Centage Learning.

Levinger, G. (1965). Marital cohesiveness and dissolution: An integrative review. *Journal of Marriage and the Family, 27*(1), 19–28.

Melchert, T. P. (2011). *Foundations of professional psychology: The end of theoretical orientations and the emergence of the biopsychosocial approach*. London: Elsevier.

Morgan, R. (2009). *Simple truth: The whole is greater than the sum of its parts*. Bloomington, IN: iUniverse.

Newman, B. M. & Newman, P. R. (2007). *Theories of human development*. Mahwah, NJ: Lawrence Erlbaum Associates, Inc.

Nichols M. P. & Schwartz, R. C. (1995). *Family therapy: Concepts and methods*, 3rd edn. Boston, MA: Allyn & Bacon.

Perilloux, H. K., Webster, G. D., & Gaulin, S. J. (2010). Signals of genetic quality and maternal investment capacity: The dynamic effects of fluctuating asymmetry and waist-to-hip ratio on men's ratings of women's attractiveness. *Social Psychological and Personality Science, 1*(1), 34–42.

Prior V. & Glaser, D. (2006). *Understanding attachment and attachment disorders: Theory, evidence and practice*. Philadelphia, PA: Jessica Kingsley Publishers.

Regan, P. C. (2011). *Close relationships*. New York: Routledge.

Regan, P. C. (2017). *The mating game: A primer on love, sex, and marriage*, 3rd edn. Thousand Oaks, CA: Sage.

Rodrigues, A. E., Hall, J. H., & Fincham, F. D. (2006). What predicts divorce and relationship dissolution? In M. A. Fine & J. Harvey (eds), *Handbook of divorce and relationship dissolution* (pp. 85–112). Mahwah, NJ: Lawrence Erlbaum.

Sabatelli, R. M. & Ripoll, K. (2004). Variations in marriage over time: An ecological/exchange perspective. In M. Coleman & L. H. Ganong (eds), *Handbook of contemporary family: Considering the past, contemplating the future* (pp. 79–94). Thousand Oaks, CA: Sage.

Santrock, J. W. (2007). *A topical approach to human life-span development*, 3rd edn. St. Louis, MO: McGraw-Hill.

Schacter, D. L. (1987). Implicit memory: History and current status (PDF). *Journal of Experimental Psychology: Learning, Memory, and Cognition, 13*, 501–518.

Simpson, J. A. (1990). Influence of attachment styles on romantic relationships. *Journal of Personality and Social Psychology, 59*(5), 971.

Stanley, S. M., Rhoades, G. K., & Whitton, S. W. (2010). Commitment: Functions, formation, and the securing of romantic attachment. *Journal of Family Theory & Review, 2*(4), 243–257.

Sternberg, K. (2014). *Psychology of love 101*. New York: Springer.

Sternberg, R. J. (1986). A triangular theory of love. *Psychological Review*, *93*(2), 119.

Sternberg, R. J. (1987). Liking versus loving: A comparative evaluation of theories. *Psychological Bulletin*, *102*(3), 331–345.

Sternberg, R. J. & Weis, K. (eds) (2006). *The new psychology of love*. New Haven, CT: Yale University Press.

Tashiro, T. (2014). *The science of happily ever after: What really matters in the quest for enduring love*. Don Mills, ON: Harlequin.

Thibaut, J. W. & Kelley, H. H. (1959). *The social psychology of groups*. New York: Wiley.

Thornhill, R., Gangestad, S. W., Miller, R., Scheyd, G., McCollough, J. K., & Franklin, M. (2003). Major histocompatibility complex genes, symmetry, and body scent attractiveness in men and women. *Behavioral Ecology*, *14*(5), 668–678.

von Bertalanffy, L. (1968). *General systems theory: Foundations, development, applications*. New York: George Braziller.

West, R. L., Turner, L. H., & Zhao, G. (2010). *Introducing communication theory: Analysis and application* (Vol. 2). New York: McGraw-Hill.

Westen, D. (1999). The scientific status of unconscious processes: Is Freud really dead? *Journal of the American Psychoanalytic Association*, *47*(4), 1061–1106.

Wilson, T. D. (2004). *Strangers to ourselves*. Cambridge, MA: Harvard University Press.

Yovell, Y. (2008). Is there a drive to love? *Neuropsychoanalysis*, *10*(2), 117–144.

PART II

Matters of the Heart
Why Do People Fall Out of Love?

Does Romantic Love Endure?

"When nothing is sure, everything is possible."

Margaret Drabble

I remember the psychology and human development courses from my undergraduate years at Iowa State in the early 1990s. The messages about love and long-term intimate partner relationships were that love changes – not if, but when. Specifically, passionate love wanes and is replaced by companionate love (Berscheid & Walster, 1978; Cancian, 1987; Coleman, 1977; D'Emilio & Freedman, 1988; Hatfield & Walster, 1978; Safilios-Rothschild, 1977; Sternberg, 1988). This viewpoint is still alive and well (Mitchell, 2002). Although it didn't strike me until recently, either romantic love wasn't discussed in my coursework or it wasn't memorable enough to remember. There is now data suggesting that romantic love, comprised of emotional connection and sexual desire, is a major player in relationships and can indeed endure, at least for some (see Ben- Zeév, 2017; Montgomery & Sorell, 1997).

For example, in a meta-analysis of 25 independent studies, Acevedo and Aron (2009) found that romantic love, including sexual attraction and intensity (without obsessive thinking of early love), can last in some long-term relationships. Further, O'Leary et al. (2012) described a random sample of 274 married adults where a whopping 40 percent of individuals married longer than ten years reported being intensely in-love, including "thinking positively about the partner and thinking about the partner when apart, affectionate behaviors and sexual intercourse, shared novel and challenging activities, and general life happiness" (p. 241). In a separate study, 29 percent of individuals in a random sample of 322 New Yorkers, also married over ten years, reported being very intensely in-love (O'Leary et al., 2012). Further, Montgomery and Sorell (1997) found romantic love present across four family life stages, including married adults with children in the home as well as those with launched children. Ultimately, "passion and friendship/companionship are not consecutive in a romantic relationship after all – rather, they appear to exist concurrently, in both dating and married life stage groups" (Montgomery & Sorell, 1997, p. 60).

Despite these promising studies, it's difficult to ignore the divorce rates discussed in previous chapters. Overall, the evidence continues to be mixed as to the longevity of romantic love. As a reminder, such love should not be confused with passionate love of first attraction, which includes anxiety, obsession, and uncertainty, generally only lasting a few weeks or a few years at best (Ackerman, 1994; Crooks & Baur, 2014; Sternberg, 1986). Worth re-stating, some suggest the historical views of romantic love's long-term failure are due to confusing definitions and terminology, mixing romantic love with passionate love (Acevedo & Aron, 2009).

Difficulties of Sustaining Romantic Love

There are several reasons why people, today, suggest romantic love cannot be sustained long-term, or at the very least is difficult to maintain. These ideas will be introduced here but flushed out in greater detail as the chapter continues. First, marriage itself may affect romantic love due to factors typical of long-term unions, such as habituation. Related is the idea that desire does not exist easily alongside deep love (Perel, 2006). Simply put, desire is *to want*, and love is *to have* – to want what you already have can be a trying paradox (Perel, 2017). A similar notion is that romance and desire are driven by sex, creating difficulty with incorporating other, more grounded elements of a relationship. As described by Mitchell (2002), "In its raw form, lust is not a pretty thing and is difficult to reconcile with other features of romantic love, such as respect and admiration" (p. 27). A second popular idea is that our emotional attachments to our partners are essential to sustaining a long-term relationship, but these attachments are often insecure, injured, or lost entirely (Johnson, 2013), making it difficult to maintain the relationship. Next, some believe the very traits we initially seek in our partners turn out to be what lead to its demise (i.e., spontaneity becomes viewed as flighty) (Felmlee, 1995). Finally, as discussed previously, some view sexual desire, a main component of romantic love, as difficult to predict and control, and not likely to last (Sternberg, 1987).

Desire and Deep Love Struggle to Co-Exist

In respect to FORL, it is possible the institution of marriage itself alters feelings of romantic love for a spouse. As discussed in previous chapters, couples are now marrying for love – specifically romantic love. Yet, some experts suggest that from the beginning of time people have struggled to combine love and commitment with desire and sexual excitement, at least for any length of time (Mitchell, 2002; Perel 2006). In fact, Sims and Meana (2010) suggest that long-term relationships have a dampening effect on sexual desire and satisfaction, even in the absence of other relationship problems, implying a natural reduction of romantic love over time. The reasons found for this wet-blanket effect include, "the institutionalization of the relationship, over-familiarity with one's partner, and the de-sexualization of roles in their relationships" (Sims & Meana, 2010, p. 364). Other researchers also regarded habituation, familiarity, and interdependence conflicts as factors causing a reduction in or loss of romantic love (Berscheid & Hatfield, 1969; Sternberg, 1986).

Further, psychotherapist Esther Perel (2006), in her popular relationship book *Mating in Captivity*, identifies a paradox between emotional intimacy and sexual desire, explaining why many couples have trouble sustaining both in long-term unions. As described by the author, the two constructs are not easily compatible. Although people yearn to truly know another and be known and feel the safety and security of spending life with their best friend, this is the very thing that extinguishes passion and desire, according to Perel (2006). The author discusses that ultimately, for many, closeness and friendship does not lead to good sex, and, unfortunately, attempts at increasing emotional intimacy often do not change the level of sexual desire. "When intimacy collapses into fusion, it is not a lack of closeness but too much closeness that impedes desire ... thus separateness is a precondition for connection: this is the essential paradox of intimacy and sex" (Perel, 2006 p. 25).

Emotional Attachment and Connection Can Be Difficult to Maintain

Love Sense: The Revolutionary New Science of Romantic Relationships, by Sue Johnson (2013), is a well-known relationship book, based on the therapeutic framework, *emotionally focused couples therapy* (EFT). Sue Johnson and Leslie Greenberg (1988) are the founders of EFT, which suggests the lack of emotional connection, caused by faltering attachment bonds, should be the focus of struggling marriages. In this view, emotional connection, or lack thereof, causes the demise of romantic love in long-term relationships. In contrast to Perel's (2006) perspective, Johnson (2013) states, "it is not good sex that leads to satisfying, secure relationships but rather secure love that leads to good-and, in fact, the best-sex" (p. 21). Chances are, both views have something to offer (see Chapter 12 on recommendations). Herein lies the tricky part for both couples and clinicians when deciding which direction to go. Just as there is not one path to FORL, there does not appear to be one way to address it.

What Goes Up, Often Comes Down

When it comes to relationships, "what comes up, often comes down" (Buss, 2006, p. 75). Sometimes, the qualities a person chooses in a mate cease to exist, and the relationship becomes dissatisfying (Buss, 2006). The term *fatal attractions* describes partner traits that appear desirable at the onset of a relationship, but later become significant problems in the union (Nicholson, 2017). In a study by leading fatal attraction researcher Diane Felmlee (1995), relationships of 300 participants were assessed and an impressive one-third of the relationships ended because of a fatal attraction. All types of partner characteristics can result in fatal attractions; however, the traits *different* or *exciting* resulted in the most fatal attractions, presumably because they were too dissimilar to their partner. These were followed by the traits *fun* and *easy-going*, likely to be seen as lacking in seriousness or maturity later on; *caring*, which was subsequently viewed as jealous and possessive; and *competent*, often perceived later as egotistical. Physically attractive traits were the least likely to result in fatal attractions, as they are thought to be somewhat more stable (i.e., nice smile), although these may also change over the long haul. *Openness* was also less likely to turn sour, as people tend to appreciate expressiveness over time. Although as stated earlier, no characteristic is immune from being a possible fatal attraction. Fatal attractions can affect romantic love by altering the level of emotional connection or sexual desire.

Sexual Desire and Attraction is Fickle

The role of attraction in the initiation of a romantic relationship has been researched extensively, yet research into attraction in long-term relationships, including change of attraction, as well as attraction as a precursor to dissatisfaction, has been meager (see Mark & Herbenick, 2014; Huston & Levinger, 1978). To complicate things even further, like love, the term attraction is often not well defined and is generally in the eye of the beholder. Further, attraction can take many forms (i.e., physical attraction, sexual attraction, intellectual attraction, general/non-specified attraction, etc.). For example, although physical traits are a significant factor in initial attraction, there are additional variables comprising attraction in long-term relationships such as honesty, intelligence, emotional stability, and desirable character (see Mark & Herbenick, 2014; Regan & Berscheid, 1997; Sprecher, Sullivan, & Hatfield, 1994).

Sexual attraction and desire often, but not always, follow physical attraction. For example, it's possible to be physically attracted to someone but not sexually attracted to them. Further, you can have passion and great sex with one person and emotional attachment but no sex with someone entirely different (Fisher, 1998). We have learned in previous chapters that sexual desire and attraction for one's partner is important for romantic love. Some evidence indicates that although romantic attraction may continue to endure in some cases, overall it fades (Fisher, 2006). And sexual desire generally declines in long-term relationships (Basson et al., 2005; see Baumeister & Bratslavsky, 1999; Fisher, 2006; Impett, Muise, & Peragine, 2014; see Muise et al., 2013), and is often variable and difficult to control (Sternberg, 1986). However, according to Acevedo and Aron (2009), even though sexual desire typically declines, it is not always inevitable. Unfortunately, although scholars know sexual desire is important in romantic relationships "almost no research has considered the factors that enable couples to maintain desire over the long term" (Muise et al., 2013).

Perhaps we too easily assume attraction and sexual desire for our partner is permanent – once attracted, always attracted. Looking back on the conversation I had with my sister in Europe about relationship vulnerability, I remember wishing there was an invisible lock on the hearts and minds of couples in love, so that nothing could ever change. If only it were that simple!

Does Romantic Love Endure? Yes, No, Maybe; it Depends

In this chapter, we have seen an abundance of conflicting information about the longevity of romantic love. Although there is some research suggesting the endurance of romantic love, there is limited information about the mechanisms by which it was sustained by the participants in those studies. A review of the common problems associated with the components of long-term romantic love make it easy to understand why it is difficult for so many to maintain. Although there is no clear answer to romantic love's staying power, perhaps the very presence of conflicting evidence provides a clue that something else may be at play. Could it be that certain elements of romantic love take on varying levels of importance at different times? Perhaps relationship expectations change, and what is considered satisfying is altered, at least for a season. For example, some research suggests that after the initial bonding phase of a relationship, when love and commitment continue to build, sexual desire and activity may no longer have the importance they once did (Hinchliff & Gott, 2004; Kotler, 1985). With that said, when a relationship is struggling in non-sexual ways (i.e., communication problems, destructive personality traits), positive sexual activity can compensate for the loss of security, providing reassurance and stability to the relationship (Birnbaum & Finkel, 2015). Ultimately, the contribution sexual desire makes "varies over the course of relationship development and across individuals and circumstances" (Birnbaum & Finkel, 2015, p. 29). This also seems to be the case with the emotional aspect of romantic love. For example, when physical intimacy is lacking, emotional intimacy and connection can help bridge the gap and stabilize the relationship. In fact, there are times in relationships where emotional intimacy and support is needed at a greater level than any other aspect (i.e., during illness, grief, and loss). Ultimately, what is needed and wanted in a long-term intimate partner relationship is person- and situation-dependent.

In the same vein of unpredictability, consider sexual satisfaction as it relates to relationship satisfaction. Sexual satisfaction and relationship satisfaction tend to be positively correlated, meaning when one goes up the other trends up, and vice versa (Yeh et al., 2006). However, some sexually unsatisfied couples still enjoy overall relationship satisfaction (Durr, 2009; Edwards & Booth, 1994). In a study consisting of open-ended interviews with 19 married women who had lost sexual desire for their spouse, many of the women reported they liked or appreciated their husbands even if they were no longer sexually interested in them (Sims & Meana, 2010). This not only suggests that emotional connection may be easier to maintain than sexual interest long-term, but that emotional intimacy may be enough – at least sometimes.

As we consider long-term love, the term *endurance* suggests permanency. However, perhaps there is a more useful way to view romantic love? For example, consider the theoretical perspectives that do not focus on the endurance of love, but instead describe occasional bursts of romantic love in long-term relationships, such as the *interruption model* (Berscheid, 1983) and the *self-expansion model* (Aron & Aron, 1986). The interruption model maintains that a temporary interruption in a relationship, such as a business trip or a short-term separation, may spark passionate love. The self-expansion model suggests that mechanisms such as trying novel experiences together and learning new things with one another can promote long-term romantic love.

It's possible that some lucky couples enjoy long-term romantic love, year after year, decade after decade, without interruption. Yet based on the information to date, that would be the exception, not the rule. Ebb and flow is a natural part of changing and evolving complex systems. It appears more likely that couples who enjoy long-term romantic love also experience stretches of emotional and/or sexual *disconnection*, bridged by the resurgence of these elements at later times, allowing for the transcendence of romantic love. This may give the illusion of seamlessness.

The key to conceptualizing long-term romantic love lies in our comparison to tornadoes (see Chapter 5). Although there are many similarities, there is one main difference between tornadoes and love in intimate partner relationships. A tornado that fizzles out is a relief; however, a dried-up love relationship is not as welcomed. Instead of viewing long-term romantic love as one massive, amazing twister requiring sustainment, maybe we should look at it as a series of mini weather systems, with periods of calm in between. In comparison to weather, *passionate love* is the unpredictable, exciting whirlwind, *companionate love* represents tranquil and stable weather patterns, and *romantic love* is a delicate balance between the two. Currently, it seems passionate love cannot last forever, companionate love can last indefinitely, and romantic love ... well, anything's possible! Ultimately, like the wind, romantic love seems to vary throughout the course of long-term relationships. Sometimes it's strong and fierce, other times it's a gentle breeze, and sometimes it's quiet and still. And maybe that's okay.

Summary

Today, there is a clash in viewpoints about what to expect from romantic love throughout the course of a relationship. For some individuals, long-term romantic love seems out of reach; alternatively, there are couples who sustain it quite well. The answer to the question, can romantic love endure, appears to be "yes," "no," and "maybe."

Based on previous literature, it seems improbable for both physical and emotional aspects of long-term romantic love to be constant, non-fluctuating features. The comparison of love and tornadoes from Chapter 5 may be useful in the discussion of romantic love's endurance. More likely, romantic love exists in vacillating amounts with emotional and physical intimacy present in varying degrees across a long-term relationship, possibly disappearing then re-appearing later. With that said, romantic love may be lost and never return. Additional research is essential to better understand the longevity of romantic love.

Further, why some individuals fall out of romantic love and others, in similar circumstances, do not deserves far more exploration. Additionally, why some individuals tolerate lower emotional or physical connection than others, yet do not experience FORL (Kayser, 1993) also deserves attention. The answer to these questions most likely includes a multitude of factors and complex differences among the individuals, the couple interaction, as well as societal and environmental forces, as illustrated by the Megatheory of FORL (see Chapter 5). Ultimately, every relationship is like a snowflake, as unique as the individuals who comprise it.

Exploration Questions

1 There are some significant differences between Esther Perel's and Sue Johnson's viewpoints, yet both relationships experts are known for their work with couples. Which stance do you align with more and why?
2 What are your thoughts on fatal attractions? Are they something more people need to be aware of? How can we educate individuals on fatal attractions?
3 Do you think it is possible for both emotional intimacy and sexual desire (i.e., romantic love) to endure in a long-term romantic relationship? Why or why not?

Key Concepts

fatal attraction

interruption model

self-expansion model

References

Acevedo, B. P. & Aron, A. (2009). Does a long-term relationship kill romantic love? *Review of General Psychology*, *13*(1), 59–65.
Ackerman, D. (1994). *A natural history of love*. New York: Random House.
Aron, A. & Aron, E. N. (1986). *Love and the expansion of self: Understanding attraction and satisfaction*. Washington, DC: Hemisphere.
Basson, R., Brotto, L. A., Laan, E., Redmonod, G., & Utian, W. (2005). Assessment and management of women's sexual dysfunctions: Problematic desire and arousal. *Journal of Sexual Medicine*, *2*, 291–300.
Baumeister, R. F. & Bratslavsky, E. (1999). Passion, intimacy, and time: Passionate love as a function of change in intimacy. *Personality and Social Psychology Review*, *3*(1), 49–67.
Ben- Zeév, A. (2017). *The underrated skills that keep couples together*. Retrieved June 3, 2018 from www.psychologytoday.com/us/articles/201705/the-underrated-skills-keep-couples-together.
Berscheid, E. (1983). Emotion. In H. H. Kelley, E. Berscheid, A. Christensen, J. H. Harvey, G. Levinger, E. McClintock, L. A. Peplau, & D. R. Peterson (eds), *Close relationships* (pp. 110–168). New York: Freeman.
Berscheid, E. & Hatfield, E. (1969). *Interpersonal attraction*. New York: Addison-Wesley.
Berscheid, E. & Walster, E. (1978). *Interpersonal attraction*, 2nd edn. Reading, MA: Addison-Wesley.
Birnbaum, G. E. & Finkel, E. J. (2015). The magnetism that holds us together: Sexuality and relationship maintenance across relationship development. *Current Opinion in Psychology*, *1*, 29–33.
Buss, D. M. (2006). The evolution of love. In R. J. Sternberg & K. Weis (eds), *The new psychology of love* (pp. 65–86). New Haven, CT: Yale University Press.
Cancian, F. M. (1987). *Love in America: Gender and self-development*. New York: Cambridge.
Coleman, S. B. (1977). A developmental stage hypothesis for non-marital dyadic relationships. *Journal of Marital and Family Therapy*, *3*(2), 71–76.
Crooks, R. & Baur, K. (2014). *Our sexuality*, 12th edn. Belmont, CA: Wadsworth.
D'Emilio, J. & Freedman, E. B. (1988). *Intimate matters: A history of sexuality in America*. New York: Harper & Row.
Durr, E. (2009). Women's experience of lack of sexual desire in relationships, and implications for intervention. *Social Work*, *45*(3), 256–274.
Edwards, J. N. & Booth, A. (1994). Sexuality, marriage, and well-being: The middle years. In A. S. Rossi (ed.), *Sexuality across the life course* (pp. 233–259). Chicago, IL: University of Chicago Press.
Felmlee, D. H. (1995). Fatal attractions: Affection and disaffection in intimate relationships. *Journal of Social and Personal Relationships*, *12*(2), 295–311.
Fisher, H. (1998). Lust, attraction, and attachment in mammalian reproduction. *Human Nature*, *9*(1), 23–52.
Fisher, H. (2006). The drive to love: The neural mechanism for mate selection. In R. J. Sternberg & K. Weis (eds), *The new psychology of love* (pp. 87–115). New Haven, CT: Yale University Press.

Greenberg, L. S. & Johnson, S. M. (1988). *Emotionally focused therapy for couples*. New York: Guilford Press.

Hatfield, E. & Walster, G. W. (1978). *A new look at love*. Reading, MA: Addison-Wesley.

Hinchliff, S. & Gott, M. (2004). Intimacy, commitment, and adaptation: Sexual relationships within long-term marriages. *Journal of Social and Personal Relationships, 21*(5), 595–609.

Huston, T. L. & Levinger, G. (1978). Interpersonal attraction and relationships. *Annual Review of Psychology, 29*(1), 115–156.

Impett, E. A., Muise, A., & Peragine, D. (2014). Sexuality in the context of relationships. *APA Handbook of Sexuality and Psychology, 1*, 269–315.

Johnson, S. (2013). *Love sense: The revolutionary new science of romantic relationships*. New York: Little Brown and Company.

Kayser, K. (1993). *When love dies: The process of marital disaffection*. New York: Guilford Press.

Kotler, T. (1985). Security and autonomy within marriage. *Human Relations, 38*(4), 299–321.

Mark, K. P. & Herbenick, D. (2014). The influence of attraction to partner on heterosexual women's sexual and relationship satisfaction in long-term relationships. *Archives of Sexual Behavior, 43*(3), 563–570.

Mitchell, S. (2002). *Can love last? The fate of romance over time*. New York: Norton.

Montgomery, M. J. & Sorell, G. T. (1997). Differences in love attributes across family life stages. *Family Relations, 46*, 55–61.

Muise, A., Impett, E. A., Kogan, A., & Desmarais, S. (2013). Keeping the spark alive: Being motivated to meet a partner's sexual needs sustains sexual desire in long-term romantic relationships. *Social Psychological and Personality Science, 4*(3), 267–273.

Nicholson, J. (March 12, 2017). *10 things that make someone a great romantic partner*. Retrieved June 18, 2018 from www.psychologytoday.com/us/blog/the-attraction-doctor/201703/10-things-make-someone-great-romantic-partner.

O'Leary, K. D., Acevedo, B. P., Aron, A., Huddy, L., & Mashek, D. (2012). Is long-term love more than a rare phenomenon? If so, what are its correlates? *Social Psychological and Personality Science, 3*(2), 241–249.

Perel, E. (2006). *Mating in captivity: Unlocking erotic intelligence*. New York: Harper.

Perel, E. (October 2, 2017). How to find the sweet spot between love and desire. Retrieved July 8, 2018 from www.youtube.com/watch?v=ierRipP-7JA.

Regan, P. C. & Berscheid, E. (1997). Gender differences in characteristics desired in a potential sexual and marriage partner. *Journal of Psychology & Human Sexuality, 9*(1), 25–37.

Safilios-Rothschild, C. (1977). *Love, sex, and sex roles*. Englewood Cliffs, NJ: Prentice Hall.

Sims, K. E. & Meana, M. (2010). Why did passion wane? A qualitative study of married women's attributions for declines in sexual desire. *Journal of Sex & Marital Therapy, 36*(4), 360–380.

Sprecher, S., Sullivan, Q., & Hatfield, E. (1994). Mate selection preferences: Gender differences examined in a national sample. *Journal of Personality and Social Psychology, 66*(6), 1074–1080.

Sternberg, R. J. (1986). A triangular theory of love. *Psychological Review*, *93*(2), 119.

Sternberg, R. J. (1987). Liking versus loving: A comparative evaluation of theories. *Psychological Bulletin*, *102*(3), 331–345.

Sternberg, R. J. (1988). Triangulating love. In R. J. Sternberg & M. L. Barnes (eds), *The psychology of love* (pp. 119–138). New Haven, CT: Yale University Press.

Yeh, H. C., Lorenz, F. O., Wickrama, K. A. S., Conger, R. D., & Elder, G. H., Jr. (2006). Relationships among sexual satisfaction, marital quality, and marital instability at midlife. *Journal of Family Psychology*, *20*(2), 339.

Pathways to FORL

The main goal of this chapter is to introduce the factors that are believed to contribute to FORL, based on my doctoral research (Hemesath, 2016; see Hemesath & Hurt, 2017). An additional objective is to ground and humanize the findings through direct quotes taken from participant responses. You may recognize elements in yourself or your personal relationships. Possessing similarities does not mean you are destined to experience FORL. The phenomenon of FORL is highly complex. Many of the factors described in this chapter are typical of healthy individuals and relationships; however, under certain circumstances they may lead to FORL.

The purpose of the study was to examine the lived experience of FORL by conducting in-depth interviews with individuals who reported FORL with their spouse. As a precursor to this study, I conducted focus groups with both mental health clinicians and other relationship professionals and individuals who have FORL. My hope was to gain a deeper understanding of this experience in order to assist professionals working in the context of relationships as well as those struggling with respect to FORL. Worth noting, there were no variations in the findings of this study after considering the participants' years of marriage, length of relationship prior to marriage, or age at the time of the marriage related to FORL.

Overview of the Research Sample

The study included a purposive sample of 15 participants (10 females and 5 males) who reported FORL with a spouse. A small, non-random sample is appropriate for an in-depth, qualitative investigation of an understudied experience. Eleven of the participants were legally divorced from their spouse at the time of the interview. Four of the participants were still married to the individual with whom they had FORL. However, three were separated and had filed for divorce, with no plans to reunite. One participant was still living with her spouse and was undecided about continuing the marriage. Ten of the participants were divorced once, three of the participants were divorced twice, and two of the participants were never divorced. Thirteen participants identified as White, one identified as biracial, and one identified as Hispanic. The participants moderately identified with a religion, with responses ranging from *don't identify* to *strongly identify*. The mean age was 46 years (range 36–63). All participants except one had children. The mean number of children was two. The children were both biological and adopted. The average length of marriage was 15 years (range 2–28 years). The average length of time the couple was in a relationship prior to marriage was two years and six months (range three months–seven years). The mean years of marriage when FORL occurred was 9 years (range 1–20 years). The mean interval of education post-high school was *some graduate school*, with responses ranging from *some college / technical school* to an *advanced degree beyond college*. This was a middle-class sample with a mean income of more than $70,000 (range $40,000 to over $70,000).

Factors Contributing to FORL

The data revealed that those who experience FORL arrive there by various *pathways*, each consisting of multiple *stepping stones* or factors. The following nine factors were identified as contributing to FORL.

1 Attributes brought to the relationship by each partner, including, but not limited to, family-of-origin issues, attachment styles, personality, self-awareness, past relationships, and experiences – which I fondly refer to as *the suitcase*.
2 Inadequate mate selection process (i.e., not knowing what to look for in a long-term relationship, minimizing or denying problems early in the relationship).
3 Minimal relationship rewards.
4 Lack of emotional and/or physical connection.
5 Extraneous stress (i.e., problems with in-laws, job loss).
6 Emerging realizations or awareness leading to negative thinking and/or feelings about self, spouse, or relationship.
7 Changes in participant or partner – *the wildcard*.
8 Participant and partner behaviors/negative incidents.
9 Coping deficits in the participant or their partner.

Individual Attributes: The Suitcase

One of the most significant contributing factors of FORL are the attributes each partner brings to the relationship. Many different items are found in our personal suitcases as we travel through life, including self-esteem, values, goals, emotional health, communication style, personality, previous relationship history, family-of-origin dynamics, role models, attachment styles, and more. For example, Allison describes what she brought into her relationship by way of several items: family-of-origin dynamics, attachment style, previous dating relationships, and self-esteem.

> My [mother] is very controlling ... my dad worked a ton and was not emotionally available ... I don't think I ever heard him say, "I love you," ever ... You know, when I was growing up, I thought my family had it all cause that's the way it was projected ... I had to be [perfect]. I had previously been in a relationship that was very unhealthy ... I was so ashamed ... so when my former spouse, "ex," shows up ... and is willing to help me work through things ... the criteria was he treated me well ... he's on one knee with this gargantuan diamond asking me to marry him and the weird part was, I knew at dinner this was coming and I didn't think I was ready, but I didn't know how to say "no" ... I didn't want to break the fairy tale.

Family-of-Origin Dynamics

A majority of participants (n = 10) described having inadequate relationship role models in their family of origin, which impacted the participants in a variety of ways. Sometimes they had little idea about how the adults in their home felt about each other, giving no guide for what an ideal romantic relationship should look like. Other times, their role models contributed to their knowledge base about what they *didn't* want in their own relationships.

Six participants noted particularly challenging family-of-origin dynamics, including abuse, neglect, and/or substance abuse. As recounted by Sandra, "I came from a really bad family where my dad was abusive to my mom. We were all abused ... so that was my baseline, which was pretty low." For Sandra, and others, these family-of-origin experiences set a precedence for what to avoid, instead of assisting them in knowing the qualities of healthy relationships. Alternatively, family-of-origin patterns can be repeated in future generations.

The Role of Attachment

As described in Chapter 5, attachment styles can be either secure or insecure (i.e., *anxious attachment, avoidant attachment*), with *secure attachments* having the best relationship outcomes. Research suggests that persons with avoidant attachments are prone to fear of intimacy, prefer distance in close relationships (Brennan, Shaver, & Tobey, 1991), and cope with stress by using denial or withdrawing (Dozier & Kobak, 1992). Alternatively, anxiously attached individuals are more likely to have obsessive tendencies toward romantic partners and express greater fear, anxiety, and low self-esteem (Collins & Read, 1990). Overall, those with insecure attachments have higher rates of relationship dissolution (Ein-Dor et al., 2010).

In childhood, insecure attachments stem from relationships where a bid for a caregiver's proximity or nurturance have been unreliable or rejected (Fearon et al., 2010). Childhood neglect or abuse can also result in insecure attachment (Baer & Martinez, 2006). Attachment styles can be malleable but often endure throughout life (Tashiro, 2014), affecting romantic relationships in adulthood (Hatfield & Rapson, 1996; Simpson, 1990), possibly contributing to FORL.

Approximately one-third of participants shared they had problems in adult relationships, such as difficulty getting close to others or anxious, reactive, or withdrawing behaviors – indicating insecure attachment styles. An example of early insecure attachment comes from Nicole, as she described her mom: "She's been married five times ... people have walked in and out of my life ... I don't get attached to people because who knows when they're going to leave." Doug offered a comparable perspective:

You know ... we had like the perfect bad fit that worked for us for a long time ... she really struggled with any kind of emotional [or] physical intimacy, connection, vulnerability, and so her pattern was to push away and kind of protect, and mine was to chase ... and earn the love ... which was very similar to me with my mom. She was very present in a real early part of my life and then because of an abusive relationship with my dad, really kind of withdrew and then I took care of her, and I kind of tried to earn her being more present again. So, it felt very familiar like that. Um, so, we lived in that pattern for a long time until we just, until I couldn't anymore.

Overall, individuals from certain family dynamics may struggle with adult relationships and relationship decisions. These findings are useful because previous research on this topic has not mentioned family-of-origin dynamics, attachment style, or lack of role models as possible contributors to FORL. Nonetheless, it is important to keep in mind that no families are trouble-free and individuals with problems are not always the result of undesirable family-of-origin dynamics, just as healthy, functioning individuals may not have been raised in a healthy family (Walsh, 1993).

Beyond family-of-origin experiences and attachment styles, individuals brought other elements to their relationships. Four participants described recently having exited abusive romantic relationships immediately prior to meeting their spouse and five participants discussed having low self-esteem. These attributes affected the participants' interactions and behaviors with their new partners, as well as their mate selection decisions.

The Role of Personality

The effects of personality are detected throughout the participant responses. There is substantial evidence to support the idea that an individual's personality can and does influence intimate relationships (see McCrae & Costa, 2008; Miller, 2012; Regan, 2017; Shpancer, 2016). *Personality traits* are distinguishing qualities represented by how an individual thinks, feels, and behaves across most situations. In fact, "The traits that a partner possesses before you ever start dating, such as his or her personality and values, are among the strongest indicators of whether a romantic relationship will be happy and stable many years later" (Tashiro, 2014, p. 5).

The Five-Factor Model of personality proposes the following basic traits, each representing a continuum of opposites inherent in all of us to varying degrees: 1) openness to experience (inventive/curious vs. consistent/cautious); 2) extraversion (outgoing/energetic vs. solitary/reserved); 3) conscientiousness (efficient/organized vs. unreliable/careless); 4) agreeableness (friendly/compassionate vs. lacking trust/detached); and 5) neuroticism (sensitive/nervous vs. non-reactive/confident) (McCrae & Costa, 1987). Of the five traits, openness to experience has the least effect on relationships (Miller, 2012).

Neuroticism, on the other hand, has the greatest effect on marital outcomes (Karney & Bradbury, 1995) by predicting marital dissatisfaction and divorce, as well as lower resilience after divorce (Shpancer, 2016). Although neuroticism gets a bad rap when it comes to relationships, each of the five traits could be considered positive or negative, depending on which end of the spectrum is expressed and in what combination with other traits. For example, neurotic individuals, strong in conscientiousness, may worry a lot, but they tend to use their anxiety for positive gain (i.e., concerns about getting heart disease lead to exercising more) (Chan, 2014).

The traits of high agreeableness, high conscientiousness, and low neuroticism, in one or both partners, are each linked to greater marital satisfaction (Dyrenforth et al., 2010). However, low agreeableness, low conscientiousness, and elevated extraversion could lead to sexual risk-taking (i.e., infidelity, sexual promiscuity) (Schmitt, 2004). Overall, individuals who wish to increase the likelihood of long-term relationship satisfaction should consider seeking a partner with higher agreeableness and conscientiousness, and lower neuroticism; openness does not make an impact one way or another, and extraversion has a mixed effect (i.e., extroverts are happier, but may lack relationship exclusivity) (Shpancer, 2016).

Personality, including the big five traits, have long been considered stable and relatively unchangeable (McCrae & Costa, 2008). However, research over the last few decades suggests that personality traits are malleable (see Hudson, Roberts, & Lodi-Smith, 2012). In new research, Damian et al. (2018) found evidence that personality is indeed *both* stable and changeable, over time, based on environmental factors, experiences, and personal genetics.

Personality is considered a significant factor in relationship success and stability (Miller, 2012; Regan, 2017; Tashiro, 2014). Providing support, several participants referenced aspects of their partner's personality as contributing to their relationship problems. However, this study did not specifically measure personality as it relates to FORL, nor did the previous studies on FORL (Hemesath, 2016; Hemesath & Hurt, n.d.; Kayser, 1990; Kayser, 1993; Sailor, 2006, 2013). More insight should be gained as to how the personality of both partners affect FORL. Interestingly, although personality certainly affects the quality of relationships, some research suggests attachment style is even a better predictor of relationship quality (Noftle & Shaver, 2006).

The Role of Knowing Yourself and Your Partner

Some individuals report their relationships did not last due to not knowing themselves well enough at the time of marriage (Wolfinger, 2015). Although self-awareness is certainly useful; individuals may think they know themselves, yet values, goals, and preferences often change greatly during young adult years – and can even change throughout life.

Knowing oneself and one's partner, inclusive of beliefs and personality, along with acknowledging how these factors contribute to relationship success is important, yet has been understated. Unfortunately, knowing your partner well is only as easy as they make it for you to do so. In early phases of a relationship, it's not unheard of for a potential suitor to represent themselves dishonestly, to increase the likelihood the relationship will continue. For instance, if a potential partner knows traveling is important to you, they may exaggerate or misrepresent their interest in traveling. Further, some individuals struggle with emotional vulnerability and connection attributable to personality, attachment styles, or other life experiences that affect how open an individual is (Reis, 1990). Waiting a reasonable amount of time before committing to long-term plans (i.e., marriage, cohabitation) is one way to reduce the risks of not knowing your partner.

Mate Selection

As described in Chapter 4, up until recently, marriage met the needs of the larger group, not the individual (Coontz, 2005). People married for practical purposes, often economic and out of family obligation, not for love. However, throughout the late twentieth century, marital roles diverted from traditional to more egalitarian (Boxer, Noonan, & Whelan, 2015; see Deutsch, Kokot, & Binder, 2007), the age of marriage increased, and people began marrying for individual happiness and love. As cultural and social roles and norms change, mate preferences shift due to differences in opportunities and resources (i.e., women gaining education, increased acceptance of divorce, children being born to single parents). Mate selection preferences are important, because they highlight the expectations individuals have for long-term relationships (Boxer, Noonan, & Whelan, 2015). (See Chapter 11 for tips on mate selection.)

Even with the freedom to select our own mates, "The process of choosing a mate is significant and often difficult for many single adults" (Cobb, Larson, & Watson, 2003, p. 222).

Misconceptions exist regarding mate selection (Lamanna & Riedmann, 2012). For example, Cobb, Larson, and Watson (2003) listed nine *constraining beliefs* about mate selection, including "opposites attract," "love is enough," and "I/my partner must be perfect." Constraining beliefs are inaccurate or unhelpful personal beliefs about mate selection, which limit a person's choices for a suitable partner. Unfortunately, important individual characteristics and relationship qualities necessary for successful long-term relationships are often not taken into account during mate selection (Lamanna & Riedmann, 2012), and many young adults are not sufficiently educated or prepared for marriage (Cobb, Larson, & Watson, 2003). Proper mate selection, important for relationship satisfaction and stability, includes factors such as partner interaction, social support, partner beliefs and attitudes, and individual personality and character traits (Kurdek, 2006).

What exactly do men and women seek in a mate? Boxer, Noonan, and Whelan (2015) report the following variables considered by both men and women as most important in long-term partner selection, listed in order of the five most popular responses: caring (i.e., sharing love, kindness, and affection), a likable personality (i.e., with a sense of humor, friendly), dependable, trustworthy, and intelligent. Similar attributes are reported by Regan and Berscheid (1997) and Sprecher, Sullivan, and Hatfield (1994). However, physical attraction is also an important feature to men and women in both dating and mating (Thao, Overbeek, & Engels, 2010).

In fact, *perceived attraction* is often the *first* indicator signaling interest in a potential partner (Huston & Levinger, 1978). However, attraction is subjective and changeable (see Lewandowski, Aron, & Gee, 2007). "For example, although physical attractiveness can be defined objectively, how attractive one perceives a particular individual depends in large part on how one happens to feel about him or her" (Hazan & Diamond, 2000, p. 197). Have you ever had the experience of someone becoming less attractive seemingly overnight after you witnessed their rude or arrogant behavior? Or alternatively, you get to know someone and notice their great personality and suddenly they seem far cuter? A romantic relationship that first starts as a friendship is not uncommon, and is less focused on attractiveness (Hunt, Eastwick, & Finkel, 2015). However, mutual attraction (i.e., believing someone is as interested in you as you are in them) is likely the key to falling in-love (Hazan & Diamond, 2000). Interestingly, although perhaps not surprisingly, the primary focus on physical attraction appears to decrease as people age (Boxer, Noonan, & Whelan, 2015).

Beyond these elements, familiarity and similarity are central factors in attraction (Bargh, 2017; see Berscheid & Reis, 1998), for example, living close in proximity to one another and having similar interests, values, and attitudes. I don't watch television often; however, when I do, I am strangely fascinated with romantic reality series. Although certainly not scientific, they are mini research experiments that tell us extraordinary information about love and human behavior. This summer, Becca, on *The Bachelorette*, had narrowed down her suitors to Garrett. During the final show, she explained that her draw to him traced back to something she wrote in a journal the first time she met him – he reminded her of home and of her dad, suggesting familiarity and similarity at work! Interestingly, various researchers suggest an unconscious attraction to romantic partners who resemble our own opposite-sex parents (see Fraley & Marks, 2010; Fugère, 2016). "In an unconscious effort to heal old wounds, we tend to fall in love with partners who are either very similar to our parents or the exact opposite of our parents" (Solomon, 2017, p. 15.) Another example comes from Doug. After his first date with his wife with whom he fell out of romantic love, he told his dad "She actually reminds me a lot of Mom"; later in the interview he commented, "I had no insight about that not being a good thing at the time."

Speaking of opposites, the cliché "opposites attract" may be true of magnets, but not of relationships. Relationship research suggests opposites (i.e., qualities, beliefs, traits) can lead to attraction but generally don't fare well over the long haul. Similarities of partners are more likely to spur attraction and dissimilar qualities in partners are more prone to dislike later (see Felmlee, 1995). Compared to complete opposite traits, complementary traits may be more useful (i.e., one partner is good at details and the other is better with the big picture), yet even complementary traits could also be detrimental if they polarize over time.

Mate selection emerged as an important element in the pathway to FORL. The reasons participants married, beginning with the most commonly cited, were as follows: (a) individual characteristics making for a solid partner; (b) physical and/or emotional connection; (c) "I am lucky you love me"; (d) "get me to a better place"; (e) drifting or progressing into marriage (i.e., sliding versus deciding); (f) common values, goals, and/or interests; (g) "things will improve"; (h) commitment; and (i) "do the right thing." At the time of marriage, each of these factors was considered significant for mate selection, as described by a number of participants. As you can see, some of these are linked to better outcomes than others. For example, selecting a mate based on physical and emotional intimacy, common values, goals, and interests combined with commitment would likely provide a solid foundation to build a healthy relationship. However, only marrying based on commitment – because you want to "do the right thing" – may not lead to a happy long-term union. Further, drifting into marriage, hoping "things will improve" or marrying because "I am lucky you love me" or with hopes the relationship "can get me to a better place" may not produce the results you are looking for in a marriage.

In respect to FORL, the reasons the participants chose to marry are important to consider because they provide useful information as to what mate selection processes may be more advantageous for a long-term, satisfying marriage. Interestingly, when marrying, eight participants reported perceiving they knew, at the time of mate selection, what they were looking for in a long-term mate, as the following comments illustrate. Jackie recalled,

> I thought I did, yeah ... well, I was 26 and I thought I knew everything. You know, I'd been out of college for two years and I had a good job and you know, I got this, I got this all figured out, you know and he was ... on a good path at the time, and, um, like I said, we were together for seven years before we got married and part of that was time for both of us to get our ducks in a row, get out of school, do what we needed to do, so that I wouldn't be 40 and divorced. Because I was going to do all this stuff ahead of time and make sure that we had this foundation. That was my thought process.

Adam said,

> I've seen, you know ... friends' parents ... how they ... treat one another ... obviously I don't know everything, right, but what I see, you know, helped set an example ... that looks like something I would like.

However, seven participants reported not really knowing what they were looking for in a long-term partner at the time of mate selection. Of these seven, three said they had no idea what they were looking for, and four had only some idea of what they were looking for in a long-term partner.

Alternatively, six participants reported knowing what they did *not* want in a long-term mate – generally based on past relationships or family-of-origin experiences. Doug said,

I have some really good examples of what not to do … my parents married each other, divorced, remarried each other, divorced, married other people, divorced, married other people [yet again], and then my dad did another time. So, I had a lot of, yeah, this is what you shouldn't be doing.

Another participant, Frank, stated,

My mother was the strong one; my father complained about everything. I don't care what it was, he bitched about it. All I knew was that I didn't want it … this is not going to be the way I'm going to do this.

Further, at the time of mate selection, ten participants did not consider the costs or rewards of the relationship. Liz stated,

I don't think at that point in my life I was really processing it in that way … I mean, there were positives and negatives on both sides of it … but I don't know that I sat down and said, "let's do this" or "let's not do this."

Finally, as described by eight participants, important details were not considered during mate selection. They married for the wrong reasons, or they simply did not think the decision through. Laura recalled,

I didn't have any kind of clearheaded analysis … at that young age, I didn't have that kind of analysis on much of anything. I was making all emotional decisions and I was making them quickly and impulsively and then picking up the pieces when everything fell apart.

Similarly, immaturity was stated by three participants as a factor in the mate selection pathway of FORL. Adam said, "looking back, yeah, there's definitely a maturity, lack of maturity on both of our parts."

Each participant listed more than one factor contributing to their mate selection decision. For example, Kelly said,

I think it was a combination of a few factors … I think it was time to get married … I felt he actually was quite a good person … I felt he would be a good husband and a good dad and that we would both be able to build a nice family, because we shared the same values.

The following illustrates two factors that Liz used in her mate selection (*individual characteristics* and *"do the right thing"*):

> I want to say the big one, for me, um, was that he was responsible ... even though we entered the whole situation kind of backwards ... there was stability ... we were poor as heck, but there was like this sense of security ... he was a hard worker, um, an absolutely wonderful dad ... we were super young, like 19 ... twins [were] born six months after we were married, so, um, the way he responded in that situation was absolutely positive ... he's a good guy and I'm pregnant and it's the right thing to do.

"Lucky You Love Me"

Three participants had children from a previous relationship at the time they met their partner. An example of *"lucky you love me"* was offered by Michelle:

> I was ecstatic, I mean, I was just absolutely ecstatic ... we got officially engaged over Thanksgiving ... everyone in my whole family was so happy ... thought I was going to be alone forever with this kid and everything else – and I was constantly told, you are so lucky, you're so lucky.

This leads one to wonder if Michelle's concerns about being alone as a single parent combined with others' enthusiasm about her finding a partner who was accepting of her child influenced her mate selection decision differently than if she had met her partner under other circumstances. Michelle's account emphasizes the importance of timing in the mate selection process, as well as factors beyond romantic love.

Sliding versus Deciding

As exemplified in excerpts through this chapter, six participants described *drifting* into marriage, also known as *sliding versus deciding*. "Sometimes we 'slide' into a situation rather than make a conscious decision" (Lamanna, Riedmann, & Stewart, 2018, p. 23). Many of us remember situations when we have been unsure of something, but we were already in too deep, so kept going. Examples range from choosing a paint color, to a college major, and even to relationships.

As illustrated by Jack:

> Well, let's see, at the time, I would say ... all of our friends were
> getting married ... Everybody goes to college at the same time
> and then everybody's getting married at the same time, so
> I figured that was what I needed to be doing, so it, uh, it made
> sense and so that was who I was in the relationship with
> then ... we'd started talking about it probably way too early in
> the relationship ... and nothing really happened to, I guess, get
> off of that direction.

Sliding versus deciding can be the result of pressure from others
(i.e., parents, friends, or society). For example, your parents talk
often about their friends having grandchildren and have asked
you a few times if you and your partner have discussed marriage.
You also know you don't want to be the proverbial *old cat lady*, so
you move forward with plans for marriage. Most of us understand
how friends and family influence our relationship decisions. However, cultural standards and influences are also at play (see
Miller, 2012; Acitelli et al., 2011). In fact, cultural standards
light the way for what is considered appropriate or popular at
any given time in history, as illustrated by the negative perception of a mature, unattached woman (i.e., the old cat lady).

Denial of Problems

All participants reported minimizing or denying problems in their
relationship. The most common reasons included wanting to
believe in the partner's goodness, having young children, and
attempting to avoid a failed relationship. Janet, for instance, said,

> There were signs along the way in the last ten years ... I just
> didn't want to see because I was too caught up in having the
> perfect life ... the house was designed and built in the perfect
> suburban neighborhood and the perfect school district and
> I was too caught up in being the perfect mom and wife and
> parent and everything else.

Concerns about the relationship, if acknowledged, were ignored or
minimized. Laura reported, "I overlooked the bad, I mean, I just
downplayed and minimized the bad."

Additionally, three participants made excuses for their partner's behavior or tried to fix them. As explained by Sandra, "as
time went by, my friends are like, he's a jerk ... you just don't

understand ... he doesn't realize he's rude, like, I made excuses ... I mean, a ton of excuses ... he'll realize, and I'll help him realize."

Denial eventually gave way to negative thoughts and feelings toward themselves, their partner, or their relationship. As such, it is possible that addressing denial early in the relationship would have been optimal before it became detrimental to the relationship; alternatively, these relationships may have ended during courtship if denial had not existed. As supported by previous research, denial is quite common in new relationships, designed to further the union (see Kayser, 1993).

Additionally, during early courtship, *positive illusions* are distorted positive perceptions of one's partner that others may not see or agree with (Murray & Holmes, 1993, 1999). Positive illusions are based on the way the individual wants the partner to be and what is needed from the relationship (Conley et al., 2009) (see more about positive illusions in Chapter 8). Interestingly, there is research suggesting we tend to idealize our current romantic partner, even after the newness wears off (Conley et al., 2009; Morry, Reich, & Kito, 2010). However, it can be dependent on relationship quality, with those more satisfied having higher partner perceptions (Morry, Reich, & Kito, 2010). Further, Barbee et al. (1996) suggest that as relationships persist, civility is sometimes lost and unpleasant behaviors (i.e., belching), which were once kept to a minimum become more commonplace. The authors noted that these unpleasant habits may cause the loss of idealization and once noticed can be difficult to ignore, possibly even leading to loss of attractiveness and passion. This leads one to question what makes some partners hold on to these denials or idealizations more easily or longer than others?

As discussed in the previous chapter, there is evidence that some marriages end because of the very same partner traits once found attractive – termed fatal attractions (see Felmlee, 1995). Situational factors, such as family stage or phase of life, may color one's perception of initially attractive features. For example, spontaneity may have been adored early on, but when having young children, a scheduled demeanor may be more appreciated. Further, other theories suggest that initial traits become the source of conflict later, based on various psychological, social, or situational processes (Felmlee, 1995). First, it's possible the couple did not know each other well to start, and other more genuine traits emerged over time. Alternatively, the couple may have known each other sufficiently, but due to the likelihood of evaluating a partner as more positive in the early stage of a relationship, the initial partner views could have been inflated and replaced by more realistic views (see McClanahan et al.,

1990; see Tennov, 1979). Regarding social factors – family and friends may influence perception of one's partner through comments made (Felmlee, Sprecher, & Bassin, 1990; Sprecher & Felmlee, 1992).

As supported by the results of this study, mate selection is complex and qualities important to successful long-term relationships are often not well thought-out prior to marriage (Lamanna & Riedmann, 2012). Further, lack of relationship education abounds (Cobb, Larson, & Watson, 2003). Although romantic love is considered ideal for most marriages, various other reasons led participants in this study to tie the knot. Together, it appears lack of knowledge or understanding pertaining to self, love, healthy relationships, and marriage, as well as needs and wants, timing, self-esteem, outside influences, sliding versus deciding, denial, and other personal factors were all components of mate selection decisions, for better or for worse. It would be useful to further study these, and other mate selection variables, in terms of long-term satisfaction and FORL.

Minimal Rewards

Many of the participants entering marriage did not consider the rewards and costs of the relationship. In fact, at the outset, several had unrealistic expectations of the relationship or none at all. Further, some overestimated their ability to change their partner and/or were in denial about concerns in the relationship. If rewards and costs would have been assessed, the participant may have chosen not to marry. However, it's possible the illogical nature of early passionate love hampered the use of logic during mate selection, further illustrating the importance of waiting to make commitment decisions.

Alternatively, all participants reported the examination of rewards and costs, as they reached FORL. The exception was one participant who continues to weigh the rewards and costs and has not yet decided about staying in her marriage. The rewards of the marriage were minimal and most often were identified as keeping children in an intact family, stable finances and lifestyle, and a shared history with her partner. As cited by Jackie, "I analyzed that to death ... I was so hell-bent on not raising them that way. I mean, my oldest is literally almost to the day the age I was when my parents split." Also, Tessa commented about lifestyle, "... here I was in this big house with a pool in the backyard and a physician husband ... but, um ... I wanted to be happy; happy is big." As Liz reasoned, "... it was a big investment that I made ... a shared history ... that first grandchild born, our daughter getting married."

About one-third of participants described the following costs of remaining in the relationship: significant emotional pain or depression by staying; emotional and/or physical abuse by the spouse; negative partner behavior such as drinking, arguing, lying, and not working; and children being hurt by the parents' continued relationship. Other costs of staying in the marriage included lack of emotional and/or physical intimacy, giving but getting nothing in return, interest in attractive alternatives, spouse's lack of motivation, intense conflict, raising children alone, and conflicting values.

The finding that costs and rewards were often not considered by the participants during their mate selection yet were considered in the decision making process to end the relationship is an important contribution to the literature. Interestingly, comparing rewards and costs was not reported by the participants as a direct *cause* of FORL, likely because it followed other contributing factors (e.g., spousal behaviors, realizations, lack of emotional or physical connection). More research is needed to flesh out how assessing costs and rewards during mate selection, as well as later in the relationship, affects FORL. For example, does the same lack of consideration take place during the mate selection processes of individuals who enjoy long-term satisfying marriages?

Loss of Emotional and/or Physical Connection

Another common pathway to FORL is the loss of emotional and/or physical connection between the participant and partner. As Adam described it,

Yeah, it was probably just an erosion, I guess ... It just got to the point where you know, the physical attraction was gone, and after all of the emotional damage had been done, I think that was probably the last straw for me.

Sexual desire and emotional attachment typify most romantic relationships, including marriage. However, like many aspects of love, sexual desire can be complex. Physical attraction often leads to sexual attraction and sexual desire. Yet, as discussed in the previous chapter, sexual desire does not have to occur inside an emotionally connected relationship, just as emotional attachment does not always include sexual desire or activity (Birnbaum & Finkel, 2015). Further, you may think someone is good looking but may not want to have sex with them. For example, Tessa shared, "I don't have a problem with sex drive ... when I look back on it, I really didn't want to have a sexual relationship with *him*. He was still a very attractive guy. He's still a very attractive guy, but any time he touched me, there was just like, ew."

As described by participants, other aspects of physical connection included reciprocal sexual desire, enjoying hugging and kissing, and other expressions of affection and sexuality with their partner, which sometimes included a physical reaction when thinking about or being physically close to them. Although there is compelling support that sexual fulfillment is an important factor in relationship satisfaction, there are many aspects to overall marital gratification (Mark & Herbenick, 2014; Sprecher & Cate, 2004). For example, feeling loved and understood, important, and cared for, and the sharing of personal information are examples of emotional connection (Reis, 1990) also significant to romantic love. Other examples of emotional intimacy described by participants included mutual appreciation, enjoying time and experiences with their partner, missing and thinking about them when apart, mutual respect, trust, sharing common interests, and feeling their partner is the right person for them. As illustrated by Joe, "In my opinion to be in love is when you just care for somebody more than you do yourself."

Jackie illustrated her perception of the importance of emotional and physical connection in romantic relationships. For her, emotional intimacy takes precedence over physical intimacy; however, both are valuable.

Ideally you would have both [emotional and physical connection]. I think if one becomes less prominent, it can still be fine ... when I'm with my boyfriend, sometimes we have sex and sometimes we don't. It's about the mood of the day. If I leave and we haven't had sex, I don't assume the relationship is doomed.

Adam illustrated the combination of both elements as magical.

I think you can love somebody on an emotional level, um, I think you can lust somebody on a physical level ... but when you have both of those, that's where the magic happens.

Likewise, Jackie illustrated, "We liked each other. We enjoyed spending time together ... so it was, you know, physical and emotional and romantic ... it was the whole deal."

The state of being in love was also frequently characterized as a special kind of love, set apart by a special connection, sexual interest, as well as a sense of inevitability. This finding is useful because it further delineates the type of love being studied and the type of relationship in which FORL is likely to occur. As Joe described, "if you don't find the person physically attractive, then you're not going to fall in love with them ... I mean, you can love your neighbor but ... you're not in-love with your neighbor." As illustrated by Jack, "I think it's maybe ... a deeper connection, uh, some sort of a stronger attraction."

Supporting previous literature citing the important facets of romantic love, the majority of participants (n = 13) reported that both emotional and physical closeness characterized the state of being in-love. Similarly, 14 participants reported the same two elements were essential for satisfaction in marriage. However, three outlying participants who believed both elements were important, were uncertain how essential physical connection was to either satisfaction in marriage or being in-love. Gaining additional information about what makes for satisfying marriage may aid our understanding of FORL.

Further, all 15 participants reported that they felt in-love with their partner early in the relationship. This is important because in attempting to understand FORL, it is useful to assess how the participants felt about their mates initially, as well as how their love changed. Although feelings of romantic love existed early in the relationship, as indicated by all the participants, the intensity varied and appears to exist on a continuum. For example, when Laura was asked if she was in love with her partner at the time of their marriage, she replied, "A little ... on my wedding day, I was ready to walk down the aisle and I saw him at the end of the aisle and I said, 'This is doable.'" Beyond romantic love, it also seems useful to regard all types of love on a continuum rather than seek their clear absence or presence (P. Regan, personal communication, August 10, 2016).

Seven of the participants reported a relatively weak connection in one or both of the dimensions of emotional and physical connection to their mate early in the relationship. Joe's example illustrates having a stronger emotional connection to a previous partner:

In college ... I can think of one ... an emotional, um, relationship that was stronger than that of my actual marriage, absolutely.

The following are examples of participants who felt stronger physical connections to past partners. Kelly stated,

> I would say, uh, attraction-wise, it was weaker than the other relationships ... here was a person in my life who I really loved so much, and I probably will always love this person ... I believe I loved that other person more ... when it comes to attraction ... but I think my husband, when I married him, I think I loved him more for ... the life and the future which you can provide together.

Likewise, in a study by Sims and Meana (2010) some women were found to have consciously chosen their spouse based on their being responsible men or good providers, "despite having felt stronger sexual desire for other men in their past" (p. 368). However, it is important to note that the women in that study were generally happy in their marriages (Sims & Meana, 2010) (see Chapter 6). Conversely, three of the participants reported the same or stronger connection, both emotionally and physically, compared to past relationships. Five participants did not describe how their love experience compared to previous relationships. The results that some chose mates whom they felt less romantic love toward than past partners leads one to consider how this affects FORL.

As referenced in Chapter 1, the results of this study confirmed that both emotional and sexual connection (i.e., romantic love) are important to the state of being in love (n = 13) and for long-term marital satisfaction (n = 14). These converging outcomes, supported by previous literature, point to romantic love and being in love as synonymous (Fromm, 1956; Grant, 1998). There was uncertainty on the part of a few participants when they attempted to articulate what it meant to be in love. For example, these participants stated, "I don't know" during their responses, or provided minimal answers. This finding informs the research about the complexity of love.

Further, all 15 participants reported that a lack of emotional and/or physical connection accompanied FORL, which was consistent with earlier literature stating FORL is likely attributed to drops in emotional connection, sexual attraction, and feelings of inevitable loss of relationship (Berscheid, 2006). Most often this lack of connection transpired over a period of time, as Kelly indicated: "I think both were fading slowly." Generally, the loss of physical and/or emotional connection happened after repeated negative actions or incidents, usually by their spouse. Though not found in the data, it is worth noting that FORL may *feel* sudden, even if the process spanned decades (W. Allen, personal communication, July 26, 2016). It's possible FORL may be sudden if there is a substantial relationship injury (i.e., revelation of sexual abuse perpetrated by spouse).

Extraneous Influences and Stressors

A few participants described extraneous factors such as high stress and exhaustion, problems with in-laws, or influence from others as contributing to their FORL. For example, Tessa noted that "eight years into the marriage [my husband] decided to go back to medical school ... which is a huge stress on him, um, and so the relationship got worse just because of the stress."

One participant described her mother's new relationship as contributing to a change in her thinking about her own marriage, suggesting the seemingly unpredictable nature of FORL.

After my dad died my mom started dating a family friend ... all of a sudden my mom's laughing and smiling and enjoying life and that, to me, made a huge impact ... you know what, I don't want to live my whole life just being kind of ... just existing.

This finding highlights outside influences, increased stressors, and insufficient coping skills as a possible pathway to FORL. Although only reported by a few participants, these outside factors are a useful and interesting finding. No other FORL research has cited these extraneous factors.

Emerging Realizations

All participants described *emerging realizations* regarding their relationship, such as negative behavior by the spouse (i.e., blaming, lying), loss of emotional and/or physical connection, lack of support, concern for safety of self and/or children, personal unhappiness, having nothing in common, that they would not be married if it were not for the kids, giving but not getting anything in return, that the spouse or situation is not going to change, and that they'd fallen out of love. These realizations developed over time and led to more negative thoughts and feelings regarding one's spouse, oneself, or the relationship. As Joe stated,

I recognized that when I was away, I was more of a punching bag for being away ... so if there was anything that was wrong, it was my fault ... I looked back, and I saw all these other spouses that were supporting their deployed military members, and I didn't receive that same type of support. And I remember thinking, "Well, this is crap."

And Sandra recognized not seeing what others do:

Yeah, when his best friend is like, "leave her alone, stop picking on her ..." if that guy thinks that ... why am I not seeing that?

The following thoughts occurred for some participants after realizations emerged: *what is going on here?*, *this isn't right, maybe it will get better, I'm not getting my needs met, I can't do anymore to fix it*, and *I can't do this anymore*. Further, some participants described beginning to think about their own importance and worth, and the possibility of alternative partners. This demonstrates the eroding relationship and shift in thoughts about self and others. Tessa hoped things would get better:

I started seeing it probably within the first, like, three or four years ... I kept thinking things were going to get better or change or something like that, once we um ... got through one hurdle and the next hurdle or what not ... After we had the first child, he ... made me nervous with his, um, moods, reactions to um, money ... different things like that.

Liz began to reflect on her own needs after her children were grown:

Yeah, when they [children] started to get pretty self-sufficient, um, we just, we grew apart ... we had nothing in common ... I was like, no, I don't, I can't, I'm not taking care of you, anymore. I'm done. I'm not going to do this anymore. My children are grown, I need to be me. I've sacrificed a lot and I love them to death, but I sacrificed a lot and you didn't.

Doug recognized feeling different years before FORL:

I realized along the way, like, wait a minute, what's happening? This feels different than before we were married ... so, there were lots of times through the years, but it wasn't until about seven years ago I think that I realized, I'm not in love anymore ... that was about ... 12 years in.

Not only did increased awareness and realizations lead to negative thoughts, but negative feelings emerged as well. Feelings were variable across participants; however, they were generally negative and directed toward one's self, one's spouse, or the relationship. The most common feelings accompanying FORL, as described by the participants in this study, included self-blame, regret, disappointment, feeling under-valued, not listened to, ashamed, heartbroken, fear, being criticized, uneasy, dissatisfied, less attracted to the partner, disrespected, anxious, hurt, nervous, confused, surprised, irritated, lost, empty, indecisive, ambivalent, hopeless, disconnected, angry, suspicious, cold, depressed, miserable, upset, sad, ill, resentful, and as if living a lie. As realized by Michelle, "We just didn't seem like we should be together." Tessa described feeling devalued by her spouse:

> My ex-husband really didn't mean to. It's just, I don't know what it was ... he just made me feel like I was, I was not that great ... his life was important and his views were important and what I was doing was not.

Frank described emerging anxiety:

> It got to the point where ... driving home, I started feeling it. I started feeling anxious and tense just pulling in my own driveway. I hadn't even gotten in the house yet ... She wants to talk about something ... eggshells. Watch how you phrase it ... I'll give you an answer, but I didn't tell you what my heart says ... That is a very big part of the falling out of love. You're protecting yourself ... To me, it's like you can look at this person you're married to and it's cold. You don't feel anything. It's gone. You could bring a boyfriend in, and I really don't care.

Doug depicted the realization that his marriage wasn't meeting his needs:

> We have always been in very different places and, and even when she was more vulnerable, more connected, more willing ... just wasn't enough ... There just wasn't enough depth, connection, intimacy. Anything.

Nicole recognized that she doesn't feel the same about her partner as he feels about her:

> He's always bringing up, how come you never chase me around? How come you never, you know, made the first move? How come you never ... finally the other day, I was like, cause I don't feel like I want to ... I have found myself becoming more

annoyed and just super irritated with things that I've always been able to overlook ... I'm not one to cry, so I've cried more in the last six months than I have in my entire life ... I mean he even, just last week he was like texting me, why don't you initiate sex anymore and I was like ... you know, it's just not there.

Gaining a more thorough understanding of emerging realizations and why they happen for some individuals and not others would be of great interest. Further, investigating how the subsequent thoughts and feelings, from these realizations, may be involved in marital satisfaction and FORL would be beneficial.

Behaviors and Negative Incidents

Spouse and participant behavior comprised yet another segment of the pathway to FORL. For simplification purposes, the behaviors listed will be broken down into three categories: common behaviors between the participant and spouse, behaviors unique to the spouse, and behaviors unique to the participant.

Common behaviors of both the participant and the spouse, as described by the participant, included an uptick in arguing, passive or withdrawing behaviors, and physical intimacy behavioral changes – generally a reduction and/or disinterest in intimacy. As stated by Laura, "We had not had sex in seven years ... but in the end it would have repelled me to even have his foot touch mine in the bed." As described by Jackie, "It got to the point where we didn't even talk. We weren't mad ... it wasn't animosity. We just plain didn't talk."

The most common spousal behavior accompanying FORL, as expressed by the participants, were repeated negative actions of the spouse, such as controlling behavior, lack of emotional support, or negative or angry moods, followed by the spouse not taking responsibility for their part in the marital problems. Additionally, three participants reported emotional and/or physical abuse from their spouse. These issues propelled the participant into a different frame of mind regarding the relationship. Terms that emerged from the data referring to the negative actions included *dominoes, realizations, big bombs, specific events, tips of the scale,* and *red flags*. As indicated by Joe, "And so you know, when did it happen, you know, the dominoes just fell." Reported by Liz, "the scales tipped ... I mean there was all kinds of these little things."

Sandra described her spouse making fun of her religious convictions,

So, he's, um, atheist ... If I mentioned God at all, I was made fun of and asked if I believe in fairies and unicorns.

Alternatively, the most commonly reported participant behaviors included passivity or not standing up for themselves, attempts to address the issues, and withdrawing. As explained by Adam, "the physical relationship kind of was non-existent, shortly after we got married ... I did feel rejected, you know, I did check out emotionally, quite a bit, because I felt like, okay, what's wrong?" Noting the tension, Tessa said, "I got to the point where I didn't share anything with him, just because I knew I would be criticized any time I did ... if I didn't follow his rules, there would be that moodiness, um, so I would find ways to skirt around it, you know."

Change: The Wildcard

A neglected aspect in the literature is the power of change in relationships, including marital relationships. It is inevitable that situations, contexts, and people change throughout life and relationships grow or dissolve (Huston & Levinger, 1978). Sure, most people know they or their partner might change, but fundamentally they may not believe the relationship will change as a result. However, it is possible these unsuspected shifts are responsible for changes in love, commitment, and satisfaction (Sprecher, 1999), despite adequate mate selection processes. I like to view change as the relationship wildcard. For example, in a poker game, if a joker is drawn it can be a game-changer – a player's hand can suddenly become a Full House.

The research results indicated changes in one or both partners (n = 11) contributing to FORL. In fact, approximately one-third of participants described that they themselves had changed in the marriage, including personal growth, change in values, or change in needs. Change was generally considered the outcome of a natural progression that could not be predicted.

An additional one-third of participants reported that their spouse had changed. As illustrated by Tessa, "I think he changed. I think he, he just slowly morphed into his parents." Some participants felt their spouse put forth more effort when dating or concealed information during courtship that came to light later in the marital relationship. For example, Allison began to feel like her marriage was "fake" based on her husband's actions not matching how he presented himself during courtship. Finally, two participants reported they both had changed. Michelle spoke of significant changes she and her partner underwent:

> I was very overweight and, um, had, I think, a lot of self-esteem problems. I still felt very bad about, um, being a single parent ... so when I met [my spouse] ... sweet guy, big guy, you know big teddy bear guy, um, he was pretty active ... I mean, I would say I was working out but ... he would run 5Ks and do things like that and that really impressed the hell out of me ... I continued to put on weight ... and I had weight loss surgery ... and, um, in that time, he's probably gained a hundred pounds ... I love to go out and do things ... I socialize a lot and, um, he's started to just kind of be the opposite and he really wasn't like that before ... I told him when we separated, you need to go see a counselor or you need to figure out what's going on. You need to empower yourself whether we end up together or not ... he's described it as he wasn't giving himself permission to have fun because he didn't think that's what parents did.

Both measurable partner changes and the interpretation of change ascribed by the other partner can affect satisfaction and potentially contribute to FORL. Interestingly, it did not appear that change itself was an issue, but it became problematic when it was not honored or celebrated between them. Overall, when the participant changed, it was perceived as change toward positive goals or personal growth; however, when the spouse changed, it was either toward stagnation or otherwise negative. These results are supported by Huston and Levinger (1978), who report that change is an inevitable part of life, resulting in relationship growth or its end. Change is an important aspect to consider as it further exemplifies its complexity and speaks to the seemingly unpredictable nature of FORL.

Coping Deficits

The results also suggested deficits among the spouses that contributed to FORL. Three participants reported that they themselves had deficits that negatively impacted their marriage. This finding is useful because it suggests that these participants shared responsibility for their relationship problems. Tessa said, "I think my ex probably wasn't okay with himself as much as he could have been, and I think I definitely didn't have the strengths I do now ... you know. It's like the old adage, I mean, I wish

I ... knew then what I know." Jack accepted his role in their break-up by explaining that he had not only changed, but didn't possess good coping skills:

> She didn't change, like she was 100 percent her, start to
> finish ... um, my reactions definitely changed over time ... I
> would have just ignored it, but now I'm like, I would notice it
> and acknowledge that I did not like it, um ... I wouldn't say
> anything to her, but I would just feel differently about it ... I
> didn't tell her everything until probably six months before
> I moved out, and then it was ... I don't want to do this anymore.
> It wasn't, here are the things we need to work on ... I convinced
> myself that it was a good thing that we didn't talk about it,
> because I remember I was with a group of, like, friends on a car
> ride, and they were talking about arguments with their wives
> and I was like completely honest with them. We never argue,
> just don't, and like, I was proud of that then, but now I realize
> that was not a good thing ... I think the relationship would
> have been saveable at any point with the right tools, which
> I did not have ... even at the end, but if I would have been able
> to communicate the feelings, like, early on, when we would
> have issues ... it would have never got to that point.

Affairs outside their marriages were also reported by some participants as a result of marital discontent (n = 3), specifically to supplement the marriage (n = 1), and following an open marriage experience, requested by the spouse (n = 1). This finding is important because those who had affairs did not condone the behavior nor did they believe they would ever participate in an affair. Again, this finding shows the unpredictable and unhelpful events that occur in the process of FORL. As Laura explained, "there's a lot of people that are ... just living in a marriage just cause they think it's good for the kids, um, but they're really out of the marriage, and I'll tell you, I did have an affair ... with an old boyfriend ... on a weekend and that was empty too." Tessa described her affair:

> I actually had an affair with my best friend, which was crazy
> cause I never thought I would do that ... I just didn't feel like
> I had a partner. I fought against it for a long time ... I think it
> was probably just to, um, actually feel like I had some worth. In
> fact ... he's been a good friend forever ... I was never attracted
> to him whatsoever ... and so ... all of that attention and all
> that, you know.

Summary

To recap, many direct and indirect elements related to the individual, partner, and couple, as well as the larger system, comprise the numerous pathways to FORL. Each individual's path consists of any number or combination of stepping stones. These stepping stones or factors include: 1) what each partner brings to the relationship; 2) poor mate selection process; 3) minimal relationship rewards; 4) lack of emotional and/or physical connection; 5) extraneous influences and stressors; 6) minimizing or denying early relationship problems; 7) emerging realizations or awareness leading to negative thinking and/or feelings about self, partner, or relationship; 8) changes in participant or partner; 9) participant and partner behaviors/negative incidents; and 10) coping deficits in the participant or partner.

Although the findings of my study suggest these elements contribute to FORL, the existence of one or more of these does not mean an individual is destined to fall out of romantic love. After all, issues and problems naturally occur in healthy relationships and many partners do not fall out of romantic love or divorce. Further, many relationship concerns can be remedied and, in the case of ongoing problems, relationships can still be satisfying and successful if they are beneficial in ways that outweigh the negative aspects.

Exploration Questions

1 *Constraining beliefs* are inaccurate or unhelpful personal beliefs about mate selection that limit a person's choices for a suitable partner. What are some examples of constraining beliefs you've seen in yourself, in other people you know, or in the media and society?

2 Think about a time you experienced *sliding versus deciding* in a situation. What internal or external factors influenced this? Were there social pressures or cultural norms that facilitated your behavior? What outcomes, positive or negative, resulted?

3 After reading the study results and quotes from individuals who identify as FORL, what aspect of FORL would you like to learn more about? What further research do you believe is needed surrounding this topic?

Key Concepts

secure attachment	anxious attachment
avoidant attachment	personality traits
Five-Factor Model	constraining beliefs
perceived attraction	sliding versus deciding
illusionary intimacy	fatal attractions
emerging realizations	positive illusions

References

Acitelli, L. K., Wickham, R. E., Brunson, J., & Nguyen, M. (2011, January). *When couples read stories about other couples' relationships.* Poster presented at the meeting of the Society for Personality and Social Psychology, San Antonio, TX.

Baer, J. C. & Martinez, C. D. (2006). Child maltreatment and insecure attachment: A meta-analysis. *Journal of Reproductive and Infant Psychology, 24*(3), 187–197.

Barbee, A. P., Cunningham, M. R., Druen, P. B., & Yankeelov, P. A. (1996). Loss of passion, intimacy, and commitment: A conceptual framework for relationship researchers. *Journal of Loss & Trauma, 1*(1), 93–108.

Bargh, J. A. (2017). *Before you know it: The unconscious reasons we do what we do.* New York: Simon & Schuster, Inc.

Berscheid, E. (2006). Searching for the meaning of love. In R. J. Sternberg & K. Weis (eds), *The new psychology of love* (pp. 171–183). New Haven, CT: Yale University Press.

Berscheid, E. & Reis, H. T. (1998). Attraction and close relationships. In D. T. Gilbert, S. T. Fiske, & G. Lindzey (eds), *The handbook of social psychology* (pp. 193–281). New York: McGraw-Hill.

Birnbaum, G. E. & Finkel, E. J. (2015). The magnetism that holds us together: Sexuality and relationship maintenance across relationship development. *Current Opinion in Psychology, 1*, 29–33.

Boxer, C. F., Noonan, M. C., & Whelan, C. B. (2015). Measuring mate preferences: A replication and extension. *Journal of Family Issues, 36*(2), 163–187.

Brennan, K. A., Shaver, P. R., & Tobey, A. E. (1991). Attachment styles, gender and parental problem drinking. *Journal of Social and Personal Relationships, 8*(4), 451–466.

Chan, A. L. (2014, April 9). *Why being neurotic could actually be a good thing.* Retrieved August 19, 2018 from www.huffingtonpost.com/2014/04/09/healthy-neuroticism_n_5035297.html.

Cobb, N. P., Larson, J. H., & Watson, W. L. (2003). Development of the attitudes about romance and mate selection scale. *Family Relations, 52*(3), 222–231.

Collins, N. L. & Read, S. J. (1990). Adult attachment, working models, and relationship quality in dating couples. *Journal of Personality and Social Psychology, 58*(4), 644–663.

Conley, T. D., Roesch, S. C., Peplau, L. A., & Gold, M. S. (2009). A test of positive illusions versus shared reality models of relationship satisfaction among gay, lesbian, and heterosexual couples. *Journal of Applied Social Psychology, 39*(6), 1417–1431.

Coontz, S. (2005). *Marriage, a history: How love conquered marriage.* New York: Viking Penguin.

Damian, R. I., Spengler, M., Sutu, A., & Roberts, B. W. (2018). Sixteen going on sixty-six: A longitudinal study of personality stability and change across 50 years. *Journal of Personality and Social Psychology.* Advance online publication. http://dx.doi.org/10.1037/pspp0000210.

Deutsch, F. M., Kokot, A. P., & Binder, K. S. (2007). College women's plans for different types of egalitarian marriages. *Journal of Marriage and Family, 69*(4), 916–929.

Dozier, M. & Kobak, R. R. (1992). Psychophysiology in attachment interviews: Converging evidence for deactivating strategies. *Child Development, 63*(6), 1473–1480.

Dyrenforth, P. S., Kashy, D. A., Donnellan, M. B., & Lucas, R. E. (2010). Predicting relationship and life satisfaction from personality in nationally representative samples from three countries: The relative importance of actor, partner, and similarity effects. *Journal of Personality and Social Psychology, 99*(4), 690–702.

Ein-Dor, T., Mikulincer, M., Doron, G., & Shaver, P. R. (2010). The attachment paradox: How can so many of us (the insecure ones) have no adaptive advantages? *Perspectives on Psychological Science, 5*(2), 123–141.

Fearon, R. P., Bakermans-Kranenburg, M. J., Van Ijzendoorn, M. H., Lapsley, A. M., & Roisman, G. I. (2010). The significance of insecure attachment and disorganization in the development of children's externalizing behavior: A meta analytic study. *Child Development, 81*(2), 435–456.

Felmlee, D. H. (1995). Fatal attractions: Affection and disaffection in intimate relationships. *Journal of Social and Personal Relationships, 12*(2), 295–311.

Felmlee, D., Sprecher, S., & Bassin, E. (1990). The dissolution of intimate relationships: A hazard model. *Social Psychology Quarterly, 53*(1), 13–30.

Fraley, R. C. & Marks, M. J. (2010). Westermarck, freud, and the incest taboo: Does familial resemblance activate sexual attraction? *Personality and Social Psychology Bulletin, 36*(9), 1202–1212.

Fromm, E. (1956). *The art of loving.* New York: Harper.

Fugère. (2016, August 2). *Why your perfect partner doesn't need to be ideal.* Retrieved September 20, 2018 from www.psychologytoday.com/us/blog/dating-and-mating/201608/why-your-perfect-partner-doesnt-need-be-ideal?amp.

Grant, D. (1998). "Desolate and sick of an old passion": The psychodynamics of falling in and out of love. *Psychodynamic Counselling, 4*(1), 71–92.

Hatfield, E. & Rapson, R. L. (1996). *Love and sex: Cross-cultural perspectives.* Boston, MA: Allyn & Bacon.

Hazan, C. & Diamond, L. M. (2000). The place of attachment in human mating. *Review of General Psychology*, *4*(2), 186.

Hemesath, C. W. (2016). *Falling out of romantic love: A phenomenological study of the meaning of love in marriage* (unpublished doctoral dissertation). Iowa State University, Ames, IA.

Hemesath, C. W. & Hurt, T. R. (2017). *Falling out of romantic love: An integrated theoretical framework* (unpublished manuscript). Department of Human Development and Family Studies, Iowa State University, Ames, Iowa.

Hemesath, C. W. & Hurt, T. R. (n.d.). *Falling out of romantic love: A focus group study*. Manuscript in progress.

Hudson, N. W., Roberts, B. W., & Lodi-Smith, J. (2012). Personality trait development and social investment in work. *Journal of Research in Personality*, *46*(3), 334–344.

Hunt, L. L., Eastwick, P. W., & Finkel, E. J. (2015). Leveling the playing field: Longer acquaintance predicts reduced assortative mating on attractiveness. *Psychological Science*, *26*(7), 1046–1053.

Huston, T. L. & Levinger, G. (1978). Interpersonal attraction and relationships. *Annual Review of Psychology*, *29*(1), 115–156.

Karney, B. R. & Bradbury, T. N. (1995). The longitudinal course of marital quality and stability: A review of theory, methods, and research. *Psychological Bulletin*, *118*(1), 3–34.

Kayser, K. (1990). The process of marital disaffection: Interventions at various stages. *Family Relations*, *39*(3), 257–265.

Kayser, K. (1993). *When love dies: The process of marital disaffection*. New York: Guilford Press.

Kurdek, L. A. (2006). Differences between partners from heterosexual, gay, and lesbian cohabiting couples. *Journal of Marriage and Family*, *68*(2), 509–528.

Lamanna, M. A. & Riedmann, A. (2012). *Marriages, families, and relationships: Making choices in a diverse society*, 11th edn. Belmont, CA: Cengage Learning.

Lamanna, M. A., Riedmann, A., & Stewart, S. (2018). *Marriages, families, and relationships: Making choices in a diverse society*. Boston, MA: Cengage Learning.

Lewandowski, G. W., Aron, A., & Gee, J. (2007). Personality goes a long way: The malleability of opposite-sex physical attractiveness. *Personal Relationships*, *14*(4), 571–585.

Mark, K. P. & Herbenick, D. (2014). The influence of attraction to partner on heterosexual women's sexual and relationship satisfaction in long-term relationships. *Archives of Sexual Behavior*, *43*(3), 563–570.

McClanahan, K. K., Gold, J. A., Lenney, E., Ryckman, R. M., & Kulberg, G. E. (1990). Infatuation and attraction to a dissimilar other: Why is love blind? *The Journal of Social Psychology*, *130*(4), 433–445.

McCrae, R. R. & Costa, P. T. (1987). Validation of the five-factor model of personality across instruments and observers. *Journal of Personality and Social Psychology*, *52*(1), 81–90.

McCrae, R. R. & Costa, P. T. (2008). The five-factor theory of personality. In. O. P. John, R. W. Robins, & L. A. Pervin (eds), *Handbook of personality: Theory and research*, 3rd edn (pp. 150–181). New York: Guilford Press.

Miller, R. S. (2012). *Intimate relationships*, 6th edn. New York: McGraw-Hill.

Morry, M. M., Reich, T., & Kito, M. (2010). How do I see you relative to myself? Relationship quality as a predictor of self-and partner-enhancement within cross-sex friendships, dating relationships, and marriages. *The Journal of Social Psychology, 150*(4), 369–392.

Murray, S. L. & Holmes, J. G. (1993). Seeing virtues in faults: Negativity and the transformation of interpersonal narratives in close relationships. *Journal of Personality and Social Psychology, 65*(4), 707.

Murray, S. L. & Holmes, J. G. (1999). The (mental) ties that bind: Cognitive structures that predict relationship resilience. *Journal of Personality and Social Psychology, 77*(6), 1228–1244.

Noftle, E. E. & Shaver, P. R. (2006). Attachment dimensions and the big five personality traits: Associations and comparative ability to predict relationship quality. *Journal of Research in Personality, 40*(2), 179–208.

Regan, P. C. (2017). *The mating game: A primer on love, sex, and marriage*, 3rd edn. Thousand Oaks, CA: Sage.

Regan, P. C. & Berscheid, E. (1997). Gender differences in characteristics desired in a potential sexual and marriage partner. *Journal of Psychology & Human Sexuality, 9*(1), 25–37.

Reis, H. T. (1990). The role of intimacy in interpersonal relations. *Journal of Social and Clinical Psychology, 9*(1), 15–30.

Sailor, J. L. (2006). *A phenomenological study of falling out of romantic love as seen in married couples* (doctoral dissertation). Retrieved from ProQuest. (UMI Number, 3238277).

Sailor, J. L. (2013). A phenomenological study of falling out of romantic love. *The Qualitative Report, 18*(19), 1–22.

Schmitt, D. P. (2004). The Big Five related to risky sexual behaviour across 10 world regions: Differential personality associations of sexual promiscuity and relationship infidelity. *European Journal of Personality, 18*(4), 301–319.

Shpancer, N. (2016, August 2). How your personality predicts your romantic life: Big Five personality traits predict marital sex, success, and satisfaction. Retrieved September 21, 2018 from www.psychologytoday.com/us/blog/insight-therapy/201608/how-your-personality-predicts-your-romantic-life.

Simpson, J. A. (1990). Influence of attachment styles on romantic relationships. *Journal of Personality and Social Psychology, 59*(5), 971.

Sims, K. E. & Meana, M. (2010). Why did passion wane? A qualitative study of married women's attributions for declines in sexual desire. *Journal of Sex & Marital Therapy, 36*(4), 360–380.

Solomon, A. H. (2017). *Loving bravely: Twenty lessons of self-discovery to help you get the love you want*. Oakland, CA: New Harbinger Publications.

Sprecher, S. (1999). "I love you more today than yesterday": Romantic partners' perceptions of changes in love and related affect over time. *Journal of Personality and Social Psychology, 76*(1), 46–53.

Sprecher, S. & Cate, R. (2004). Sexual satisfaction and sexual expression as predictors of relationship satisfaction and stability. In J. H. Harvey,

A. Wenzel, & S. Sprecher (eds), *The handbook of sexuality in close relationships* (pp. 235–256). Mahwah, NJ: Lawrence Erlbaum.

Sprecher, S. & Felmlee, D. (1992). The influence of parents and friends on the quality and stability of romantic relationships: A three-wave longitudinal investigation. *Journal of Marriage and the Family, 54*(4), 888–900.

Sprecher, S., Sullivan, Q., & Hatfield, E. (1994). Mate selection preferences: Gender differences examined in a national sample. *Journal of Personality and Social Psychology, 66*(6), 1074–1080.

Tashiro, T. (2014). *The science of happily ever after: What really matters in the quest for enduring love.* Don Mills, ON: Harlequin.

Tennov, D. (1979). *Love and limerence: The experience of being in love.* New York: Stein and Day.

Thao, H., Overbeek, G., & Engels, R. E. (2010). Effects of attractiveness and social status on dating desire in heterosexual adolescents: An experimental study. *Archives of Sexual Behavior, 39*(5), 1063–1071.

Walsh, F. (1993). Conceptualization of normal family processes. In F. Walsh (ed.), *Normal family processes*, 2nd edn (pp. 3–69). New York: The Guilford Press.

Wolfinger, N. (2015, July 16). *Want to avoid divorce? Wait to get married, but not too long.* [Web log comment]. Retrieved July 27, 2018 from family-studies.org/want-to-avoid-divorce-wait-to-get-married-but-not-too-long/.

The Secret Word

My sister and cousins were my favorite playmates when I was growing up. One of the things we enjoyed most was playing house using an old refrigerator box. To be admitted you had to know *the secret word*. We would take turns coming up with the secret word, but it was usually something brilliant, like "poopyhead." Recently, I shared this story with my 16-year-old daughter and she replied, "yeah, we used secret words too, but we called them *passwords*." That dates the Generation Xers, but makes perfect sense! Today, passwords are needed for everything from bank accounts to social media and medical accounts.

Do you want to know the secret word when it comes to long-term love? Commitment. For relationships, commitment is a form of protection, just like passwords safeguard our most valuable information. Commitment is what gives relationships staying power. This extra measure of security is invaluable; after all, most happy couples experience distress and difficult times (Gottman & Silver, 1999). Further, commitment early in a relationship functions to transform romantic relationships from uncertainty to stability. Therefore, without commitment, few unions would get off the ground to begin with! This chapter discusses commitment, a critical factor for romantic relationship formation, maintenance, and outcomes. Commitment is also useful for identifying those who are willing to put more into their relationship, or, for better or worse, stay in a dissatisfying relationship.

The definition of *commitment* in romantic relationships is an intention to maintain a relationship long-term (Rosenblatt, 1977; Stanley, Rhoades, & Whitton, 2010) and to persevere through difficulties because the relationship is viewed as valuable (Amato et al., 2007; Lamanna & Riedmann, 2012). Simply put, commitment implies "a future" (Rhoades, Stanley, & Markman, 2010, p. 10). Further exemplifying the importance of commitment (see Chapters 1 and 5), consummate love (sexual desire, emotional intimacy, plus commitment) is the most sought-after type of love for long-term relationships according to Stermberg's Triangular Theory of Love.

Commitment is related to the quality of relationships (see Clements & Swensen, 2000) and is considered fundamental by many (Mace & Mace, 1991). Beyond the importance of emotional and sexual intimacy in contemporary relationships, commitment has become equally necessary for marital stability due to the lack of economic, structural, or social constraints, that were present in past marriages (Teachman, Tedrow, & Hall, 2006). Regarding marital quality, commitment reflects shared goals rather than individual goals, with importance placed on maximizing joint outcomes (Stanley, Rhoades, & Whitton, 2010). Further, commitment helps to shelter relationships from infidelity and allows spouses to focus on long-term gain through sacrifice, even if it may interfere with individual gain in the moment (Stanley, Rhoades, & Whitton, 2010).

Although individuals strong on commitment are more likely to put forth greater effort and time into their relationships, high commitment does not automatically guarantee a more satisfying union or guard against FORL. Commitment can be the very thing that keeps *unhappy* marriages intact. Ultimately, commitment influences if the relationship will endure (Regan, 2011), regardless of relationship happiness. (See recommendations for sustaining commitment in a relationship in Chapter 12.) For example, an individual could fall out of romantic love with a partner in a romantic relationship lacking commitment (i.e., dating, cohabitating, affair) or high in commitment (marriage). On the other hand, a partner may fall out of romantic love and remain highly committed to their significant other (i.e., stay married).

Commitment is based on several psychological processes, some of which are not rational, starting with *positive illusions* about one's mate, which help to preserve commitment by reducing anxiety and doubts about the relationship (Berscheid & Regan, 2005) (see Chapter 7). In fact, Conley et al. (2009) found that people are happier in their relationships when they idealize (i.e., positive illusions) their partner, and this research extends to lesbian, gay, heterosexual cohabitating and married couples. Murray and Holmes (1993, 1999) cited several studies that show that those in romantic relationships tend to have idealistic and positive views of their partner, which are not seen by others outside the relationship. Further examples of positive illusions include the tendency for individuals to view their relationship as superior to others, when it is not objectively justified (Van Lange & Rusbult, 1995) and to have improbable optimism about the durability of their relationship despite the high divorce rates (see

Fowers et al., 2001; Fowers, Veingrad, & Dominicis, 2002). Positive illusions of our partners may protect ourselves from outside negativity or self-doubt about our partner being the wrong mate (Murray, Holmes, & Griffin, 1996). According to Conley et al. (2009), "people project their ideal image of a relationship partner (i.e., their image of a perfect relationship partner) onto their current partners, which leads to enhancement of the partner's positive traits" (p. 1418), somewhat like a self-fulfilling prophecy.

Researchers have struggled to define commitment as a static or variable construct (Berscheid & Regan, 2005). There are many individual predictors of commitment, including attachment style, with secure attachment being associated with willingness to commit, and avoidant attachment style less likely to commit (Davis, 1999). However, other factors also influence commitment, such as the effect each partner's level of commitment has on the other partner (Berscheid & Regan, 2005). According to Adams and Spain (1999), commitment is indeed a dynamic process that changes over time and situations. For example, an individual may have a high commitment to the original marital relationship, but when children are born and a new dynamic develops between the spouses, commitment for the emerging, post-child relationship may be lower. Berscheid and Regan (2005) observed what appears to be conditional commitment:

> Some contemporary brides and grooms revise the traditional marriage vows to specify more exactly the kind of relationship they are committing themselves to – that is, they commit themselves to the partner and the relationship not "so long as we both shall live" but rather "so long as we both shall love," foreseeing the possibility that the present relationship may change into one which they do not wish to commit themselves to continuing.
>
> (p. 211)

Related, Cherlin (2002) describes marital commitment as waning because of the trend toward individual goals instead of communal goals in relationships. Further, some commitment theorists view commitment as a variable based on ever-changing costs and rewards that can increase or decrease commitment levels. Kelley (2002) reported that when the pros outweigh the cons, commitment will persist. Like love, perhaps the construct should be viewed on a continuum instead of an absolute absence or presence. Still others believe commitment is a skill set couples need to learn and practice, and demonstrate daily, not unlike conflict resolution and communication skills (see Goddard, 2007).

Key Elements of Commitment

Theorists argue that to truly understand romantic relationship development and quality, commitment must also be understood (Rhoades, Stanley, & Markman, 2010). Scholars have identified aspects of commitment that are quite similar yet differ in terms and categorical breakdown. Like the taxonomies of love, described in Chapter 1, various commitment theories are useful for expanding our understanding of how and why relationships endure or end.

Modern commitment theories grew out of exchange theories, which are based on attraction forces and barrier forces (i.e., rewards and costs) (Rhoades, Stanley, & Markman, 2010). It is important to briefly outline the research of the main commitment scholars, Johnson (1973), Rusbult (1980), and Stanley and Markman (1992). First, Michael Johnson's (1991) commitment framework posits three distinct components of commitment: *personal commitment*, wanting to stay married, *moral commitment*, feeling morally obligated to stay married, and *structural commitment*, feeling constrained to stay married. Personal and moral commitment are functions of an individual's attitudes and values, while structural commitment refers to constraints that make it difficult or costly to leave the relationship (Johnson, Caughlin, & Huston, 1999). Johnson and his colleagues believed that all three types must be included in an overarching view of commitment because of their mutual effects on relationship endurance (Johnson, Caughlin, & Huston, 1999). In support, the major research to date regarding marital commitment tends to view the concept as multi-faceted.

Similarly, Caryl Rusbult (1980) described how, at times, people persist in marriage for reasons other than happiness. Specifically, Rusbult conceptualizes commitment from the viewpoint of the *investment model*. In the investment model, Rusbult (1983) suggests that commitment rests on three factors: 1) *level of relationship satisfaction*, based on perceived relationship rewards and costs and what the person believes they deserve; 2) *quality of alternatives*, represented by another individual, hobby, job, pet, etc. or no relationship at all; and 3) *investment size*, referring to the importance of the resources attached to the relationship that would be lost if it were to end (Rusbult, Martz, & Agnew, 1998). Rusbult (1983) notes the investment model can predict both the development and deterioration of satisfaction and commitment in relationships; including the causes of individuals staying, even when a relationship is not gratifying (Rusbult, 1983; see Rusbult, Martz, & Agnew, 1998). The investment model appears to apply to all ethnic groups, both men and women, and heterosexual and homosexual orientations (Regan, 2011; see Le & Agnew, 2003). Beyond Johnson (1973) and Rusbult et al. (1998), Stanley and Markman (1992) view commitment as comprised of two key elements, dedication and constraint. *Dedication* is described as a personal desire to be with a loved one for the joint benefit of both parties. *Constraint* is defined in terms of values and beliefs, such as *finish what you started*, as well as by internal or external pressures, amount of investment, and perceived difficulty of ending a relationship regardless of quality (Stanley, Rhoades, & Whitton, 2010). The public nature of marriage, including interest of family and friends in the continuance of the marital contract, as well as joint partner endeavors, such as childbearing and financial growth, are constraints and barriers to terminating the marriage (Musick & Bumpass, 2012). Stanley, Rhoades, and Whitton (2010) described that most marriages are likely to be unsatisfying at times, and constraints help the union to persist; in fact, poor-quality relationships often continue due to constraints. In other words, pressures to remain together are sometimes responsible for the continuation of a relationship, instead of a true desire to be with the partner (see Stanley, Rhoades, & Whitton, 2010). To illustrate, some participants in my study stayed in the marriage for many years, despite being dissatisfied. Doug stayed for six additional years after recognizing he had fallen out of romantic love. Laura remained 17 years after realizing in the first year of marriage that she had fallen out of romantic love.

However, many couples have weakened commitment from the beginning of their relationship, due to *sliding versus deciding* (i.e., initially *sliding* into a relationship rather than *deciding* to be in a long-term union) (Stanley, Rhoades, & Whitton, 2010). For instance, cohabitation or having children prior to a commitment can create difficulty for couples in achieving a solid commitment, often resulting in a higher likelihood of divorce or an enduring unhappy marriage (Stanley, Rhoades, & Whitton, 2010).

What the Data Say about Commitment

Laura reported being *a little in-love* prior to marriage, but was more focused on commitment and someone loving and needing her, as well as fulfilling her goal of having a family. Interestingly, only three participants in my study named commitment as a significant factor in their mate selection. With that said, all participants made the decision to marry, indicating commitment. It is worth considering that commitment is an implied feature of marriage, which may account for the small number of participants who specifically identified commitment as important to their mate-selection process. Two of the three participants discussed continuing their commitment to their partner, despite negative thoughts and feelings. For instance, Doug tried for many years to get his wife's love and attention, but eventually shifted the narrative from what he hoped for in marriage to simply being a good husband and father. He stayed in the marriage 12 years after FORL. Laura reported FORL one year into her marriage; however, she was married a total of 18 years, hoping things would change. She described trying hard to make the relationship work but made a significant number of excuses for her spouse. The third participant recounted significant denial during the process of FORL. Her spouse was abusive; therefore, she left the marriage upon the realization of FORL. These findings support other research suggesting commitment continues even during bad times, keeping the marriage intact longer than it would have otherwise. Although commitment often includes working harder and persevering, it may also contain aspects of denial and minimizing.

Along with the loss of emotional and/or sexual intimacy, commitment to the relationship was also eventually lost by all participants of the study – except for one, who was undecided about continuing her marriage. The participants described the pain of remaining in an unsatisfying marriage. Despite this, their marriages continued unhappily, for some time, due to commitment. It is uncertain how long a marriage or other romantic relationship can rest on commitment alone, without the rewards of emotional or physical connection. As discussed in Chapter 7, participants in this study fell out of romantic love with their partner an average of 9 years into the marriage, with the average length of marriage being 15 years. Based on these results, and as reported in previous literature, there is evidence that commitment maintains the marriage longer than the union would have continued otherwise (Stanley, Rhoades, & Whitton, 2010).

As mentioned earlier, those who drift into marriage or have children prior to marriage tend to have lower levels of commitment (Stanley, Rhoades, & Whitton, 2010). In my study, one couple was pregnant prior to marriage and four participants, or their mates, had children from previous relationships. Pregnancy prompted the one participant to marry, while others developed close relationships with their partner's children, motivating their commitment. Additionally, six participants described *sliding* into marriage. Thus, many participants either had children involved in the relationship prior to marriage and/

or drifted into marriage. More research is needed to investigate how factors such as children being present prior to relationship commitment or *sliding instead of deciding* affects long-term commitment and FORL.

So how does commitment relate to FORL? Commitment is both a blessing and a curse. It's a blessing because as discussed previously in this chapter, it gives relationships staying power when the going gets rough. It's also what we all yearn for during the enchantment and splendor of that special kind of love that makes us smile from ear to ear. Although these loving feelings are amazing, they can also be anxiety-provoking. We want assurance that the person we're smitten with not only feels the same, but that there is a future we can count on. Further, the more time you spend with this person, the greater your attachment and "the more you become attached, the more you have to lose" (Perel, 2007, p. 9). Ultimately, we crave security.

As described by Perel (2007), it feels great to have the security that comes with habits you can count on and endearing "pet-names" you give your partner, but there is a downside to commitment. Unpredictability is what fuels excitement. "Your high resulted from the uncertainty, and now, by seeking to harness it, you wind up draining the vitality out of the relationship" (Perel, 2007, p. 10). We compound that with our incredibly high expectations of modern-day marriage, and our lack of outside resources, and it creates a difficult paradox. We want commitment and security in order to have more control of ensuring that love lasts forever, but by doing so, we feel less in control of keeping it. Thus, commitment appears to be a bit of a necessary evil. As I tell my kids, there is both good and bad with most everything in life. Can we contain the possibility of a stale and boring marriage, or, worse yet, FORL, while we enjoy the positives that commitment can bring? Suggestions on how to do this can be found in Chapter 12.

One point to consider is that commitment could potentially be what gets you from FORL back to romantic love again. For example, some scholars report that romantic love can resurge (i.e., after children are raised). Because we can't predict the future and we have deduced that anything is possible with romantic love, it could be plausible that a couple who fell out of romantic love when children are younger could fall back into love as empty-nesters. The problem is, the couple would have to spend many years in a less-than-ideal marriage to see if that might happen, and there are no guarantees it will. It's a risk that many are not willing to take.

As describe by Finkel (2018), Americans don't spend nearly the amount of time with friends and relatives outside our marriage as we did in past decades. As discussed previously, we rely on just our spouse to provide everything that once was provided by our larger social networks and extended family. When it comes to love, there are two camps of people, romantics and realists. Esther Perel (2007) describes it nicely: romantics are looking for "the one," true love that never dies. Realists, on the other hand, would tell a romantic to "grow up." They tend to believe that excitement morphs into companionship and anything else is wishful thinking. "Romantics value intensity over stability. Realists value security over passion. Both are often disappointed, for few people can live happily at either extreme" (Perel, 2007, p. 3). It seems the best place to be is in between.

To commit to marriage, in light of the current divorce rate, "is so hazardous that no totally rational person would do it" (Glenn, 1991, p. 269). This sentiment is understandable considering that, at least for some, commitment appears to be variable and based on relationship costs and rewards (Kelley, 2002). Despite this, commitment is still a significant safeguard for relationship stability (Stanley, 2015). Additional research would be useful in determining strategies and techniques to bolster commitment levels.

Summary

Commitment, the intention to continue a relationship and to persevere through difficult times, has emerged as a critical factor for identifying those who continue in unhappy marriages rather than leave them (Johnson, Caughlin, & Huston, 1999; Kayser, 1993; Rusbult, Martz, & Agnew, 1998; Stanley, Rhoades, & Whitton, 2010). With that said, the role of commitment is valuable to the institution of marriage and long-term relationships, in general. If commitment did not exist, many relationships would end, even those that are largely satisfying, because even the happiest relationships have problems.

Most commitment theorists believe it is an important factor in the stability of long-term relationships. However, different theorists offer various frameworks for commitment (i.e., Johnson, 1973; Rusbult, 1980; Stanley & Markman, 1992). For example, Stanley and Markman (1992) view commitment as comprised of dedication and constraint. Individuals remain committed for a combination of reasons, including obligation, costs of ending the relationship, and enjoying rewards of the relationship (Goddard, 2007).

Finally, commitment, the intention to continue a long-term relationship (Rosenblatt, 1977; Stanley, Rhoades, & Whitton, 2010) and to persevere through difficult times (Amato et al., 2007; Lamanna, & Riedmann, 2012) appears to be a protective factor for marriage and is necessary for enduring, long-term relationships. Although commitment can drive hard work and encourage joint goals instead of individual pursuits, commitment is variable and can wane. Individuals higher on commitment are more likely to put forth greater effort or time into their marriage versus those lower on commitment (Stanley, Rhoades, & Whitton, 2010); however, high commitment does not automatically guarantee a more satisfying union. Ultimately, commitment dictates if a marriage endures or ends. However useful, commitment may not prevent FORL.

Exploration Questions

1 After reading about commitment, what are three benefits of commitment in a relationship? Can you think of situations where commitment could be problematic?
2 This chapter discusses sliding, rather than deciding to move forward with a long-term relationship. It was noted that sliding can occur when there is a pregnancy. In your opinion, what other instances might facilitate sliding rather than deciding?
3 Three frameworks of commitment were reviewed: Johnson (1973), Rusbult (1980), and Stanley and Markman (1992). Each has value; however, which framework resonates most with you? Why?

Key Concepts

commitment	sliding versus deciding
personal commitment	moral commitment
structural commitment	the investment model
dedication	constraint

References

Adams, J. M. & Spain, J. S. (1999). The dynamics of interpersonal commitment and the issue of salience. In J. M. Adams & W. H. Jones (eds), *Handbook of interpersonal commitment and relationship stability* (pp. 165–179). New York: Kluwer Academic/Plenum.

Amato, P. R., Booth, A., Johnson, D. R., & Rogers, S. J. (2007). *Alone together: How marriage in America is changing.* Cambridge, MA: Harvard University Press.

Berscheid, E. S. & Regan, P. C. (2005). *Psychology of interpersonal relationships.* Upper Saddle River, NJ: Pearson Education.

Cherlin, A. (2002). *Public and private families.* New York: McGraw-Hill.

Clements, R. & Swensen, C. H. (2000). Commitment to one's spouse as predictor of marital quality among older couples. *Current Psychology,* 19(2), 100–119.

Conley, T. D., Roesch, S. C., Peplau, L. A., & Gold, M. S. (2009). A test of positive illusions versus shared reality models of relationship satisfaction among gay, lesbian, and heterosexual couples. *Journal of Applied Social Psychology,* 39(6), 1417–1431.

Davis, K. E. (1999). What attachment styles and love styles add to the understanding of relationship commitment and stability? In J. M. Adams & W. H. Jones (eds), *Handbook of interpersonal commitment and relationship stability* (pp. 221–238). New York: Kluwer Academic/Plenum.

Finkel, E. J. (2018). *The all-or-nothing marriage: How the best marriages work.* New York: Dutton.

Fowers, B. J., Lyons, E., Montel, K. H., & Shaked, N. (2001). Positive illusions about marriage among married and single individuals. *Journal of Family Psychology,* 15(1), 95.

Fowers, B. J., Veingrad, M. R., & Dominicis, C. (2002). The unbearable lightness of positive illusions: Engaged individuals' explanations of unrealistically positive relationship perceptions. *Journal of Marriage and Family,* 64(2), 450–460.

Glenn, N. D. (1991). The recent trend in marital success in the United States. *Journal of Marriage and the Family,* 53(2), 261–270.

Goddard, H. W. (2007). Commitment in healthy relationships. *The Forum for Family and Consumer Issues,* 12(1), 1–8.

Gottman, J. M. & Silver, N. (1999). *The seven principles for making marriage work.* New York: Crown.

Johnson, M. P. (1973). Commitment: A conceptual structure and empirical application. *Sociological Quarterly,* 14, 395–406.

Johnson, M. P. (1991). Commitment to personal relationships. In W. H. Jones & D. W. Perlman (eds), *Advances in personal relationships* (pp. 117–143). London: Jessica Kingsley.

Johnson, M. P., Caughlin, J. P., & Huston, T. L. (1999). The tripartite nature of marital commitment: Personal, moral, and structural reasons to stay married. *Journal of Marriage and the Family,* 61(1), 160–177.

Kayser, K. (1993). *When love dies: The process of marital disaffection.* New York: Guilford.

Kelley, H. H. (2002). Love and commitment. In H. H. Kelley, E. Berscheid, A. Christensen, J. H. Harvey, T. L. Huston, G. Levinger, E. McClintock,

L. A. Peplau, & D. L. Peterson (eds), *Close relationships* (pp. 265–314). Clinton Corners, NY: Percheron Press.

Lamanna, M. A. & Riedmann, A. (2012). *Marriages, families, and relationships: Making choices in a diverse society*, 11th edn. Belmont, CA: Cengage Learning.

Le, B. & Agnew, C. R. (2003). Commitment and its theorized determinants: A meta–Analysis of the investment model. *Personal Relationships*, *10*(1), 37–57.

Mace, D. & Mace, V. (1991). *Marriage enrichment: The life and work of Drs. David and Vera Mace* (L. Roth, ed.). Winston-Salem, NC: The Association for Couples in Marriage Enrichment.

Murray, S. L. & Holmes, J. G. (1993). Seeing virtues in faults: Negativity and the transformation of interpersonal narratives in close relationships. *Journal of Personality and Social Psychology*, *65*(4), 707.

Murray, S. L. & Holmes, J. G. (1999). The (mental) ties that bind: Cognitive structures that predict relationship resilience. *Journal of Personality and Social Psychology*, *77*(6), 1228–1244.

Murray, S. L., Holmes, J. G., & Griffin, D. W. (1996). The benefits of positive illusions: Idealization and the construction of satisfaction in close relationships. *Journal of Personality and Social Psychology*, *70*(1), 79–98.

Musick, K. & Bumpass, L. (2012). Reexamining the case for marriage: Union formation and changes in well-being. *Journal of Marriage and Family*, *74*(1), 1–18.

Perel, E. (2007). *Mating in captivity: Unlocking erotic intelligence*. New York: Harper.

Regan, P. C. (2011). *Close relationships*. New York: Routledge.

Rhoades, G. K., Stanley, S. M., & Markman, H. J. (2010). Should I stay or should I go? Predicting dating relationship stability from four aspects of commitment. *Journal of Family Psychology*, *24*(5), 543–550.

Rosenblatt, P. C. (1977). Needed research on commitment in marriage. In G. Levinger & H. L. Rausch (eds), *Close relationships: Perspectives on the meaning of intimacy* (pp. 73–86). Amherst, MA: University of Massachusetts Press.

Rusbult, C. E. (1980). Commitment and satisfaction in romantic associations: A test of the investment model. *Journal of Experimental Social Psychology*, *16*(2), 172–186.

Rusbult, C. E. (1983). A longitudinal test of the investment model: The development (and deterioration) of satisfaction and commitment in heterosexual involvements. *Journal of Personality and Social Psychology*, *45*(1), 101.

Rusbult, C. E., Martz, J. M., & Agnew, C. R. (1998). The investment model scale: Measuring commitment level, satisfaction level, quality of alternatives, and investment size. *Personal Relationships*, *5*(4), 357–387.

Stanley, S. (2015). Seven ways to make yourself divorce-proof. Retrieved October 14, 2018 from www.psychologytoday.com/us/blog/sliding-vs-deciding/201503/7-ways-make-yourself-divorce-proof.

Stanley, S. M. & Markman, H. J. (1992). Assessing commitment in personal relationships. *Journal of Marriage and the Family*, *54*(3), 595–608.

Stanley, S. M., Rhoades, G. K., & Whitton, S. W. (2010). Commitment: Functions, formation, and the securing of romantic attachment. *Journal of Family Theory & Review*, 2(4), 243–257.

Teachman, J., Tedrow, L., & Hall, M. (2006). The demographic future of divorce and dissolution. In M. Fine & J. Harvey (eds), *Handbook of divorce and relationship dissolution* (pp. 59–82). New York: Routledge.

Van Lange, P. A. & Rusbult, C. E. (1995). My relationship is better than – and not as bad as – Yours is: The perception of superiority in close relationships. *Personality and Social Psychology Bulletin*, 21(1), 32–44.

Common Dimensions of FORL

In Chapter 7, factors believed to contribute to FORL were outlined. The goal of this chapter is to review the five properties or dimensions common across FORL experiences (Hemesath, 2016; Hemesath & Hurt, 2017). Falling out of love appears to be a process occurring over time, comprised of loose *patterns* that were consistent among participants. Additionally, the existence of a *point of no return* is indicated, which signifies the moment when the lost love was acknowledged by one or both spouses and the chance of reconnecting are slim. Further, a variety of *efforts* to remedy dissatisfaction in the marriage were attempted. *Considerable emotional pain* was described as part of FORL. Finally, FORL is thought to be a relatively *common experience* (see Box 9.1).

Box 9.1 Common Dimensions of the Process of FORL

- *Patterns.* There are four patterns to FORL: (a) red flags; (b) efforts; (c) indifference; and (d) completion – FORL had occurred and participants were considering the viability of the relationship.
- *The point of no return.* A majority of the participants indicated a point of no return in the marital relationship, defined as a point where acceptance of FORL had taken place by the participant and there was no plan or desire to reconcile the relationship.
- *Efforts made.* Various individual and partnered attempts to resolve marital issues ensued throughout the process of FORL, including: (a) individual therapy; (b) couple's therapy; (c) pastoral care; (d) communicating directly with spouses,

family, or friends about problems; (e) being kind to the spouse; (f) providing support to the spouse; (g) personal soul-searching; (h) reading self-help books; (i) attempting to fix the situation themselves; (j) agreeing to an open marriage; (k) entering into an extramarital affair; (l) trying harder; (m) ignoring their own feelings; or (n) changing their expectations.

- *Emotional struggle.* The participants expressed emotional struggle throughout the process of FORL regarding: (a) concerns about children; (b) not having the family unit together; (c) not wanting to be divorced; (d) regret for not seeing warning signs prior to marriage; (e) not leaving sooner; (f) feeling judged; (g) being uncertain about their decision; and (h) feeling hurt or concern for their spouse. The emotional pain was significant, and included feelings such as self-blame, regret, shame, guilt, confusion, hope-lessness, exhaustion, anger, and sorrow.

- *Advice.* The participants shared advice regarding various aspects of FORL. The most common advice given for profes-sionals, such as marriage therapists, was to meet the client where they are. Advice given for individuals in early roman-tic relationships included: (a) know yourself; (b) go slow; (c) know your mate; (d) be healthy emotionally; (e) pay atten-tion; (f) be honest with yourself; (g) make decisions by both thinking and feeling; (g) don't ignore warning signs or intui-tion; (i) get educated on healthy relationships; and (j) know what to look for. Advice cited for those already in marriage included: (a) know yourself; (b) put each other first; (c) expect change; (d) work hard; (e) engage in the process; (f) pay attention; (g) don't ignore your feelings; and (h) commu-nicate. Last, some participants recommended individual or couple's counseling, both before *and* during marriage.

Patterns

FORL generally does not happen overnight (Hemesath, 2016; Hemesath & Hurt, 2016, 2017; Kayser, 1990; Sailor, 2006). In other words, most people do not go to bed in-love and wake up out of love. This brings about questions regarding the process of FORL. When the prospect of stages was investigated in this study, the results were mixed. Six participants expressed there were not stages, whereas nine participants reported the likelihood of stages, but had difficulty naming them. Adam loosely reflected on the stages he experienced:

> There probably [were] stages that I went through. I can't put any labels or tell you what they were, but yeah ... I felt the rejection ... that led into other things ... not talking effectively about things, not working through things ... and ultimately ... not even really liking each other.

Together, the data from all 15 participants revealed similar patterns, over a period of time, indicating a process. The common patterns were: a) red flags – "warnings," "realizations"; b) efforts to remedy the concerns – "trying to re-engage," "last-ditch effort to fix it," "trying to please"; c) indifference – "ambivalence," "I don't care," "acceptance that this is how it will be"; d) completion, FORL has occurred – "giving up," "I'm done," "I've decided we need to separate." An illustration of a *red flag* came from Joe, who was ready to leave on military deployment:

> I remember saying to her ... "I don't know how to say this, but something feels strange about this" ... I think that was my first acknowledgement that this isn't working. I'm ready to get on a plane. She's nice enough to drop me off ... the trouble I'm having is leaving [child] and [child]. My trouble is not leaving her.

The notion of FORL as a process, inclusive of patterns, seems to fit with Kayser's (1990, 1993) work on marital disaffection. In fact, the results of this study are quite similar to Kayser's (1990) three stages of marital disaffection: a) *disappointment*, comprised of disillusionment (i.e., turning points), leading to increased anger, hurt, negativity, thoughts of leaving, and withdrawal emotionally and physically; b) *between disappointment and disaffection*, consisting of continued anger, hurt, negativity, assessing rewards and costs, trying to change the marriage, thoughts of leaving, and withdrawal emotionally and physically; and c) *reaching disaffection*, comprising apathy and indifference and a possible decision to end the marriage (Kayser, 1990, p. 259). Further, "red flags," as found in this study, are equivalent to "turning points," found by Kayser (1990, 1993).

Hemesath and Hurt (2016) found mixed support for the existence of formal stages of FORL. Sailor (2013) noted two general patterns, a gradual decline in romantic love, followed by a pivotal moment of knowing the love was gone. Due to inconsistencies between studies, it is too soon to draw formal conclusions regarding specific stages. At the very least it appears FORL follows a similar pattern for most individuals. Future research on the process of FORL would be enormously useful in terms of conceptualization, assessment, and treatment. For instance, if we can better pinpoint timing and specific key events, treatment would likely be more successful.

It is an important reminder that although FORL generally occurs over a period of time, there are instances where it may occur suddenly, such as if there has been an extraordinary breach of trust. For example, it would be possible to fall out of love with your partner instantly if you discovered they were abusing your child. It is also possible you may continue to have romantic love for that individual, despite a revelation of this magnitude.

The Point of No Return

Most participants (n = 13) indicated a *point of no return*, which was loosely defined as a point in the relationship where acceptance had taken place and the participant had no plan or desire to reconcile their love. The point of no return aligned with the completion of FORL. At the point of no return, the participant and spouse were still married, but many were considering separation or divorce. The point of no return was accompanied by the sentiment that once romantic love was gone, it would be too difficult to resurrect, the drive was not there, and there was nothing either the participant or their partner could do to reverse the loss of romantic love.

One participant explained reaching the point of no return in a counseling session when sharing his concerns about the relationship. Adam noted,

I think I probably knew at that point it's really over ... but falling out of romantic love probably happened earlier than that in terms of a consistent feeling.

Tessa spoke of points of significant dissatisfaction several times throughout the course of her marriage, eventually reaching the point of no return, despite her commitment to making it work.

But he [spouse] tried for a period, there was that honeymoon period of about three or four years where he stopped doing that kind of stuff and then it just went back ... then there was another point where I was just like done, and I still kept trying cause I wanted to stay together for the kids' sake ... I'm going to stay until my youngest daughter is out of high school, but then I just hit that point again where, I'm just ... done.

These findings were supported by Hemesath and Hurt (2016), Kayser (1990, 1993), and Sailor (2006, 2013). For example, Kayser asserted (1993), "Even in cases in which the partner made substantial changes, the respondents described a 'point of no return,' that is, a point beyond which feelings could no longer be restored" (p. 88). Sailor's (2013) alternate term for the point of no return was a "pivotal moment," of knowing the romantic love is gone. The point of no return is an important consideration for assessment and treatment purposes because it can indicate where an individual is in the process of FORL and guide clinicians to implement the interventions that may be most useful. (See Chapter 12 for clinical suggestions regarding what to do when one or both partners have fallen out of romantic love.)

Efforts to Save the Marriage

The participants employed both individual and partnered attempts to remedy their marital dissatisfaction. The majority of participants sought couple's therapy (n = 11) and/or individual therapy (n = 12), and a few sought pastoral support (n = 3). Other efforts to address the problems included communicating with their partner directly, and less-common tactics such as offering kindness or support to their partner, engaging in personal soul-searching, negotiating with the spouse, reading self-help literature, and trying to fix the problems on their own. Because all participants eventually experienced FORL, it may be tempting to conclude the uselessness of the strategies – or, worse yet, to wonder if the strategies themselves caused FORL. Although possible, this is not probable, because the tactics employed by the participants are generally considered helpful.

Individual Therapy

Of those who participated in *individual therapy* (n = 11) all but one reported greatly benefiting, generally described in terms of processing thoughts and feelings, personal growth, or healing. Specifically, participants noted understanding oneself, their contribution to the state of the relationship, and feeling validated. Consider Allison's explanation of how individual therapy was useful for her:

The biggest thing was helping me process and heal. Processing what I did to contribute to the end of the relationship and how that, working together with the issues we had as a couple, contributed to each other. It was also a validation. Sometimes when I was in the thick of it, I would start to second-guess my reality. Therapy helped me to get grounded around that and really process things from a centeredness space instead of a chaos space.

The only participant who reported not benefitting from individual counseling described that he had attended Christian counseling for only one visit, but didn't continue due to feeling judged.

Couple's Therapy

Out of the 11 participants who sought *couple's therapy*, six participants found it to be helpful regardless of their eventual experience of FORL. Therapy efforts described as effective earlier in the marriage included communication, working through affairs, and rebuilding. Despite those gains being lost over time, longer-lasting benefits included a better understanding of themselves, their spouse, and the relationship. Frank noted gaining insight from couples counseling:

"I can't say coming to me will keep you married or get you a divorce, but you're going to learn." And that's the person [therapist] I learned a lot from about relationships ... I could have stayed married. If I had ... changed ... I think she gave up ... 'cause she didn't want to change either.

The participants who were not benefited by couple's therapy described poor results as being caused by the spouse and/or participant not wanting to take part in therapy, or the participant feeling they could not be honest about what was really going on in the relationship (i.e., abuse, affairs). Adam described his counseling attempts and outcome:

I mean, we worked on some action items and tasks ... during that therapy ... we did have better intimacy and better emotional connection. And yeah, we did work on, um, some of those things, and you know, it helped in our relationship for that period of time, and then once we didn't go anymore, it was like we just reverted back ... then she decided to stop going when it came time to talk about what [I] needed her to do differently ... I could have probably forced the issue if maybe I had wanted it more myself, and I own that too, that we didn't go.

Interestingly, none of the participants who attended couple's therapy used the phrase "falling out of love" in their sessions to describe their situation. This suggests a few possibilities: the participant may have been unfamiliar with the phrase or they may not have identified themselves as falling out of love, at the time. Additionally, FORL may not have been mentioned because it could be perceived as a significant negative blow to the marriage and contraindicated for the goals of couple's therapy. These results support my own experience as a clinician, as FORL is often not mentioned as the presenting problem in couple's sessions. More commonly it is brought up in individual sessions. This finding is important because it suggests providers need to assess for FORL in couple's therapy by listening closely for contributing factors, even if FORL is not specifically referenced.

Pastoral Care

Of the three participants who used *pastoral care* to address their relationship concerns, one found it somewhat helpful and two found it unhelpful. For example, as Frank described,

> I listened and tried to think I was keeping an open mind ... but I also somewhat discredited it [because the priest had never been married] ... it was a lot more of the Biblical version of marriage. They don't care if you don't like it anymore, you're married.

More research would be greatly beneficial to understand how pastoral care may assist individuals and couples affected by FORL.

Direct Communication with Spouse

Fourteen participants said that they *communicated with their spouse* directly about the problems. As illustrated by Doug,

> Occasionally, I would come out with "I'm not satisfied, something needs to change" and whenever I would do that she would try and show differently, but it would only last like a couple weeks.

Talking to the partner about their concerns was not effective long-term. Some spouses attempted to change or repair problems discussed by the participant, but these attempts were largely unproductive. Based on participant responses, it is likely the communication may not have been effective for a variety of reasons. For instance, the participant may have brought the topic up too late in the process of FORL when too much damage had already been done. The participant may not have been clear about their concerns, or the spouse may not have understood the seriousness of the situation. Alternatively, the spouse may not have felt the problems presented by the participant were valid or didn't share the same feelings. Finally, the spouse or participant may not have been interested in or able to make changes to adequately address the concerns. Delving further into the process of communication would be beneficial for understanding its role in FORL.

Communication with Family or Friends

About half of the participants (n = 7) *communicated with family and friends* about their relationship problems. These confidants were considered members of their support system. Such sharing was not identified as contributing to their FORL. One participant reported that her parents' acceptance and understanding of her decision to divorce was helpful.

Overall, family and friends were supportive of the participants, and sometimes had quite a substantial influence on their decision to leave the relationship. For example, in a few cases, the family or friends were concerned for the safety of the participant, and in another case, the extended family felt the participant's spouse was taking advantage of the participant. The reasons some participants gave for not talking to their family or friends about their marital struggle included issues of privacy or not feeling comfortable.

Investing Patience and Time

It was clear from the responses most participants *invested patience and significant time* into their marital relationships. As noted by Liz:

I was married 28 years, and so that time span was all focused on children ... doing the right thing for 28 years.

The participants indicated they experienced FORL with their spouse an average of 9 years into the marriage (range of 1–20 years). Interestingly, they indicated beginning thoughts of unhappiness an average of 3 years into the marriage (range of 0–14 years). Therefore the average time frame from the first inklings of FORL to the end of the relationship was approximately 6 years. Because FORL does not appear to be a hasty process, there may be time to stop damage from occurring if interventions are begun sooner rather than later (more on this in Chapter 12). In support of these findings, Kayser (1990) reported that the length of the process of disaffection among her participants varied from 1 to 38 years, with an average of 11 years. Sailor (2006) did not report the specific timing of FORL in her study, although describes FORL as happening over time. These results suggest FORL does not generally occur quickly, nor is taken lightly. Although much time was spent in these relationships, what is done with that time is likely of great importance. Gaining additional details about what both partners were doing, or not doing, throughout the course of the relationship would be helpful to the study of FORL.

Other Efforts

Many participants initially blamed themselves and attempted to fix the situation by trying harder, ignoring their feelings, or changing their expectations, which appeared to work for a while. Additional strategies included showing kindness, providing support for the spouse, personal soul-searching, or reading self-help books. Kelly focused on supporting her spouse:

> I kept working harder and harder to help him ... so I put aside myself, my feelings ... I was trying to be there for him and do things how he wanted, how he would like ... and I was trying to help take any chores ... he could just focus on fixing his life ... I really wanted to save the family.

Liz consulted self-help books:

> Well, yeah, I read books, but that was again, one sided. I mean, there was lots of times when I would be looking at some sort of self-help book to figure out, like communicating ... here's what I have to say and how he's going to respond according to the book, and it didn't work.

Laura scheduled getaways for her and her partner:

> I would plan getaways ... I said, every six weeks I want us to go somewhere, so I got a beautiful bed and breakfast in La Jolla, a cozy little place, and we flew there. We flew to Hawaii and never had sex ... I was constantly trying to re-ignite that, constantly trying to take us away.

One participant reported having an affair as an attempt to supplement or stabilize her marriage. Two participants noted that they and their spouse agreed to try an open marriage arrangement to remedy their marital problems. The participants indicated that neither tactic was beneficial over the long term. Although they did provide some stabilization or met some of the participants' needs, they caused other problems such as guilt or jealousy. Doug described their attempt at open marriage:

> She suggested open marriage ... she's like, "I'm tired of not being able to give you what you need. I want us to work and if you can get some of this emotional intimacy that you're talking about with someone else then, maybe, maybe we can be okay." So, she set me up with her friend ... it was weird ... it didn't work out with the friend ... but you know what it did do, what I really appreciated, was that it made our relationship, um, equal cause we had to talk about everything ... we had to trust each other. We had to respect each other, we had to, um, be vulnerable and it made [her] show up in a way that she never had before and I just, I've really appreciated that part of it ... and in that way it was really good for us. I started dating and had an instant, like emotional connection to her, and it was just really great. It was meeting some of those needs and she got really, really jealous ... and we were still doing the open marriage thing and had been for a while and ... it was working fine, um, but when she could see that I was getting some of those needs met elsewhere, it was really hard on her and she got, she started getting really mean.

In support of the findings on effort, Kayser (1990) described numerous problem-solving actions of participants, including talking to the partner about their concerns, attempts to please their partner, marriage counseling, and actions to dissolve the marriage (i.e., contacting an attorney, saving money, seeking alternate housing). Hemesath and Hurt (2016) reported remedies that included self-help books, talking with the spouse, friends, or extended family about their concerns, individual counseling, temporary separation, attempts to re-engage with their spouse through couple's counseling, spending quality time together (i.e., date nights, trips), and having a child. Worth noting, if couple's therapy took place after the "point of no return" had been reached, it was not done to repair the relationship, but for other reasons (i.e., end the marriage with professional assistance, cope with pressure from the spouse or others). This finding was also supported by Kayser (1993), who reported that 27 percent of participants sought professional counseling in the last phase;

however, it was not done for the purpose of repairing the marriage. Sailor (2006, 2013) did not address remedies or problem-solving actions. Overall, the efforts of the participants were not able to thwart the eventual experience of FORL. Understanding which strategies, under what conditions, benefit and protect intimate partner relationships would be enormously useful. However, it is important to remember that factors prior to meeting a potential long-term partner influence the possibility of FORL, such as mate selection and attachment styles.

Significant Emotional Pain

All participants reported that they struggled emotionally throughout the process of FORL. The most common aspects of this emotional struggle were concerns about children (i.e., wanting to protect them, not wanting to hurt them, concern about their welfare), not having the family unit together, and not wanting to be divorced. As illustrated by Liz,

> I really think adult children don't deal with divorce as easily as the little children do. It's so traumatizing for them and my son had just gotten married and it was so traumatizing ... my boys didn't speak to me for, from May to September, it was really difficult.

As described by Janet, "I felt so terrible that I failed again." Laura described sticking it out for 17 years, knowing that her marriage was over:

> How long do I wait? What do I do? ... I'll just stay in this hell hole. Even though we're not really in a marriage ... then you're playing out all sorts of dysfunctional sick crap ... I think just sort of takes your soul away.

Other struggles included regret for not seeing warning signs prior to marriage, not leaving sooner, feeling judged, being uncertain about the morality of their decision (self-care versus being selfish), and feeling hurt or concern for their spouse due to still caring for them or loving them, despite the loss of romantic love. As indicated by Janet, "I still had feelings for him, but ... what was totally necessary for a good marriage and to be healthy and stay together wasn't there." Laura described sadness for her spouse:

> I always felt sorrow for him that he could never get the courage to face his stuff, because I think there was a deep nugget of

a really beautiful human being that he never uncovered and never had the courage to let shine.

Nicole described feeling tremendous guilt:

> He would do absolutely anything for me ... I'm a terrible person because I have what most people would die for and ... I don't even want it.

To reiterate, a dominant pattern among the participants was that of emotional struggle. They had painful feelings toward themselves (i.e., self-blame, regret, guilt, and shame), toward the relationship (i.e., indecision, ambivalence, surprise, confusion, hopelessness, exhaustion, sorrow), and toward their spouse (i.e., under-valued, not listened to, criticized, less attracted, disrespected, anger). See Chapter 7 for more information on feelings.

The findings associated with the emotional pain of FORL were also supported by Hemesath and Hurt (2016) who described guilt, shame, confusion, anger, tiredness, fear, regret, apathy, and failure. Additionally, Sailor (2006) reported emotional pain including grief, exhaustion, devastation, fear, feeling unloved, anger, and low self-esteem, describing "the emotional pain of falling out of romantic love with one's spouse was intense, penetrating, and unrelenting" (p. 152). Finally, Kayser (1990, 1993) discussed that disaffection included anger, hurt, disillusionment, loneliness, hopelessness, hurt, ambivalence, and pity. Although hardship is expected from the partner on the receiving end of FORL, these findings are useful because it provides a more complete understanding of the emotional pain on the road to FORL.

Participant Advice on Romantic Relationships

Neither Kayser (1990) or Sailor (2006) reported advice given by participants in their research. Alternatively, 14 of the participants in this study offered words of advice for both professionals (i.e., couple counselors, clergy) and individuals in romantic relationships. The most common suggestion for professionals was to meet the client where they are at. Allison shared her experience with a marriage counselor:

> Marriage counselors, I don't know, I only know one personally, like, that I've been in front of, and he's, he's an amazing soul, um, funny, when I made my decision and I went back to him and I'm like, I made my decision, I'm done. You know, and he celebrated with me and he gave me permission to celebrate.

And he was like, he just, the look on his face, to know that I was free, freeing myself ... he meets you where you're at and that's what I'm trying to do for people in my life, right now ... People just need permission sometimes, to be ... And it's about the being and it's not about the doing ... but learning how to be comfortable in being, but also knowing that someone's there for your "being self," even if it's ugly and hideous and gut-wrenching, that they're still there. I mean, that's to me what a counselor provides – no matter how horribly you show up.

Advice for individuals in romantic relationships was provided by the participants for two separate time frames, *prior* to marriage and *during* marriage. The most common advice given by the participants before marriage was to know yourself, followed by recommendations to go slow, know your mate, be healthy emotionally, pay attention, be honest with yourself, make decisions by both thinking and feeling, don't ignore warning signs or intuition, gain education on healthy relationships, and know what to look for. As suggested by Laura, "I would advise anybody, clearheaded thinking, clearheaded thinking ... the perfect balance of clearheaded thinking and emotional thinking." Adam offered this view:

I would have slowed down. If I could talk to myself at that point, I would say, don't rush into it. You know ... you're caught up in the moment, caught up in the feelings of this is perfect, this is right, let's do it, but ... we didn't have any reason to rush into it, so I think I would have told myself to slow down, spend some more time getting to really know this person ... Make sure that you share the values. Make sure that you share the same life goals ... how do you see the roles ... once you start living together. I think it's probably having dialogue around those things. And talking about, um, you know, what's important to each person and I don't think we really did that a lot. We talked superficial-level stuff at that age, and at that point we didn't really get into the deep level of really understanding what was really important to us at the core, both of us ... I think part of it too is really each person knowing themselves completely ... And I don't know if you know yourself ever completely 100 percent. It's a process too, right? I'm definitely a different person now than I was when we got married. I'm different, I'm at a different level of maturity in terms of relationships and what I know I can give and how I want things to be and what my ideal definition would be now ... of a spouse versus what it was then.

Frank described paying attention was primary:

> Pay attention ... you need to pay attention to what your mind tells you. So many people put it off. Oh, I'm not going to pay attention to that ... Oprah Winfrey once made a statement ... "humans are the only animal that will run toward danger." The others know better. We ignore it. I thought, that's quite a statement. You need to get back to realizing that this is what it is. You have to pay attention to what you feel.

The participants' most common recommendations to individuals *during* marriage were to know yourself, put each other first, expect change, work hard, engage in the process, pay attention, don't ignore your feelings, and communicate. Liz spoke of her spouse changing during the course of their marriage:

> I think both parties have to be open to ... the other person is not who they were when you first got married. I was not that 19-year-old person that you saved from a terrible childhood ... I'm not that person. Thank God. There's lots of healing and growing, and they have to grow in the same direction. They can't grow in two separate directions, which is what happened ... growing parallel ... you keep checking in and you're, um, respectful and, um, encouraging ... More than what's for supper, I mean more like, how are you feeling?

Finally, most participants had some kind of therapy and found it beneficial, with three specifically recommending individual or couple's therapy, both before and during marriage, to understand oneself and the relationship, suggesting sources of positive, outside support.

The nuggets of advice offered by the participants are especially useful because they come from those who have lived the experience of FORL, first-hand. However, providing recommendations on the topic of intimate partner relationships was not always easy, highlighting its complexity, and the need for further research. For example, Tessa noted, "try to marry your best friend, you know, or try to be with your best friend, but ... a lot of times there's no attraction there ... so it's hard to say." Jack gave his advice:

> Oh just like lots of hours [of] therapy, and, um, you know, figuring why I react to certain things in certain ways, figuring out what it is I'm looking for in a relationship, and, um, what I do, you know, when I'm stressed, or ... all my triggers ... if I was advising myself, I mean, pretty much every decision was the

wrong one … so, um, I would have lots of advice for myself. Um … I mean, for other people, it's just, um, figuring out how to understand what you're feeling and then just communicating that directly and then dealing with, um, I guess what that means.

FORL as a Common Experience

Fourteen participants indicated that FORL is a common experience. These results suggest that FORL is something worth investigating as it is not a rare phenomenon. As judged by Adam, "I don't think it's unique, I mean, I guess I can't comment on anybody else, specifically, but I mean, I can't imagine I'm the only person that's gone through this." Tessa agreed:

> Oh my, everybody but their dog … that's been married for a while, um, has fallen out of love with their spouse, and then there's the other half … they're still madly in love with their spouse, but they don't know their spouse is a dog, um, you know … like you wonder if people are clueless or whatever, but yeah, I know people that are still married that have fallen out of love with their spouse.

These findings corroborate related research suggesting that "a lack of loving feelings" ranks highest in problems presented in couple's therapy by way of frequency of presentation, difficulty treating, and level of damage to the relationship (Whisman, Dixon, & Johnson, 1997). Hemesath and Hurt (2016) also found FORL to be a relatively common experience. Kayser (1990) and Sailor (2006) did not specifically address the commonality of FORL. Because there is very little research on this phenomenon, the commonality of the experience needs to be examined further. See Table 9.1 for a summary of the findings from this chapter and Chapter 7.

Summary

Although distinct stages were not identified, FORL is generally a process, occurring over time, with several typical dimensions, including emerging patterns (i.e., red flags, indifference). Additionally, the existence of a point of no return was identified, signifying the moment when the lost love was acknowledged by the participant and the chance of reconnecting was slim. Further, a variety of efforts to remedy marital dissatisfaction were made by the participants, but FORL occurred despite these efforts. Considerable emotional pain appears to be an unavoidable aspect of FORL. As a result of the participant's experiences several suggestions were

Table 9.1 Summary of Findings from Qualitative Analyses of Married
Individuals (n = 15) Who Experienced FORL with their Spouse

Findings	*Percentage of Participants*
Elements of Romantic Love and Marital Satisfaction	
Emotional and physical connection essential for romantic love	87%
Emotional and physical connection important to marriage	93%
Were in-love early in the relationship	100%
Weak emotional or physical connection early in the relationship	47%
Felt stronger emotional or physical connection to previous mates	47%
Pathways to FORL	
What an individual brings to the relationship – *the suitcase*	
Poor role models	67%
Family-of-origin struggles (participant)	40%
Insecure attachment characteristics	27%
Inadequate mate selection process	
Did not know what to look for in a long-term mate	47%
Did not consider costs and rewards of the relationship	67%
Married for wrong reasons/right things not considered	53%
Costs eventually outweighed rewards	100%
Lack of emotional and/or physical connection	100%
Outside influences/stressors	20%
Minimizing or denying earlier relationship problems	100%

(Continued)

Table 9.1 (Cont.)

Findings	Percentage of Participants
Emerging realizations leading to negative thinking	100%
Someone changed after marriage	
Participant changed	27%
Spouse changed	33%
Both changed	13%
Negative behaviors/actions/incidents of spouse	100%
Coping deficits of participant	20%
Dimensions of FORL	
Point of no return	87%
Multiple efforts to remedy FORL	100%
Significant emotional struggle	100%
FORL is a common experience	93%
Advice offered by participants regarding FORL (i.e., before marriage, during marriage, for professionals)	100%

provided to assist others in their romantic relationships. Finally, FORL is believed to be a relatively common experience, although the phrase "falling out of love" may not be used to describe it. Many of the results are supported by previous research.

Exploration Questions

1 This chapter notes that no specific stages were discovered through the research for this book; however, many of the findings align with Kayser's (1990) three stages. Further research is needed to establish any formal conclusions regarding stages of FORL. When thinking about the future research and also what was shared by the participants of this study, what hypothesis can you make regarding the likelihood of formal stages of FORL? Do you believe there are formal stages or that every experience of FORL is

relative to the individual's life circumstances? Explain your answer.

2 Many participants made attempts to mend their romantic relationships, but the efforts did not prevent FORL. What ideas do you have on why these efforts were not successful? Looking at your own relationship difficulties, or relationships of those close to you, give examples of efforts you believe are vital to implement to ensure the relationship stays on track.

3 This chapter shared recommendations made by participants for individuals both prior to marriage and during marriage. The most common was the notion of "knowing yourself." List three things that everyone can actively do, to better understand who they are as an individual.

Key Concepts

patterns	efforts made to save marriage
emotional struggle	advice
point of no return	individual therapy
couple's therapy	pastoral care
communication with spouse	communication with friends or family
investing patience and time	FORL as a common experience

References

Hemesath, C. W. (2016). *Falling out of romantic love: A phenomenological study of the meaning of love in marriage* (unpublished doctoral dissertation). Iowa State University, Ames, IA.

Hemesath, C. W. & Hurt, T. R. (2016). *Falling out of romantic love: A focus group study* (unpublished manuscript). Department of Human Development and Family Studies, Iowa State University, Ames, IA.

Hemesath, C. W. & Hurt, T. R. (2017). *Falling out of romantic love: An integrated theoretical framework* (unpublished manuscript). Department of Human Development and Family Studies, Iowa State University, Ames, IA.

Kayser, K. (1990). The process of marital disaffection: Interventions at various stages. *Family Relations, 39*(3), 257–265.

Kayser, K. (1993). *When love dies: The process of marital disaffection.* New York: Guilford Press.

Sailor, J. L. (2006). *A phenomenological study of falling out of romantic love as seen in married couples* (doctoral dissertation). Retrieved from ProQuest. (UMI Number, 3238277.)

Sailor, J. L. (2013). A phenomenological study of falling out of romantic love. *The Qualitative Report, 18*(19), 1–22.

Whisman, M. A., Dixon, A. E., & Johnson, B. (1997). Therapists' perspectives of couple problems and treatment issues in couple therapy. *Journal of Family Psychology, 11*(3), 361–366.

PART III

So Now What?

When Romantic Love Ends

I remember attending a wedding of a friend when I was 25, and engaged to be married myself. During the ceremony the pastor talked at length about the difficulties of marriage, to the point where I was thinking, "Wow, he sure is putting a damper on this happy occasion!" After 21 years of marriage, I understand how daily life and certain developmental stages (i.e., the birth of a baby) can and will bring about stress and frustration with a spouse. Many of these tense moments are replaced by warmth. However, when of longer duration and intensity, relationship satisfaction can be hindered. Eventually the hope of emotional connection and/or physical interest returning in a way that is gratifying can be lost.

What makes for a happy, satisfying marriage? Although the conditions and factors responsible for happiness are subjective, Halford, Kelly, and Markman (1997) defined a long-term, healthy relationship as,

> a developing set of interactions between partners which promotes the individual well-being of each partner and their offspring, assists each partner to adapt to life stresses, engenders a conjoint sense of emotional and sexual intimacy between the partners, and which promotes the long-term sustainment of the relationship within the cultural context in which the partners live.
>
> (p. 8)

The loss of romantic love is not what most individuals want or expect out of their marital relationship. With that said, it is important to differentiate between the kind of fleeting unhappiness that is typical in a healthy marriage – and the longer-term, more profound sense of unhappiness that comes with FORL. For example, all long-term romantic relationships go through ups and downs, and change is natural for human beings. That being said, I have provided ten signs indicating you *may* be experiencing FORL (see Box 10.1).

Box 10.1 Ten Signs You May Have Fallen Out of Romantic Love

1 I have lost emotional connection with and/or physical desire for my partner.
2 The costs of my relationship seem to outweigh the rewards.
3 My partner and/or I have changed in significant ways.
4 I experience my partner's behavior as increasingly frustrating, annoying, or poor.
5 Emerging realizations have led me to have negative feelings about myself, my partner, and/or our relationship.
6 I no longer feel my relationship with my partner is special.
7 Single life has become more appealing to me and/or I have interest in other romantic partners.
8 I have struggled with feelings of sadness, hopelessness, and/or indifference about the relationship.
9 I have no desire or plans to work on the relationship and/or I am considering ending the relationship.
10 There is nothing more my partner or I can do to change our situation.

Note: it is common for individuals who have FORL to experience *more than one* of these signs; however, the presence of one or more of these items does NOT mean FORL has or will occur. For example, change is typical and natural for human beings. The more items you agree with, the higher the likelihood you could be on the path to FORL.

Can There be Satisfaction in the Absence of Romantic Love?

Can a romantic love relationship be happy without romantic love? This implies an oxymoron. The obvious answer is "no," right? Not so fast. Some scholars say companionate love, comprised of commitment and emotional intimacy, is satisfying and can sustain some marriages, with anything more being unrealistic. Yet companionate love is often insufficient for many (Sternberg & Weis, 2006). A challenge some companionate relationships face is "degeneration into a brother-and-sister relationship" (Berscheid & Regan, 2005, p. 427). Yet, other research maintains some partners are quite happy, even with the loss of sexual intimacy or desire (Sims & Meana, 2010).

It is unknown how likely it is for couples to become satisfied again after a period of unhappiness (see Acevedo & Aron, 2009; Berscheid & Hatfield, 1969; Buss, 2006; Montgomery & Sorell, 1997; O'Leary et al., 2012; Sims & Meana, 2010; Sprecher & Regan, 1998; Sternberg, 1987; Tucker & Aron, 1993). However, it would seem the longer an individual has been dissatisfied, the more unlikely it would be for satisfaction to return (Hawkins & Booth, 2005). Yet, it is challenging to form this conclusion because of the plethora of complex events and processes involved in romantic relationships. For example, some studies incite hope that couples can reconnect following the launching of children (Sims & Meana, 2010). Overall, it appears easier to repair marriages where there was once a strong romantic love compared to minimal love, or no romantic love to begin with (Kayser, 1993).

The simple answer to the question many have asked – "is marital satisfaction a possibility when FORL has occurred" – is a resounding *it depends*. If your values, goals, and needs are in line with ideals such as a shared history, financial security, raising children, and stability, then marriage can indeed be satisfying, even if romantic love has been replaced with a different form of love (i.e., companionate love). However, one of the complexities of human relationships is that values, goals, and needs can and do shift over time, often unexpectedly. So, although commitment may keep you married, it may not be satisfying in the absence of romantic love unless your values and goals align with other aspects of the relationship deemed valuable.

Remember our discussion in Chapter 5 about social exchange theory and its application to entering relationships by weighing of rewards and costs? People considering divorce process rewards and costs in a similar fashion. In fact, although most research on relationship dissolution has been on marital relationships, even long-term non-marital relationships appear to have the same dynamics (Kamp Dush, 2011). Research shows that generally, care or concern for children, religious values, and finances are considered the greatest deterrents or costs of divorce (Previti & Amato, 2003). Specifically, child-related reasons can be enough to delay or thwart an impending divorce (Poortman & Seltzer, 2007). Many often wonder if they would be happier if they ended the marriage. Unfortunately, no one can know that answer for certain, because there is no crystal ball and the future can be difficult to predict.

Often, leaving a committed relationship, no matter how unhappy you are, is incredibly difficult. Understandably, quitting and failure are challenging for many people, including when it comes to marriage and other intimate partner relationships. In fact, in my clinical work, I see the struggle with perceived failure as one of the greatest hurdles for clients considering divorce. No doubt, hard work and persistence are significant contributors to success in everyday life and relationships. Important values such as religion, commitment, kindness, children, and extended family can encourage people to keep trying. Ideally, all efforts would be exhausted prior to a decision to exit the relationship. Not only is this important for giving the relationship the best shot at success, but it sends a message to your partner that you took it seriously. It also gives the individual who has FORL assurance they have done all they can and lessens the possibility of regret. I have seen people who appear to walk away without much soul-searching or effort given. However, more often, I have seen individuals try for years, holding steadfast to their values and ideals, while their dissatisfying marriage continues, hoping it will change.

Living our best life includes honoring our values and being true to them. When we don't, we usually don't feel very good about ourselves or the situation. Beyond children, religious beliefs, commitment, and other personal values, most people also value life satisfaction. Considering our relationships add significant meaning to our lives, it's easy to see how unhappy relationships can sometimes cause major values conflicts within us. But what happens when living one value means going against another? – anxiety, stress, confusion, sadness, and overall feeling pretty lousy. Often, values conflicts show up during the process of FORL. (See Chapter 12 for information on addressing values conflicts.)

Is it Best to Divorce?

The literature regarding dissatisfied couples remaining married or getting divorced is mixed. Hawkins and Booth (2005) noted the significant lack of attention research has given to long-term, unhappy marriages, and the individual and societal costs of staying in them. Their study focused on a nationally representative longitudinal sample of unhappily married individuals who had experienced continuous dissatisfaction at four separate points for at least 12 years. It seems likely that marriages that have been unhappy long-term may not be as recoverable as those of a shorter-term unhappiness (Hawkins & Booth, 2005). Furthermore, the results indicated that, despite the negative aspects associated with divorce, "Divorced individuals who remarry have greater overall happiness, and those who divorce and remain unmarried have greater levels of life satisfaction, self-esteem, and overall health, than unhappily married people" (Hawkins & Booth, 2005, p. 462). Ultimately, staying in an emotionally dead or unfulfilling marriage can be just as painful and damaging as the dissolution of a marriage (Kayser, 1993).

Alternatively, Waite and colleagues (2002) conducted a study of 645 spouses drawn from a nationally representative database who rated themselves as unhappy in their marriages in the late 1980s, and were interviewed five years later. Of the spouses who stayed together, two-thirds said they were happy five years later; for those who did divorce, most were not much happier following divorce (Waite et al., 2002). There are some limitations to consider. It is important to note that these findings and the strength of the study's conclusions have been criticized by some scholars. Further, it is unknown how long the couples in this study had experienced unhappiness.

Tips for Decision Making

How is a person to decide if they should stay or go in the midst of an unhappy marriage? As described by Solomon (2017), the following issues suggest a poor prognosis for the outcome of a relationship: untreated addiction, abuse, patterns of dishonesty and betrayal, or lack of love. However, if you have fallen out of romantic love, you might still "love" your partner, or have other vested interests or values that make it difficult to make the decision to stay or go. I have a few tips to offer. These suggestions are useful for marriage or any type of long-term intimate partner relationship. Several of the suggestions come from "How to cope with a difficult dilemma" by Russ Harris (2013), a leader in acceptance and commitment therapy, one of my favorite theoretical frameworks used in my practice. More tips can be found in Chapter 12.

Before continuing, if you are in a relationship where you do not feel safe, FORL should be addressed at a later time. Your safety comes first. Regardless of love or lack thereof, abuse or intimate partner violence of any kind is not acceptable. Contact a trusted family member, friend, medical or mental health professional, or the authorities to assist you. You can come back to other issues when the safety concerns have been resolved.

Tip 1: try not to get hung up on the idea that deep romantic love is the only way to be satisfied in a relationship. For example, if your marriage is not emotionally all you want it to be or, conversely, everything you were hoping for sexually, remember that a marital relationship can be sexless and wonderful or alternatively, intensely passionate, erotic, and sexual but horrible in other respects (P. Regan, personal communication, August 8, 2016). Also, it's important to keep in mind that relationships, like people, are ever-changing. The marriage you have now will not be the marriage you have five, ten, or 20 years from now, which may provide optimism. What matters is that you and your partner are working toward a relationship that is mutually beneficial, despite what elements exist at a given time.

Tip 2: recognize there may be no quick fix (Harris, 2013). First, major life decisions are nothing to make hastily. Further, some struggles in life have no easy solution. I, of all people, do not enjoy perpetual mental or emotional battles with myself. But, know you are not alone; "many people consider leaving their marriages or their careers for several years before they finally do it" (Harris 2013, p. 79).

Tip 3: give yourself time to reflect, as well as time to let it go. Make sure you are balancing the amount of time you are thoughtfully considering your situation and taking a break from everything swirling around in your mind. Too much of either can be detrimental to decision making. It's certainly important to reflect about the situation on a regular basis, with no distractions or interruptions; however, it can be difficult to know how much time to spend processing the situation. A common misconception is that we must think about something continually until we find the solution. The adage "too much of a good thing" applies here. Sometimes we think so much that we get overwhelmed and confused. Taking a few days away from the topic and coming back later can provide much-needed perspective and clarity. Further, writing thoughts down or making lists can be useful for some.

Tip 4: identify your personal values and goals in your intimate partner relationship, as well as your life in general. Although we need to know our values in order to make a solid informed decision, I suspect FORL has much to do with goals and values, in a number of cases. During our lives our goals and values change, sometimes in unpredictable ways. Further, it's not uncommon for the goals within us to compete with one another or, alternatively, to conflict with our values. For instance, if my goal is to be the highest-paid prosecuting attorney in New York City, despite my values, I may take on cases that morally or ethically I wouldn't typically take. For humans, goals are high driving forces in unconscious activity, and behavior. In fact, we will sometimes break our values and morals for a goal. Afterward, people might think, "gosh, that was a crappy thing to do," "or that isn't something I would normally do." Behavior and decisions that do not seem to be in line with a person's general tendencies can be confusing and unsettling. However, when viewed in the context of meeting a goal, we begin to understand how relationships can be an unintended casualty. Understanding your goals and values, as well as how they impact your relationships, is an important consideration (see Chapter 12 for information). Many people have a difficult time readily identifying their goals and values, therefore getting someone to assist in this effort can be enormously useful.

As described by Harris (2016), values and goals are not the same and should be differentiated.

"Goals" describe what I want to have, complete, achieve, or do ... values describe the personal qualities I want to embody in my actions; the sort of person I want to be; the manner in which I want to treat myself, others, and the world around me.

(Harris, 2016, pp. 2–3)

Also, as recommended by Harris (2016), goals and values should be narrowed to a specific life realm (i.e., health, career, relationships). Assessing them one realm at a time will decrease confusion as you sort things out. For example, in the area of health, a goal could be to go to the gym three times a week, whereas a value could be self-care. Goals and values should be assessed regularly because, "It is true, however, that people can focus on some goals and values during one part of their lives, then turn their attention to different ones at other times" (Lamanna, Riedmann, & Stewart, 2018). Once values and goals are known, individuals should consider if their relationship fits within them – in other words, can the relationship coexist with your goals and values, or are they in direct conflict? Are there any deal-breakers? Meaning, could the presence or absence of a specific ingredient end the relationship? An example of a deal-breaker is drug use. For some people, if their partner used illegal drugs, it would be a deal-breaker and their relationship would end based on drug use going against their values and goals. In a second example, let's assume you have the value of healthy living and goal of physical activity and recreation; how might it be possible to experience these with your partner, even if you are not currently? You might reflect on a more satisfying time in the relationship, and the aspects you appreciated about your partner and the situation, then. If you experienced recreation before with your partner, who or what do you believe is responsible for any changes? Are these goals attainable? Sometimes biological, social, or financial factors block us from achieving our goals (Tsaousides, 2018). For instance, are you or your partner experiencing health-related issues that could be interfering with your goals? Assess the obstacles and determine if you have any control over them. "The more control you have over the factors that contribute to success, the more likely that your goal is attainable" (Tsaousides, 2018, p. 2). If there is something you can do, move forward by taking steps to resolve these issues (i.e., see a physician or offer to go with your partner to one).

If you are feeling stuck, ask yourself if you can get some aspects of the goal met in a different way than you had imagined. In other words, is there an alternate way to achieve your goal, satisfactorily, that you both can agree on (i.e., training with a friend at the gym)? This may not be possible, but it is worth considering the options. It can be helpful to consider conflicting values as "both/and" instead of "either/or." For example, if you value kindness, you can honor this value and express kindness, even if it means divorce. You can still be kind to your partner, even if you decide to part ways.

Tip 5: take a good look at your own contribution to the state of the relationship. In my two decades of providing couple's therapy, there have certainly been situations where one partner is causing more than their fair share of problems in the relationship. However, more often, both partners have contributed to the marital discontent. It's easy to point out the faults of others but identifying our own misgivings and taking responsibility for them is when true change happens. Note: abuse of any kind, verbal, emotional, physical, or sexual, is always wrong and never deserved. You may wonder why I keep bringing up the topic of abuse. I have seen too many individuals with abusive partners take the blame and the responsibility. Yet, the bar keeps moving higher, creating a situation where nothing you do will be good enough.

Tip 6: ask yourself if you have done everything you can to create or find satisfaction in the relationship (i.e., have you gone to marriage or individual therapy, have you made changes in yourself to support a positive outcome, have you communicated your feelings with your partner)? If the answer is "yes", proceed to Tip 7. If the answer is "no," it is worth your time to invest in this consideration. After all, how can you be sure the marriage cannot be what you need and want if all avenues have not been considered and exhausted? If you believe you have worked as hard as you can at your marriage, make sure you are working smart, not just hard (Goddard, 2007). Consulting a relationship professional can ensure you are coming at this from an angle that is most likely to produce positive results.

Tip 7: consider who and what is involved in your decision making. Do you suffer from depression or other mental or physical health concerns? Health problems can drastically interfere with the ability to be your best in all areas of your life, including relationships. Are you unhappy in your career or struggling with finances? Significant stress can contribute to a host of health and interpersonal problems. Are you taking advice from others? Do you feel pressured? If so, how and by whom? A family member or close friend who shares your values and is supportive of you/your relationship is a better choice to confide in than someone who would like to see your relationship end for their own benefit. Ideally, you would not be in a relationship with anyone else (i.e., affair) when you are making this decision. Metaphorically speaking, Hawaii will always look better than Iowa, especially in the new phases of a relationship. In other words, bills, childcare, work schedules, housekeeping, and laundry are the types of things new relationships generally do not have to deal with. If you are unable or unwilling to give the other person up, recognize that your current spouse is likely not getting a fair shake at winning your heart and you are not able to fully invest in your relationship. Therefore, you may be in for an unfulfilling marriage longer than is necessary or desired. It is possible the other relationship will fizzle out, and there will be room for reconnection with your partner; however, there is risk of losing the opportunity should the affair be revealed.

Tip 8: the decision may not feel right, no matter which choice you make. Although some individuals have an easy time making the decision to leave a long-term committed relationship, most do not. I have often heard clients say some version of the following statement: "maybe this isn't the right decision, because it is so painful." That is certainly something to consider. However, when someone is miserable in a relationship, neither the decision to stay or leave feels particularly good. "Anxiety and self-doubt are guaranteed, whichever option you choose" (Harris, 2013). Further, feeling less than happy, possibly even crummy, about a decision does not necessarily mean it's the *wrong* decision. All you can do is assess the information you have available today, taking responsibility for your role in the state of the relationship, making sure you are doing all you can, and living your values with utmost kindness and respect.

Tip 9: acknowledge that not choosing means you *are* choosing (Harris, 2013). In other words, "there is no way not to choose" (Harris, 2013, p. 79). If you are still in your marriage today, then you have decided to stay, at least for the time being. Sitting on the proverbial fence is not a fun place to be. Sometimes viewing the present moment as a little more black-and-white, instead of gray, can be useful. **Tip 10: make peace with the present.** Continuing from Tip 9, go with the decision you have made for that day, and make the most of it. Whatever you are doing is okay for today. Maybe tomorrow, you will make a different choice. In other words, "acknowledge today's choice" and try to live by it (Harris, 2013).

Tip 11: take an inventory of the costs and rewards (Harris, 2013). Beyond mulling them over in your head, it can be helpful to write them down. Perhaps you have done this in the past. Consider participating in this exercise from time to time because things may have changed since the last time you assessed costs and rewards.

Tip 12: do not compare your relationship to others. Focus on reasonable expectations and not comparing your relationship to others. First, what you see in other relationships is not always accurate, especially when it comes to social media. Most posts on Instagram, Facebook, Snapchat, and other social media sites are the highlights of life and a snapshot of what users want others to see. Yet, many of us find ourselves being sucked into a misleading vortex of private reality versus public image. We start to wonder, what's real? Ultimately, "when we compare our partners at their worst with acquaintances at their best, the marriage is likely to suffer" (Goodard, 2007, para. 16).

Tip 13: practice self-compassion (Harris, 2013). There is no doubt that experiencing FORL, from the giving or receiving end, will create self-doubt, low self-esteem, and other undesirable mental states. It's important to remember that most people would not choose this experience. Yes, you are here, in this place, today. But you are trying to figure it out. Show yourself compassion and kindness; you are human, after all.

Other Considerations

Michelle Weiner-Davis (2009) suggests there are five stages of marriage, represented by a U-shaped curve, which she coined the *Marriage Map*. For some, this can be a useful way to view the situation, keeping in mind it is certainly not the only way to view marriage and may not apply to all unions. Weiner-Davis describes these marital phases as typical, yet misunderstood by couples, often creating over-reactions. Stage 1: passion – everything is perfect. This stage includes the infatuation, butterflies, and excitement of early relationships. Stage 2: disillusionment – what was I thinking? This stage marks the end of passionate love and the recognition of partner flaws. Stage 3: you need to change – I'm right, you're wrong. This marks a time when couples view their own perspective as the "correct" one and wish the other would change. Stage 4: coming to terms – that's just the way you are. Here, the partners realize that their spouse is who they are and there is more acceptance. Stage 5: coming full-circle – appreciation and security. In this stage, the couple is no longer trying to change the other. Often, by this time, children are grown so they can spend more time together. "Since you are no longer in a struggle to define who you are and what the marriage should be, there is more peace and harmony. You start 'liking' your spouse again" (Weiner-Davis, 2009, para. 16). This may result in the rekindling of old feelings and coming full-circle.

Weiner-Davis suggests that if couples can traverse these difficult times, they will come out with greater love and commitment in their relationship. Although this line of thinking deserves merit, many couples do not make it to stage four or five. In this view, there could be 20-plus years of potential dissatisfaction (assuming Stage 2 to 4 last from the end of passionate love to when children are launched). Further, it seems specific personality traits would be necessary for successful couples to reach Stage 5, such as patience, altruism, and selflessness. Pre-existing issues of attachment, poor mate selection, family-of-origin dynamics, and lack of coping skills could also derail the relationship over the course of all five stages.

Weiner-Davis (2009) makes a wise point, however, stating that nothing lasts forever, including the phases of marriage. Difficulties of marriage might be endured more easily if there was hope for something different to come. For example, FORL may occur, but partners might decide to stay in the relationship, with the hope of renewed love. Similarly, it's possible your measure of rewards and costs may morph over time, or your values and goals will change – also creating a more satisfying situation – or at the very least a different dynamic. Of course, other considerations also need to be taken into account, such as the level and depth of unhappiness and discontent. If a partner is miserable, waiting for the tide to turn may not be a good option (P. Regan, Personal Communication, August 8, 2016). One of the potential hazards for couples *waiting it out* is that there are no guarantees. As described by Perel (2007), "It's a story that they are writing together, one with many chapters, and neither party knows how it will end" (p. 219).

Recommendations When on the Receiving End of FORL

When someone we deeply love no longer reciprocates our feelings, the pain can be unbearable (see Chapter 3). It's noteworthy that not all partners react the same in response to their spouses' FORL – some withdraw, and others hold on even tighter. For example, Michelle wanted to disengage, while her partner held on:

> He was like crying, sobbing, and wanted me to have sex with him, right now. So, I had sex with him while he was sobbing … I will never do that again … I don't owe anyone sex or anything … that did not feel good.

Although it's natural to grasp on to whatever we can, holding on tighter can drive the object of our affection even further away. For years, and relevant to all types of cases, I have been teaching clients about the pursuer-distancer dynamic (Lerner, 2012). Exactly as it sounds, the pursuer in the relationship pursues and the distancer distances. Have you ever seen the old Looney Tunes cartoons of Pepé Le Pew and Penelope Pussycat? Pepé Le Pew, a smitten skunk, is forever in pursuit of love with the black cat, Penelope, who accidentally, yet perpetually, has a white stripe painted down her back. For example, Penelope might scamper under a newly painted white fence, making Pepé Le Pew even more attracted to her white-striped skunk appearance. Penelope is always seen in the cartoons desperately trying to avoid Pepé. The harder and faster she runs, the more Pepé pursues. In fact, it's not uncommon for Pepé to bound along effortlessly while Penelope is bolting away as fast as she can. Invariably, Pepé is waiting for her with roses before Penelope can even get to her hiding spot. The pattern the cartoon characters display is not far off from what happens in the life of some couples. In fact, the pursuer-distancer dynamic is present in most relationships, at least to some degree, and it is not unusual for the roles to shift between partners. This dynamic isn't problematic unless it becomes polarized and habitual. In more entrenched situations, the pursuer is most likely to be the partner with the most distress about the relationship distance, leading to even more pursuing (Lerner, 2012). The goal for the pursuer is to gain love, affection, or attention from the distancer. The distancer may be unhappy in the relationship and will likely do little to stop distancing when a partner is in hot pursuit. The best thing the pursuer can do is to stop pursuing and the distancer to stop distancing. Because the pursuer is the most motivated to change the pattern, it makes sense to start there (see Lerner, 2012). Although the rejection and pain of being on the receiving end of FORL certainly makes it difficult to do, ending the pursuit can help stop the pattern, give the distancer the space they need to consider their options, and allow them the opportunity to stop distancing or perhaps even make pursuing gestures. Although easier said than done, it can help to remind yourself that if you keep doing what you're doing, you'll keep getting what you've gotten. Although the outcome cannot be certain, it is more likely for the pursuer to have the results they are hoping for when they stop pursuing. Either the distancer will make changes of their own, leading to a healthier, more balanced relationship, or they will continue to distance, allowing you the insight to make decisions of your own. For more information, the Gottman Institute offers a helpful summary of how to avoid the unhealthy pursuer-distancer patterns, here: www. gottman.com/blog/how-to-avoid-the-pursuer-distancer-pattern-in-your-relationship/.

Healing from Unrequited Love

Sometimes nothing you do will change your partner's feelings. Countless days, months, years, and even lives are lost to clinical depression, suicide, or homicide in response to unrequited love. Some say time is the only healer of a broken heart (Regan, 2017), but what you do with that time matters. Here are some recommendations.

- Focus on positive people and things. Surround yourself with positive friends and family or other support systems such as a religious group. Although you might not feel like socializing, being around others who can provide support is essential. Additionally, it's important to keep active both physically and mentally (being careful not to overdo it).
- Take a few minutes to take stock and to assess the situation. Allow yourself to process how you feel. Naming your emotions (i.e., I feel disappointed, I feel sad) can calm the strength of the emotion (Boyes, 2018). One of the many normal feelings you may have is sadness or regret – perhaps you stayed in the relationship too long or wish you would have done something different. It's important to remember you may not have been able to do anything to change the outcome; and even if you made a mistake, have compassion for yourself – you're only human (Boyes, 2018).
- If it has been a few weeks and you are not feeling any better, consider professional help from a qualified mental health provider. If you feel like hurting yourself or someone else, seeking help is the top priority. If you don't know how to find these services, contact your primary care provider for recommendations, or go to

your local emergency room or walk-in clinic for assistance. Often, therapy or medication alone will be enough to get you back where you want to be, but the combination of medication and therapy together is the best strategy for a one-two punch.

• Be careful how much time you spend talking or thinking about the loss, or your former partner. Although sharing your feelings is extremely important for healing, spending too much time hashing out a problem can make you feel worse and contribute to rumination. Rumination tends to be the nail in the coffin of an already painful experience. It keeps us stuck in a circular pattern of wondering what we did wrong, why our partner doesn't love us anymore, what we can do to get them back, repeatedly exposing us to self-blame and self-doubt. As you have learned in previous chapters, FORL is extremely complex. Thinking about it all day, every day for weeks, months, or years will likely not lead to an "aha moment" of how and why this happened. Hopefully, reading this book will provide insight, but repeatedly drowning yourself in the what-ifs and the whys of your lost relationship won't make you feel better. I understand that it's easier said than done – after all, I'm the thinking queen! One strategy that can be helpful is to carve out 30 minutes a day committed to journaling about your thoughts, feelings, and the experience. When your mind drifts there at other times of the day, gently tell yourself that you will think about it later – during the time set aside. This provides a nice forum for processing but is also time-limited. Further, it can be useful to take the journal to therapy sessions where you can follow up with these thoughts and feelings with your counselor without them filtering through your brain in the meantime. Overall, it's essential to neither ignore feelings nor constantly keep them in the forefront of your mind. As nicely stated by Boyes (2018),

Human emotions are a signaling system. A traffic light isn't useful if either red or green are permanently lit up. The light is only a useful signal if it changes to give you information. Emotions are like that. They're designed to come on and then go away. When emotions become sticky, it's usually because we're feeding them in some way, through rumination, harsh self-criticism or avoidance.

(para. 15)

• Sometimes we are thinking and don't even know it! Have you ever been folding laundry and suddenly realize you've been thinking about something unpleasant for the past 20 minutes? It doesn't make us feel very good! Thoughts and feelings have a way of sneaking up on us. Occasionally, we need to check the background noise in our minds and make sure it's not doing us a disservice.

- Set new goals for yourself! This is one of my favorite recommendations, because it can be so empowering. Make sure your goals are SMART (specific, measurable, attainable, relevant, and time-bound) because goals with these characteristics are accomplished easier. Ask yourself if there is something you have always wanted to do. Maybe you always wanted to play tennis – make a plan and sign up for lessons! Once you have new goals, put your energy and resources toward the goals, instead of the old relationship/partner. Bettering yourself will always result in more positive feelings and will lead you to a more satisfying place, no matter what transpires in the relationship.

- When in love, we have an uncanny way of remembering things better than they were – often ignoring any negatives. It can be helpful to write a list of the things in the relationship that posed values conflicts for you, were not healthy, or made you unhappy. Keep this note where you can easily retrieve and review it when you are having weak moments or when all you can recall are the wonderful qualities and amazing times you shared. You might be thinking, "shouldn't we try to remember the good times?" – there will be time to reflect on those later. Now, it's about you getting to a better place and healing. If you do focus on the positive, you also need to give fair attention to what wasn't good.

- Similarly, if friends attempt to keep you updated on your previous partner – with kindness, let them know it's best for you to focus on other things. If your former partner has a change of heart, you will hear from them again (in your absence of contacting them), at which time you should consider keeping the relationship at bay until you have fully processed and determined the risks and rewards of a possible future relationship with this person.

- Unless you have children together or must communicate with your former partner for other reasons, healing is easier when there is no contact, at least while things feel raw and painful. This can be incredibly difficult, considering most people not only feel they lost a life partner or lover, but a best friend. We form attachments to them and it's not as simple as just not caring anymore. Be patient with yourself, but as much as we think talking to our beloved will help, it can make us feel worse. This is when it is most useful to reach out to friends or remind yourself of that list you wrote about why you might be better off without the relationship!

- If you were blindsided by the end of the relationship or offered no explanation, you might be frustrated, confused, and wanting to talk to your former partner for closure. When people talk about closure, Solomon (2017) describes it nicely: "They want the opportunity to hear the other person validate their story of the relationship" (p. 177). People usually seek closure to feel better. I think true closure, and the healing that comes along with it, comes from within. What really matters is *your* view of the relationship, and knowing that for whatever reason (right or wrong), your partner no longer shares the same view or at least is no longer willing to continue the relationship. However, if you are struggling with closure in the relationship you might consider asking your former partner for a conversation (assuming it's really for closure and not a way to extend the relationship). Prior to making that decision you need to remind yourself: (a) there is a chance they won't agree to communicate; (b) they could be hurtful or unkind; (c) the conversation could bring more questions than answers; (d) sometimes there is nothing the former partner can say that will make what happened okay or make it less painful. If you believe any of these are likely, it would be best not to entertain a conversation. If you decide to move forward, you need to be mentally prepared for any or all of these things to happen. Only proceed if you feel there is something to be gained. Although it's best for most discussions to take place in person, in this instance, you might consider talking by phone or by real-time video applications. This tends to lessen your emotional vulnerability. Email or letters are an option; however, there are drawbacks – they could be shared with others and are one-dimensional – meaning the richness of a traditional conversation is lost. Limit your contact to only one conversation. Again, although someone who has hurt you can sometimes provide assistance with closure when there is ambiguity surrounding the end of the relationship or with a sincere apology when appropriate, this is best done when you don't have to twist their arm to get it. It is very possible to heal without ever interacting with the former partner and sometimes that is best – especially when they are not able or willing to provide what is needed to move forward in a positive direction. Most often you will know the answer to that before you ever pick up the phone. Expect there will be times when the urge to reach out will feel overwhelming. Reassess the situation in 24 hours before you make any decisions.

I wish there were more sure-fire ways to heal quickly from the pain of lost love. Certainly, additional research needs to be done on recovering from unrequited love. Interestingly, Fisher et al. (2016) recommend the possibility of addiction treatment modalities to address issues that sometimes coincide with unrequited love (i.e., depression, suicide, obsession). The author's reasoning is that intense, romantic love has many of the same features as addiction, "including euphoria, craving, tolerance, emotional and physical dependence, withdrawal and relapse" (p. 1). Further, brain scans show that areas of our brains are activated in similar ways when in love and during addiction states (i.e., dopamine-rich areas, and the ventral tegmental). Perhaps what assists in treating addictions issues would help to combat negative mental health outcomes related to unrequited love. Likewise, could this correlation to addiction somehow give clues to FORL itself? Additional research in this area would provide a wealth of new treatment modalities.

Summary

It is suspected that relationships are easier to repair when there was once a strong romantic love compared to those where romantic love was lacking from the start (Kayser, 1993). However, there is virtually no information on the likelihood of partner satisfaction following a period of dissatisfaction (see Acevedo & Aron, 2009; Berscheid & Hatfield, 1969; Buss, 2006; Montgomery & Sorell, 1997; O'Leary et al., 2012; Sims & Meana, 2010; Sprecher & Regan, 1998; Sternberg, 1987; Tucker & Aron, 1993). As described in Chapter 6, periods of decreased emotional and/or sexual connection are typical of healthy, long-term romantic relationships. Of importance are whether these elements return to the relationship in a way that provides satisfaction to both partners. Despite romantic love's loss, or the elements therein, some individuals remain satisfied in the relationship (Sims & Meana, 2010). The possibility of continued marital happiness in the absence of romantic love appears to depend largely on the goals and values of the individuals involved, as well as changes in the system, which may unexpectedly shift over time.

Many individuals struggle with relationship dissatisfaction and the important decision of ending a marriage or other committed relationship. Several considerations are recommended as part of the decision-making process. For instance, marriage is described by some as a U-shaped curve, beginning with amazing love, transitioning to annoyance and frustration, eventually reaching acceptance, leading to the rewarding sweet spot of coming full-circle complete with peace and stability (Weiner-Davis, 2009). In this view, it seems the key to finishing the race is enduring the rough spots. Although worth considering, this model may not apply to all marriages or other long-term committed relationships. A dissatisfying relationship may or may not improve; however, you can increase the chances of making a solid decision about the union by following the tips found in this chapter. To fall out of romantic love and come to a conclusion about how to proceed in a relationship is difficult – as are the emotional processes of those being rejected. Although there is not a quick fix, hopefully the tips and suggestions provide some relief and optimism for those contending with unrequited love. You can and will feel better.

Ultimately, more research would be useful for drawing conclusions about the likelihood of satisfaction following a period of dissatisfaction or after FORL; as well as the possibility or means by which falling into love may occur again with a spouse. Further, additional research would be useful for decision making in respect to relationship dissatisfaction. Finally, although some individuals on the receiving end of FORL recover quickly, others wrestle with it substantially. New research suggests treatment modalities used for substance abuse may be beneficial in this arena. Investigating this hypothesis would provide useful information for future direction on FORL and unrequited love.

Exploration Questions

1 The Marriage Map (Weiner-Davis, 2009), inclusive of five stages, is one way to view the course of marriage. What are your personal views about the course marriage takes? Would you say the same of long-term, non-marital romantic relationships?
2 As stated, there is virtually no information on partner satisfaction after dissatisfaction has taken place. What would you hypothesize plays a factor in the return of satisfaction?
3 Many individuals have a difficult time identifying the difference between goals and values. In your own words, what is the difference? Write down three values you hold, as well as three goals you have for yourself.

Key Concepts

ten signs of FORL

tips for decision making

the Marriage Map

References

Acevedo, B. P. & Aron, A. (2009). Does a long-term relationship kill romantic love? *Review of General Psychology, 13*(1), 59–65.

Berscheid, E. & Hatfield, E. (1969). *Interpersonal attraction*. New York: Addison-Wesley.

Berscheid, E. S. & Regan, P. C. (2005). *Psychology of interpersonal relationships*. Upper Saddle River, NJ: Pearson Education.

Boyes, A. (2018). Five tips for coping with regret. *Psychology Today*. Retrieved September 20, 2018 from www.psychologytoday.com/us/blog/in-practice/201808/5-tips-coping-regret?amp&__twitter_impression=true.

Buss, D. M. (2006). The evolution of love. In R. J. Sternberg & K. Weis (eds), *The new psychology of love* (pp. 65–86). New Haven, CT: Yale University Press.

Fisher, H. E., Xu, X., Aron, A., & Brown, L. L. (2016). Intense, passionate, romantic love: A natural addiction? How the fields that investigate romance and substance abuse can inform each other. *Frontier in Psychology, 7*, 1–10.

Goddard, H. W. (2007). Commitment in healthy relationships. *The Forum for Family and Consumer Issues, 12*(1), 1–18.

Halford, W. K., Kelly, A., & Markman, H. J. (1997). The concept of a health marriage. In W. K. Halford & H. J. Markman (eds), *Clinical handbook of marriage and couples interventions* (pp. 3–12). New York: Wiley.

Harris, R. (2013). How to cope with a difficult dilemma. Retrieved on August 4, 2018 from www.actmindfully.com.au/wp-content/uploads/2018/06/2018_COMPLETE_WORKSHEETS_FOR_RUSS_HARRIS_BOOKS.pdf.

Harris, R. (2016). How to deal with "values conflicts". Retrieved on October 16, 2018 from www.actmindfully.com.au/upimages/How_to_deal_with_values_conflicts_-_Russ_Harris.pdf.

Hawkins, D. N. & Booth, A. (2005). Unhappily ever after: Effects of long-term, low-quality marriages on well-being. *Social Forces, 84*(1), 445–465.

Kamp Dush, C. M. (2011). Relationship-specific investments, family chaos, and cohabitation dissolution following a nonmarital birth. *Family Relations, 60*(5), 586–601.

Kayser, K. (1993). *When love dies: The process of marital disaffection*. New York: Guilford Press.

Lamanna, M.A., Riedmann, A., & Stewart, S. (2018). *Marriages, families, and relationships: Making choices in a diverse society*. Boston, MA: Centage Learning.

Lerner, H. (2012). *Marriage rules: A manual for the married and the coupled up*. New York: Gotham.

Montgomery, M. J. & Sorell, G. T. (1997). Differences in love attributes across family life stages. *Family Relations, 46*, 55–61.

O'Leary, K. D., Acevedo, B. P., Aron, A., Huddy, L., & Mashek, D. (2012). Is long-term love more than a rare phenomenon? If so, what are its correlates? *Social Psychological and Personality Science, 3*(2), 241–249.

Perel, E. (2007). *Mating in captivity: Unlocking erotic intelligence*. New York: Harper.

Poortman, A. R. & Seltzer, J. A. (2007). Parents' expectations about child-rearing after divorce: Does anticipating difficulty deter divorce? *Journal of Marriage and Family, 69*(1), 254–269.

Previti, D. & Amato, P. R. (2003). Why stay married? Rewards, barriers, and marital stability. *Journal of Marriage and Family*, *65*(3), 561–573.

Regan, P. C. (2017). *The mating game: A primer on love, sex and marriage*, 3rd edn. Los Angeles, CA: Sage.

Sims, K. E. & Meana, M. (2010). Why did passion wane? A qualitative study of married women's attributions for declines in sexual desire. *Journal of Sex & Marital Therapy*, *36*(4), 360–380.

Solomon, A. H. (2017). *Loving bravely: Twenty lessons of self-discovery to help you get the love you want*. Oakland, CA: New Harbinger Publications.

Sprecher, S. & Regan, P. C. (1998). Passionate and companionate love in courting and young married couples. *Sociological Inquiry*, *68*(2), 163–185.

Sternberg, R. J. (1987). Liking versus loving: A comparative evaluation of theories. *Psychological Bulletin*, *102*(3), 331–345.

Sternberg, R. J. & Weis, K. (eds) (2006). *The new psychology of love*. New Haven, CT: Yale University Press.

Tsaousides, T. (2018). Is it time to give up on your dreams? The costs and benefits of abandoning a goal. *Psychology Today*. Retrieved September 30, 2018 from www.psychologytoday.com/us/blog/smashing-the-brainblocks/201805/is-it-time-give-your-dreams.

Tucker, P. & Aron, A. (1993). Passionate love and marital satisfaction at key transition points in the family cycle. *Journal of Social and Clinical Psychology*, *12*, 135–147.

Waite, L. J., Browning, D., Doherty, W. J., Gallagher, M., Luo, Y., & Stanley, S. (2002). *Does divorce make people happy? Findings from a study of unhappy marriages*. New York: Institute for American Values.

Weiner-Davis, M. (2009). The marriage map. Wouldn't it be nice if marriage came with directions? *Psychology Today*. Retrieved August 24, 2018 from www.psychologytoday.com/us/blog/divorce-busting/200902/the-marriage-map.

11

Mate Selection Roadmap

The important task of partner selection will be the focus of this chapter. Mate selection refers to the process of choosing a partner for a long-term, intimate partner relationship. Recommendations will be provided for individuals who are interested in entering romantic relationships in the future or are in the early phases of one now. These suggestions are intended to assist in making the best decisions possible when choosing a long-term partner. Mate selection processes appear to be a major player in secure and satisfying marriages and other long-term committed relationships. Further, mate selection is thought to be one of the variables that significantly influence FORL (see Chapter 7) (Hemesath, 2016; Hemesath & Hurt, 2016, 2017). This chapter covers the following suggestions: become happy and healthy prior to mate selection; educate yourself about love and relationships; get to know yourself; take your time; decide, don't slide into a relationship; increase awareness of social pressures; consider non-conscious processes; look for specific partner traits; know your deal-breakers; participate in couple's counseling or other couple's education; keep your sense of self; and reflect on the relationship if it doesn't work out.

Making Informed Decisions in Mate Selection

For most people, thinking about mate selection recalls features such as attraction and common interests. However, the best mate selection decisions begin before ever laying eyes on a potential partner. Believe it or not, the groundwork to a successful long-term relationship starts with you! What's more, elements that influence our mate selection decisions often happen outside our awareness (i.e., attachment style, biological factors) and begin even before we are born (i.e., social and environmental forces).

Chapter 9 contained recommendations from the research participants for individuals in romantic relationships who had not yet married. To recap, they included: know yourself; go slow; know your mate; be healthy emotionally; pay attention; be honest with yourself; make decisions by both thinking and feeling; do not ignore warning signs or intuition; gain education on healthy relationships; and know what to look for. I compared their suggestions to the list of recommendations for mate selection I compiled over the years and it is quite similar! Suffice to say, it appears the participants' experience led them to suggestions that seem to be on target. The following suggestions come from my clinical experience, training, education, and research and expound on the participants' recommendations.

Get to a Good Place

It is important to work toward being a healthy, happy, and self-assured individual before seeking a long-term partner. Boyfriends or girlfriends are the icing on the cake of life, not the cake. In other words, significant others add sweetness and beauty to our lives, but you are the main attraction. If the icing doesn't turn out, the cake will still be amazing on its own. Being unhealthy emotionally at the time of mate selection could lead to poor decisions and outcomes (see Chapter 7). Further, the type of person we attract often depends largely on what we feel we deserve, so being in a positive state, within yourself, is important! Healthy self-esteem is essential.

Educate Yourself

Informed decisions require education. Our society does an incredibly poor job of educating our youth (and adults) about romantic relationships, which is ironic considering the high importance relationships hold for Americans. It's important to learn about the pros and cons of relationships (Lamanna, Riedmann, & Stewart, 2018; see Meyer, 2007). Relationship education can be useful in numerous ways, before, during, and after a romantic relationship. For example, it is important to realize that struggles are inevitable with long-term relationships. For starters, education can assist with learning about how to develop appropriate boundaries and expectations, setting you and your future relationship up for success. Additionally, when entering a long-term relationship, it is helpful to understand how love works. An awareness of the difference between early courtship love (i.e., passionate love) and other types of love in long-term relationships (i.e., romantic love, companionate love) is useful. Passionate love's natural tendency to be illogical, obsessive, and full of unrealistic partner idealizations highlights the importance of waiting at least a year to decide if the relationship is right for marriage. To assist with education, although I wish there were more offered, try to find a relationship course to take in high school or college. Alternatively, look for reputable online sources pertaining to relationship topics, or pick up a good relationship self-help book. I highly recommend *Loving Bravely*, by Alexandra Solomon (2017). Solomon teaches a rare but highly important relationship course, called "Building Loving and Lasting Relationships: Marriage 101," at Northwestern University. I believe this type of course is exactly what every high school and college should offer! Solomon's book focuses on what she teaches in her course about building the relationship you are looking for, starting with what occurs before you even meet your spouse. She offers practical tips and exercises for this important self-discovery work. This leads to the next recommendation.

Know Yourself

Solomon (2017) describes relational self-awareness as the key to healthy intimate relationships. "Self-awareness means knowledge of your own history, character, feelings, motives, and desires ... and understanding in a deep and heartfelt way how you 'show up' for love" (Solomon, 2017, p. 3). Preparation for mate selection also includes becoming familiar with items such as your past relationships, family-of-origin dynamics, personality, goals, values, self-esteem, attachment styles, and current phase of life. I refer to this as our *personal suitcase* that we carry throughout life (see Chapter 7). Consider how each of these items impacts what you want in your future, and how each may influence your mating or dating choices and outcomes. It is imperative to recognize and understand our emotions, because, "Whatever we are doing with our emotions will not be clear until we know them well" (Masters, 2013, p. 1). You might be surprised about how many of us do not have an awareness of our emotions or alternatively will try to avoid them. There are many reasons for this, some of which include having poor role models who expressed emotion in unhealthy ways, experiencing negative outcomes from expressing your emotions, societal views of gender and emotional expression, and other factors such as neurodevelopmental disorders (autism spectrum disorders). To our detriment, our educational system does not prioritize emotional intelligence (Masters, 2013). Robert Masters (2013) does an excellent job of explaining emotions and how to connect with them in his book *Emotional Intimacy: A Comprehensive Guide for Connecting with the Power of Your Emotions.* Although learning about ourselves is a lifelong process, waiting to get to know yourself until *after* you have committed to a long-term relationship will not be as effective. First, you will not have a sense of your boundaries, expectations, or values. Further, if the relationship ends, you may not have a clear sense of who you are as an individual, which can limit healthy recovery. Finally, it is important to see yourself as a valuable, special person, outside the context of a romantic relationship. Special note: as you reflect on your personal attributes and what you bring to a relationship, it is understandable to be concerned if you have life experiences that put you at greater risk of relationship instability. As wisely stated by Scott Stanley (2015), it is important to "Consider the hand you were dealt and play that hand as well as you can" (para. 16). Being aware of these obstacles and doing the best you can to address them is far better than ignoring them and trying to pick up the pieces later; remember, no one has a flawless set of circumstances.

Take Your Time

Go slow. Don't rush. It is possible you have met the person you would like to spend the rest of your life with, who is also a good fit. However, as discussed in the previous section, due to the features of passionate love, you may not be in the best position to notice the details necessary for making an informed decision. (Warning, you won't believe me if you are in the throes of passionate love.) If the relationship is what you think it is, your partner will still be there a year from now. You will both feel good about having the opportunity and time to assess relationship dynamics and prepare for a solid future, together. Savor the experience!

Let Go of Misconceptions and Unrealistic Expectations

Constraining beliefs are misconceptions regarding mate selection that hinder our decision-making process and can lead to poor relationship outcomes (see Chapter 7). Examples are, "opposites attract," "love is enough," or "I/my partner must be perfect," to name a few. Being aware of these misconceptions and replacing them with more realistic views is important to finding the best fit and satisfaction long-term. Related to letting go of misconceptions is the importance of having realistic expectations. *Marital expectations* are beliefs one has about what will happen in the marriage. As described by Stanley (2015), "some very sound marriages fail because one or both partners expected a level of acceptance, passion, or perfection that is just not possible or exceedingly rare" (para. 15).

Further, Seidman (2016) describes the importance of fostering realistic marital expectations by mentally preparing for the natural decrease in satisfaction experienced by most couples. One example of an unrealistic expectation is the idea of eternal happiness and marriage. Sometimes people marry because they are tired of dating. For those who have dated for any length of time, this can be relatable. The motivation to marry and get out of the dating grind is fine, if mixed with a relationship containing the elements necessary for a long-term, successful union. Although it's true the commitment of marriage may protect against relationship instability and encourage hard work, it does not promise happiness and the absence of problems. In other words, marriage does not eternally preserve a happy dating relationship (The School of Life, n.d.). "Happiness doesn't come in year-long blocks ... we should be ready to appreciate isolated moments of everyday paradise whenever they come our way, without making the mistake of thinking them permanent" (The School of Life, n.d., para. 40).

Decide, Don't Slide into a Relationship or Commitment

Deciding instead of sliding into a relationship has been touched on in previous chapters. Instead of going with the flow in a relationship, it is important to assess your current situation, weigh the future implications or consequences of each choice, and factor these into a conscious decision. The goal is to avoid going down a path that seems easiest in the moment but is not in your long-term best interest. For example, let's say your boyfriend stays most weekends at your place. Your coffee-maker breaks, but your boyfriend's parents bought him a new one a few months ago, so he offers to bring it over. At the same time, he mentions he never uses his grill, so he's bringing that over to your place, too, because it may as well get some use! Over time, your boyfriend has left his toothbrush there and a stash of clothes. One day he tells you his lease is up with his roommate, but he has been too busy to find a new place. One thought may be, "well, we spend a lot of time together already and his stuff is here already, so he may as well move in!" Instead of *just letting it happen*, now is the time to consider all potential options and outcomes. It may be a good decision to have your boyfriend move in, but as stated earlier, decisions need to be accompanied with thinking and anticipating potential positive and negative consequences.

While we are on the topic, according to Manning (2016), two-thirds of couples live together prior to marriage and many believe cohabitation is part of the marriage process (Guzzo, 2009). Even though several early studies suggested cohabitation generally increases the chance of divorce, more recent studies report the relationship between cohabitation and divorce has weakened and may be disappearing (see Lamanna, Riedmann, & Stewart, 2018). With that said, couples use cohabitation for different reasons (i.e., trial marriage, instead of marriage, and even without a reason at all) (Bianchi & Casper, 2000). Using cohabitation as a trial marriage (i.e., to see how it goes) may be the worst reason, according to Stanley (2015), because it is much more difficult to get out of a relationship when living together. And if the relationship is based on low commitment, it is likely to end. As if that isn't bad enough, it could put you in a situation of *sliding* into an unhappy marriage. The key to decreasing the risk of cohabitation appears to be commitment, ahead of cohabitation. As reported by Manning and Cohen (2012), when an agreement to marry precedes cohabitation there is a lower risk of divorce. This makes sense because the couple is in agreement about the plans for the relationship, long-term. One thing scholars seem to agree on is that, "the longer people cohabit, the less enthusiastic about marriage-and the more accepting of divorce-they become" (Miller, 2012, p. 12).

Increase Awareness of How Societal Pressures Contribute to Decisions

"In a very real way, we and our personal decisions and attitudes are products of our environment" (Lamanna, Riedmann, & Stewart, 2018, p. 23). As discussed in Chapter 7, pressure from family, friends, or current societal norms can impact romantic relationship decisions. Keep in mind, people may not be pressuring you intentionally – they might believe they know what is best for you. Remember the story about the woman who wanted to avoid being the *old cat lady*? In our society, being female, older, single, and owning an abundance of cats is not the most desirable situation. Alternatively, parents and friends may not want their loved one to be the *old cat lady*. All of these entities may encourage her to enter into a marriage with a less-than-ideal partner.

> Sometimes people decide that they agree with socially accepted or prescribed behavior ... Other times, people decide that they strongly disagree with socially prescribed beliefs, values, and standards. Whether or not they agree with such standards,

once people recognize the force of social pressure, they can choose whether to act in accordance with them.

(Lamanna, Riedmann, & Stewart, 2018, p. 23)

Recognize There are Non-Conscious Processes at Play

Thus far we have talked about recommendations for decision making on a conscious, thinking level. However, this discussion would not be complete without addressing intuition and gut feelings. "Cognitive psychologists now know that intuition, gut feelings, chemistry, and 'vibes' are manifestations of the workings of the extraordinarily efficient and powerful human mind" (Berscheid & Regan, 2005, p. 228). Psychologist John Bargh (2017) describes there are times when you should listen to your gut and times you should not – the reason being that current goals and motivations influence our gut reactions, significantly. Depending on the motivation in the moment, our gut feelings could lead us to good or bad choices. Alternatively, Solomon (2017) discusses that anxiety can masquerade as gut feelings and vice versa. To sort it out, she recommends tuning into how your body feels when you have symptoms of anxiety so you can compare them to gut feelings.

To me (and many others), anxiety feels like tightness in my chest and pressure in my head. Anxious, frantic thoughts and stories flood and swirl around in my brain. By contrast, data that comes from my gut feels more raw, primary, and unfiltered.

(p. 95)

For the best decision making results, individuals should consider both their thinking brain (conscious processes) and their intuition (non-conscious processes), because each have strengths and weaknesses (Bargh, 2017). I would also suggest we consider our emotional brains. For example, I had a client recently express sick feelings after her boyfriend told her he hoped to get engaged, soon. In our previous sessions she had shared how well the relationship was going. Now, she was wondering if a gut feeling was trying to tell her that he wasn't right for her. This particular client also struggles with anxiety and a touch of perfectionism. She recalled that she never wanted or expected to get married until she was over 30 (the client is only 28). She determined that the feelings were likely anxiety related, instead of a gut feeling that he was wrong for her.

The following excerpt describes the use of both conscious and non-conscious processes. When it comes to decision making, cognitive biases, referring to the biases each of us possess, are believed to be responsible for important split-second decisions, as well as decisions that don't always seem rational (see Chapter 5). As described by Comaford (2017), our unconscious minds utilize these inherent biases to filter information. To make the best decisions, she recommends spending time understanding and checking our biases. For instance, perhaps we rely too much on an "anchoring bias," and focus too heavily on one trait or characteristic to make a decision, or an "availability bias" where we focus on similar situations that are easily recalled in memory. An example of anchoring bias comes from a female client with a very abusive up bringing. She selected her spouse on an anchoring bias – he was a good fit, simply because he wouldn't hit her. Unfortunately, they are now struggling in their marriage because they have nothing in common and have very different goals and values. Slowing down, considering all your options, and getting an outside opinion can make all the difference when it comes to making good decisions (Comaford, 2017).

Although it's true that many relationships are developed and maintained only when we anticipate or experience positive rewards or profitability from the relationship, it is not always that simple. In sum, mate selection is likely guided by an automatic, non-conscious, neural process, which has more to do with our partner choice than we might think.

Pay Attention to Partner Traits

Partner characteristics and traits are important to mate selection, but equally relevant to FORL. As wisely stated by Stanley (2015), "Look for someone who can commit and grow and sacrifice" (para. 15). Partner characteristics comprise what each partner brings to the relationship in individual attributes (e.g., self-esteem, needs and wants, values, emotional health, communication style, coping skills), previous relationship history (e.g., past romantic relationships), and family-of-origin dynamics (e.g., poor role models, abuse, conflict resolution patterns, attachment style). It is necessary for couples to make room for individual partner characteristics, but equally essential to acknowledge and discuss the positive and negative effects of these characteristics on overall relationship dynamics (see Chapters 5 and 7).

When seeking an enduring romantic partner, Tashiro (2014) notes three necessary considerations: personality, attachment style, and behavior. Additionally, it's important to select a partner with whom you share common interests and values. Other desirable traits to seek in a long-term partner include kindness, affection, likability, friendliness, dependability, trustworthiness, and intelligence (see Chapter 7). It's also valuable to select a partner who has a positive social network of friends and/or family, demonstrates healthy problem solving and communication skills, as well as participates in gainful employment or schooling (Cotton, Burton, & Rushing, 2003; see Lamanna, Riedmann, & Stewart, 2018). Additionally, it is wise to consider substance use or abuse because excessive drinking is associated with infidelity, conflict, violence, and divorce (Roberts, 2005), and the same is true for other types of substance use (Kaye, 2005).

It is also important to take into consideration the traits that you admire most in your partner, because what is once positive, sometimes can become negative (see fatal attractions in Chapter 6). In other words, "attractive and unattractive qualities often mirror each other" (see Nicholson, 2017, para. 6). Unfortunately, the traits most often admired in the beginning (i.e., easy-going or relaxed) may end up being the very things you dislike about your partner (i.e., undependable) (Felmlee, 1995).

Similarly, some believe we seek partners that can give us what we were not given as youngsters – in other words, our mate's strengths are our weaknesses (see Perel, 2017). This can be a good thing, because we can complement each other; however, it can also be the very thing that drives us away from our partners. For example, if we came from an unstable childhood, we seek a stable partner, but this also may leave us frustrated because it is not what we find familiar or are good at navigating.

Finally, Tashiro (2014) recommends seeking a mate you like more than you sexually desire. Although more research is required to determine the best combination of these qualities for enduring love, there may be something to be said for putting kindness ahead of spark. If the relationship doesn't last, most people would rather have someone who wants the best for you and your children than someone who would do anything they could to see you crash and burn at any expense. However, this is not to discount the attributes of attraction and sexual desire. Overall, it appears best to select a mate you both like and are sexually attracted to.

Look for Negative Patterns

Further, it's essential to examine the patterns you see, not only in your partner individually, but in the interactions between you and your partner. *Patterns* are repetitive acts or behavior. I'm sure my kids get sick of hearing me say "look for patterns" when we discuss any type of social relationship (i.e., friend, teammate, boyfriend/girlfriend). Patterns are a sign of what's to come. We cannot assume that someone is going to suddenly change their ways when their typical behavior has been consistent. Consider you are on a first date with a guy, who takes you to dinner. When the server accidentally spills water on your table, he says to the server, "are you stupid?" – in the next breath he tells you how nice you look. You notice his insensitive comment to the server, but the rest of the night went well, so you assume it's a one-time incident. You agree to go on a second date, the following week, to the state fair. As you are in line for lemonade, the counter server announces there will be a ten-minute wait because they are out of sugar. Your date proceeds to march to the front of the line and demand to be served immediately, because they shouldn't be so stupid to not have sugar. At this time, it would be wise to consider this behavior an emerging pattern. Likewise, if he were to inter-act with you (instead of the server) in a similar fashion, the same would apply. It is likely this type of behavior would lead to poor outcomes in a long-term relationship. In fact, Markman et al. (2010) found that when negative patterns are present during courtship, less-satisfying marriages ensue. Further, "for relation-ships to flourish in the long term, couples need to be not only physically and emotionally compatible but also intellectually, ideologically, and spiritually compatible" (Lamanna, Riedmann, & Stewart, 2018, p. 124; also see De La Lama, De La Lama, & Wittgenstein, 2012).

Know Your Deal-Breakers

The likelihood of any one person finding the *perfect mate* to meet our exact yet ever-changing needs is not likely (Shah, 2009). Knowing that perfection is improbable can be helpful to keep partner frustrations in perspective. Does the good in the relation-ship outweigh the bad? With that being said, it's important to know what your deal-breakers are (see Chapter 10). *Deal-breakers* are components of relationships that are non-negotiable to the continuance of the relationship. If deal-breakers appear in dating relationships, they should be considered serious red flags. For example, someone may not consider a relationship with another who is a smoker because they find the odor and other aspects of the habit offensive, may be allergic to smoke, or concerned about health-related illness.

Deal-breakers are strongly linked to our values. As you are learning about yourself and your values, write a list of your personal deal-breakers. Then check in with this list, occasionally, as you experience new relationships. Due to wonder of new love, your original gut feelings about deal-breakers, such as smoking, may disappear. If you are blinded by love, hopefully your list of deal-breakers will remind you of your values.

Couple's Therapy or Couple's Education Prior to Significant Commitment

By and large, the study participants did not address the costs and rewards when entering into marriage (i.e., drifting or sliding into marriage), which pointed to the need for greater thought and care going into their decision making process. Further, even if they had reviewed costs and rewards, most did not know what they should be looking for due to lack of knowledge.

Couple's therapy or other relationship education is highly recommended prior to a commitment for marriage or cohabitation. As discussed previously, a major problem in our society is that we do not properly educate teens or young adults about committed, long-term relationships. We know marriage and other intimate partner relationships are highly valued, yet the lack of educational opportunities gives the impression that no education is needed. It's true – the initial stage of romance seems as natural and easy as breathing. However, as we have seen throughout this book, relationships are incredibly complex and most long-term relationships face difficulties and obstacles. Although not all problems can be avoided by early education, it could undoubtedly save people from significant hardship. Reputable online educational programs such as ePREP (Braithwaite & Fincham, 2011) are highly recommended. ePREP is a research-based, self-paced couple's education program that takes as little as one to three hours to complete.

The goal of *pre-marital therapy* is for the couple to communicate expectations and thoughts about the upcoming marriage, as well as to improve the relationship, through skill building, generally offered by a trained professional. Many topics are discussed during pre-marital therapy such as extended family, finances, and conflict resolution. Traditional pre-marital therapy (sometimes required through religious organizations) is certainly useful and recommended, but often does not occur until after engagement to be married. Unfortunately, once a couple is engaged or living together, revelations about potential issues may not be acknowledged and the relationship may continue, despite new insight. In fairness, it can be difficult to call off a wedding that has been paid for, or to move out of a place you just bought together. Therefore, if you and your partner have discussed the possibility of marriage or living together, now would be a good time to begin meeting with a relationship professional. Unfortunately, partners may be reluctant to participate in couple's therapy if they are concerned it will highlight problems in the relationship they would like to see continue; or alternatively, couples may believe they only need to attend therapy if they see significant concerns. Further, the negative stigma of mental health or related services may play a role in reduced participation. Remember, healthy, everyday people attend therapy and benefit greatly. Therapy and counseling services are most effective BEFORE issues become significant. It will likely only take a few sessions to get what you need and is a good opportunity to make sure you are on the same page and have the skills for a great start!

Keep Your Sense of Self

Have you ever been around couples who do everything together, or alternatively, will not do anything their partner isn't? It can be fulfilling to have a close connection with your significant other. However, there can be too much closeness in a relationship – a concept called *enmeshment*. Enmeshment refers to the blurring of boundaries between partners, often creating over-involvement, thereby stifling individual autonomy and self-direction (Goldberg & Goldberg, 2012). Further, a sense of self does wonders not only for the relationship itself, but by providing resiliency if the relationship should end (Gunther, 2017, para. 27).

When it Does Not Work Out

If a relationship doesn't work out, it's worth spending some time asking yourself how things came to be as they are. You may not find an answer that feels good, but you will gain valuable insight you didn't have before. Some relationship problems are caused by enduring patterns within one or both partners. These patterns may be caused by any number of factors: lack of education, poor examples growing up, insecure attachment relationships in childhood, poor self-esteem, insufficient coping skills, personality, mental health issues, substance abuse problems, or simply bad habits. Alternatively, relationship problems can be limited to the dynamics of the relationship at hand, and not a long-standing interpersonal pattern. Examples of this might be stress that is unique to the current situation or acute mental health issues. If it's a personal pattern, individual therapy would be helpful for halting the patterns and ensuring healthier future relationships.

Alternatively, if it is determined to be a problem within the relationship itself, couple's therapy (as well as individual therapy, depending on the specific situation) may be the most beneficial. Although reflection on the issues that ended the union is recommended, it's okay if it takes a while to understand the relationship dynamics. After all, if the issues were easy to see, you may not be in the situation to begin with!

Summary

Making good decisions about mate selection is one of the best strategies an individual can take to secure a satisfying, long-term relationship. Because we have considerable control over mate selection, it is important to recognize and understand the steps that appear to limit the risk of poor relationship outcomes. These include: getting to a good place, educating yourself, taking your time, knowing yourself, letting go of misconceptions and unrealistic expectations, deciding not sliding into a relationship, increasing awareness about how societal pressures contribute to decisions, recognizing there are non-conscious processes at play in decision making, paying attention to partner traits, looking for negative patterns, knowing your deal-breakers, participating in couple's therapy or gaining couple's education prior to commitment, and keeping your sense of self. The pitfalls most often associated with mate selection are sneaky and happen when we least expect it. When falling in love everything you thought you knew can go out the window and it can be difficult to think logically enough to follow the recommendations offered. Although adhering to these suggestions cannot guarantee preventing FORL, keeping them in mind and implementing them to the best of your ability is a good start.

Exploration Questions

1 This chapter details many components in making an informed decision regarding mate selection. In your own perspective, what aspect of mate selection do you find most vital? Why do you view this as the most important?
2 Stemming off question #1, which component of mate selection do you feel you are already successful at? Elaborate. Which component do you have the most difficulty with? Elaborate.
3 One of the preparations for mate selection includes reflecting on your "personal suitcase." Write about a few items in your own suitcase that are important pieces of your life to be mindful of when seeking a partner.

Key Components

mate selection	deal-breakers
informed decision	pre-marital therapy
personal suitcase	enmeshment
marital expectations	patterns

References

Bargh, J. A. (2017). *Before you know it: The unconscious reasons we do what we do*. New York: Simon & Schuster, Inc.

Berscheid, E. S. & Regan, P. C. (2005). *Psychology of interpersonal relationships*. Upper Saddle River, NJ: Pearson Education.

Bianchi, S. M. & Casper, L. M. (2000). American families. *Population Bulletin, 55*(4), 3–43. Washington, DC: Population Reference Bureau.

Braithwaite, S. R. & Fincham, D. (2011). Computer-based dissemination: A randomized clinical trial of ePREP using the actor partner interdependence model. *Behaviour Research and Therapy, 49*(2), 126–131.

Comaford, C. (2017). *Why smart people make stupid decisions*. Retrieved July 20, 2018 from www.forbes.com/sites/christinecomaford/2017/03/11/why-smart-people-make-stupid-decisions/#4f83385f5405.

Cotton, S. R., Burton, R., & Rushing, B. (2003). The mediating effects of attachment to social structure and psychosocial resources on the relationship between marital quality and psychological distress. *Journal of Family Issues, 24*(4), 547–577.

De La Lama, L. B., De La Lama, L., & Wittgenstein, A. (2012). The soul mates model: A seven-stage model for couple's long-term relationship development and flourishing. *The Family Journal, 20*(3), 283–291.

Felmlee, D. H. (1995). Fatal attractions: Affection and disaffection in intimate relationships. *Journal of Social and Personal Relationships, 12*(2), 295–311.

Goldberg, H. & Goldberg, I. (2012). *Family therapy: An overview*, 8th edn. Belmont, CA: Centage Learning.

Gunther, R. (2017). *Ten reasons why some people just can't let go*. Retrieved August 10, 2018 from www.psychologytoday.com/us/blog/rediscovering-love/201708/10-reasons-some people-just-cant-let-go-ex.

Guzzo, K. B. (2009). Marital intentions and the stability of first cohabitations. *Journal of Family Issues, 30*(2), 179–205.

Hemesath, C. W. (2016). *Falling out of romantic love: A phenomenological study of the meaning of love in marriage* (unpublished doctoral dissertation). Iowa State University, Ames, Iowa.

Hemesath, C. W. & Hurt, T. R. (2016). *Falling out of romantic love: A focus group study* (unpublished manuscript). Department of Human Development and Family Studies, Iowa State University, Ames, Iowa.

Hemesath, C. W. & Hurt, T. R. (2017). *Falling out of romantic love: An integrated theoretical framework* (unpublished manuscript). Department of Human Development and Family Studies, Iowa State University, Ames, Iowa.

Kaye, S. (2005). *Substance abuse treatment and child welfare: Systematic change is needed.* Family Focus on Substance Abuse across the Life Span: FF25: F15-F16. Minneapolis, MN: National Council of Family Relations.

Lamanna, M. A., Riedmann, A., & Stewart, S. (2018). *Marriages, families, and relationships: Making choices in a diverse society.* Boston, MA: Cengage Learning.

Manning, W. D. (2016). *Trends in cohabitation: Over twenty years of change, 1987–2010.* Retrieved July 31, 2018 from www.bgsu.edu/con tent/dam/BGSU/college-of-arts-and-sciences/NCFMR/documents/FP/ FP-13-12.pdf.

Manning, W. D. & Cohen, J. A. (2012). Premarital cohabitation and marital dissolution: An examination of recent marriages. *Journal of Marriage and the Family, 74*(2), 377–387.

Markman, H. J., Rhoades, G. K., Stanley, S. M., Ragan, E. P., & Whitton, S. W. (2010). The premarital communication roots of marital distress and divorce: The first five years of marriage. *Journal of Family Psychology, 24*(3), 289–298.

Masters, R. A. (2013). *Emotional intimacy: A comprehensive guide for connecting with the power of your emotions.* Boulder, CO: Sounds True.

Meyer, J. (January 22, 2007). Making good decisions. *Omaha World Herald*, pp. 01B.

Miller, R. S. (2012). *Intimate relationships*, 6th edn. New York: McGraw-Hill.

Nicholson, J. (March 12, 2017). *10 things that make someone a great romantic partner.* Retrieved June 10, 2018 from www.psychologytoday.com/us/ blog/the-attraction-doctor/201703/10-things-make-someone-great-roman tic-partner.

Perel, E. (October 2, 2017). How to find the sweet spot between love and desire. Retrieved September 17, 2018 from www.youtube.com/watch? v=ierRipP-7JA.

Roberts, L. J. (2005). *Alcohol and the martial relationships.* Family focus on substance abuse across the life span: FF25: F12-F13. Minneapolis, MN: National Council of Family Relations.

Seidman, G. (2016). This is why some couples are destined to split. Retrieved October 15, 2018 from www.psychologytoday.com/us/blog/ close-encounters/201602/is-why-some-couples-are-destined-split.

Shah, M. (2009). Falling out of love? *Berkeley Scientific Journal, 12*(2). Retrieved September 5, 2018 from https://escholarship.org/uc/item/ 58v0q3qr.

Solomon, A. H. (2017). *Loving bravely: Twenty lessons of self-discovery to help you get the love you want.* Oakland, CA: New Harbinger Publications.

Stanley, S. (2015). Seven ways to make yourself divorce-proof. Retrieved October 14, 2018 from www.psychologytoday.com/us/blog/sliding-vs-deciding/201503/7-ways-make-yourself-divorce-proof.

Tashiro, T. (2014). *The science of happily ever after: What really matters in the quest for enduring love.* Don Mills, ON: Harlequin.

The School of Life (n.d.). *How we end up marrying the wrong people.* Retrieved October 15, 2018 from http://thephilosophersmail.com/rela tionships/how-we-end-up-marrying-the wrong-people/.

12

Clinical Recommendations for Professionals

> Love, and the lack of it in a relationship expected to provide
> it, has been a "forgotten variable" in marital therapy even
> though, as Roberts (1992) wrote, most couples marry because
> they have "fallen in love" and tend to divorce when they "fall
> out of love."
>
> (Berscheid & Regan, 2005, p. 429)

Although almost three-quarters of couples receiving treatment
gain positive results (Lebow et al., 2012), resources and interventions regarding the lack of romantic love presented in clinical
work are limited at best (Berscheid & Regan, 2005; Roberts,
1992). Many of the traditional techniques utilized by couple's
therapists are not effective, because they are not specifically
designed for those who are falling out of love (Kayser, 1993;
Roberts, 1992). Further, many clinicians do not know how to
assess FORL because it has not been properly conceptualized or
even defined.

The goal of this chapter is to provide clinical support and
recommendations for couple's therapists and other professionals
working with those who may be affected by FORL, either now or
in the future. This chapter would likely also be useful for the
general reader, as many of the suggestions refer to discussions
found in previous chapters. Reviewing this information may also
provide insight to potential clients who are considering working
with a relationship professional.

The recommendations are listed in no particular order. An
informed clinician can decide what best fits each case. Unfortunately, due to space limitations, detailed explanations of all
treatment modalities, frameworks, or interventions are not possible. However, it is likely that many relationship professionals are
familiar with these techniques or can learn about them through
the reference list provided at the end of each chapter, the plethora

of online resources and books, or through continuing educational opportunities.

Before proceeding, it is essential to remember that relationships, in line with all open systems, are dynamic and in constant flux. At times, for both the clinician and the couple, relationships and their issues can seem like moving targets. One method or approach may not benefit a specific couple, or an approach or technique that was effective in the past may not work at a different time with the same couple. This requires clinicians to be flexible in their thinking and willing to change course when appropriate. It is also important to keep in mind that individuals who are on the verge of FORL or have already fallen out of romantic love may not benefit from some of these recommendations. As Kayser (1990) suggested, therapy has different goals depending on the phase of FORL.

The following recommendations are a result of my research and clinical experience (Hemesath, 2016; Hemesath & Hurt, 2016, 2017) and corroborate and extend previous work conducted by Kayser (1990, 1993) and Sailor (2006, 2013). Assessment and treatment planning recommendations will be reviewed, followed by clinical interventions and techniques. Additionally, therapeutic frameworks will be outlined, both generally as well as specific to emotional intimacy, sexual desire, and commitment. Finally, suggestions will be offered for individuals and couples who are leaning out of the marriage or have decided to divorce. First, however, two general recommendations will be offered that prepare professionals for addressing FORL and related issues.

Gain Additional Education and Peer Support

Clinicians should educate themselves about various types of love, as well as FORL. Bergner (2000) summed it up nicely,

> Because love holds such a central place, it becomes vitally
> important that psychotherapists possess a strong
> understanding of its nature, so that they will be able to bring
> such an understanding to their work with the many clients who
> are struggling, in one way or another, with love relationships.
>
> (p. 1)

By reading this book you are well on your way!

Clinical consultation is also recommended. Consulting with other professionals provides alternate ways to view a case, which can be extremely beneficial when clients (or clinicians) are stuck. Peer consultation and support is especially useful in the case of

FORL because of the limited resources available (Hemesath & Hurt, 2016).

Meet Them Where They Are

The experience of FORL often comes with confusion, shame, and other painful emotions. It is important for helping professionals to provide validation and support as clients work through their thoughts and feelings. Research participants valued therapists who were able to provide a judgment-free space to discuss their thoughts and feelings (Hemesath & Hurt, 2016). This was the only recommendation for providers given by participants who had fallen out of romantic love, thus it appears to be worth taking into consideration.

Clinical Assessment and Treatment Planning

When it comes to FORL, one size does NOT fit all. Accurate assessment is essential because it informs treatment. Those struggling with FORL may present to a helping professional individually or as a couple. In either case, it is important to conduct a full assessment of each presenting party. Partners attending couple's therapy should come separately for the individual portion of the assessment. Individual time with the clinician is an important assessment tool because different information may be gathered compared to what is shared in a couple's session. Further, assessing for safety is especially important in this context considering the potential outcomes of unrequited love (i.e., suicide, homicide). Note: be sure to address secret-keeping policies at the start of couple's work.

Assessment

The assessment should be comprehensive and include standard mental health evaluation items such as: current relationship history; family-of-origin information; early attachments; personality; mental health and substance abuse; coping skills; values; needs; expectations; self-esteem; psychosocial history (i.e., previous romantic relationships, stressors, occupational issues, social supports, spirituality); strengths and growth areas; physical health; and treatment goals. For couples, all areas of the relationship would be assessed based on each partner's perspectives (i.e., relationship expectations, relationship roles, parenting and children, sexuality, communication, conflict resolution, financial issues, etc.). If treating a couple, it is useful to incorporate a research-based couple's assessment, such as the PREPARE (unmarried couples) or ENRICH (married couples) (Olson & Olson, 1999). These can be easily and inexpensively administered online and provide a wealth of information and treatment planning resources.

Clarify Terminology

Love terminology is confusing (Berscheid, 2006) and many individuals struggle to articulate love (Carter, 2013; see Hemesath, 2016; Hemesath & Hurt, 2016). Ensure you are speaking the same language, conceptually (i.e., what is meant by "intimacy," how is "love" defined). In my practice I have seen many examples of miscommunication based on assumptions about what is meant by a word or phrase, calling for increased clarity of terminology.

Romantic Love and Commitment

In cases where FORL is presented or suspected, it is important to home in on the three main aspects of long-term romantic love – emotional intimacy, sexuality, and commitment. Use the diagram of Sternberg's Triangular Theory of Love (see Figure 1.2 in Chapter 1) to assess and discuss these three elements of long-term romantic love with clients. It can assist them in identifying and talking about what they may be experiencing in their relationship. I utilize this often in my work with both couples and individuals. Presenting Sternberg's Triangular Theory of Love with couples can be a nice way to open dialogue on sensitive topics in their relationship. It can also be a great assessment tool.

Relationship Changes

Consider all possibilities that may explain changes in the relationship. The decline of sexual attraction, desire, or emotional connection may not have anything to do with the state of the relationship but may be a result of change in the physical or mental state of the individual (Regan, 2017). For example, illness, mental health issues (depression, anxiety, grief, stress), hormones, chronic pain, and substance abuse can all impact an individual's ability or motivation to seek intimacy, either emotional or physical (see Regan & Berscheid, 1999).

Family of Origin and Attachment Style

The client's family-of-origin information is important to uncover. "Family patterns, loyalties, and legacies are strong, and unless you are willing to explore your past, you are at risk of having old patterns in the driver's seat of your love life, rather than you" (Solomon, 2017, p. 13). A specific technique offered by Solomon (2017) in her book *Loving Bravely* is to ask the client to list three aspects of their family life growing up that were precious, beneficial, and valuable, and three that were destructive, hurtful, or unhelpful. "These lists will reveal the beliefs, values, patterns, and traditions that you want to carry on in your own life, as well as the ones that you are probably eager to leave behind" (Solomon, 2017, p. 19). As discussed throughout this book, attachment style is also an important area of assessment with respect to FORL. For example, Shah (2008) posits that partners can inaccurately attribute the decline in satisfaction to their partner's shortcomings, when the cause could be their own unconscious processes related to attachment needs not being met. As noted in Chapter 5, the following empirically based web questionnaires are useful for assessment purposes. To measure attachment style across a variety of close relationships (mother, father, romantic partner, and friend) go to: www.yourpersonality.net/relstructures/ (Fraley, n.d.b.). For attachment style, specific to a romantic partner, go to: www.web-research-design.net/cgi-bin/crq/crq.pl (Fraley, n.d.a.).

Goals and Values

It is essential to identify what really matters to each of us, considering the multitude of differences in attitudes, beliefs, and objectives. Chapter 10 (Tip 4) reviewed changing partner goals and the impact on FORL. However, *values* are also important because they represent the core of who we are and how we define ourselves. Compromising our values to please another person is likely to end with resentment. Interestingly, many people are not aware of their own values. The best way I have found to assist clients in identifying their values is with a values-sort exercise. Instructions to a values-sort exercise can be found at: www .praxiscet.com/blog/guiding-valued-based-choices-rft-theory-and-card-deck (Drake, 2017). You can find values cards to purchase online or you can make your own!

It is not uncommon to have conflicting values, within yourself, especially when it comes to dissatisfied relationships. Conflicting values are emotionally uncomfortable, often causing a great deal of anxiety and stress. For example, consider the values of integrity (i.e., honoring your marriage vows) and self-care (i.e., divorce), in regard to a marital relationship. Russ Harris (2016), acceptance and commitment therapy guru, does a great job of addressing how to deal with values conflicts. See www.actmindfully.com.au/upimages/How_to_deal_with_values_conflicts_-_Russ_Harris.pdf.

Harris suggests identifying the difference between goals and values to be sure you really have a values conflict (see Chapter 10). If there is indeed a values conflict, Harris (2016) recommends the following steps: 1) identify the life domain where values conflict (i.e., marriage); 2) identify the two main values that conflict (i.e., integrity vs self-care); 3) think of values as being like the continents on a globe. When you spin the globe, you are unable to see all the continents at once. Like the continents on a spinning globe, throughout the day, you often cannot see all your values because they are continually shifting to the front or back; 4) think of all the different ways – in this specific domain of life (i.e., marriage) – that you can live value A (i.e., integrity) by itself, value B (i.e., self-care) by itself, and both values A and B simultaneously. At this point, many people can view their situation a little differently and may have addressed their values conflict. However, there is one more step; 5) is there still a dilemma you need to address? Even though your values may be workable, there may be two choices that conflict. In the example given, the dilemma is, "do I stay married or should I divorce?" Although these dilemmas present tremendous difficulty, great insight is offered in Chapter 10, under the section "Is it Best to Divorce?"

Stages of Change

Finally, I recently discovered a promising new assessment tool for professionals working with troubled relationships (including FORL). The Stages of Change in Relationship Status (SOCRS) questionnaire, developed by Ritter, Handsel, and Moore (2016), is a reliable and valid tool for evaluating an individual's decisional process regarding the end or continuance of a romantic relationship (Ritter, Handsel, & Moore, 2016). This promising new measure is based off the well-known *stages of change* model (Prochaska & DiClemente, 1982), proposing that any major life change occurs in five predictable stages; precontemplation, contemplation, preparation, action, and maintenance. The SOCRS scale is particularly useful because it is specific to the decision making process of romantic relationship dissolution, which can be loosely applied to the general course of FORL.

The ability to accurately assess an individual's stage of change is highly advantageous for clinicians because it informs which treatment strategies are most likely to be beneficial. For example, if a client is in the first stage, precontemplation, they likely have not yet fallen out of romantic love, which means strategies such as skill building (i.e., communication and conflict resolution) may be enormously useful in attending to relationship problems. Alternatively, if in the fourth phase of action, meaning they could be considering the end of the relationship and may have fallen out of romantic love, a relatively new modality of treatment, called discernment counseling, would be indicated (more to come later in this chapter) (see Box 12.1).

Box 12.1 Stages of Change in Relationship Status (SOCRS)

Factor 1: Precontemplation (No Change Being Considered in Relationship)

1 I am happy with my relationship as it is.
2 My relationship is fine; there is no need to change it.
3 My relationship is not that bad.
4 There is no need for me to do anything about my relationship.

Factor 2: Contemplation (Beginning to Ponder Relationship's End)

5 Sometimes I think I should end my relationship.
6 I believe that my relationship is not healthy for me.
7 I'm beginning to see that my relationship is a problem.
8 I'm beginning to feel the harmful impact of my relationship.

Factor 3: Preparation (Making Plans to End Relationship)

9 Although it is difficult to end my relationship, I am making plans to do it anyway.

10 I have started working on ending my relationship, but I would like some help.
11 I intend to end my relationship within the next month.
12 I intend to end my relationship very soon but am not sure the best way to do it.

Factor 4: Action (Movement Toward Relationship's End)

13 I have told my partner that I am ending the relationship.
14 I talk less to my partner when we're together.
15 I have started spending more time with other people and less time with my partner.
16 I find myself thinking about my partner less and less.

Factor 5: Maintenance (Continuing With the End of Relationship)

17 I changed my daily routine to avoid any association with my partner.
18 I avoid places where I know I will see my partner.
19 I have thrown away items that belong to my partner or taken steps to get rid of things that remind me of him/her.
20 I will never return to my partner.

Source: Ritter, K., Handsel, V., & Moore, T. (2016). Stages of change in relationship status questionnaire: development and validation. *Journal of College Counseling, 19*(2), 154–167.

The researchers used a likert-type response scale ranging from 0 (do not agree at all) to 8 (completely agree). Although no specific instructions were given on scoring, it would seem appropriate in a clinical setting to have clients answer the 20 questions using a response of 0 (do not agree at all) to 8 (completely agree). Sum the four scores in each of the five areas, then compare each of the five scores. The higher the score, the more likely the individual is currently in that stage of change. An individual could have similar scores across stages, suggesting they may fit in more than one stage or be between stages. Overall, results indicated that participants who identified with one of the later stages of change on the SOCRS reported experiencing less satisfaction, investment, commitment, and relationship adjustment; having a higher quality of alternatives; and taking more steps toward leaving a relationship compared with those who identified with one of the earlier stages of change.

(Ritter, Handsel, & Moore, 2016, p. 164)

View of the Problem

In order to address problems adequately, first they must be recognized (see Chapter 10 for more information). Once physical and mental health reasons have been ruled out, ask each partner if they can assess the source of their relationship issues, including their own responsibility in the current relationship dynamics. To assist in this process, we might consider the concept of core issues. Core issues are created by experiences in your family of origin, school, with friends, and/or past relationship and are always stirred up by intimate partner relationships (Solomon, 2017). *Core issues*, in Solomon's view, are "negative themes that recur in our life stories ... a wound in need of healing or at the very least, a still-tender scar" (p. 23). The key to addressing core issues is to know them, anticipate them, and practice a healthy reaction so when they come up in your romantic relationship, they don't cause irreparable damage.

Treatment Planning

Once the assessment is complete, the clinician will have an understanding of client goals. From here recommendations for therapy can be developed, as well as a treatment plan. Depending on who presented for treatment (individual or couple) and the assessment results, the recommendations may include couple's therapy, individual therapy, both couple's and individual therapy, or something entirely different, such as discernment counseling.

Treatment plans are important because they provide a clinical road map from where the client is now to where they want to be at the conclusion of therapy. Treatment planning is informed by the client's goals and will contain therapeutic objectives that outline each step in achieving the goals. Depending on the treatment plan goals and objectives, the following techniques, interventions, and frameworks may be useful in assisting clients with their treatment goals related to FORL.

Therapeutic Frameworks and Clinical Interventions

Many relationship professionals, and couples alike, believe the best way back to marital satisfaction is to fix the problem areas. For example, as described by Montgomery and Sorell (1997) "interventions which encourage exclusive commitment to the partner, partner-supportive attitudes, sexual intimacy, and the passionate valuing of the partner and the relationship are most likely to enhance the partners' mutual satisfaction" (p. 60). Although this makes sense, there are few treatment recommendations specific to FORL. Treatment interventions and strategies employed are only going to be effective under certain conditions. For example, many models will likely not be productive near the conclusion of FORL because the decision to end the relationship may have already occurred. Additionally, it is important to remember that conscious processes such as logic may not be effective for problems of an emotional nature (Atkinson, 2005, 2014). Emotional issues, such as fostering emotional intimacy, are best addressed by working through perceptions and anxieties rather than skill building (Reis, 1990).

Although there are many empirically based therapeutic frameworks to date, a comprehensive model that adequately addresses all aspects of FORL has not emerged. Some models or techniques seem in direct conflict with others. For example, relationship science leader Esther Perel (2007) suggests too much emotional intimacy kills sex and desire; however, Sue Johnson (2013), co-founder of emotionally focused couples therapy, describes lack of emotional intimacy as the cause of relationship problems, suggesting a strong emotional connection is the only way to good sex. Both frameworks have merit. A model may not fit a specific situation in the present; however, the model may apply to the same couple later, or an alternate couple with different presenting features of FORL. Until additional research is available, it is warranted to be eclectic and open-minded in our use of therapeutic strategies, techniques, and treatment models.

Clinical Techniques and Interventions

Below you will find multiple recommendations from various schools of thought that show promise in addressing FORL. The following recommendations comprise a sample of what may be useful. There are likely other techniques that may be equally helpful.

Promote Skill Building

"Good marital skills, including self-repair, are necessary to prevent or change direction once negative patterns of interaction begin (Fincham, Stanley, & Beach, 2007)" (Sailor, 2013, p. 16). Learning new relationship skills can benefit a couple in respect to many issues, such as conflict resolution, poor communication, role confusion, or parenting or financial concerns. However, as mentioned earlier, it should be cautioned that utilizing skill-based interventions is typically ineffective for issues of an emotional nature (Reis, 1990), as often found with FORL. Skill building can be very useful but is recommended for cases where FORL has not already occurred.

Encourage Positive Partner Affect

Robert Sternberg (1987) highlights the importance of action in maintaining the ideal love components of commitment, intimacy, and passion. For effective action, it is essential to have positive affect. Well-known psychologist John Gottman discovered it is not the presence of negative affect or arguing that predicts marital dissatisfaction and divorce, but the *absence* of positive affect (Gottman & Levenson, 2000). Therefore, it is recommended couples respond with *positive affect* (i.e., warmly and with interest), not only in daily communication, but also in disagreements. Gottman (1994) concluded that four specific types of negative affect (contempt, criticism, defensiveness, and stonewalling) were the most destructive to marriage, which he termed the Four Horsemen of the Apocalypse. Later, Gottman et al. (1998) added belligerence to the list. Ultimately, contempt, criticism, defensiveness, stonewalling, and belligerence are predictive of marital unhappiness and divorce (Gottman & Levinson, 2002). Lamanna, Riedmann, and Stewart (2018) provide a nice description of these constructs:

> Rolling one's eyes indicates contempt, a feeling that one's spouse is inferior or undesirable. Criticism involves making disapproving judgements or evaluations of one's partner. Defensiveness means preparing to defend oneself against what one presumes is an upcoming attack. Stonewalling involves resistance-refusing to take a partner's complaints seriously ... Avoiding or evading an argument is an example of stonewalling ... belligerence, a behavior ... challenges the other's power or authority.
>
> (pp. 280–281)

Reduce Stress

As we saw through the participant interviews, stress from both inside and outside the marriage caused or added to marital dissatisfaction. Although it is impossible to eliminate stress, look for ways to reduce stress as much as possible (see Lamanna, Riedmann, & Stewart, 2018). Not only can stress cause physical and emotional health problems, but it can cause communication breakdown through ineffective word choices and overall tone when stressed and strained.

Expect Occasional Bumps

Life, as well as love, is like flying in an airplane – we experience unexpected turbulence among patches of smooth air. I haven't been on a flight yet where there was an absence of turbulence. Expecting a few bumps on the way keeps us from being paralyzed when they happen. And they will happen.

Identify and Share Marriage Expectations

It is important to identify and share your expectations for the relationship with your partner (Bachand & Caron, 2001). Discussing expectations from time to time is useful, because they may change. Expectations are good to have – without them, there would be no direction or boundaries for the relationship (see Montgomery & Sorell, 1997). However, it is important to be realistic as well as honest with yourself about what your partner (or any partner) can and can't provide. Ultimately, expectations themselves are not a problem; it's when the expectations go "unmet" that issues arise (Seidman, 2017).

Acknowledge that Some Level of Denial is Good

Infatuation and other psychological and biological processes of new love seem to block logic, leading to *denial*. However, having at least a moderately elevated view of one's partner is healthy for relationships and predicts relationship satisfaction (Conley et al., 2009). (See Chapter 8 for more information about the benefits of positive illusions.) Positive illusions may help relationships to form and can assist the maintenance of long-term committed relationships – as long as "realizations" don't set in. As discussed in Chapter 7, realizations were identified as a stepping stone to FORL. It appears that denial is positive for relationships, when used within reason. However, denial could be detrimental if significant negative traits are being ignored.

Addressing Emotional Intimacy and Attachment Issues

The following frameworks may be useful for addressing attachment issues and other causes of emotional disconnection and can be implemented in either individual or conjoint therapy.

Emotionally Focused Therapy

Specific to insecure attachments, *emotionally focused therapy* (EFT), co-founded by Sue Johnson and Leslie Greenberg (see Greenberg & Johnson, 1988; Johnson & Greenberg, 1985), rests on attachment bonds being the single most important aspect in marriage. The book, *Love Sense: The Revolutionary New Science of Romantic Relationships* (Johnson, 2013) is a recommended read for couples and clinicians alike. One shortcoming of this approach is the loss of sexual attraction and desire between partners may not be adequately addressed, yet is often a major force of marital dissatisfaction and FORL. Additionally, although there are many benefits to the techniques used in EFT, "underneath the emotional connection, romantic relationships are still social exchanges intended to meet the needs of both partners" (Nicholson, 2017, para. 10).

Emotional Intelligence

Brent Atkinson's (2005) notion of *emotional intelligence* is a couple's therapy friendly therapeutic model that attends to the subconscious mind, as well as behavior. This framework is based on neurobiology, and the work of relationship expert John Gottman (Atkinson, 2014). Other contributions to this framework come from "narrative, cognitive-behavioral, emotionally focused, and Bowenian" approaches (Mansfield, 2010, p. 362).

There is emerging evidence that many of our decisions, including mating and dating decisions, are out of our conscious control (Atkinson, 2005, 2014) (see Chapter 5). These powerful non-conscious processes may explain why some people fall out of romantic love or cannot easily fall back into love, despite their best efforts.

Atkinson also related his emotional intelligence framework to attachment theory, claiming that individuals may react unconsciously in a relationship based on their hard-wired preconceived notions that self-protection and safety can be obtained through withdrawing, expressing anger, clinging, or other maladaptive behavior (see Chapter 5). This model provides support for emotionally focused couple's therapy framework. In couple's therapy, Atkinson suggests utilizing *mindfulness*, being present, not reacting to protective impulses that have been hard-wired within us (Atkinson, 2005, 2014).

Dialectical Behavior Therapy

Dialectical behavior therapy (DBT) is intended to reduce intense emotional reactions, and assist clients in tolerating distress and more effective interaction with others. For example, if there is a pattern of intense negative emotional reactions, such as those often present in anxious attachments, work on reducing the intensity of the reactions so they are no longer detrimental to the relationship.

As its name suggests, DBT is influenced by the philosophical perspective of dialectics: balancing opposites. The therapist consistently works with the individual to find ways to hold two seemingly opposite perspectives at once, promoting balance and avoiding black and white – the all-or-nothing styles of thinking. In service of this balance, DBT promotes a *both-and* rather than an *either-or* outlook.

(*Psychology Today*, n.d., para. 6)

This recommendation is supported by Sailor (2013): "assisting clients in developing healthy emotional regulation could help to decrease the negative focus and flow of emotions that develops when clients begin to report marital distress" (p. 16).

Internal Family Systems

Consider utilizing *internal family systems* (IFS), developed by Richard Schwartz (1995), in either couples or individual work. IFS combines systems theory with the idea that each individual contains three main "parts" – managers, exiles, and firefighters, which although having positive intent can sometimes create problems in our lives by trying to protect us in ways that are not helpful (i.e., protecting us from traumatic or painful feelings through alcohol or drug abuse or distancing from others). IFS views the self as separate from these parts with the goal of assisting clients in tapping into the healing qualities of the self and disentangling themselves from any protective, yet destructive, elements of the different parts. This framework could be particularly useful for attachment issues.

Addressing Issues of Sexual Intimacy and Desire

Research indicates that it is typical for sexual desire to decline in long-term relationships (Basson et al., 2005; see Baumeister & Bratslavsky, 1999; Fisher, 2006; Impett, Muise, & Peragine, 2014; Muise et al., 2013). Although leading scholars and psychotherapists offer suggestions for keeping romance alive in long-term relationships, baring sexual dysfunction recommendations, there are minimal solutions offered for couples where sexual attraction or desire is exceedingly low or absent. In fact, as described by Muise et al. (2013), "Few studies have investigated the factors that promote sexual desire, especially in the context of established relationships" (p. 272).

Between emotional intimacy and sexual desire, the latter appears to be more challenging to address based on its difficulty to predict and control (Sternberg & Weis, 2006). In fact, Sternberg views individuals as having at least some degree of conscious control over their emotional intimacy, and a higher degree of control over commitment to a relationship, but almost no control over the passionate or sexual component. To date, there is no known, reliable way to ensure unending desire or to get it back once it's gone. Because of the central place sexual intimacy holds in romantic love and intimate partner relationships, it's absence could be a deal-breaker for some (see Chapter 11). Luckily, sexual attraction and desire are not essential in all phases of a relationship, or to all people. There may be other aspects of the relationship that may be satisfying. It is important to talk with couples about their expectations and needs. Overall, it seems prudent to enter a long-term relationship with *intact* sexual attraction and emotional connection. Even when both dimensions are present from the beginning, issues can arise over the course of a relationship. This raises the question of what to do to help individuals who have fallen out of romantic love because the passionate or physical/sexual component is missing.

The Paradox of Desire

If there are concerns about sexual desire, it may be useful for the clinician to work from Esther Perel's (2007) perspective of the paradox of desire in her best-selling book, *Mating in Captivity*. I also recommend her 40-minute YouTube video, How to find the sweet spot between love and desire (2017b), found in the reference section. As described by the author, security and passion have difficulty co-existing at the same time in the same relationship. Thus, too much emotional connection can squelch desire. Her recommendation is to create space, novelty, and surprise within your marriage or long-term relationship. The thought behind this is that our needs are different than our desires (Perel, 2017b). Acknowledging there are natural periods in all relationships where desire is dormant, Perel (2007) recommends couples cultivate playfulness and enhance independence and mystery in the relationship to nurture eroticism and desire.

The "Eww" Factor versus "I'm Just Not into It"

In my quest for seeking information on how to better address individuals who have absent or low sexual desire for their partner, Melissa Fritchle, sex therapist, educator, and author of *The Conscious Sexual Self Workbook* (2014), has much to offer. First, Fritchle supports the recommendation of assessing the partners individually, highlighting the importance of gaining an honest perspective about how each view themselves and their partner sexually. For example, there is a difference between a partner feeling: (a) completely turned off/disgusted – we'll call it the "eww" factor; or (b) "it's fine and I like you, but I'm just not very interested." As you can imagine, there is far more that can be done with the latter (M. Fritchle, personal communication, September 13, 2018).

Grieve What is Missing

Fritchle recommends considering grief work to mourn the changes in themselves and/or their partner, creating a situation where sexual desire is not what it once was or hoping it would be. We are taught not to grieve, especially about something like sexuality, yet this can be a helpful process (see Epstein, 2019).

Foster Transparency

Invite the struggling partner to consider what used to attract them to their partner (M. Fritchle, personal communication, September 13, 2018). How might that look, today? Across all aspects of the relationship, this recommendation is supported by Kayser (1990), who suggested vague descriptions of complaints or dissatisfactions are not helpful and need to be made more explicit. Open yet gentle and kind discussion among the couple about what may assist in building or regaining attraction, as well as realistic expectations, can be useful. With that said, these conversations can be painful for both partners. To decrease the risk of resentment it is important to frame these conversations in a safe and loving context where both partners are longing to move forward and regain intimacy.

Develop Curiosity

Can the low-desire partner develop a curiosity about what could happen in their relationship sexually (M. Fritchle, personal communication, September 13, 2018)? If they are willing, begin with focusing on the sensation of physical touch, not desire itself. This may include practicing mindfulness, slowing down, and looking at subtle details of an experience – being *more* self-focused can lead to positive outcomes for both partners.

Explore New Ideas

Fritchle recommends inquiring if the low-desire individual is willing to endure awkward feelings while exploring options. For instance, have they considered using fantasy during sex? Maybe fanaticizing about an earlier time when they were sexually attracted to their partner, or even fanaticizing about something/someone else may be helpful if they are comfortable.

Lighten it Up

Perhaps looking at sex in a lighter, less serious way, knowing it doesn't have to be great for both partners every time, can take pressure off and provide a fresh perspective (M. Fritchle, personal communication, September 13, 2018). For example, providing physical intimacy could be an "act of service," not unlike making a nice meal for your partner, because you know your partner enjoys it even if you are "not in the mood." However, to be clear, sexual relations should not be recommended or expected if they are unwanted (see Muise, Impett, & Desmarais, 2013). Ultimately, it is likely to be unhelpful and can do more harm than good (P. Regan, Personal Communication, August 8, 2016).

Other Means of Experiencing Relationship Satisfaction

Referring back to the "eww factor," if there is no sexual interest or if it was never strong to begin with, it may not be a realistic goal to expect sexual satisfaction from the relationship (P. Regan, personal communication, August 8, 2016). If sexual desire and satisfaction remain elusive, Fritchle suggests inquiring if there are other enjoyable or positive aspects of the relationship that make up for lack of sexual satisfaction. Further, ask if the couple is okay with a non-sexual relationship. If not, is monogamy the only option? In other words, if the couple wants to stay married, but sexual intimacy is important, are there other ways to make it work that are acceptable to both partners (M. Fritchle, personal communication, September 13, 2018)? The goal for the clinician is to come from a place of being open-minded and not assuming. Romantic love is not the only way to find satisfaction in a long-term intimate partner relationship.

Scheduling Sex

In regard to sexual desire, some believe that especially for women, desire comes *after* good sexual relations are underway (Basson, 2000). In other words, desire may be the *result* of sex, not the *cause* (Castleman, 2012). Instead of waiting for desire to initiate sex, one possible solution is to schedule sex (see Castleman, 2012; Perel, 2007) by planning intimate time in advance. Scheduled sex can also have the benefit of anticipation. However, scheduling sex can be negatively perceived by some due to the importance of spontaneity.

Consider Communal Strength

Some suggest seeking a partner who is high on communal motivation for the purpose of keeping sexual desire alive for the long haul (see Muise et al., 2013). Individuals strong in *communal strength* are motivated to meet their partner's sexual and other needs without expectation in return (Muise et al., 2013). These individuals have greater sexual desire in long-term relationships compared to those who are lower in communal strength (Muise & Impett, 2015). Higher sexual desire increases overall relationship satisfaction (Brezsnyak & Whisman, 2004) and those with higher sexual desire are also less likely to think about leaving their relationship (see Muise et al., 2013; Regan, 2000). Some scholars suggest applying communal relationship strategies to long-term relationships in hopes of sustaining desire, thereby increasing satisfaction and relationship stability (Muise et al., 2013; Muise & Impett, 2015).

Traditionally, more sex was thought to lead to greater relationship satisfaction (see Laumann et al., 1994). However, beyond the altruistic nature of communally motivated partners, research indicates the underlying reason for having sex is what matters. For instance, someone who engages in sex because they want to increase closeness or provide pleasure for their partner (i.e., approach-motivated) is going to reap more benefits for themselves, their partner, and the relationship than one who has sex with their partner to avoid their partner being disappointed or upset (i.e., avoidance-motivated) (Muise et al., 2013; Muise, Impett, & Desmarais, 2013; Impett et al., 2008). Therefore, being motivated to meet a partner's sexual needs to gain something (i.e., enhance closeness), not avoid something (i.e., disappointment, conflict), may be the key to enduring sexual-desire (Muise, Impett, & Desmarais, 2013; Muise et al, 2013).

Although this is a fascinating area worth investigating, it poses the question about the fit of communal goals against the backdrop of an increasingly individualized society. Those higher on communal strength tend to be more supportive, emotionally expressive, and helpful than those lower in communal strength (see Muise, Impett, & Desmarais, 2013), suggesting a cluster of specific personality characteristics. Perhaps if individuals could work toward increasing the traits typical of those high in communal strength, there could be an increase in communal relationships and potentially an increase of relationship satisfaction and long-term sexual desire.

Couples can encourage sexual communal strength and possibly promote long-term sexual desire in an ongoing relationship by expressing gratitude to one's partner (Lambert et al., 2010; see Muise et al., 2013) and providing self-disclosure about sexual needs and wants (Clark & Mills, 2010; Muise et al., 2013). One feature missing from the literature on communal relationship strategies is loss of physical attraction or desire for one's partner and the related effects.

Addressing Commitment

Commitment is viewed as essential to long-term intimate partner relationships (see Chapter 8). If an individual or couple is struggling with commitment, it could be addressed in a variety of ways. For example, Goddard and Olsen (2004) suggest putting the relationship first with the help of boundaries and rituals, for enduring commitment (i.e., scheduling a regular date night). Further, if commitment has waned and needs bolstering, consider customizing the treatment plan based on what speaks most to the individuals regarding the relationship (Goddard, 2007). For example, if stability and financial security matter most, it may be helpful to focus on the benefits of those rewards in the relationship, as an anchor of commitment.

Finally, consider motivational interviewing for addressing commitment. *Motivational interviewing* was developed by clinical psychologists William Miller and Stephen Rollnick, in 1991, primarily for problem drinking. Motivational interviewing is a directive, client-centered approach, aimed at exploring and resolving ambivalence, in hopes of eliciting behavioral change (Rollnick & Miller, 1995).

Other Clinical Recommendations

In respect to FORL, presenting issues generally include concerns regarding emotional or physical intimacy; however, the following frameworks would be useful for a wide variety of other couple's issues such as conflict resolution, communication, problem solving, or parenting concerns, which may be *stepping stones* to FORL (see Chapter 7). The therapeutic models listed below are recommended for individuals and couples who are experiencing marital distress in any of these areas. Many of these recommendations are likely to be most effective earlier in the process of FORL (even if FORL is not yet a concern); however, depending on the context and the therapeutic goals, these frameworks may be useful in a variety of ways. For example, ACT is particularly versatile.

Acceptance and Commitment Therapy

Acceptance and commitment therapy (ACT) was developed by Steven Hayes in the 1980s and has roots in behavioral therapy as well as cognitive therapy. Hayes (2005) views psychological inflexibility, the inability to adapt to life's problems, as the main source of suffering. The premise of ACT is that by accepting inevitable difficulties of life, as well as changing our behavior accordingly, we will have better outcomes than if we try to ignore or avoid problems. ACT differs from cognitive behavioral therapy. The main goal of CBT is to control or change thoughts and feelings, whereas ACT has the goal of accepting them for what they are, while moving toward something more positive, and in line with your values (see Hayes, Strosahl, & Wilson, 2012). The techniques used include expansion and acceptance, mindfulness, cognitive defusion, values clarifications, and committed actions (Harris, 2007). Examples of the usefulness of ACT were identified in Chapter 10, throughout the decision making tips and in this chapter regarding values conflicts. I find ACT to be one of the most effective frameworks for addressing the emotional pain, internal conflict, and decision making pieces of FORL. Based on the behavioral components, it may also be effective for addressing commitment and sexual intimacy issues.

Cognitive-Behavioral Therapy

Cognitive-behavioral therapy (CBT) focuses on changing undesirable behaviors and distorted thinking, as well as gaining coping skills, to treat a variety of problems. "CBT is based on the scientifically supported assumption that most emotional and behavioral reactions are learned. Therefore, the goal of therapy is to help clients unlearn their problematic reactions and to learn a new way of reacting" (Newman & Newman, 2007, p. 147). This approach is supported by Kayser (1990), who noted the importance of positive behavioral exchanges in dissatisfied relationships as well as reframing the perceived causes of the problem. Similarly, *cognitive-behavioral couple therapy* (CBCT) focuses both on negative behavior as well as the interpretation of the behavior that creates discord between partners (Baucom & Epstein, 1990). CBCT uses *cognitive restructuring* to address maladaptive thoughts and assumptions about each other and the relationship, as well as communication and problem solving skills training (Regan, 2011). Additionally, it can be helpful to discuss with clients the idea that thoughts create feelings, which is a prominent feature of cognitive therapy (Leahy, 2003). For example, if we think positively about our partner and our relationship, our feelings may follow (see Kayser, 1990).

Solution-Focused Therapy

If clients are presenting earlier in the process of FORL, consider utilizing techniques from solution-focused therapy. *Solution-focused therapy* was coined in the 1980s by married-couple's therapists Steve de Shazer and Insoo Kim Berg. Solution-focused therapy is credited for not only shortening the length of therapy but for also focusing on solutions and offering a forward, positive momentum. "Do something different" is one of my favorite techniques from this style of therapy (see De Shazer & Dolan, 2007). I often tell my clients, if something isn't working and you've been doing the same thing over and over and getting the same results, do something different. Sometimes we are not sure what change is needed to get the results that are desired. That's okay – as we have learned, relationships are complex. Consider the options you might try, select one from your list, and take note of the effects. It may take two to three weeks to see the effects of what you are doing differently. If you don't like what you get from the choice you made, go back to the drawing board and pick a different selection to try. Through trial and error of these "mini experiments" you will gain perspective of what you need to do more or less of in order to get closer to your goals. Other techniques that can be helpful from solution-focused framework are *the miracle question* – "If tonight while you were asleep a miracle happened, and it resolved all the problems that bring you here, what would you notice different tomorrow?" (see De Shazer & Dolan, 2007). This question is helpful with the topic of FORL because it clarifies what is needed in the relationship, from the client's perspective. Likewise, it's good to *look for exceptions* by investigating what is happening when things are more satisfying with one's partner (either currently or in the past). Maybe some of those things still happen, from time to time, and can be built on. Consider recommending behaving in loving ways, because sometimes action leads to feelings (i.e., "act as if" strategy from solution focused therapy) (Weiner-Davis, 1993). Behaving in positive ways may get us to the feeling we are hoping for. Although solution-focused techniques are very useful, this framework is present and future-oriented. Research suggests there also needs to be assessment and attention to the past when working with the phenomenon of FORL due to important constructs such as early attachment formation (Hemesath, 2016; Hemesath & Hurt, 2016, 2017). After all, "the past shapes how you love" (Solomon, 2017, p. 12).

Positive Psychology

Unpredictable life stressors can wreak havoc on even stable relationships. Consider utilizing *positive psychology* (see Seligman et al., 2005). "Positive psychology emphasizes the pleasant emotions of happiness and joy. The cognitive outlooks of optimism and hopefulness, and the adaptive, creative behaviors that result in mastery and efficacy" (Newman & Newman, 2007, p. 147). Davis (2018) describes that with practice, we can learn to see the good in most any situation through a process called *positive reappraisal*. Alternatively, negatives or losses in a relationship can simply be viewed as an inevitable part of compromise, relationships, and life. Instead of learned helplessness in response to uncontrollable stress, individuals can develop learned resourcefulness through skill building and self-regulation (Newman & Newman, 2007; Seligman, 1974). Often, good coping skills can lessen the negative effects of stress.

When One or Both Partners are Leaning Out of the Relationship

Many traditional couple's strategies are ineffective for FORL because the goal for the partners may be separation or divorce. For example, traditional marriage therapy is not appropriate when one or both partners is seeking a divorce or is not interested in working on the marriage.

Discernment Counseling

Discernment counseling is a unique, one-to-five-session model designed specifically for couples who are on the fence about the relationship, where one spouse is leaning in and the other spouse is leaning out of the marriage (Doherty, 2011). Discernment counseling is a relatively new technique developed by scholar and couple's therapist William Doherty. Discernment counseling is indicated when one or both partners are ambivalent about continuing the relationship or contemplating divorce (see Doherty, 2011). When a couple is considering divorce, discernment counseling can reduce negativity among divorcing couples, encourage collaboration, and ensure both parties are confident about their decision to divorce (see Doherty, Willoughby, & Peterson, 2011). As noted by Kayser (1990) "Spouses in the late phase of disaffection may primarily need assistance in making a decision about repairing the marriage or dissolving it" (p. 264). I have utilized this model in my practice and have found it useful in cases where FORL has occurred or is in process.

Discernment counseling is NOT marriage therapy. It is especially helpful in opening communication when traditional couple's therapy is not indicated. The goal is to take the pressure off the marital situation by discussing what they have both brought to the relationship, how they each view the situation, and what they would each like to do. Through discernment counseling, clinicians assist individuals in formulating their own working model of the meaning of love in marriage, the role of commitment, or alternative benefits to marriage, etc. It is possible that some form of love (possibly not romantic love) or purpose strong enough to sustain the marriage will emerge. The end goal is to come to one of three decisions: end the marriage; continue the status quo (not ready for decision); or move toward marriage therapy and actively work on the relationship. In cases where it has been decided by one or both partners that the union should end, a process called collaborative divorce is highly recommended and worth considering (more to come in this chapter).

Marital Separation

In the late phase of FORL, when deciding whether to divorce, some couples elect to have a *marital separation* (see Kayser, 1990). Separation provides time and space for the spouses to assess their relationship (Tumin, Han, & Qian, 2015). If marital separation is decided upon, most relationship experts recommend a structured separation with ample communication and clear expectations regarding dating, finances, child rearing, and length of separation (Gadoua, 2010). Many spouses try to reconcile during separation (Weinberg, 1996); although some couples get back together, most trial separations end in divorce (Manning & Smock, 2005). This is not surprising considering significant marital distress generally precedes separation.

When Divorce is Imminent

When one or both partners have decided divorce is the best option, collaborative divorce might be considered over traditional divorce. Collaborative divorce was founded in 1990, by Stuart Webb, an attorney in Minneapolis, Minnesota. Webb was reportedly frustrated by settling divorce issues in court (Collaborative Divorce.Net, 2017, para. 1). *Collaborative divorce* is a respectful divorce process that strives to preserve the emotional and financial resources of the entire family (Iowa Collaborative Divorce, n. d.). Collaborative divorce is a cooperative divorce model where both parties agree not to litigate. The model's intent is to set the couple on an upward trajectory. It is often far less expensive and less time-consuming than traditional divorce. The process is respectful, creating shared solutions, without having the courts decide (International Academy of Collaborative Professionals, 2018). I highly recommend collaborative divorce where possible. Collaborative divorce is not recommended where there has been a history of domestic violence or when the couple cannot get along well enough to sit in the same room and "collaborate."

The collaborative divorce model is built on a team of professionals, many of whom may be part of the couple's divorce process. Professionals on the collaborative divorce team include collaboratively trained family law attorneys; licensed mental health providers serving as divorce coaches and child specialists; financial specialists; and family law mediators. Research supports these recommendations as both providers and clients believe avoiding negative dynamics among partners is important following divorce (Hemesath & Hurt, 2016).

Although this concludes my clinical recommendations, I encourage fellow scholars or students to explore the wide-open topic of FORL. Your input is needed! I also recommend that clinicians and scholars work more closely together, because each has a unique vantage point with much to offer (Hemesath, 2016). More research specific to FORL conceptualization, treatment, and intervention is necessary for future advancements in this area.

Summary

A major goal of this chapter was to provide direction for mental health providers and relationship professionals in regard to FORL. Providers express uncertainty regarding adequately treating FORL (Hemesath & Hurt, 2016). Additional research on the dynamics of FORL is sorely needed, including a focus on provider training, inclusive of a range of supportive tools and strategies. We know couple's therapy is beneficial for many presenting problems. However, minimal research and clinical literature on FORL has led to providers being inadequately equipped to address this issue. New research and theoretical frameworks for couple's therapy, with respect to FORL, are desperately needed. In the meantime, providers are advised to seek peer consultation and professional support. Although the recommendations in this chapter support long-term relationship satisfaction, there does not seem to be a "one size fits all" solution.

Ideally, the information in this chapter will provide a useful conceptual framework for professionals, as well as incite appropriate interventions that are hand-picked for the couple and/or individual. The recommendations listed were generated by my research findings and 20 years of experience as a licensed marriage and family therapist and mental health counselor. Additional research needs to be conducted to test these recommendations with respect to FORL.

Exploration Questions

1 Denial is often viewed as negative. However, in relationships it is said to be healthy, at least to some extent. Explain how denial can be healthy for relationships and give an example. Also, give a specific example of how denial could be unhealthy in a romantic relationship.

2 The SOCRS questionnaire is a new measure to assess the stage of change in the decision-making process of relationship dissolution. How might the SOCRS be useful for assessing and treating FORL?

3 Many clinical assessment and treatment recommendations were offered. Because the study of FORL is in its infancy, more research needs to be conducted; however, what recommendations resonate with you? Can you think of therapeutic frameworks, models, or techniques not listed that may be beneficial?

Key Concepts

assessment	acceptance and commitment therapy
stage of change	cognitive-behavioral therapy
SOCRS	cognitive-behavioral couple's therapy
treatment plan	solution-focused therapy
denial	positive psychology
emotionally focused therapy	positive affect
emotional intelligence	positive reappraisal
mindfulness	discernment counseling
dialectical behavior therapy	marital separation
internal family systems	collaborative divorce
communal strength	core issues
motivational interviewing	

References

Atkinson, B. (2005). *Emotional intelligence*. New York: Norton.

Atkinson, B. (2014, January/February). The great deception: We're less in control than we think. *Psychotherapy Networker*. Retrieved July 5, 2018 from www.psychotherapynetworker.org/magazine/article/142/the-great-deception.

Bachand, L. L. & Caron, S. L. (2001). Ties that bind: A qualitative study of happy long-term marriages. *Contemporary Family Therapy, 23*(1), 105–121.

Basson, R. (2000). The female sexual response: A different model. *Journal of Sex & Marital Therapy, 26*(1), 51–65.

Basson, R., Brotto, L. A., Laan, E., Redmonod, G., & Utian, W. (2005). Assessment and management of women's sexual dysfunctions: Problematic desire and arousal. *Journal of Sexual Medicine, 2*, 291–300.

Baucom, D. H. & Epstein, N. (1990). *Cognitive-behavioral marital therapy*. New York: Brunner/Mazel.

Baumeister, R. F. & Bratslavsky, E. (1999). Passion, intimacy, and time: Passionate love as a function of change in intimacy. *Personality and Social Psychology Review, 3*(1), 49–67.

Bergner, R. M. (2000). Love and barriers to love: An analysis for psychotherapists and others. *American Journal of Psychotherapy, 54*(1), 1–17.

Berscheid, E. (2006). Searching for the meaning of love. In R. J. Sternberg & K. Weis (eds), *The new psychology of love* (pp. 171–183). New Haven, CT: Yale University Press.

Berscheid, E. S. & Regan, P. C. (2005). *Psychology of interpersonal relationships.* Upper Saddle River, NJ: Pearson Education.

Brezsnyak, M. & Whisman, M. A. (2004). Sexual desire and relationship functioning: The effects of marital satisfaction and power. *Journal of Sex & Marital Therapy, 30*(3), 199–217.

Carter, J. (2013). The curious absence of love stories in women's talk. *The Sociological Review, 61*(4), 728–744.

Castleman, M. (2012, April 16). Which comes first? Desire? Or sex? Retrieved July 25, 2018 from www.psychologytoday.com/us/blog/all-about-sex/201204/which-comes-first-desire-or-sex.

Clark, M. S. & Mills, J. (2010). A theory of communal (and exchange) relationships. In P. A. M. Van Lange, A. W. Kruglanski, & E. T. Higgins (eds), *Handbook of theories of social psychology* (pp. 232–250). Thousand Oaks, CA: Sage.

Collaborative Divorce.Net (2017). History of collaborative divorce. Retrieved October 18, 2018 from www.collaborativedivorce.net/history-of-collaborative-divorce/.

Conley, T. D., Roesch, S. C., Peplau, L. A., & Gold, M. S. (2009). A test of positive illusions versus shared reality models of relationship satisfaction among gay, lesbian, and heterosexual couples. *Journal of Applied Social Psychology, 39*(6), 1417–1431.

Davis, T. (2018). *How positive reappraisal can boost happiness.* Retrieved on October 17, 2018 from www.psychologytoday.com/us/blog/click-here-happiness/201807/how-positive-reappraisal-can-boost-happiness.

De Shazer, S. & Dolan, Y. (2007). *More than miracles: The state of the art of solution-focused brief therapy.* New York: Routledge.

Doherty, W. J. (2011, November/December). In or out? *Psychotherapy Networker.* www.psychotherapynetworker.org/magazine/article/315/in-or-out.

Doherty, W. J., Willoughby, B. J., & Peterson, B. (2011). Marital reconsideration interest of divorcing parents: Research and implications for practice. *Family Law Forum, 19*, 48–52.

Drake, C. (2017). Guiding values-based choices with rft theory and a card deck. Retrieved on October 16, 2018 from www.praxiscet.com/blog/guiding-valued-based-choices-rft-theory-and-card-deck.

Epstein, S. (2019). Four types of grief nobody told you about. *Psychology Today.* Retrieved May 4, 2019 from www.psychologytoday.com/us/blog/between-the-generations/201904/four-types-grief-nobody-told-you-about.

Fincham, F. D., Stanley, S. M., & Beach, S. R. (2007). Transformative processes in marriage: An analysis of emerging trends. *Journal of Marriage and Family, 69*(2), 275–292.

Fisher, H. (2006). The drive to love: The neural mechanism for mate selection. In R. J. Sternberg & K. Weis (eds), *The new psychology of love* (pp. 87–115). New Haven, CT: Yale University Press.

Fraley, R. C. (n.d.a). *Attachment styles and close relationships.* Retrieved September 18, 2018 from www.web-research-design.net/cgi-bin/crq/crq.pl.

Fraley, R. C. (n.d.b). *Relationship structures – Attachment styles across relationships.* Retrieved September 19, 2018 from www.yourpersonality.net/relstructures/.

Fritchle, M. J. (2014). *The conscious sexual self workbook*. North Charleston, SC: CreateSpace Independent Publishing Platform.

Gadoua, S. (2010). Can a temporary separation make a relationship stronger? *Psychology Today*. Retrieved on October 17, 2018 from www.psychologytoday.com/us/blog/contemplating-divorce/201004/can-temporary-separation-make-relationship-stronger.

Goddard, H. W. (2007). Commitment in healthy relationships. *The Forum for Family and Consumer Issues*, *12*(1), 1–8.

Gottman, J. (1994). *What predicts divorce? The relationship between marital process and marital outcomes*. Mahwah, NJ: Erlbaum.

Gottman, J. M., Coan, J., Carrere, S., & Swanson, C. (1998). Predicting marital happiness and stability from newlywed interactions. *Journal of Marriage and the Family*, *60*(1), 5–22.

Gottman, J. M. & Levenson, R. W. (2000). The timing of divorce: Predicting when a couple will divorce over a 14-year period. *Journal of Marriage and Family*, *62*(3), 737–745.

Gottman, J. M. & Levenson, R. W. (2002). A two-factor model for predicting when a couple will divorce: Exploratory analyses using 14-year longitudinal data. *Family Process*, *41*(1), 83–96.

Greenberg, L. S. & Johnson, S. M. (1988). *Emotionally focused therapy for couples*. New York: Guilford Press.

Harris, R. (2007). *The happiness trap: Stop struggling, start living*. Boston, MA: Trumpeter Books.

Harris, R. (2016). How to deal with "values conflicts." Retrieved on October 16, 2018 from www.actmindfully.com.au/upimages/How_to_deal_with_values_conflicts_-_Russ_Harris.pdf.

Hayes, S. (2005). *About ACT*. Retrieved on October 17, 2018 from https://contextualscience.org/about_act.

Hayes, S. C., Strosahl, K. D., & Wilson, K. G. (2012). *Acceptance and commitment therapy: The process and practice of mindful change*, 2nd edn (p. 240). New York: Guilford Press.

Hemesath, C. W. (2016). *Falling out of romantic love: A phenomenological study of the meaning of love in marriage* (unpublished doctoral dissertation). Iowa State University, Ames, IA.

Hemesath, C. W. & Hurt, T. R. (2016). *Falling out of romantic love: A focus group study* (unpublished manuscript). Department of Human Development and Family Studies, Iowa State University, Ames, IA.

Hemesath, C. W. & Hurt, T. R. (2017). *Falling out of romantic love: An integrated theoretical framework* (unpublished manuscript). Department of Human Development and Family Studies, Iowa State University, Ames, IA.

Impett, E. A., Muise, A., & Peragine, D. (2014). Sexuality in the context of relationships. *APA Handbook of Sexuality and Psychology*, *1*, 269–315.

Impett, E. A., Strachman, A., Finkel, E. J., & Gable, S. L. (2008). Maintaining sexual desire in intimate relationships: The importance of approach goals. *Journal of Personality and Social Psychology*, *94*(5), 808–823.

International Academy of Collaborative Professionals (2018). What is collaborative practice. Retrieved on October 18, 2018 from www.collaborativepractice.com/.

Iowa collaborative divorce. (n.d.). Retrieved October 22, 2018, from www.iowacollaborativedivorce.com/.

Johnson, S. (2013). *Love sense: The revolutionary new science of romantic relationships*. New York: Little Brown and Company.

Johnson, S. M. & Greenberg, L. S. (1985). Differential effects of experiential and problem-solving interventions in resolving marital conflict. *Journal of Consulting and Clinical Psychology*, 53(2), 175–184.

Kayser, K. (1990). The process of marital disaffection: Interventions at various stages. *Family Relations*, 39(3), 257–265.

Kayser, K. (1993). *When love dies: The process of marital disaffection*. New York: Guilford Press.

Lamanna, M. A., Riedmann, A., & Stewart, S. (2018). *Marriages, families, and relationships: Making choices in a diverse society*. Boston, MA: Cengage Learning.

Lambert, N. M., Clark, M. S., Durtschi, J., Fincham, F. D., & Graham, S. M. (2010). Benefits of expressing gratitude: Expressing gratitude to a partner changes one's view of the relationship. *Psychological Science*, 21(4), 574–580.

Laumann, E. O., Gagnon, J. H., Michael, R. T., & Michaels, S. (1994). *The social organization of sexuality: Sexual practices in the United States*. Chicago, IL: University of Chicago Press.

Leahy, R. L. (2003). *Cognitive therapy techniques: A practitioner's guide*. New York: Guilford Press.

Lebow, J. L., Chambers, A. L., Christensen, A., & Johnson, S. M. (2012). Research on the treatment of couple distress. *Journal of Marital and Family Therapy*, 38(1), 145–168.

Manning, W. D. & Smock, P. (2005). Measuring and modeling cohabitation: New perspectives from qualitative data. *Journal of Marriage and Family*, 67, 989–1002.

Mansfield, T. R. (2010). A review of "Emotional Intelligence in Couples Therapy: Advances from Neurobiology and the Science of Intimate Relationships." *Journal of Couple & Relationship Therapy*, 9(4), 362–363.

Montgomery, M. J. & Sorell, G. T. (1997). Differences in love attributes across family life stages. *Family Relations*, 46, 55–61.

Muise, A. & Impett, E. A. (2015). Good, giving, and game: The relationship benefits of communal sexual motivation. *Social Psychological and Personality Science*, 6(2), 164–172.

Muise, A., Impett, E. A., & Desmarais, S. (2013). Getting it on versus getting it over with: Sexual motivation, desire, and satisfaction in intimate bonds. *Personality and Social Psychology Bulletin*, 39(10), 1320–1332.

Muise, A., Impett, E. A., Kogan, A., & Desmarais, S. (2013). Keeping the spark alive: Being motivated to meet a partner's sexual needs sustains sexual desire in long-term romantic relationships. *Social Psychological and Personality Science*, 4(3), 267–273.

Newman, B. M. & Newman, P. R. (2007). *Theories of human development*. Mahwah, NJ: Lawrence Erlbaum Associates, Inc.

Nicholson, J. (2017, March 12). *10 things that make someone a great romantic partner*. Retrieved September 8, 2018 from www.psychologyto day.com/us/blog/the-attraction-doctor/201703/10-things-make-someone-great-romantic-partner.

Olson, D. H. & Olson, A. K. (1999). PREPARE/ENRICH program: Version 2000. In R. Berger & M. Hannah (eds), *Preventative approaches in couples therapy* (pp. 196–216). Philadelphia, PA: Brunner/Mazel.

Perel, E. (2007). *Mating in captivity: Unlocking erotic intelligence.* New York: Harper.

Perel, E. (2017a). *The state of affairs: Rethinking infidelity,* 1st edn. New York: Harper.

Perel, E. (2017b, October 2). How to find the sweet spot between love and desire. Retrieved July 20, 2018 from www.youtube.com/watch?v=ier RipP-7JA.

Prochaska, J. O. & DiClemente, C. C. (1982). Transtheoretical therapy: Toward a more integrative model of change. *Psychotherapy: Theory, Research & Practice, 19*(3), 276–288.

Psychology Today (n.d.). Dialectial behavior therapy. Retrieved September 25, 2018 from www.psychologytoday.com/us/therapy-types/dialecti cal-behavior-therapy.

Regan, P. C. (2000). The role of sexual desire and sexual activity in dating relationships. *Social Behavior and Personality, 28,* 51–59.

Regan, P. C. (2011). *Close relationships.* New York: Routledge.

Regan, P. C. (2017). *The mating game: A primer on love, sex, and marriage,* 3rd edn. Thousand Oaks, CA: Sage.

Regan, P. C. & Berscheid, E. (1999). *Lust: What we know about human sexual desire.* Thousand Oaks, CA: Sage.

Reis, H. T. (1990). The role of intimacy in interpersonal relations. *Journal of Social and Clinical Psychology, 9*(1), 15–30.

Ritter, K., Handsel, V., & Moore, T. (2016). Stages of change in relationship status questionnaire: Development and validation. *Journal of College Counseling, 19*(2), 154–167.

Roberts, T. W. (1992). Sexual attraction and romantic love: Forgotten variables in marital therapy. *Journal of Marital and Family Therapy, 18*(4), 357–364.

Rollnick, S. & Miller, W. R. (1995). What is motivational interviewing? *Behavioural and Cognitive Psychotherapy, 23*(4), 325–334.

Sailor, J. L. (2006). *A phenomenological study of falling out of romantic love as seen in married couples* (doctoral dissertation). Retrieved from ProQuest. (UMI Number, 3238277.)

Sailor, J. L. (2013). A phenomenological study of falling out of romantic love. *The Qualitative Report, 18*(19), 1–22.

Schwartz, R. C. (1995) *Internal family systems therapy.* Needham Heights, MA: Guilford Press.

Seidman, G. (2017). Are romanticized expectations good or bad for relationships? Retrieved July 18, 2018 from www.psychologytoday.com/us/blog/close-encounters/201707/are-romanticized-expectations-good-or-bad-relationships.

Seligman, M. E. P. (1974). *Helplessness: On depression, development, and death.* San Francisco, CA: W. H. Freeman.

Seligman, M. E., Steen, T. A., Park, N., & Peterson, C. (2005). Positive psychology progress. *American Psychologist, 60*(5), 410–421.

Shah, M. (2008). Falling out of love? *Berkeley Scientific Journal, 12*(2). Retrieved from https://escholarship.org/uc/item/58v0q3qr.

Solomon, A. H. (2017). *Loving bravely: Twenty lessons of self-discovery to help you get the love you want.* Oakland, CA: New Harbinger Publications.

Sternberg, R. J. (1987). Liking versus loving: A comparative evaluation of theories. *Psychological Bulletin, 102*(3), 331–345.

Sternberg, R. J. & Weis, K. (eds) (2006). *The new psychology of love.* New Haven, CT: Yale University Press.

Tumin, D., Han, S., & Qian, Z. (2015). Estimates and meanings of marital separation. *Journal of Marriage and Family, 77*(1), 312–322.

Wallace Goddard, H. & Shoup Olsen, C. (2004). Cooperative extension initiatives in marriage and couples education. *Family Relations, 53*(5), 433–439.

Weiner-Davis, M. (1993). *Divorce busting: A step-by-step approach to making your marriage loving again.* New York: Fireside.

Wineberg, H. (1996). The resolutions of separation: Are marital reconciliations attempted? *Population Research and Policy Review, 15,* 297–310.

13

Conclusion

Throughout my 20 years of practice, I thought, surely, I must be missing a secret repository of scholarly manuscripts and journal articles ripe with information on falling out of love. Although I often searched for these holy grails, I came up disappointed and empty-handed. But there HAD to be information on the topic I saw regularly in my practice, right? I mean it isn't rocket science, is it? Little did I know ... it's likely far more difficult than rocket science. Berscheid and Regan (2005), leaders in the field of relationship science, explain why.

> People want behavioral scientists to refine their actuarial predictions to the extent that they can make reliable point predictions – predictions custom-tailored to each individual case and its unique circumstances. This, it should be noted, is a difficult, almost impossible, task. Other scientists are not expected to make point predictions about natural phenomena outside of the laboratory. For example, no one ever expected Isaac Newton to predict exactly which apple would fall off the tree and hit him on the head and when it would do so. Physical scientists know that such predictions usually are too difficult to make outside the laboratory because they depend on too many unknown, interacting, and hard-to-measure events. Moreover, such predictions require the application of laws from several domains (e.g., gravity, wind pressure) but there is no known law – in the material sciences or the behavioral sciences – that can describe the sequence in which several causally connected events are likely to occur.
>
> (pp. 71–72)

Although accurate and insightful, this is one of those things in life I'm glad I did not fully realize until later. Had I understood the overwhelming complexity prior to embarking on my several-year stint as a full-time FORL detective, I'm afraid I would have run the other way. However, I am glad I stayed the course. The knowledge gained has been extraordinary, not just with respect to FORL, but related topics as well. The information will be tremendously useful in my practice. From the beginning, that's what I set out to do – better assist the clients I sit in the trenches with, every day.

That being said, there is something that strikes me about the knowledge I gathered pertaining to FORL. I noticed a consistent thread weaving throughout – one of *opposites*, and *contradictions*. For instance, denial serves relationships both positively and negatively; it is not uncommon to select our mates based on the very traits that end up frustrating us the most; our personal values are often incongruent, yet we should live according to our values; we convince ourselves (and others) we will never change, but sometimes we do – even when we don't want to; people tell us to know ourselves, but how can we know ourselves (much less others) when unconscious processes out of our awareness are influencing our thoughts, feelings, and behaviors; we are blinded by passionate love but expected to have our eyes wide open; and the list goes on.

During the process of researching FORL, I became frustrated with these incongruencies and would think to myself, "How can anyone understand FORL when contradictions are everywhere? None of this makes sense!" (Not unlike my participants' or clients' experience.) As I trudged through the data and thousands of pieces of research and literature, I began to look at these contradictions differently. Per my usual advice to others, I had been looking for patterns. But I was discarding one pattern that holds an abundance of insight. *The pattern of contradiction.*

I had been viewing these incongruencies as annoyances, getting in the way of what I was really supposed to be seeing. However, the pattern of contradictions holds an important place just like any other emerging pattern of FORL. To some extent, incongruencies are inherent to romantic love relationships. As with all complex systems, we cannot escape contradictions and unpredictability. As soon as I started to accept these frustrations as *part* of the answer, researching FORL became much easier and more enjoyable. (As a trained systems thinker and acceptance and commitment therapy groupie it's embarrassing to admit it took me so long.)

Life evolves in a process of ebb and flow (Mager, 2018), and I believe love is no different. My advice for scholars, partners, and professionals is to lean into uncertainty, learn to embrace it. This skill can be game-changing. After all, life is full of uncertainty, incongruency, and paradox. Consider the Chinese philosophy of yin and yang – two seemingly opposite forces working together to create a dynamic system (i.e., light and dark or water and fire). Although unsettling and uncomfortable, tolerating ambiguity is a valuable skill underlying contentment – it is a calming force, allowing you to take more in, fostering flexibility and experimentation (Mager, 2018).

There is a Spanish proverb, *donde hay amor, hay dolor*, which means where there is love, there is pain. We have seen the complexity of love, relationships, and FORL. Because of this, some may want nothing to do with love and marriage, for fear of pain or divorce. However, I do not believe that is the answer. As poignantly stated by Scott Stanley (2015), "To really avoid the possibility of such pain, one would need to completely avoid love, sex, and children" (para. 4). Love and relationships are too meaningful. They provide the sweetness of life.

To be sure, the ability to predict the future of relationships is difficult, if not impossible, due to ever-changing human behavior, societal norms, beliefs, and goals (see Teachman, Tedrow, & Hall, 2006; see Berscheid & Regan, 2005). Because relationships are complex systems, there may never be a fail-proof method of preserving romantic love or preventing FORL. That aside, I have used the following story many times in my sessions. I wish I could remember who shared it with me, because I would thank them. There was an elderly man and woman who had been married many years. On their 70th wedding anniversary someone asked them their secret to such a long marriage. The old man smiled and looked at his wife. In his shaky voice, he replied, "we didn't fall out of love at the same time." This beautifully illustrates the difficulty and complexity of long-term intimate partner love, but it also instills hope. This couple made it. They may have fallen out of romantic love, but it implies they may have fallen back in-love. It reminds us that anything is possible.

Every relationship is like a snowflake, as unique as the individuals who comprise it. Ultimately, why some individuals fall out of romantic love and others do not deserves far more exploration; however, it is likely due to a conglomeration of factors including what each partner brings to the relationship, complex differences between the partners, the couple interaction, societal and environmental factors, as well as non-conscious, biological forces (see the Megatheory of FORL in Chapter 5). Although relationship outcomes cannot be known for sure, we can get closer to the results we want by making informed decisions. Combining the personal and relationship information we have access to in each moment with current research is the best strategy to obtaining our desired outcome.

For those who fall out of romantic love, as well as the partners on the receiving end, I'm hopeful a main takeaway from this book includes less self-blame. People do not intend to fall out of romantic love. It is painful for all involved. But it's important to remember, you are valuable, and this single relationship does not define you. In the multitude of variables involved – you are just one star in the constellation of factors.

As wisely stated by Esther Perel (2017), there are no true romantic relationship "experts," only individuals who have thought an awful lot about the topic. Expertise, after all, suggests knowing everything there is to know about a topic. I do not claim to know the melody that will mesmerize every serpent who tries to choke the life out of my clients, but I have a heck of a lot more music to choose from than I used to. My goal for this book was to be a useful resource in the clinical toolbox as we wait for research to embrace romantic love and the risk of FORL in long-term intimate partner relationships. As stated at the outset,

> I promise to give you the most up-to-date, empirically based information that I have, shored up with the knowledge gained from being in the trenches with amazing people like you. At the very least, I believe I can provide insight into many of the pressing questions about FORL.

We have gained a new integrated theoretical framework to assist in the conceptualization of FORL. We know the basics about how and why love forms and are beginning to understand the factors thought to be involved in FORL. We are also making ground on the process by which FORL occurs. Assessment and treatment recommendations guided by clinical experience, practice, and research have been provided. Although we have more to discover, I did my best to keep my promise.

We have seen and continue to see the importance of relationships, marriages, and families; however, Americans, like many others, are stuck in a vortex. We can't go back to marrying for land and wealth or to the *Leave it to Beaver* era. We have moved on to a place, individually, socially, and culturally, where personal fulfillment and love reigns. As humans, we yearn for love and stability, possibly now more than ever. This ups the ante for romantic love. The time has come to catch up with ourselves. As a society and as individuals, we are poised to create a more informed and prepared future to better support our goals for modern-day intimate partner relationships. I am filled with anticipation for what lies ahead! Let's keep the conversation going!

Exploration Questions

1 What are your predictions for the future of FORL research? Do you think it will flourish or do you think it will continue to be meager? Explain your views.
2 Although romantic love is one of the most important considerations for Americans when it comes to long-term intimate partner relationships, society has not done a good job of promoting education, knowledge, or resources for success. What might be done to bolster these efforts?
3 For you, what were the three biggest take-aways from reading this book? How will this information assist you personally or professionally?

Key Concepts

the pattern of contradiction

References

Berscheid, E. S. & Regan, P. C. (2005). *Psychology of interpersonal relationships*. Upper Saddle River, NJ: Pearson Education.

Mager, D. (May 31, 2018). *Can you be okay with uncertainty?* Retrieved September 25, 2018 from www.psychologytoday.com/us/blog/some-assembly-required/201805/can-you-beokay-uncertainty.

Perel, E. (October 2, 2017). *How to find the sweet spot between love and desire*. Retrieved October 1, 2018 from www.youtube.com/watch?v=ier RipP-7JA.

Stanley, S. (2015). *Seven ways to make yourself divorce-proof*. Retrieved July 23, 2018 from www.psychologytoday.com/us/blog/sliding-vs-deciding/201503/7-ways-make-yourself-divorce-proof.

Teachman, J., Tedrow, L., & Hall, M. (2006). The demographic future of divorce and dissolution. In M. Fine & J. Harvey (eds), *Handbook of divorce and relationship dissolution* (pp. 59–82). New York: Routledge.

Index

Page numbers in *italics* refer to figures. Page numbers in **bold** refer to tables.

Printed in the USA
CPSIA information can be obtained
at www.ICGtesting.com
LVHW010541050424
776421LV00001B/208

9 781138 327559

The Place of Stone

DOUGLAS HUNTER

The Place of Stone

Dighton Rock and the Erasure
of America's Indigenous Past

The University of North Carolina Press *Chapel Hill*

© 2017 Douglas Hunter
Set in Arno Pro by Westchester Publishing Services
Manufactured in the United States of America

The University of North Carolina Press has been a member of the
Green Press Initiative since 2003.

Library of Congress Cataloging-in-Publication Data
Names: Hunter, Doug, 1959– author.
Title: The place of stone : Dighton Rock and the erasure of America's indigenous past /
    Douglas Hunter.
Description: Chapel Hill : University of North Carolina Press, [2017] |
    Includes bibliographical references and index.
Identifiers: LCCN 2016051985 | ISBN 9781469634401 (cloth : alk. paper) |
    ISBN 9781469634418 (ebook)
Subjects: LCSH: Dighton Rock (Mass.)—Historiography. |
    Petroglyphs—Massachusetts—Dighton Rock—History. |
    Indians of North America—Government relations.
Classification: LCC F74.D45 H86 2017 | DDC 974.4/85—dc23
    LC record available at https://lccn.loc.gov/2016051985

Cover photograph: Daguerreotype of Seth Eastman at Dighton Rock, July 7, 1853, by Horatio B.
King (digital image courtesy of the J. Paul Getty Museum's Open Content Program).

publication supported by
Figure Foundation

by the ley of the lasting land

For Deb

Contents

Figures and Map

Acknowledgments

I wish to thank the Social Sciences and Humanities Research Council and the Government of Canada for support that made this book possible, and Carolyn Podruchny, Boyd Cothran, Marlene Shore, Colin Coates, and Gordon Sayre for their advice and insights. I am indebted to Gilberto Fernandes for sharing his research in Portuguese archives on Dighton Rock and Manuel Luciano da Silva.

Abbreviations

AAAS	American Academy of Arts and Sciences
AAS	American Antiquarian Society
AES	American Ethnological Society
DRC	Dighton Rock Collection, Old Colony Historical Society
HUA	Harvard University Archives
MCRMS	Miguel Corte-Real Memorial Society
MHS	Massachusetts Historical Society
NYHS	New-York Historical Society
OCHS	Old Colony Historical Society
PACL	Portuguese-American Civic League
RIHS	Rhode Island Historical Society
RSNA	Royal Society of Northern Antiquaries

The Place of Stone

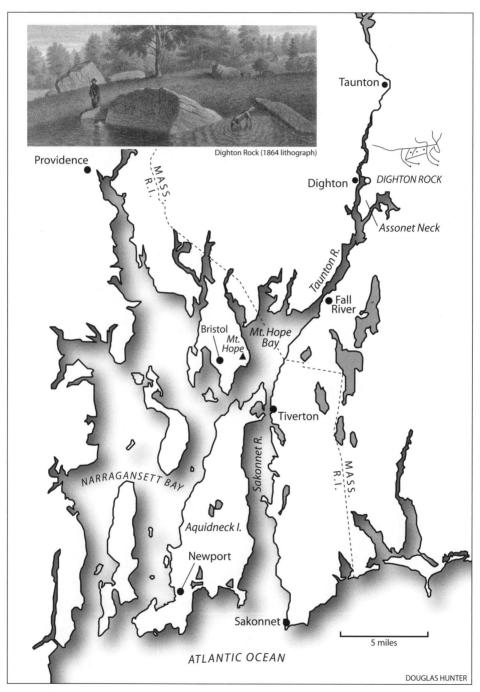

Dighton Rock (1864 lithograph)

Taunton

Providence

DIGHTON ROCK

Dighton

Assonet Neck

Taunton R.

MASS.
R.I.

Fall
River

Bristol
Mt.
Hope

Mt. Hope
Bay

NARRAGANSETT BAY

Tiverton

Sakonnet R.

MASS.
R.I.

Aquidneck I.

Newport

Sakonnet

5 miles

ATLANTIC OCEAN

DOUGLAS HUNTER

Dighton Rock and its environs.

Introduction

A Lost Portuguese Explorer's American Boulder

"Every man will see something different from every other."
—Edward Augustus Kendall, "Account of the Writing-Rock
in Taunton River," 1809

"It is easy to imagine as present on the rock almost any desired letter of the
alphabet, especially of crude or early forms; and that, starting with almost any
favored story, he can discover for it, if he looks for them eagerly enough,
illustrative images to fit its various features, and initial letters or even entire
words or names."
—Edmund Burke Delabarre, "Recent History of Dighton Rock," 1919

On Saturday, September 24, 2011, several hundred Americans of Portuguese
descent gathered on the shaded grass of Dighton Rock State Park in Berkley,
Massachusetts, on the east bank of the Taunton River to celebrate "500 years in
southern New England" for the Azorean people. The rallying point of the
festivities, organized by the government of Portugal's autonomous region of
the Azores in cooperation with the park's shoreside museum and local
Portuguese-American groups, was Dighton Rock, a forty-ton boulder housed
within the museum.[1] The rock's western face, eleven feet long and five feet
high, is covered in enigmatic markings said to record a visit by a lost Portuguese explorer from the Azorean island of Terceira. Miguel Corte-Real was last
seen sailing into the Atlantic in 1502, probably in the direction of Newfoundland. No one knew what had become of him until February 1919, when Edmund Burke Delabarre, a psychology professor at Brown University in nearby
Providence, Rhode Island, announced he had detected amid the boulder's
tangle of lines, figures, and fissures the date 1511, along with Corte-Real's name—
and on further study, an abbreviated Latin inscription indicating he had become a leader of the local Indians. Nine years after departing Portugal, Miguel
had reappeared by means unknown on the upper reaches of the shallow, som-
nolent Taunton River, a tidewater tributary of Narragansett Bay, some thirty
miles north of the Atlantic Ocean. As the celebration proclaimed, Miguel
Corte-Real had placed the Portuguese in New England more than a century

before the Pilgrims had set foot on the other famous rock of Massachusetts, at Plymouth.

The idea that Dighton Rock is a Portuguese relic has never been unanimously held in the Portuguese-American community, much less among Portuguese historians, as I will address in chapter 10. Yet that Saturday celebration in September 2011 saw a new generation of Portuguese Americans embracing the rock as a touchstone of cultural pride and continuity, even if it cannot be said for certain that they all regarded it without question as a 500-year-old talisman of the brave if doomed Miguel Corte-Real. Serving as an ethnic rallying point was not a new role for the contested rock. After its markings were first described in 1680, its provenance was debated for centuries to wildly varying ends, the arguments supported by drawings that could never agree on what was inscribed on its surface. Dighton Rock may not enjoy the notoriety it did in the eighteenth and nineteenth centuries, when it was one of the most debated curiosities in the world, but archaeologist Stephen Williams has called it "the most frequently documented artifact in American archaeology."[2] Depending on how finely the theories are sliced, anywhere from twenty to more than thirty proposals of who made the markings have included Phoenicians, pirates, the Lost Tribes of Israel, Egyptians, an expedition from Atlantis, and Norsemen. *Antiquitates Americanae*, published by the Royal Society of Northern Antiquaries (RSNA) of Denmark in 1837, made the first comprehensive case for an eleventh-century Norse presence in eastern North America by locating the name of Thorfinn Karlsefni of the Vinland sagas on Dighton Rock, in the process supporting a Gothicist interpretation of American history that made the hardy, freedom-loving Norse the ancestors in spirit and ethnic fact of Anglo-American New Englanders (see below and chapters 6 and 9). The Norse attribution never found widespread critical favor, and by the end of the nineteenth century the Karlsefni theory was committed by most serious inquirers, including the RSNA, to a scrap heap of daring voyagers associated with the rock. By the mid-nineteenth century, such transoceanic migrationist explanations had largely given way to the Native American attribution, which might have continued to hold broad sway until today, were it not for Delabarre's Corte-Real theory of 1919 (see chapter 9). Delabarre's reading, once it had been embraced by Portuguese-American community members, dominated popular interpretation thereafter and led to the creation of the state park in 1954 and of the museum in 1978, with an interpretation heavily slanted to the Corte-Real interpretation (see the conclusion).

The greatest proponent of the Corte-Real theory after the Second World War, Manuel Luciano da Silva, a Bristol, Rhode Island, doctor who emigrated from Portugal as a teenager, once accused a local heritage professional of lacking "guts" in not unequivocally accepting the Portuguese provenance of Dighton Rock. In the spirit of the late Dr. Silva's remonstrance, I will state that he and Delabarre, and all who have shared their essential view, were (and are) wrong in attributing Dighton Rock to Miguel Corte-Real—as wrong as the Danish scholar Carl Christian Rafn was in attributing its markings to Thorfinn Karlsefni. These theories were as wrong as every other theory has been, save one: the markings, as they were initially observed in 1680, were made at some unknown point(s) in the past, to an end that may never be fully understood, by Indigenous people—if not specifically the Wampanoag who lived in the rock's vicinity in the seventeenth century, or the collective Algonquian-speaking peoples of southern New England, the *Ninnimissinuok*, or their ancestors,[3] then a broad cultural class incorporating different historic tribal and language groups that archaeologists call Eastern Woodlands.

I base my pronouncement of an Indigenous provenance not on any expertise on my part in interpreting glyphs, or on some exciting technological breakthrough in examining the rock's surface, but on noting that this provenance was apparent from the beginning of European and Anglo-American inquiries, was the least cumbersome and most plausible explanation, and was repeatedly asserted by individuals familiar with Indigenous glyphs and inscribed stones in eastern North America. Advocates of alternate theories have had more than 300 years to make an interpretation stick to the satisfaction of scholarly peers, and have failed repeatedly and resoundingly. As Harvard historian Samuel Eliot Morison memorably quipped in 1954, if given enough time he could find "Kilroy Was Here" or "To Hell With Yale" inscribed upon the boulder. The only recent academic effort that supported a Portuguese reading was that of George F. W. Young in 1970, which inspired the interpretive approach of the museum, but, as I state in the conclusion, Young's analysis ignored the case for Indigeneity. For more than 300 years, the rock has not only been studied, it also has been vandalized by graffiti, and its inscriptions probably have been altered by people making them clearer for illustration and photography, seeking clues to buried treasure, or for their own amusement. Offending graffiti in the past was chipped away, and the surface was further damaged in 1955 by a chain in an abortive attempt to drag the boulder to higher ground in creating the state park. The greatest damage, however, has been inflicted on its Indigenous provenance, and on Native Americans in general, through the explanatory theories.

I came face to face with Dighton Rock in July 2013, finding it housed in a windowless concrete bunker of a building, having been raised in 1963 from its original position in the river. In its natural state it was completely submerged twice daily at high tide, and investigators had to scrub away marine growth and dirt to get a proper look at the shallow markings. So too must we scrub away the surficial arguments to see beneath the ostensibly rational hypotheses and facts and recognize the harsh presumptions behind many interpretations. It is not possible within the limits of this book to assess the historiography of Dighton rock in full detail; Edmund Burke Delabarre alone produced hundreds of pages of analysis in the early twentieth century. But I am less concerned with the minutiae of the many theories than I am with the thread of disdain toward and lack of interest in Indigenous people and culture that runs through them. Dighton Rock has been a mirror that reflects the prejudices and ignorance of everyone who has preferred not to see what is actually here. One of the more extraordinary aspects of the long history of misinterpretation is that Delabarre, a renowned experimental psychologist, was a pioneer in inkblot tests. Only late in his studies did Delabarre acknowledge that he might be staring at the greatest inkblot he had ever encountered, but he never realized he was employing it to conduct a revealing study of his own cultural prejudices.

Stephen Williams has argued that Dighton Rock, in its long history of competing theories, "has something of the quality of litmus paper for testing the tides of current archaeological interpretation."[4] Indeed, as my examination of the succession of theories shows, Dighton Rock's ever-changing interpretation was in lock step with (and contributed to) the shifting Western ideas of Native American origins. And even if, amid the many Indigenous glyphs that the most ardent supporters of alternate theories have conceded are there, a few markings truly could be translated into some Old World script, the premise of this book would remain unchanged. Regardless of what you choose to believe is inscribed in the rock, studying how Dighton Rock has been interpreted at any given time allows us to understand how Indigenous peoples themselves have been interpreted.

I have entitled this book *The Place of Stone* because of the multiple meanings of the phrase. Dighton Rock is located on the shore of what was once called the Assonet River, on Assonet Neck, and was often referred to as Assonet Rock. *Assonet* in Algonquian languages can be translated as "the stone place" or "the place of [the] stone." The rock's place today is more than physical, although its initial, violent removal from its original location, dragged in chains, and virtual captivity today within a bunker-like museum structure, form a gateway to broader, more urgent meanings. "The place of stone" speaks to the role of stone in general and boulders in particular in Indigenous cosmology, and in the relationship between living people, their human and other-than-human ancestors, and the landscape, which have largely eluded understanding in Dighton Rock theories. More important to this book is how "the place of stone" conveys the role an Indigenous artifact occupies in Western intellectual inquiries into American antiquity, including the artifact's utility in advancing and justifying colonization and conceptualizing hierarchies of humanity. Dighton Rock's place encourages us to consider the place of all artifacts in that inquiry, their use and misuse in defining ancient and living peoples. The story of Dighton Rock gathers in other places, other artifacts, and illuminates the much larger and more consequential story of how a colonizing society (through its most educated and politically empowered elite) has defined Indigenous people at both the biological and cultural levels, and to what ends. The ever-changing versions of American antiquity and racial hierarchies spawned under colonization served to disenfranchise Native Americans from their past, and in the process from their lands, while at the same time advancing northern Europeans as the rightful claimants to those lands. The story of Dighton Rock—the story of Dighton Rock's many stories and storytellers— uniquely illuminates processes of belonging, possession, and dispossession from the first decades of the colonial period to the present day.

THIS BOOK IS not about Indigenous cultural survival. A growing body of literature addresses the endurance of Native American peoples, communities, and cultures in defiance of colonialist assurances of their disappearance, and I cite a number of authors to that end where New England tribes are concerned. Although I cite anthropologist Craig N. Cipolla on the enduring importance of stones to Indigenous peoples of New England, the modern Indigenous relationship specifically with Dighton Rock remains to be explored, and perhaps even to be forged. Indigenous peoples have been disenfranchised from Dighton Rock for so long that I am not aware of any scholarly effort to make or record an interpretation of it from their cultural perspective, apart from a problematic one in Edward J. Lenik's *Pictured Rocks*.[5] Nor am I aware of any attempts to reassert formally an Indigenous sovereignty over the rock by the two federally recognized tribes in Massachusetts, although to that end it must be remembered that the Wampanoag Tribe of Gay Head (Aquinnah) and the Mashpee Wampanoag Indian Tribal Council only secured recognition in 1987 and 2007, respectively. Further complicating the contemporary Indigenous relationship with Dighton Rock is the effort by the Mashpee Wampanoag to establish a casino resort in nearby Taunton.[6] In asserting their historic connections to the region, the Mashpee Wampanoag at the time of my visit to the rock in 2013 seemed to be avoiding any public claim to Dighton Rock—a politically deft move, as the controversial casino plan had required the approval of a plebiscite at the local level in 2012 and faced another one at the state level in 2014. With Portuguese Americans accounting for anywhere from 28 to 50 percent of the population of nearby municipalities, the casino advocates would not have done their cause any favors by trying to take Dighton Rock away from Miguel Corte-Real.[7] A representative (with a Portuguese surname) of the self-identifying Assonet Wampanoag (who had nothing to do with the casino plan) adopted a conciliatory approach to the rock's provenance in a public talk at Dighton Rock Museum in October 2013. While asserting the Indigeneity of markings, he cautioned: "I'm not saying someone else didn't write on it. This is probably the first case of graffiti in what became called the United States."[8] The utility of Dighton Rock to contemporary Indigenous culture is charged with great possibility. As this book went to press, I was informed by Ellen Berkland, an archaeologist with the Massachusetts Department of Conservation and Recreation, of a 3-D imaging project for Dighton Rock. "The carvings are definitely Native American," she told me. I am hopeful that changes will be made to the museum interpretation that I describe in the conclusion.

This book also is not a conventional work of rock art scholarship. Dighton Rock does not speak in this book in the sense of conveying a message from an Indigenous antiquity. Rather, it speaks in the voices of its many Western interpreters. Theorists from a multifaceted colonizing culture have employed the rock in a never-ending act of cultural ventriloquism. Only rarely, if we listen carefully, can we hear Indigenous voices, as in the case of the story of the four Mohawk sachems in chapter 4, or in Henry Rowe Schoolcraft's interpretation of the reading by the Ojibwa (Ojibway, Ojibwe, Chippewa; Anishinabe) spiritual and political leader Shingwauk in chapter 7. Even then, Indigenous voices are heard through a Western voice, and we cannot be confident the original message was clearly understood, or has been presented accurately. Sometimes Indigenous voices (as in the case of the story of the wooden ship related in chapters 1 and 4) appear spurious, a colonialist tradition. Edward Augustus Kendall (chapter 4) questioned Native Americans of southern New England on the rock's images, but his Eurocentric ideas about pictorial composition caused him to discard whatever he learned without reporting it to his readers. No unfiltered Indigenous account of the meaning or purpose of the rock's markings is available.

The petroglyphs of southern New England, according to Kathleen J. Bragdon, "have received little scholarly attention. Their age is unknown, and no ethnographic accounts survive that explain their meaning or creation."[9] Dean R. Snow's *The Archaeology of New England* (1980) only addresses one example of rock art, the Solon petroglyphs in Maine.[10] I am not about to attempt to remedy this scholarly deficit by interpreting Dighton Rock's Indigenous meaning(s), beyond addressing the role stones are known to have played (and still play) in linking living people to human and other-than-human ancestors, and in fixing that relationship within the landscape. We have no idea of its age, and based on similar imagery can only assign it to that broad cultural class of pre-Contact peoples called Eastern Woodlands. Although I reference other examples of rock art and sacred boulders, and provide evidence for the rock's Indigeneity and the possible nature of some of its imagery (especially the horned quadruped), I make no effort to lift from the rock a concrete "message." I am not sure we will ever know one, and scholars should be wary about attempting to determine one. Western inquiry has always been ill at ease with the idea of the permanently and intrinsically unknowable, instead determined to "decipher" what is recorded on the stone. Note that where rock art is concerned, I avoid the word "inscription" and instead use "markings," unless I am conveying a perspective within the historiography. "Inscription" implies a unified textual message made by a person or group at a particular time in accordance with an alphabetic or glyphic writing system.

The unknowable, which I have chosen to embrace with Dighton Rock, is consistent with the "percept ambiguity" described by anthropologist Mary B. Black in an ontology ("an inventory of the things people perceive to exist in the world"[11]) she constructed from a foundation of Algonquian language structure and ethnographic fieldwork among the Ojibwa by herself and by A. Irving Hallowell. Ambiguity in rock art produced according to this ontology can be due to interpretive uncertainty—a circle image might be a mégis shell used by shamanic healers, an egg, or a solar or lunar symbol—and because we do not know the artist's intentions (or his/her specific culture), we cannot be sure which one of them it is. This ambiguity might also be deliberate and metaphoric, reflecting the instability of form for living and other-than-living entities in the artist's ontology and the use of images with multiple meanings that are at once literal and symbolic. Seeking clues to meanings of the Maine petroglyphs in Penobscot traditions of shamans and their associated ontology, Dean Snow noted: "when dealing with the supernatural there is no need for either precision or permanence, because the entities described are capable of endless transformation. This characteristic of traditional Penobscot belief makes shambles of modern efforts to impose a rigid structure upon it.

It must also be kept in mind in any analysis of petroglyph motifs."[12] Accompanying this physical ambiguity is metaphoric richness in language. According to Grace Rajnovich: "The Ojibways emphasize the shape-changing capacity of both manitous and powerful medicine men and women through the generous use of metaphor, a poetic figure of speech whereby one object becomes another."[13] An image such as a boat can have multiple meanings. It could be a boat, a journey, and a vision quest, all at the same time.[14] Above all, I am mindful of the fact that rock art images produced by Eastern Woodlands peoples most likely were deeply personal, a record of a vision quest or an exchange with other-than-human entities in order to acquire "power" or medicine. As such, these images were never meant to be public messages, readily understood by anyone.

An interpretation of rock art by modern Indigenous people may not reflect what the original artist intended, or even be important to them. Anishinabe anthropologist John W. Norder has argued that for Indigenous communities in northwestern Ontario, rock art sites "are typically not remembered in terms of their specific meanings or even origins. Their importance emerges as part of the historicity and agency of landscape. These sites are remembered as places of engagement between people and the spirits, and remain within social memory as places of power where contemporary First Nations peoples can still go to in order to pray and re-engage with these spirits through these places."[15] Much like oral traditions, they fulfill an important social utility for contemporary Indigenous communities, which may be distinct from whatever purpose they served when created.

Australian rock art researcher Robert G. Bednarik has criticized scholarly efforts to interpret rock art images worldwide. The readings by researchers are themselves of interest to a scientist because from them we can learn "the perception of the person interpreting the art."[16] In the spirit of Bednarik's proposal, I examine the European and Anglo-American scholarship and folklore constructed around Dighton Rock (and other Indigenous rock art). I analyze the ethnographic reactions to (and for the most part, the misunderstanding and appropriation of) an alien material culture, and weigh the utility of those reactions within an overarching framework of colonization.

I DO NOT MEAN to accuse the proud Portuguese Americans who gathered at Dighton Rock State Park on September 24, 2011, of any particular malice toward Indigenous people. It is possible to be proud of one's ethnic heritage without denigrating the heritage of others. Nevertheless, the celebration (and the state of interpretation in the museum at the time of my visit) was the end product of a long and corrosive exercise in denying Indigenous provenance, and in demeaning and otherwise ignoring Indigenous cultures and peoples in advancing alternative interpretations. Plymouth Rock may have been where the Pilgrims landed, but Dighton Rock was a departure point for many untenable notions still among us, including the persistent idea that Indians were too lazy and stupid to ever have carved markings in rocks, as Harvard professor Isaac Greenwood argued in 1730 (chapter 2). Dighton Rock in particular deserves much credit for the birth in the late eighteenth century of the notion that Native Americans were descendants of barbarian hordes who were not the continent's original inhabitants and had nothing to do with the antiquities of a young nation, and as such should make way for white colonizers.

Dighton Rock's interpretation, as noted, speaks to three related themes inextricable from colonization: *belonging, possession,* and *dispossession.* The long-standing dispute over Dighton Rock's authorship fundamentally has been one of attribution: to what people, what culture, and perhaps what event do its markings belong? *Belonging,* however, operates on multiple dimensions, as do possession and dispossession, in this book, and they form a continuum that ranges from scholarly attribution to private property to identity theft. In particular, the process of attribution has been dependent on possession and dispossession, and these factors can be applied widely and defined in broad dimensions in ethnographic study.[17] Access to an artifact might facilitate study, but *control* of an artifact ensures unfettered interpretation and attribution. A forty-ton boulder like Dighton Rock is not easily carried away to an anthropology department or a museum collection. Nevertheless, plans were hatched in the late nineteenth century to move Dighton Rock alternately to Copenhagen and Boston (see chapter 9), where it could be celebrated as a Norse artifact. Ultimately, the boulder was elevated from tidewater and had its museum built around it, sealing it within an all but undeniable Portuguese provenance (chapter 10, conclusion). Long before experiencing a physical repositioning that disconnected it from a riverside location that likely was critical to its Indigenous significance, Dighton Rock's interpretation was inseparable from its possession, and by "possession" I mean a range of conditions that arose through conquest and colonization. These conditions include the incorporation of the surrounding countryside into the future states of Massachusetts and Rhode Island following King Philip's War, the associated removal of the Wampanoag in 1676, and the subsequent legal ownership of the rock and the surveyed property on which it rested. By the twentieth century, possession of legal title to the rock and the surrounding lands had become a key factor (perhaps *the* key factor) in determining to whom the enigmatic markings belonged in the sense of attribution, as scholarship was consigned a role secondary to physical possession and political power. I extend the place-making that Keith Basso observed through the Western Apache relationship with the land to the rock's role in New England colonization and the twentieth-century Portuguese-American immigrant experience. I also associate place-making with the "home-making" described by Orm Øverland, by which immigrant groups claim America as a place where they rightfully belong. Both place-making and home-making were at work in the Scandinavian-American and Portuguese-American efforts to claim Dighton Rock, as I show in chapters 9 and 10.

Dispossession was (and remains) the operative concept of colonization, and was grounded in the fifteenth-century principle of *terra nullius*.[18] Where my analysis of Dighton Rock is concerned, dispossession extends beyond the recognized tools of colonization in the Americas—violence, coercion, and failed treaty promises—and engages it as a process of erasure. I am going beyond Roy Harvey Pearce's contention in *Savages of America* that following the War of Independence, Americans determined the Indian "belonged in the American past and was socially and morally significant only as part of that past. . . . He belonged in American prehistory, or in the non-American history of North America."[19] In the historiography of Dighton Rock, Indigenous peoples are not so much consigned to America's past as disenfranchised from their own past by being denied their ancestral relationship to archaeological materials, while also being denied an existence in their own present. Theorists also dispossessed Indigenous peoples of their identity and culture by transforming them into their oppressors in what amounted to cultural and biological identity theft. Through what I call *White Tribism*, theorists turned Indigenous peoples in whom they detected intellectual and cultural capabilities into whites, or at least into Indigenous peoples who must have been improved in the past by the superior cultures, technologies, and blood of Europeans. This was also a form of possession, with the bodies and cultures of ancestral Native Americans colonized by newcomers.

Belonging is at the root of the most essential questions that studies of Dighton Rock have posed. The fundamental question of to whom America originally belonged is of long-standing interest to ethnology and anthropology (and its subdiscipline of archaeology). Theories of the peopling of the Americas have evolved and been contested since Columbus set foot in the Bahamas in October 1492, as I outline in chapter 1. Well into the nineteenth century, these theories were answerable to scriptural hermeneutics that traced all living peoples, through migration patterns, to Noah's three sons, and in the case of Native Americans also considered the fates of the so-called Lost Tribes of Israel. Such theories created proto-racial hierarchies that made Europeans the progeny of a favored son of Noah, Japheth, and often considered Native Americans the offspring of Noah's cursed grandson, Canaan, who, according to prophecy, were subservient to the Japhetite lineage.

The biological question of *belonging* for Native Americans was intertwined with the issue of who had the right to possess the continent. Theorists asked whether Native Americans were fully human, descended from the progeny of Noah (and ultimately from Adam and Eve). Did they qualify as "natural" slaves in the Aristotelian model, intrinsically (and irreversibly) inferior and subservient to Europeans? As the eighteenth-century Enlightenment began to consider humanity in more ostensibly scientific terms, two competing arguments of belonging persisted. The monogenic one, reliant on scriptural hermeneutics, posited humanity as one species descended from the Creation of Genesis, with Native Americans one of several variants or races. The polygenic one, claiming freedom from religious dogma, argued on the purported basis of scientific evidence that monogenism's races were in fact distinct human species that arose in different geographic locales. The monogenism–polygenism dispute, as I show in chapter 8, informed and complicated the mid-nineteenth-century debates surrounding Dighton Rock and the Mound Builders.

Belonging and *possession* were further expressed in theories of *migrationism* (population movements) and *diffusionism* (the spread of cultural traits), both of which endure as concepts in modern anthropology.[20] Theorists employed migrationism to argue for racial privilege—white privilege—for modern peoples determined to belong to the descendants of Japheth, who were charged by God with overspreading the Earth after the Flood, and conversely for racial subservience for those peoples—among them Native Americans— who could be assigned to the ranks of the progeny of Noah's cursed grandson, Canaan. Diffusionism was enlisted in earnest in the eighteenth century, as I discuss in chapter 2, in theories of a "golden age" from which all civilization emerged. Theorists sought affinities between Indigenous peoples of the Americas and Old World cultures through language and cultural practices. They debated whether Native Americans ever received a diffusion of wisdom in ages past, or had possessed it only dimly and imitatively, or had once been privileged by it but through degeneration (cultural as well as biological) had lost their grip on it. As I explain in chapter 2, this idea of a root wisdom turned both esoteric and scientific in the eighteenth century, as the concept emerged of an exceptional northern European race/culture/lineage linked to both the Japheth migration and root-civilization diffusionism, which would give rise to Gothicism and Aryanist white supremacy.

As I discuss in chapter 2, theorists beginning with Menasseh Ben Israël in 1650 and Jean-François Lafitau in 1724 articulated a profoundly important concept for the populating of the Americas that I call the *multiple-migration displacement scenario*. A more advanced people arrived first, generally from Asia; later, a less sophisticated people, who were broadly identified by theorists as "Tartars" and considered ancestors of Native Americans, eradicated the first arrivals or drove them southward. The multiple-migration displacement scenario, usually employing what we now call Beringia as a transit locus, was further developed by a variety of eighteenth-century writers, including Pehr Kalm and his English translator, Johann Reinhold Forster, and Thomas Pennant. I show the underappreciated influence of Philipp-Johann Strahlenberg on efforts (including the decipherment of Dighton Rock) to link northern Asiatic peoples to ancestral Native Americans.

Most theorists I discuss fall into the intertwined categories of British and American, although a few crucial Scandinavians and continental Europeans appear. Enlightenment ideas about race and human antiquity led to the construction of a privileged Whiteness, and that Whiteness in turn was indebted to a romantic, esoteric, and pseudoscientific idea of a superior northern European people and culture that scholars call Gothicism. As I show in chapter 2, the Gothicism initially articulated by Sweden's Olf Rudbeks gained influential form through works of the French Swiss, Paul Henri Mallet, in the mid- to late eighteenth century. Rudbeks also influenced the Baron de Montesquieu's *De l'Esprit des loix*, which in turn was a major influence in the American colonies. Rudbeks was also a mentor to Linnaeus, who created the enduring system of species classification for all life on earth, including *Homo sapiens*, for which he contrived a superior form called Europaeus. Mallet's and Montesquieu's writings were cited by the German philosopher and historian Christoph Meiners, who in furthering the Linnaean scheme conceived of "Caucasian" as a superior racial category that is identifiably Gothicist in Meiners's use of Celts (as per Mallet) as the most elite Caucasian form. Meiners evidently inspired Johann F. Blumenbach to include *Caucasoid* in his five-race system, which dominated nineteenth-century archaeology. While a variety of European theorists engaged the antiquities of the Americas, including Dighton Rock, their ideas were incorporated into a particular Anglo-American discourse. In the nineteenth century these colonizers routinely conceptualized themselves as the superior Gothic northern European race and culture, positioned in opposition to the inferior Other of Native Americans.

Belonging became an urgent question in the late eighteenth century for the new republic of the United States. Settlement pressures west of the Appalachians led Americans to justify incursions into lands already peopled by Native Americans. Settler encounters with impressive and puzzling archaeological sites in the Ohio and Mississippi valleys coincided with fresh theorizing on the multiple-migration displacement scenario of Indigenous origins. Dighton Rock was an elemental and unrecognized stepping-stone in the process of crafting a confrontation in America of two rival migrations. As I show in chapter 3, in 1786 a prominent Anglo-Irish antiquarian, Charles Vallancey, held that the rock's markings were the work of a more advanced, initial migration out of Asia that gave way to a brutish Tartar "horde," the ancestors of present-day Native Americans. This crystallizing of the multiple-migration displacement scenario at the dawn of American scientific archaeology gave rise to the concept of an original, superior people, the Mound Builders, in a flurry of theorizing from 1786 to 1789 by a network of American theorists associated with Dighton Rock's most committed American student, Ezra Stiles. American antiquaries and the archaeologists who followed them conceptualized a vanished founding people. Regardless of where the Mound Builders were thought to have originated—China? Carthage? Israel? the land of the Great Khan?—they had been displaced by the savage horde of later arrivals, the ancestors of Native Americans. Ergo, America did not belong to Native Americans because their ancestors had violently seized it from a superior people. Colonization employed the language and methodology of science to turn the displaced into the original displacers, the victims of conquest into the original aggressors, and to justify their removal. The scientific certitude of the Mound Builders found explicit and devastating utility in the Jacksonian policy of forced removal that led to the Trail of Tears and the deaths of thousands of Cherokee in 1838, and many more tribes suffered the consequences of its logic.

The idea that the Mound Builder theory served colonization is not new. Bruce Trigger, for one, considered Mound Builder theories of the nineteenth century a classic expression of "colonialist archaeology," which arose from the presumption that Indigenous people were "inherently unprogressive and incapable of adopting a civilized pattern of life," with archaeology from the beginning assuming that it would reveal little evidence of change or development. When evidence of cultures strikingly different from peoples known in historic times was found, as in the case of the Mound Builders, they were assigned to a "lost race" that was distinct from North Americans and had been either destroyed or driven out of North America by them. "Archaeology thus identified the Indians not only as being unprogressive but also as having willfully destroyed a civilization; which made their own destruction seem all the more justifiable."[21] In my approach to Dighton Rock theories and the associated interpretations of the Mound Builders, I apply Trigger's framing of early American archaeology, but extend its colonialist nature into the specifics of methodology, while taking account of what Steven Conn has described as its "object based epistemology," as I discuss in chapter 5. I argue that the emergent American archaeology was militarized in perspective and methodology, born out of the conquest of Indigenous lands and allied with their surveying and settlement. Trigger's definition was most concerned with the colonial mentality, while here I am proposing archaeology as an intrinsic part of the colonizing project, reflecting its military and surveying character, for example.

By the late eighteenth century, Dighton Rock was also being enlisted in esoteric ideas about civilization's rise. Dighton Rock's inscription was assigned to the Phoenicians by the leading French Freemason and esotericist, Antoine Court de Gébelin, in 1781 (chapter 3). Freemasonry was enormously popular among the leading citizens of colonial and early Republican America and advanced the idea of an ancient knowledge possessed and perpetuated by a secret order. Through Freemasonry and related esoteric initiatives, the root culture shared by all peoples, as advocated by Lafitau in the early eighteenth century, became a foundational knowledge of civilization's arts in the possession of a privileged and secretive few, and of the greatest benefit to whites who preserved and propagated it among themselves. In the early nineteenth century, Edward Augustus Kendall, as I show in chapter 4, argued by appropriately esoteric means that, contrary to the beliefs of American Freemasons, Dighton Rock indicated that ancestors of Native Americans had at least been exposed to the ancient brotherly wisdom at the heart of all great civilizations, but he was doubtful they ever possessed it.

The historiography of Dighton Rock informs another question of belonging: Who belongs in America? This was a multidimensional issue that engaged divine will, race destiny, constructions of ethnicity, and, in the twentieth century, U.S. immigration policy. Ezra Stiles was a pioneer in articulating what I have called *Transatlantic Gothicism*. Stiles in his Election Sermon of 1783 (see chapter 3) itemized multiple pre-Columbian migrations of northern European descendants of Japheth. Stiles's Japhetite multiple migrations answered the questions of to whom America belonged, as well as of who belonged in America: it was a place of white destiny, with New Englanders fulfilling God's will to create a New Canaan in America and displace the Indians/Canaanites they found in their way.

Transatlantic Gothicism figured in the early work of Benjamin Smith Barton, a correspondent of Stiles, who imagined Bronze Age Europeans as the architects of America's mounds. Barton's disowned scenario was largely appropriated after his death by Samuel Latham Mitchill (chapter 5). Recognizably Gothicist pre-Columbian adventurers crossed the ocean to attempt a colonization that in Mitchill's case could be cited as a rightful European claim to North America that predated the arrival in New York State by ancestors of Native Americans. By the time Mitchill and his close associated De Witt Clinton were writing in the second decade of the nineteenth century, two rival migrations to the Americas had been constructed. One was the trans-Beringian invasion by Tartarian hordes who were ancestors of Native Americans, and who had displaced or destroyed the superior earlier arrivals, the Mound Builders. The other migration was the Gothic one of northern European whites (Mitchill actually used the term "Gothick"), who asserted the most rightful claim to these lands.

Transatlantic Gothicism was the basis of efforts to place the Vinland of the Icelandic sagas in southern New England, with Dighton Rock reinterpreted as a record of the expedition of Thorfinn Karlsefni in one of the most influential historical works of the nineteenth century, *Antiquitates Americanae* of 1837 (chapter 6). The publication's chief author, Carl Christian Rafn, was assisted in his misappropriation of Indigenous culture by an American antiquarian, Thomas Webb, who was adamant that no inscribed rocks in New England were the work of Indians. In his continuing researches, Rafn relied on White Tribism in asserting that Norsemen colonized New England for centuries and improved the local Indians through interbreeding. Along the way, a typical Indigenous burial of the mid-seventeenth century near Dighton Rock at Fall River, Massachusetts, was declared alternately to be pre-Norse European by Rafn or (in the estimation of the leading Harvard historian, Jared Sparks) Phoenician, while the Harvard professor Henry Wadsworth Longfellow, in the grip of Gothicist romanticism, immortalized the remains as a tenth-century Viking with the poem "The Skeleton in Armor."

The leading American ethnologist of the mid-nineteenth century, Henry Rowe Schoolcraft, engaged Dighton Rock in his struggle to define both American antiquity and Native Americans in a way that was scientific as well as answerable to scriptural hermeneutics and his arch-Presbyterianism. As I show in chapters 7 and 8, Schoolcraft's writings addressed multiple facets of belonging in mid-nineteenth-century debates, not only over Native American descent from the Mound Builders, which he supported, but also over their essential humanity, which he endorsed (albeit as inferiors to whites), in the midst of a resurgence of polygenism that was embraced by Schoolcraft's peers in the American Ethnological Society, Ephraim George Squier and John Russell Bartlett. Schoolcraft's ideas about American antiquity were exacerbated by his acceptance as genuine the fraudulent Grave Creek stone and its multilingual Old World gibberish. I dissect Schoolcraft's curious philological/racial terminology, showing how labels like Algic, Ostic, and Abanic, which he inadequately explained, reveal the undercurrents of his conceptualizing of Native Americans through Old World analogues that were in part scriptural, in part reflective of the period's ferment of migrationist theories. I also ask how much of the published interpretations of Dighton Rock (and the Cunningham's Island petroglyph) that Schoolcraft credited to Shingwauk in fact belonged to Schoolcraft.

Schoolcraft repeatedly reversed himself on a Norse attribution for Dighton Rock, ultimately ruling against it. His Indigenous interpretation of Dighton Rock prevailed with late nineteenth-century scholars, and found widespread favor in no small part because the rock's utility for colonizers had reversed polarity. Where Vallancey had proposed that the rock's markings were the product of a superior, initial migration wave, the same markings were now considered the work of the barbarous hordes that displaced those earlier migrants. The rock provided proof of Indigenous inferiority and the necessity of their displacement in America's westward settlement plans.

In the late nineteenth century, as I show in chapter 9, an enthusiasm for the Gothicist idea that Americans shared with Norse adventurers a freedom-loving spirit and daring, a commitment to republicanism, as a well as a shared superior racial heritage, resulted in a plan by leading New England citizens to move Dighton Rock to Boston as part of a memorial to Leif Eiriksson. This plan failed, but the question of who belonged in America as revealed by Dighton Rock was becoming more explicitly associated with (and dictated by) who possessed the rock in a legal sense. The rock's deeded title, which had been granted to Denmark's RSNA in 1860, was transferred in 1887 to the Old Colony Historical Society (OCHS) of Taunton, Massachusetts, which was determined to ensure it would never again be threatened with removal as a Norse relic. However, it would be under the society's protection that Dighton Rock was transformed into a Portuguese relic.

In the early twentieth century, Edmund Burke Delabarre's Corte-Real theory for Dighton Rock (chapter 9) disrupted any possibility that the boulder might at last settle undisturbed into its rightful identity as an enigmatic if somewhat vandalized Indigenous artifact of uncertain age and meaning. Delabarre's new interpretation likely would have passed into the annals of the very historiographical eccentricity he had so carefully documented, were it not for an urgent new question of belonging in America. As I explore in chapter 10, eugenicist concerns over the nation's racial fitness produced the immigration quota system of 1924 that favored northern Europeans. For Portuguese Americans of southeastern New England, who were made second-class citizens and undesirable immigrants, Delabarre's Corte-Real interpretation became a way for them assert a role as the original European discoverers (and colonizers) of America. Portuguese Americans, who formed a social, economic, and quasi-racial underclass, belonged in America because Dighton Rock's inscription proved that America by discovery originally had belonged to them. In the Corte-Real theorizing that Delabarre continued to pursue into the 1930s, White Tribism figured prominently. Corte-Real and his companions colonized the Native Americans, creating a mixed-blood population superior in character and capability to the original inhabitants. Manuel da Silva, the most ardent proponent of the Corte-Real theory after the Second World War, similarly cast the Indians as an improved mulatto Wampanoag-Portuguese population whose language and place names were full of Portuguese inspirations.

A final question of belonging asks: Who belongs in history? Historians of the nineteenth century were confident that Indigenous people lay outside of it, both in their own pasts and in their present experiences. In the context of Dighton's Rock's historiography, Indigenous culture lay beyond the interests of academic history because it did not meet the profession's objective of describing humanity's progressive ascent to civilization. If living Native Americans had any relationship with civilization, it was their presumed cultural and/or biological degeneration from a semicivilized people in antiquity, their culpability in having destroyed or displaced those semicivilized people, and their continuing, sometimes violent resistance to the just colonization movement of their civilized superiors. Dighton Rock's persistent repurposing as a relic of one Old World people after another was consistent with a Western view of history that considered the rock interesting only if it could be related to a people like the Phoenicians, the Norse, the Lost Tribes of Israel, Portuguese explorers, or an esoteric root civilization of antiquity like Atlantis. Delabarre's eleventh-hour breakthrough in ascribing the rock's markings to the lost Corte-Real expedition, as I describe, was an epiphany that was also a kind of deliverance for the professor. He could now assert a heroic European past for a boulder that otherwise was of no historic interest. In doing so, he crafted a portrait of Native Americans as demeaning as anything in the long history of the rock's interpretations.

Dighton Rock's interpretations have been a tour de force of colonization. The rock was heralded as a territorial claim marker—a statement of conquest—in the Norse interpretation of *Antiquitates Americanae,* while other arguments have seen the European newcomers who allegedly created its inscriptions colonize the gene pool and languages of Indigenous people in what I call White Tribism. To the legalistic enclosures that removed the rock from Indigenous territory I add its capture by the epistemology of Western rationalist inquiry that used a veneer of objectivity and scientific and scholarly method in the service of colonization, disenfranchisement, and the colonizers' ever-shifting priorities of belonging.

First Impressions and First Arrivals

Colonists Encounter Dighton Rock

Dighton Rock was a war prize. After the Native American rebellion remembered as King Philip's War was put down in 1676—after the burnings, the massacres, and the mutilations; after the head of the Wampanoag sachem "Philip" (Metacom, Pumetacom, Metacomet) was displayed on a pole in Plymouth, Massachusetts; after the head of Weetamoe, the widow of Philip's slain brother Alexander, was displayed on a pole in Taunton—New Plymouth exacted retribution in colonization's most meaningful currency: real estate. It seized from the banished Wampanoag people a 1,100-acre triangle of land, called Assonet Neck, at the confluence of the Taunton and Assonet rivers. In 1677 the colony sold the land to compensate its defenders. Six local men purchased Assonet Neck and divided it among themselves.[1] James Walker, a prominent Taunton citizen whose house burned in the opening days of the uprising, acquired a share at the north end, which fronted on the east bank of the Taunton River where it widens for a spell, opposite the town of Dighton, on its way to Narragansett Bay.[2] Along Walker's shore was a large boulder, a glacial erratic, that twice daily emerged fully at low tide. At some point, someone—presumably Walker himself—discovered that the side of the boulder facing the river was covered in strange markings.

In October 1680, twenty-year-old John Danforth, a son of the late Reverend Samuel Danforth of Taunton, made the first known drawing of the markings (figure 1). John Danforth would begin ministering in the Boston suburb of Dorchester in 1682, and his drawing came into the hands of Cotton Mather, the leading Puritan minister and pastor of First Boston Church.[3] The boulder today known as Dighton Rock was about to become one of the most enigmatic relics of American antiquity.

As an artifact in its own right, Dighton Rock became an artifact machine that churned out artistic renderings, photographs, alleged Indian lore, eyewitness descriptions, and above all, theories as to what the markings meant and who made them. People who never came within a thousand miles of the boulder made confident pronouncements on its nature, offering interpretations based on the interpretations of others. No two drawings would ever be the same: every rendering was an act of interpretation, as was every

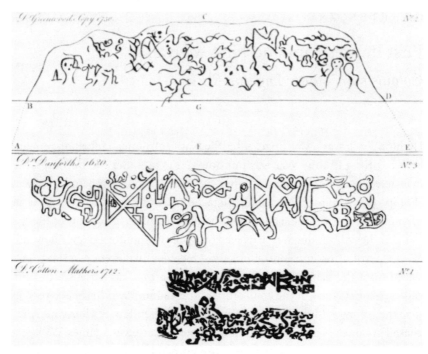

FIGURE 1 Drawings of Dighton Rock by Isaac Greenwood, 1730 (top), John Danforth, 1680 (middle), and Cotton Mather, 1712 (bottom), as depicted in *Archaeologia* 8 (1787).

photograph, for what was perceived depended on lighting, and especially on decisions made in chalking (or painting) the markings that the artist or the camera then recorded. The historic succession of image recordings also was likely documenting to some degree physical changes in the markings, beyond natural processes of erosion. Over time the markings would have been reshaped subtly by repeated chalking and cleaning of the tide- and ice-scoured rock, and doubtless more insistently by people with sharp instruments who wanted to clarify the muck-encrusted incisions—that is, when people weren't vandalizing the rock with their own contributions. The Danforth drawing, then, as the first evidence of Dighton Rock's markings, should have been its best evidence, its best hope of being understood, or at least of being recognized for what it was—a Native American petroglyph of uncertain antiquity and meaning.

A protégé of Cotton Mather, Isaac Greenwood, sent what may have been the original Danforth drawing to a fellow of the Royal Society of London in 1730 (see chapter 2).[4] A slip of paper accompanying the drawing, which seems to have originated with Danforth as well, explained:

The Uppermost of yᵉ Engravings of a Rock in yᵉ river Assoonet six miles below Tau[n]ton in New England. Taken out sometime in October 1680. by John Danforth. It is reported from the Tradition of old Indians, yᵗ yʳ came a wooden house (& men of another country in it) swimming up the river Asonet, yᵗ fought ye Indians, & slew yr Saunchem. &c.

Some recon the figures here to be Hieroglyphicall. The first figure representing a Ship, without masts, & a meer Wrack cast upon the Shoales. The second representing an head of Land, possible a cape with a peninsula. Hence a Gulf.[5]

In reporting "the Tradition of old Indians," John Danforth did not make it clear whether he collected that tradition from them, or if instead the source was fellow colonists who reckoned the inscription to be "Hieroglyphicall." The "wooden house" story might have been a folkloric transplant from a notorious incident on the nearby Connecticut River in 1633, in which Pequot attacked and killed the eight-man crew of a trading vessel.[6] Also unclear was whether the inscription was an Indigenous hieroglyphic record of the alleged visit by foreigners, or if survivors among these unknown strangers left the puzzling record for posterity. The natives-or-strangers questions Danforth's terse note raised defined the debates over the nature of the rock in the coming centuries.

The cause of comprehending Dighton Rock not only as an Indigenous relic, but also from an Indigenous perspective, was lost from the moment of its discovery. The people who would have known it best would, at the least, have been able to explain that the Algonquian place name "Assonet" essentially meant "the stone place" or "place of [the] stone." The very fact that the triangle of land had a name was significant. As Ojibwa scholar Brian D. McInnes has written, a place name for Indigenous people fundamentally "is a symbol and reminder of relationship. . . . The existence of a place name shows how important that site was to the lived experience of the people or the spiritual legacy of the land itself."[7] But when Danforth drew and described the markings, the Wampanoag had just been defeated and removed in a bloody uprising that traumatized both sides.[8] The region around Dighton Rock had figured prominently in King Philip's War. Metacom initially had agreed to a peace with colonists in 1671 in the town of Taunton, six miles upstream from the rock, and the land that formed the town as well as the greater township had been purchased from Metacom and his father, Massasoit, the Wampanoag leader who had all but saved the original Plymouth colony by striking an alliance with the Pilgrims.[9] A number of Taunton residents died in the uprising, or like Walker had their homes torched. Metacom was killed in

August 1676 near Mount Hope, about twelve miles downstream from Dighton Rock, where the Taunton River reaches Narragansett Bay. Anawan Rock, about six miles west of Taunton, was where tradition holds that Metacom's chief captain, Anawan of the Wampanoag, was captured two weeks after Metacom's death, thus ending the uprising.[10] And, as noted, the severed head of Weetamoe was displayed on a pole in Taunton.[11]

Most of Metacom's closest followers were killed, but several enclaves of pro-English Indigenous groups and Christian converts remained throughout southeastern Massachusetts as well as on the islands offshore. Beginning in the late seventeenth century, these Wampanoag enclaves either coalesced or disappeared, leaving two principal communities, one at Gay Head at the west end of Martha's Vineyard and the other at Mashpee on Cape Cod, where there was already a township of Christian Indian freemen.[12] In the absence of the defeated and banished Wampanoag, the inscribed rock was discovered on the seized land of Assonet Neck. In more than 300 years of debate over the nature of the rock's markings that followed the Danforth drawing and description, only one person, Edward Augustus Kendall, apparently ever sought out the remaining Wampanoag and asked them what they thought or knew of it, but not even Kendall (as we will see in chapter 4) published what they told him. Nor would Edmund Burke Delabarre, its most thorough and obsessed investigator, consider how King Philip's War might have affected the way colonists responded to questions of its provenance and meaning. When John Danforth examined it, the atrocities of King Philip's War were all too fresh, for colonist and Native American alike. Although accounts of the war that almost immediately began to see publication focused on the suffering of colonists, Native Americans had been traumatized and violently displaced. The Great Swamp near West Kingston, Rhode Island, was the site of a massacre in December 1676 in which colonial militia shot or burned to death hundreds of Narragansett and Wampanoag. Colonists wiped out about 70 percent of the people allied with Metacom, and as many as 1,200 were enslaved.[13] When Weetamoe's head was displayed in Taunton, in the words of Bristol County historian Duane Hamilton Hurd, "the sad and barbarous spectacle caused great lamentations among the Indian prisoners, her former subjects."[14] The surviving Wampanoag would have had little interest in sharing with colonists their traditions or insights regarding Dighton Rock and Assonet Neck after their own traumas of war and removal.

Even before the war with the colonists, epidemics had devastated Indigenous numbers and doubtless imperiled collective cultural memories. By 1650, Indigenous numbers in southern New England were probably one-tenth of their pre-Contact strength.[15] Some stories conveying traditional culture endured and would be recorded in the early twentieth century, but Christianity became the cultural norm. Christian Indians of Massachusetts had been literate in their own language from the seventeenth to the late eighteenth centuries, but their writing was limited mainly to public records and did not preserve traditions. Fidelia Fielding of Mohegan was the sole person in southern New England to record religious experience and folklore in her own Algonquian language.[16] Any specific knowledge of Dighton Rock's meaning appears to have been lost to ethnographic neglect and submerged in successive tides of European and Anglo-American interpretation. On the colonial front, those interpretations were rooted in traumatizing violence, in a hardening conviction that Native Americans were bloodthirsty savages incapable of becoming civilized, and incapable by inclination, technology, or skill of ever having made markings in stone.

Christine DeLucia has asked: "How do individuals and communities reckon with a past of almost unspeakable cruelties and dispossessions, the effects of which have persisted through centuries of racialized thinking and policy making? How do they—we—conceive of ourselves as complicit in these violences, or as witnesses, victims, survivors of them?"[17] In the immediate aftermath of King Philip's War, the reckoning for colonists involved the erasure of a defeated enemy—removal, enslavement, and condemnation, with redemption only possible through their conversion to Christianity. The succession of American theorists who ventured an array of interpretations of Dighton Rock would not have felt obligated or motivated to seek interpretations from surviving Wampanoag because, in the narrative of the triumphant colonies, Native Americans like the Wampanoag ceased to exist, despite evidence to the contrary in surviving communities, however dramatically reduced their numbers. Thomas L. Doughton has called this the "disappearance model" of official New England history, in which "traditional" culture vanishes along with the people themselves after King Philip's War.[18]

Jean O'Brien has framed the assumed rather than actual extinction of the Indigenous peoples of New England through the terms "firsting and lasting." In southern New England, she argues, colonists and their historians made the boldest claims to "firsting," which "in essence asserts that non-Indians were the first people to erect the proper institutions of a social order worthy of notice."[19] "Lasting" was the penchant of local historians to treat Native Americans as a vanished people, and these local stories informed a national narrative of the "vanishing Indian" that created "a narrative of Indian extinction that has stubbornly remained in the consciousness and unconsciousness of Americans."[20]

One consequence of "lasting," according to O'Brien, has been to deny Indians a place in the modern world, to "purify the landscape of Indians."[21] Colonists thought of Natives as timeless, as incapable of change; it was colonists who brought change and modernity (however you wish to define it) to the western hemisphere. For O'Brien, "The assertion of modernity is made through the seemingly mundane erection of churches and roads, entirely eliding the dynamic world of Indian spirituality and elaborate network of trails and place-names rooted in history."[22] Dighton Rock occupies a peculiar place in this eliding. We cannot blame the erasure of the rock's Indigenous nature on a penchant of writers (as Roy Harvey Pearce has stated) to assign the Indian to prehistory or "the non-American history of North America."[23] If this were the case with Dighton Rock, the many learned men (and they were all men) who began to pronounce on the nature of its markings soon after King Philip's War would have adhered to the standard script of departed savages. They would have recognized the rock as an Indigenous artifact and included it in their narratives of vanquished and vanished peoples. Instead, most theorists denied Indians any responsibility for it, and in the process banished them not only from the landscape, but from their own past as well. Not even antiquity was a safe haven. Such revisionist displacement was (and continues to be) a retroactive ethnic cleansing of the Americas.

Other boulders and rock faces in similar waterside locales would be found, some in the general vicinity of Narragansett Bay, that were marked with peculiar visual symbols, or glyphs. These markings may still defy absolute interpretation, but because of their sinuous lines, similar motifs, and anthropomorphic and zoomorphic forms, they seem to be all of a kind, which some rock-art scholars have placed in the category of "Eastern Woodlands" and generally associated with Algonquian-speaking peoples.[24] Dighton Rock was the largest, the most complex, and the first such set of markings to be found *and* described. The fact that for about a century it was the only petroglyph known in New England added to its exceptionality and gave it cultural momentum that left similar regional petroglyphs behind. Dighton Rock's fame made it a natural attractor for students of American antiquity, who tended to consider it in isolation from similar artifacts, even after these became known as well. In the centuries that followed John Danforth's initial, ambiguous assessment, Dighton Rock's Indigenous provenance was periodically and authoritatively asserted, but to little or no avail. As a war prize, Dighton Rock was quickly put to more practical uses than understanding a culture whose people were considered incapable of ever having produced it.

THE COLONIZERS WHO TOOK the initial interest in Dighton Rock and other ancient puzzles of the Americas were known as antiquaries or antiquarians. The first dictionary of English slang, published in 1699, skewered the *Antiquary* as "a curious Critick in old Coins, Stones and Inscriptions, in Worm-eaten Records, and ancient Manuscripts; also one that affects and blindly doats, on Relicks, Ruins, old Customs, Phrases and Fashions."[25] Among the men who instilled the antiquarian enthusiasm in the new American colonies was the Reverend Cotton Mather, who made the first published mention of Dighton Rock in 1690: "Among the other Curiosities of *New-England*, One is that of a mighty *Rock*, on a perpendicular side whereof by a River, which at High Tide covers part of it, there are very deeply Engraved, no man alive knows *How* or *When*, about half a score *Lines*, near Ten Foot *Long*, and a foot and half *broad*, filled with strange Characters; which would suggest as *odd Thoughts* about them that were here before us, as there are *odd Shapes* in that Elaborate Monument; whereof you shall see, the *first Line*, Transcribed here."[26]

Mather was wrong in saying the markings were organized into anything like ten horizontal lines of text. His illustration was a crude, thick-lined woodcut a little more than three inches wide, which scarcely did justice to markings that filled the face of a boulder eleven feet wide. Delabarre reasonably would conclude that it was based on the Danforth drawing (which would not be published until 1787), and he doubted that Mather ever ventured thirty miles south from Boston to see the rock himself.[27] Mather offered no further comment on who might have created the inscription or to what end, and his remarks in the same volume's "Memorable Providences" illustrate why he would have had no interest in seeking out a Native American explanation. He decried the "miserable heathen" who had risen up against the colonists, reserving particular venom for the "Monster" Metacom.[28]

As Jill Lepore has remarked on the aftermath of King Philip's War, English colonists in New England defined themselves against two "others," the savage Indians and the cruel Spaniards of the Americas. Between them, "the English in New England attempted to carve out for themselves a narrow path of virtue, piety, and mercy. Out of the chaos of war, English colonists constructed a language that proclaimed themselves to be neither cruel colonizers like the Spaniards nor savage natives like the Indians."[29] After King Philip's War, J. H. Elliott notes, there was a growing consensus among colonists "that the Indians were, and always had been, degenerate barbarians."[30] The Indian College at Harvard, established in 1655 to educate and assimilate Native American children, was considered a failure, and was torn down in 1693.[31] As David J. Silverman has written, King Philip's War "permanently broke the back of Indian power in southern New England and reinforced English suspicions that Indians were irredeemable savages. It also set the terms for a postwar racial order in which repeated wars and war scares on the frontier and the colonists' subjugation of New England's surviving Indians hardened racial identities."[32]

Dighton Rock's interpretation and the attitude toward Native Americans of men like Cotton Mather must be understood in the context of their particular remembrance of King Philip's War and earlier conflicts, as well as the brutal ongoing clashes on the colonial frontiers marking British, French, and Indigenous territories, which included raids associated with the European conflict known as King William's War.[33] Both Cotton Mather and his father, the Puritan minister Increase Mather, wrote histories of the conflicts that were drenched in the blood of colonists and that propagandized the barbarity and cruelty of Native people. Cotton Mather depicted King Philip's War as a triumph by colonists favored by God, who "extinguished whole Nations of the Salvages at such a Rate, that there can hardly any of them now be found under any Distinction upon the Face of the Earth."[34] As he pondered the authorship of Dighton Rock's markings, Cotton Mather, not surprisingly, failed to consult people, however savage, he asserted had virtually disappeared.

In 1691, Dighton Rock was mentioned in the letter book of Samuel Sewall, who would be appointed justice of the superior court of judicature in Massachusetts in 1692 and participate in the Salem witch trials that year.[35] Sewall had been a party, perhaps reluctant, to atrocities that followed the defeat of Metacom. After an Indian captive was executed in Boston, Sewall assisted with his dissection. A companion reached into the split body cavity, fetched the heart, and mockingly declared it to be the stomach.[36] Sewall's entry for February 24, 1691, read: "Memorand. to write to Mr. Danforth to take the writing off the Rock and send it."[37] He may have been referring to John Danforth (who more formally should been called Reverend Danforth), but Sewall also knew his uncle, Thomas, whose various posts included the treasurer of Harvard College from 1650 to 1669, deputy governor of Massachusetts from 1679 to 1692, and president of the district of Maine from 1681 to 1692 (in both cases except for the troubled 1686–89 governorship of Sir Edmund Andros). In December 1692 Thomas Danforth would be appointed a judge of the superior court alongside Sewall.[38] Delabarre would propose that Sewall might have been seeking evidence to support a Ten Lost Tribes origin of Native Americans.[39] So it was that Dighton Rock, within a year of first being described publicly by Cotton Mather, was conscripted into a debate that has still not ended over the origins of Native Americans and the true identity of the first peoples of the Americas.

FROM THE MOMENT Christopher Columbus was greeted by Arawaks on a Bahamian beach in October 1492 and considered their resemblance to the Guanches of the Canary Islands, the origins of the Indigenous peoples of the Americas became the subject of intensive study and speculation by Europeans and the colonists who settled the novel lands. Two questions of "belonging" were raised for Native Americans in the initial stage of inquiry. First, theorists asked if Indians even belonged in the human family descended from Adam and Eve and the "second Adam," Noah.[40] Second, theorists who were satisfied that Native Americans were fully human asked to which Old World peoples their ancestors belonged. The second question was inseparable from the mystery of how they got to the Americas—once it was understood the Americas were distinct landmasses from Asia. As a celebrated relic of unknown provenance, Dighton Rock's interpretation became bound up in the larger questions of Native American origins and the contested history of American antiquity.

The Western recognition of Asia and North America as distinct landmasses separated by a strait began to gel in the mid-sixteenth century.[41] The gap (which first appeared as the Strait of Anian in the Bolognino Zaltieri map of North America in 1566), would not be confirmed until the conclusion of the second Russian expedition of Vitus Bering, in 1743.[42] By the late eighteenth century, the Bering Land Bridge, or Beringia, would become the dominant theory/route for the pre-Contact peopling of the New World.[43] Although modern Beringian migration theories are grounded in archaeology and genetic mapping, the migration route, whether by land or water, adhered to a Judeo-Christian scriptural worldview for the better part of 200 years. Researchers have grafted the case for a Beringian migration onto the original one of Old Testament diasporas. While this fact does not negate current scholarship, it contextualizes Beringia as a long-standing construction project that also served colonization objectives. Theories of migration and human origins, not to mention descriptions of living peoples, also were shaped by antiquaries and other armchair scholars who often had little or no actual experience among the peoples on whom they pronounced. These theorists operated within a European and Anglo-American culture that considered its own members a race favored by God, with a divine mission to overspread the world and displace or absorb lesser peoples. Their studies of the past often served to justify the present.

Theorists who were satisfied that Indigenous peoples of the Americas were fully human were concerned with how ancient peoples got from the classical known world of Europe, Asia, and Africa to the novel landmasses separated from them by water. The Judeo-Christian story of humanity was migrationary, regardless of the known configuration of continents, because all people could be traced to a single couple, Adam and Eve, in a single locus, the Garden of Eden. The German humanist Johann Boem, in *Omnium gentium mores* (1520), endorsed the idea that all of *living* humanity, post-Flood, originated with Noah's three sons and thus had a shared Edenic origin. Noah's sons, Shem, Ham, and Japheth (Japhet), and their wives were the choke point through which all humans must have passed. Genesis 9:19 tells us that after the Flood, "of them was the whole earth overspread."

In Colin Kidd's memorable phrase, any effort to trace the lineal descent of humanity from some seventy branches of Noah's offspring described in Genesis to the peoples recorded by classical scholars "runs into sand."[44] A great deal of what Kidd calls "early modern anthropology" thus involved "the reconstitution of the lineages of peoples between the petering out of scriptural ethnography and the start of the classical record."[45] For these early scholars, race and ethnicity "involved questions of pedigree: did an ethnic group descend from the line of Ham or Shem or Japhet?"[46] Noachic migration scenarios and ethnic identities were supported by *Commentaries on Works of Various Authors Who Speak of Antiquity*, a post-Deluge history fabricated by an Italian Dominican friar, Giovanni Nanni (Annius). His sham chronicle of the world's repopulation by Noah's descendants, first published in 1498, was enormously influential, with at least eighteen printings in the original Latin appearing by 1612, as well as translations into major European languages.[47] For many Protestant Anglo-American scholars in particular, well into the nineteenth century, a narrative based on successive generations descended from Noah formed the armature on which human history (and prehistory) had to be arranged.[48] The distinctions in lineal descent were critical, as the descendants of Japheth and Shem were favored by God, whereas the descendants of Ham's son Canaan had been cursed by Noah after Ham looked upon Noah, drunk and naked, and failed to shield him from his humiliation.

According to Noah's curse (Genesis 9:25–27), Canaan would become "a servant of servants unto his brethren," and specifically to the descendants of Shem and Japheth. As well, God was to "enlarge Japheth." For early modern scholars, the descendants of Shem (Shemites, or Semites) were the Jews;

Shem was "the father of all the children of Eber" (Genesis 10:21), the Hebrews, and the progenitor of the Abrahamic line. Europeans in general were considered to be the descendants of Japheth, who were the Gentiles, as the King James Bible (Genesis 10:5) described them. John Wesley, a founding figure in Protestant evangelism, suspected Japheth was Noah's most favored son, possibly his firstborn.[49] The progeny of Ham included the cursed descendants of his son Canaan, the Canaanites, as well as the darker races, among others.[50] The Puritan missionary in New England, John Eliot, circa 1650 expressed a common opinion that Europeans were the progeny of Japheth and Africans the progeny of Ham.[51]

Whether or not the branch of humanity occupied by living Native Americans could be traced to a particular Noachic progenitor, the Tartars (Tatars) from Tartary (Tartaria) in Asia were early contenders for their ancestors. In a letter describing his contested first voyage to South America of 1497, Amerigo Vespucci said the Indigenous people had unappealing faces and looked like Tartars, and followed a very barbarous way of life.[52] The Scyths, or Scythians, a people described by Herodotus who lived north of the Black Sea, also became a popular choice for Native American origins. Scythians were first compared to peoples of the Americas in the early sixteenth century, in Pietro Martire D'Anghiera's *De Orbe Novo*. Martire reported that the 1499–1500 voyage of Vicente Yañez Pinzón encountered in coastal Brazil "a vagabond race similar to the Scythians."[53] Richard W. Cogley notes that Scythians "had epitomized unlettered barbarism in western sources at least since the time of Herodotus," and this made them natural ancestors to Tartars.[54] Strabo advised that Scythians were the northern peoples known to the ancient Greeks, whom Homer also called Nomads; the ones to the west the Greeks called Celts, Iberians, or Celtiberians or Celtoscythians, "the several peoples being classed under one name through ignorance of the facts." The term "Tartar" no less ignorantly combined a diversity of peoples.[55] In Nicolas Sanson's world map of 1691, *Grande Tartarie* stretched from the frontiers of eastern Europe and Turkey to the Arctic Ocean in the north and to the easternmost reaches of Asia, incorporating Russia and China. Enlightenment geographers produced exhaustive subregions of Tartary and also of Tartar peoples, speculating over their relationship to ancient Scythians and the various regions once considered Scythia.[56]

The chief distinction of people variously described as Tartars was their barbarity, as nomadic horse people, warriors, and herders, compared to the neighboring urbanized civilizations of Europe, China, Mogul India, and ancient Persia. Europeans could be indiscriminate in using different Tartar ethnologies in drawing comparisons with other living peoples. As Lee E. Huddleston has written of mid-seventeenth-century theorizing, "Europeans assumed that whatever held true for near-Tartary also held true for far-Tartary."[57] Fundamentally, if Native Americans were considered migrant Tartars, and Tartars were considered former Scythians, then Native American biological and cultural roots had to lie in Scythia.

Not everyone accepted a Scythian or Tartarian ancestry for Native Americans. Humphrey Gilbert argued in 1576 that there was no evidence of either group in North America (although he had never been there), which meant the continent must be an island, separate from Asia.[58] José de Acosta, however, did not see an insurmountable gap. The Spanish Jesuit missionary in 1590 proposed a land bridge or narrow strait between Asia and northwestern North America, but also between North America and Europe, as Greenland was considered the end of a westward-arcing peninsula of northern Europe or Asia.[59] It was in the northeastern reaches of Asia, in what Sanson labeled the land of *Tartares de Kaimachites*, that Native Americans increasingly would be presumed to have originated from Tartar peoples of specific tribal identities, although eighteenth-century theorists sometimes generalized about Native American character based on the Tartars of central Asia.

In the seventeenth century, with northern European countries like England and the Netherlands accelerating their transatlantic colonization efforts, Protestant newcomers closely considered the origin of Native Americans. In addition to the questions raised by the movements of Noah and his offspring, a key line of inquiry took up the fates of all the members of the twelve tribes descended from the twelve sons of Joseph, grandson of Abraham. For some theorists, Native Americans solved the problem of the fate of the ten "lost" tribes that disappeared after the conquest of the northern Kingdom of Israel by the Assyrians around 722 B.C.[60] Still another theory considered the fate of the Canaanites expelled by Joshua. The French Catholic lawyer Marc Lescarbot, who visited the Port Royal colony of the Protestant (Huguenot) Sieur de Mons in Nova Scotia in 1606–7 (and never ventured beyond it), aired the idea that Native Americans were Canaanites punished by God. As Lescarbot proposed in *Histoire de la Nouvelle France* (1609), when driven from their lands by the children of Israel, the Canaanites took to their boats and, at the mercy of the seas, were tossed to America.[61] Thomas Thorowgood, an Anglican priest in Norfolk, England, noted in *Iewes in America* (1650) how some thought the Indians were "a remnant of those Cananites that fled out of that Land when the feare of Israel approaching thither fell upon them."[62]

Lescarbot concurred with Acosta, acknowledging it was possible the Americas were populated by Old World peoples who, expanding little by little, spread to these lands, from either the east or the north (an apparent nod to a crossing from Europe via Greenland).[63] Lescarbot alternately argued for an ancient transatlantic migration, and employed prototypic ethnology (comparative ethnography) in venturing that both the *sauvages* and the Canaanites were cannibals and leaped through fire in worshiping their gods. His expanded third edition of *Histoire* (1617) is rife with allusions to or comparisons of Indigenous peoples to Old World cultures."[64] Lescarbot's theorizing included what would prove to be the important concept of degeneration: Indigenous peoples of the Americas had a more sophisticated Old World origin, but had undergone a cultural deterioration not unlike French colonists left on Sable Island by the Marquis de la Roche in 1598. Surely if Frenchmen could be reduced to wearing sealskins in five years, Native Americans could be the degenerate descendants of more advanced transatlantic ancestors.

Lescarbot's understanding of the actual events at Sable Island was poor—it was a penal colony that La Roche failed to resupply in one year, not five consecutive years.[65] But between Lescarbot's example of European degeneration and Thomas Harriot's earlier equivalency of Native Americans with European barbarians of yore in *A Briefe and True Report of the New Found Land of Virginia* (1588), the basic issues of Indigenous character and potential were stated. Lescarbot supposedly had shown that civilized Europeans could degenerate rapidly into a savage state in the New World, which meant that Native Americans could have degenerated over a much longer period of time from more advanced Old World cultures. Harriot's illustrated comparisons of savage Native Americans to ancient tattooed Picts had offered hope that, through the example and influence of civilized Europeans, Indians could rise from the primitive state they had either always occupied or into which they had fallen. King Philip's War may have shattered that optimism in New England, but hopes for their Christian salvation did not die entirely. Redemption nevertheless hinged on where Native Americans originated, and whether they were fully human.

In a work published posthumously in London in 1614, the antiquarian Edward Brerewood asserted that Native Americans could not be from Africa or Europe but instead must have been from Asia. Brerewood specifically chose Tartary—"Because in America there is not to be discerned, any token or indication at all, of the arts or industry of China, or India, or Cataia, or any other civill region, along all that border of Asia."[66] Brerewood's *Enquiries* contains the first gleam of a migration theory focused on Beringia. In 1642, the Dutch jurist Hugo Grotius published the terse *De origine gentium Americanarum dissertatio.*[67] Grotius was skeptical that Tartars or Lost Tribes populated the Americas, and instead believed the New World had been peopled from a multitude of directions: North America north of the isthmus of Panama had been populated almost entirely by Norwegians or Norsemen (*Noruuegiae* in the original Latin text[68]) and Yucatán from Africa (*Aethiopia*[69]), as Grotius noted that Columbus's chronicler, Pietro Martire, had supposed. While Grotius was amenable to the idea that South Asians from the region of Java and New Guinea had crossed the Pacific to populate South America, the advanced state of Peruvians (the Inca) convinced him they arrived separately, from China. Grotius claimed that place names like Cimatlan, Coatlan, and Guecoslan, which the Spanish had adapted from Indigenous peoples, were all Germanic in origin and hence were Norse. Spaniards had modified the original Germanic words by dropping the last letter. (The Nahuatl suffix *-tlan* thus would have derived from *-land*.)[70] He also found parallels between German or Norwegian and the Indigenous language of Mexico, as well as shared customs.[71] Grotius was not the first person to make such language comparisons. Thomas Morton, who had arrived in New England in 1622, assured readers of *New English Canaan* (1637) that Native Americans "doe use very many wordes both of Greeke and Latine."[72] Morton supposed "the Natives of New England may proceede from the race of the Tartars, and come from Tartaria into those partes, over the frozen Sea,"[73] but also ventured that they might have crossed the Atlantic as "scattred Trojans."[74]

Grotius's ideas were rejected in 1643 by Joannes de Laet, in what became a bitter internecine dispute of Dutch intellectuals.[75] The details are less important to this book than the fact that by the mid-seventeenth century, as the colonial discovery of Dighton Rock approached, several core tools of prototypic ethnology were in use: interrogating place names, probing languages for affinities (and dissimilarities), and citing shared cultural practices. While none of these tools were necessarily incorrect, early theorists were asserting European and other Old World origins for Indigenous languages and place names when they did not understand the grammar and polysynthetic root-stem structure of languages like those of the Algonquian group. Instead, drawing on early lexicons full of best-guess phonetic spellings, they cherry-picked words in Indigenous languages to make analogies with purported Old World sources. The strategy was discredited by a new structural and grammatical approach to the study of Indigenous American languages pioneered in the early nineteenth century by Peter Stephen (Pierre Étienne) Du Ponceau, John Pickering, and Albert Gallatin, and was condemned by Alexander von

Humboldt in Volume 2 of *Cosmos* in 1847.[76] But it persisted as a pseudohistorical tool into the twentieth century, wielded by theorists who were determined to assign Dighton Rock's markings to Old World adventurers.

ACOSTA IN 1590 had dismissed the idea that Native Americans were wandering Jews, but in the mid-seventeenth century, the Lost Tribes theory enjoyed a resurgence among English Protestants.[77] The theory would persist for centuries in debates over Native American origins and the provenance of petroglyphs, including Dighton Rock.

Thomas Thorowgood's *Iewes in America* (1650) may have been the first original English-language work to embrace the Lost Tribes theory for Native Americans.[78] He suspected all the Lost Tribes ended up in the Americas, probably by crossing the Strait of Anian, and represented a single colonizing migration that made them ancestors to Native Americans. Thorowgood never visited America, but in forming his ideas he corresponded with theologian Roger Williams, who in 1636 had purchased land for his Rhode Island colony from the Wampanoag leader Massasoit, father of Metacom (King Philip). Williams endorsed the theory, and among those Thorowgood influenced was the missionary John Eliot.[79] Eliot, in a letter to Thorowgood included in the revised edition and expanded edition, *Jews in America* of 1660, which was published to support Eliot's proselytizing, said he believed the "first planters of America, to be not only of Sem, but Ebrewes of Eber."[80]

Menasseh Ben Israël of Amsterdam's Jewish community presented his own Lost Tribes theory in *Miqveh Yisrael* (*The Hope of Israel*), a work first published in 1650.[81] While Menasseh's work is normally confined to discussions of Lost Tribes theories and millenarianism, he deserves recognition for the foundational proposal of what I call the multiple-migration displacement scenario. This was a profoundly important scenario for Native American origins, which would come to dominate nineteenth-century American archaeology and race theory. It contended that a more culturally sophisticated people were the initial colonizers of the Americas, only to be supplanted in a later arrival by less sophisticated, violent Tartars who swept across the Bering Strait or the land bridge that would be called Beringia and were ancestral to living Indigenous peoples.

The idea that there were "white" people in the Americas had been around since the time of Columbus, long predating the formulation of racial categories that codified whiteness in quasi-scientific terms. In the first Decade of *De Orbo Novo*, Pietro di Martire related a report he had gathered from Columbus of Indigenous peoples in present-day Venezuela. Although the people the

Genoese explorer encountered on his third voyage (1498) lived at the same latitude as Africans, they were strikingly different: "The Ethiopians are black and have curly, woolly hair, while these nations are on the contrary white and have long, straight, blond hair."[82] As Columbus went to his grave insisting the new lands were part of Asia, Martire's report was not as radical as Menasseh's Lost Tribes assertions. Like most anyone considering the story and fate of the Lost Tribes, Menasseh relied on (among other scriptural sources), 2 Esdras (4 Ezra) in the Apocrypha for clues to their eastward migration.[83] As for proof that they made it all the way to the Americas—and could still be found there—Menasseh endorsed a story brought to Amsterdam in 1644 by a Spanish marrano, Antonio de Montezinos, of people practicing Judaism in the Andes, along with other accounts from the Spanish Americas of bearded white men. Menasseh concluded that some of the Lost Tribes had been the first people to populate the Americas, proceeding from Tartary to China, and then across the Strait of Anian. Some might have sailed across the strait; alternatively he wondered if there had been a land bridge that, after the Lost Tribes passed across it, was inundated, perhaps intentionally by God.[84] Menasseh thus managed to articulate the theories of a Beringian land bridge *and* a Beringian ocean crossing in one short volume, long before they became staples of scientific studies of human arrival in the Americas. Most important, unlike Thorowgood, Menasseh did not believe Native Americans were descendants of the Lost Tribes, but rather were their "persecuting Tartars" in the Americas.[85] Descendants of the tribe of Reuben continued to exhibit their Judaic culture, portions of which had been adopted by neighboring, Tartar-derived Indians. These wandering Hebrews were otherwise forced by the less sophisticated Indians into mountain refuges in the Andes, where they awaited an opportune messianic time to reemerge.[86]

The influence of Menasseh on the multiple-migration displacement scenario as it would emerge in the late eighteenth century is difficult to judge. *The Hope of Israel* was popular among contemporary Protestants who believed a millennial or messianic kingdom on Earth was at hand, and that the requisite conversion of Jews to Christianity was already under way in the 1650s, as prophecy foretold. The Protestant millenarian movement, however, was fading by the 1670s, and the emerging natural sciences of the eighteenth century avoided the scriptural hermeneutics that propelled Lost Tribes theories. Still, *Miqveh Yisrael* was one of the most widely distributed books in modern Jewish history, with around three dozen editions and translations in Spanish, Latin, English, Dutch, Yiddish, Hebrew, and French.[87] Menasseh's work clearly remained known for more than a century among New England

Protestants pondering Native American origins—critically so, I will note in the case of migration theorist Ezra Stiles. There was also enough interest in his ideas to encourage a fresh English edition of *The Hope of Israel* in 1792, and again in 1850 and 1901.[88]

Menasseh relied on evidence that was part of a longer (and ongoing) tradition of strangers in a strange land that I call *White Tribism*. (I am using "white" in a broad cultural and biological sense, and not in the narrower definition that privileged northern Europeans as some strains of race science began to gel in the late eighteenth century.) I define three strains of White Tribism. The first strain proposes that the original Native Americans were either migrants from Europe or were descendants of some Asiatic-Oriental-Mediterranean people of antiquity with whom whites aligned themselves. This is White Tribism in its most inclusive form, an effort to make Native Americans members in full standing of humanity, albeit perhaps a version that had degenerated culturally or biologically. The second strain, involving white isolates, posits that biologically distinct descendants of Europeans (or Jews descended from the Lost Tribes) endured as intact communities surrounded by Indigenous savagery in the Americas, as in the case of Menasseh's Lost Tribe of Reuben in the Andes. The third strain imagines a comingling of newcomers and savages, resulting in enigmatic Indian tribes, sometimes called White Indians, which have been improved in every possible way by contact with European strangers. Bear in mind that White Tribism is distinct from actual cases of ethnogenesis or otherwise mixed populations of Indigenous peoples and Europeans. It involves writers and theorists largely trading in *imagined* migrations, and *imagined* infusions of White or European genes.

Crediting Indigenous achievements to outsiders is not limited to whites and their biological or cultural kin. Theories of Chinese, Japanese, Buddhist, Egyptian, and Mongol origins for (or influences on) Indigenous cultures abound, as do arguments that black Africans seeded Mesoamerican civilizations. The second and third strains especially of White Tribism, however, were symptomatic of a colonialist perspective that sought to define Indigenous peoples as inferior in every sense, except where an injection of white blood— ultimately colonists' ancestral blood—and a transfer (diffusion) of white culture and technology could explain their purported exceptionalities. Native Americans otherwise were routinely labeled as lazy, ignorant, and ugly, and incapable of improvement. White Tribism also has enjoyed a unique utility in supporting the contention that whites (as opposed to a specific nationality, like the English) have long been in the New World and thus enjoy as much of a claim to it as living Native Americans—possibly an even greater claim.

White Tribism employs five categories of evidence. The first category is physiological. Observations of racial typology—light hair and skin, blue eyes, physical beauty by European standards—suggest interbreeding or European isolates. The second category is ethnological, along the lines of Grotius: interrogating place names, probing languages for affinities (and dissimilarities), and citing shared cultural practices, including "civilized" behaviour. The third category is semiotic or pictographic. Indigenous glyphs, chiefly in rock art, were used to show that Indigenous people were familiar with Old World concepts (including Freemasonry). Alternately, glyphs have been interpreted as entirely Old World in origin to argue the presence of ancient visitors.

The fourth category concerns material culture. Indigenous grave goods, weapons, and other archaeological finds have been interpreted either as Old World in origin or as proof that Indigenous peoples had through interbreeding or diffusionist inspiration adapted Old World technologies. A subcategory of material culture is fraudulent archaeological finds like the Grave Creek stone and the Michigan relics of the nineteenth century, which can also fall under the third (semiotic/pictographic) category. The fifth category is anecdotal. Writers and explorers claimed to have gathered from Indigenous sources stories of peoples that did not sound Indigenous, or were said to be like the newcomers.

White Tribism reflects in part the gendered narrative of the conquest of Native Americans, as Philip J. Deloria has described. "In one set of narratives, Indian women, linked to the land itself, gave themselves metaphorically to colonizing white men, engendering a peaceful narrative of cross-cultural harmony in which whites became Indigenous owners of the continent through sexualized love and marriage stories such as that of Pocahontas. Another set of narratives—and sometimes the two could be woven together—relied on the masculinist imagery of violent conflict."[89] In brief, the newcomers bred with the women and fought with the men; the men were defeated, and the women gave themselves, and metaphorically their lands, over to the conquerors. In White Tribism, the gendered encounter narrative exhibits an explicitly racial (and racist) agenda. It constructs a lost encounter in the shadows of the unrecorded past, previous to the standard colonizing history that concerns Deloria. Any supposed advancement in Native Americans beyond savagery detected by European newcomers in recorded history was due to some past interaction with and/or a mixed-blood descent from more civilized and biologically superior adventurers. The Indians of White Tribism were noticeably superior to their Indigenous neighbors—more civilized in their manners, politics, social organization, culture, and technology, and more physically refined according to Eurocentric standards. Purported evidence included the very ability to create rock art, which could only have arisen through improvement by a superior outside race and culture. Time and again, White Tribism would be enlisted to explain the origin and meaning of Dighton Rock.

WHEN THE REVEREND Danforth first described Dighton Rock in 1680, the issues of belonging, possession, and dispossession were in abundant evidence, both for the provenance of the rock and for Native Americans. The process of erasing Native Americans from the landscape of southern New England was already underway. Devastated by epidemics earlier in the century, Indigenous communities in southern New England were crushed and scattered by King Philip's War, which made the rock a possession of colonists. The idea that America belonged providentially to colonists, and was without a place for irredeemable savages, was hardening. The process of "firsting and lasting," as described by Jean O'Brien, began writing Native Americans out of existence in the unfolding colonial narrative. Interpretations of Dighton Rock would rapidly move in the direction of denying its Indigenous provenance. Even as Native Americans began to be written out of existence in southern New England, conflicts with Indigenous peoples on the frontiers of colonial settlement were ample reminders that the Indian was far from disappearing from the larger geopolitical picture. The atrocities of those conflicts reinforced the impression of Native Americans as savages. As violence persisted into the eighteenth and nineteenth centuries on the ever-moving frontier of colonization, it would become easier to pronounce Indigenous peoples incapable of having produced markings that theorists were determined to treat as an alphabetical or hieroglyphic inscription.

Dighton Rock was being conscripted into answering the main questions of human arrival in the Americas, which hinged not only on an emergent European understanding of global geography but also on determining to which Old World source population Native Americans belonged. The essential Bering Strait/Beringia theory for humanity's arrival in the Americas was forming by the late sixteenth century, while allowing for possible additional transoceanic visits by Mediterranean peoples of classical antiquity and advanced Asian cultures, a combination that proved durable. Hugo Grotius in 1642 employed a fundamental template for comparative inquiry, encouraging theorists to seek Old World precedents in Indigenous languages, place names, and cultural practices that demonstrated where Native Americans originated. Cotton Mather's allusions to the Lost Tribes of Israel arose from that long-standing origins debate, and cross-cultural comparisons tended to override autonomous Indigenous identity and made Native Americans inferior or degraded versions of Old World peoples. English colonial proselytizers like John Eliot and Cotton Mather, who suspected that Native Americans were descendants of the Ten Lost Tribes in accordance with Thomas Thorowgood's 1650 proposition, had hoped to convert them to Christianity, to transform in spiritual belief what already existed in body and soul. King Philip's War, and the ongoing frontier violence, turned many colonists against the proselytizing endeavor. Theorists considering the provenance of Dighton Rock would wonder who else other than the ancestors of living Native Americans already had visited the New World, perhaps even changing them for the better. The ensuing theories that I call White Tribism expressed several forms of possession. The white-isolates variant would contend that Europeans had settled in the Americas long before Columbus and gave whites an a priori claim to the new lands that overrode Indigenous sovereignty. White Tribism otherwise would seek retroactively to turn the conquered into the conquerors from within, to prove that long before English colonists arrived in the New World, Europeans had established an occupational beachhead within Native American societies that was cultural as well as biological.

CHAPTER TWO

Altogether Ignorant
Denying an Indigenous Provenance
and Constructing Gothicism

In November 1712, Cotton Mather wrote thirteen letters on the natural history of New England—seven to John Woodward, professor of physics at Gresham College, and six to Richard Waller, secretary of the Royal Society of London. Waller was sufficiently impressed to propose Mather as a candidate for membership in the society, and notified him in December 1713 that he had been admitted.[1] The letters were summarized in the January 1, 1714, edition of *Philosophical Transactions*, the society's unofficial house organ.[2] Amid Mather's observations on plants, lightning, thunder, earthquakes, birds, the bones of antediluvian giants near Albany, "Antipathies, and the Force of the Imagination," and "*monstrous Births,*" he made occasional mention of Native Americans. Mather also addressed Dighton Rock. As he described in his original letter:

> At o[r] *Taunton* by the side of a Tiding River, part in, part out, of the River, there stands a large Rock; on the perpendicular side of which Rock next to the River, there are seven or eight Lines, seven or eight foot long, and about a foot wide, each of them in unaccountable characters. It is generally taken for granted that they are Artificial; and there they stand *Graven in the Rock forever*; but no man as yett has been a Zaphnath Poaneah enough to know any more what to make of them, than *who* it was that *graved* them. I have not yett been able to gett all y[e] Lines; which, I hope, ere long I shall, when they will be at your Service. But will here give you two of them.[3]

The woodcut of the two lines was printed in *Philosophical Transactions,* along with an abridged version of the letter (figure 1). The top part of the illustration was much the same as the one Mather had printed in 1690. It is unclear where Mather got his information for the lower part. Edmund Burke Delabarre would determine that this appended area had been printed upside down in both *Philosophical Transactions* and a broadside Mather printed around this time. If Mather never saw the rock himself, it is easy to understand how he made such a major error in reproduction. He thought the petroglyph was organized into lines of script, and his broadside presented the drawings (as the label read) as "TWO Lines of Un-accountable Characters."

In Mather's letter and broadside, he neither raised nor dismissed the possibility that the script was Indigenous in origin. The fact that he could not assert Native American ignorance of it reinforces the impression that no one had asked a member of the southern New England peoples for their opinion. Mather had illustrated and discussed an inscription he had never seen that was made by ancestors of people he had never consulted. His mention of "Zaphnath Poaneah" (which did not survive the abridgment process for *Philosophical Transactions*) was a biblical reference: "And Pharaoh called Joseph's name Zaphnathpaaneah" (Genesis 41:45). The name is considered alternatively to mean "the man to whom mysteries are revealed," "one who reveals mysteries," and "a finder of mysteries."[4] This preacher's literary allusion may only have been appropriate to what was thought to be an undeciphered alphabetic or hieroglyphic script, but it also placed the puzzle of Dighton Rock's meaning within the context of ancient Israel, and Mather was familiar with Thomas Thorowgood's ideas about Native Americans representing the Lost Tribes.

The intellectual labor in disenfranchising Native Americans from a past preserved in Dighton Rock was taken up by a Mather protégé. Isaac Greenwood had begun studying theology in the fall of 1722 under Mather, who in a diary entry in July 1724 resolved to treat Greenwood as a son.[5] In May 1727 Greenwood became the first holder of the chair of Hollisian professor of mathematics and natural philosophy, which was endowed by a London merchant, Thomas Hollis. Greenwood was a precocious talent: the first science professor at Harvard, the first mathematics professor to teach calculus in the American colonies, and the author of the first mathematics text, *Arithmetick Vulgar and Decimal* (1729), written in English by a native-born American.[6] David C. Leonard has called Greenwood an important transitional figure between the puritanism of Mather and "heterodox deism" of the American Enlightenment's Benjamin Franklin, Thomas Jefferson, and Thomas Paine.[7]

Unlike his mentor Mather, Greenwood visited and sketched Dighton Rock in September 1730. That December, the twenty-eight-year-old Greenwood wrote to John Eames, a fellow of the Royal Society, with the first detailed discussion of the rock's provenance.[8] His enclosed drawing depicted it partly submerged, with the markings more finely delineated than Danforth or Mather had managed, albeit with the lower part of the inscribed surface hidden (and unknown to him) under water (figure 1). Greenwood was the first of many learned men who would assert that the rock was not the handiwork of Indians, due to their deficient nature.

Greenwood's main objective may not have been to solve the riddle of an inscription but rather to defend his mentor's reputation by countering William Douglass, a Boston physician from Edinburgh, who did not think the rock's markings were made by any human hand—or at least was prepared to say so to humiliate Mather. Douglass's interest in the rock appeared to be due the fact he had made a lifelong enemy of Mather (and most likely Greenwood) over Mather's initiative to introduce inoculation against smallpox in Boston when an outbreak panicked the city in 1721.[9] Among more than 100 Bostonians inoculated by Dr. Zabdiel Boylston in November 1721 was Greenwood. Greenwood injected himself into the resulting inoculation pamphlet war in February 1722 with his first publication, *A Friendly Debate*, which defended Mather and Boylston and savaged their opponents in a work of thinly veiled pseudonyms. "Greenwood's little tract was not even-handed or subtle," according to Leonard: "He characterized Douglass as a semi-literate Scotchman."[10] Greenwood had already made himself a powerful friend and mentor in Mather, and was now also joined to him as an enemy of Douglass.[11] Thus Greenwood's letter to Eames and the Royal Society regarding Dighton Rock in 1730 ought to be considered a continuation of the vicious and enduring enmity between Mather and Douglass born of the inoculation controversy. In 1747 Douglass would publish an attack on Mather's interpretation of Dighton Rock in *Philosophical Transactions* in 1714, but Douglass's opinions probably were not so belatedly formed.[12] As Greenwood's 1730 letter is structured like a response to the future Douglass diatribe, Greenwood likely was defending Mather from criticisms already being circulated by Douglass that would only take on a published form seventeen years later.

In his opinion printed in 1747, Douglass maintained the inscriptions in Dighton Rock were an entirely natural phenomenon. The Indians, he argued,

> had no Characters, that is, *Hieroglyphics*, or letters; they had a few Symbols or Signatures, as if in a *Heraldry* way to distinguish Tribes, the principal were the *Tortoise*, the *Bear*, the *Wolf*.[13] There was not the least Vestige of Letters in *America*; some Years since a certain credulous Person, and voluminous Author, imposed upon himself and others; he observed in a tiding River, a Rock, which, as it was not of an uniform Substance, the ebbing and flowing of the Tide made a Sort of *vermoulure*, Honeycombing or etching on its face; here he imagined, that he had discovered

the *American Indian* Characters, and overjoy'd, remits some Lines of his imaginary Characters to the Royal Society in *London: See Philosophical Transactions, No. 339.* [Douglass quoted here from Mather's contribution to the 1714 *Philosophical Transactions.*] This may be supposed wrote *Anno 1714*: At present *Anno 1747* by the continued ebbing and flowing the Honey-combing is so altered as not in the least to resemble his Draught of the Characters.[14]

Douglass may have misstated Mather's position, as Mather had not credited the Indians with the inscription in *Philosophical Transactions.* Mather had ventured that someone familiar with "Oriental characters" had made the markings, although if Mather suspected the Indians were descendants of the Lost Tribes of Israel, such characters would have been expected. Yet a Douglass attack—unpublished at that point—must have been Greenwood's motivation for visiting the rock himself, making a detailed drawing, and rallying to Mather's cause through what had become a favorite medium for both sides: letters to prominent members of the Royal Society of London. The American colonies would not have a comparable fellowship until Benjamin Franklin established the American Philosophical Society in Philadelphia in 1743.[15]

Greenwood began his letter to Eames by rejecting the idea that the marks were entirely natural, the contention Douglass would publish in 1747.[16] Some people "look upon it as the work of Nature," Greenwood explained, but they "are little acquainted with her Operations and have made but a cursory Observation hereof." Surely that was payback for an unkind characterization of Mather by Douglass. Two popular opinions remained, according to Greenwood. The first was that the markings were "the undersigning and artless Impressions of some of the Nations, out of meer [*sic*] curiosity or for some particular Uses." The second was they were "a Memorial in proper Sculpture of some remarkable Transactions or accident." Greenwood doubted the Indians would have created the inscription out of "meer Curiosity," as they were "altogether ignorant of Sculpture & the use of Iron. And tho' they had some Stone Instruments none that ever I have seen are capable (in much better hands than theirs) of forming so accurate an Inscription." Even if they were capable of such work, Greenwood expected there would be "other Sketches of the same or a like Nature" in New England, which he assured Eames was not the case. He dismissed the possibility that the marks were the result of Indians sharpening their arrows or axes: "If this were their usual Custom, we should find these Traces & Indentions very probably on many Rocks of the same Nature as this; and if it was political (a customary preparation to confirm & encourage one another in their Intention or prosecution of War) no doubt but kindred & confederate Tribes would have had their respective Standards." Further, if Indians were to make any markings or drawings, "One would think their Curiosity would have lead them to the Representation of Birds, Bears, Fishes, Trees &c which we have since found to be their prevailing Genius, & not to figures quite different from the Objects of their Senses."

Greenwood's trump argument was that Indians "were a Nation too idle and irresolute for a work of so much Industry and appeared Design." In addition to Indians lacking the necessary characteristics of civilized people, he as much as said that they lacked the mental capacity to conceive of the inscription. Greenwood was the first to make the "too lazy and stupid" argument against the idea that Indigenous people inscribed Dighton Rock, but he would not be the last, and the idea that Native Americans were an inferior branch of humanity (if not a distinct species), or were held back by sloth, was hardly new or unique to Greenwood. William Wood, while believing Native Americans were equipped with "quick wits" and capable of improvement, had advised in *New England's Prospect* (1635): "Much good might they receive from the English, and much might they benefit themselves, if they were not strong fettered in the chains of idleness."[17]

Greenwood had no particular suggestion as to the inscription's authors, but he did echo Mather in noting the "Oriental Characters." Greenwood and Mather made their "Oriental" suggestions at a formative period of the scholarly discipline of Orientalism, when it was focused on biblical studies.[18] Greenwood suggested that a resolution to the puzzle would require "the extraordinary Skill and Ingenuity of Mr. La Croze in the alphabet both ancient & modern of the Oriental Tongues." Mathurin Veyssière de La Croze was a former Benedictine monk who converted to Calvinism after the revocation of the Edict of Nantes. Most of his *Histoire du christianisme des Indes* (1724) was a polemical attack on the Jesuits' treatment of the Nestorian Christian communities of southern India.[19]

Greenwood was partial to what he called the second popular opinion on Dighton Rock's inscription: it was "a Memorial in proper Sculpture of some remarkable Transactions or accident." Greenwood suspected that whoever made it was at the heart of the "tradition" held by Indian elders related by John Danforth in 1680. Greenwood quoted from the first part of the Danforth description: "That there came a wooden house (and men of another Country in it) swimming up the River of assoonet (as this was then called) who fought the Indians with mighty success etc." As noted, however, this tradition likely came from colonists rather than the Wampanoag. Greenwood proposed: "This

I think evidently shews that this Monument was esteemed by the oldest Indians not only very antique, but a work of a different Nature from any of theirs."[20] Greenwood thus advanced what John Danforth had only intimated: the inscription actually was made by more cultured invaders in some distant age.

GREENWOOD HAD ASSESSED the provenance of Dighton Rock—and the lowly character of Indians—soon after the French Jesuit Joseph-François Lafitau published a landmark work of ethnology, *Moeurs des sauvages Améri-quains, comparées aux moeurs des premiers temps* (1724). Gordon M. Sayre has associated Lafitau with a *"premier temps* trope," a "backward-looking historical view that placed the *sauvage américain* in comparison with various peoples of the ancient world."[21] According to Lafitau's modern editor and English translator, William Nelson Fenton, to Lafitau, *premiers temps*, or the "First Times," was the great age of antiquity in which humanity shared a belief in one true God, a heritage that underpinned a "uniformity of sentiments of all nations."[22]

Unlike many European intellectuals who pronounced on the nature and origins of Indigenous peoples, Lafitau actually had spent time among them, living for about five years with Christian Mohawk at Caughnawaga (Kahnawà:ke) near Montréal. Lafitau refuted notions that ancient Europeans, Mediterraneans, or any culture in the Oriental category had anything to do with colonizing the New World. Native American languages bore no resemblance to virtually any known languages of the Old World, he advised, although he thought a few people in Novaya Zemlya in the Russian arctic spoke "la Huronne."[23]

Lafitau noted that most theorists believed Native Americans migrated from Asia, and he agreed this was probably correct. He ventured that they arrived soon after the Flood, using a land bridge that had once joined the easternmost lands of Tartary with North America. By comparing the customs of Native Americans with Asians, Thracians, and Scythians, he hoped to prove that America had been peopled by migrants from easternmost Tartary.[24] The greater part of the Native American population, and perhaps the Five Nations of the Iroquois Confederacy (Haudenosaunee) and the Iroquoian-speaking Huron (Wendat) in particular, were descended from early Greeks ("Pélas-giens & d'Helléniens"), but had lost their root language over the long period of a movement from the Old World to the New.[25] Lafitau made a strained attempt to draw links between cultures based on survivals in vocabulary, including similarities between some Iroquoian and Thracian words.[26] Lafitau believed that less sophisticated, more recent arrivals drove before them the more sophisticated, older migrant nations, so that the most "civilized" (*policée*) societies were found in Mexico and Peru.[27] Whether or not Lafitau was aware of Menasseh Ben Israël's pioneering work in the mid-seventeenth century, he had advanced the same multiple-migration displacement scenario for the peopling of the Americas from Asia.

Greenwood showed no familiarity with Lafitau's (or Menasseh's) ideas. Nor did the enigma of Dighton Rock's inscription spur him to advance his knowledge of the Indigenous nations whose ancestors were the most obvious candidates for its creation, as by his own admission the area around Dighton Rock "was one of the most considerable Seats of Indians in this part of the World."[28] Greenwood's analysis affirmed that an Indigenous provenance had to be discounted before some other candidate for the inscription's creation was advanced, and Greenwood did so by declaring that Native American tools, minds, and characters were not up to the task.

Greenwood offered to make a more detailed study of Dighton Rock if Eames thought it worthwhile, but nothing came of his initiative.[29] Greenwood's investigation of Dighton Rock having been abandoned, his analysis and drawing were forgotten for some fifty years, until they were made public by Michael Lort (along with the Danforth materials) in *Archaeologia* in 1787 (see chapter 3). Greenwood's career was soon placed in jeopardy by his drinking: he was censured by the Harvard Corporation in 1737 and removed from his chair in 1738, replaced by his best student, John Winthrop, who would have his own history with Dighton Rock.[30]

An attribution of Dighton Rock to Native Americans would have its supporters before the century was out, but once Indigenous people were accepted to be physically, mentally, and culturally inferior to Euro-Americans, in accordance with Greenwood's reasoning, other avenues of argument opened. The deemed inferiority of Native Americans could be leveraged by White Tribism: any sign of advanced capability, which would otherwise negate the inferiority argument, could be used as proof that some superior outside civilization had changed them for the better. Greenwood may not have been the first person to question the intelligence of Native Americans, but he earns the distinction of having been the first person to go on record asserting they were incapable of making marks on a boulder, without any apparent attempt to judge for himself how simple it would be to peck glyphs in relatively soft rock with a stone tool.

ISAAC GREENWOOD MAY HAVE made an ignominious exit from the Dighton Rock debate, but the Hollisian chair he was forced to abandon helped to keep scholarly interest in it alive. At an unknown date John Eames, Greenwood's correspondent at the Royal Society, made a request of a fellow Royal Society member, Timothy Hollis, whose family oversaw the fund for the Hollisian chair. Hollis was to ask Greenwood's Hollisian successor, John Winthrop, to visit Dighton Rock and make a fresh drawing of it for an unnamed German philologist.[31] Winthrop would do so in the company of Samuel Danforth, a prominent son of the Reverend John Danforth, who had produced the first drawing and description of Dighton Rock in 1680.[32]

A pioneering figure in American natural sciences, mathematics, and astronomy, John Winthrop was a member of one of New England's most esteemed families. He was descended from the first governor of the Massachusetts Bay colony and author of *The City on the Hill* (1630), whose name he shared. Winthrop made his acquaintance with Samuel Danforth no later than September 1741. A Harvard graduate and former schoolteacher, Samuel Danforth was a member of the governor's council, a position he would hold until 1774, when his royalist leanings cost him his various public offices. In July 1741, two months before Winthrop recorded their first trip together, Danforth was named a judge of the court of common pleas for Middlesex County, which encompassed Cambridge.[33] He lived on an estate close by Harvard Square, and Winthrop joined him for a number of trips over the next few years, mainly between Boston and Cambridge, sometimes sharing Danforth's sedan chair. Presumably, Dighton Rock figured in their conversations, although Winthrop's general curiosity was aimed more skyward, as he studied sunspots, auroras, and lightning, and kept meticulous daily weather records.

In 1743, Winthrop and Danforth committed to an investigation of Dighton Rock together. They set out for Dighton on an "excessive hot day" on July 25, stopping over in Easton. The following day they reached Dighton. On July 27 (overcast with light rain), Winthrop recorded: "Went to see y famous *rock*." Winthrop and Danforth spent another day in Dighton, as Winthrop attempted a drawing of the markings, before returning to Cambridge on July 29.[34]

Winthrop's Dighton Rock investigation led nowhere, possibly because he was dissatisfied with his drawing.[35] Timothy Hollis never heard back from Winthrop, and John Eames died in 1744. So did Isaac Greenwood. After attempting to establish a private academy with the assistance of Benjamin Franklin, Greenwood's downward spiral ended with a chaplaincy in the Royal Navy. Discharged from service in Charleston, South Carolina, in May 1744, he drank himself to death five months later.[36] Scholarly interest in Dighton

Rock achieved complete disarray three years later, when William Douglass printed his attack on Cotton Mather's interpretation and asserted the so-called inscription was entirely natural. Almost twenty years would pass before interest in Dighton Rock was reignited.

IN THE LULL that followed John Winthrop's abandoned drawing of Dighton Rock, Isaac Greenwood's death, and William Douglass's insistence that any human markings were figments of Cotton Mather's imagination, there appeared three influential works by French authors (none of whom ever set foot in the Americas) that had a major bearing on conceptions of Native Americans and the race destiny of Anglo-American colonizers. The first was the Baron de Montesquieu's *De l'Esprit des loix* (1748); the second was the Comte de Buffon's third volume of *Histoire naturelle* (1749); the third was Paul Henri Mallet's *Monumens de la mythologie et de la poesie des Celtes* (1756).

Montesquieu and Mallet expanded on earlier efforts by the Swedish physician, botanist, and scholar Olf Rudbeks (or Olof Rudbeck), who, at virtually the same time English colonists first took notice of Dighton Rock, had promoted a heroic and racialized view of human history that championed the innate superiority of northern Europeans. Called Gothicism by modern scholars, Rudbeks's version of European antiquity informed Enlightenment theories about race and culture that figured critically in European and Anglo-American approaches to American antiquity, and would come to dominate theories about Dighton Rock's markings in the nineteenth century.[37]

In the first volume of *Atland eller Manheim* (*Atlantis, or Manheim*), published in 1677, Rudbeks began crafting his hyperdiffusionist mythology of Scandinavia as the root source of civilization and humanity's supreme form. Sweden was Plato's Atlantis, the true home of the descendants of Noah's son, Japheth, the homeland of most European peoples, and the source of Greek mythology. Rudbeks's Gothicism had its own roots in *Gothorum Sveonumque historia* (1554) by the archbishop of Uppsala, Johannes Magnus, and his brother Olaus Magnus's *Historia de gentibus septentrionalibus* (1555), with Johannes positing Sweden as superior to all other kingdoms and its Goths as the descendants of Gog and Magog, the latter a son of Japheth (Genesis 10:2).[38] Rudbeks relied on imaginative philology to assert Scandinavian influences on Greek mythology: Venus derived from *wen* ("friend"), while Hercules was a Swedish name, formed from *här* (army) and *kulle* ("leader" or "head").[39] Such word-hunting, already employed earlier in the seventeenth century by Grotius and others in their theories of Indigenous origins, would become a fundamental tool of Dighton Rock theorists. Rudbeks extended the relevance of the Icelandic sagas beyond the Scandinavian world to apply more generally to northern Europe, and his particular Gothicism became an intellectual project of Enlightenment Europe.

Charles-Louis de Secondat, Baron de Montesquieu, was respectfully aware of Rudbeks, even if he did not have a copy of *Atland eller Manheim* to consult, when he proposed his ideas of inherently superior northern peoples in *De l'Esprit des loix* in 1748: "I don't know if the famous *Rudbeck*, who, in his *Atlantis*, has so glorified Scandinavia, spoke of this great privilege that must place the Nations there above all the world's people; they have been the source of the Liberty of Europe, that is to say, of nearly all of it today among men."[40] Montesquieu adhered somewhat to polygenism, the idea that distinct races had experienced separate creations, as opposed to being descended from a single Edenic creation that passed through Noah's progeny, as per monogenism. He employed environmental determinism to argue for innate differences in peoples and nations. Heat enervated the strength and courage of peoples, whereas cold climates exerted an influence on the body and spirit that made northern peoples capable of actions that were extended, physically demanding, grand, and bold.[41] Differentiating the characters of peoples along a north–south gradient is traceable to Aristotle; already the French royal geographer André Thevet had employed this gradient in describing the people of Canada in 1557.[42] Montesquieu used differences in local geography to explain why Europe had developed people superior to Tartars in the same climatic zone in Asia, and referenced Rudbeks in making northern peoples innately freedom-loving rather than innately enslaved.[43] Montesquieu's view of Tartars recalled sixteenth-century European debates about whether or not Native Americans qualified as Aristotle's "natural slaves," who were intellectually and morally deficient, innately subservient to the rest of humanity, and in need of rule by force.[44]

Montesquieu had little to say about the Indigenous peoples of the Americas: his chapter "De l'Afrique & de l'Amérique" totaled sixty-seven words.[45] Montesquieu only stated that what he had written about Asia and Europe with respect to the climatic influence on the character of nations applied equally to Africa and America. Montesquieu thus failed to connect the Tartars via the established Bering-crossing theories with Indigenous peoples of the Americas, possibly because he had not yet learned of Vitus Bering's discovery of his namesake strait, which began to gain wider understanding in France through the efforts of Joseph-Nicolas Delisle two years after Montesquieu published.[46] *De l'Esprit des loix* nevertheless left abundant room and inspiration for others to ruminate on the Americas and their Indigenous peoples. Montesquieu's ideas about the innate inferiority of Tartars and their natural state of enslavement (and the applicability of these ideas to peoples of the Americas) would have been absorbed by the many American (and European) intellectuals who read him for his wisdom on the evolution of law and constitutional government.[47] In America, they tended to be the people in positions of authority wondering how to deal with—or wondering how to justify the way they dealt with—Indigenous peoples in the course of westward colonization.

Our second significant mid-century work was by Georges-Louis Leclerc, Comte de Buffon. A giant of natural history elected to the Académie française in 1753, Buffon in Lisbet Koerner's estimation was the chief rival (and a bitter public one) to Sweden's Carolus Linnaeus (Carl de Linné), in claiming the title of the eighteenth century's most famous naturalist.[48] In the third volume of his *Histoire naturelle* (1749), Buffon took up Montesquieu's ideas on environmental determinism and ventured into fresh terrain on the degeneration theory. He also elaborated on Montesquieu's idea that the Tartars were an inferior Asiatic people, both naturally enslaved and enslaving.

Buffon's theory was proto-evolutionary, holding that life forms, including humans, could degenerate under different climates. Buffon decided that a temperate Eurozone between latitudes 40 and 50 north was where the ideal human form of beautiful, light-skinned people was found, along with the world's civilized countries. This allowed him to ignore the British Isles and Scandinavia, but naturally to include France.[49] Where Montesquieu proposed that Native Americans exhibited the same inferior characteristics as Tartars because they arose in a similar but separate northern environment, Buffon made Native Americans the direct descendants of Tartars. Buffon did not doubt that Native Americans were "the same as us," at least in being human.[50] Their resemblance to Tartars suggested they left this Asian population long ago, and the recent discoveries made by the Russians (a nod to Bering), Buffon advised, left no doubt as to the possibility of a migratory connection between the continents, although Buffon also imagined transpacific migrations. The Tartars were a degenerated type; the ones that lived around latitude 55 along the Volga River were "rude, stupid, and brutal," and had almost no concept of religion.[51] Native American groups descended from Tartars might vary in being "more or less savage, more or less cruel, more or less brave," but they were all "equally stupid, equally ignorant, equally lacking arts and industry."[52] The climate and people's diets in the Americas varied little, and so they had no means to degenerate, or to improve.[53] Buffon believed that as Native Americans had only a very small number of ideas, they also had only a very small number of expressions, so that they could only deploy the most general words and address the most common subjects.[54] Buffon appeared to be distorting, without citation, Lafitau's observation in *Moeurs* that missionaries faced difficulty teaching the gospel to Native Americans because their languages lacked European concepts, an idea traceable to the Récollet missionary Gabriel Sagard, who in 1632 published an account of his time among the Huron-Wendat in 1623–1624.[55]

Buffon might not have held Scandinavians in special regard, but Gothicism found its foremost proponent of the mid- to late eighteenth century only a few years after the appearance of the third volume of *Histoire naturelle*. Paul-Henri Mallet was a French Swiss scholar who served as a professor of belles-lettres at the Royal Academy at Copenhagen from 1752 to 1760 and as a preceptor to the future king, Christian VII. The presiding king, Frederick V, engaged Mallet to write a history of Denmark, in French, which was published at Copenhagen as the two-volume *Histoire de Dannemarc* in 1758.[56] Mallet prefaced the main work with two additional volumes. The first, *Introduction à l'histoire de Dannemarc* (1755), included a chapter summarizing the Icelandic sagas generally known as the Vinland sagas, which recounted the Norse exploits around A.D. 1000 in searching for and attempting to colonize lands to the west of Iceland and Greenland. Mallet's second prefatory volume, *Monumens de la mythologie et de la poésie des Celtes, et particulièrement des anciens Scandinaves* (1756), hewed to Montesquieu's division between northern and southern Europe in positing a "Religion Celtique" shared by ancient Britons, French Gauls, Germanic peoples, Scandinavians, and Scythians, based on a translation of the Icelandic saga *Snorra Edda*.[57] Both of Mallet's prefatory works were issued in 1770 as a two-volume English translation, *Northern Antiquities*. The translation broadened the appeal of the romance of Gothicism, which celebrated the northern Europeans Mallet collectivized as "Celts" as hardy, adventurous, freedom-loving peoples.[58] A third edition of *Monumens* (issued as *Edda, ou Monumens de la poésie des anciens peuples du nord*), was published in 1787. A fresh printing of the English translation in Edinburgh in 1809 testifies to Mallet's enduring popularity.

The construction of Gothicism's protean northern European whiteness was entwined in the construction of overlapping nomenclatures of racial and ethnic identity, language groups, and Noachic lineages. The inventor of our binomial system of species nomenclature, Linnaeus, was a protégé of Olf Rudbeks's son, Olf (Olaf) the Younger. While Linnaeus did not pursue the philological interests of the Rudbeks family, according to Lisbet Koerner, he was a Gothicist in his concern for identifying "a primeval language of nature," and in the pursuit of this knowledge his biblical fundamentalism and Gothicism merged.[59] In his masterwork, the tenth book of *Systema naturae* of 1758, Linnaeus revealed a more explicit Gothicist influence in his ideas of racial hierarchy. For his newly defined *Homo sapiens*, Linnaeus defined four basic races: Americanus, Europaeus, Asiaticus, and Afer. Linnaeus reserved special praise for Europaeus, describing its members as "white, gracious, and governed by reason," whereas (Native) Americans were "reddish, single-minded, and guided by tradition."[60]

IN THE FALL of 1766, Dighton Rock gained fresh intellectual currency as it captured the imagination of thirty-nine-year-old Ezra Stiles, a Congregationalist minister in Newport, Rhode Island, after he was shown a copy of the Mather broadside of around 1714. Stiles was the main author of the charter for Rhode Island College in Providence, forerunner of Brown University, in 1764. He received a doctorate of divinity from Edinburgh University through the influence of Benjamin Franklin in 1765, and declined the presidency of Yale University in 1766, a post he would accept in 1778.[61]

Stiles would be the first theorist to draw Dighton Rock into a Gothicist concept of history—he in fact appears to have been the first theorist to articulate a version of American history that we can call Transatlantic Gothicism, as we will see in chapter 3. At the beginning of his investigations, though, Dighton Rock, the Ten Lost Tribes, and Native Americans were bound up in his theorizing. Dighton Rock is about thirty miles north of Newport, and Stiles visited and drew the "Writing Rock" three times in the summer of 1767, after he had become determined in May to learn Hebrew from members of the Jewish community in Newport.[62] His interest in Hebrew seems to have arisen from a concern with the fate of the Ten Lost Tribes.[63] He also became familiar at some point with Menasseh Ben Israël's ideas, as he praised Menasseh's character in lamenting the death of a Jewish merchant in Newport in 1782.[64]

Stiles was the first person to study inscribed rocks in southern New England—the first person to be aware that Dighton Rock was not an anomaly—and was chasing them down in 1767 and 1768. Native Americans also captured his interest. He probably taught some members of the Narragansett tribe to read and write, and he made considerable notes about Indigenous life and culture for a book he never did write.[65]

After his second visit to Dighton Rock on June 6, 1767, he recorded in his letter book: "Spent the forenoon in Decyphering about Two Thirds the Inscription, which I take to be in Phoenician Letters & 3,000 years old."[66] Jean-Jacques Barthélemy's decipherment of Phoenician script in 1754 had given antiquarians a new diagnostic tool in probing purported inscriptions for ancient mysteries.[67]

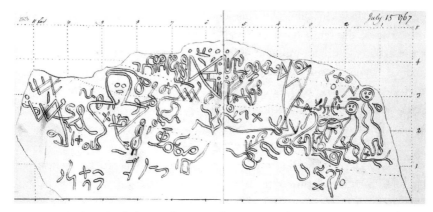

FIGURE 2 Dighton Rock drawing by Ezra Stiles, 1767, in Stiles, Itineraries II. Beinecke Rare Book and Manuscript Library, Yale University.

After sketching the rock's markings on July 15, 1767 (figure 2), Stiles enlisted the aid of Elisha Paddack of Swansea in hopes of securing a full-size drawing. In a letter to Stiles in August 1767, Paddack referred to the "Phoenitian rock."[68] Arising in Tyre in the eastern Mediterranean, Phoenicians and their descendants (including the Punics) were considered the first great Western civilization of maritime trade and colonial expansion, and some believed they were descendants of the Canaanites of the Old Testament.

In June 1768 Stiles visited Harvard, lodging with Stephen Sewall, who had been appointed the Hancock Professor of Hebrew and Other Oriental Languages in 1765; he also spent an hour with John Winthrop.[69] Stiles was close to both men—Winthrop, according to Stiles's son-in-law, was "a most valuable friend and correspondent"[70]—and they were all close to Benjamin Franklin. Franklin arranged Stiles's doctorate in divinity from Edinburgh in 1765, and that same year, Franklin wrote Stiles from London, confiding he had proposed their mutual friend Winthrop as a fellow of the Royal Society.[71] Sewall was a scholar in Hebrew, Aramaic, and Greek, and compiled *An Hebrew Grammar* for instruction at Harvard in 1763, on which Stiles must have relied in his Hebrew studies. Surely Stiles discussed with Sewall and Winthrop his consuming interest in inscribed stones of the previous two years. Winthrop, as we have seen, had his own history with Dighton Rock, and Stephen Sewall was the grand-nephew of Judge Sewall, whose interest in Dighton Rock surfaced in his letter book in 1691. Whatever Stiles confided about Dighton Rock compelled Sewall to engage its mystery at an unprecedented level. In 1768 Sewall visited it, and with the aid of four local men made a life-size drawing of the markings, perhaps achieving for Stiles what Paddack could not (figure 3).

FIGURE 3 Dighton Rock drawing by Stephen Sewall, 1768, as depicted in *Archaeologia* 8 (1787).

What is striking about Stiles's investigations of Dighton Rock and other inscribed stones around Narragansett Bay is that nowhere in his diaries does he mention asking the various Native Americans he met and tutored what if anything they knew of the markings. His fascination with inscribed rocks seemed to be contained within his newfound interest in Hebrew and other ancient scripts, and he was persuaded from the beginning that Dighton Rock was the work of Old World visitors. Sewall, however, demurred. On his drawing of 1768 appeared the words: "I imagine it to be the work of the Indians of North America," created, he thought, for amusement rather than any serious purpose.[72] In 1769 Sewall wrote Stiles: "I confess I have no faith in the significancy of the characters. There is indeed in some of the figures an appearance of design:—I mean that some of the figures seem to be representations of some things that the engraver previously had in mind; for instance, of human faces, & bodies, &c. But the strokes in general appear to me to be drawn at random: So I cannot but think the whole to be a mere *lusus Indorum* [an Indian game]."[73]

John Winthrop was no more enthusiastic about a non-Indigenous interpretation. In November 1774 Winthrop at last reported back to the Royal Society (which had accepted him as a fellow on Franklin's recommendation in 1765), informing them that he had gone to see the rock "above 30 years ago, and then took an imperfect copy of the inscription, and saw it again last spring." Rather than send along his old, imperfect rendering, Winthrop in 1774 enclosed a scaled-down copy of the life-size drawing Stephen Sewall had made in 1768, "the most exact copy of [the rock's markings], that I believe was ever taken." Contrary to William Douglass's opinion, Winthrop had no doubt the inscription was man-made, as there seemed to be human figures (which Greenwood's 1730 drawing first suggested), as well as "some resemblance of a quadruped with horns."[74] He thought the inscription had visibly deteriorated over thirty years. Greenwood had reported the same weathering phenomenon in his 1730 letter to Eames: "The figures are not all so well defined as I have expressed them. Time has gradually impaired them; and an old man of the town told me, he remembered them more perfect."[75] Winthrop was sure that Native Americans were responsible for the markings: "Whether this was designed by the Indians as a memorial of any remarkable event, or was a mere *lusus* [game] at their leisure hours, of which they have a great number, I cannot pretend to say. 'Tis certain it was done before the English settled in this country."[76] Stiles was not persuaded, and the Phoenicians remained strong contenders for the rock's authorship.

IN 1770, shortly after Stiles and Sewall were drawn into the puzzle of Dighton Rock, Johann (John) Reinhold Forster published *Travels into North America*, the first English translation of Swedish naturalist Pehr (Peter) Kalm's account of his journeys in 1748–1749, *En Resa til Norra America*.[77] Within a travelogue interspersed with natural history and life sciences, Kalm offered an enigmatic story of inscribed stones, deep in the American continent, that was amplified by Forster and would help inspire one theorist to decouple Dighton Rock from its Native American ancestry. Between them, Kalm and Forster also advanced a variation on the multiple-migration displacement scenario that relegated Native American ancestors to the role of inferior migrants from Tartary.

Pehr Kalm was a friend and student of Linnaeus, and was named a docent of botany in 1746 and a professor of economy in 1747 at the University of Åbo in what was then Sweden (now Turku, Finland).[78] Kalm traveled to the British colonies of North America in 1748 to serve as the "eyes and ears" of Linnaeus, under instructions from the Royal Swedish Academy of Sciences, which had admitted him as a member in 1746.[79] His English translator, Johann Forster, was a naturalist in his own right.[80] Born in Prussia, Forster arrived in London in October 1766, quickly built connections with the scientific and scholarly communities, and began translating works of scientific interest. Perhaps his greatest newfound friend and supporter was Thomas Pennant, a renowned Welsh antiquarian, naturalist, travel writer, and patron of science, who was elected a fellow of the Society of Antiquaries in 1754 and of the Royal Society (along with Forster) in 1767. Pennant helped Forster out of financial scrapes and encouraged him to undertake translations of works by Kalm and other Linnaean disciples who had made international journeys. As we will see in chapter 3, Pennant would become a major if largely forgotten figure in the development of the Beringia migration theory, and would directly inspire fresh theories about Dighton Rock and ancient America.

Kalm in translation stated that the history of North America before the arrival of Europeans "is more like a fiction or a dream, than any thing that really happened. In later times there have, however, been found a few marks of antiquity, from which it may be conjectured, that *North-America* was formerly inhabited by a nation more versed in science, and more civilized, than that which the *Europeans* found on their arrival here; or that a great military expedition was undertaken to this continent, from these known parts of the world."[81]

Kalm offered what he supposedly had learned from Pierre Gaultier de Varennes, Sieur de La Vérendrye, at Quebec in August 1749 of his explorations beyond Lake Superior.[82] The French encountered "on a large plain, great pillars of stone, leaning upon each other." They also found "a large stone, like a pillar, and in it a smaller stone was fixed, which was covered on both sides with unknown characters. This stone, which was about a foot of French measure in length, and between four or five inches broad, they broke loose." They took it back to Canada, "from whence it was sent to France," and given to Jean-Frédéric Phélypeaux, Comte de Maurepas, the secretary of state. Nothing more was heard of this stone, which in Kalm's telling was assumed still to be in the Comte de Maurepas's possession, but Jesuits in Canada "unanimously affirm, that the letters on it, are the same with those which in the books, containing accounts of *Tataria*, are called *Tatarian characters*."[83]

La Vérendrye left behind nothing that would support the Kalm anecdote,[84] which, along with his initial reports, probably from the Cree, that the Mandans were light-skinned and lived in dwellings like the French, helped to fuel White Tribism ideas that would plague accounts of these peoples. La Vérendrye may have exaggerated (or Kalm may have garbled) an encounter with Chippewa/Ojibwa or Dakota grave markers, which were planks of wood inscribed with glyphs and which would be documented in the early nineteenth century by Henry Schoolcraft. Kalm's account, with its standing stones and reference to "Tatarian characters," did have a strange resonance in the inscribed standing stones of Siberia recently documented by Philipp-Johann von Strahlenberg.

Strahlenberg was a Swedish military officer (likely born in Germany) who was captured by the Russians in the Great Northern War and spent thirteen years in western Siberia as a prisoner of war.[85] His *Das nord- und ostliche Theil von Europa und Asia* (1730) appeared in English in 1738 as *An Historo-Geographical Description of the North and Eastern Parts of Europe and Asia.* Its illustrations included inscribed rocks and standing stones, which would soon find their way into the interpretation of Dighton Rock. It is peculiar that Kalm would show no awareness of a significant work that had been published in Sweden (beyond making a vague reference to "books, containing accounts of Tataria") and that, in addition to its examples of inscribed rocks and standing stones, proposed affinities between Siberian and Native American languages. Strahlenberg had produced the first ethnographic resource that would make it possible to suggest links between the shamanic complexes of Siberia and the Americas.[86]

Johann Forster was inspired to make his own contribution to speculations about the peopling of the Americas. In a lengthy footnote to Kalm, Forster proposed that the ships of Kublai Khan sent eastward to conquer Japan, as mentioned by Marco Polo, had carried on across the Pacific and erected the stones La Vérendrye allegedly had seen, then turned south and founded the Aztec empire in Mexico. Forster asserted there was "a great familiarity between the figures of the *Mexican* idols, and those which are usual among the *Tartars*, who embrace the doctrines and religion of the *Dalaï-Lama*, whose religion Kublai-Khan first introduced among the *Monguls*, or *Moguls*."[87]

Leaving aside the fact that Forster conflated Kublai Khan's thirteenth-century Mongol warriors with the Muslim Mogul empire founded in India in 1526, Forster crucially did not think the "savage Indians of North-America" were from the same migration that produced La Vérendrye's inscribed stones. Instead, they were probably descended from "the *Yukaghiri* and *Tchucktchi*, inhabitants of the most easterly and northerly part of Asia, where, according to the accounts of the Russians, there is but a small traject to America. The ferocity of these nations, similar to that of the Americans, their way of painting, their fondness of inebriating liquors . . . and many other things, show them plainly to be of the same origin." He otherwise thought South America, especially Peru, was populated from Africa, "the great unknown fourth continent."[88]

The Forster translation of Kalm aired in a popular work another multiple-migration variation on American antiquity. *Travels* reversed the order of arrival proposed by Menasseh and Lafitau, with the more primitive ancestors of Native Americans from easternmost Tartary arriving first and outlasting a more sophisticated Tartarian people, the Mongols of Kublai Khan. Its treatment of La Vérendrye's inscribed stones reinforced the idea that Native Americans were descended from inferior Asiatic brutes from easternmost Tartary who could never be held responsible for any American antiquity that suggested cultural sophistication. Someone else must have arrived and produced them. Unfortunately, no one could testify to having actually seen La Vérendrye's stones, and no drawing of them existed, especially the small one featuring Tartarian characters that was supposedly taken to France. The leading antiquaries would need a more concrete relic on which to pin their migration theories. Dighton Rock would continue to fulfill that role.

IN 1772, two years after publishing his translation of Kalm's *Travels*, Johann Forster was engaged as the lead naturalist (assisted by his son George, who had handled most of the Kalm translation) on the second Cook expedition. Forster's account, *Observations Made during a Voyage round the World* (1778), had a significant impact on race theory, and ultimately on theories about the relationship between Native Americans and North America's antiquities. Forster proposed two "varieties" or "races" in the islands of the South Pacific, based on skin color, hair type, build, and temperament.[89] The anatomist Johann F. Blumenbach in his influential dissertation *De generis variatate nativa* (1775), published in 1776 as *On the Natural History of Mankind*, had employed a system of four human varieties similar to that of Linnaeus. Forster's voyage account moved Blumenbach to revise his system in his third edition of 1795. He defined mankind's original, superior form as Caucasoid, and itemized four degraded racial variants: Mongolian, Ethiopian, American, and Malay, the latter category inspired by Forster's observations.[90] This five-race scheme would dominate American anthropology, archaeology, and race science of the nineteenth century, with the Malay race figuring prominently in migration theories addressing the Mound Builders.

In Blumenbach's racial scheme, degeneration was specific to a European standard of physical beauty, and he rejected ideas of racial intellectual inferiority.[91] He evidently borrowed without credit the term (if not the precise meaning of) *Caucasoid* from a colleague at the University of Göttingen, the philosopher and historian Christoph Meiners, who had deployed it initially in *Grundriss der Geschichte der Menschheit* (*Outline of the History of Humanity*) in 1785, which Bruce Baum has called the "ur-text of 'Caucasian race' theory."[92] Meiners made Tartars and Caucasians members of one superior race, and classified the rest of humanity as inferior Mongolians. Caucasians had two branches, the Celtic ("richer in spiritual gifts and virtue") and the lesser Slavic.[93] Meiners in 1790 identified Germans as the superior people among the superior Celts, for their "dazzling white skin, blond curly hair, and blue eyes; courage and love of freedom, that never finds itself submissive to other nations, inexhaustible invention, and an unbounded talent for the arts and sciences."[94] His pioneering scientific racism was derided in print in Germany in 1792 by Forster, a progressive and an abolitionist.[95] Unmoved, Meiners re-vised his race terminology in the second (1793) edition of *Grundriss der Ge-schichte der Menschheit*. His Caucasians became "white and beautiful," and he continued to define their supreme form as Celts, who were cast as the origi-nal non-Finnish, non-Slavic peoples of Europe, "the most noble branch of mankind."[96]

Meiners's terminology echoed the Gothicist theorizing of Mallet, and he repeatedly cited Mallet's *Introduction à l'histoire de Dannemarc* and *Edda*.[97] In addition to his praise of Germanic Celts' courage and love of freedom, Mein-ers's ideas about why some nations were naturally rulers and others were ser-vants, along with other notions about the exceptional qualities of European nations, recalled Montesquieu's *De l'Esprit des loix*, which he also cited re-peatedly.[98] By the early nineteenth century, the sentiment of a Gothic/Celtic northern European supremacy would be entrenched in the process of shap-ing the concept of "white," as disparate terminology borne of different intel-lectual disciplines tracked toward a common meaning. *Japhetite*, which arose from biblical hermeneutics and was central to Rudbeks's conceptualization of superior Scandinavians, became synonymous with the *Caucasian* of race science and the *Indo-European* of philology.[99] In the mid-nineteenth century, the myth of an "Aryan" race that originated in Persia gained popularity as the basis of European superiority, and provided another synonym for "white."[100]

Theories in support of the innate superiority of "whites" were endlessly variable and revisable, both inclusive and exclusive, and with gradations of excellence answerable to larger social and political imperatives. In America in the nineteenth century, Gothicism would acquire a particularly Anglo-American dimension, a heritage mapped to Scandinavia through the French Norman conquest of England. The Normans were Norse in origin; hence, so were the English, post-1066, in their racial and cultural roots—and by ex-tension so were Americans who traced their own migrationist heritage to England. These particular Gothic northerners were the elite of the white/ Caucasian/Aryan racial elite. Mallet's discussion (however unenthusiastic) of the possible location of a historic Vinland in North America, based on the Icelandic sagas and the unpublished speculation of Pehr Kalm (see chap-ter 6), presaged the nineteenth-century flourishing of this transatlantic Anglo-Norse Gothicism, for which Dighton Rock would be an evidentiary showpiece.

IN THE LATE EIGHTEENTH century, the matter of to whom Dighton Rock belonged in a historical, ethnographic sense was about to be pressed into the service of addressing the larger, more consequential issue of to whom America belonged. Gothicist theorizing was informing the new theories of race and shaping the self-conception of European colonizers and their conception of Native Americans. Gothicism was a potent fusion of race destiny, Noachic lineage, culture, republican liberty, and civilization. Least appreciated has been the way Gothicism became a migrationist counterpoint to the Asiatic multiple-migration displacement scenario of Native American origins. Gothicism positioned northern Europe as the source of an out-migration of the most refined example of humanity's supreme form, which bore with it the world's greatest civilization, while eastern Asia was being cast as the source of an out-migration of some of humanity's least admirable peoples, who happened to stand in the way of America's westward expansion. Refining and articulating arguments in favor of the justness of American colonization, with the necessary dispossession of Indigenous lands, was about to become a major intellectual enterprise. Within and without that enterprise, antiquaries on both sides of the Atlantic would continue to turn to Dighton Rock as evidence.

CHAPTER THREE

Multiple Migrations

Esotericism, Beringia, and Native Americans as Tartar Hordes

On the morning of Wednesday, April 7, 1778, François-Marie Arouet—better known by his pen name, Voltaire—was led blindfolded to his induction into the French order of Freemasonry, the Grand Orient, at the Neuf soeurs lodge of Paris. After Voltaire answered moral and philosophical questions to everyone's satisfaction and delivered his own address, the eighty-three-year-old philosopher was crowned with a laurel wreath. As Charles Monnet drew Voltaire's portrait, the lodge's secretary, Antoine Court de Gébelin, delivered a short lecture on ancient Elysian mysteries from the first volume of his new work, *Monde primitif*.[1] Voltaire would die the following month, but Court de Gébelin would carry on composing the magnum opus that he had begun writing in 1773 and that would reach nine volumes in 1782. He was assisted in his researches by Benjamin Franklin, a pioneering figure in American Freemasonry who led the blindfolded Voltaire in his Neuf soeurs induction and would become president of the Paris lodge the following year.[2]

By *monde primitif*, Court de Gébelin meant a root or primal age preceding the recorded history of the Greeks and Romans that was the source of global culture and knowledge. He was determined to reconstruct this golden age through language, mythology, and symbology, and his quest shortly would bring him into contact with Harvard's Stephen Sewall, who in turn would lead him to the impenetrable mystery of Dighton Rock. Court de Gébelin never crossed the ocean to view the markings himself, but the prominent French Freemason would not be deterred from inducting them into his esoteric worldview. With an imaginative extravagance not yet witnessed in the rock's interpretation, Court de Gébelin would turn a Native American relic into a symbolically verbose work of Phoenician adventurers.

Court de Gébelin's reading came on the eve of an explosion of new theorizing about Native American origins and American antiquity. Court de Gébelin published his Dighton Rock interpretation in 1781, in the midst of the American Revolution—Franklin had been in Paris in the late 1770s to secure financial and military assistance for the Second Continental Congress when he became involved in local Enlightenment and Masonic activities. Two years after Court de Gébelin's Dighton Rock interpretation was published, the United States wrested its independence from Britain. As America began pressing westward into fresh territories wrested in turn from Native Americans, new archaeological discoveries demanded explanations—demanded, in fact, a new domestic discipline of archaeology. At the same time, reports from the latest European explorations in the Pacific influenced new theories of race science and inspired ideas about America's past and the role of ancestral Native Americans in it. Dighton Rock, America's oldest and most contested antiquarian puzzle, would find fresh currency in a debate increasingly charged with Enlightenment concepts of human migration and racial fitness that still embodied convictions of white destiny rooted in biblical hermeneutics. Esotericism would figure in that debate because it was entwined with Enlightenment inquiries ostensibly propelled by reason, as the connections Court de Gébelin forged with the American scholarly community reiterate.

ANTOINE COURT DE GÉBELIN began researching *Monde primitif* in 1773, and joined Neuf soeurs around 1776, when the Masonic lodge was founded as a learned society. Originally trained in a Protestant seminary at Lausanne founded by his father, his interests encompassed an array of esoteric subjects, including divination and astrology.[3] The esoteric movement was a search for new modes of spiritual enlightenment that arose in tandem with the moral and philosophical Enlightenment that began in early eighteenth-century France. As Joscelyn Godwin has described, "*esoteric* and its derivatives *esotericist, esotericism*, always presuppose the existence of a corresponding *exoteric* body of knowledge or doctrine, such as a scriptural text or a religious ritual. The esotericist's object is to penetrate the surface meaning in order to reach a secret and superior knowledge."[4] According to Margaret C. Jacob, the "mentality" of official Freemasonry in Europe during the Enlightenment embodied a taste for science, a craving for order and stability, a worldly mysticism expressed in fanciful rituals, passwords and mythology, a love of secrecy, and above all "a religious devotion to higher powers, be they the Grand Architect, the king or the grand master."[5] The convergence of rational inquiry and mystical or occult interests has been called the "Dark Enlightenment" because of the association with dark arts, but some scholars have proposed to recast as the "Super-Enlightenment" on the basis that its participants "saw themselves as engaging in the same intellectual projects as their more conformist peers."[6]

Court de Gébelin would best be remembered for turning the old French card game of tarot into a system of prognostication in the eighth volume of

Monde primitif, published in 1781, as the card symbols were (to his mind) rooted in Egyptian mythology. But it was his effort in that same volume to incorporate Native Americans into his root-civilization vision of human history that concerns us. He compared Native American and Old World languages in an attempt to show that all of the world's languages shared a deeper root in the primal age. Court de Gébelin knew Lafitau's scholarship, as he cited him as a source on the Indigenous languages of Canada.[7] The similarity between Lafitau's concept of *premier temps* and Court de Gébelin's *monde primitif* is impossible to overlook, particularly when *Monde primitif* asserted that solar worship was the foundational religion, and Lafitau had already compared the role of the sun in Indigenous beliefs and Old World classical mythology.[8] However distant the worldview of a Masonic Protestant with occult interests might otherwise have been from that of a French Jesuit, Court de Gébelin must have known that he shared with the late Lafitau an interest in proving a golden age at the root of all human culture.

In 1781 the Neuf soeurs lodge opened a *musée* (aka Musée de Paris) under Court de Gébelin's direction, offering students a program in the humanities, at which he taught ancient philosophy.[9] With the help of Franklin, who was among the Paris *musée*'s initial membership of fifty, Court de Gébelin forged a close relationship between the *musée* and the American Academy of Arts and Sciences (AAAS), chartered by the Massachusetts legislature in 1780.[10] The two institutions were "virtually twins," according to Frank E. Manuel and Fritzie Manuel, and Court de Gébelin was admitted to the American Academy in 1781.[11]

Franklin provided Court de Gébelin with a Delaware grammar, which must have been a copy of the Moravian missionary David Zeisberger's German manuscript.[12] By no small coincidence, Zeisberger's work would be published for the first time as *Grammar of the Language of the Lenni Lenape or Delaware Indians* (1827), an English translation by Peter Stephen (Pierre-Étienne) Du Ponceau, who had spent "six or eight months" in 1777 as secretary to Court de Gébelin in Paris before departing for America as an eighteen-year-old aide to Baron von Steuben in 1778.[13] Du Ponceau was a gifted linguist who would spur the recognition of the polysynthetic structure of Native American languages, which rendered obsolete the sort of word-hunting that antiquaries had long used to propose Old World origins for Indigenous peoples. Du Ponceau would recall of Court de Gébelin: "He was in the zenith of his fame when I became his secretary. He was an excellent man, and I cannot but remember with pleasure, the time I spent with him. He was to me as a father. . . . But though I sincerely loved him, and admired his talents, I did not agree with him in his philological opinions. He was endeavouring to find the primitive language, which I considered as impossible."[14]

Court de Gébelin reached beyond Franklin in seeking the assistance of Americans. The Marquis François de Barbé Marbois, the French embassy official in Philadelphia who provided to Thomas Jefferson at this time the questionnaire that inspired *Notes on the State of Virginia* (1787), helped with the introductions.[15] One way or another, Stephen Sewall came to his aid around 1780 and was able to assist Court de Gébelin to a degree that touched the French mythographer. Sewall recommended Court de Gébelin to John Adams for his AAAS membership; Court de Gébelin shared with Sewall details of the founding of the *musée* and expressed his hope for close relations between his new society and the AAAS.[16] Sewall sent him Indigenous vocabularies or grammars compiled by missionaries to the Wampanoag, William Mayhew (who had been a regular traveling companion of John Winthrop) at Martha's Vineyard and Gideon Hawley at Nantucket (to whom we will return in chapter 4).[17] In March 1780, Court de Gébelin informed Sewall that the Hawley material was helping him show affinities not only between Native American languages, but also between those languages and the *Langes d'Orient*.[18] At some point around 1780 Sewall also sent Court de Gébelin a copy of his 1768 drawing of Dighton Rock.[19]

A migrationist link between Phoenician and Native Americans, based on the Dighton Rock inscription, was already circulating at least privately among American antiquaries, as the diary and correspondence of Ezra Stiles has shown, but Antoine Court de Gébelin was the first person to make the assertion in print, when he published his interpretation, accompanied by a labeled drawing, in the eighth volume of *Monde primitif*. He quoted the letter (in French) that accompanied Sewall's drawing.[20] The convenience of the anchorage and the ease with which the Taunton River (which Court de Gébelin misread as "Jaunston") could be navigated made Sewall think the inscription was the work of Phoenicians who had been blown there from European shores. Others, Sewall said, thought that the inscription was hieroglyphic rather than alphabetic, and so perhaps was the work of Chinese or Japanese voyagers.[21]

Sewall's opinion is surprising, as in the late 1760s, as we have seen, he seemed confident the markings were Native American. However, a damaged transcription of a lost label, once attached to Sewall's full-size drawing when it hung over the door of Harvard's department of mineralogy, was so near to

Court de Gébelin's transcription (albeit minus the Phoenician opinion) in its decipherable phrasing that it seems possible that Sewall came around to the Phoenician interpretation, which his friend Stiles advocated.[22]

Volume 8 of *Monde primitif* was already printed when Court de Gébelin informed Sewall in August 1781 (in a letter that would not arrive until November 1783) that he had made an engraving of Sewall's drawing (along with one of the "rough and extravagant" Mather woodcut published in 1714) for the new volume. He reported that this "incontestable Carthaginian monument has caused a remarkable sensation throughout Europe," and that his reading divided it into three scenes, devoted to past, present, and future. He would say no more; Sewall could find everything in the eighth volume.[23] There, Court de Gébelin assured readers they would be surprised by the striking similarity between Dighton Rock and the Phoenician inscriptions he reported as having been discovered at Mount Horeb (Mount Sinai), where Moses was said to have received the Ten Commandments. The Dighton inscription could not be the work of Indians because the nations of Canada, from what he understood from the writings of Jean de Thévenot (he must have meant André Thevet) and Baron de Lahonton, had nothing approaching an alphabet.[24] Court de Gébelin thus applied a simple proof: the marks on Dighton Rock were alphabetical; Indians did not have an alphabet; therefore Dighton Rock was not the work of Indians. Yet Court de Gébelin translated it not by reading the Sewall drawing as an alphabetical inscription, but rather as a tableau of pictographic glyphs intermingled with a few alphabetical letters. His glyphs qualified as semasiography, or writing by signs. This is a "languageless" system, comparable to road signs warning of falling rocks with silhouettes of tumbling boulders, which could be interpreted by anyone.[25]

Court de Gébelin's reading of Dighton Rock has more details than we need to review. He imagined (that is the only word) the rock as a triptych, with panels devised by the Phoenicians in right-to-left order devoted to the past (their arrival in America), the present (their alliance with the people of the country), and the future (their plans to return home). He found an owl, which he explained was the symbol of Minerva, Isis, and Astarte, deities of wisdom and the arts. There was also a hawk, which he said symbolized to the Egyptians and Phoenicians the north wind necessary for the return voyage. A bull—John Winthrop and Stephen Sewall had thought there was a horned quadruped—symbolized agriculture. (I will return to the issue of the horned quadruped in chapter 4.) On the far left, near a ship preparing to depart, was a bust of the Oracle, on whose right arm was a butterfly, symbol of resurrection and return. In the center panel Court de Gébelin could detect a vessel, complete with prow, mast, stern deck, and steering rudder. He somehow teased from the lines of Sewall's drawing symbols for each nation: a horse (which was also linked to Neptune) for the Phoenicians, and a beaver for the local people; the two animals were carrying banners or streamers that floated in the wind.

There is something endearing about the way Court de Gébelin's interpretation was wholly unlike the approaches taken by other Western interpreters. Learned New Englanders stressed the ignorant savagery of Indians, and were intrigued by a secondhand story of a battle between Indians and strange men in a floating house on the Taunton River. Court de Gébelin, as wrongheaded as he was, instead saw amity and equal standing between the two groups. The goodwill between the horse and the beaver, he explained, was proof of the intelligence of both nations. The favorable welcome of the strangers was due to the hospitality and virtue in all nations, as well as to how wondrous these strangers appeared in the eyes of *des Sauvages de l'Amérique*. So it was, Court de Gébelin lectured, that when the Spanish arrived, these same *sauvages* regarded them as gods, but these Spaniards were beneath those who left us this rare monument.[26]

Court de Gébelin's interpretation can be read as an expression of Rousseauian idealism in its portrayal of Native Americans as peace loving, intelligent, and noble in their goodwill. Yet with Court de Gébelin's attack on the Spanish in the New World, one can also read the translation effort as an elaborate anti-Catholic diatribe. In 1763 Court de Gébelin had published *Les Toulousaines*, which condemned the persecution of Protestants by the Parliament of Toulouse, in particular the merchant Jean Calas, who was executed in 1762 after being accused of murdering one of his children who reputedly had converted to Catholicism. Calas's case was also taken up by Voltaire, and his innocence was declared posthumously by the Conseil du roi in 1765.[27] Gébelin's condemnation of the Spanish exploitation of Indigenous people in the Americas would not have been out of character for a Protestant Freemason who had written *Les Toulousaines*. Still, however kindly he treated Native Americans, Court de Gébelin's interpretation was true to the trend of erasing the rock's Indigenous past and overwriting it with an inscription better suited to European and Anglo-American priorities.

SAMUEL WILLIAMS APPEARS to have inherited a curiosity in Dighton Rock that had been attached to the Hollisian chair at Harvard since the inquiries of its original holder, Isaac Greenwood. Williams had assumed the chair after Stiles's friend, John Winthrop, died in 1779; in May 1782, Williams asked Ezra

Stiles for his thoughts on Court de Gébelin's opinion that the inscription was Punic or Phoenician. Stiles's antiquarian standing had risen considerably since he first considered the rock's markings in 1766. He had become president of Yale College in 1778, and was also made a counselor of the American Philosophical Society and a fellow of the AAAS in 1781.[28] Stiles noted his reply to Williams in his diary: "I doubt it, havᵉ compared it with all the oriental Paleography."[29] Stiles presumably had accepted Winthrop's assessment that Dighton Rock's markings were plausibly Native American.

Stiles's reversal was momentary. He never seemed to doubt that people of the ancient eastern Mediterranean had once visited America: it was a matter of finding the right evidence. In December 1771, Stiles had received a third-hand report from the Ohio country of an arresting relic, related to him by David McClure, a Yale graduate of 1769. The report originated with Samuel Kirkland, a missionary to the Oneida, who in turn attributed it to Indians visiting his mission. The report told of an enormous boulder in the Ohio country, with a surface thirty by forty feet covered in "Characters, Emblems, and Hieroglificks," including Hebrew letters and a symbol that appeared to indicate the regiment or legion of whoever made the marks. Two similar, smaller boulders were nearby. Native Americans "endeavor to keep all Europians [*sic*] from viewing it," McClure reported, and "from a religious devotion, frequently visit those Rocks and offer up sacrifices near them, and say that a sight of them makes them feel devout."[30] The story was as strong an endorsement of a Lost Tribes origin for Native Americans as one could imagine.

While Stiles was hesitant to accept a Lost Tribes scenario, he remained convinced of a civilized Mediterranean presence in American antiquity. Only a year after rejecting Court de Gébelin's Phoenician attribution for Dighton Rock, Stiles was embracing it, in his "Election Sermon" (aka "The United States Elevated to Glory and Honor") to the General Assembly of Connecticut, on May 8, 1783.[31] Stiles crafted a theory of American antiquity that brought biblical hermeneutics, Gothicism, and Dighton Rock to bear on the nature of Native Americans and the God-given destiny of the new American republic, "God's American Israel."[32]

Stiles's ideas probably were informed by Samuel Mather. A son of Cotton Mather, Samuel was a Boston preacher as well as a tireless pamphleteer who published *An Attempt to Shew, That America Must Be Known to the Ancients* (1773).[33] Mather's textual influences belonged to previous centuries, and he appears to have relied substantially on *The American Traveller*, published without an author attribution in London in three printings from 1741 to 1745.[34] This orphaned intellectual work (which, for all we know, Samuel Mather might have written) offered a plethora of scenarios for the peopling of the Americas, including a Phoenician one. It was mostly derivative of the survey of theories on Indigenous origins (including those of Grotius and de Laet, as well as classical writers) by the German scholar Georgi Horni (Georg Horn, Georgius Hornius) in *De originibus Americanis*, which was initially published in 1652 and expanded in 1669 and was never translated from Latin. As such, *The American Traveller* deserves credit for popularizing among English-speaking readers ideas of Horni that otherwise might have remained obscure. It may have influenced Kalm and his translator, Forster. Kalm was in London only a few years after it was published, preparing for his journey to America. Kalm's idea of a military invasion, and Forster's more specific reference to a Mogul fleet invading Japan before sailing on to America, were anticipated by *The American Traveller*, which offered a story from Diodorus of an invasion fleet of 15,000 Tartar ships.[35]

Samuel Mather thought some theorists "injudiciously" contended the Canaanites scattered by Joshua had fled to America.[36] He was confident, however, that the Phoenicians were descended from the Canaanites, and that perhaps after interbreeding with Japhetite Europeans, they had crossed the Atlantic and colonized America. This migration was only one among many, from a scattering of Old World sources. The initial peopling of the Americas after the Flood had been by Tartars descended from Scythians, who in turn were progeny of Japheth's son Magog. They had crossed the Strait of Anian by boat or canoe, or on foot when it was frozen over. These original inhabitants then migrated southward and westward as new peoples arrived— Norwegians and Icelanders in the manner of Grotius's proposal, as well as Chinese. Finally, the Phoenicians appeared, and "became very well settled; and vast Numbers of People were found in this *Western World*, when *Columbus, Americus* [Amerigo Vespucci] and succeeding Voyagers came to it."[37] Thus the Phoenicians gave rise to many if not all Native Americans.

In his variant on multiple migrations and displacement, Mather was unable to provide any physical evidence of the original Phoenician presence in America. His failure to even consider Dighton Rock is surprising, given that his father had devoted so much energy to publicizing the markings and had considered the rock face to contain lines of script in unknown characters. Stiles moved in to fill the evidentiary void, now that Court de Gébelin and apparently Sewall had endorsed the idea that Dighton Rock was a Phoenician relic.

Noah's curse upon Canaan had specified: "God shall enlarge Japheth." Stiles explained that Scythia had been the residence of the family of Japheth. One branch spread westward into Europe, while another branch became the ancient kingdoms of Media and Persia. Stiles identified "a new enlargement" for Japheth "in the country *where Canaan shall be his servant,* at least unto tribute."[38] This new enlargement was the colonization of America. As for the subservient Canaanites: "I rather consider the American Indians as Canaanites of the expulsion of Joshua."[39]

Stiles had praised Menasseh Ben Israël's character in his diary in January 1782 and essentially agreed with *The Hope of Israel* in rejecting the idea that Native Americans were descendants of the Lost Tribes, which had recently been promoted by James Adair in *The History of the American Indians* (1775). Stiles also implicitly agreed with Menasseh that Native Americans were Tartar migrants, whose origins Stiles stretched back to the cursed Canaanites. It was important to Stiles to herd all Native Americans into the role of Canaanites cursed by Noah to be subservient to the Japhetite whites, and also to not have them be descendants of the Lost Tribes, which would have implied that they were capable of redemption and improvement, and would also have strengthened their right to lands coveted by the new republic. According to Stiles, one branch "of the canaanitish expulsions might take the resolution of the ten tribes."[40] Native Americans were *not* these ten Lost Tribes, but they conformed to the migrationist scenarios of Lost Tribe theorists. Some became "the Tchuschi and Tungusi Tartars about Kamschatka and Tscukotskoinoss in the north-east of Asia: thence, by water, passing over from island to island through the northern Archipelago to America, became the scattered Sachemdoms of these northern regions."[41] All American Indians, Stiles held, from the Arctic to Tierra del Fuego, were one kind of people, and they were the same as the people still found in northeast Asia.

Other Canaanites became Phoenicians, as was generally believed, and in a scenario already familiar from *The American Traveller* and Mather, some of them "wafted across the Atlantic, land in the tropical regions, and commence the settlements of Mexico and Peru."[42] Still other Canaanite-derived Phoenicians "charged the Dighton rock and other rocks in Narragansett-bay with Punic inscriptions, remaining to this day. Which last I myself have repeatedly seen and taken off at large, as did Professor Sewall. He has lately transmitted a copy of his inscription to M. Gebelin of the Parisian academy of sciences, who comparing them with the Punic paleography, judges them punic, and has interpreted them as denoting, that the ancient Carthaginians once visited these distant regions."[43] Notwithstanding Court de Gébelin's elaborate interpretation, Stiles preferred to leave the Phoenician inscription undeciphered. Stiles did not say whether these migrants were ancestors of New England's Native Americans, but that would have been consistent with Mather's idea.

Stiles added a novel twist to the idea of colonizing migrations to America, founding what amounted to Transatlantic Gothicism. The multiple migrations of special interest to him were made not by ancestral Native Americans, but rather by ancestral whites of northern Europe. Mather had aired a theory that the Welsh prince Madoc had colonized South America as well as Mexico "and left Monuments *there* both of *the British Language and British Usages*."[44] Mather addressed other purported pre-Columbian European arrivals, but where he preferred to focus on "*more ancient Times and Things*," including the Atlantis myth, Stiles crafted an identifiably Gothicist series of Japhetic outmigrations.[45] Stiles recounted several waves of Japheth: the visit of Madoc in 1170, "the certain colonization from Norway, A.D. 1001, as well as the certain Christianizing of Greenland in the ninth century," and the ongoing colonization of America from Europe.[46]

Stiles was describing and justifying a *second* expulsion of the Canaanites by Joshua, this time in the promised land of "God's American Israel." He stopped short of calling for the extermination that God had commanded Joshua to inflict upon the original Canaanites, in the original promised land, and limited himself to the idea of their subservience due to the curse of Noah upon his grandson, Canaan, in the manner of natural slavery described by Aristotle and imposed upon Tartars (and their New World analogues) by Montesquieu. Stiles certainly was a literalist where Indigenous subservience was concerned. In an indenture drawn up on June 10, 1782, Ruth Waukeet (or Wauket), "an Indian Squaw Widow," agreed to bind her nine-year-old son Aaron to Stiles until age twenty-one.[47]

Stiles was also a land investor, and as he assured his audience, "The protestant Europeans have generally bought the native right of soil, as far as they have settled, and paid the value ten fold; and are daily increasing the value of the remaining Indian territory a thousand fold; and in this manner we are a constant increasing revenue to the Sachems and original Lords of the Soil."[48] Although Stiles estimated that the blood of whites had been "transfused" into two million Native Americans, he was confident that the demographic growth of pure whites would overwhelm them, as well as blacks. Stiles had published an antislavery pamphlet, *A Dialogue Concerning the Slavery of the Africans*, in 1776, but owned a West African slave whom he had acquired as a ten-year-old boy in 1756 through shipping rum to the Guinea coast. After freeing the slave in 1778, he would have the man's son bound to him at age two.[49]

"We are increasing with great rapidity; and the Indians, as well as the million Africans in America, are decreasing as rapidly," Stiles preached to the Connecticut assembly. "Both left to themselves, in this way diminishing, may gradually vanish: and thus an unrighteous SLAVERY may at length, in God's good providence, be abolished and cease in the land of LIBERTY."[50] Stiles was looking forward to the day when African Americans and Native Americans vanished, leaving the continent a promised land for the white descendants of Japheth.

ON MAY 16, 1783, eight days after delivering his Election Sermon, Stiles noted in his itinerary: "Visited Dighton Rock charged with Inscriptions & Character which M. Gebelin of the Acad^y of Paris says is Phoenecian or Carthaginian."[51] The Reverend Michael Lort, a member of the Royal Society and a vice president of the Society of Antiquaries of London, would mount an assault on the Phoenician attribution with a paper read before the Society of Antiquaries on November 23, 1786.[52] Lort wrote nothing about Ezra Stiles's support for the idea; he was concerned with Court de Gébelin's interpretation. When Lort first saw Court de Gébelin's version of Sewall's drawing, "I own I could conceive of it as nothing more than the rude scrawls of some of the Indian tribes, commemorating their engagements, their marches, or their hunting parties, such as are to be seen in different accounts of these nations, and very lately exhibited to this Society by a member of it."[53] Lort was referring to a letter from William Bray read before the Society of Antiquaries on March 1, 1781, which discussed a dendroglyph, a glyphic message carved in a blazed tree trunk by a Delaware warrior.[54] Lort proposed that Court de Gébelin had been in the midst of his researches to prove the Phoenicians reached all parts of the globe when he received the drawing and letter from Sewall: "He therefore falls into raptures on receiving this additional proof and support of his system."[55] Lort, in contrast, heralded the efforts to decipher Dighton Rock by Charles Vallancey, "a learned member of this Society."[56]

Even by the relatively liberal theorizing standards of the late eighteenth century, Charles Vallancey held eccentric historical ideas. Many contemporaries doubted his scholarly judgment and Phoenician notions. Sir William Jones, who established Orientalism as a serious philological discipline and helped Vallancey with scholarship on India, thought his work "very stupid."[57] Norman Moore, who wrote Vallancey's entry in the *Dictionary of National Biography, 1885–1900,* dismissed entirely his works on Irish history: "Their facts are never trustworthy and their theories are invariably extravagant." Moore consigned him to a school of writers "who have had some influence in retarding real studies, but have added nothing to knowledge."[58] Regardless, Vallancey commanded the attention of his scholarly contemporaries, was admitted to the leading philosophical, scientific, and antiquarian societies, and would influence perceptions of Native Americans and the development of the multiple-migration displacement scenario through his interest in Dighton Rock.

Vallancey spent his entire career in the British military as an engineer, rising to the rank of lieutenant general in 1798.[59] As an ensign in the 10th regiment of foot, Vallancey had been sent to Ireland around 1750, where he settled for life and developed a romantic attachment to the past of his adopted land. Like so many theorists addressing Native Americans in general, Vallancey never visited North America, but he held a membership in the American Philosophical Society and was convinced of pre-Columbian connections between the Old World and the New. In *An Essay on the Antiquity of the Irish Language* in 1772, Vallancey argued for the Phoenician roots of the Irish language, the result of Ireland's invasion by Carthaginians. In a revised and expanded version, issued as *A Grammar of the Iberno-Celtic or Irish Language* in 1773, he made a more ambitious case for "Iberno-Celtic" being the basis of languages worldwide, including the Algonquian language family. Vallancey could have been inspired to revisit the *Essay* so quickly as the *Grammar* by Samuel Mather's pamphlet advocating a Phoenician visit to America, which was published the same year. Still, the idea of a Phoenician visit to America had been debated for more than a century.

Vallancey asserted: "Father Lafitau has endeavoured to show, from an affinity, or rather an agreement of customs, that some of the Americans are descended from the *Pelasgi*; which is still coming to the same point, for the Pelasgi were of Phoenician extract."[60] This Vallancey sentence, however, was a near-verbatim lift from "A Dissertation on the Peopling of America" in *Additions to the Universal History* of 1750.[61] If Vallancey actually read Lafitau's *Moeurs*, he did not heed his warnings about the reliability of Indigenous vocabularies in Baron de Lahonton's *Mémoires de l'Amérique septentrionale* (1703).[62] Vallancey relied on Lahonton in comparing Irish words and the language "understood by all the Indian nations, except two," to prove that Algonquian was related to the old "Iberno-Celtic, or *bearla feni*," which in turn, he asserted, was derived from Phoenician. "The Algonkins say, they are the most ancient and most noble tribe on that continent: their name in Irish indicates as much, *cine algan*, or *algan cine*, i.e. the noble tribe; *all gain cine*, i.e. the most renowned nation, which is derived from three Phoenician words of the same signification . . . *al gand gins*."[63]

Lafitau had been agreeable to the idea that Phoenicians had reached the Americas, but did not see them as progenitors of the Indigenous inhabitants. Lafitau thought it possible that humankind had peopled the Americas before the Flood, and otherwise was certain that the Americas were occupied soon after it, long before any Phoenicians came along.[64] Seconding the opinions of Georgi Horni in *De originibus Americanis* (1652) and the Dutch scholar Roberti Comtei Nortmanni (Robert Comte) in *De Origine Gentium Americanarum Dissertatio* (Amsterdam, 1644) that the Phoenicians made several voyages to America (as *Additions to the Universal History* noted in the case of Horni), would prove awkward for Vallancey in the 1780s.[65]

In the *Grammar*, Vallancey included Pehr Kalm's observations from the recent Forster translation, paraphrasing him: "That North America was formerly inhabited by a nation more versed in science, and more civilized than the present, is certain from the late discoveries of Mons. Verandrier and his companions." Kalm's descriptions of stone pillars, wrote Vallancey, "perfectly answers to our Clogh-oirs, at this day visible all over Ireland," and he recounted the discovery of the smaller inscribed stone that was sent to France for study.[66] Vallancey wasn't quite sure yet what to make of all this, and he had experienced a theoretical near miss with Lafitau. If he read any of Lafitau closely, it was volume 4, which made cross-cultural comparisons based on language, but Lafitau in the first few dozen pages of volume 1 had made his case for multiple migrations out of Asia across a Bering land bridge, with newcomers displacing earlier, more sophisticated arrivals.

By 1786, Vallancey had significantly revised his ideas, with Dighton Rock as his inspiration. "Observations on the American Inscription," which so impressed Michael Lort, was read before the Society of Antiquaries on February 9, 1786, and printed in *Archaeologia* in 1787. Vallancey was at the height of his scholarly authority: he had received an LL.D. from Dublin University in 1781, and was elected a fellow of the Society of Antiquaries of London in 1784 and a fellow of the Royal Society in 1786.[67] Vallancey also developed a reputation for treating his critics arrogantly. In 1802 Edward Ledwitch wrote a fellow Irish antiquarian, Bishop Thomas Percy (the English translator of Mallet), despairing of "Vallancey's ungentlemenlike treatment of every writer dissenting from him, and his monstrous absurdities."[68] In "Observations," Vallancey rained contempt on Court de Gébelin over his Phoenician theory for Dighton Rock, but also made a major error. He could not believe the French mythographer had read Isaac Greenwood's 1730 letter that accompanied his drawing of Dighton Rock, "or M. Gebelin would not have hazarded an explanation so repugnant to all history. Many letters passed between me and Gebelin on this subject; at length he acknowledged his doubts; in short, tacitly gave up the point."[69] But Court de Gébelin had worked from Stephen Sewall's 1768 drawing, not Greenwood's of 1730. There is further reason to doubt Court de Gébelin ever capitulated to Vallancey. Court de Gébelin died in failing health in May 1784 in the Paris home of the healer Franz Anton Mesmer, who promoted the concept of animal magnetism, and therefore was in no position to refute Vallancey's haughty and triumphant contention in 1786. It is difficult even to imagine a lively exchange of "many letters" between Vallancey in Ireland and Court de Gébelin in France in the midst of the American Revolution, when Britain and France were enemies, and when Vallancey was engaged as a British military engineer in ensuring Ireland was prepared for a French invasion. A single letter in August 1781 from Court de Gébelin in France to Sewall in the American colonies, which were allied in revolution, took more than two years to be delivered. However extensive their actual exchange, Vallancey allowed that Court de Gébelin wrote: "You have proved the Algonkin language of America (now almost lost[?]) to have been the same with the old Scytho-Irish, and *that* you have proved to be Punic; ergo the Punic and the Algonkin were the same." The argument, Vallancey stated, "is futile and puerile."[70] This was extraordinary, as Court de Gébelin had just summarized Vallancey's own argument in the *Grammar* in 1773, a work Vallancey had reissued unaltered in 1782. Vallancey probably felt he had no choice but to disown his own work, including his endorsement of Horni's assertions that Phoenicians had sailed to America (and was loathe to admit he had changed his mind), as he was confronting the considerable critical and popular success of volume 1 (1784) of the ground-breaking work of natural history, *Arctic Zoology* by Johann Forster's friend, Thomas Pennant.[71]

The possible role of the Bering Strait in human migration to the Americas had already gained greater currency in the English-speaking world with the appearance in 1761 of *Voyages from Asia to America*, Thomas Jefferys's translation of the report by Gerhard Müller, the co-leader of the academic contingent of the second Bering expedition. The case became far more persuasive and topical with the discoveries of the third Cook voyage (1776–79) in the northern Pacific. Pennant argued that because of the recent Cook expedition's findings, "every other system of the population of the New World is now overthrown . . . [I]n the place of imaginary hypotheses, the real place of migration is uncontrovertibly pointed out."[72] Pennant was not the first theorist to posit a multiple-migration scenario out of Asia or to conclude that these migrations had employed the Bering Strait, but he packaged these ideas as a scientifically respectable proposition, shorn of biblical hermeneutics.

Moreover, in discussing human migrations in a book devoted to zoology, he placed human history within the context of natural history. Pennant leveraged Cook's discoveries in asserting there was one route, with multiple migrations, and gave no space to wandering Israelites. While leaving open the possibility (as Lafitau and Forster had) that a few migrants may have arrived from other routes, including Japan, Pennant argued that the Americas could only have been populated via the Bering Strait, whether by boat or across a land bridge that he proposed was later destroyed by volcanism, and only by waves of migrants at different times from different Old World nations: "It is impossible, with the lights which we have so recently received, to admit that *America* could receive (at least the bulk of them) from any other place than eastern *Asia*."[73] Pennant made the same comparisons between the scalping practices of Scythians and Native Americans that Lafitau had in 1724, but relied additionally on observations of the "newly-discovered *Americans* about Nootka Sound,"[74] which had been visited by Cook's expedition in 1778 and described in Captain James King's official voyage account in 1784.[75] Pennant suggested the "Five Nations" (Haudenosaunee; actually Six Nations by then, with the addition of the Tuscarora) derived from the *Tschutski*, who were "from that fine race of Tartars, the Kabardinski, or inhabitants of Kabarda."[76]

Arctic Zoology was a formidable rebuke to transatlantic-migration theorists and their reliance on classical authors like Diodorus, and (without addressing it) to the progeny-of-Japheth, multiple Transatlantic Gothicist migrations recently extolled by Stiles. Having missed or failed to grasp the utility of the multiple-migration displacement scenario when Lafitau proposed it in the first volume of *Moeurs*, Vallancey abandoned his transatlantic Phoenicians and presumably took inspiration from Pennant to forge a fresh explanation for the origin of Dighton Rock. First, he had to deal with the nuisance of Court de Gébelin's Phoenician theory. Vallancey turned to the crude Mather woodcut reproduced by Court de Gébelin and observed: "In this drawing there are no human figures, or any thing that could possibly lead M. Gebelin to the explanation he has given. It is evidently an inscription free from hieroglyphics." As for the story of the wooden house full of strangers coming up the Taunton River, it must have referred to the later arrival of English colonists rather than Phoenicians.[77]

If Vallancey knew Isaac Greenwood's drawing, then he also knew his conclusion that Native Americans were too stupid and lazy to have carved the inscription. Vallancey proposed that the inscription was "the work of a race of people who arrived on this great continent prior to the present race of Indian savages." Vallancey disingenuously buried his own work in remarking, "I have read somewhere of an obelisk and inscription having been discovered many days journey N. W. of Quebec," which was a reference to his own quotation in the *Grammar* of Pehr Kalm's La Vérendrye story. Had he cited the *Grammar*, which he had so recently reissued, he might well have triggered antiquarian memories of his Algonquian-Phoenician theory that Court de Gébelin had flung back at him.

The problem with Kalm's La Vérendrye story, as we have seen, is that not even a drawing existed of the stone pillars, and most importantly of the Tartarian characters on the stone allegedly sent to France. Kalm had left an evidentiary vacuum that other relics needed to fill. Vallancey moved on to a recording of an "inscription made by a priestess of the Michmac Indians" that had been copied in 1766, which was further proof "that letters or characters did once flourish with this people." Vallancey floated the possibility that the Mi'kmaw pictographic system may have been created by proselytizing Jesuit missionaries, but he believed the hieroglyphic aspects originated with the Mi'kmaq and evidently thought this pointed in the direction not of Egyptian visitors but rather of a diffusionist Old World heritage borrowed from a learned people who had migrated across the Bering Strait and left the script behind for the Mi'kmaq to use.[78]

Vallancey maintained that Armenian Scythians spread eastward into Tibet and then into Siberia, eventually crossing over to America from Kamchatka. Pennant too had pointed to the Scythians and a crossing from eastern Siberia, but Vallancey was mute on this precedent. In addition, rather than grant the Welshman an iota of credit where the application of Cook's discoveries were concerned, Vallancey claimed to have discussed them directly with Captain James King, which seems doubtful: King had relocated to Nice in 1783 to seek relief for his tuberculosis, and died there in November 1784.[79]

Vallancey then turned to Dighton Rock. He selected one plate from Strahlenberg's book (figure 4) "which bears so strong a resemblance of the New England inscription" that "there can be little doubt of their being written by the same people. These are also written on perpendicular rocks, forming the banks of rivers; a strong instance of that people having been navigators."[80] Beyond the fact that the inscription on the Siberian stone in the Strahlenberg plate bore no resemblance to Dighton Rock, Vallancey lacked the ethnographic resources from America to notice the resemblance between Native American pictographs and Strahlenberg's illustration of a Siberian shaman's drum.[81]

Vallancey concluded that Dighton Rock was carved by "the same race of people, who formerly possessed Siberia, and passed from hence to the great

FIGURE 4 "Tartarian" inscription from Philipp-Johann von Strahlenberg's *An Historico-Geographical Description of the North and Eastern Parts of Europe and Asia* (1738), reprinted by Charles Vallancey in *Archaeologia* 8 (1787), because of its alleged resemblance to Dighton Rock.

continent of America; and that these were a lettered people, and skilled in all the sciences of those ages, but have been mostly destroyed, in the northern part of America, by great hords [*sic*] of rambling Tartars, who followed them, and now form the savage Indians; and that many of the original people are to be found in South America."[82] Whether either Lafitau's or Menasseh's multiple-migration displacement scenario influenced him is open to question, but Vallancey probably was familiar with the work of Montesquieu, as his Tartar hordes might have wandered out of *De l'Esprit des loix* on another binge of brutish, enslaved, and enslaving conquest.

Vallancey's Dighton Rock theory arrived with fortuitous timing, as the discovery of the so-called Mound Builder ruins of the Ohio and Mississippi valleys made both pressing and consequential the question of from whom Native Americans were descended. Any theorist who wished to classify ancestral Native Americans as brutish Tartars who had nothing to do with any impressive relic of American antiquity would have welcomed Vallancey's new theory for Dighton Rock, and some of them evidently did.

IN 1772, David Zeisberger made one of the earliest observations of mounds west of the Appalachians. The Moravian missionary came upon the earthworks at the confluence of the Muskingum and Ohio rivers as he laid out a settlement near present-day New Philadelphia, Ohio, for a group of Christian Indians he had led west from Pennsylvania.[83] They would become known as the Marietta mounds, in honor of the town that mostly obliterated them. Zeisberger had no difficulty associating present-day Native Americans with an ancestral people who created the mounds. However, as American settlement spread westward following American independence, doubts about their affinity grew as colonizers confronted more mounds, some of them cones or platform and ridge pyramids, some of them animal-shaped, some of them with burials and grave goods. "Though few of these earthen heaps were impressive as individual sights," according to Robert Silverberg, "they had a cumulative effect. There were so many of them—ten thousand in the valley of the Ohio alone—that they seemed surely to be the work of a vanished race that had thrown itself into the task of construction with obsessive fervor."[84]

We now consider these archaeological survivals to be the remnants of several different cultural complexes ranging across a vast area and many centuries, from 1000 B.C. to as recent as A.D. 1750.[85] But in the late eighteenth and the nineteenth centuries, these earthworks (and the cultural materials buried within them) struck antiquaries as the remnants of a single mysterious, ancient culture. Whoever these people were, they appeared to have been far more sophisticated, far more industrious, far more *civilized*, than present-day Indians. The erroneous idea that the Mound Builders were expert metallurgists, arising from a misunderstanding of items worked in copper, persisted until 1883.[86] One explanation for the existence of the mounds—and the apparent nonexistence of their creators—was that the Native Americans known to colonists had degenerated from the people who had created the earthworks. However, theorists quickly began to abandon the degeneracy model and to disenfranchise Native Americans from their past, by coming up with candidates other than ancestral Native Americans to fill the role of the ancient people who came to be known as the Mound Builders. Not until the publication in 1894 of a comprehensive report on the mounds for the U.S. Bureau of Ethnology by Cyrus Thomas would scholars discard the idea there had been a single "Mound Builder" culture, unrelated to contemporary Indians.[87]

The essence of Vallancey's Dighton Rock theory was applied with remarkable simultaneity to the Mound Builders question. Vallancey's paper had been read before the membership of the Society of Antiquaries in London in February 1786. That same month, Samuel Holden Parsons, who had been a major general in the Continental Army and was a member of the Connecticut General Assembly, had a plan made of the Marietta earthworks. Parsons had been sent west that winter as an Indian commissioner, as the United States claimed lands as far west as the Mississippi by right of conquest. With Richard Butler he compelled the Shawnee to accept under threat of arms the Treaty of Fort Finney in January 1786, by which they surrendered all their land in what is now southern Illinois and southeastern Ohio.[88] In July 1787 Congress passed the Northwest Ordinance, which established a government for the Northwest Territory in the western Great Lakes, west of the Ohio River and east of the upper Mississippi, and outlined the process for granting statehood to what would become Ohio, Indiana, Illinois, Michigan, Wisconsin, and Minnesota. Parsons's work had been essential to this expansion plan, which faced resistance from Indigenous nations. The questions of Native

American ancestry and the moral right of westward colonization were becoming more pressing.

Parsons also visited the conical Grave Creek mound in the Ohio River Valley. On April 26, 1786, having returned to Connecticut, Parsons called on Ezra Stiles and showed him his Marietta plan, of which Stiles made a copy.[89] Parsons assured Stiles the mounds he had seen in the Ohio country, which he interpreted as military works (Zeisberger concluded the same), long predated the coming of Europeans: "The present Inhabitants having no Knowledge of the Arts or Traditions respecting the fortifications leaves a Doubt whither the former Inhabitants were Ancestors of the present."[90] The fact that individual living Native Americans were not walking repositories of knowledge about the deep and broad ethnohistory of North America made it easy to conclude that what they could not explain could not have anything to do with their ancestors. The Marietta complex is now considered to have been a ceremonial center of the Hopewell culture (200 B.C.–A.D. 400), while the Grave Creek mound has been assigned to its predecessor, the Adena culture (600–200 B.C.).

Stiles recalled in his diary that Parsons was "convinced that the Region thereabout has once been inhabited by a civilized People different from the present Indian Inhabitants in this country." Stiles went on in a progeny-of-Japheth, multiple-migration vein, drawing parallels with the lost Greenland colony, once inhabited by "civilized people" but "destroyed & obliterated by the aboriginals," and the conflicts in New England in the seventeenth century, including King Philip's War, in which the Indians "resolved to extirpate" the English colonists. Stiles then ventured into White Tribism, holding that a settlement by the Welsh prince Madoc in Kentucky "might have at length alarmed surrounds Indians & been attended with an Extirpation." A remnant group of Welshmen escaped up the Missouri, "where it is s^d there is a Tribe that speak Welch to this day & have a Writing rolled up in Skins," a reference to the Mandan. "Gen. Parsons however goes into none of these Ideas, but believes there have been civilized People at Muskingham in former & very distant past ages."[91] In Stiles's reckoning, Native Americans had been committing ethnic cleansings of superior northern Europeans for ages, and continued to do so, as Stiles's days were marked by stark reminders of attacks by British-allied Indigenous forces during the American Revolution.[92]

As Stiles was an active antiquary with a long-standing interest in Dighton Rock, he could have learned quickly of Vallancey's new theory presented in February 1786 in London. However, Stiles's diary makes no mention of Vallancey or Dighton Rock in association with the Parsons visit of April 1786, and it does seem that at this stage Vallancey, Stiles, and Parsons had tapped a zeitgeist of complementary ideas about Native Americans as primitive displacers or exterminators of superior peoples, as captured in the multiple-migration displacement scenario proposed by Menasseh and later advanced by Lafitau. Stiles for one was aware of Menasseh's *The Hope of Israel*. Parsons did not go as far as Vallancey in linking his superior peoples and their inferior conquerors specifically to multiple migrations out of Asia in the Pennant model: Parsons's Mound Builders could have been transatlantic colonizers. Stiles (along with Benjamin Franklin) was among the first members admitted to the AAAS in 1781, and he likely elicited from Parsons his longer missive to the corresponding secretary of the society in October 1786, which would be published in 1793 (four years after Parsons's death).[93] Writing of Grave Creek, Parsons concluded: "On the whole, I am of [the] opinion, that country has been thickly peopled, by men to whom the necessary arts were known in a much greater degree than to the present native Indians of that region."[94] Parsons ventured that the usurpers, ancestors of modern Indians, arose from a Lost Tribes or implicitly Canaanite migration.[95]

The officer who appears to have conducted the Marietta survey for Parsons, Captain Jonathan Heart, published a simple plan and a basic site description in the May 1787 issue of *The Columbian*. Heart was skeptical about its Native American origin, despite finding graves that contained their arrows. "Nothing is yet found which can lead to a discovery, when, or by whom those works were constructed, or the design of the different parts; the accounts of Indians are irregular and inconsistent, and carry more fable than appearance of tradition—but the uniform regularity, and prodigious extent of the works, as well as their former height . . . are convincing proofs that they were constructed by a people not only numerous, but well acquainted with the art of fortification and defence."[96]

Migration and displacement theories continued to swirl around the mounds and Dighton Rock, evolving rapidly, and Ezra Stiles was a conduit—a distributive hub, even—for the discussion. In late 1787 Noah Webster, who had studied under Stiles at Yale, wrote him on Benjamin Franklin's idea the de Soto expedition had left behind the Marietta mounds as military fortifications.[97] Webster published to that end in the December 1787 issue of the *American Magazine*.[98] In a letter to Stiles on January 20, 1788, Webster revisited the issue of the Marietta earthworks, having now read Captain Heart's article.[99] He had also absorbed Thomas Jefferson's recent comments on earthworks and Native Americans in *Notes on the State of Virginia* (1787). Jefferson had participated in mound excavations in Virginia, but the findings did not affect his ideas on Native American origins. He was more intrigued by the implications of the third Cook expedition in the Pacific, and by the diversity of Native American languages. Like Pennant and Vallancey, Jefferson reflected on the third Cook expedition's survey of the Kamchatka Peninsula of eastern Siberia, and suspected that Native Americans more likely had migrated from Asia than from Europe. However, based on differences between Native American languages, he presumed the "red men of America" were "of greater antiquity than those of Asia," thus raising the possibility that the ancient migration had occurred in reverse while leaving unanswered what he thought of the relationship of Native Americans to humankind in general.[100]

Persuaded in part by Jefferson's observations, Webster now concluded that the mounds were of Native American origin. Their apparent similarity to British mounds and barrows further suggested to Webster that Native Americans were descended from primitive Britons and Celts, and had reached America over time through Greenland, an idea "by no means obviated by Capt Cooks' [*sic*] late discoveries in the Pacific Ocean." Webster, however, was not (yet) a Transatlantic Gothicist: he made clear to Stiles that he did not think ancient Britons migrated directly to America.[101]

Webster's sudden interest in British as well as Danish mounds was suspiciously reminiscent of a circa-1787 work by another Stiles correspondent, a young Benjamin Smith Barton, then studying medicine in Edinburgh.[102] Barton's *Observations on Some Parts of Natural History* was labeled Part I; a further four parts were promised. The pamphlet did not address natural history at all, but instead was given over entirely to the mystery of the Mound Builders. Barton was born into an intellectually rarefied American family: his father, the Reverend Thomas Barton, corresponded with Linnaeus and was a member of the American Philosophical Society; his maternal uncle was the second president of the society; his older brother William, a lawyer, to whom he dedicated *Observations*, preceded him in securing a society membership. Barton would become a professor of materia medica (pharmacology), natural history, and botany at the University of Pennsylvania, securing his initial appointment in 1789 when he was only twenty-three, and he acquired memberships and fellowships in organizations such as the Society of Antiquaries of Scotland, the Massachusetts Historical Society, the American Philosophical Society, and the AAAS. Barton would also correspond with Jefferson, dedicate a book to him, and serve as an advisor to the Lewis and Clark expedition.

Barton may have been aware of Vallancey's recent works, as his pamphlet opened with a discussion of Pehr Kalm's account of La Vérendrye's stone monuments and inscriptions, which had so captivated Vallancey. Barton also spared a few words of invective for Corneille de Pauw, "the most angry and most petulant of philosophers."[103] De Pauw was a Dutch intellectual who served for short periods at the court of Prussia's Frederick the Great; in *Recherches philosophiques sur les Américains*, initially published in 1768–69, he amplified and distorted the degeneration theory of the Comte de Buffon.[104] De Pauw was another European intellectual expounding on Native Americans who never crossed the Atlantic Ocean, but this did not prevent his ideas from having considerable impact, or at least in gaining considerable notoriety. De Pauw asserted that the climate was deleterious to any plant or animal species or race of human being introduced to North America. A great deluge had altered the land and the climate, and left it in the possession of a young, inferior, savage people who could never improve.[105] They were more like orangutans or apes than human beings.[106] His work ignited outrage, inviting a harsh rebuke even from Buffon, who in 1777 charged that his portrayal of the weakness and general inferiority of Native Americans had "no foundation."[107] Buffon for his part earned an acute rebuke from Thomas Jefferson in *Notes on the State of Virginia*, a rejoinder that, according to John C. Greene, earned him "the everlasting gratitude of his countrymen."[108] (In this close-knit intellectual world, Jefferson met with Stiles in New Haven in 1784 and then wrote him to seek his help in rebutting Buffon on "a theory in general very degrading to America."[109]) Jefferson praised the physical and intellectual character of Native Americans in his rebuttal of Buffon. But unlike Jefferson, Barton had nothing good to say in *Observations* about present-day Native Americans. Barton thought the mounds were the work "of a people differing, in many respects, from the present savage nations of America."[110] He proposed "there has formerly existed in some of the *higher* (as well as in the *lower*) latitudes of AMERICA, a people who had made advances towards civilization, and improvements in war, as an art, unknown to the present NATIVE inhabitants of those regions."[111] In an unpublished essay from this time, Barton criticized contemporary European scholars who were "content to meditate in their closets." None of them, he contended, "had ever seen either the country or its inhabitants whose history they have attempted to give." But Barton's own experience with Native Americans was limited if not equally secondhand.[112]

Stiles evidently had shared with Barton some of Parsons's opinions on the Mound Builders, and most obviously his own copy of Parsons's plan of the Marietta "fortress," as Barton included an unattributed version in *Observations* (figure 5). The similarity to the unpublished Parsons plan rather than the

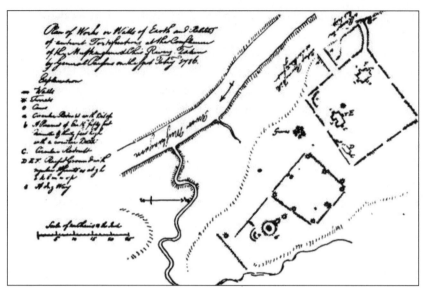

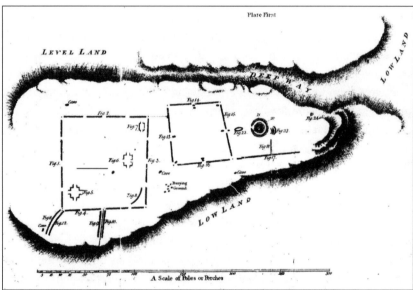

FIGURE 5 Top: Copy made by Ezra Stiles of a 1786 plan by Samuel Holden Parsons of the Marietta earthworks. Bottom: Benjamin Smith Barton's drawing of the Marietta earthworks in *Observations on Some Parts of Natural History* (c. 1787). Barton obviously made unattributed use of the Parsons plan, redrawing it upside down and with a scale in poles or perches rather than the chains of the original.

published Heart plan is plain. Barton attempted to hide his appropriating tracks by redrawing it upside-down and contriving a different scale, in poles or perches rather than the chains of the original.[113] Echoing Parsons (as well as Heart), Barton maintained that Native Americans lacked the capacity to have conceived of or constructed the Ohio relics. When Europeans discovered America, they found the Indians "attentive MERELY to the necessaries of life ... and hence the minds of the savages continued PASSIVE, perhaps for ages."[114]

In the final pages Barton made a daring, Transatlantic Gothicist gambit. Comparing Ohio earthworks with Irish examples, which he understood were constructed by invading Danes, he concluded the Mound Builders were one and the same people.[115] He imagined a band of Danish adventurers landing in Labrador and, over the course of several centuries, working their way toward Mexico.[116] Barton also pointed out the "amazing similitude of the *Iroquois* to some of the nations inhabiting the north-east parts of Asia," which likely came from Pennant's *Arctic Zoology*.[117] Although his ideas were not fully formed, Barton was constructing a multiple-migration displacement scenario in which superior inhabitants, whether or not they arrived first, came from northern Europe, while the hordes from which present-day Native Americans arose were from Tartary. *Observations* prompted a letter from Stiles on Dighton Rock, which Barton had not addressed, but Stiles failed to motivate the young scholar to investigate it.[118] Barton soon came to his senses, and so regretted his precocious *Observations* that he apologized to his brother for the dedication and abandoned plans for further installments.[119]

The critical year for the adoption of the multiple-migration displacement scenario for the Mound Builders appears to have been 1789, two years after Vallancey's Dighton Rock theory appeared in *Archaeologia*. Stiles had returned to Dighton Rock in October 1788 to make a new drawing.[120] Unsatisfied with this effort, he turned to the Reverend John Smith of Dighton to arrange for another. Smith wrote Stiles in July 1789 with a progress report on the drawing. As Smith was reporting on the latest effort to decipher Dighton Rock, it should not be surprising if Vallancey's 1787 interpretation was the inspiration for his more general comments on ancient America. Smith's speculations also could have owed a debt to Menasseh's multiple-migration displacement scenario for Lost Tribes that had taken refuge in the Andes, knowledge easily imparted to Smith by Stiles. "Was N. America once inhabited by a people from Asia who were skilled in hierogliphicks," Smith proposed, "who used the shield and helmet, who worshiped on high places & who gradually receding before the more northern tribes from Siberia settled themselves in the southern continent?"[121]

The drawing overseen by Smith identified a bird that suggested the origins of the rock's inscribers, or at least a country through which they had passed. As Smith explained: "Capt Walter Haley who has resided seven years in China, not knowing our conjectures, declared the bird to be the Casur or Casuar of China; one of which he saith he owned several years."[122] This presumably was a species of cassowary (genus *Casuarius*), a large flightless bird related to the emu, which actually is found in New Guinea and nearby islands.

Noah Webster tendered a version of multiple migrations and displacement similar to Barton's (with echoes of Samuel Mather) in a letter to *The American Museum* in September 1789, which was published in 1790. Webster first abandoned publicly the de Soto explanation for the Marietta mounds. He now proposed that "Carthaginians or other European nations" made their way to the Americas by an unstated route and were the ancestors of the more advanced peoples of Mexico and Peru, as well as the builders of the Marietta mounds. These nations had become "more civilized, than the present northern Indians," whose ancestors, perhaps 400 or 500 years ago, were "Siberian Tartars" who "found their way to the North West parts of this country, and pushed their settlements till they met the southern and more ancient settlers." The Tartar newcomers were "accustomed to a colder climate and more hardy and active life," and were the "Goths and Vandals of North America" who "drove the more ancient settlers from their territory."[123]

Webster's proposal that Tartars were the equivalents of Goths and Vandals resonated with the common belief in the cycle of history and the idea that, like the higher civilization of Rome with which the early American republic identified, the United States was under threat from savage tribes. It also harkened back to Thomas Harriot's comparisons of Native Americans to Picts in *A Briefe and True Report* (1588), which endured in similar comparisons by the Scottish Enlightenment's Adam Ferguson in *An Essay on the History of Civil Society* (1767) and was the basis of the belief that living Native Americans could provide insights into the cultures of ancient, pagan Europeans. But as the Transatlantic Gothicism pioneered by Stiles polished pagan northern European tribes as heroic ancestors of Christian northern European (white) colonizers of America's deep past as well as its present, it was difficult for ancestral Native Americans to be both the equivalent of Gothic tribes overcoming a more advanced but corrupt southern regime *and* a brutish, inferior people who needed to make way for Gothic Anglo-American colonists—just as it was difficult for the young republic to identify with the glory of ancient Rome *and* condemn Rome as an oppressive and corrupt southern regime that deserved to be overthrown by the Gothic northerners with whom American colonists identified. Still, Webster's scenario hinted at a knockout playoff format, in which the Tartars defeated Carthaginian Mound Builders in America, while in Europe the Goths and Vandals overcame the corrupt Romans, culminating in a final, ongoing showdown in America between the Transatlantic Gothic Europeans and the Tartarian Native Americans.

In June 1790, Stiles drafted a manuscript addressing the inscribed rocks of New England, which he provided to his friend Stephen Sewall, who in turn forwarded it to James Bowdoin, a former governor of Massachusetts and a founder and first president of the AAAS.[124] Stiles held that the letters *I HOWOO* could be discerned on one end of Dighton Rock (to what purpose he did not explain), and he now looked to the colonizers of Atlantis, under their first king, Atlas, as the source of the markings:

> There was a period previous to the Age of Atlas, when the maritime shores of Europe, on this side the pillars of Hercules, around up to the Baltic, were colonized by all the various languages of *Scythia* & *Japhet*, & some Phoenician Navigators of the Derivation of Shem. It was in this period I conjecture those navigated over to America who made these Inscriptions. . . . There seems to be a mixture of Phoenician or antient *Punic* letters, with symbol, & perhaps *ideal character*, in the inscriptions at Narragansett. ATLAS, after the first discovery of his great insular Continent, sent over four ships of settlers to colonize upon it; which on their return, carried back the report, that the island was overwhelmed & *submersa ponto*. One of these Vessels of *Atlas* might have been shipwreckt at Narragansett.[125]

Thus in his final analysis Ezra Stiles espoused a fusion of ideas about transoceanic migration that were not inconsistent with Antoine Court de Gébelin's wandering Phoenicians and the Punic language roots of Algonquian in Charles Vallancey's *A Grammar*. Stiles was so blinded to an Indigenous attribution for Dighton Rock by this point that he was willing to enlist the apocryphal lost Atlantis that Rudbeks had made fundamental to Gothicism and had also figured in Samuel Mather's Phoenician theory. In Stiles's final interpretation of Dighton Rock, he did not try to link the Atlantean Phoenicians back to the cursed Canaanites. Instead, they were descended from one of Noah's favored sons, Shem, progenitor of the Hebraic line. This 1790 summation of Stiles's life's work on New England's inscribed stones was never published by the AAAS.

Around this time, Benjamin Smith Barton, established as a leading academic in Philadelphia, corresponded with Jonathan Heart—now promoted to major—on ancient earthworks. Major Heart wrote Barton on January 5, 1791, from Fort Harmer, whose construction he had overseen, opposite the Marietta site. By then Heart had also examined the mound at Grave Creek. Heart was certain no one from Europe, Africa, or Asia had arrived since Columbus and constructed these earthworks, but he also advised: "They were not constructed by the present Indians or their predecessors."[126] Heart's speculations on Native American ancestry ended abruptly the following November, when was killed at the rout of General St. Clair's army by an alliance of northwestern nations at the Wabash River. The idea that Native Americans were descendants of a brutish Tartar horde that had wiped out a superior civilization in the Ohio country had acquired a visceral currency.

Barton gave Dighton Rock a pass when he returned to the subject of American antiquity in *New Views of the Origins of the Tribes and Nations of America* in 1797. In his preliminary discourse, he quoted Strahlenberg on the importance of the languages of northern Asia to understanding the "nice and ticklish Point" of the "transmigration of Nations," acknowledged *Arctic Zoology* and "my learned and much-valued friend Mr. Pennant" (who was elected to the American Philosophical Society in 1791), and built on Pennant's limited comparative ethnography as he left his Transatlantic Gothicist idea of Danish Mound Builders in his own deep past.[127] Barton instead turned to Beringia to posit multiple migrations for the arrival of Native Americans. He now believed modern Native Americans were a degenerate cultural form of the Mound Builders, and that they could recuperate. "Let it not be said," he wrote Jefferson (president of both the United States and the American Philosophical Society) in the dedication, "that they are incapable of improvement."[128] Natural history, Barton continued in the dedication, "teaches us, a mortifying truth, that nations may relapse into rudeness again; all their proud monuments crumbled into dust, and themselves, now savages, subjects of contemplation among civilized nations and philosophers. In the immense scheme of nature, which the feeble mind of man cannot fully comprehend, it may be our lot to fall into rudeness once more. There are good reasons for conjecturing, that the ancestors of many of the savage tribes of America are the descendants of nations who had attained to a much higher degree of polish than themselves."[129]

Barton's conception of a Native American rise and fall was part of a dawning sense of American exceptionalism, a hope that the young republic could break history's cycle and progress ever upward.[130] Two years after publishing

New Views, Barton reiterated to the Reverend Joseph Priestley his case for cultural degeneration, maintaining that the American earthworks had been created by "the ancestors of some of the present races of Indians."[131] Barton's opinion, however, proved to be a minority view, and the term *horde* used by Vallancey for ancestral Native Americans would find telling currency in the nineteenth century.

THE ANTIQUITIES of the New World were a New World of their own to eager theorists who rushed to colonize them with their learned scenarios. Many of them negotiated the same narrow land bridge of prejudice and ignorance where Native American peoples were concerned. Alone in his interpretation of Dighton Rock, Antoine Court de Gébelin had been willing to grant Native Americans equal moral and intellectual standing with an Old World civilization. His eccentric reading of the inscription as Phoenician would not withstand scrutiny, and his elevated view of Indigenous people (albeit based on no personal experience) largely vanished with it in the ongoing debate over American antiquities. Ezra Stiles's faith that Dighton Rock was Phoenician (or perhaps Hebrew) may not have withstood close inspection for long, either, but his Election Sermon showed how deeply rooted ideas of racial supremacy, linked to biblical hermeneutics, were in the conscience of the new nation, and in its antiquarian logic. Stiles had brought Gothicism across the Atlantic to cast Protestants of northern Europe as descendants of Japheth who in the New World were fulfilling prophecy in enlarging their territory, while Native Americans were the children of Canaan, condemned to eternal servitude to the progeny of Japheth.

Charles Vallancey, in adapting Thomas Pennant's value-neutral theory on Beringian multiple migrations and perpetuating a dim Enlightenment view of Tartars, encouraged antiquarians to think of Native Americans as brutish usurpers of an earlier, semicivilized migration from Asia that had carved Dighton Rock. It is unclear whether Vallancey was aware of the theoretical precedent set by Menasseh Ben Israël and Jean-François Lafitau for the multiple-migration displacement theory. It is also unclear whether Americans enchanted by the theory had been inspired by Vallancey, Menasseh, or Lafitau—or by all three of them—in the rich ferment of theorizing that swirled around Stiles between 1786 and 1789. Regardless, the explanation Vallancey used for Dighton Rock proved to be readily applicable to the much larger and more pressing puzzle of the Mound Builders.

In New England, possession of Dighton Rock and the surrounding country had long been decided. With an ongoing westward land rush placing the mounds firmly in the colonizers' possession, the Tartarian "hordes" scenario would find compelling, irresistible utility in justifying Native American dispossession. The idea that pre-Columbian visitors unrelated to present-day Native Americans were responsible for America's perplexing antiquities continued to gain momentum, and in Dighton Rock's case was headed in both Gothicist and esoteric directions in the nineteenth century.

CHAPTER FOUR

Stones of Power

*Edward Augustus Kendall's Esoteric Case
for Dighton Rock's Indigeneity*

On a visit to Harvard in October 1789, George Washington (an original member of the AAAS) happened upon a drawing of Dighton Rock. Washington's guide, John Lathrop, would recall twenty years later that it was a life-size one made in 1788 by James Winthrop (son of John), who served as Harvard's librarian from 1782 to 1787. Alternatively, it may have been the one made in 1768 by Stephen Sewall, which hung above the entrance to the mineralogy department. Lathrop launched into an explanation of the Phoenician theory. When he was done, as Lathrop recounted,

> the President smiled, and said he believed the learned Gentlemen whom I had mentioned were mistaken: and added, that in the younger part of his life, his business called him to be very much in the wilderness of Virginia, which gave him an opportunity to become acquainted with many of the customs and practices of the Indians. The Indians he said had a way of writing and recording their transactions, either in war or hunting. When they wished to make any such record, or leave an account of their exploits to any who might come after them, they scraped off the outer bark of a tree, and with a vegetable ink, or a little paint which they carried with them, on the smooth surface, they wrote, in a way that was generally understood by the people of their respective tribes. As he had so often examined the rude way of writing practiced by the Indians of Virginia, and observed many of the characters on the inscription then before him, so nearly resembled the characters used by the Indians, he had no doubt the inscription was made, long ago, by some natives of America.[1]

John Lathrop recounted Washington's response in an 1809 letter to John Davis, a federal district court judge for Massachusetts who had been Washington's comptroller of the treasury. Judge Davis was a member of the Massachusetts Historical Society, the American Philosophical Society, and served as the recording secretary of the AAAS.[2] Davis too was persuaded Dighton Rock's inscription was Indigenous—he thought it depicted a hunting scene similar to one using enclosures illustrated by Pierre-François-Xavier de Charlevoix, which in turn drew on the observations of Samuel de Champlain. Davis shared his opinion in a letter around 1809 to Samuel Webber, who held the Hollisian chair at Harvard from 1789 to 1806 and was the president of the college from 1806 until his death in 1810.[3]

In his letter to Webber, Davis mentioned "Mr. Kendal's drawing."[4] Edward Augustus Kendall (or Kendal, in his early publishing years) was a British subject who had become intrigued by the mystery of Dighton Rock and other inscribed rocks while touring the American states east of the Hudson River in 1807–8. Davis assisted Kendall in his researches, and as recording secretary of the AAAS elicited from Kendall in October 1807 a letter outlining his initial thoughts on Dighton Rock, which was published by the academy in 1809 as "Account of the Writing-Rock in Taunton River." Kendall revisited and summarized his ideas in *Travels through the Northern Parts of the United States* (1809), the three-octavo record of his tour. Kendall agreed with Davis on cultural affinity, and made the most detailed and persuasive case of any investigator for the rock's Indigenous provenance.

With Kendall, the debate over the nature of Dighton Rock, now more than a century old, appeared to have found a firmly rationalist footing that could steer clear of transatlantic Gothicism, Phoenician adventurers, and Dark Enlightenment esotericism. However, Kendall's analysis shows how pervasive esotericism was in intellectual circles at the turn of the nineteenth century. His initial writing on Dighton Rock was steeped in Masonic allusions that have gone unnoticed, as his analysis brought the rock (and with it, Native Americans) into a Masonic diffusion of ancient hermetic knowledge. Kendall did so in association with prominent American antiquarians who were also well-known Masons. Through Freemasonry and related esoteric initiatives, the root culture shared by all peoples, as advocated by Lafitau in the early eighteenth century, became a foundational knowledge of civilization's arts in the possession of a privileged and secretive few, and of the greatest benefit to whites who preserved and propagated it among themselves. The egalitarian reading of Dighton Rock by the esotericist Antoine Court de Gébelin, which presented the Indians and Phoenicians as nations of equals, was about to take a far different Masonic turn with Kendall.

FREEMASONRY WAS NOT so much a secret society as it was a society with secrets, although it is not possible to confirm that everyone involved in Dighton Rock's Kendall episode, including Kendall himself, belonged to the fraternal order of "speculative" Freemasonry, the esoteric cousin of "practical" freemasonry, the trade of stonemasons.[5] George Washington was the most prominent

American Freemason. At the dedication of the United States Capitol building in 1793, Washington wore the Masonic apron and placed a silver plate on the cornerstone, covering it with the Masonic symbols of corn, oil, and wine.[6] Two figures involved in Kendall's researches of Dighton Rock were leading American Freemasons. One was a Unitarian minister, William Bentley of Salem, Massachusetts, a "passionate defender of Masonry and a Freemason himself," according to J. Rixey Ruffin.[7] ("We have but one Lodge in Salem, which has a good character," Bentley wrote in his diary regarding the Essex lodge in 1804, "but this is not derived from masonic zeal or masonic duty. It is an association of sober men, who admit no liquor into the Lodge & want none out of it. The severe scrutiny & the frequent rejection of Candidates keeps the number small.")[8] The other figure was Thaddeus Mason Harris, chaplain to the Grand Lodge of Massachusetts, an active antiquary whose published works included *Ignorance and Prejudice Shewn to be the Only Enemies to Free Masonry* (1797).

Steven C. Bullock has argued that American Freemasonry was more concerned with promoting a universal fraternal brotherhood than it was with esoteric knowledge, and that its "links to impenetrable mysteries" were "virtually ignored by colonial brothers."[9] American Freemasonry also was unique in striving to identify the fraternity with the scientific knowledge of learned men of the past and fostering ongoing, progressive learning, which included public education.[10] The Masons with whom Kendall associated in New England, the Reverend Bentley in particular, adhered to utopian, republican civic ideals of the eighteenth-century English Masonic tradition, while still embracing esoteric knowledge and practices, especially in communicating among themselves.[11] "The knowledge of Masonry is not contained in any of the present known languages of the world (for as I observed, it has a language peculiar to itself) but in emblems, hieroglyphics, signs, tokens and words," explained Abraham Lynsen Clarke, a church rector in Providence, Rhode Island, in 1799.[12] Kendall's effort to understand the rock—and to express that understanding—precisely reflected the Masonic penchant for rational inquiry alongside esoteric beliefs and obscure or metaphorical communication that included semiotics. Kendall was concerned with what could be perceived and described, what might be lurking within the obscure or hidden that was esoteric or hermetic, and perhaps what should remain obscure to all but initiates in the brotherhood. In the best practice of Freemasonry, Kendall's discourse conveyed subtextual meanings to anyone familiar with Masonic concepts.

An important aspect of Masonic doctrine where Dighton Rock is concerned is that its imaginative version of human history was a blend of diffusionism (the spread of a universal root wisdom) and migrationism (the movements of ancient peoples, in accordance with the Noachic repopulating of the Earth). *Diffuse* is a word that regularly crops up in Masonic literature of this period, and Kendall employed the concept as well as the term in his writings. Josiah Bartlett, grand warden of the Massachusetts Grand Lodge (and an associate of Bentley) in Boston, described in a 1793 discourse how Masonry flourished successively in Assyria, Judea, Persia, Egypt, Greece, Rome, and Italy. From there it "diffused" through the greater part of Europe and Asia, "and is not unknown in the more informed kingdoms of Africa." Absent from this ancient diffusion of wisdom were the Americas. The founding fathers, Bartlett explained, settled an "inhospitable wilderness."[13] With his investigation of Dighton Rock, Kendall was about to challenge the idea that the "Royal Art" only arrived in America with the English colonists.

EDWARD AUGUSTUS KENDALL was a prolific writer, but we know virtually nothing about his personal life beyond the fact that he died in Pimlico in central London in 1842 at age 66. He may have had Irish Protestant roots, and he spent a few years in the civil service in Canada, probably after publishing *Travels* in New York in 1809.[14] Although nothing came of the initiative, he also formed the Patriotic Metropolitan Colonial Institution in 1817, "for assisting new Settlers in His Majesty's Colonies," which took special interest in "establishing New and Distinct Colonies for the Relief of the Half-Casts of India, and Mulattoes of the West Indies."[15] Most of his early books, including *A Pocket Encyclopedia* (1802), were for children; some remained in print long after his death, and today these anchor his reputation. He founded the weeklies *The Literary Chronicle and Weekly Review* (1818–28) and *Olio* (1823–33), which, according to Gordon Goodwin, were conceived with "the object of providing cheap and good literature for the people."[16] He also produced works on political economy and jurisprudence, as well as translations of French prose and poetry.[17] For those interested in life in the northeastern United States in the early years of the republic, his main literary legacy is *Travels through the Northern Parts of the United States*.

Kendall's appraisal of Dighton Rock was augmented by what appears to have been a well-executed oil painting that would enter the collection of Harvard's Peabody Museum, where it unfortunately has gone missing, the image preserved only through two engravings (figure 6).[18] (No biographical account mentions his artistic talents.) Kendall's initial "Account" for Judge Davis bears many similarities to the chapter addressing the rock in *Travels*, but the former is a distinctly Masonic interpretation that all but confirms a

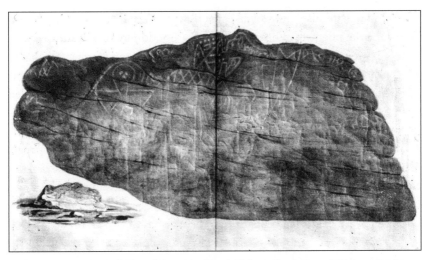

FIGURE 6   Engraving of Edward Augustus Kendall's lost oil painting of Dighton Rock, 1807, plate 28 in Edmund Burke Delabarre's "Middle Period of Dighton Rock History," *Publications of the Colonial Society of Massachusetts*, vol. 19 (1918).

fraternity membership for Kendall, and his writing embodied the tension between the mystical and the rational in the English Masonic tradition. As Margaret C. Jacob has remarked on eighteenth-century English Masonic literature: "Uniformly these writers claim to represent an ancient, generally Egyptian and Hermetic wisdom, rediscovered and augmented by the new useful learning of their age."[19] Kendall likely was fully charged with the energy and ephemera of Egyptology when he arrived in America, as he had contributed an essay on the French invasion of Egypt to an English translation of Vivant Denon's official account of the associated scientific discoveries.[20]

Kendall never explained why he made his American tour, which began in New York in May 1807, but seeking out inscribed rocks may have been his primary motive. His curiosity could have been piqued by James Winthrop's drawing of Dighton Rock, published as a foldout by the AAAS in 1804. In the letter accompanying the drawing's publication, Winthrop described his effort to pull a life-size impression of the markings using printer's ink. He ventured no interpretation of its meaning or origin.[21] Kendall also was captivated by the *Poems of Ossian*, which had charged Charles Vallancey's enthusiasm for the Celtic past. This popular epic cycle, first published in the 1760s by James Macpherson, allegedly was based on a manuscript Macpherson discovered and on oral traditions he gathered from Scottish Highlanders. They were Scotland's answer to the Icelandic sagas embraced by Gothicism, and they raised immediate suspicions of fakery.[22] Macpherson died in 1796, but a new edition of the poems had been published in London in 1807. If the new edition did not inspire Kendall that same year to seek out American analogues for megalithic circles in the Ossian poems, the poems at least spurred his ideas on the universalities of paganism as expressed through what he called "Stones of Power" and stone circles, which, as we will see, consumed six discursive chapters of *Travels*.

Judge Davis arranged for Kendall to examine Stiles's unpublished papers at Yale on inscribed rocks, and Kendall strove to see firsthand the examples Stiles documented. Kendall realized there were numerous examples, including ones recently reported across the Appalachians, and even painted rocks observed by fur traders in Canada. "My own wish is to visit all the sculptured rocks," Kendall informed Davis, but admitted: "This I may never be able to accomplish."[23]

Over the course of about one week Kendall inspected Dighton Rock (and chipped away a sample), compared the inscription to four previous drawings dating back to Cotton Mather (of which he thought Stephen Sewall's was the best, although it was "performed with a feeble and hesitating hand"[24]), executed an oil painting, and recorded local traditions of colonists. While the more learned preferred a Phoenician attribution, he reported, the unlearned "believe that the rock was sculptured by a pirate, either Captain Kyd or Captain Blackbeard, in order to mark the site of buried treasure; and the shore, for more than a hundred fathom on a side, has been dug, in hope of a discovery."[25]

The idea that the rock was associated with buried treasure belonged to a widespread phenomenon in the northeastern United States of treasure hunting, steeped in supernatural practices and fears, which had been flourishing since about 1780.[26] Treasure-digging fever had gripped Maine's Kennebec Valley in 1804, and as Kendall remarked: "The settlers of Maine, like all the other settlers in New England indulge an unconquerable expectation of finding money buried in the earth."[27] Kendall was unaware that in the town of Dighton, notions of buried pirate treasure, with supernatural associations and occult search methods, extended beyond the rock. The Richmond house was said to be haunted, and more than one party dug up the cellar under the direction of clairvoyants who said large sums of money were buried there.[28]

Kendall gathered previously unrecorded local stories that supposedly accounted for the rock's inscription, beyond pirate treasure. One held that one of the first English vessels to visit America spent a winter anchored there, and its crew made the rock's markings; another proposed that the rock recorded the stranding of an English vessel. In support of both stories was still another story, of ship's timbers and an anchor once seen on the shore. There was also a more elaborate version of the purported Indian tradition related by Greenwood: "that in some ages past, a number of white men arrived in the river, in a *bird*; that the white men took Indians into the *bird*, as hostages; that they took fresh water for their consumption at a neighboring spring; that the Indians fell upon and slaughtered the white men at the spring; that, during the affray, *thunder* and *lightning* issued from the *bird*; that the hostages escaped from the *bird*; and that a spring, now called White Man's Spring, and from which there runs a brook, called White Man's Brook, has its name from this event." Dighton Rock thus was "a monument of the adventure of the slaughter of the white men of the *bird*."[29]

The bird was supposed to be portrayed on Dighton Rock. As we have seen, the Reverend John Smith of Dighton had reported to Ezra Stiles in 1789 that a new drawing being prepared included a bird, which a local captain identified as a cassowary. Kendall was assisted by two brothers, Major Hodijah Baylies, a former aide de camp to Washington, and Dr. William Baylies, a judge of the county court of common pleas. Judge Baylies had assisted with the life-size drawing made by Stephen Sewall in 1768, and supervised a more recent drawing that became known in Dighton Rock historiography as the Baylies-Goodwin drawing of 1790.[30] Now the bird was supposed to be a crane. Despite discussing the bird with Judge Baylies and inspecting the rock over the course of six or seven days, Kendall could not find the bird, nor could anyone point it out.[31]

The Indian story of the "white bird" ship, whatever the truth of its origins, had not imprinted itself on the rock, except in the imagination of Judge Baylies's team of local artists. As for the spring, it was about a quarter-mile northeast of the rock, on the property of a farmer, Asa Shove; the farm had been in his family since George Shove acquired the land as one of the original purchasers of Assonet Neck after King Philip's War. Kendall could learn nothing there about the Indian tradition. Shove's son instead told him the spring and the brook had been named in memory of a white hunter, who "being heated with the chace [*sic*], drank freely at the spring, and died in consequence, upon the spot. In regard to the spring, one neighbour had told me that it was a hot spring; and another, that it was remarkable for its intense coldness; and I found it neither warmer nor colder than springs in general."[32]

Kendall was the first person to understand the perceptual challenge in depicting the inscription. James Winthrop's use of printer's ink to lift an impression "shows only the congeries of disjointed members; whereas in the original, the whole is connected and complete," according to Kendall. Chalking the inscriptions "is deceitful in its promises of accuracy; I tried it myself, and found that I falsified the figures at every touch."[33] Kendall did not claim in *Travels* that his own effort was perfectly accurate, but he did adhere to two useful principles that he said his predecessors did not follow: "the first is that of aiming to make the copy neither worse nor better than that of the original; the other, that of being content to leave obscure and nearly indistinct in the copy, that which is obscure and nearly invisible in the original. . . . My wish is, not to show what the same design would have been, in the hands of a skilful [*sic*] artist, furnished with proper tools; but what it really is, in the hands of the artist that performed it."[34]

In October 1807 Kendall visited Salem to show his painting to the prominent local Freemason, the Reverend William Bentley. Kendall in turn was made aware of a revival (or perpetuation) of the Hebrew theory for the rock's inscription, advanced by a young Bostonian and Bentley protégé, Samuel Harris, whose scholarly genius was thought to bear the greatest promise of the age.

IT IS DIFFICULT to know what to make of the extravagant claims for Samuel Harris's brilliance, any more than one can be comfortable with extravagant claims for his friend and mentor, the Reverend William Bentley, pastor of East Church in Salem. Bentley supposedly could read more than twenty languages, including Latin, Greek, Hebrew, Arabic, and Persian, and was fluent in most of the major languages of Europe.[35] In addition to his prominence in Freemasonry, Bentley was a model antiquarian, keen on natural history as well as a collector of coins and rare books, and he knew the leading educators and antiquaries of greater Boston. In Salem, he kept close watch on the comings and goings of its ships, which ranged the world, gathering from them artifacts for his cabinet of curiosities. When the Treaty of Paris of 1783 opened the world to American shipping, the globe's "curiosities" fueled an American enthusiasm for these displays, which could be as large as entire rooms.[36] Bentley also contributed specimens to the cabinet of curiosities of the East India Marine Society (which became the Peabody Essex Museum).[37]

In October 1805 Bentley was visited by one of the Boston area's far-ranging American sea captains, Obadiah Rich, who made passages to the East Indies, studied conch shells, and gathered hard-to-find publications. Rich was accompanied by Samuel Turell (or Turrell), who had opened a cabinet in Boston stocked in part with Native American materials loaned to him in 1802 by the Massachusetts Historical Society (MHS).[38] Bentley had toured Turell's cabinet in 1803: "I see something like taste, & science, but a man impoverished by his genius & industry."[39]

Turell told Bentley he wanted to propose a young friend, Samuel Harris, for membership in the MHS. Harris was twenty-two, an engraver who lived in Boston's north end.[40] Harris would be said to have attended two schools at age ten, such was his thirst for learning, but his modest background had denied him a higher education.[41] Even before meeting Harris, Bentley was primed to expect greatness from the young man: "Who can say that I shall not see American genius ripen in my own times?"[42] Bentley noted after the visit by Rich and Turell that Harris "has displayed taste in his profession & an inclination for Oriental Literature."[43] Harris, Turell, and Rich were part of a circle or club that supported each other's antiquarian enthusiasms, Bentley noted. "They have all engaged the public notice by their efforts without a public education."[44] After Joseph T. Buckingham launched *The Polyanthos*, an illustrated miscellany, in Boston that December, Harris began contributing portraits.[45]

There was a clear yearning for an American genius in the hopes Bentley expressed for Harris before they had even met. Americans had been stung by the criticisms of Guillaume-Thomas Raynal, who in 1774 contended that America had not produced a good poet, a clever mathematician, or a man of genius in a single art or science. There were skills aplenty, but no decided talent in anything.[46] Raynal was rebuked by Jefferson in *Notes on the State of Virginia* and by Thomas Paine in 1791.[47] Harris seems to have been something of a project, a virgin-soil genius to be elevated and refined as a living rejoinder to the slander of Raynal. Harris's chief supporter was soon the Reverend Bentley, as Rich died November 25, 1805, mere weeks after alerting Bentley to Harris's great promise.[48] (As for Turell, he had a serious falling out with the MHS when he refused to return the Native American items on loan to him.)[49] After *The Polyanthos* ceased publication for five years, following the July 1, 1807, issue, Harris around September 1807 began preparatory studies for Harvard, supported by "a number of individuals," of whom Bentley would have been one, that funded him so that he could leave his engraving work and focus on his education.[50] Surely Bentley (who had been a tutor in Latin and Greek during his own Harvard studies) also assisted Harris in his preparations for the admission examination he would undergo in 1808.

Edward Kendall called on the Reverend Bentley on October 13, 1807. "He gave me the best view I had ever had of the Dighton Rock," Bentley noted of Kendall's painting in his diary. "He exhibited the shape of the rock, of the fissures & the shade of the figures that such as were most visible might be easily known."[51] Bentley in turn shared a drawing and a written explanation by Samuel Harris. Kendall was unimpressed. Harris had never seen the rock, instead relying on James Winthrop's drawing, which Kendall considered a poor representation. Kendall left Harris nameless, identifying him only as a "Hebrew scholar, in Boston" in *Travels*. Perhaps this was merciful, for Harris had produced an interpretation (now lost to us) as fanciful as the Phoenician triptych of Court de Gébelin. As Kendall recounted, "he shows that one of the figures is a king; another, his throne and canopy; a third a priest; a fourth an idol, a fifth a foreign ambassador, &c. and, in the intervening parts, he points out Hebrew characters, composing words, which words explain the figures; as *the king—the priest—the idol*. But this gentleman has misemployed his ingenuity, and a single glance at the rock would have robbed him of all disposition to support the hypothesis. There is not, in reality, the smallest reason to doubt, that these sculptures are of Indian work."[52] In his diary, Bentley stated: "I shewed [Kendall] Mr. Harris' letter & the authority of the Palmyrine Characters to which the Marks were compared. Mr. Kendall saw no resemblance of the letters."[53] By "Palmyrine," Bentley meant the script of an Aramaic dialect associated with the Palmyrene Empire of the third century A.D. ruled by Queen Zenobia, which gives some clue as to who Harris thought carved Dighton Rock, and when.

Kendall may not have thought much of Samuel Harris's interpretation of Dighton Rock, but the young Boston engraver could have been responsible for the engraving of Kendall's painting that was published in 1809. The engraving accompanied the letter Kendall wrote to Judge Davis on October 29, 1807—sixteen days after Kendall met with Bentley—when it was published by the American Academy of Arts and Sciences. This initial engraving is less refined than the one made for the Colonial Society of Massachusetts and which was published in 1918. The differences underscore the essential problem with all rock art of achieving an objective representation without resorting to subjective interpretation. Already, Kendall's two-dimensional painting was an artistic interpretation of a three-dimensional rock. Both engravings, in black and white, were in turn interpreting a painting in color. The engravers disagreed on how to depict some of the markings that Kendall rendered in oils with atmospheric obscurity. Kendall in his "Account" for the AAAS noted: "If you find yourself obliged to approach close to some of my figures, and can at last arrive at no certainty as to their outlines, I must beg you to remember, that this will always be your situation, when examining the rock itself."[54] As for the striking differences in various renderings over time, including his own, Kendall advised they were not always "to be attributed to the fault of the copyists, but often to the obscurity of the sculpture, in which every man will see something different from every other. Under these circumstances no perfect copy can ever be made."[55]

Bentley showed Kendall a recent book by Thaddeus Mason Harris, who apparently was no relation to Samuel Harris. Thaddeus Harris graduated from Harvard in 1787 and was poised to become the private secretary of George Washington on graduation when he was disqualified by a bout of smallpox. He returned to Harvard to earn a theology degree in 1789, served as Harvard's librarian from 1791 to 1793, and became the Unitarian minister of the First Parish Church in Dorchester.[56] As noted, he served as chaplain to the Grand Lodge of Massachusetts and published a defense of Freemasonry in 1797. Harris visited the Ohio country in 1803 and published *The Journal of a Tour into the Territory Northwest of the Alleghany Mountains,* an early account of its mounds and petroglyphs, in 1805. An excerpt published in the first issue of *The Polyanthos,* on December 1, 1805, described the mound at Grave Creek. Harris wondered at its maker ("some renowned prince or warrior") and concluded: "we cannot but regret that the name and the glory it was designed to perpetuate are gone—LOST IN THE DARKNESS OF THE GRAVE!"[57] Bentley mentioned in the diary entry for his meeting with Kendall, "the Ohio rocks with marks are in the same position" as Dighton Rock, meaning along a river's edge, and further asserted "these rocks [Kendall] intends to visit."[58]

In December 1808, Thaddeus Harris wrote a curious letter to John Adams, the Boston lawyer, one-term American president, and president and corresponding secretary of the American Academy of Arts and Sciences, to whom Stephen Sewall had recommended Antoine Court de Gébelin for AAAS membership. The letter touched upon the Ohio mounds and rock art, Dighton Rock, and Native American origins. Thaddeus Harris claimed to have come upon road workers in Medford, Massachusetts, in 1787 who had found a cache of square copper coins under a stone. Their design purportedly was that of Tartary coins illustrated in Strahlenberg's volume. Coins rank among the most easily faked archaeological finds, simple to plant and readily available through numismatists. Indeed, Harris's friend Bentley was a coin collector, and Johann Forster coincidentally had sold some Tartarian coins he had collected during a Volga assignment to help make ends meet when he arrived in London.[59] Harris's find alternatively could have been a legitimate oddity of discovery during a period of copper coin counterfeiting and numerous copper minting schemes in the former colonies following the Revolution.[60] Wherever the coins originated, they allowed Harris to assert connections between the Siberian/Tartarian peopling of America, the Ohio mounds, and "inscriptions on rocks on the banks of the Ohio and at Taunton," by which he meant Dighton Rock.[61]

KENDALL'S 1807 LETTER to Judge Davis differed from the *Travels* of 1809 in being so steeped in Masonic allusions that it might as well have been a discourse to a lodge membership. "I was greatly struck with the regularity of its features," he wrote, transforming the boulder into a flat-topped, three-sided pyramid.[62] Even before the excitement generated by Napoleon's invasion of Egypt in 1798, pyramids were *ne plus ultra* expressions of the Masonic craft. Kendall also remarked that a few inches beneath the sand the rock "is terminated suddenly by an horizontal ledge. . . . Precisely indeed, as every block of stone, partly exposed, and partly hidden, is treated by a mason."[63] Kendall's description brings to mind a frontispiece illustration in the 1781 regulations of Neuf soeurs lodge, which depicted an elongated pyramid set atop a pedestal.[64] Kendall noted the nature of chisel marks with terminology a mason would understand. His awkward analogy of linked elements of the inscription as being *joining-hand* in nature is a dead giveaway to Freemasonry's handshakes of recognition between members. Kendall also ventured less opaquely: "if, as there may be reason to believe, the pyramid is a figure in masonry, originating in Egypt out of local circumstances," then the fact that that the rock was a hand-crafted pyramid "may be made to give support to theories, false or true, of the transatlantic origin of the inscription."[65] While he decided that the rock's shape was natural, he ventured that it had been selected for the inscription because it was in a ready-made pyramidal form.

Kendall observed in his "Account" that the authorship of the rock's inscription came down to two candidates: Native Americans ("the savage follower of the fishery and the chase . . . the inhabitants of the surrounding forests") or migrationist voyagers ("learned circumnavigators . . . sojourners from the ancient seats of arts and civilization").[66] Kendall concluded that Dighton Rock, like other inscribed rocks he had seen or read about, was incontrovertibly the work of Indians, with an inscription much older than a date merely preceding the European arrival in America.[67] Still, Kendall proposed, "the design has proceeded from an artist not unacquainted with pen or pencil; or at least from one, whose taste has been influenced, though possibly without his knowledge, by the use of those instruments, in other hands than his."[68] There was more in this vein of cryptic influence. He also thought that three figures with human heads were portrayed standing on some kind of base or pedestal.[69] Whoever inscribed the rock "was not unacquainted with works of art, of a better and higher character," and he reiterated the artist's imitations of "pen writing, drawing, and statuary." The artist "has evidently intended to describe equilateral angles, planes parallel to the horizon, and right and perpendicular lines; but he has failed in almost every instance." He "wished to imitate figures, determined with the precision of the rule and compasses."[70] Kendall could not have been more blatant about invoking the core Masonic symbols of the compass and square as well as the geometric precision of "practical" masonry. Kendall was insinuating that either the secret arts of ages past, now preserved by Freemasons, had once been known to the Indians' forebears—this was the degeneration theory for Native Americans in its most esoteric form—or, more likely, that the Indians who carved Dighton Rock were crudely imitating ancient works left behind by the original, more advanced migrants to America, to whom they were unrelated, without understanding the arts of their vanished influencers. It was no wonder Kendall intended to head west, in the direction of the mysterious mounds and petroglyphs that Thaddeus Harris had described.

IN HIS LETTER to Judge Davis, Kendall mentioned an alleged reading of the inscription by "some Mohawk Indians" who were shown a drawing while in Boston. Kendall offered no dates or names for the reading, nor did he reveal how he gathered the anecdote. The Mohawks "declared its meaning to be, that a dangerous animal, represented by the animal on the rock, had been killed at the place immortalized; that the human figures represented the persons, whom the animal killed; and that the others denote other parts of the affair."[71] Kendall did not doubt that the animal was depicted: "its character is strongly, and it may be presumed faithfully marked."[72]

As Isaac Greenwood's drawing of 1730 only depicted the top half of the inscription (the rest being under water when he visited), the first surviving drawing to show this figure was Stephen Sewall's of 1768, and every rendering that followed, including the engravings of Kendall's painting, depicted it in similar style. Edmund Burke Delabarre called "a peculiar quadruped with horns" one of the few images on the rock that viewers agreed on, and he thought there were two, side by side.[73] Delabarre proposed that a drawing of Dighton Rock had been shown to four Mohawk chiefs who visited Boston in 1744.[74] When Britain declared war on France in 1744, a delegation of Haudenosaunee, led by four sachems, did visit Boston. Hendrick Peters Theyanoguin, a Mohawk, was accompanied by two Cayuga, remembered as James and Jonathan, and an Onondaga, Joseph.[75]

There is sound reason to believe that these four sachems were the basis of the Mohawk story. John Winthrop had attempted his drawing, now lost to us, in July 1743. Winthrop in his 1774 letter to Timothy Hollis noted: "on the lower side, near the middle, there seems to be some resemblance of a quadruped with horns."[76] Winthrop must have depicted this animal figure in his 1743 attempt. The Haudenosaunee delegation spent several days in Boston and Cambridge in early July 1744, entertained by leading citizens, among them Governor Jonathan Belcher, who certainly could have included Winthrop and/or Judge Danforth.[77] Unfortunately, no pages for Winthrop's itinerary survive from May to August in his 1744 almanac. Still, an examination of his drawing by the delegation may have been why Winthrop preferred an Indigenous provenance.

Delabarre would relegate the Mohawk story to "an extraordinary collection of theories clustering about the old rock like barnacles."[78] Neither Kendall nor Delabarre knew enough about Indigenous traditions to recognize the potential significance of the Mohawk account. Most theorists concluded the drawing depicted a deer, but Kendall, who inspected it closely, noted its hybridity. "Its body is crossed, in near equal divisions, with bars or stripes. It is spotted. Its head is long and delicate. It wears horns. Its feet are paws.—Already we see reason to suspect, that this is a creature of fancy, made up of the members of different animals; and this assuredly must be the case, if the line above its back, and which is wanting in all the previous draughts, forms, as it strikes the eye, the wing of an insect."[79] This glyph more than likely depicted a major other-than-human entity in the cosmology of Eastern Woodlands peoples. In the Ojibwa/Anishinabe and greater Algonquian belief system, the Great Cat (or Panther or Lynx) is Michipeshu (Mishipizheu, *mishi-bizhii*), who is depicted with horns (which signify power) and travels in the company of a horned snake (Ginebik, *mshi-ginebig*).[80] In some traditions, the Great Cat and the Horned Snake are manifestations of the same entity.[81]

According to F. Kent Reilly, Eastern Woodlands peoples divided the world into at least three levels: the Above World, the Beneath World, and the Earthly Plane: "The Great Serpent not only dwelt in the Beneath World as the master of beneath and underwater creatures but reigned as Lord of the Realm of the Dead. This powerful supernatural presence was envisioned as a netherworld being who could assume the form of a Great Panther. With its elongated tail, this Great Panther could roil the waters of lakes, rivers, and ponds into whirlpools and thus caused many deaths among humankind. Nevertheless, this fearsome creature's power could help an individual courageous enough to seek and channel it."[82] The noticeably long tail in the Sewall drawing, in this riverside location, does give the viewer pause and would seem to discount a deer, as does Kendall's confidence that it had wings.[83] Michael Pomedli also notes that, to the Ojibwa, "serpents had ambivalent characteristics: on the one hand, they were sources of disease and dread, and on the other . . . they exhibited curative powers."[84] Dighton Rock's stripe-bodied horned quadruped was not unlike the Great Cat depicted in 1830 by an American interpreter at Sault. Ste. Marie, John Tanner, in the song of an Ojibwa shaman, Chi-ah-ba. As Tanner explained: "The wild cat here figured has horns, and his residence is under the ground; but he has a master, Gitche-a-nah-mi-e-be-zhew (the great under-ground wild cat,) who is, as some think, Matche-Manito himself, their evil spirit, or devil."[85] Variants in the form assumed by the underwater spirit or Cat Monster in so-called Mississippian and Southeastern Ceremonial Complex art include winged, antlered serpents and long-tailed quadrupeds.[86]

A Mohawk man seeing the drawing would have understood the Eastern Woodlands cosmology, as the northern Iroquoian mythical reality was essentially the same as that of their Algonquian- and Siouan-speaking neighbors.[87] Teiaiagon, a Seneca village at Baby Point in present-day Toronto, yielded to archaeologists a comb dated to the 1680s that depicted the horned, long-tailed panther.[88] As George R. Hamell has described the role of "long-tails" in the Iroquoian Huron-Wendat and Seneca cultures, the water's edge was a threshold between the physical and spiritual worlds where someone could seek a vision or an exchange in the form of charms or medicines with other-than-human beings considered to be kin, or grandfathers: "These potent grandfathers are characteristically sleek of body and long of tail. Their dwelling place is the underwater realm where the chiefs of supernatural game animals hold council, and which is inhabited also by the underwater panther, the great serpent, and the dragon (i.e. composite panther-serpent). These beings control the waters, and their antlered or horned appearance signifies their chiefly status and power. They may also serve as personal guardian spirits, animal medicine society patrons, and protectors of the people."[89] The Mohawk interpretation of "a dangerous animal" that had killed several people depicted elsewhere on the rock's surface was consistent with this potentially lethal spirit entity. In addition, the apparent X shapes above and to the left as well as other hourglass shapes on the rock could have depicted the thunderbeings (*animikiig*, also *nimkiik*) and thunderbirds (*binesiiwag*) of the sky world, as art historian Ruth B. Phillips has shown that the angular forms of the hourglass, triangle, and chevron are used to depict them in Anishinabe material culture.[90]

With the detection of a horned quadruped on the face of Dighton Rock that was covered for parts of the day by tidewater, the first opportunity arose to understand the significance in Eastern Woodlands cosmology of such marked stones. But the Mohawk anecdote Kendall heard probably was garbled by colonists, and was not understood to convey a deadly encounter with a major spirit entity. Kendall doubted the Mohawk interpretation because, to his artistic eye, the horned figure was placed too insignificantly to be the center of a dramatic narrative. He did not understand that if the horned quadruped depicted a beneath-world entity, its location might have been deliberately placed below the tideline in defiance of a Eurocentric notion of pictorial composition, so that it would emerge twice daily with the receding tide. Kendall asked for explanations of the rock from Native Americans, but "Indians themselves, even those of the same language and country as those by whom it was probably executed, are unable to offer any explanation of its meaning. From such Indians, I have in such instances obtained conjectures as to particular parts, but never any satisfactory glimpse of the whole."[91] Were it not for his determination to hear a unified translation of the entire surface, Kendall might have gathered useful insights for individual glyphs, or groups of glyphs, from Native Americans. Instead, he disregarded whatever he heard, sharing none of it in print.

KENDALL NEVER MADE IT to the Ohio territory to see its inscribed rocks and earthen mounds, and was left to summarize what he had learned about inscribed stones based solely on his New England tour. His ideas had evolved significantly when he published *Travels* in 1809. His account of Dighton Rock was drained of all Masonic allusion and innuendo; not even its alleged pyramidal form was worthy of mention. Instead, Kendall incorporated Dighton Rock into a "psycho-theology" theory of paganism.

Kendall was concerned with the role of stones worldwide in supernatural beliefs, and his discussion of these stones began with an account of the Sacrifice Rocks on the roadside between Plymouth and Sandwich:

One of them may be six feet high, and the other four; and both of ten or twelve feet in length: and they differ in nothing, as to their figure, from the masses of granite and other rock, which are scattered over the surface of all the adjacent country. All that distinguishes them is the crowns of oak and pine branches which they bear, irregularly heaped, and of which some are fresh, some fading, some decayed. These branches the Indians place there, from motives which they but obscurely explain, and for doing which their white neighbours therefore generally suppose that they have no reason to give. When questioned, they rarely go further than to say, that they do so because they have been taught that it is the right to do it, or because their fathers did so before them: if they add any thing to this, it is, that they expect blessings from the observance of the practice, and evils from the neglect.

But to whom is this worship offered? To a *manito*; and by *manito*, through the religious prejudices of the whites, is usually understood *a devil.*[92]

On the road from Plymouth to Sandwich, Kendall passed through the Native American community at Herring Pond, one of several Pokanoket (Wampanoag) communities on upper Cape Cod that were under the guidance of Christian missionaries and Indigenous ministers and teachers.[93] As Ives Goddard and Kathleen Bragdon have noted, "No history of the Native peoples of the upper Cape, the Pokanoket nation, is available."[94] Kendall's visit, however brief, thus stands as a rare firsthand account of these "Christian Indians" only a few decades after the American Revolution.

Kendall was challenged in his perceptions of what a North American Indian ought to be. As throughout Massachusetts, the Indians here "are said to be mixed, that is, to have the children of Europeans and Africans among them." He met several on the road to Sandwich, "particularly women, half Indian and half negro," who were not recognizably "Indian" to him: they were well dressed, with good, clean shoes and stockings. He thought one woman was more black than Indigenous, in both physical appearance and conviviality, "for the unmixed Indian is what he has often been described, serious and taciturn, and shy of access." His walking companion "descanted on the condition of her *nation* (for it is thus the Indians always denominate their communities) in that language of submission to the evil that is inevitable, and of enjoyment of the good that offers, which appears to me to characterize the negro; but proclaimed herself an Indian, at the same time."[95] Here was an empathetic Westerner captured in the full confusion of a confrontation with a living Native American of New England who defied his expectations of what an "Indian" should be. In spite of being in the extended conversational presence of a member of the Pokanoket Wampanoag, Kendall did not report any conversation about the Sacrifice Rocks, or about Dighton Rock, which was located in the lands occupied by the Pokanoket before the diaspora caused by King Philip's War. The only question he recorded asking her was "whether or not she thought that the Indians were really more disposed to drunkenness than the whites, or only more easily affected by liquor."[96]

Instead, Kendall questioned the missionary and pastor at Mashpee on Nantucket about the Sacrifice Rocks. Gideon Hawley was a Yale graduate who had served at a missionary station to the Haudenosaunee at Ononhagh-wage (Onondaga) before the outbreak of the Seven Years War, and had been at Mashpee since 1758 under the sponsorship of England's Society for Propagating the Gospel among the Indians. Hawley died one month shy of his eightieth birthday on October 3, 1807, soon after Kendall met him.[97] As we have seen, Stephen Sewall had provided Antoine Court de Gébelin with a Wampanoag grammar composed by Hawley, but there is no reason to believe Kendall was aware of the missionary's past connection to Court de Gébelin's work. Hawley recounted for Kendall having once seen two Indian women dragging a young pine tree to place it atop one of their Sacrifice Rocks. "It was so large and heavy, that the undertaking almost exceeded their strength."[98] The missionary, Kendall reported, "saw the Indian sacrifices as they ought to be seen. They are offered to the overruling providence, wherever it may reside, and by whatever name it may be called."[99]

Anthropologist Craig N. Cipolla has drawn connections between stone, memory, and ancestors among New England peoples. He notes that Frank Speck recorded the Mohegan-Pequot gloss for stone as *sun*, with *sunjum* meaning sachem, or tribal leader, and that the practice of heaping stone and brush had been observed in 1624 by Edward Winslow, who called these assemblages "memory piles." According to Cipolla, "Most tribal groups of the Northeast currently refer to stones as either 'grandmothers' or grandfathers.'" Leaving offerings on (or with) stone may have been part of "the process of easing the recently dead into the community of ancestors in deep time, a process of symbolic petrification."[100]

Sacred rocks otherwise were widespread in Algonquian-speaking lands. The German traveler Johann Georg Kohl, in recounting his experiences around Lake Superior in the late 1850s, would report a stone called *rocher de Otamigan*. A young Ojibwa, Otamigan, had paused to rest on a trail, and as he "regarded the rock opposite him, it seemed as if it were oscillating, then advanced to him, made a bow, and went back again to its old place . . . he straightaways felt the greatest veneration for the rock, and ever after considered it his 'protecting god.' Now, I am told, he never goes past it without laying some tobacco on the rock as a sacrifice."[101] Kendall found an account of a place of offering in the writings of the eighteenth-century fur trader and explorer Alexander Mackenzie. Mackenzie had reported that Portage du Bonnet at the south end of Lake Winnipeg "derives its name from the custom the Indians have of crowning stones, laid in a circle on the highest rock in the portage, with wreaths of herbage and branches."[102] Kendall was confident that the practice he had seen at the Sacrifice Rocks between Plymouth and

Sandwich was part of a larger, enduring Algonquian cultural tradition. Despite his own reticence to engage Native Americans directly on questions of their enduring culture, Kendall's writing revealed that some 130 years after the trauma and dislocation resulting from King Philip's War, not only Native Americans, but their traditional beliefs as well, could be discovered in southern New England, if one only looked for them. Unfortunately, where Dighton Rock specifically was concerned, Kendall declined to record those beliefs.

Kendall left unaddressed the long and unhappy experience of Native Americans corralled onto the island "plantation" administered by Hawley, where their freedoms had been repeatedly restricted and rescinded by the state.[103] The imposition of a Board of Overseers at Mashpee in 1788 had deprived the Indians of civil rights, and as a member of the board, Hawley received a "donation" of 200 acres from the tribe.[104] Kendall may have absorbed the wisdom of Hawley as to the degenerative state of his Indian charges, as Hawley once recalled how on his arrival at the Mashpee mission, "The Mashpee Indians were clad according to the English mode: but a half-naked savage was less disagreeable than Indians who had lost their independence."[105] If Kendall's acceptance of the Pokanoket as genuine Indians was at best reluctant, one can appreciate how New Englanders could persuade themselves that there was nothing genuine about such mixed-blood (especially *Negro* mixed-blood) communities, and that these communities were not worth protecting or preserving. The Wampanoag at Mashpee would at last secure federal tribal recognition in 2007, after the Wampanoag at Aquinnah (Gay Head) achieved the same in 1987.[106]

THE SACRIFICE ROCKS LAUNCHED Kendall into his six chapters on the universalities of paganism as expressed in "Stones of Power," which he associated with hallowed stones of antiquity, including the Black Stone at Mecca, the stones that Jacob used for a pillow in his dream of a ladder to heaven and then assembled into a commemorative pillar (Genesis 28:10–18), and the sacred stone of Delphi.[107] If Kendall was building a case for a golden-age source from which all human knowledge migrated or diffused, he failed to articulate it precisely, although he did declare that Stones of Power and stone circles "are of a remoter date than the druids themselves, and of a much wider diffusion."[108] Druids were favorites of Gothicism as well as Freemasonry, and were renowned for tree worship, but Kendall never claimed that Native American examples of stones with sacrifices or offerings of branches and trees had an Old World or root-civilization origin.[109] Rather, Kendall's statement that "paganism teaches what may be called a psycho-theology" suggests the essence of his argument.[110] The supernatural power vested in stones was a universal human response to the natural world. Kendall may have been far ahead of his time in proposing a theory of parallelism, of independent origins of similar beliefs and cultural practices, based on fundamental human psychology, that precluded the need for migrationist or diffusionist explanations. We will never know, as Kendall did not return to the subject. Despite being a fellow of London's Society of Antiquaries, he never contributed to *Archaeologia*. An oddity of Kendall's extended discussion of Stones of Power is that he did not address the standing stones allegedly found by La Vérendrye, as Pehr Kalm had related, despite being aware of (and citing) Kalm's *Travels into North America* on the subject of Fort Saint-Frederic in volume 3.[111]

Kendall had an epiphany at Bellows Falls in Rockingham, Vermont (which he had not yet visited when he wrote the "Account" letter to Judge Davis), where petroglyphs first noticed in 1789 provided "conclusive evidence" that Dighton Rock was a Native American artifact.[112] "Unlike the sculptures of the [Dighton] Writing Rock," Kendall wrote, "they are parts of no connected work, but are scattered over the face of the rock, in the most even and eligible places."[113] Why Kendall did not also regard Dighton Rock as a gathering of unconnected images is a mystery. Where Isaac Greenwood had thought Dighton Rock was beyond the capability of idle, primitive people without higher motivations, Kendall now argued that only such primitive people would have produced such inscriptions. The markings at Bellows Falls were "too rude, too insignificant, and too evidently without depth of meaning, to be attributed to Phoenicians or Carthaginians. No person will carry European vanity so far, as to contend, that there is any thing here, above the level of Indian genius. But, if Indians were the authors of these sculptures, then Indians were the authors of the [Dighton] Writing Rock also. The style of drawing is the same; the style of sculpture is the same."[114] A further lesson was that the Indians at Bellows Falls obviously had tools and techniques that could remove granite, which meant that the softer stone of Dighton Rock was well within their carving capabilities.[115]

In his initial assessment of the rock in 1807, Kendall ventured that "it was wrought on some solemn occasion, or for some solemn purpose, either civil, military, or religious. It may be a memorial, a monition, or an offering of piety."[116] Kendall in *Travels* still believed the markings were very ancient but now argued that Native Americans made them for reasons known only to themselves. That the markings were Indigenous was incontrovertible. "Though the Writing Rock is a monument as rude as it is unintelligible, yet it deserves attention, as well for what it really is, as for what various observers have supposed it to be: it is not a monument of the Phoenicians, nor of the Carthaginians, nor of the lost tribe of Israel, nor of Prince Madoc, nor of Captain Blackbeard, nor of Captain Kyd; but it is a monument of the sculpture of the ancient inhabitants of America, whether Narragansetts or others."[117] He added: "There is not, in reality, the smallest reason to doubt, that these sculptures are of Indian work."[118] Whether he still believed more than that is another matter. Garlands and laurel wreaths were fixtures in Masonic imagery. The frontispiece drawing for the regulations of Neuf soeurs depicted the elongated pyramid entwined in garlands; Voltaire had been crowned with a laurel wreath at his Neuf soeurs induction. The coincidence of greenery laid by Native American on stones of sacrifice and the festooning leaves of Freemasonry must have registered with Kendall. But he said no more.

EDWARD AUGUSTUS KENDALL had found Dighton Rock fully immersed in Yankee folklore. In ascribing meanings to its markings, American colonists behaved like Native Americans who interpreted elements of their landscape in the process Keith Basso has called "place making." With this universal tool of the imagination, historical knowledge is produced and reproduced; historical understandings are altered and recast. This widespread form of imaginative activity, says Basso, is also a form of cultural activity.[119] In the case of Dighton Rock, the process of Euro-American place-making was also a form of appropriation. The landscape (including the rock) that was once a locus of the Wampanoag people had been seized by colonists, and along with physical and legal possession came an ongoing process of cultural dispossession. The rock was being reimagined and denuded of Indigenous significance, save for "Indian traditions" that may only have been colonial fictions and as such were an erasure of actual cultural memory.

The efforts by Kendall and Judge Davis to interpret the rock as an Indigenous artifact underscored the ongoing issue of the distinction between affinity and meaning: it was possible to be correct (in a general sense) about the identity of the culture that produced such rock art, that it was Indigenous, without necessarily being correct in one's interpretation of the inscription—in Davis's case, that it depicted a hunting scene. While Kendall was correct in his assessment of affinity, to make his case in *Travels* that the markings were Indigenous, he resorted to the same stereotype of Native Americans that had served Greenwood in arguing to the contrary. Kendall allowed his ignorance of Indigenous culture to lead him to conclude that Indigenous people themselves were ignorant, and that there was nothing worthy of inquiry behind the images. Because he expected the rock to bear a single, unified inscription, he disregarded whatever Native Americans told him about individual elements. The significance of the horned quadruped eluded him, as it did everyone else who recorded it. In Kendall's painting and account, Michipeshu may well have surfaced, only to disappear unrecognized, much as the image on Dighton Rock was revealed for parts of every day by a diurnal tide.

Initially, in the "Account," Kendall had stressed: "Whatever be its origin or signification, it belongs to the history of America, and perhaps to that of the world," and he urged that the rock be removed to Boston for preservation and further study. "The rock and its inscription are but little valued in their own neighborhood," he assured his readers, and proposed that treasure hunters might dynamite it in search of pirate gold. Failing that, he feared it could be buried beneath a wharf or shipyard.[120] Kendall was the first person to argue for the rock's relocation, but two years later, in *Travels*, there was no such pleading. "The Writing Rock is by far the most important of the sculptured rocks in New England," he concluded, but left unanswered *how* it was important. Kendall probably thought that if it was a mere Indian inscription, then it was rude, unintelligible, and uninteresting. But if it was an imitative record by Indians of esoteric knowledge possessed by an ancient people—who were either the ancestors of the Indians, or a superior culture they once encountered in ages past—then to his mind Dighton Rock mattered. Kendall left an impression that would become more explicit in historical inquiry by the turn of the twentieth century: Native Americans had no history worth recording or preserving, and in fact could not possess a history, as they lacked G. W. F. Hegel's preconditions of written records and a state.[121]

For all his faults, Kendall deserves credit for coming closer than anyone to grasping the relationship between markings and stone in Dighton Rock, to understanding that there might be something sacred about the stone itself. With every other reproduction but those of Kendall's painting before the advent of photography, the artist aimed to lift an inscription from a rock's surface and present it as black lines on paper, treating it as a challenge for translation. Kendall, in contrast, saw a boulder that existed in three dimensions in a particular environment, from which the markings were inseparable.

In his "Account" of 1807, Kendall wondered about the significance of marks on rocks in riverside locations that were at times submerged, and that seemed to face in the same direction, but he did not pursue these intriguing commonalities as he gave over his analysis to Stones of Power in *Travels*. A mind less inclined to conclude that the markings "evidently were without depth of meaning" might have asked what significance there could be in these sites, as we now understand the sacred significance of places where rock, sky, and water converge in Eastern Woodlands cosmologies. As much as he recognized the persistence of an "Algonquin" practice of "sacrifice" of branches at sacred rocks in Massachusetts, too little was known about Indigenous belief systems for Kendall to make the leap across the threshold at which he was perched. A profound irony of Kendall's analysis was that in his concern with esoteric Masonic symbolism, he was ignorant of the esotericism of shamanic Algonquian rock art, with its layers of multiple meaning, literal and figurative, and its ambiguity or instability of identity and form in living and nonliving beings. Kendall left Native Americans of the past as ignorant savages without a history worth contemplating, and the ones of the present-day in southern New England as perplexing mulattoes. He handed Dighton Rock back to Native Americans in *Travels* because it was beneath the arts and minds of more civilized peoples who were heirs to an ancient root wisdom embodied by Freemasonry. But because Native Americans were not on hand at Dighton to receive or defend the rock, other Western theorists would step forward with fresh acts of place-making.

CHAPTER FIVE

Colonization's New Epistemology

American Archaeology and the Road to the Trail of Tears

Samuel Harris passed his Harvard entrance exam and was admitted with advanced standing as a Junior Sophister in October 1808.[1] His eccentric reading of Dighton Rock had no apparent bearing on his reputation—perhaps it was even enhanced—and he was on the verge of graduating, with an oration in Hebrew assigned to him for Commencement, when he drowned while bathing in the Charles River on July 7, 1810.[2] "I expected in him the Greatest Orientalist our Country has ever produced," a devastated Reverend Bentley wrote that day. "From no man had I greater expectations as my attentions during his life abundantly prove. In a moment our thoughts perish."[3] When Harris's body was recovered and buried three days later, Bentley noted: "The public mind is not insensible to the real worth of this man & scholar."[4] Eight days later, Bentley was still reeling: "Mr. Harris had more genius than could be found in the government of the University."[5]

This extraordinary regard for Harris was not limited to Bentley. When *The Polyanthos* resumed publishing in 1812, a portrait of Harris appeared on the cover, and a tribute to him from *The Harvard Lyceum* of July 28, 1810, was reprinted.[6] The *Lyceum's* article was rapturous in its estimation of Harris. His language skills defied belief, and there was no area of study in which Harris did not deserve the highest rank. He was a master of both modern and ancient astronomy, and as a historian, "he was intimately acquainted with every important fact in the chronology of Asia, Europe, and America. His conjectures respecting the migrations and settlements of ancient nations were extremely ingenious, and seldom unsatisfactory."[7]

Native American languages, the *Lyceum* article continued, had claimed "a considerable share of his interest and attention . . . had he lived, the result of his labours in this department would have been a copious and systematical grammar of the Indian languages of North America. The specimen he has left of this intended work, is a proof of his success in these investigations."[8] Bentley, to the contrary, observed on July 18, 1810: "I am told that Mr. Harris had prepared a Hebrew Grammar for the press as the first part of his researches."[9] The Hebrew and Native American grammar projects may not have been unrelated. Delabarre searched for Harris's papers in Harvard's library a century after his death, and could find nothing of the supposedly copious materials, save a single worksheet devoted to his Dighton Rock interpretation, with letterforms arranged in three columns. Harris seems to have been hunting for them in the 1804 Winthrop drawing. The first column was labeled "Siberian," which may have been inspired by image examples in Strahlenberg; the second was labeled "Iceland," and thus was runic. The third was called "American," and, as Delabarre noted, "It is evident that Harris regarded them as ancient Phoenician forms of Hebrew letters."[10] At the least, Harris seemed to have been following Vallancey's lead and was planning to argue that the Algonquian language was a form of Hebrew-derived Phoenician, which would have upheld Stiles's apparent belief that Dighton Rock was carved by Phoenicians ancestral to local Native Americans.

Samuel Harris's genius may have been as much a hallucination as his Dighton Rock interpretation, a product of almost hysterical wishful thinking by mentors like the Reverend Bentley who hoped to answer the criticisms of Raynal with a virgin-soil American genius. Harris's death came at a time when interest in philology (the structure, historical development, and relationships of languages) and semiotics (the study of signs and symbols), and especially decipherment, were at an apex. The discovery of the Rosetta Stone in Egypt in 1798, with a single message repeated in three scripts, had launched a multinational race to decipher it that would be won by France's Jean-François Champollion in 1822. Harris's stillborn studies of Dighton Rock, with the worksheet of three scripts, sound suspiciously like an attempt to turn Dighton Rock into an American Rosetta Stone.

Had Harris lived, he may have outgrown his youthful exuberance, but he may also only have done further harm to an already problematic understanding of Native American culture and antiquity. Harris died two years before the formation of the American Antiquarian Society (AAS) at Worcester, Massachusetts, in 1812.[11] Its library received a bequest of more than 900 volumes from Harris's mentor, the Reverend Bentley, who also furnished its cabinet with curiosities.[12] Given Harris's friends and mentors, he would have been a prime candidate to contribute to the first volume of the society's influential *Archaeologia Americana*, which appeared in 1820, and his ideas on Native American origins surely would have engaged the Mound Builders with "a certain ingenuity and originality of conjecture," as the *Lyceum* article had praised his work. In the absence of Harris, theories of American antiquity still managed to strike out in adventurous directions. Those theories were concerned fundamentally with the mystery of the so-called Mound Builders, which dominated the first volume of *Archaeologia Americana*, but theorizing over Dighton Rock continued to be a catalyst for how the continent's past was hypothesized to the point of unassailable fact, only now with fatal implications for many living Native Americans.

IN 1816, another theory surfaced in France for Dighton Rock, more bizarre than that of Antoine Court de Gébelin's Phoenicians or Samuel Harris's Palmyrenes. In 1816 Charles-Léopold Mathieu had published at Nancy a purported translation of a Chinese poem in a twenty-eight-page monograph, *Le printemps*, into which Mathieu insinuated the Dighton Rock inscription.[13] Mathieu's effort might have remained buried in antiquarian obscurity, but for the skeptical attentions of Samuel Latham Mitchill, who took considerable interest in American antiquity and the nature of Native Americans. The American-born Mitchill bore impeccable intellectual credentials: he was trained as a physician in Edinburgh and then as a lawyer in America. He was a professor of chemistry and natural history at Columbia College from 1792 to 1801 and at the New York College of Physicians and Surgeons from 1808 to 1820, and of botany and materia medica from 1820 to 1826. He was cofounder (and chief editor for more than twenty-three years) in 1797 of a leading scientific journal, *The Medical Repository of Original Essays and Intelligence, Relative to Physic, Surgery, Chemistry, and Natural History*. And he was founder and president (1817 to 1823) of the Lyceum of Natural History of New York City.[14] Mitchill was "an avid dabbler in many areas of science, from chemistry and mineralogy to biology and a host of applied sciences," and his own research led to improvements in gunpowder, detergents, and disinfectants.[15] He was also active in politics as a congressman and senator from New York.

Mitchill probably learned of the obscure French tract through his interest in mineralogy and explosives, as there was a Charles-Léopold Mathieu who was a French expert in mining, gunpowder, and pyrotechnics.[16] This individual was unlikely to have been the author of *Le printemps*.[17] But as the two Mathieus shared a name, were both from Nancy, and the gunpowder expert evidently was an older man, they could have been father and son. The Charles-Léopold Mathieu of *Le printemps*, born in 1756, was a deputy of the Parlement de Nancy under the prerevolutionary monarchy, a professor at the *écoles centrales* of Tulle and Autun, and a lawyer at the royal court of Nancy under the Restoration of 1814 and *la monarchie de Juillet* of 1830. This Mathieu earned the honorific *homme de lettres* by publishing at Paris and Nancy between 1799 and 1834 a series of brochures, *Le Printemps* among them, that were in Paul Durrieu's estimation "rather ridiculous . . . a heap of veritable nonsense."[18] Mitchill, alert to the works of Charles-Léopold

Mathieu the explosives expert, probably happened upon the pseudohistorical fantasies of Charles-Léopold Mathieu the lawyer and Louis XVIII acolyte.

Mitchill discussed Mathieu's Dighton Rock interpretation in a College of Physicians and Surgeons discourse in November 1816, then addressed it in the August 1817 issue of *The American Monthly Magazine and Critical Review*. Mathieu made no mention of his countryman Court de Gébelin's interpretation, based on the Sewall drawing, but relied instead (as Samuel Harris had) on James Winthrop's 1788 drawing, published in 1804. Winthrop had not offered an opinion as to its provenance or meaning, an omission Mathieu rectified with an extravagance seldom witnessed in the history of the rock's interpretation. Mathieu's interpretation, as indicated by its full title, *Le printemps, chant du poëme chinois des Saisons, traduit en vers français et mêlé d'allusions au règne de Louis XVIII*, was an elaborate if roundabout paean to the Bourbon king. Like Ezra Stiles in his unpublished 1790 paper and Olf Rudbeks in his pioneering Gothicism, Mathieu enlisted the myth of the lost continent of Atlantis. In an explanatory note to his translation of the Chinese poem (it is beyond the scope of this book to determine whether the original Chinese poem existed), Mathieu contended the Chinese numerical system was the same as that employed in Atlantis. An Atlantean expedition led by In, the son of In-dios, king of Atlantis, had created the Dighton Rock inscription in the year of the world 1902. The Atlanteans had arrived at the rock "for the purpose of concluding a treaty of 'commerce and amity' with the Americans," as Mitchill explained Mathieu's interpretation—which sounded like Court de Gébelin's memorial to peace and friendship between the Phoenicians and the Native Americans. According to Mathieu, Prince In of Atlantis went on to found a distinguished family in China, and was still alive in the time of Yao, "in the year 2296, being 48 years after the utter submersion of the island of Atlantis in the *Ogygian* deluge."[19] There was more in this vein, and as Mitchill remarked dryly, "We may safely recommend it to the reader to believe as much of it as he can."[20]

At the same time Mitchill was disparaging Mathieu's Dighton Rock fantasy, Mitchill's insatiable and varied curiosity was confronting the puzzle of the Mound Builders. In 1820 Mitchill contributed to *Archaeologia Americana* multiple letters and lectures on the provenance of the mounds and the nature of Native Americans. The appearance of the American Antiquarian Society's first volume of "transactions and collections" has been hailed as marking the beginning of the discipline of American archaeology.[21] Bruce G. Trigger argued that "scientific" archaeology "originated early in the nineteenth century in Scandinavia and diffused from there to Scotland and Switzerland and eventually throughout Europe," while "prehistoric" archaeology "developed in America within the context of an awareness of what was happening in Europe."[22] However you wish to date it, the emergence of the American discipline was driven by the exploitation of the vast resources attributed to the Mound Builders. The Ohio Valley's mysteries alone were made use of "by a veritable Who's Who of American science in the nineteenth century," according to Stephen Williams.[23] Most of the first volume of *Archaeologia Americana* was devoted to Caleb Atwater's comprehensive 154-page illustrated report on the earthworks of Ohio and other locales, and contributions by society members like Mitchill addressed them as well.

If archaeology as an emerging discipline was fundamentally about basing interpretations on rigorous processes of excavation and site recording, which set it apart from occult-tinged treasure hunting, the men who practiced it (or held forth on its results) were still antiquaries at heart. And while American archaeology may have been striking westward, beyond Dighton Rock, the theories this relic inspired retained intellectual currency as the second decade of the nineteenth century witnessed a coalescing of trends in the multiple-migration displacement theory. The "Tartarian hordes" scenario, which divorced ancestral Native Americans from any remarkable American relic and had been argued initially for Dighton Rock by Vallancey, became scientific fact through the Mound Builder investigations in *Archaeologia Americana*. The preface to volume 1 considered "confirmed" that the earthworks "were erected by a race of men widely different from any tribe of North American Indians, known in modern times."[24]

To understand the contribution of Samuel Latham Mitchill to this theorizing, we need to begin with his close associate, De Witt Clinton. Best known perhaps for his promotion and completion in 1825 of the Erie Canal, Clinton was a United States senator from New York from 1802 to 1815 and governor of New York from 1817 until his death in 1828.[25] Clinton was also a prominent Freemason who in 1806 pronounced the fraternity "co-extensive with the enlightened part of the human race."[26] Such enthusiasm for science and education saw brethren sponsor educational endeavors that reached beyond the ranks of the lodge, in pursuit of a post-Revolutionary vision of "an enlightened society built around equality and openness," according to Bullock.[27] Clinton's support of the public good through voluntary organizations has been called "fanatical."[28] He was a founding member of the New-York Historical Society in 1804, and by 1815 was president of the Literary and Philosophical Society, the American Academy of Arts, and the Free School Society, second vice president of the New-York Historical Society, a director of the Humane Society, and a trustee of New-York Lying-In Hospital. His interest in natural sciences and archaeology earned him memberships in the Linnaean Society of London, the Wernerian Society of Edinburgh, and the Academy of Natural Sciences of Philadelphia.[29]

Clinton's educative efforts included American archaeology's most pressing mystery, the Mound Builders, on which he was a hypermigrationist.[30] Clinton was working against the grain of the wisdom of James Madison, the first Protestant Episcopal bishop of Virginia, who in a letter to Benjamin Smith Barton published by the American Philosophical Society in 1809 refuted the idea that the mounds were military fortifications; all evidence indicated that ancestors of Native Americans were their creators.[31] Clinton was of a much different mind. In an 1811 address to the New-York Historical Society, Clinton laid out his own scenario for ancient America.

Theorists like Clinton could not bring themselves to reject transatlantic migrationism, a door on the east Lafitau and others had left open, in explaining the origin of at least some Native Americans, although Clinton was willing to slam it shut on ancient Gothicist and other speculative European migrations. Clinton thought it "not improbable" that Phoenicians were ancestral to some Native Americans, implicitly upholding the plausibility of the Dighton Rock interpretation advanced by Ezra Stiles (and for that matter, by Antoine Court de Gébelin).[32] But he called "incorrect and fanciful" the ideas that ancient earthworks in western New York and the Ohio country had been made by Spaniards, Welshmen, or any other Europeans. Rather, they were erected "a long time before the discovery of America," some of them in New York along an ancient Lake Erie shore that was much higher than at present. They were "totally variant from European fortifications."[33] But it was "equally clear that they were not the work of the Indians."[34] Clinton perpetuated the unkind estimation of Isaac Greenwood (expressed for the carving of Dighton Rock) in stating: "The erection of such prodigious works must have been the result of labor far beyond the patience and perseverance of our Indians."[35]

Clinton took up the accumulating theories that favored multiple migrations from Asia across the Bering Strait, with their hierarchies of civilization and barbarity, and contrived a dramatic narrative. At some remote age, "A great part of North America was then inhabited by populous nations, who had made considerable advance in civilization. These numerous works could never have been supplied with provisions without the aid of agriculture. Nor could they have been constructed without the use of iron or copper: and without a perseverance, labor, and design, which demonstrate considerable progress in the arts of civilized life."[36] Clinton cited Pennant on multiple migrations, but appeared to owe an unspoken debt to Vallancey in arguing there was an initial arrival in America of people who lived in peace and developed an advanced civilization: "In course of time, discord and war would rage among them, and compel the establishment of places of security. At last, they became alarmed by the irruption of a horde of barbarians, who rushed like an overwhelming flood from the North of Asia."[37] "Horde," of course, was a term from Vallancey's "Observations," and to Clinton, present-day Indians were those barbarians.

Clinton's terminology had a crucial heritage. The sixth-century Romanized Goth historian Jordanes (a key source for Olf Rudbeks) had called northern Europe *Humani generis officinam*—the factory of the human race. Johannes Magnus called Sweden the *vagina nationum* in his mid-sixteenth century celebration of Scandinavian superiority, a cause taken up by Rudbeks in positing Scandinavia as the Gothic root of all European culture.[38] Montesquieu in *De l'Esprit des loix*, noting that Jordanes had called northern Europe the factory of the human race, commented: "I would rather call it the factory of the instruments that broke the shackles forged in the South," thus binding northern Europe, in place, culture, and ethnicity, with humanity's highest qualities as he saluted the defeat of Imperial Rome by these northern freedom fighters.[39] Thomas Pennant made a veiled nod to these sources when he proposed: "I see no reason why the Asiatic north might not be an *officina vivorum*, as well as the European."[40] Just as northern Europe had been the *Humani generis officinam*, or factory of humanity, discharging from Sweden the outmigration wave of Goths, so too northern Asia had been the *officina vivorum*, the living factory, which produced the outmigration of Tartars (and a variety of animal species) to the Americas. Clinton in his 1811 "Address" cited this passage from Pennant's *Arctic Zoology* to argue that Europe became a factory of humanity supplying the New World, just as Asia once had been.[41] Clinton thus endorsed and popularized two contrasting, even oppositional factories in the peopling of the Americas: the original one, which had churned out multiple migrations of Indigenous peoples in eastern Asia according to Pennant's Bering-Strait analysis, and the European one, which had delivered North America the Gothicist civilization through Anglo-American colonization.

Clinton in 1820 elaborated on his theory for ancient earthworks in western New York in a public address that was published to provide maximum educative benefit: "The old fortifications were erected previous to European intercourse. The Indians are ignorant by whom they were made; and in the wars which took place in this country it is probable that they were occupied as strongholds by the belligerents. . . . It is remarkable that our ancient forts resemble the old British and Danish. . . . The Danes as well as the nations which erected our fortifications, were in all probability of Scythian origin. According to Pliny, the name of Scythian was common to all the nations living in the north of Asia and Europe."[42]

Clinton has been misunderstood as advocating a Norse presence in the heart of America.[43] Clinton never proposed any such thing, and he was firm in rejecting pre-Columbian European arrivals. His 1820 statement of the resemblance of ancient American forts to British and Danish ones was a retreat from his 1811 assertion that the earthworks bore no resemblance to European examples. Nevertheless, he held that these American fortresses only *resemble* Danish and British examples because Danes *as well as the nations which erected our fortifications* shared a Scythian heritage. Except for perhaps a few wandering Phoenicians, the nations that had populated the Americas arrived from Asia, across the Bering Strait, as Pennant had argued. Clinton's scenario was consistent with Vallancey's theory for Dighton Rock, in which the Armenian Scythians branched in two directions: one into Europe and the British Isles, the other into Asia and eventually the Americas.

The distinction between diffusionist similarities in fortification types and transoceanic migrating Danes was lost on Samuel Latham Mitchill, a member of Clinton's inner political circle and an original member of the New-York Historical Society's standing committee.[44] The beachhead for pre-Columbian Transatlantic Gothicism, established by Stiles in his Election Sermon of 1783, was reoccupied by Mitchill, by misconstruing Clinton and reanimating the theory proposed around 1787 and later abandoned by Benjamin Smith Barton.

Late in life, Barton revealed himself to be a hyperdiffusionist as well as a fence sitter on polygenesis (as Jefferson was). As Barton wrote in 1809, "I do not positively contend . . . that all mankind constitute but *one species.*"[45] Still, by the time of his death in late 1815, Barton was far removed from the process of labeling Native Americans as the barbaric and unworthy usurpers of a vanished greatness rather than as its direct descendants, whatever one thought of their present condition and their capacity for recovery or improvement. That did not prevent Samuel Latham Mitchill from taking up the essential points of the now-departed Barton's disowned *Observations* and crafting a Transatlantic Gothicist explanation for America's perplexing mounds in western New York.

NOTWITHSTANDING THE INCLUSION of his theories in *Archaeologia Americana*, Samuel Latham Mitchill was not an archaeologist: neither he nor De Witt Clinton conducted any fieldwork or formal survey of the mounds of western New York. Mitchill's postulations were consistent with the

"Antiquarian" name of the society that published *Archaeologia Americana*. His writings, in that volume and elsewhere, testified to the persistence of eighteenth-century theorizing and cabinet-of-curiosities curating alongside archaeological fieldwork and race-based science.

Steven Conn has noted "a new reliance on objects as the place where knowledge inhered," or what he has called an "object-based epistemology," in the American antiquarian turn toward archaeology in the early nineteenth century.[46] "The archaeologists of this era traded on a widespread belief in the explanatory power and epistemological transparency of objects, specimens, things," in contrast with the "textual business" that had defined the practice of history in the eighteenth and early nineteenth century.[47] Another element of this turn "was the conviction that objects constituted a permanent record of Native American history, while language disappeared with the speakers, and that by the middle of the nineteenth century, those speakers did indeed seem doomed to disappear."[48] Mitchill had argued precisely the irrelevancy of semiotics and philology in disentangling the truth of American antiquity in his dismissal of Mathieu's Dighton Rock interpretation: "But what need is there of all this etymological research and grammatical conjecture? The features, manners and dress, distinguishable in the North American natives of high latitudes, prove the [Native American] people to be of the same race with the Samoieds and Tartars of Asia. And the physiognomy, manufactures and customs of the North American tribes of the middle and low latitudes, and of the South Americans, show them to be nearly akin to the Malay race of Australasia and Polynesia."[49]

Investigators relied on physical experience of and interaction with evidence. Cabinets of curiosities were being filled with global material culture gathered by travelers, especially American seafarers. Having these materials in hand, in combination with the excavated findings in mounds, made it possible for theorists like Mitchill to make intuitive leaps in ethnology that drew connections between cultures on a global scale and supported migrationist and diffusionist theories for the peopling of the Americas. Mitchill and others were also active in natural history and mineralogy, which entailed gathering, describing, and categorizing specimens according to global schemes; additionally, the medical training of Mitchill and others (including Barton) required them to diagnose illness based on directly observed symptoms. I would additionally argue that antiquarian philology was as much object-based as it was text-based. Individual words, removed from the context of their structural and grammatical environments, were collected and pinned to

tables of comparison like beetles in an entomologist's display case in an attempt to prove affinities between far-flung peoples.

Another important aspect of the emergent American archaeology was the
reliance on surveying: on maps of sites and on drawings of excavations, including cross-sections, which suggest an additional epistemology of observational precision, which approached a fetishist faith in the ability of to-scale
representations to preserve and reveal historical truths. This dedication to
two-dimensional verisimilitude had already been seen in the eighteenth-
century efforts of Stephen Sewall and James Winthrop to map the inscribed
surface of Dighton Rock at full scale, and to then reduce the master drawing for reproduction. Such refined recording and observation was the close
cousin of land surveying (Ezra Stiles produced numerous maps and plans, in
addition to drawings of marked rocks[50]), and we must also recognize the role
of military conquest and associated surveying in the emergent archaeology
and theories about Native American origins. The methodological archaeology that inspired Britons and Americans had been established in the early
nineteenth century in Denmark, in surveys and precisely documented excavations of barrows and ring forts. Charles Vallancey was a military surveyor,
for whom the barrows and ring forts of Ireland helped to stimulate his interest
in antiquities. Those European earthworks in turn were natural analogues to
the Mound Builder relics, and American theorists were influenced by publications such as Richard Twiss's *A Tour of Ireland* (1776) and James Douglas's
twelve-volume *Nenia Britannica* (1786–93). In the Ohio country, the early
surveys of the Marietta earthworks—Heart's and Parsons's in 1786, Rufus Putnam's around 1788—were military not only in execution, but in interpretation
and consequence as well. They helped to define and apportion for settlement
land that had only recently been wrested, by violence and by treaties signed
under duress, from Native Americans. American archaeology thus arose to
a significant degree from military conquest, and accompanied colonization,
dispossession, and displacement. As with Dighton Rock, the interpretation
of the mounds was an act of possession, an assertion of domain, both legal
and intellectual. Having secured dominion over the landscape on which the
mounds rested, antiquarians and educators reserved the right to determine to
whom these relics belonged in an ethnographic sense.

Ezra Stiles's migration theories had been the products of semiotic and
philological misadventures with Indigenous petroglyphs like Dighton Rock,
and such misadventures would persist into the twentieth century. Kendall, as
we have seen, was exceptional in maintaining the rock and the markings as a

unified whole. Inscribed stones otherwise might have been objects, but their data value to theorists was script-based. Such investigations presumed that rock markings *were* inscriptions, as opposed to an array of symbols or glyphs that may have been created at different times by different Indigenous peoples within a single culture or from successive ones, without any intention of "writing" a unified message. And while Mitchill in general championed object-based material culture over language in sorting out America's past, he shared the late Stiles's passion for advancing the Transatlantic Gothicist idea of pre-Columbian migrations of white people out of Europe.

In a discourse delivered at the College of Physicians and Surgeons in November 1816, set down in letter form in January 1817 and reproduced in volume 1 of *Archaeologia Americana*, Mitchill recounted a recent conversation with Clinton, which inspired his own theory of a dramatic clash of cultures in what until recently had been the territory of the Onondaga in western New York. Clinton, according to Mitchill, believed that "a part of the old forts and other antiquities at Onondaga and the adjacent territory, were of *Danish* character."[51] While that did not mean Clinton ever thought they were of Danish *origin*, Mitchill nevertheless recounted: "In the twinkling of an eye, I was penetrated by the justness of his remark. An additional window of light was suddenly opened to me."[52] For his 1816 address, Mitchill experienced an unacknowledged Transatlantic Gothicist flashback to Barton's idea of Danish Mound Builders, and crafted a pre-Columbian expedition of European colonizers. He ignored the earlier objections of Pennant and Clinton to such theorizing and Barton's own abandonment of the idea. With Barton having only recently died, Mitchill may have considered his disowned Danish-invaders scenario free for the taking.

Mitchill was not satisfied with limiting himself to roving Danes. The Welsh of the fabled Prince Madoc, who had supposedly reached America in A.D. 1170, also begged to be included. The descendants of Madoc roamed widely in antiquarian theories, but were most often attached to the Mandan people of Missouri. The Mandan had been the subject of White Tribism speculation since 1733, when the Sieur de La Vérendrye (of mysterious standing stones fame) gathered a story, probably from the Cree, that indicated they had light hair and lived in dwellings similar to the French.[53] Madoc had been featured in the Gothicist-Japhetite migrations of Ezra Stiles in 1783's Election Sermon, and Stiles was referring to the Mandan when he noted in his diary in 1786 that up the Missouri "there is a Tribe that speak Welch to this day & have a Writing rolled up in Skins."[54] Barton in *Observations* took his cue directly from Pennant in discounting the entire Madoc story.[55] But Madoc was not to be denied. An Englishman, John Williams, popularized the Madoc story in 1791 with a White Tribism argument that the Delaware and Tuscarora as well as some tribes west of the Mississippi, including the Mandan, were of Welsh descent, the result of interbreeding with the 120 men who had crossed the ocean with Madoc, or *Madog*, as Williams called him.[56] In the winter of 1796–97, a young Welshman, John Thomas Evans, visited the Mandan, hoping to meet his distant relations, but heard not a word of his own language.[57] No matter: The British poet Robert Southey romanticized the idea of a Madoc colonization of America in an epic poem in 1805 that found a popular audience in the United States. Southey in his preface asserted: "There is strong evidence that [Madoc] reached America, and that his posterity exist there to this day, on the southern branches of the Missouri, retaining their complexion, their language, and, in some degree, their arts."[58]

Clinton rejected Madoc where the origin of earthworks was concerned in 1811.[59] Moses Fiske of Tennessee, in an 1815 letter published in *Archaeologia Americana*, ridiculed the idea that the Mound Builders originated in Wales.[60] But Mitchill could not resist the hoary romance and included in his Gothic "band of adventurers" Madoc's band of Welsh colonizers, along with Scandinavians who, having colonized Iceland and then Greenland in the ninth and tenth centuries, had pressed on for the New World.[61]

Mitchill's band reached the St. Lawrence River, where they left "Peunic inscriptions."[62] Mitchill thus was not averse to relying to some degree on semiotics and comparative languages, regardless of his disdain for "etymological research and grammatical conjecture." While he did not explain why medieval northern Europeans would carve messages in a Phoenician script, he must have known the work of Vallancey, who had posited that Celtic languages had Phoenician roots. Mitchill's adventurers presumably had brought Vallancey's Iberno-Celtic script with them. Mitchill made confused use of any number of possible sources on Pehr Kalm's account of La Vérendrye's discovery, including Vallancey as well as Barton, who opened *Observations* with it. Where an inscribed stone was supposedly discovered by La Vérendrye far to the west and brought back to Quebec, Mitchill had a Punic (not Tartarian) stone inscribed *at* Quebec. In any event, Mitchill's newcomers carried on until they reached the country south of Lake Ontario, and along the way they gathered an additional identity as "Esquimaux," on which he did not elaborate.[63] One cannot help but notice that Barton in *Observations* had cited Pennant in refuting a linguistic connection between the Welsh and the Esquimaux.[64] The more one considers Mitchill's scenario, the more it seems that he reworked the recently departed Barton's *Observations*, keeping whatever he found interesting, regardless of the objections Barton had mounted even within it.

An explanation for the Esquimaux identity can be found in Mitchill's 1816 theory of the structure of the human race and the peopling of America. Mitchill believed that human beings comprised a single species. One variant was "the *white* man, inhabiting naturally the countries in Asia and Europe, situated north of the Mediterranean Sea; and, in the course of his adventures, settling all over the world. Among those I reckon the Greenlanders and Esquimaux."[65] (He even considered the idea, ventured by Jefferson, that humanity had originated in the Americas and spread to Asia.)[66]

In *The Medical Repository* of February 1817, Mitchill merged the emergent American archaeology whose development was being fueled by the Mound Builder mystery with the established cabinet-of-curiosities practice of gathering material culture from around the world through American shipping, and ventured into comparative ethnography. Recently discovered grave goods, including woven materials from Copperas Cave in Tennessee and Mammoth Cave in Kentucky, "all have a perfect resemblance to the fabricks of the Sandwich, the Caroline, and the Fegee [Fiji] islands."[67] Mitchill was using an object-based epistemology to compare cultural materials plucked out of their ethnographic context in the Old World and the New. In practice, this was not much different from the way men like Vallancey and Barton had drawn links between languages based on the phonetics of gathered specimens of words.

Mitchill divided Native American ancestors into two Asiatic subgroups that conformed to a multiple-migration displacement scenario, while also adopting Blumenbach's five-race scheme that included Malays. The more advanced Malay group from Asia's south crossed the Pacific, while the less advanced, warlike group from the north swept across the Bering Strait. Mitchill counseled: "colonies of Australasians, or Malays, landed in North-America, and penetrated across the continent, to the region lying between the Great Lakes and the Gulph of Mexico. There they resided, and constructed the fortifications, mounds, and other ancient structures, which every person who beholds them admires." Mitchill did not send his Malays as far east as Dighton Rock, but otherwise echoed Vallancey in proposing: "They have probably been overcome by the more warlike and ferocious hordes that entered our hemisphere from the north-east of Asia. These Tatars of the higher latitudes have issued from the great hive of nations, and desolated, in the course of their migrations, the southern tribes of America, as they have done to those of Asia and Europe. The greater part of the present American natives are of the Tatar stock, the descendants of the hardy warriors who destroyed the weaker Malays that preceded them."[68]

Mitchill categorized the Asian Tatar/Tartar factory as a *hive*, which carried the connotation of a menacing swarm, an idea that was closely allied with Vallancey's *horde*. To satisfy himself that descendants of the swarming Tartars were present-day Native Americans, Mitchill inspected Chinese sailors from a ship that had arrived in New York harbor from Macao. He concluded they resembled the Mohegans and Oneidas.[69] Sidi Suleiman Melli Melli, the Tunisian envoy to the United States, Mitchill further assured, "in 1804 [*sic*], entertained the same opinion, on beholding the Cherokees, Osages, and Miamies, assembled at the city of Washington, during his residence there. Their Tartar physiognomy struck him in a moment."[70]

In Mitchill's estimation, the transpacific Malays who were not destroyed had been driven into cave refuges in Kentucky and Tennessee. Mitchill believed the Iroquoian-speaking nation known as the Erie had been of this Malay migration, which seemed at odds with his conviction that the neighboring, Iroquoian-speaking Oneida were of Tartar stock. The Tartars, having conquered the Malay/Erie, had "probably a much harder task to perform. This was to subdue the more ferocious and warlike European colonists, *who had already been intrenched* [*sic*] *and fortified in the country, before them* [italics added]. There is evidence enough that long and bloody wars were waged among the tribes. In these, the Scandinavians or Esquimaux seem to have been overpowered and destroyed in Newyork [*sic*]. The survivors of the defeat and ruin retreated to Labrador, where they have continued secure and protected by barrenness and cold."[71] Mitchill marveled at "what a memorable spot is our Onondaga, where men of the Malay race from the southwest, and of the Tartar blood from the northwest, and of the Gothick stock from the northeast, have successively contended for supremacy and rule; and which may be considered as having been possessed by each before the French, the Dutch, and the English visited the tract, or indeed knew any thing whatever about it."[72]

Mitchill was one of the most learned and intellectually influential men of his time, and his fanciful theorizing was neither idle nor harmless. His ideas rationalized a contemporary ethical dilemma of Indigenous displacement. Mitchill escalated the savagery of Tartarian Native Americans by having them destroy or displace not only the Malay Mound Builders but the original pre-Columbian "Gothick stock" settlers as well. Mitchill also ensured that these original European colonizers had reached western New York before the Tartarian Native Americans did. Mitchill in 1788 had been appointed a state commissioner to negotiate the acquisition of a six-million-acre tract of Onondaga land in western New York.[73] Mitchill appeared to be assuring himself (and his audience) that this acquisition, not to mention the coerced surrender of

Indigenous lands beyond the Ohio, was a just displacing of the displacers. It is important to note in this regard that White Tribism did not factor into Mitchill's theory. The "Gothick stock" that had arrived with their Esquimaux brethren were vanquished militarily by the Tartar savages and forced to retreat to Labrador. There was no chance that a drop of white blood might have been left behind among the savages who were ejected from their lands by the later wave of European arrivals of recorded history. The Tartars's descendants were now being removed, militarily as well as by coercive treaty and purchase, by the descendants of the whites whom the Tartars had earlier repelled from western New York. Mitchill's scenario was an argument of just deserts, foundational in the construction of the idea that Native Americans had an unworthy claim to their lands, and prescient of theories of early Caucasian arrivals in the New World (including the controversy surrounding Kennewick Man in our time[74]) that negate Indigenous assertions of sovereignty.

CALEB ATWATER's "Description of the Antiquities Discovered in the State of Ohio and other Western States" in volume 1 of *Archaeologia Americana* was the first concerted study of so-called Mound Builders. Atwater turned decades of speculation into an interpretive standard in asserting that the Mound Builders had nothing to do with living Native Americans. In the words of Francis P. Weisenburger, Atwater was "a rather aggressive, eccentric Circleville lawyer"—Circleville, Ohio, having been named for its Hopewell formations.[75] Atwater's expertise was diverse if elusive on the anthropological front: born in Massachusetts, he was the proprietor of a school for young women while he was studying theology, and was ordained as a Presbyterian minister; he was also ruined financially by a glass factory venture and was admitted to the New York bar. After relocating to Ohio in 1815, he initially attempted to build a law practice before securing a postmaster's appointment in 1817; he was elected to the state House of Representatives in 1821.[76] In 1826 the visiting duke of Saxe-Weimar, after spending an evening in Atwater's company, would write: "He is a great antiquarian, and exists more in the antiquities of Ohio, than in the present world."[77]

Atwater declared in *Archaeologia Americana*: "The skeletons found in our mounds never belonged to a people like our Indians. The latter are a tall, rather slender, strait limbed people; the former were short and thick."[78] Atwater believed some artifacts indicated Hindu worship. European (particularly English) studies of the languages, culture, and religions of India were blossoming in the school of Orientalism pioneered by Sir William Jones, whose identification of the Indo-European language family has been hailed by Bruce Trigger as "the beginning of comparative philology."[79] This new fascination with India (and in particular Hinduism) extended long-standing ideas of cross-cultural influences in ancient civilizations in a rich Oriental direction and would lead to the foundation of the Royal Asiatic Society in 1823.[80]

Atwater diverged slightly from the Vallancey model of multiple migrations, and was more aligned with Kalm and Forster. He posited that northern Tartars, who were ancestors of present-day Native Americans, arrived first and settled on the Atlantic coast. The Hindus and southern Tartars, who possessed more advanced cultures—a variant on the Malays of Mitchill's theory—followed and became the Mound Builders of North America. Through further migration the Mound Builders became the Aztecs of Mexico and the Inca of Peru. Orientalism was creating a cultural affinity under the Indo-European umbrella between Gothic northern European colonizers and the Malay/Hindu/southern-Tartar migrants that American theorists were proclaiming as ancestral to the Mound Builders.[81] Atwater's assertion that the Mound Builder bones "resemble the Germans" hinted at a biological as well as a cultural Indo-European connection. In the broadest, Orientalist sense, the ongoing Gothicist colonization was a cycle-of-history *reconquista*, avenging the original displacement by Tartarian hordes of Indo-European civilization in the New World.

Atwater viewed the idea that all American antiquities belonged to ancestors of present-day Indians (which Barton had championed) as a flawed rejoinder by American theorists to nameless Europeans—he did not even have to identify Buffon, de Pauw, and Raynal—who contended that "our climate was debilitating in its effects upon the bodies and minds of the people of America, and that nature belittled every thing here."[82] In Atwater's mind, allowing Indians to lay ancestral claim to the archaeological marvels of the mounds would only provide further support to a poisonous European view of the Americas, as the low state of modern Indians could be seized upon as proof that the climate had caused them to degenerate from more advanced ancestors. Far better for a proud American like Atwater in a newly settled state like Ohio that Indians arrived on the continent fully degenerate as Tartars who had displaced a more refined Hindu-Malay people with whom Europeans shared a deep cultural and even biological heritage and who were responsible for the continent's most impressive antiquities. Benjamin Smith Barton had scarcely been buried, and his defense of living Native Americans as descendants of the Mound Builders was being buried with him.

Only three years after the appearance of *Archaeologia Americana*, Joseph Smith discovered the plates in upstate New York that revealed to his eyes the Book of Mormon. Smith's translation, completed in 1830, extended the Old

Testament narrative to America. The descendants of Lehi of the tribe of Joseph in their long migration to the New World split into the Nephites and the Lamanites. The Nephites were favored by God and established a civilization in upstate New York, where they thrived until the Lamanites arrived and destroyed them in A.D. 400. In Mormon teachings, Native Americans were from the brutish Lamanite stock. Colin Kidd has noted the parallels to the Lost Tribes theorizing of Ethan Smith (no relation) in *View of the Hebrews* (1823), but the scenario is also reminiscent of Mitchill's writings on the antiquity of the Ohio Valley and upstate New York published in 1817/1820, and consistent with the ascendance of multiple-migration Beringian theories since the end of the American Revolution.[83]

THE EMERGENT AMERICAN ARCHAEOLOGY may have been scientific in its aspirations, but in function it reflected and served the colonizing agenda of the new American republic, and in interpretation it remained beholden to eighteenth-century antiquarian frameworks. The process of cultural erasure witnessed in New England in the early history of Dighton Rock's interpretation became a national one of disenfranchisement in the early nineteenth century, as some of America's leading educators and political leaders, in concert with new learned societies devoted to public education, applied to the Mound Builders the multiple-migration displacement scenario that Vallancey had already applied to Dighton Rock: the ancestors of Native Americans were a brutish "horde" that swept into America from Siberia, displacing more sophisticated, earlier migrants. A leading authority like Samuel Latham Mitchill could skewer the esoteric nonsense of Charles-Léopold Mathieu's Atlantean theory for Dighton Rock while mounting his own Transatlantic Gothicist colonization fantasy in resuscitating the Danish Mound Builder theory advanced and then abandoned by Benjamin Smith Barton. In puzzling over the identity of Dighton Rock's inscribers and the Mound Builders, learned and influential men on both sides of the Atlantic were assigning Native Americans to precarious roles in the narratives of both humanity and the United States—if they were willing to grant them full membership in the human race. Indigenous people became but one of a succession of immigrant groups to the Americas, and as a Tartarian horde the least admirable one at that, in a self-justifying thread of logic in support of colonizing dispossession.

On May 28, 1830, ten years after the appearance of the first volume of *Archaeologia Americana*, which disseminated Mitchill's and Atwater's learned opinions on the unhappy fate of the Mound Builders (and pre-Columbian European colonizers) at the hands of Tartarian hordes, President Andrew Jackson signed into law the Indian Removal Act, which empowered him to grant tribes unsettled land west of the Mississippi in exchange for their lands within settled states.[84] In making his case for removal of the Five Civilized Tribes in his second annual address before Congress on December 6, 1830, Jackson stated:

> Humanity has often wept over the fate of the aborigines of this country, and Philanthropy has been long busily employed in devising means to avert it, but its progress has never for a moment been arrested, and one by one have many powerful tribes disappeared from the earth. To follow to the tomb the last of his race and to tread on the graves of extinct nations excite melancholy reflections. But true philanthropy reconciles the mind to these vicissitudes as it does to the extinction of one generation to make room for another. *In the monuments and fortifications of an unknown people, spread over the extensive regions of the West, we behold the memorials of a once powerful race, which was exterminated or has disappeared to make room for the existing savage tribes* [italics added].[85]

A multiple-migration displacement scenario that Charles Vallancey had ventured for Dighton Rock, which had then migrated to the Mound Builder mystery, had brought intellectual inquiry to the doorstep of genocide. Without ever setting foot in America, Vallancey had turned Native Americans into descendants of brutish Tartarian hordes, which suited the needs of the republic's colonization project. Brian W. Dippie argues that a "humanitarian rationale" was the cornerstone of the general removal policy, which predated Jackson.[86] Jackson's presidential predecessor, James Monroe, had stated in 1825 that removal "would not only shield . . . [Native Americans] from impending ruin, but promote their welfare and happiness."[87] Nevertheless, Jackson (a former Indian fighter) could contend, with the support of the emergent American archaeology, that Native Americans had displaced a more advanced people. Their own time had come for displacement. Jackson argued that his proposed removal was progressive, inevitable, and consistent with the "general interest of the human race."[88] Jackson's logic was a combination of the irresistible cycle of history, multiple-migrationism that disenfranchised Native Americans from their past, the justness and desirability of what he called "white" westward expansion, and a confidence the removal would be benign—notwithstanding the fact that some four thousand Cherokee would die on the Trail of Tears in 1838.[89]

CHAPTER SIX

Vinland Imagined

The Norsemen and the Gothicists Claim Dighton Rock

American antiquaries continued their fascination with Dighton Rock as a Phoenician relic, regardless of the Indigenous attribution by Edward Augustus Kendall in 1809. The most influential advocates were John Vann Ness Yates and Joseph W. Moulton, who gave over a large part of their first volume of *History of the State of New-York* (1824) to theories of pre-Columbian arrivals in America. Yates was the American secretary of state and Moulton was a lawyer, and they were sympathetic to Mound Builders theories advanced by their fellow members of the New-York Historical Society (NYHS), Clinton and Mitchill. The authors visited Dighton Rock in 1821, and declared a trident of Neptune "plainly visible," advising: "we are inclined to believe that the Dighton inscription is of Phoenician origin."[1]

In *Antiquities of America Explained* (1831), Ira Hill contended that the Phoenicians—he preferred Tyrians, from the city of Tyre—were descendants of Noah's son Shem (as Ezra Stiles contended in his unpublished 1790 work), migrating in every direction and serving as the root of all the world's civilizations. The Tartars who others thought resembled Native Americans were simply another company of wandering Phoenicians and had never crossed the Bering Strait to America. Hill argued a combination of Tyrians and Jews crossed the Atlantic together three thousand years earlier, in the time of Solomon—in his estimation, wherever the Tyrians went, as Shemites of the Abrahamic line some Jews went with them. They made their colony at Nova Scotia or New England, and Dighton Rock "must have been at, or near their head quarters."[2] From there, they populated the Americas through further migrations. In addition to accounting for the identity of the Mound Builders, these Tyrian-Jews created all of the petroglyphs in eastern North America. "From lake Champlain to the Potomac river, at every important pass, and on every conspicuous place, there are figures carved on the rocks indicative of their march, and a hand pointing to the West, showing the direction of their journey."[3]

Dighton Rock was a commemoration of the original crossing from Tyre. The record in stone was so detailed that Hill was able to determine that "in the second month of the tenth year of the reign of Solomon, the Tyrians and

Jews formed a bond of union on the American shore, one year and two moons after they left their native shores."[4] Here was another interpretation of Dighton Rock as a record of amity in the Court de Gébelin vein, only now the expressed amity was between two peoples who had just arrived. The inscription indicated that, after suffering three months of tyrannical rule in the New World, the colonists killed their king with an arrow to the head.[5] Hill resorted to a standard tactic of White Tribism in providing a list of about fifty words from "various dialects or tongues" of Native Americans that corresponded with Hebrew.[6] As for how the continent ended up in the possession of savages, Hill enlisted degeneration and a variation on displacement: "the Indians which filled our forests when our predecessors first came to these shores, were but the relics of a more powerful and enlightened people who had gone before them, and who had long since left these realms for milder climes." All that remained were "wandering barbarous tribes, that filled our forests, and dragged out a miserable existence in the wilds of America."[7]

The Phoenician attribution for Dighton Rock was proving persistent, but a Gothicist explanation was on the rise. Around 1823 a Scottish professor of geology and mineralogy, John Finch, visited Canada and the United States. Finding America lacking a storied past comparable to that of Europe, Finch, in an 1824 article in the *American Journal of Science and Arts*, proposed the means for Americans to "elucidate the history of their native country" more effectively than the "genius of Buffon."[8] It was their duty to refute the "groundless accusation" that their country had no antiquity worth mentioning. He proposed that antiquarians repurpose Native Americans as descendants of ancient Celts, for the good of America.

Having read Edward Augustus Kendall's descriptions of the Sacrifice Rocks and Dighton Rock, among other sources, Finch detected abundant raw material for asserting a Celtic past for America. "Who is there within the limits of the wide world, that has not heard of the name and fame of the Druids, of their religious sacrifices, and of their instruments of gold, with which they severed the sacred mistletoe from the venerable father of the forest, the wide-spreading oak," Finch proposed. Finch asserted that Native Americans were descended from "all the tribes who departed from the land of Scythia," and imagined that "in ages long since past, perhaps at the same instance of time, though under different skies, the Druids of England, and the priests of Cuzco, the astronomers of Ireland, Hudson, and Winnipigon, seated upon the lofty hills, and surrounded by their sacred circles of stone, were calculating the progress of the seasons, the revolutions of the planets, and the eclipses of the sun, by the same formulae which their ancestors had first practiced in the central plains of Asia." Finch's ideas foreshadowed the twentieth century's pseudohistorical obsession with an alleged Bronze Age Celtic presence in North America that gave rise to the Early Sites Foundation in 1954 and the New England Antiquities Research Association (NEARA) in 1964. Finch differed critically from most of his twentieth-century counterparts in proposing that Native Americans were part of a global, Scythian, root-culture hyperdiffusion. Latter-day theorists like Barry Fell were only satisfied with actual Bronze Age Celts crossing the Atlantic and leaving their standing stones and ogham inscriptions behind, while also leaving Native Americans in the chasm of prehistory that Finch had attempted to fill by making their ancestors a worthy foundation to a young nation's history.

Americans, however, were not interested in embracing as distant cousins the Native Americans they were displacing, as Finch proposed. Finch himself abandoned the Celtic fantasy when he published *Travels in the United States and Canada* in 1833. What was more, Finch argued that Americans should not be expected to share the land with primitive Indians. "This would be, in effect, as if an Englishman should desire that the painted Celts and Picts should take possession of the flourishing islands of Britain, erect their huts of wood, feed their cattle in the fertile valleys, and amuse their leisure hours by making war upon the neighboring tribes. Such a state of things would not be desirable in England, neither would it be in America."[9] Extending the presence of a superior northern European race and culture to pre-Columbian North America, as Stiles and Mitchill had attempted, required another champion. Already, the greatest proponent of Transatlantic Gothicism had emerged, and he would soon enlist Dighton Rock in the cause, with the aid of American antiquaries.

IN THE LATE 1820s, American antiquaries began to learn of a striking new scholarly project. As the November 28, 1828, edition of *Niles' Weekly Register*, published in Baltimore, reported (reprinting a notice in Philadelphia's *National Gazette and Literary Register*), "A distinguished savant of Copenhagen has addressed a letter, containing very curious historical information, to a gentleman of this city. He is engaged in the composition of a work on the voyages of discovery to North America, undertaken by inhabitants of the north of Europe, before the time of Columbus. They furnish various and unquestionable evidence, not only that the coast of North America was discovered soon after the discovery of Greenland, towards the close of the tenth century, by northern explorers, a part of whom remained there, and that it was again visited in the 11th, 12th, and 13th centuries, but also that Christianity was introduced among the aborigines."[10]

This announcement seemed all the more surprising as it challenged the idea of Columbus as discoverer of the New World just as Washington Irving published his popular (if factually unreliable) biography of the admiral.[11] The unnamed correspondent was Carl Christian Rafn, secretary of the Royal Society of Northern Antiquaries (RSNA) of Copenhagen, which Rafn had organized in 1825 with the historian and linguist Rasmus Christian Rask under the sponsorship of Frederick VI.[12] The result of Rafn's labors, *Antiquitates Americanae* (1837), was one of the most important scholarly works on American antiquity of the nineteenth century. In 1892, Daniel Wilson, the prominent Scottish-Canadian professor of history and English literature at the University of Toronto (and who rose to the university's presidency), proclaimed *Antiquitates Americanae* the cause of "a revolution," adding "some five centuries to the history of the New World. From its appearance, accordingly, may be dated the systemic aim of American antiquaries and historians to find evidence of intercourse with the ancient world prior to the fifteenth century."[13] Douglas R. McManis in 1969 heralded *Antiquitates Americanae* as the beginning of modern scholarship on Vinland. Since its publication, McManis argued, no important critic had argued that the Vinland voyages were folk myth, as the leading American historian George Bancroft had in 1834.[14]

Rafn's foremost accomplishment in *Antiquitates Americanae* was publishing the relevant Vinland sagas in their original Old Norse, as well as in Danish and Latin, in concert with an Icelandic expert, Finnur (Finn) Magnussén. However, for all the praise Rafn and Magnussén secured for legitimizing the idea of a Norse presence in the Americas some 500 years before Columbus, they overreached in striving to prove the historicity of the sagas by firmly locating Vinland on the American shore. Dighton Rock became a centerpiece of a major scholarly enterprise that was in fact an elaborate project of Transatlantic Gothicism. The rock acquired a new guise, as a Norse inscription declaring possession of the lands. White Tribism marred the researches pursued by Rafn and American members of the RSNA, as an assortment of other supposed curiosities in New England (which were not very curious at all and included Native American remains and artifacts) secured an enduring place in the pseudohistorical canon through their initial miscasting as Norse relics. Rafn's Norse adventurers did more than temporarily colonize New England: the Norse remained for centuries, intermarried with the Indigenous peoples, and improved them, and, moreover, were preceded by Irish Christians who

occupied a colony that sprawled all the way from the Chesapeake Bay to Florida, called White Men's Land.

"THERE IS NOT A Vinland; there are many Vinlands," Douglas R. McManis
wrote in 1969 of the long-standing quest to prove the place mentioned in the
Vinland sagas was a historic fact.[15] Rafn's effort to prove the historicity of *his*
particular Vinland must be understood in the context of the main streams of
antiquarian investigation in the early nineteenth century. A major stream was
what Bruce Trigger has called "nationalist archaeology," of which nineteenth-
century Danish efforts were exemplary. Denmark's national pride, according
to Trigger, had taken a drubbing during the Napoleonic period and would
suffer further in conflicts with Germany. The Danes "turned to history and
archaeology to find consolation in thoughts of their past national greatness.
In particular, they took pride in the fact that Denmark, unlike its southern
neighbours, had not been conquered by the Romans. They were also powerfully attracted to the Viking period."[16] This nationalist archaeology lay on a
patriotic continuum with the Gothicism of Olf Rudbeks, which celebrated a
superior northern Gothic people who had never been subjugated by south-
erners. Danish archaeology's methodologies were adopted in Britain, which
had similar ring forts and shared Gothicist objectives, and migrated to the
United States, where the enigmatic mounds encouraged the same archaeological approaches and even interpretations. Where Rudbeks's evidence was
primarily linguistic and mythopoetic, the new nationalist archaeology was
object-based, as was the American enthusiasm for material culture, collected
from around the globe for cabinets of curiosity and in archaeological digs.
Rafn's investigations synthesized all of the main streams in antiquarian investigation: philology, archaeology, oral tradition, and semiotics. While nothing
immediately around Dighton Rock prompted an archaeologist to excavate,
the investigations it inspired did encompass archaeology as an Indigenous
burial at nearby Fall River was drawn into Rafn's theorizing.

The idea that Vinland existed somewhere in North America was not radical when Rafn began his researches in the 1820s. Paul-Henri Mallet made a
curious promise in 1755 that Pehr Kalm was about to propose that Vinland
was somewhere around the Strait of Belle Isle, between Newfoundland and
Labrador. While Kalm never published to this effect, the hunch as to the location was a remarkable foreshadowing of Helge Ingstad's discovery of Norse
ruins—the only such ruins in the Americas broadly accepted by archaeologists and historians—at L'Anse Aux Meadows in northern Newfoundland
in 1960.[17] Like Mallet, Thomas Pennant did not doubt the Norse reached

America, but he was certain for reasons unexplained they did *not* colonize it, or that they saw more of it than "barren" Labrador.[18]

The idea of a Norse presence (however temporary) in the Americas was plausible but abstruse to eighteenth-century writers: it mattered little to the construction of a Gothic sensibility in Europe. Mallet proposed in 1756 that Vinland was a Norse colony in Newfoundland or Labrador, but that attempting "to ascertain the exact fate, extent and fortune of the establishment, would be a fruitless labour."[19] And a Norse arrival, if it ever happened, was too far north, in Labrador or Newfoundland (and without any resulting colony, according to the influential Pennant) to matter to the contested narrative of America, where Anglo-Americans were constructing Transatlantic Gothicism as a race-based justification for colonization. For Vinland to factor in assertions about America's past and the race destiny of its present, the Norse exploits of the sagas would have to be located much farther south, in the United States.

DECADES BEFORE HEINRICH SCHLIEMANN relied on Homer's *Iliad* to locate a historical Troy, Carl Christian Rafn was certain the Vinland sagas could lead him to a historic Norse presence in North America. The chief sources and inspiration of all such searches have been two family narratives, called *Graelendinga Saga* (Greenlander's Saga) and *Eiriks Saga Rauda* (Eirik the Red's Saga).[20] They told—with varying degrees of concurrence, contradiction, and fantasy—the adventures of an assortment of voyagers, all but one of the leaders Greenland Norse, who sighted or attempted to colonize new lands to the west around A.D. 1000. The main voyages of interest to modern Vinland seekers were those of Leif Eiriksson and an Icelandic merchant, Thorfinn Thordsson *karlsefni* (a nickname or byname meaning "the stuff a man is made of"), generally known as Thorfinn Karlsefni.[21] Leif's voyage left a temporary settlement in Vinland called Leifsbúdir (Leifsbooths, a collection of huts). Karlsefni married Gudrid, widow of Leif's brother Thorstein, who had died shortly after returning from an attempt to reach the new lands. Gudrid and Karlsefni, with three ships, 160 colonists, and cattle, settled at a place called Hóp. The colonists battled with the local people the sagas called *skroellings* or *skraelings*, the settlement was abandoned, and the colonists returned to Iceland and Greenland. Thus ended the saga accounts of the attempts to explore and settle Vinland.

The Vinland sagas were not written down until more than two centuries after the events described. Different versions of the individual sagas survive, and they otherwise provide discordant accounts of voyages.[22] Scholars have accepted that the sagas, although a mass of contradictions and filled with elements of legend, are based on historical events. Rafn deserves much credit for the acceptance of their essential historicity. His pioneering investigations, however, were shaped, and compromised, by several factors: the scholarly novelty of the sagas; the inaccessibility and limited knowledge of geography in pertinent northern latitudes; his determination to conduct his geographical and archaeological research from the comfort of Copenhagen; and his reliance on American antiquarian informants for gathering research materials. These informants were clustered in urban centers of the eastern United States and were prone to providing him with potential evidence from their immediate surroundings. Moreover, these antiquaries already had produced an inventory of mysteries in seeking Old World explanations for the continent's past. In addition, because *Antiquitates Americanae* was an editorial project that relied on subscribers, Americans were far more likely to fund it if its Vinland evidence pointed to the United States. As it happened, Rafn's Gothicist impulse was to link the northern Protestants of the Old World with their descendants and relatives in the New World along America's populous eastern seaboard. All of these factors drove Rafn's Vinland search into the heart of southern New England, more than 1,000 miles southwest of L'Anse Aux Meadows.

Rafn was assisted and encouraged in producing *Antiquitates Americanae* by the leading American Scandinavianist, George Perkins Marsh. Marsh's Nordic enthusiasm, according to David Lowenthal, was rooted in part in "analogies between the solemn grandeur of Scandinavia and stern and rockbound New England, and between the moral excellences of the Goths and the Puritans," which "evoked in Marsh, as in some of his fellow-countrymen, both national and regional pride, and encouraged them to steep themselves in a stew of Gothicist romance and Scandinavian antiquities."[23] Rafn probably was at least initially assisted by another leading American Scandinavianist, Henry Wheaton, who had arrived in Copenhagen in 1827 as the first dedicated ambassador (chargé d'affaires) of the United States to Denmark.[24] Rafn also contacted the MHS, which elected him as a corresponding member in February 1829.[25] In June 1829, Rafn wrote the Rhode Island Historical Society (RIHS) in Providence, similarly seeking assistance, and Wheaton, who had strong personal connections to Providence, may have been the conduit.[26]

Evidence for the relationship thereafter between Wheaton and Rafn where *Antiquitates Americanae* is concerned is elusive, if nonexistent, which might have been due to differences in their attitudes toward Gothicism. Wheaton generally agreed that Anglo-Americans enjoyed some broad measure of Scandinavian roots, for, as he wrote in 1828, "even to us, the literature of the

North must have its interest,—since we deduce our origin, our language, and our laws, from the Scandinavian and Teutonic races."[27] But he was not interested in extending Gothicism across the Atlantic, especially in the broad terms asserted by Rafn in his society's 1836 report to British and American members. Rafn waxed romantic on the ancient connections between Angles, Saxons, Jutes, Scandinavians, and Scottish Highlanders. He asserted that Christianity had arrived in Norway from England, which would mean that the Christian Norse of Greenland who reached America in the sagas owed their soul's salvation to the English.[28] Wheaton in *History of the Northmen, or Danes and Normans* (1831) devoted only ten pages to the Vinland sagas and their historicity and said little more than Mallet had.[29] Had Rafn (and Magnussén) been forced to rely solely on Wheaton's cooperation, the most controversial aspects of the RSNA's researches would never have come to pass. But Rafn had been able to connect with the antiquaries of Rhode Island, likely with Wheaton's assistance. Through them American antiquity was changed, in many ways for the worse, and with Dighton Rock as the evidentiary centerpiece.[30]

Rafn would concentrate on three strategies of proof for Vinland's location in southern New England: assigning Indigenous cultural materials, including rock art, to the Norse (or making them of Norse inspiration); asserting Norse origins for Indigenous place names and legends; and assuming that Norse intermarriages during a long-standing presence in America produced a hybridized people that accounted for Indigenous intellectual capabilities and skills. Rafn's Gothic project, in short, was fundamentally reliant on appropriating Indigenous material culture and identity as Norse in much the same way that John Finch had wanted to make them Druidic. It was a tour de force of White Tribism. And in popularizing the sagas, *Antiquitates Americanae* validated a Gothicist racial hierarchy of handsome, capable Scandinavian men and women, in contrast with small, weak, ugly, and shifty Native American *skraelings* that was already encoded in the race science of Linnaeus and Meiners. *Antiquitates Americanae* also fueled a race longing, a sense that the Norse *should have* succeeded in colonizing America, which their Gothicist Anglo-American descendants were now achieving in their name and spirit, in the same lands, by overcoming the same unworthy, primitive people.

Rafn was assisted by an American whose contributions were so significant as to qualify him as a collaborator. Thomas Hopkins Webb was not yet twenty-eight when, as secretary of the RIHS, he made the first response to Rafn's 1829 request for input. After investigating Dighton Rock in 1830 with an initial RIHS committee, Webb assumed the chair of the society's Committee on the Antiquities and Aboriginal History of America, formed in April 1833 to assist Rafn.[31] Through Webb, the inscribed rocks of southern New England, foremost among them Dighton Rock, were brought to Rafn's attention. Private letters show that Webb was even more indispensible to Rafn's quest to locate Vinland in southern New England (and to engineer a popular and critical reception of Rafn's work in America) than the official societal correspondence from Webb to Rafn reproduced in *Antiquitates Americanae* might indicate.[32] The private letters also reveal the full extent of Rafn's reliance on White Tribism to assert a Norse presence in New England.

In an 1882 memoir of Webb, J. P. Quincy confessed: "To say the truth, I find that the sixteen years which have elapsed since his death have somewhat blurred his personality even to eyes that are in search of it."[33] Quincy left an impression of Webb as an enabler rather than an independent scholar or thinker. He was born in Providence in 1801, and after earning his medical degree from Harvard in 1825 established a practice in Providence, although his passions lay beyond medicine. He joined Brown University's Franklin Society, which was dedicated to literary and learned matters, and reported on local mineralogy in *The American Journal of Science and Arts*.[34]

Webb's fellow members of the RIHS Antiquities and Aboriginal History committee were Albert Gorton Greene and John Russell Bartlett. Greene, a founding member of the RIHS in 1822, does not figure significantly in the records of the committee's activities.[35] Bartlett had a limited education but had worked his way up from a position in his uncle's dry goods business to become prominent in banking in Providence. Bartlett, like Webb, was a member of the Franklin Society, and Webb, Greene, and Bartlett were all involved in running the Providence Athenaeum, a private library and reading room established in 1831, where Bartlett indulged his love of books as its first treasurer, librarian, and cataloguer.[36] By 1833 the young trio were senior figures in the historical society, with Webb serving as the society's secretary and Bartlett its treasurer. Bartlett occasionally wrote Rafn directly (although the letters do not survive), and (as I will explain in chapter 8) would cofound the American Ethnological Society (AES) in New York. Webb, as chair of the RIHS committee, took the lead in dealing with Rafn.

Webb would claim in 1854 that he had proceeded with "the greatest caution" in his fact gathering for Rafn, especially in trying to determine "whether Indians were, or had been, in the practice of making Rock Inscriptions." He recalled writing letters to the few authorities he could identify, among them Henry Rowe Schoolcraft and Lewis Cass, to whom I will return in chapter 7. "They all sent similar replies; which were in substance that they knew of, and to the best of their opinion and belief there existed *no Indian Rock Inscrip-*

tions."[37] Webb's lengthy response to Rafn's June 1829 request for assistance, however, written in September 1830, made no mention of such consultations, and if they happened they probably came later. Webb was forthright in a manner Schoolcraft never would have been, especially in disassociating living Native Americans from American antiquities. Webb assured Rafn: "That the existence of the Continent of America was known to European Nations at a period anterior to the Voyages of Columbus has long been the received opinion of many of our most learned Antiquaries."[38] Webb testified to the "numerous and extensive mounds" similar to ones in Scandinavia, Tartary, and Russia, as well as fortifications "that must have required for their construction, a degree of industry, labour and skill, as well as an advancement of the Arts, that never characterized any of the Indian tribes."[39] There were also inscribed rocks, and Webb flexed his amateur mineralogy to assert that it was "almost impossible" for Indians to have engraved on them without the aid of iron or some other hard metal instruments. The Indians, he assured Rafn, "were ignorant of the existence of these rocks," and only learned to work with iron tools from Europeans, after the English had settled the country.[40]

Webb had visited Dighton Rock with the initial RIHS committee in February 1830 and, as he explained to Rafn, "No one, who examines attentively the workmanship, will believe it to have been done by the Indians. Moreover, it is well attested, that no where, throughout our wide spread domain, is a single instance of their recording or having recorded their deeds or history, on Stone."[41] In asserting that Native Americans had nothing to do with the storied mounds of the Ohio country, Webb had the temerity to cite Benjamin Smith Barton, who actually had argued for a Native American provenance for them.[42] Webb relied heavily on the researches of Ezra Stiles on the inscribed rocks of New England, and otherwise was indiscriminate in relating possible evidence. Among the scattergun bits Webb offered was Thaddeus Mason Harris's account of copper coins found at Medford, Massachusetts, whose designs resembled Tartarian characters illustrated in Strahlenberg. Webb lamented to Rafn the loss of many inscribed rocks. The farmer who cleared wild lands "sees in those rocks nothing but unmeaning scrawls of, as he supposes, the idle Indian, who has spent his time in this lazy manner."[43] Rafn could not have found a more like-minded, more enabling and more cooperative collaborator than Webb in appropriating an Indigenous past so as to locate the events of the Vinland sagas in southern New England.

HENRY WHEATON MADE a tentative effort to locate Vinland in *History of the Northmen*. Rafn or Magnussén probably had shared with Wheaton material from their early researches. Wheaton made the offhand observation that if the sun rose at 7:30 and set at 4:30 in Leif Eiriksson's Vinland, as the sagas supposedly indicated, "it must have been in the latitude of Boston."[44] The idea that the length of the day mentioned in the sagas could be determined in hours, and that a latitude figure could be distilled from it, had been around for more than a century.[45] The latest iteration of this speculative method probably was Magnussén's doing, and would have been shared with Wheaton close to Wheaton's publication date of 1831, as Wheaton appended the information in a footnote.[46]

In 1828, when Rafn sought to enlist the aid of American antiquaries, he had cast a reasonably wide net as to the location of Vinland, from the Gaspé Peninsula to the Carolinas, but by 1831, the location had narrowed to the latitude of Boston. Magnussén's astronomical analysis probably did not lead Rafn to the Boston area, but rather Rafn's determination to place Vinland in the Boston area led Magnussén to produce a supportive interpretation of its latitude. Rafn in 1830 had received his first (and highly detailed) response from Thomas H. Webb about the possible evidence carved into stones around southern New England, especially in the long-debated Dighton Rock, about thirty miles south of Boston. Webb's September 1830 letter thus was fundamental in directing Rafn's researches. Once Rafn had decided southern New England and Dighton Rock presented his best hope of offering definitive physical proof for a historical Vinland, he (and Magnussén) focused on producing evidence that fit the theory, and where need be, on making that evidence fit.

After receiving Webb's letter of September 1830, Rafn let several years lapse in silence, not acknowledging receipt of the previous materials until September 1833.[47] In May 1834 Rafn informed Webb that he was confident he could decipher Dighton Rock. He submitted twenty-five questions about the rock and the surrounding geography, flora, and fauna, which were inspired by details in the Karlsefni story. Rafn also asked for "a view of the rock (the side of it where the inscription is) as seen when highest out of the water, with a view to its being engraved for our work."[48] The Rhode Island society had already provided Rafn with two unpublished drawings, the one by Baylies and Goodwin in 1790 and a more recent one by a local farmer, Job Gardner, made in 1812. Webb's committee produced two drawings of its own: one of the inscription, and the other, by Bartlett, depicting the rock in its natural setting. These new drawings, along with copies of the better-known earlier ones, were sent to Rafn in January 1835.[49]

The drawings proved critical in transforming Dighton Rock into a Norse relic, but equally critical was a comment Webb made in an addendum to his response to Rafn of November 30, 1834: "Mount Hope, or *Haup* as the Indians termed it."[50] Mount Hope lies on the west shore of Mount Hope Bay, within present-day Bristol, Rhode Island, where the Taunton River widens a dozen miles downstream from Dighton Rock as it empties into Narragansett Bay. Webb must have gathered the fact that Hope allegedly derived from *Haup* from Jedidiah Morse's *The American Universal Geography*, as the source is otherwise unknown.[51] Morse also was Webb's likely source for an "Ethiopian" inscription at Rutland, Vermont, to which he alerted Rafn in 1830.[52] Kendall had read about this inscription in Morse's 1805 edition, and on investigation found it to be nothing more than a natural line of white quartz interspersed with black crystals in a chunk of granite lodged in a barn foundation.[53] Rafn would still be asking Webb about the Rutland inscription in April 1835.[54] As for Mount Hope, Morse described both *Mount Haupe bay* and *Mount Haup*, which "was once the capital of the Wampanoags, and the residence of Philip [Metacom]."[55] For Rafn, this was an astounding revelation.

Rafn had been scouring modern maps since at least 1828 for clues to the presence of Norsemen among Indigenous peoples. As the notice published in Philadelphia and repeated in Baltimore asserted: "In the names of the northern American places, traces of the Scandinavian descent of the early settlers are found." Rafn would assert in *Antiquitates Americanae* that *Hope* was an English colonial corruption of the Native American *Haup*. Rafn then had to turn the Native American term into a corruption of a Scandinavian term, *hóp*, pronounced *hope*. As Rafn explained, *hóp* "may either denote a small recess, or bay, formed by a river from the interior, falling into an inlet from the sea, or the land bordering on such a bay."[56] The sagas tell us that after Karlsefni spent an initial winter at a place called Straumfjord ("Current Fjord") somewhere north of Vinland, he sailed southward along the land for a long time until reaching a *hóp* where a river flowed down from the land and into a lake separated from the sea by large sandbars. Karlsefni appropriately named the place Hóp and made a settlement there, but abandoned it after fighting with the skraelings. The sagas tell us nothing about how far or in precisely which direction Karlsefni had sailed to reach Hóp, and so there is still plenty of leeway for speculation as to its location.

It must have seemed almost too good to be true to Rafn that the body of water through which the Taunton River flowed toward the sea, so close to Dighton Rock, originally was called *Haup* by Native Americans. Rafn was also impressed by the tradition that Dighton Rock commemorated a battle between Native Americans and strangers who came up the river in a wooden boat. Rafn asked Webb if there was enough water in the Taunton River for a European vessel of the Middle Ages to navigate it. Webb assured him ten feet of water could be found in the channel to Dighton.[57] But Mount Hope Bay, which is some fifteen miles from the sea, only dimly qualifies as a *hóp*, provided we imagine one of its outlets, the narrows at Tiverton at the north end of Aquidneck Island, once created a partial embayment at a time when sea levels were lower than today. Rafn also made Leif Eiriksson's Leifsbúdir and Karlsefni's Hóp one and the same place, on the western shore of Mount Hope Bay.[58] However, no reading of the sagas would agree with this concordance. Leifsbúdir and Straumfjord probably were one and the same, on the evidence of the Greenlander's Saga, but Hóp lay a good sailing distance away.[59]

Using the statement in the Greenlander's Saga about the length of the midwinter day in Vinland, Rafn (or rather Magnussén) concluded with astounding precision that Vinland lay in the vicinity of 41 degrees, 24 minutes, 10 seconds latitude north, which aligned with the ocean's entrance to Narragansett Bay.[60] Thus the key saga events involving Leif Eiriksson and Thorfinn Karlsefni at Leifsbúdir and Hóp had occurred in the northeastern reaches of Narragansett Bay at Mount Hope Bay, downstream from Dighton Rock.

FINN MAGNUSSÉN ALREADY was interpreting Dighton Rock's markings largely on the basis of the Baylies-Goodwin drawing before the drawings made by Webb's committee had arrived. *Antiquitates Americanae* would devote nineteen pages to analysis by Magnussén that can safely be called fevered and of a piece with the pictographic fantasies of Antoine Court de Gébelin, Samuel Harris, Charles-Léopold Mathieu, and Ira Hill.[61] He arrived at his Dighton Rock reading around the same time that he produced a catastrophic misinterpretation of Sweden's Runamo Rock. Magnussén declared in 1833 the rock was inscribed in runes with a poem about the Battle of Bråvalla. In 1836, the Swedish chemist, Jakob Berzelius, determined the "runes" were natural markings.[62] On Dighton Rock, Magnussén detected a tableau of images relating to the Karlsefni voyage. For example, Karlsefni had taken cattle to Hóp, and to Magnussén the horned quadruped figure recounted the saga episode of one of Karlsefni's bulls frightening away the skraelings. Magnussén also saw Karlsefni being showered with skraeling arrows, the figure of Karlsefni's wife, Gudrid, and their child Snorri, a shield with an inverted helmet that symbolized peace, a ship, and figures of skraelings.

Magnussén found an inscription, a combination of Roman letters and runic writing. He teased from the horizontal XXX pattern "CXXXI," for the number of people in Karlsefni's company. The sagas, however, told of a party of 160 (including five women), whereas the Roman numerals totaled only 131. Magnussén decided the "C" represented the Scandinavian "great hundred" of twelve decades to the hundred, or 120, and so the total was actually 151. As nine members of Karlsefni's party led by Thorhall the Hunter sailed off on their own in Eirik the Red's Saga, subtracting them from 160 neatly arrived at 151, the true number of Karlsefni's company at Hóp. Magnussén, however, miscounted: Thorhall left *with* nine men, and so Magnussén should have subtracted ten from 160, which would have left him at 150.

Magnussén's efforts to place Karlsefni's name in the rock are too complex to relate, but suffice it to say that he found the mash-up of runic and Latin letters ÞRFIŊS, or Thorfins. Other letters, some of them abbreviations, allowed Magnussén (and Rafn) to extract a message: "Thorfins and his 151 companions took possession of this land."[63] Using a drawing of the inscribed rock at nearby Tiverton supplied by Webb, they also found runic letters indicating Leif Eiriksson and a German companion, Tyrkir the Southerner, left their single-initial marks.[64] Such was the excitement generated by the idea that Dighton Rock was a Norse relic that a new theory tabled in 1838 by France's Moreau de Dammartin, proposing the inscription was an Egyptian sky map ("a fragment of the oriental celestial sphere, or an astronomical theme for a given moment, i.e., for December 25th at midnight, epoch of the winter solstice"), sank more promptly than it might have otherwise.[65]

Edmund Burke Delabarre secured a photograph of the original 1834 RIHS drawing in the collection of the Royal Society of Northern Antiquaries, and concluded that Magnussén and Rafn had added critical elements, especially alphabetic ones, without making clear that they were publishing a composite of different drawings, and had mislabeled the end product as the work of the RIHS in 1830, when the drawing actually was done in 1834. Their treatment fell short—barely—of scholarly fraud. In 1854, Thomas H. Webb recounted how the RIHS committee used "dots and cross lines" to distinguish indistinct features from the solid lines indicating clear features.[66] Delabarre concluded that the Danish scholars too used some shading to add features, and noted that in engraving and printing the drawing, all distinction was lost between what was original and what was added, with the subtleties of dotted lines and shading otherwise either lost or discarded. No extant drawing, on its own, made possible the detection of Karlsefni's name. And unlike the sagas, based on an irrecoverable past, Dighton Rock could be inspected to confirm Rafn's and Magnussén's interpretation. Bartlett was the only member of the Rhode Island committee that created the original drawing to make a public objection to the version Rafn printed. Even at that, Bartlett's protest did not appear in print until 1873, and he refrained from accusing Rafn and Magnussén of misrepresenting the committee's work (see chapter 8). Delabarre would write: "Opinion is almost unanimous that there is nothing there that at all resembles ThORFINS."[67] Unfortunately for scholarship on American antiquity, the truth as to the RIHS drawing would not emerge through Delabarre's research until some eighty years after its publication in *Antiquitates Americanae*, and even now the Rafn-Magnussén version continues to be reproduced uncritically, even in scholarly works.

Despite the skepticism expressed by learned American reviewers of *Antiquitates Americanae* and by other antiquaries as to the Karlsefni inscription (see chapter 7), the larger assertion that Narragansett Bay was the heart of Vinland was considered sound. The Norse claim that Rafn staked to Dighton Rock—by making its markings a Norse claim-staking to America—proved lasting, aided by popularizing English-language works by RSNA members Joshua Toulmin Smith and Ludlow North Beamish. The most influential effort, Beamish's *The Discovery of America by the Northmen, in the Tenth Century*, summarized the Dighton Rock evidence in less than four pages, although the controversial drawing was included and Beamish assured readers: "Professor Rafn has gone into elaborate dissertation upon this inscription, proving by unanswerable arguments its Scandinavian origin."[68] As Beamish's late-nineteenth-century biographer Henry Manns Chichester praised, "Beamish's modest volume not only popularised the discovery by epitomising the principal details in Rafn's great work, 'Antiquitates Americanæ' (Copenhagen, 1837), but it contains, in the shape of translations from the Sagas, one of the best summaries of Icelandic historical literature anywhere to be found within an equal space."[69] Beamish's volume was reissued by the Prince Society of Boston in 1877, and it may deserve the lion's share of credit for the widespread acceptance of the idea not only that the Norse reached North America, but also that Vinland was in southern New England, with Dighton Rock providing incontrovertible proof.

CARL CHRISTIAN RAFN ESTABLISHED an enduring strain of White Tribism in *Antiquitates Americanae* by turning saga references to Hvítramannaland, or White Men's Land, into a historical fact. In Eirik the Red's Saga, Karlsefni's party on their return journey to Greenland capture two skraeling boys in Markland, who tell them "there was a country across from their own land where the people went about in white clothing and uttered loud cries and carried poles with patches of cloth attached. This is thought to have been Hvítramannaland."[70] The Hauksbók version of Eirik the Red's Saga notes that Hvítramannaland was also called Greater Ireland.[71] White Men's Land also appeared in the story of Are Márson in the Landnámabók (the book of land-taking), the saga describing the settlement of Iceland. Márson's ship is blown by storm to this land, and Márson is baptized there.[72] Rafn ignored the fact that Hvítramannaland was a mere six days from Ireland in the Márson story. Casting it as *the Land of the White Men* or *Great Ireland*, settled by Irish Christians prior to A.D. 1000, Rafn gave the colony a sprawling locale, from Chesapeake Bay south to Florida. In support, Rafn alluded to an alleged Shawnee tradition "that Florida was once inhabited by white people, who were in possession of iron implements."[73] John Johnston, an Indian agent at Piqua, Ohio, had related the tradition in an 1819 letter to Caleb Atwater published in volume 1 of *Archaeologia Americana*. Johnston held that the Shawnee had migrated to Ohio from west Florida only sixty-five years earlier. "The people of this nation have a tradition that their ancestors crossed the sea. . . . It is a prevailing opinion among them that Florida had once been inhabited by white people, who had the use of iron tools. Black Hoof affirms, that he has often heard it spoken of by old people, that stumps of trees covered with earth, were frequently found, which had been cut down by edged tools."[74]

Johnston subscribed to the Ten Lost Tribes explanation for Native Americans origins, as his letter to Atwater reiterated, which undermines the credibility of a Shawnee tradition that otherwise has no apparent ethnographic basis.[75] Scholarship has been nearly unanimous in regarding Hvítramannaland as most likely a fiction based on an Irish tradition that had insinuated itself into Eirik the Red's Saga.[76] White Men's Land nevertheless became a staple of popular and pseudohistorical accounts of pre-Columbian discovery, perhaps the most literal expression of the colonizers' opinion of to whom North America truly belonged.[77]

ANTIQUITATES AMERICANAE WAS ONLY the beginning of Dighton Rock's new role as a Norse antiquity anchoring a Gothicist enthusiasm for a pre-Columbian presence in North America. Further investigations and speculations about Norsemen (and early Europeans in general) in North America were captured and promoted by the Royal Society of Northern Antiquaries' journal, *Mémoires*.

Rafn had much unfinished business in his White Tribism inclinations, even before *Antiquitates Americanae* was published. He suspected more place names than Mount Haup were Norse and had been remembered imperfectly by Native Americans and then adopted by English colonists. In an April 1835 letter to Webb, Rafn wanted to know if Brattleboro, in Vermont, Truro, at the northern tip of Cape Cod (and Cape Cod itself), and Assonet, the site of Dighton Rock, were Indian names.[78] While he did not include his list of purported Norse place names in *Antiquitates Americanae*, he began revisiting it with Webb in 1839, hoping to publish an article in *Mémoires*.

Rafn was fluent in Danish, English, and French, and wrote scholarly works on runes, but his ignorance of Indigenous languages was profound. In June 1835, Rafn sent Webb a variety of publications, including "some minor publications in the Greenland tongue. It may perhaps be worth while to direct attention to the language spoken by the Esquimaux of Greenland, with a view to a comparison between it and the Esquimaux dialect of America."[79] That Rafn thought there was an *Esquimaux* dialect that would have a bearing on place names in New England was revealing. On Rafn's death, Webb would recall sending Rafn *A Key into the Language of America* (1643) by Roger Williams, assuredly in the form of its RIHS reprinting. As Williams did not discuss place names in his rough assembly of Algonquian words and phrases, Rafn probably did not consider Williams of much use.[80] Webb turned for help to one of the foremost experts on Native American languages, John Pickering, who had overseen the RIHS republication of the Williams lexicon. Pickering was "the only scholar hereabouts, within my knowledge, properly qualified to sit in judgment on the case," Webb recalled. "I communicated Professor Rafn's conjectures, which struck him with much surprise. He said that the subject was one deserving a thorough, critical examination. I consequently furnished him with a copy."[81]

We can only guess at the degree of disbelief Pickering experienced in examining Rafn's ideas. In a letter to Webb on April 26, 1839, Rafn asserted that place names ending in *-et* (a suffix that signified a place in the Algonquian dialects of southern New England) were Norse. As well, all of the place names with the suffix *-nessit* or its variants, including Nauset, became *Nesit* in old Norse or *Nassit* in modern Danish (whose meaning he did not explain, although how the Danish word for "messy" or "gooey" should have applied defies understanding). According to Rafn, *Pocconaset* derived from a proper name, Pocka, which could be found in records of Iceland, Greenland, and Norway. *Poppinnessit* or *Poponesset* possibly derived from Poppa, "one of the earliest preachers of Christianity in Denmark . . . which name has subsequently been given to many persons in our northern countries." Rafn's discussion of place names consumed most of three dense pages in this single letter, and included an assertion that Mashpee was Másby, "from Más, the name of a man, gen. Más, and byr, by, a town or farm," and Assonet was Esiones, "from *esia*, gen. *esio*, a marshy district."[82] Place names made for an extended discussion between Rafn and Webb. Rafn wrote on April 21, 1840: "You ask me if I consider the names *Moswetuset* and *Aquiday* to be of Old Danish original. I think it not unlikely that they may be." Rafn turned Moswetuset into Mosveduset, a combination of the words *Másvidr* ("Mar's wood") and *húset* ("the house") and Aquiday into Hvítay ("pronounced nearly *a Kvitay*"), meaning "on white island."[83]

Rafn was also inclined to find traces of Norse influence in Native American traditions, much as Rudbeks saw Gothic roots in Greek mythology. Webb had sent Rafn a number of volumes on New England history, which Rafn evidently mined to gain some knowledge of Indigenous lore, and he combined this with his word hunting in explaining the origin of Seaconnet.[84] Rafn bent it into Seáconunesit, which meant Mermaid Cape in Old Norse. Rafn was crafting his own version of the well-known Indigenous tradition of the giant Maushop and his wife, Squant, who were associated with Nantucket and whaling. In a variation related by James Freeman in 1815, Maushop retreated to parts unknown at the arrival of the English, and threw his wife onto Seaconnet Point, where she became a misshapen rock.[85] Rafn was en route to equating Maushop with the pagan Thorhall the Hunter of the Karlsefni voyage. In Eirik the Red's Saga, Thorhall performs a rite atop a seaside cliff, and boasts to the starving expedition that a whale that has washed ashore to feed them was a reward from his namesake, Thor.[86] Thorhall soon disappeared from the saga, departing with nine companions to seek Vinland. The saga has them swept away by a storm to Ireland, where they are enslaved. The Maushop story, however, seemed to suggest to Rafn the White Tribism influence of the Norse. If Thorhall was Maushop, and he had a wife, then Thorhall must have sired Indian progeny with Norse blood, and been worshipped at least in memory.

Rafn suspected a much more extensive and extended presence of the Norse among Native Americans. As he informed Webb in 1840: "As far as I can judge, these local names furnish a proof that the ancient Northmen have *during several centuries* inhabited your district."[87] Rafn expanded on his White Tribism convictions in 1841: "As the Scandinavians were settled for a considerable time in your country, and as it is highly probable that the Indians of Massachusetts and Rhode Island were a mixed race partly derived from them, it becomes easy to explain how skill in the cutting and delineating of inscriptions was transmitted from this race to the other tribes and thus diffused over

North America, assuming as we may do, that the pure Indian races acquired the art from that which was mixed with the Scandinavians."[88] (The idea there were Native Americans of mixed descent from Norsemen had been proposed as early as 1796 by Christoph Girtanner, a writer on natural sciences at Göttingen.)[89] In short, while the Norse newcomers did not create all the rock inscriptions to be found in North America, the example provided by the Norse, and the racial improvements afforded by an infusion of their blood, made Native Americans capable of creating them.

Rafn pressed Webb repeatedly for Pickering's verification of his word-hunting ideas, as he was reluctant to publish without it.[90] They were still waiting for Pickering to comment when Pickering died in 1846. Pickering's repeated assurances that he would get to Rafn's ideas when he could secure "a release from a portion of his professional and other duties" may have cloaked a mortified response to Rafn's linguistic eccentricity.[91] Rafn's Lost Tribism where Native American place names were concerned might have remained far from public consumption were it not for Webb. In writing of his experiences with Rafn after Rafn's death in October 1864, Webb quoted at length from Rafn's letters in the Massachusetts Historical Society's *Proceedings* of 1864–65.[92] Rafn had never published this material, not having secured the informed scholarly opinion he had desired. Webb, however, considered the material too interesting not to share with the public, without any comment as to its validity, and so the Lost Tribism word hunting that saw proof of Transatlantic Gothicist adventuring preserved in Native American words finally found a way to daylight.

RAFN'S DETERMINATION TO PROVE a Norse presence in eastern North America extended to the object-based epistemology of archaeology. The discipline was sufficiently established through the Mound Builders that Americans were accustomed to excavating literal mounds of buried evidence for mysterious peoples of the pre-Columbian era. Rafn and Magnussén, through a new committee of the Royal Society of Northern Antiquaries devoted to the "Ante-Columbian History of America," encouraged investigations for such evidence where early European visitors were concerned, and naturally created the demand for it. Without such additional physical proof, it was difficult to sustain Rafn's idea of a prolonged and influential Norse presence. The society's *Mémoires* thus became an important propagator of pre-Columbian fringe history.

Rafn and Webb were like-minded about the Old Stone Mill of Newport, Rhode Island, which would become better known to pseudohistory as the

Newport Tower. In a series of letters that Webb began writing to Rafn in May 1839 and that were published that year in *Mémoires*, Webb asserted that the stone structure, a cylinder-shaped ruin with Romanesque arches at its base, "has, for a long time, been an object of wonder to beholders, exciting the curiosity of all who visit it, and giving rise to many speculations and conjectures, among both the learned and unlearned. But nothing entirely satisfactory has ever been decided about it; it still remains shrouded with mystery."[93] Nothing better illustrates the fact that this "mystery" was a recent product of either local enthusiasms for *Antiquitates Americanae* or Webb's own imagination than the complete lack of interest shown in the tower by Ezra Stiles, who lived in Newport and was determined to prove ancient Old World visitors had trod this very ground. Rafn in his commentary and through illustrative plates turned the shell of the old mill into a Norse church. Charles Timothy Brooks demolished this idea in 1851, linking the mill to Rhode Island's seventeenth-century governor, Benedict Arnold, and all but proving it was built no earlier than 1657. Brooks showed that its Romanesque design was strikingly similar to a mill built in Chesterton, England, in 1632, a few miles from where Arnold grew up.[94] In 1951 the mill was firmly dated to the colonial era by the presence of seventeenth-century materials beneath its foundation.[95]

More pertinent to the White Tribism inclinations of Rafn was the so-called "skeleton in armor" discovered at Fall River, only a few miles downriver from Dighton Rock, in April 1831. Jared Sparks drew attention to the burial in an article in the *American Monthly Magazine* of January 1836 (figure 7).[96] The Harvard-educated Sparks was the only American historian, in the judgment of an 1867 memoir, to equal the scholarly efforts of George Bancroft.[97] He would be appointed McLean Professor of Ancient and Modern History at Harvard in 1839, and was later elected president of Harvard. Sparks's status is important to bear in mind when reading his article on the Fall River skeleton, as he fully subscribed to the multiple-migration displacement scenario that cast Native Americans as brutish usurpers of the superior original inhabitants, which President Andrew Jackson had cited in justifying his Indian Removal Act of 1830. The tragedy of the Trail of Tears was but two years away.[98]

The burial was a typical Indigenous one of the 1620–70 period in southern New England.[99] "That the body was not one of the Indians, we think needs no argument," Sparks nevertheless declared.[100] The body belonged either to "one of the race who inhabited this country for a time anterior to the so called Aborigines . . . or to one of the crew of some Phoenician vessel, that, blown

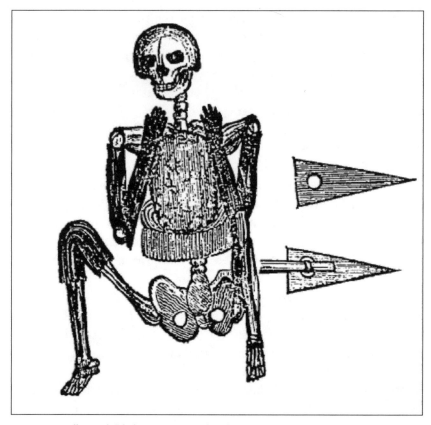

FIGURE 7 Fall River's "skeleton in armour," as depicted in an article by Harvard historian Jared Sparks in *American Monthly Magazine,* January 1836. Sparks argued the typical seventeenth-century Indigenous burial was Phoenician.

out of her course, thus discovered the western world long before the Christian era."[101] Sparks preferred the Phoenician interpretation, noting that the burial was in "the immediate neighborhood of 'Dighton Rock,' famed for its hieroglyphic inscription, of which no sufficient explanation has yet been given."[102] Sparks stated that near the rock "brazen" (brass) vessels had been found, which was a novelty in the Dighton Rock historiography. Sparks ventured these Phoenician mariners, "the unwilling and unfortunate discoverers of a new world—lived some time after they landed; and have written their names, perhaps their epitaphs, upon the rock at Dighton, died, and were buried by the natives."[103]

Webb investigated the Fall River burial at Rafn's request. While this did not involve an actual dig, Webb made a credible, careful assessment of the site and the recovered artifacts. He sent Rafn samples of tubes that formed a belt or necklace, metal arrowheads, and most of what survived of a rectangular "breast plate."[104] Webb's report was noncommittal about a possible ancient European provenance, but Rafn responded with intransigent conviction in *Mémoires*. The belt "bears a great resemblance to belts that have been found in our regions of the North in connexion with antiquities from the times of paganism."[105] Rafn had the breastplate analyzed, which returned an analysis of 70 percent copper and 28 percent zinc. The metal was brass, and so could not have been created by Native Americans. But Rafn was oblivious (or hostile) to the most logical explanation: given the Indigenous nature of the burial and the fact that flesh still remained on the bones, the body would have dated from the early colonial period of the seventeenth century, before King Philip's War. The brass materials would have been secured through trade from the European newcomers and fashioned into traditional items that prior to Contact had been made of annealed North American copper. A metal plate or plaque, suspended around the neck, would have indicated a man's high status. Such ornaments were widespread among peoples east of the Rockies. The Coronado expedition in 1542 met the Wichita people in what is now Kansas, and as the narrative of Pedro Castañeda recounted, "Their lord wore a copper plate on his neck and prized it highly."[106] Gabriel Archer's account of the 1602 Gosnold voyage to New England described an encounter on upper Cape Cod with a Native American who "had hanging about his necke a plate of rich Copper in length a foot, in breadth half a foot for a brest-plate."[107] The artist John White had portrayed a Roanoke chief or *werowance* wearing such a rectangular copper plaque. Rafn (or anyone else) could have consulted Theodore de Bry's popular engraved version of White's painting in *A Brief and True Report* (1590) and seen this particular plaque for himself.[108]

Sparks asserted that the method of constructing the Fall River arrows from copper "was never practiced by the Indians," but Rafn admitted the metal arrows bore no resemblance to anything found in Europe.[109] Rafn nevertheless was not going to leave this burial to the Phoenicians, as Sparks proposed. Rafn stressed that Fall River "is situated precisely at the spot which, in the Map of the Vinland of our ancestors, I have assigned as the position of Leifsbúdir."[110] As for how these items came to be part of a burial at Fall River, Rafn proposed: "on many occasions such antiquities may reasonably be assumed to originate from the descendants of the ancient Scandinavian colonists, who, on the cessation of all communication with the mother country, would naturally get intermingled with the wild natives. In this view, we are not on all occasions to suppose that the articles, so found, are actually Scandinavian, but more frequently that they have been fabricated after Scandinavian prototypes."[111]

The Fall River skeleton and the Newport Tower were immortalized through the Gothicist enthusiasms of Henry Wadsworth Longfellow, who had been among the first Americans to make the pilgrimage to study history at Göttingen, where the historian and philosopher Christoph Meiners had crafted his Gothic-tinged racial scheme of humanity. His poem "The Skeleton in Armor" was completed by December 1840, when Longfellow informed Samuel Ward that it "is connected with the Old Round Tower at Newport. The skeleton in armor really exists. It was dug up near Fall River, where I saw it some two years ago. . . . I suppose it to be the remains of one of the old Northern sea-rovers, who came into this country in the tenth century. Of course I make the tradition myself."[112] In a preface to the poem, published in 1842, Longfellow made clear his indebtedness to Rafn and the material on the Newport Mill in the first volume of *Mémoires*.[113] Longfellow's poem may not have proved important over the long term to historical theories of early New World visitors, but it was crucial in fusing a romantic literary Gothicism with the scholarly efforts of Rafn and like-minded Americans such as Webb, and in popularizing the idea of daring Old World visitors to New England. "The Skeleton in Armor" outlived the skeleton that inspired it, as it was destroyed in a museum fire around 1843.

THROUGH *ANTIQUITATES AMERICANAE*, Gothicism brought hardy northern European Christians into the Taunton River more than 600 years before Metacom's uprising was defeated, to inscribe on Dighton Rock a statement of claim ("Thorfins and his 151 companions took possession of this land"), which became an a priori assertion of European entitlement to the New World. Rafn's arguments for an earlier Irish Christian colony called White Men's Land in eastern North America was as clear a statement as could be made about entitlement and belonging. An Indigenous inscription was recast as a Norse commemoration of Indigenous savagery, as arrows flew against Thorfinn Karlsefni's colonists and forced them to retreat to Iceland and Greenland. A burial at Fall River of an Indigenous leader (who likely would have known Dighton Rock) became a Scandinavian one, or at least evidence of the Norse improvement of the skraelings. Mount Hope, where Metacom was cornered and killed in 1676, became Hóp, the homestead of the Karlsefni colony as well as the site of Leif Eiriksson's Leifsbúdir. By Rafn's logic, the people led by Metacom during King Philip's War, called the *Pocanoket* in a 1671 document, some of whose descendants were the Pokanoket of Cape Cod whom Kendall met, were sporting a name that was derivative of *Pocka* and indicated a Norse bloodline.[114] Indigenous lands and identity thus were possessed by their Gothic superiors, who made a biological improvement of the original Tartarian migrant stock. Metacom's ancestors, the skraelings of the sagas, may have succeeded in driving away Karlsefni in Rafn's version of American antiquity, but the northern European strangers returned in much larger numbers as English, in a fresh wave of the Japhetic migration that asserted possession over the land as well as over the past. Karlsefni had been at Mount Hope and left behind the markings on Dighton Rock because Anglo-Americans who claimed through romantic Gothicism to have sprung from the same root stock as Karlsefni were prepared to agree with Rafn that it was so—and were free to say so because they possessed the rock, its surrounding territories, the great institutions of education, the learned societies, and the publishing operations that disseminated their convictions.

CHAPTER SEVEN

Shingwauk's Reading
Dighton Rock and Henry Rowe Schoolcraft's Troubled Ethnology

In the summer of 1839, Henry Rowe Schoolcraft, the superintendent of Indian affairs for the Michigan Territory, arrived at his post at Michilimackinac, the island on the strait between lakes Michigan and Huron. Schoolcraft had been active in ethnology and philology in the United States for almost two decades, and the publication of his two-volume *Algic Researches* that same year secured his reputation as an authority on Native American oral traditions and beliefs.[1] He was carrying a copy of *Antiquitates Americanae*, which he had just reviewed for *The American Biblical Repository*. Its interpretation of Dighton Rock as a Norse inscription had not impressed him, and he was curious about what he might learn of its markings from an Indigenous perspective. No one else publishing on Native American culture likely had as much experience as Schoolcraft did in the "picture writing" of Native Americans, and for Dighton Rock he wanted to hear from the most authoritative Ojibwa man he knew on that subject. Shingwauk was a prominent political and spiritual figure among the Ojibwa around the American post at nearby Sault Ste. Marie.[2] He was now living on the Canadian side of the border, at St. Mary's, and Schoolcraft sent him an invitation to visit so that he could show him the drawings in *Antiquitates Americanae*.[3]

After almost 180 years, Shingwauk's interpretation remains the only firmly documented "reading" of Dighton Rock by an Indigenous authority. While Shingwauk's recognition of the Dighton Rock markings as Indigenous can be accepted, his interpretation remains contestable. Shingwauk was an Ojibwa from the upper Great Lakes, not a member of a New England Indigenous community, but his reading is most problematic because it came to us through Schoolcraft, who repeatedly revised his own opinion of Dighton Rock.

Schoolcraft's writings on Dighton Rock, and on Native Americans in general, must be placed in the context of evolving theories and practices of ethnology and the emergence of American anthropology, and especially in the context of the ferment of debate about Native American origins. Twelve tumultuous years also transpired in Schoolcraft's life between securing Shingwauk's interpretation in 1839 and publishing it in 1851. To understand Shing-wauk's reading of Dighton Rock, then, we need to begin by understanding the life of Henry Rowe Schoolcraft, his intellectual milieu, his marriage into a prominent Ojibwa family, and his struggles with competing ideas about, and evidence of, American antiquity.

BORN IN 1793 in upstate New York, Henry Rowe Schoolcraft was privately tutored in chemistry, geology, and mineralogy while receiving what Richard G. Bremer has called a "smattering" of formal education.[4] Schoolcraft's life was marked by repeated efforts to secure (and retain) political appointments and favors. He attached himself as a mineralogist to the 1820 expedition of Lewis Cass, who served as governor of the Michigan Territory from 1813 to 1831 and was appointed governor of the Northwest Territory in 1818. Cass's expedition was to reconnoiter what is now northern Wisconsin and Minnesota. Schoolcraft recounted his experiences traveling with Chippewa (Ojibwa) guides and meeting a variety of peoples, including Dakota, with whom the Chippewa were sporadically at war, in *Narrative Journal of Travels through the Northwestern Regions of the United States* (1821).

Cass became a close friend and mentor to Schoolcraft. In 1823 Cass published *Inquiries Respecting the History, Traditions, Languages, Manners, Customs, Regions, etc., of the Indians*, which demonstrated his considerable knowledge of Indigenous cultures and languages.[5] In 1830 Cass publicly reversed his position on allowing the tribes of the Old Northwest to remain on their lands. He now supported Andrew Jackson's plan for the forcible relocation west of the Mississippi of the so-called Five Civilized Tribes in favor of Anglo-American settlement (and he would be appointed Jackson's secretary of war, with oversight of Indian matters). A polygenist, Cass expressed some of the lowest possible opinions of Native Americans. The two races on the continent, whites and Indian, Cass wrote, "cannot exist in contact, independent of each other."[6] Cass believed in a divinely ordained destiny, and offered a racialized interpretation of Noah's curse on Canaan ("God shall enlarge Japheth") in Genesis 9: "the race of pale men *should increase and multiply*, and *they did increase and multiply*."[7] Schoolcraft for his part advocated Indian removal as early as 1829.[8] Arranging and encouraging the removal of tribes from the Old Northwest would become Schoolcraft's objective as an Indian agent and superintendent in the 1830s.

Schoolcraft expressed his own low estimation of Indigenous people in his 1821 *Narrative Journal*: "The savage mind, habituated to sloth, is not easily roused into a state of moral activity, and is not at once capable of embracing and understanding the sublime truths and doctrines of the evangelical law."[9] He found the songs and dances of "untutored savages" to be "particularly tedious, and it is a severe tax upon one's patience to sit and be compelled, in order to keep their good opinions, to appear pleased with it."[10] One aspect of Indigenous culture that did impress him was pictographic communication. On decamping one morning in northern Minnesota, the Chippewa in his party left a glyphic message on birch bark, which was inserted in a pole and left for other tribal members to find.[11] The message conveyed information about events on their journey and their anticipated arrival at Sandy Lake in three days. Schoolcraft was depicted as a figure with a hammer. (Earlier in the journey, his Chippewa companions had called him *Paw-gwa-be-caw-e-ga*, which Schoolcraft said meant "destroyer of rocks," a name inspired by his method of gathering mineral samples.[12]) "I had no previous idea of the existence of such a medium of intelligence among the northern Indians," Schoolcraft confessed. "All the travellers of the region, are silent on the subject.... [H]ere was a historical record of passing events, as permanent certainly as any written record among us, and full as intelligible to those for whom it was intended."[13] Later, Schoolcraft's party encountered a birch-bark message left by a party of Dakota who had hoped to negotiate peace with the Chippewa.[14] The Dakota message showed that Indigenous peoples who spoke completely different languages were able to communicate through pictographic conventions.

Schoolcraft's response revealed his lack of reading, as by 1820 there had been several examples of such pictography in antiquarian and scientific literature.[15] The birch-bark messages nevertheless indicated to him the essential intelligence and capability of Indigenous people. Rich oral traditions were another surprise. He recounted two legends in *Narrative Journal*, but the breadth and depth of traditions only became clear after he secured (with Cass's help) his appointment as the U.S. Indian agent at Sault Ste. Marie in 1822. Schoolcraft boarded with John Johnston, a prosperous Irish fur trader who had married the daughter of a prominent Ojibwa leader, Waubojeeg (the White Fisher). In 1823 Schoolcraft married the trader's daughter, Jane, who brought with her a substantial dowry of £2,000, or about $10,000.[16] An additional asset was Jane's knowledge of Ojibwa culture. Jane and her siblings gathered, translated into English, and vetted for Schoolcraft the traditional knowledge of the many Ojibwa visitors to the Johnston home, which was the center of social life in the community. The English traveler Anna Brownell Jameson met the Schoolcrafts at Michilimackinac in 1838 and found a close friend in Jane: "The most delightful as well as the most profitable hours I spend here, are those passed in the society of Mrs. Schoolcraft. Her genuine refinement and simplicity, and native taste for literature, are charming. . . . While in conversation with her, new ideas of the Indian character suggest themselves; new sources of information are opened to me, such as are granted to few."[17] Schoolcraft had long harbored literary as well as political ambitions, and Ojibwa traditions promised publishing success that to date had been denied to him, not to mention that had impoverished him. Schoolcraft was determined to accomplish with Native American lore what James Macpherson had with (alleged) Celtic oral traditions in *Poems of Ossian*. As he never mastered Ojibwa and was a stranger to the community, Schoolcraft would not have managed on his own the access he enjoyed to Indigenous culture that Jane and her family provided.[18]

In 1827 Henry and Jane Schoolcraft were devastated by the death from croup of their child, Willy, after only a day of illness.[19] While two more children followed, their relationship, which appears to have been a close and happy one, never recovered from the loss. Schoolcraft took refuge in a forthright embrace of Presbyterianism. He ascribed the death of Willy to God's punishment for their "idolatry" in loving Willy too much.[20] The following years were especially hard on Jane; he questioned her upbringing and moved the family to Michilimackinac so the children could attend a Presbyterian school. As a "half-breed," Jane was shunned there by white women, and Henry lost most of their money—Jane's dowry money—in land speculation when real estate values collapsed around Detroit as part of the larger 1837 financial crisis.[21]

After his embrace of Presbyterianism, Schoolcraft believed Christianity held out the only hope of salvation for the Ojibwa and other Indigenous peoples. His religion became the lens through which he viewed their cultures, but his faith may at least have saved him from a serious scholarly misstep. Although polygenism (already present in his friend Cass's worldview) enjoyed a resurgence of scientific respectability among Schoolcraft's peers in the 1840s, he could never accept the idea that Indians were a distinct human species. Schoolcraft held firmly to the biblical model of an Edenic origin and a post-Deluge global diaspora by the progeny of Noah. Schoolcraft's faith did mean he could accept racial degeneration as an explanation for the condition and character of Indigenous peoples, as he found and judged them.[22]

IN 1837 SCHOOLCRAFT SECURED his appointment as superintendent of Indian affairs for the Michigan Territory and published a highly favorable review of Albert Gallatin's landmark work on Indigenous languages, "A Synopsis of the Indian Tribes of North America," which dominated the second volume of *Archaeologia Americana* of 1836.[23] The review allowed Schoolcraft to argue the value of philology over the object-based epistemology of archaeology in understanding the Indigenous past: "By far the most enduring 'monuments' which our native tribes possess, are to be sought in the sounds and syntax of their languages."[24]

Schoolcraft's choices in labeling Indigenous languages (and the people who spoke them) are an unappreciated aspect of how he interpreted American antiquity. He differed with Gallatin's nomenclature; Schoolcraft had an established habit of attempting to impose his own terminology and ignoring or disparaging the work of predecessors. In his first major article on Indigenous language and culture in 1828, a review of J. C. Beltrami's *La Découverte des Sources du Mississippi, et de la Rivière Sanglante* (which Schoolcraft could not have read, as he did not know any European language other than English), he called the compound structure of Chippewa words "transpositive" and asserted that the term was provided by the "older philosophers."[25] This was ten years after Peter Stephen Du Ponceau had introduced the definitive term, "polysynthetic."[26] Du Ponceau for his part admired the materials on the Chippewa language in Schoolcraft's *Narrative of an Expedition through the Upper Mississippi to Itasca Lake* (1834), informing a friend, "his description of the composition of words in the Chippewa language is the most elegant that I have yet seen. At the same time he appears to be (as far as his book shews) a selfish, morose man. . . . It seems he wishes to occupy the whole ground alone."[27] In "Synopsis," Gallatin introduced "Algonquin-Lenape" for what is now generally called Algonquian. Schoolcraft in his review called it a "compromise term."[28] He imposed mid-review his own term, *Algic*, which he explained was an adjective "derivative from *Algonquin*, and is introduced for brevity's sake."[29]

In 1839, Schoolcraft formally introduced his term in *Algic Researches*. He gave a peculiar explanation for *Algic*: "Derived from the words Alleghany and Atlantic, in reference to the race of Indians anciently located in this geographical area, but who, as expressed in the text, had extended themselves, at the end of the 15th century, far towards the north and west."[30] Equally curious, he lumped Iroquoian-speaking groups ("Tuscaroras, Iroquois and Wyandots") into "a generic language, which we shall denominate Ostic." He contended that his renaming of the recognized Iroquoian group derived from the Algic word *Oshtegwon*, "a head, &c."[31] Schoolcraft's explanations of his Algic and Ostic terminology are unconvincing, Ostic least of all. He also created the term *Abanic* for Siouxan languages and claimed it denoted "occidental. From

Kabeyun the west."[32] This etymology was even less credible than the ones he offered for Algic and Ostic.

Schoolcraft's coining of labels was not unlike C. S. Rafinesque's eccentric contemporary efforts—for example, calling the Huron and Iroquois the *Ongwi* in *The American Nations* (1836).[33] Schoolcraft was playing subtextual word games, constructing esoteric meanings beneath his exoteric nomenclature. Schoolcraft had wondered aloud about Sioux origins in *Narrative Journals*, calling them "a distinct race of people" and comparing them to the Chinese, especially in the sound of their language (how much Chinese had Schoolcraft heard?).[34] Schoolcraft apparently then looked southward in Asia for his Sioux root stock, as his *Abanic* may have been inspired by *abangan*, a Javanese term that was short for *wong abangan*, "red people." Schoolcraft's knowledge of *abangan* would have been unusually early, but its use would have been consistent with ideas of a transpacific South Asian origin for the Mound Builders, who were Malays according to Samuel Latham Mitchill, and Hindus or southern Tartars according to Caleb Atwater.[35]

Daniel Garrison Brinton, whom Franz Boas would identify as a cofounder of American anthropology, would reject Schoolcraft's "manufactured" term *Algic*, insisting there was "no occasion to accept it" in lieu of *Algonkin*.[36] As for how Schoolcraft actually manufactured it, we have already met a term suspiciously similar in Charles Vallancey's ideas. Schoolcraft shared Vallancey's fascination with the Ossian poems, and as Vallancey contended in the *Grammar*, the Algonquin name derived from the Irish "*cine algan*, or *algan cine*, i.e. the noble tribe," which in turn derived from the Phoenician *al gand gins*.[37] This correlation between Schoolcraft's *Algic* and Vallancey's *algan* might be coincidental, given that both men were working from the same inspiration of Algonquin/Algonkin. However, Schoolcraft most certainly got his term *Ostic* from the literature devoted to allegedly brutish Old World peoples and their possible connections to New World Indians. Both Buffon and Strahlenberg called a warlike subgroup of Tartars the Ostiaks; Strahlenberg pronounced them "one of the most stupid Nations in Siberia."[38] Schoolcraft would incorporate Strahlenberg's illustrations into volume 1 of his magnum opus, the six-volume Congressional report, *Historical and Statistical Information Respecting the History, Condition and Prospects of the Indian Tribes of the United States* (1851–57), and essentially agreed with Strahlenberg's assertion (seconded by Benjamin Smith Barton) that languages were key to linking Native Americans to Asiatic source populations.

Leaving the Abanic Sioux to the west, Schoolcraft organized the Indigenous people of eastern North America into two clashing, contrasting races,

Algics and Ostics, for in his assessment language was equated with race. Schoolcraft's conception of Native American origins agreed with the predominant multiple-migration displacement scenario, in which a more advanced people arrived first, only to be displaced by brutish hordes. Regardless, Schoolcraft was largely in sympathy with Barton's ideas of Native Americans as degenerated descendants of the Mound Builders. Barton's conviction that Native Americans could be traced back across the Bering Strait to biblical lands, through alleged traces of Persian in their language, was echoed in Schoolcraft's proposal the Algic were descended from "a race of shepherds or pastoral nomads," while the Ostic were "from a line of adventurers and war-like plunderers." The Algic race was "mild and conciliating," the Ostic "fierce and domineering."[39] Algic pictographs, or "hieroglyphics," bore "quite a resemblance to the Egyptian," and the language was "of a strongly Semitic cast."[40] Schoolcraft's assurance that Algic was Semitic undermined his purported linguistic expertise. He might have subscribed to the Lost Tribes origins of Native Americans, a conviction that was widely held in the Lake Superior region, where Schoolcraft served as an Indian agent and superintendent, and suggests the wide influence of the trader James Adair's *The History of the American Indians* of 1775. In traveling the region in the 1850s, Johann Georg Kohl would remark: "It is very curious that I meet so many persons here still adhering to the belief in the Jewish descent of the Indians, not merely among the American clergy, but also among the traders and agents."[41] Schoolcraft at this point was also a cultural degenerationist and environmental determinist. In *Algic Researches* he wondered if the Algics, rather than not having advanced at all, in fact "fell back. . . . It may be doubted whether the very fact of the immensity of an unoccupied country, spread out before a civilized or half civilized people, with all its allurements of wild game and personal independence, would not be sufficient, in the lapse of a few centuries, to throw them back into a complete state of barbarism."[42]

Schoolcraft did not directly engage the Mound Builders mystery in *Algic Researches*, but in his 1839 review of *Antiquitates Americanae* he rejected the idea that anyone other than Native Americans was responsible for the mounds. In *Algic Researches* he implicitly identified the Mound Builders as ancestors of the Algics, who had entered the modern boundaries of the United States from the southwest and were "followed by the Ostic, the Muskogee and the Tsallanic [Cherokee] hordes." The Ostics, in the first wave, were the invaders by whom the Algics "were driven, scattered, and harassed, and several of the tribes not only conquered, but exterminated."[43] After driving off the Algics, the Ostics initially occupied the Ohio Valley before assuming "a most commanding and central position in Western New-York."[44] School-craft's pre-Columbian history of North America, as conveyed in *Algic Researches*, was a narrative of ceaseless conquest and displacement, with his "warlike and jealous" Iroquoian Ostics the progenitors of territorial change.[45] As for cultural change, there was none, except in the direction of degeneration.

IN APRIL 1839, Henry Schoolcraft's review of *Antiquitates Americanae* appeared in *The American Biblical Repository*, a "learned and weighty" monthly magazine, according to Frank Luther Mott.[46] Schoolcraft had entered the intellectual fray about a year late, as major, supportive reviews had already been organized, in large part by Thomas H. Webb, and written foremost by the brothers Edward and Alexander Everett and by George Folsom.[47] An English-language abstract from the volume had also been printed as an offset in New York as *America Discovered in the Tenth Century* in 1838. A striking curiosity was that the offset made no mention of Dighton Rock, which may indicate how late in the composition of *Antiquitates Americanae* Rafn and Magnussén composed their Dighton Rock evidence. American reviewers generally were complimentary of the main work, persuaded of the historicity of the saga accounts and that Vinland was in southern New England. Reviewers were regrettably convinced that the RIHS drawing of Dighton Rock as published in *Antiquitates Americanae* was the most accurate yet. However, they left an impression that Rafn and Magnussén had overreached in asserting the Norse provenance of Dighton Rock. Suspicions also were circulating that Webb's RIHS committee had concocted a drawing that would satisfy the Danish antiquarians' desire to locate the name of Thorfinn Karlsefni. Webb would recount how one opponent of the decipherment "boldly & shamelessly asserted, that knowing what the Danish Society wished to find there, or to make out, we, the suppliant tools, formed & fashioned characters accordingly."[48]

As with his critique of Gallatin, Schoolcraft used the *Antiquitates Americanae* review to promote his theories about the Algic language and race, which he published that year in *Algic Researches*. His review was otherwise a reasoned rebuttal of the Norse provenance for Dighton Rock. While he thought the work "seems to place beyond doubt that the Northmen made repeated voyages into the northern Atlantic, early in the 10th century, and visited and wintered at various points on the New England coast," he was unsatisfied with the volume's Indigenous evidence.[49] He assumed the skraelings were the "Esquimau race," and doubted (with good reason) they had ever lived in New England. At the time of the Pilgrims' arrival, he asserted, "the Algic race possessed the entire coast." He did not believe that "Hope" derived

from the Scandinavian *Hóp*. While accepting that *Mounthaup* was an Indigenous term, he thought it to be "rather a derivative from the name of one of
the gods of Algic mythology," without explaining which god that might be.[50]
He was more on the mark when he wondered why Native Americans would
replace their own place names with ones made up by invaders they had driven
off.[51] Schoolcraft could not know that Rafn harbored a White Tribism notion
that the Norse had remained in the country for centuries, interbreeding with
Native Americans, altering their culture, and inspiring their place names.

As for the inscription on Dighton Rock, Schoolcraft in making his critique
of *Antiquitates Americanae* was unaware of George Catlin's letter to the *New-
York Mirror*, published December 29, 1838. Catlin was establishing himself as
an artist specializing in portraits of Native Americans, and met Edward Everett (who was the governor of Massachusetts and a historian trained at Göttingen) when his tour of paintings took him to Boston in 1838. Everett's review
of *Antiquitates Americanae* the previous January had been generally favorable,
but as to a Norse inscription on Dighton Rock, "We own that we remain
wholly unconvinced. . . . The representations of the human figures and animals appear to us too rude for civilized artists in any age, erecting a public
monument."[52] On December 1, the *Mirror* reported that at one of Everett's
Boston lectures on *Antiquitates Americanae*, Everett recounted asking Catlin
whether he had ever seen inscriptions like those on Dighton Rock "in the Indian country." Catlin purportedly had replied that "he had seen hundreds of
them on white quartz rock, and that if he had copied all of them, they would
have filled a volume of more than a thousand pages."[53]

Catlin wrote to the *Mirror* from Philadelphia on December 11 to contest
the idea that Dighton Rock was "an *anomaly* which needs to be explained and
understood."[54] Catlin quashed two antiquarian conceits: that Native Americans did not make rock carvings, and moreover, that carvings were made in
rocks too hard to be worked with anything other than metal tools, and so
could not have been made by people who did not possess them.[55] Of Dighton Rock, Catlin ventured: "These inscriptions (I should think myself entirely safe in saying) are the works of Indian hands. I advance this opinion
with confidence, because I have met many similar productions in the western
country, and I have seen the Indians busily *at work*, recording *his own totem*,
or mark, among those of his ancestors."

Catlin's description of the "Red Pipe-stone Quarry" on the Coteau des
Prairies appears to be the first recorded reference to petroglyphs at the sacred
quarries in southwestern Minnesota at what is now Pipestone National Monument.[56] Catlin's account of his visit is a remarkable firsthand report of a

major site that includes testimony from Native Americans still contributing markings. Although some of the figures might represent historic events or traditions, Catlin was sure most were totems (*doodems; dodems*) made by thousands, if not tens of thousands, of individuals, their families, and tribes, a kind of tagging by visitors over the course of centuries. Catlin estimated there were 500 figures of animals and birds. Catlin examined the petroglyphs with several Dakota men "who took great pleasure in pointing out their own marks or *totems,* and also those of their friends. Quite an old man (and a *medicine-man* withal) took great pains to show me the totems of the Chippeways, his enemies; but he revered their marks, for 'those (said he) are *wakons,*' (spirit or medicines)." Catlin proposed Dighton Rock "had been, perhaps, the site of an ancient Indian town, or famed for some battle or other remarkable scene, and this rock, having a conspicuous position and a suitable surface for such marks, became gradually covered on its face with the strange and unintelligible entries which we now find upon it, and about which a thousand different theories may be formed, and each one for ever resting, in my humble opinion, on evidence equally vague and uncertain."

Catlin was subjected to an outrageous assault in *The Northmen in New England,* Joshua Toulmin Smith's enthusiastic promotion of *Antiquitates Americanae.* An English barrister who was living in Roxbury, Massachusetts, when he prepared the book, Smith constructed it in the form of dramatic dialogues between fictional characters in Newport, Rhode Island.[57] Smith's characters have the following exchange about Dighton Rock that put Catlin in his place:

> But I have heard it stated, observed Mr. Cassall, that Mr. Catlin says it is an Indian inscription.
> Mr. Catlin! exclaimed the doctor, in amazement; do you mean Mr. Catlin, the Indian traveller?
> The same.
> What, in the name of goodness, has he to do with anything about inscriptions?[58]

Smith in a flight of rhetoric maneuvered Catlin *in absentia* into expressing an opinion he never held: that Dighton Rock most certainly was *not* the work of Indians. Smith claimed he had "positive and immediate knowledge of the fact, that Mr. Catlin distinctly stated, to two highly respectable gentlemen, by whom the question was directly put, that *he never had seen any Inscription like the Assonet Rock.*"[59] Smith also dismissed the relevance of Catlin's opinion with a firm conclusion from one of his characters, Dr. Dubital: "how any body could seriously quote [Catlin's] authority with respect to an inscription asserted to be Runic, is past my comprehension to understand."[60]

Catlin's observations survived the eccentric slander of Smith. They are most valuable in indicating that a complex example of rock art like Dighton Rock, as with the pipestone quarries petroglyphs, could be a palimpsest of glyphic images, recorded by different individuals over a lengthy span of history. They also could be individuals from different tribal peoples separated considerably in time or actively contesting the site's control, as the Dakota and Chippewa/Ojibwa had at the Coteau des Prairies. In such a case there could be no single, coherent *message* that qualified as an inscription awaiting decipherment.

In assessing Dighton Rock's provenance, Schoolcraft too could draw on personal experience with Indigenous pictography. He examined the nine drawings reproduced in *Antiquitates Americanae* for his 1839 review. The earliest three (Danforth, Mather, and Sewall) he pronounced "of no historical value, unless it be to denote how the preconceived theories of men may lead them to distort facts, even where the data, if properly recorded, would not militate against such theories."[61] Like every other reviewer, he was unaware of the doctoring of the RIHS drawing when he remarked: "It is only to be regretted that the care and precision bestowed upon the latter, could not have been applied, in getting an accurate impression, a century earlier."[62] But he rejected the idea that any part of the inscription was Norse: "We consider the characters hieroglyphics of the Algic stamp. They are not Runic characters."[63] Schoolcraft ventured the letters R, I, N, and X first appeared in the engraving of Kendall's 1807 painting published by the AAAS in 1809, and so were a recent addition: "we think it would be hazarding little to suppose that some idle boy, or more idle man, had superadded these English, or Roman characters, in sport. These alphabetical marks certainly spell nothing in the ordinary Runic, either backward or forward."[64] Schoolcraft called Magnussén's interpretation "far-fetched, in some respects cabalistic, and thoroughly overstrained; and after all, nine tenths of the whole inscription is unintelligible, and is left unexplained. We admire his learning and ingenuity, but rise from the perusal unconvinced."[65]

In support of his Algic interpretation, Schoolcraft made one of his first extensive comments on Native American pictographic forms. Nothing was "more characteristic of the mental peculiarities of the Algic race, than their mythology and the system of hieroglyphics, by which they appear, at all times, to have perpetuated events and names."[66] He explained how personal glyphs were carved into or painted on cedar posts or other materials to mark the graves of chief and warriors, and how symbols were carved into blazed tree trunks or recorded on strips of birch bark. Schoolcraft also revealed that he had inspected and collected a large number of glyphs of the type seen on Dighton Rock, made on wood and bark—a reference in part to the birch-bark song scrolls from which he would extract copious illustrations and analysis in volume 1 of *Historical and Statistical Information*.

As a mineralogist, Schoolcraft noted (citing Webb from his November 30, 1834, letter to Rafn in *Antiquitates Americanae*) that Dighton Rock was "a species of fine-grained graywacke." This stone, Schoolcraft advised, was "so much inferior in hardness to most of the silicious stones, that there could have been but little difficulty in making the impressions with sharp pieces of hornstone or common quartz, such as arrow-heads were chipped with."[67] And as similar inscriptions had been found elsewhere in the eastern United States, Schoolcraft was confident that Native Americans were capable of making them. Schoolcraft also had seen stones in waterside locations employed as shrines, with offerings of tobacco.[68] In his *Narrative* of 1834, Schoolcraft mentioned a gneiss boulder at Lac Travers marked with a red circle, which his companions called Shingaba Wossin, and which he translated as Image Stone.[69] "Offerings are usually left at such rude altars," he explained.[70]

Through Shingaba Wossin, Schoolcraft experienced a near miss in reinforcing the Indigeneity of Dighton Rock. The second word, Wossin, was usually spelled *assin* (or *asin*, among other English and French variants), which means stone.[71] As we have seen, Dighton Rock was located on the shore of what was once called the Assonet River, on Assonet Neck, and *assonet* can be translated as "the stone place," or "the place of [the] stone." The name was strong evidence that Dighton Rock long had been an important part of the local landscape for the Wampanoag. Schoolcraft noted in the review that the rock was located "on the shore of 'Assonet Neck,' so called."[72] That he did not recognize the significance of the place name "Assonet" was a telling statement on his actual knowledge of Algonquian dialects.

IN THE SUMMER of 1839, following his review of *Antiquitates Americanae*, Schoolcraft pursued his own investigations of Dighton Rock's inscription by turning to Shingwauk. He had an uncertain European father and was a member of the prominent Crane clan, which Schoolcraft misunderstood to be a local tribe.[73] Schoolcraft first met Shingwauk in 1822, and as Schoolcraft would recall, he was renowned as a war chief, a councilor, and an orator; he was also a *djiskui*, a practitioner of the shaking-tent ritual, and a member of the Midéwiwin and the Wabanowin medicine societies.[74] Shingwauk had figured prominently in often-tense negotiations at the Sault rapids between the Americans (including Schoolcraft) and the Ojibwa, who did not trust the expansionist ambitions of the United States. As Janet Chute has written, some of the chiefs at the Sault "seemed to demonstrate a Machiavellian flair for diplomacy which won Schoolcraft's grudging respect."[75] By the late 1830s, political maneuvering in the upper Great Lakes had made Shingwauk a chief on the British side of the international border, at St. Mary's. The Anglican minister at St. Mary's, William McMurray (whose spouse, Jane Schoolcraft's sister Charlotte, served him as an interpreter), helped win over Shingwauk to Christianity by praying over his ailing son, who became a convert as well.[76] Shingwauk's lodge became a site for Anglican prayer meetings.[77] It was in a new role for Shingwauk, as a Christianized "good Indian" in the eyes of the British, that the American Schoolcraft sought his aid in interpreting Dighton Rock.

"Naturally a man of a strong and sound, but uncultivated mind, he possesses powers of reflection beyond most of his people," Schoolcraft would write of Shingwauk. "He has also a good memory, and may be considered a learned man, in a tribe where learning is the result of memory, in retaining the accumulated stores of forest arts and forest lore, as derived from oral sources."[78] As Schoolcraft further related, when he assumed his Indian agency post in 1822, "I observed this man to be expert in drawing the Indian signs and figures."[79]

When Shingwauk arrived at Schoolcraft's post with four companions in the summer of 1839, Schoolcraft showed him two drawings of Dighton Rock from *Antiquitates Americanae*, the one by Baylies and Goodwin that initially had inspired Magnussén, and the so-called RIHS drawing. Schoolcraft claimed to provide only basic information: the inscription was on a rock in New England, the rock was washed twice daily by the tide and might have had some figures obliterated, and the drawings were made at different times. It is not clear how Schoolcraft concluded the glyphs were made at different times (which also meant they did not form a unified inscription), and we will revisit this issue in chapter 8. He asked Shingwauk: "Was the inscription made by Indians, or by others? What is your opinion?"[80]

In volume 1 of *Historical and Statistical Information* (1851), Schoolcraft at last published the interpretation Shingwauk provided in 1839. Shingwauk had studied the drawings for some time with his Ojibwa companions before making a preliminary judgment: "It is Indian; it appears to me and my friend, to be a *Muz-zin-na-bik*, (i. e., rock writing.) It relates to two nations. It resembles the *Ke-ke-no-win-un*, or prophetic devices of an ancient class of seers, who worshipped the snake and panther, and affected to live underground. But it is not exactly the same. I will study it." Schoolcraft did not explain, but

Shingwauk was referring to the two major figures of the Eastern Woodlands cosmology's beneath worlds, known to the Anishinabe Ojibwa/Chippewa as the giant serpent Chignebik and the Great Cat (or Panther or Lynx), Michipeshu, who traveled in company.

Shingwauk and his companions returned the next morning with a final pronouncement. Shingwauk's reading (assisted mainly by a hunter named Zha-ba-ties) was as elaborate as anything offered by Court de Gébelin and the other interpreters maintaining an Old World provenance. Without saying why, Shingwauk relied on the Baylies and Goodwin drawing, and explained it was a unified one, albeit divided into two scenes. The drawing was the product of a shamanic vision as well as a record of a historical event. The imagery involved a war between two nations of *Un-ish-in-á-ba*, or Indian people. (By this Shingwauk did not mean they were specifically Anishinabe in a modern political-cultural sense, but rather that neither party depicted was non-Indian.) On the left side of the drawing Shingwauk identified "an ancient prophet and war captain," accompanied by his sister, "his assistant and confidant in some of his prophetical arts." She was also "held out, as a gift, to the first man who shall strike, or touch a dead body in battle." There was a shaman's lodge, a war club, dots representing the passage of time in moons, "an anomalous animal, which probably appeared in his fasts to befriend him," a figure denoting the number forty next to a dot denoting skulls, a sun that served as the clan symbol of the prophet, a loon that represented the prophet, named Mong, a war camp, "a wooden idol, set up in the direction of the enemy's country, and within sight of the prophet's lodge," and more. On the right side were two human figures, representing the enemy ("drawn without arms, to depict their fear and cowardice"), three decapitated men, a belt of peace, and symbols denoting boasting, doubt, and preparation for war.[81] As for the horned quadruped, Shingwauk read the Baylies-Goodwin version as "a symbol of the principal war-chief of the expedition against the enemy. He led the attack. He bears the totemic device of the Pizhoo, which is the name of the northern lynx. (L. Canadensis.)." Schoolcraft added: "The same word, with a prefix denoting great, is the name of the American cougar, or panther."[82]

Schoolcraft seemed not to understand that the "great panther" was not a Linnaean classification for a species but rather was Michipeshu, the major cosmological figure. The fact that Schoolcraft reported Shingwauk initially saying the rock reflected worship of "the snake and the panther" suggests Schoolcraft did not understand what Shingwauk was surmising. In the horned quadruped Shingwauk may have seen a glyph denoting a long-tail "grandfather" that protected a war chief. Schoolcraft's failure to grasp these essential points casts doubt on his claim that Shingwauk not only had instructed him in the "medicine and mystical songs" and the meaning of song-scroll images, but also that "I became, according to his notions, a member or initiate of the Medicine Society, and also of the Wabeno Society."[83] Consider that John Tanner, who was raised by the Saultaux and the Odawa, served as an interpreter under Schoolcraft, and made important early recordings of song-scroll images, never wrote about the Midéwiwin medicine society or its more secretive offshoot, the Wabanowin. George Woodcock suspected Tanner was excluded from the Midéwiwin.[84]

Schoolcraft proposed that Shingwauk's reading might be related to a tradition gathered by Schoolcraft's brother-in-law, George Johnston, of a Nipigon war leader, the king-fisher, Kish-kemanisee, who pursued a course of war that carried him all the way from northern Lake Superior to the Atlantic coast. "His hieroglyphics have been discovered on one of the islands in Boston Bay," Johnston related, and in printing this narrative in volume 1 of *Historical and Statistical Information*, Schoolcraft noted: "This may possibly be an allusion to the inscription on the Dighton Rock."[85]

It is difficult to know what to make of Shingwauk's elaborate reading, as it is problematic on multiple levels. To begin, Shingwauk could only "read" what had been drawn by Anglo-Americans. Translation was another problem. Schoolcraft's lack of fluency in Ojibwa was underscored by the fact that he made sure he had on hand a translator, Henry Conner, "the most approved interpreter of the department," in addition to two unnamed members of Schoolcraft's relations (probably drawn from the siblings Jane, Charlotte, and George).[86] Even if these interpreters were faithful to Shingwauk's words, before the information reached the printed page it had to be filtered through Schoolcraft, and he published his reading nine years after the death of his most valuable informant, his wife Jane.

In addition, Shingwauk and his companions may not have been *translating* an inscription, but rather infusing with meaning a set of pictographs of an unknown antiquity, far from where they lived. Indigenous peoples can give cultural materials like rock art of unknown origin fresh relevancy by assigning them interpretations that fulfill cultural objectives in memory and place-making. An important factor in assessing whether this was the case with Shingwauk's reading is that Dighton Rock was not the only example of glyphs Schoolcraft had Shingwauk read for him. Shingwauk provided birch-bark drawings of Lake Superior rock paintings that he explained depicted a prophet and war chief named Myeengum, or the Wolf of the Mermaid, who dispatched canoes on a successful war party and recorded his success on both sides of the lake. Reading Schoolcraft's account of Shingwauk's Myeengum explanation in the same volume, one is struck by the thematic similarities to Shingwauk's Dighton Rock interpretation.[87] Further, when another sculptured rock was discovered, on Cunningham's Island in Lake Erie, Schoolcraft had a drawing made and presented to Shingwauk for interpretation. Shingwauk's reading for Schoolcraft (see chapter 8) was of a kind with the Dighton Rock interpretation: a multipart composition involving chiefs who were also shamans, and depicting war narratives. As such, these readings, including the Lake Superior pictographs, were a reflection of Shingwauk's life and standing. These readings may also fall into a pattern of "militarized" interpretations of cultural materials, including rock art and earthworks, by Indigenous people in the nineteenth and twentieth centuries, which may reflect both a gender bias in researchers collecting interpretations from men, and the honoring of past military feats being a cultural priority at a time of great dislocation.

We must also question how much of Shingwauk's reading of Dighton Rock and other glyphic works was shaped by what Shingwauk suspected Schoolcraft wanted to hear. Shingwauk, as noted, was a shrewd politician, and although he had settled on the British side of the border, he may have wished to make himself useful to the American superintendent. Schoolcraft's vision of American antiquity was of multiple migrations and bloody clashes, and depictions of warfare between different Indigenous groups would have been made to order for him.

Finally, we must question how much of Shingwauk's readings actually was the work of Schoolcraft. Schoolcraft's shaping (and reshaping) of his Indian legends for publication (and republication) has been explored by a number of scholars.[88] There should be little doubt that he took the information he gleaned from Shingwauk and composed a literary narrative as much as an ethnographic report. Nothing Shingwauk is quoted as saying should be considered a verbatim record. More problematic is the possibility that Schoolcraft allowed his own interpretations to masquerade as Shingwauk's explanations. This possibility is especially acute with the Cunningham's Island interpretation, as we will see in chapter 8.

We must also keep in mind that in the case of Dighton Rock, considerable time—twelve years—passed between Schoolcraft gathering Shingwauk's reading and publishing his account. These were major years in the development of American ethnology and Schoolcraft's ideas on the continent's past. In many ways, the Schoolcraft who sought Shingwauk's help in 1839 was not the Schoolcraft who published his findings on petroglyphs in the early 1850s.

CHAPTER EIGHT

Reversing Dighton Rock's Polarity

Henry Rowe Schoolcraft, the American Ethnological Society, and the Grave Creek Stone

In August 1847, Henry Schoolcraft was rowed across the Taunton River to view the most contested inscription in America. The previous November, he had persuaded the NYHS, of which he was a leading member, to form a committee to investigate Dighton Rock. The NYHS committee filled the boat: joining Schoolcraft (and the local youth at the oars) was Marshall S. Bidwell as well as John Russell Bartlett, whose involvement with Dighton Rock investigations dated back to the RIHS committee formed in 1833 to assist Carl Christian Rafn in his researches.[1]

Eight years had passed since Schoolcraft had secured Shingwauk's interpretation of Dighton Rock's markings. Another four years would pass before he actually published it. The previous March, Congress had yielded to several years of Schoolcraft's lobbying and authorized (under the aegis of the secretary of war) his multivolume study of Native Americans.[2] Based in part on statistical data from Native American populations, *Historical and Statistical Information* would be issued in six rambling volumes between 1851 and 1857, with Shingwauk's reading appearing in the first one.[3] When Schoolcraft visited the rock in 1847, he was not only beginning his multivolume effort: he was also attempting to make sense of American prehistory, of Indigenous identity and culture, in one of the most energized and controversial periods of American science and ethnology. Polygenism had surged into respectability through the efforts of naturalist Samuel George Morton and his circle of skull measurers. Schoolcraft's companion in the boat being rowed across the Taunton River, Bartlett, harbored polygenic sentiments. The new star of American archaeology, Ephraim George Squier, who was about to copublish an acclaimed study of the Mound Builders that firmly disenfranchised them from Native American ancestry, was a polygenist who was championed by Bartlett. Although Schoolcraft was friendly with Squier, his own firm monogenism and certainty that the Mound Builders were ancient Native Americans (as well as a difference of opinion over the authenticity of the Grave Creek stone) could not avert an imminent, bitter break in their relationship. Yet Schoolcraft still managed to remain married to a virulent polygenist and slave owner from South Carolina, Mary Howard. Widowed by the death of Jane in 1842, Schoolcraft had married Howard in January 1847, after assuring her he accepted the institution of slavery.[4]

Amid this intellectual and personal upheaval, and increasingly less mobile after the first of a series of paralytic strokes in 1845, the newly remarried Schoolcraft had made the pilgrimage to Dighton Rock.[5] It was as if he could not move forward on his massive new undertaking on Native Americans, in a climate of pronounced discord over America's past and a resurgent doubt that Native Americans even belonged to the human species, without coming to a personal reckoning with this long-standing enigma. Schoolcraft was foremost a philologist and mythographer, but in this age of objects-as-epistemology, the man who had held the Grave Creek stone and gauged the weight of its authenticity needed to confront the massive physical fact of Dighton Rock. Regardless of what Shingwauk had told him could be read on its surface, Schoolcraft had to experience the rock for himself before he could place it in the rubric of the nation's—and humanity's—past. Schoolcraft's confounding changes of opinion about the provenance of the inscription would play out over the course of several volumes of his new study, as struggles over American antiquity, race, and ethnology ran their own confounding courses.

AFTER CONSULTING SHINGWAUK on the meaning of Dighton Rock's markings in 1839, Henry Rowe Schoolcraft's life passed through a series of traumas and dislocations. *Algic Researches* sold well and ensured his reputation, but Schoolcraft had assumed the financial risk and the work failed to turn a profit.[6] Worse, in 1841 he lost his position as superintendent of Indian affairs at Michilimackinac. Schoolcraft, an ardent Democrat, was dismissed after the Whig candidate, William Henry Harrison, won the 1840 presidential election. The Schoolcrafts relocated to New York and Henry traveled to England in unfulfilled hopes of securing a publishing deal for a multivolume study of Native American ethnography, *Cyclopedia Indianensis*. While he was away in 1842, Jane, who had contracted whooping cough in 1835 and become dependent on laudanum, died suddenly.[7] Schoolcraft never returned to the upper country of the Great Lakes. Between his dismissal as Indian superintendent and the death of Jane, Schoolcraft lost direct personal connection with the communities that made possible his reputation as an authority on Indigenous cultures.

Schoolcraft returned to New York and entered the circle surrounding philologist Albert Gallatin in the NYHS. That circle included Bartlett, who had relocated from Providence to New York in 1836. After enduring various business struggles, Bartlett turned to his love of books and with Charles Welford established a business, Bartlett & Welford, in the Astor House. The bookstore and publishing house became an informal salon for men interested in ethnology and archaeology, and in November 1842 Schoolcraft, Gallatin, Bartlett, and others founded the American Ethnological Society (AES).[8] The society operated practically as an adjunct of the NYHS, with Schoolcraft, Gallatin, and Bartlett holding leading positions in both organizations.[9]

Antiquitates Americanae loomed over interpretations of American antiquity, and initially it had enjoyed Bartlett's support. He was one of the American contacts for subscribers, and he arranged to have the English abstract *America Discovered in the Tenth Century* published in New York in 1838. But by October 1841, Bartlett had drifted away from Rafn's ongoing project to prove a Norse presence in New England, as Rafn informed Webb that he had not heard from Bartlett for "a long time."[10] In an address on the "progress of ethnology" read before the NYHS in late 1846, Bartlett would state: "I am aware that many believe the sculptures on the Dighton rock to contain several alphabetic characters. Prof. Rafn in his learned and ingenious memoir on this inscription, supports this view."[11] Bartlett, however, did not, and "ingenious" was consistent with its common use as a backhanded compliment for something considered clever rather than factually credible, and echoed Edward Everett's categorization of the Dighton Rock reading as "the learned and ingenious commentaries of our friends in Copenhagen."[12] Late in life, Bartlett remained confident that Norsemen had visited North America and that Narragansett Bay was a good fit for Vinland. But as for the infamous inscription, "although I was instrumental in calling the attention of the Danish savans to the Dighton Rock, I never believed that it was the work of the Northmen or of any other foreign visitors. My impression was, and is still, that it was the work of our own Indians."[13]

Although volume 1 of *Historical and Statistical Information* in 1851 would be Schoolcraft's first effort to use the 1839 interpretation from Shingwauk, he already may have tried to persuade the Royal Society of Northern Antiquaries to include an article on Dighton Rock in its *Mémoires* around 1841. In spite of harsh passages in his 1839 review of *Antiquitates Americanae*, Schoolcraft had joined Rafn's society.[14] The society's concerns with mythopoetic tradition, the historicity of the sagas, and runic writing were too close to Schoolcraft's interests in Native American oral traditions and picture writing to ignore, and leading American figures in antiquarian and philological studies were also society members, whatever misgivings they might have had over some evidentiary interpretations of *Antiquitates Americanae*.[15] Thomas Webb, as noted, would assert in 1854 that he consulted Schoolcraft at the beginning of his researches on Dighton Rock, but it seems more likely Schoolcraft initiated contact when he became interested in Dighton Rock and *Antiquitates Americanae*. In a letter to Webb on October 22, 1841, Rafn commented on a theory for Dighton Rock that Schoolcraft evidently had shared with Webb. Rafn's letter raises an important question about Schoolcraft's opinion of Dighton Rock soon after—or even at the time of—Shingwauk's reading in the summer of 1839.

A key factor in Schoolcraft's ever-changing ideas about Dighton Rock is a rejoinder to his review of *Antiquitates Americanae* of April 1839, which appeared in *The American Biblical Repository*'s July 1839 issue, at the very time Schoolcraft was seeking the help of Shingwauk.[16] The Reverend A. B. Chapin of New Haven, Connecticut, challenged Schoolcraft's conclusion that the Roman lettering on Dighton Rock was likely a schoolboy prank.[17] Chapin pointed out that the letters CXXXI at least in portions had appeared in several drawings that preceded Kendall's rendering, and must be genuine. Chapin proposed the inscription at the center of the rock relating to Karlsefni was made by the Norse, and that the Indians added their drawings later, around it.[18] Had Schoolcraft already read Chapin's riposte when he consulted Shingwauk in the summer of 1939? Chapin's influence could explain why Schoolcraft would recall telling Shingwauk the glyphs were made at different times, which otherwise was mere conjecture, and why Schoolcraft wanted Shingwauk to tell him if the markings were made "by Indians, or by others." Rather than having Shingwauk say whether the markings were Indigenous or not, Schoolcraft probably wanted him to say if the markings were *only partly* by Indians.

In speaking or corresponding with Webb around 1841, Schoolcraft seems to have been considering Chapin's proposal that an authentic Norse inscription existed on the rock. Rafn's letter to Webb of October 22, 1841, stated: "Mr. Schoolcraft's explanation of the figures in Assonet Rock agrees with the opinion expressed by me, that a representation is intended of a battle (a meeting or a convention) between the Scandinavians and Aborigines."[19] Rafn, however, had a way of imposing his own conclusions on the opinions of others, and Schoolcraft may only have reported to Webb that Shingwauk had interpreted the markings as a battle scene, not that Norsemen were in it. And if Schoolcraft firmly believed there was a Norse inscription on the rock at this time, it is difficult to imagine Rafn not agreeing to publish something from him to that effect in *Mémoires*.

Instead, Rafn chose to publish (and comment upon) in *Mémoires* letters from Schoolcraft that addressed the Grave Creek stone. Schoolcraft's gullible fascination with this fraud and his possible overture to write about Dighton Rock in *Mémoires* may not have been unrelated. Schoolcraft circa 1841 could have been inclined to offer an interpretation of Dighton Rock that also accounted for whichever Old World adventurers allegedly left behind the Grave Creek stone. For now, Schoolcraft's published analysis of enigmatic inscribed stones in America was reserved for Grave Creek.

Schoolcraft was an unwitting champion of the Grave Creek fraud after visiting the excavation and examining the inscribed stone for himself in 1838.[20] He gave notice of the find to the Royal Geographical Society in London in 1841; Schoolcraft's letters to Rafn in January and June 1842 and Rafn's comments were published in *Mémoires* in 1844. Schoolcraft then published a longer report on Grave Creek, incorporating his analysis in *Mémoires* as well as Rafn's essential comments, in the first volume of *Transactions of the American Ethnological Society* in 1845. Schoolcraft assigned its twenty-two characters, crudely inscribed in three lines, to eight different Old World scripts. Rafn agreed with Schoolcraft that the script most resembled Celtiberic. Although the inscription was gibberish, Rafn ventured it was evidence of a pre-Norse visit to America by "tribes from the Pyrenean peninsula, who in very remote ages may be supposed to have visited the Transatlantic part of the world; or to inhabitants of the British Isles sojourning in this remote country before the close of the 10th century."[21] As Schoolcraft stated in *Transactions*: "The early and common impression of the preoccupancy of the country, by a people having some further claims to civilization and art than the existing Red Race, is thus revived and strengthened."[22]

The stone may have shaken, but it did not topple, Schoolcraft's conviction that the mounds of the Mississippi and Ohio valleys were the work of the ancestors of Native Americans.[23] As to how the anomalous inscribed stone got into the Grave Creek mound, Schoolcraft was convinced "there was a period of adventure and migration to this continent, having its impulse from the East, towards the Atlantic coasts—that it proceeded from the European coasts, in the infancy of navigation, and was born hither on the Western breeze."[24] But this early migration "was evidently limited in numbers, and went down, either by the sword or amalgamation in the more powerful native races."[25] This explanation made more sense to him than proposing that Native Americans had degenerated from such a high plateau of culture that they had once possessed Old World alphabets.[26] The scenario recalled Samuel Latham Mitchill's Transatlantic Gothicist conquest in western New York. Schoolcraft must have known Mitchill's theory, for in addition to its popularization through *Archaeologia Americana*, Schoolcraft was raised and educated in New York State and was made an honorary member of the NYHS in 1819, at the height of Mitchill's theorizing as a leading member.[27] Schoolcraft supposed the Grave Creek stone arrived at its final resting place through the capture of its makers or its inheritance by Native Americans as a treasure.[28] But where Mitchill wanted the mounds to be the work of wandering Gothic Europeans, Schoolcraft in the first volume of *Historical and Statistical Information* in 1851 remained steadfast in his views that Native Americans were not a product of an ancient, transatlantic culture, and that the mounds could not have been left behind by such a foreign culture.[29] He considered it no great feat of civilization to arrange large volumes of dirt into tidy piles.[30] Cultural materials otherwise indicated to him "no art or degree of civilization superior to that possessed by the present race of Indians. They give no countenance to the existence, in these regions of a state of high civilization."[31]

Schoolcraft deserves some credit for holding to his convictions that Native Americans were descendants of the Mound Builders, especially as Ephraim George Squier was setting new standards in American archaeological rigor while contending that Native Americans not only were unrelated to the Mound Builders, but also did not even belong to the same human species as those people—or as white Americans. Squier (a newly arrived newspaper editor in Chillicothe, Ohio) and Edwin Hamilton Davis (a local doctor) excavated 200 mounds and surveyed about 100 earthworks from 1845 to 1847. Their report, *Ancient Monuments of the Mississippi Valley*, was the first monograph in the *Contributions to Knowledge* series issued by the new Smithsonian Institution in 1848.[32] "The work of Squier and Davis long served as a model of empirical observation and reporting," Terry A. Barnhart has observed.[33] Steven Conn has noted that their study "quickly became the standard reference work on the topic of mounds, displacing Caleb Atwater's 'Description,'" and that *Ancient Monuments* "still stands as a remarkable archaeological achievement."[34] Their methodology in excavation, surveying, and recording was superior to anything yet demonstrated in the new American archaeology.

Their sprawling study included a survey of petroglyphs, and one example near Steubenville, Ohio, impressed them with the "striking resemblance" of figures on the lower right-hand face with figures in the same position on Dighton Rock.[35] They observed how numerous inscribed rocks of similar character "are scattered over the West, occurring chiefly upon or near the banks of streams." It was "very apparent that they are all the work of the same race: there is a family likeness in their style and workmanship, and a coincidence in position, which admits of no dispute, and seems to be conclusive at this point."[36] Squier and Davis were confident that Native Americans had carved Dighton Rock and these other petroglyphs. But they could not believe the "mound builders" (a term they employed and thus perpetuated through the notoriety of their volume in the nineteenth century) were the same race. Mound Builder cultural materials were too sophisticated to their eyes: the "elaborate and laborious, but usually clumsy and ungraceful, not to say unmeaning, productions of the savage can claim but a slight approach."[37] They viewed the Mound Builders as a single people, "essentially homogeneous in customs, habits, religion, and government," who were connected to semicivilized peoples of Mexico, Central America, and Peru.[38]

Squier's ideas about American antiquity were informed by polygenism, which was enjoying a surge of fresh interest and scientific respectability. Samuel George Morton in 1839 had published *Crania Americana* on Native Americans, and was actively pronouncing on Indian moral and mental deficiencies.[39] In *Crania Aegyptica*, published by the American Philosophical Society in 1844, Morton presented cranial evidence purporting that human races had been unaltered since antiquity, which pointed to separate creations. Theoretical allegiances in the New York circle of the AES (which Squier joined) under its firmly monogenist president Gallatin were complex and contradictory. The monogenic Schoolcraft's marriage to a polygenic southern slave owner in January 1847 underscored those contradictions. Bartlett supported Schoolcraft in viewing the Grave Creek stone as authentic, but otherwise was a transatlantic diffusionist with undertones of polygenism. With his partner Welford, Bartlett published Squier and Davis's landmark Mound Builder study, and he agreed with Squier that the Mound Builders were not the ancestors of Native Americans. The discovery of the Grave Creek stone had opened a new field of inquiry for philologists, Bartlett advised in *The Progress of Ethnology*, the final published version of his two-part address before the NYHS in late 1846. It could provide "the means to unravel one of the most difficult questions connected with the origin of the American race, and the means by which they reached this continent, for we never have been among those who believed that America derived the mass of her population, her men and animals, from Asia, by the way of Behring's Straits."[40] Bartlett did not say *where* he thought Native Americans came from, if indeed they came from anywhere, and he appears to have embraced polygenism. Bartlett looked back across the Atlantic for the source of advanced Mound Builder cultures, citing works published in France that the Grave Creek stone's inscription was Phoenician, or was consistent with inscriptions in the heart of Africa, as well as in Algiers and Tunis.[41] Bartlett also delivered a paper before the AES on evidence for the Welsh visit by Prince Madoc in 1170.[42]

He ventured further into White Tribism with stories of blond-haired and "white" Indians in the western United States, including a trapper's tales of a tribe, called the Mawkeys, that "had 'light, flaxen hair, blue eyes and skins of the most delicate whiteness.' "[43]

Polygenism and monogenism did not fall into neat categories where attitudes toward Native Americans and other ethnic (nonwhite) populations were concerned. A monogenist could hold Noachic migration convictions that produced harsh, racist views of peoples who were preordained to be subservient to whites. Advocates of polygenism derived much intellectual mileage from attacking the monogenism of men like Schoolcraft who accepted on unscientific faith that humanity descended from the sons of Noah.[44] Monogenists also could harbor ideas (to which Schoolcraft subscribed) of degeneration of certain racial stocks, while a polygenist like Squier could view the different branches of the multispecies human family as equals. As Robert E. Bieder has written, Squier "was sharply critical of the derogatory and pessimistic views that polygenists held of Indians,"[45] and found "particularly obnoxious" denials of the Indian's potential for progress.[46] Schoolcraft the monogenist, on the other hand, had come to look down on the Indigenous heritage of his own offspring. As he had explained to Jane in a letter in 1839, his hopes for their children rested in "that mixture of the Anglo-Saxon blood which they derive from their father, with the *eastern mind* so strongly exemplified in the Algic race. Without the *former*, the result is a want of *foresight*, and *firmness*—two traits that man cannot spare and excell in the sterner duties of human life."[47]

IN HENRY SCHOOLCRAFT'S ANNIVERSARY address to the NYHS in November 1846, he declared that, except for the Grave Creek stone, "there is no monument of art on the continent, yet discovered, which discloses an alphabet, and thus promises to address posterity in an articulate voice."[48] Yet Dighton Rock appeared to be unfinished business—perhaps not proven to be an alphabetic inscription, but not entirely disregarded, either. In November 1846, the NYHS adopted Schoolcraft's resolution that a committee be appointed "to investigate the character and purport of the ancient pictorial inscription of symbolic figures of the (so called) Dighton Rock," and to report back "at the earliest convenient time."[49] If Schoolcraft reported back, there is no record of it. Instead, he saved his analysis for his forthcoming *Historical and Statistical Information*, the multivolume project rooted in his failed proposal for *Cyclopedia Indianensis*, which Congress approved in March 1847.

Like everyone engaged in ethnology, Schoolcraft was wading through the puzzles (and frauds) of American antiquity. In volume 1 of *Historical and*

Statistical Information he would pronounce the "skeleton in armor"—actually, all of the burials found at Fall River—to have been "Indians who may possibly have lived during the time of Philip's wars, or a few years earlier," which was a sound conclusion that archaeologists and ethnologists would agree with today.[50] He was aware of a burgeoning trade in inscribed fakes (some of which he attributed to the Mormon prophet Joseph Smith), but assured that "these pretended discoveries have been so bunglingly done as not for a moment to deceive the learned, or even the intelligent portion of the community."[51] The bungling was not as easy to detect as he thought, as he continued to treat the Grave Creek stone as genuine in volume 1 of *Historical and Statistical Description*, in terms that rendered the discoverers innocent of hoax.[52] Nor was he aware that the most authoritative drawing of Dighton Rock was a deceptive pastiche, or that Rafn, upon whose opinion he was relying in determining the authenticity and cultural affinity of the Grave Creek stone, was partly responsible for it.

Of Dighton Rock, Schoolcraft would write in volume 1 of *Historical and Statistical Information*: "It has been easy, at all times, to distinguish the true from false objects of archaeology, but there is no object of admitted antiquity, purporting to bear antique testimony from an unknown period, which has elicited the same amount of historical interest, foreign and domestic, as the apparently mixed, and, to some extent, unread inscription of the Dighton Rock."[53] Schoolcraft knew nothing of the long historiography of the rock's interpretation, as he alleged, "It is certain that it was not regarded in any other light than the work of Indian hands" before the Royal Society of Northern Antiquaries took an interest in it.[54]

On his visit to the rock with his fellow members of the NYHS committee in August 1847, he found that the youth who rowed them across the Taunton River already had chalked the main elements. "The first impression was one of disappointment," Schoolcraft confessed in volume 1. "As an archaeological monument, it appeared to have been over-rated."[55] Schoolcraft related the interpretation by Shingwauk, and provided his own firsthand assessment. He noted minor discrepancies between the Baylies-Goodwin drawing of 1790 and the so-called RIHS drawing of 1830 in *Antiquitates Americanae*. The letters shown in the latter drawing were "either imprecise or wholly wanting" in the rock itself. Nevertheless, Schoolcraft came to a startling conclusion: "there were two diverse and wholly distinct characters employed, namely, an Algonquin and an Icelandic inscription."[56] Without alluding to it, Schoolcraft had accepted the hypothesis proposed by the Reverend Chapin in 1839. A Norse message at the center of the rock face was surrounded by Indian glyphs.

Schoolcraft had firm grounds on which to reject any Norse contribution to Dighton Rock. Shingwauk had told him the three X shapes in the Baylies-Goodwin drawing (which became CXXXI in the doctored RIHS drawing) represented decapitated bodies. Schoolcraft's own examples of pictographs in volume 1 (including his own portrait in the 1820 birch-bark message) showed the X was a common core form for depicting human bodies, and for body shapes in general, including figures like the thunderbird. When Schoolcraft had pointed out to Shingwauk the C and I and a compound character for "men" before and after the Xs in the doctored RIHS drawing, Shingwauk "promptly threw them out, saying that they had no significancy in the inscription." But Schoolcraft put them right back in, along with the Xs: "It would seem by every fair principle of interpretation, that these six characters should be construed together." Schoolcraft's strange logic was that denying Shingwauk the three Xs as Indigenous symbols only cost Shingwauk's interpretation "the adjunct fact of an acknowledged loss of three men in the attack, while it restores to the Scandinavian portion, what is essential to it." This Solomonic wisdom, which divided the inscription between Native and Norse as if it were contested property, was hardly scholarly, but it upheld Magnussén's core reading of "CXXXI men," with the inscription below being "manifestly either the name of the person or the nation that accomplished this enterprise." Yet Schoolcraft not only admitted he could not find the name "Thorfins" as the purported RIHS drawing promised, but also observed that the runic figure Þ for *Th* "is some feet distant from its point of construed connection [to 'orfins'], and several other pictographic figures intervene." Regardless, Schoolcraft called this area "the presumed Icelandic part of the inscription," and advised that further scrutiny was invited.[57]

Schoolcraft may have accepted that at least part of the rock's markings was "Icelandic" to restore his good relations with those (including Rafn) who believed in the Karlsefni reading. The reversal also may have been due to the souring of his friendship with E. G. Squier. Their relationship had managed to rise above their differences on polygenism, but the Grave Creek stone was a serious stumbling block. Squier and Davis doubted its authenticity in their *Mound Builders* study.[58] In *Transactions of the American Ethnological Society* that same year, Squier suggested the Grave Creek stone was a hoax and sarcastically offered a White Tribism theory for how it might have gotten there: "It is quite feasible, by a single effort of imagination, to transport a sturdy Celt across a trackless ocean, through a wilderness infested by savages and wild beasts, and upon the banks of the Ohio invest him with a chieftaincy among the mound-builders; who, it is also easy to suppose, in memory of so renowned an adventurer, reared over his remains a huge earth structure,—a mode of sepulture eminently congenial to an individual accustomed to similar practices in his native land!"[59]

Despite Squier's boisterous sarcasm, his "sturdy Celt" would become precisely the archetype of purported Dighton Rock inscribers in the twentieth century—vastly outnumbered European adventurers who somehow commanded the fealty of Native Americans. Squier did not name Schoolcraft as one of the true believers in the Grave Creek stone, but Schoolcraft was offended that Squier had been permitted to express an opinion "offensive to truth" in the publication of a society in which Schoolcraft was a leading member. Schoolcraft complained to Squier's leading supporter in the AES, Bartlett, who otherwise shared Schoolcraft's conviction the Grave Creek stone was authentic.[60] Schoolcraft and Squier finally broke over Squier's publication in early 1851 of *The Serpent Symbol*. Schoolcraft's collections of Native American traditions had inspired Squier to explore religion and mythology, but Squier angered Schoolcraft by advancing polygenism and condemning the influence of Noachic lineages on ostensibly scientific explanations of human racial differences and the peopling of the Americas.[61]

In April 1851, soon after the publication of *The Serpent Symbol*, Squier was condemning the ideas promoted by the Royal Society of Northern Antiquaries in his rebuttal to a paper delivered to the AES by Christian Augustus Adolph Zestermann of Leipzig. Zestermann unwisely employed Davis and Squier's *Ancient Monuments* to make the White Tribism argument that the mounds and artifacts were evidence of a visit by ancient Europeans who taught arts and religion to the Indians. Squier began his retort by deriding recent theories for Norsemen in the New World. The evidence put forward by "the Antiquaries of Copenhagen" for a Norse presence in Rhode Island "is incapable of supporting a critical analysis; and the stress which has been laid upon it has contributed to weaken, rather than to sustain, the original proposition." Dighton Rock, Squier assured, "has almost exact counterparts in various parts of our country, which are well known to be of Indian origin: the Fall River Skeleton, in its mode of burial, cranial characteristics, and in the ornaments found with it, is clearly that of an Indian; and the 'Old tower' at Newport, it is now demonstrable, has an antiquity of not more than two hundred years."[62] If Squier insisted there was nothing Scandinavian about Dighton Rock, then Schoolcraft in his anger with Squier may have been prepared to consider that there was. In volume 4 of *Historical and Statistical Information* in 1854, Schoolcraft conducted his own housecleaning of untenable ideas in

American ethnology and archaeology, condemning Squier and *The Serpent Symbol* along the way.[63]

HENRY SCHOOLCRAFT'S EXPLANATION of the Cunningham's Island petroglyph over the course of several volumes of *Historical and Statistical Information* raises issues about Schoolcraft's ideas on American antiquity, and especially about his scholarship. There is ample reason to question how much of the interpretation of this petroglyph should be attributed to Shingwauk. Schoolcraft made passing mention of it in volume 1 of *Historical and Statistical Information* in 1851, and published drawings by Captain Seth Eastman (a military officer and artist assigned to the project) along with a preliminary description in volume 2, in 1852.[64] Shingwauk's interpretation did not appear until the third volume, in 1853. Schoolcraft did not interview Shingwauk personally, as the men were now far removed from each other. Shingwauk was deeply involved in difficult negotiations with the Canadian colonial government over territorial rights on the north shores of Lake Superior and Lake Huron, was seriously ill, and died in March 1854.[65] Schoolcraft did not return to the upper Great Lakes after his dismissal as Indian superintendent in 1841. After his first paralytic stroke in 1845, Schoolcraft had difficulty traveling—his 1847 visit to Dighton Rock was a rare bit of fieldwork.

Schoolcraft wrote in volume 2 that as a drawing of the Cunningham's Island petroglyph was awaiting interpretation by Shingwauk, "It would be premature, therefore, to attempt its reading in the present state of the question."[66] But Schoolcraft already seemed to have decided what it portrayed. "Its leading symbols are readily interpreted. The human figures—the pipes; smoking groups; the presents; and other figures, denote tribes, negotiations, crimes, turmoils, which tell a story of thrilling interest, in which the white man or European, plays a part. . . . The whole inscription is manifestly one connected with the occupation of the basin of this lake by the Eries—of the coming of the Wyandots—of the final triumph of the Iroquois, and the flight of the people who have left their name on the lake.[67]

Shingwauk's reading was secured by Schoolcraft's brother-in-law, George Johnston.[68] The fidelity of Johnston's reportage is unknowable, but Schoolcraft likely primed Johnston to secure a reading (as he promised in volume 2) that reflected the history of the Erie. Schoolcraft volunteered in volume 3 that the symbols "related to tribes and transactions [Shingwauk] knew little or nothing of."[69] Shingwauk nevertheless purportedly "expressed the opinion that he believed the inscription related to the wars and history of the Eries, after the Indians became acquainted with the white."[70]

Schoolcraft may have interpreted the Cunningham's Island petroglyph largely himself. He had assured readers of volume 2 that the petroglyph's "leading symbols are readily interpreted" before he had even received Shingwauk's reading. In volume 1 he had intimated that he was qualified to interpret images on his own, as Shingwauk had revealed to him the meaning of song-scroll glyphs and inducted him into the medicine societies. Schoolcraft could have shaped Shingwauk's readings of pictographs as recordings of dramatic historical events to address a deficit that, as Robert E. Bieder noted, Schoolcraft found exasperating. Schoolcraft "lamented that Indians had no history because they had no historians; they had no records that could throw light upon their past before European contact. Schoolcraft considered their legends too fabulous and their picture writing insufficient for constructing real histories."[71]

Schoolcraft did not make clear in volume 2 who he thought were the white men or Europeans in the Cunningham's Island petroglyph. Might they have been the Gothic Europeans of Mitchill's scenario or the inscribers of the Grave Creek stone, or instead were they the colonists of recorded history? Schoolcraft only promised they would "play a part" in the thrilling narrative forthcoming from Shingwauk. When Schoolcraft finally delivered Shingwauk's alleged reading in volume 3, whatever Gothicist fever Schoolcraft might have suffered had subsided. He placed the events in a conventional historical setting, after the arrival of the Dutch and other Europeans in the seventeenth century. Schoolcraft asserted the petroglyph was a record of events related to the Iroquois' expulsion of the Erie, who he proposed in retreat became the Catawba.[72]

Understanding Shingwauk's (purported) readings, and Schoolcraft's reportage of them, is critical not only to the long-standing dispute over Dighton Rock's provenance, but also to the entire field of study of glyphic Native American communications. Schoolcraft's efforts to document examples, especially images in Ojibwa song scrolls, in volume 1 of *Historical and Statistical Information*, were an important milestone in ethnographic study, a comprehensive attempt to draw connections between rock art, song scrolls, and gravesite glyphs, which included references to (and reproductions of) Strahlenberg's images from Siberia. Schoolcraft proposed a cognitive root in China for the glyphs and favored the Bering crossing theory: "Idle, indeed, would be the attempt, at this day, to look for the origin of the American race in any other generic quarter than the eastern continent," which was a gloss of

Pennant's *Arctic Zoology*.[73] His drawings of song-scroll "hieroglyphs" were admired by J. G. Kohl, who made his own recordings of images and interpretations (including a number explained to him by Shingwauk's son) and adopted the term *Algic*.[74] Garrick Mallery, in his major survey, "Pictographs of the North American Indians" (1886), noted a case of forgery in which someone created a ceremonial pipe stem using images recorded by Schoolcraft.[75] Researchers continued to rely on Schoolcraft's depiction and explanation of glyphs.

Through Shingwauk, Schoolcraft proposed a nomenclature for Indigenous rock art. Rock art (or as Schoolcraft put it, rock writing) was known as *Muzzinnabik*, and picture writing in general fell into two classes: *Kekeewin*, which consisted of images understood by everyone and incorporated messages written in the course of travels; and *Kekeenowin*, which was an esoteric system reserved for shamanic practices and encompassed (as Schoolcraft defined them) medicine, necromancy, revelry, hunting, prophecy, war, love, and history.[76] While the general term for rock paintings, *mzinabiginigan*, has retained currency among the Anishinabeg, the nomenclature set down by Schoolcraft generally has not endured.[77] At a meeting of the Anthropological Society of Washington, DC, in 1881, Garrick Mallery delivered a paper, "Dangers of Symbolic Interpretation."[78] Mallery wished to "protest against the misapplication of symbols in studies of North American ethnology. Few writers on the pictographs, customs or religious rites of the North American Indians have successfully resisted the temptation to connect them, through a correspondence of symbols, with those of certain peoples of the eastern hemisphere," he charged. Among his transgressors were Schoolcraft, whose "ponderous tomes are rich in symbols of the most abstract character, such as 'power,' 'deity,' and 'prophecy.' "[79] In his major survey published in 1886, Mallery made limited use of Schoolcraft and ignored his terminology. Mallery nevertheless relied on Schoolcraft's final pronouncement of Dighton Rock's Indigeneity and called Dighton Rock "merely a type of Algonkin rock carving, not so interesting as many others."[80]

ON APRIL 28, 1854, John Ordronaux of Taunton wrote to Thomas H. Webb, posing five questions about the preparation of *Antiquitates Americanae* and the interpretation of Dighton Rock.[81] Ordronaux was a law student who would become a professor of law and medical jurisprudence at Columbia College in New York; he had been elected corresponding secretary of the Old Colony Historical Society (OCHS) of Taunton when it was founded in May 1853. Presumably, he was interviewing Webb on behalf of the new organization, although nothing was published.[82] Ordronaux's questions were an interrogative bookend to the ones Carl Christian Rafn had submitted to the Rhode Island Historical Society in June 1829. Webb's confident initial response of 1830 had launched Dighton Rock into its most recent and contested incarnation, as a Scandinavian relic. Twenty-four years later, writing a second reply to Ordronaux on May 27, 1854, Webb was defensive over his reasoning and researches, recounting the early advice he allegedly received from Cass, Schoolcraft, and others that there were no Indian rock inscriptions in America.[83]

Webb's life since the publication of *Antiquitates Americanae* had undergone dislocations and traumas to rival those of Henry Schoolcraft. Webb had married in 1833 and moved to Boston around 1839, following the example of John Russell Bartlett in New York in entering publishing. He joined Marsh, Capen, & Lyon and worked on the *Common School Journal* under editor Horace Mann.[84] Something then went terribly awry in his life, but J. P. Quincy only remarked in his obituary for Webb: "Financial and family troubles, unnecessary to particularize, followed hard upon this new occupation; they gave Dr. Webb that experience of the tests and trials of life which it is probably not wholesome altogether to escape."[85] In 1850, Webb's old friend, Bartlett, who had just moved back to Providence, came to his rescue. The politically connected Bartlett secured from U.S. President Zachary Taylor the post of American commissioner for the United States and Mexico Boundary Commission. Bartlett hired Webb as his secretary, and Webb performed additional duties as one of four collectors in Bartlett's biology unit, although Webb's focus was on mineralogy.[86] Webb served on the commission for the duration of its existence, from 1850 to 1853, exploring the American southwest from the Gulf of Mexico to California on horseback.

The most remarkable part of Webb's letter to Ordronaux was Webb's recollections of his experiences with rock art in the American southwest. "In various portions of this vast tract, I saw many rocks in situ, and many boulders, whose surfaces & perpendicular sides were highly charged with markings. Most of these were isolated forms or figures, and may have been Indian figures." Passing through Hueco Tanks, a dramatic uplift about thirty miles southeast of El Paso, he saw on a rock face "a very extensive inscription, painted in colors," that depicted men on horseback in pursuit of game, an "enormous serpent," and other images. "The idea flitted through my mind was, that these were the work, through thoughtlessness, or by way of a joke, of some emigrant who had journied [*sic*] that way." Webb had all too briefly seen one of the major rock-art sites in North America: over 3,000 images, which were not formally studied until 1939, have been documented at Hueco Tanks State Historic Site.[87]

Webb also spotted petroglyphs along the Gila River in passing through Yuma territory. Bartlett drew and published examples from both areas and attributed no historical value to them.[88] But where Bartlett was convinced they were the work of Indians, which helped to reinforce his certainty that Dighton Rock was an Indian monument, Webb remained stubborn about denying Native Americans almost any credit for rock art, anywhere he found it. Every example Webb saw in the southwest appeared very old to him. "Very probably, most, if not all of these, like those spoken of by Catlin, were the work of the former inhabitants, or earlier wanderers thro' these regions. But I have yet to learn that any Indian of the present day has made such inscriptions, and if the reverse be the fact, it far from settles the great question at issue." If Webb was referring to Catlin's comments on the sacred pipestone quarries, he ignored Catlin's statement that he had witnessed Dakota men making glyphs, and, contrary to Webb's contention that the images at Hueco Tanks were of great antiquity, they are considered to be Mescalero Apache paintings, which were still being created at the time of Webb's visit.[89] Webb had been granted a privileged early view of some of the most extensive Indigenous rock art in the United States, to complement what he had seen in Dighton Rock and other New England examples, and he still could not be shaken from his conviction that few if any Native Americans had produced such works.

Webb objected to Squier's assertion in *Ancient Monuments* of the similarity between the petroglyph near Steubenville, Ohio, and Dighton Rock—"it is a fancied one, merely"—and frowned on an address Squier had given to a British association in which he "commented somewhat severely, if not unhandsomely, upon the doings of the Royal Society of North. Antiq. and its collaborators. He of course considered the Assonet [Dighton] Inscription no great affair, & decided it to be the work of Indians." After a lengthy condemnation of Squier, Webb cited Schoolcraft's "great Work," the first volume of *Historical and Statistical Description*. Webb may not have been happy that Schoolcraft had used the testimony of an "Algonquin Chief... who professes to have deciphered as *Indian*, all but that portion which Prof. Magnusen conjectured to be Runic," but at least an Icelandic attribution for Dighton Rock had survived Schoolcraft's scrutiny.

Webb then noted for Ordronaux that while in Washington in March 1853 he had met with Schoolcraft, who told him he was arranging to have a daguerreotype made of Dighton Rock. Webb informed Schoolcraft that he had arranged a daguerreotype himself in 1840.[90] What became of this extremely early American daguerreotype is unknown, but according to Webb, Schoolcraft explained that he wanted a new one of his own, and Captain Seth Eastman would supervise it. Webb promised to assist Eastman, but they failed to connect.

Webb next revealed that in the very course of writing this letter, Schoolcraft's fourth volume of *Historical and Statistical Information* had arrived. As that volume revealed, Captain Eastman indeed visited the rock and enlisted a Taunton daguerreotypist, Horatio B. King, who took the first surviving photographs in July 1853 (figure 8). Schoolcraft could see no evidence in King's prints for the Icelandic inscription he previously had persuaded himself was there. Schoolcraft thus reversed himself *again* on Dighton Rock in volume 4. The rock represented "a uniform piece of Indian pictography. . . . It is entirely Indian, and is executed in the symbolic character which the Algonquins call Kekeewin,—i.e., teachings. The fancied resemblances to old forms of the Roman letters or figures, which appear on the Copenhagen copies, wholly disappear."[91]

Schoolcraft dismissed both Dighton Rock and the Newport Tower (whose purported mystery Webb had thrust upon the world) as "fallacious proofs" of a Norse presence, thus bringing his opinions in line with those of Squier, although he was still accepting the Grave Creek stone as genuine.[92] Webb's apoplexy unfolded in real time as he continued his letter to Ordronaux. Schoolcraft "thinks the question is now conclusively settled, that no Scandinavian or Runic record was ever made on the rock." Webb insisted the volume's daguerreotype "settles nothing," condemning it as an "imperfect representation, and by no means a complete facsimile of the original. I regret more than ever that I did not accompany Capt. E." It angered Webb (not without cause) that the inscription had been chalked for the daguerreotype. None of the subtleties that his RIHS committee had striven to capture in their drawing could possibly be shown without proper lighting.

After his tirade had run its course, Webb abruptly rationalized that Dighton Rock could be discarded as a Norse relic. The evidence for the Norse voyages to New England, he reasoned, was strong enough without it. He then made an extraordinary pirouette. Having tirelessly insisted that Native Americans were not responsible for the many pictographs and petroglyphs he had seen, having never expressed a word of concern over appropriating a cultural heritage he had so steadfastly denied since 1830 (and indeed, right up until the argumentative preceding paragraphs in this letter), he delivered this burst of sentiment: "But allowing [Dighton Rock] to be an Indian Monument, it

FIGURE 8   Daguerreotype of Seth Eastman at Dighton Rock, July 7, 1853, by Horatio B. King. The Getty Museum.

should be none the less highly prized, and carefully preserved, not only as a precious Aboriginal relic, & valuable specimen of the redman's pictography, but as *the* one which has aroused attention in the present day to this class of memorials and thus proved the means of rescuing from utter oblivion many such which otherwise would have been soon destroyed by the corroding tooth of time, or the more rapidly devastating march of modern 'improvement,' and the heavy blows unsparingly dealt to the right and left by the vigorous arm of young America."

Thus ended the record of Thomas Hopkins Webb's involvement with Transatlantic Gothicism and Dighton Rock.

SHINGWAUK PRONOUNCED ON the Indigeneity of Dighton Rock because he was asked to by Henry Rowe Schoolcraft, and we in turn must ask ourselves how much of Shingwauk's reading can be accepted. Schoolcraft may have been fooled by Rafn and Magnussén's reworking of the Dighton Rock drawing attributed to the RIHS, and by the perpetrators of the Grave Creek fraud, but he may also have fooled untold others with the interpretations of Dighton Rock and the Cunningham's Island petroglyph he attributed to

Shingwauk. Still, Shingwauk's confidence that Dighton Rock was the work of *Un-ish-in-á-ba* deserves our own confidence. Beyond affinity, meaning remains contestable, and probably irresolvable, in part because of Schoolcraft's reliability as a faithful recorder of Shingwauk's interpretation. For all its problems, Shingwauk's reading is a rare example of an Indigenous voice being sought and heard, however garbled or miscast, in the studies of Indigenous material culture, including the Mound Builder relics.

Although Schoolcraft, aided by Shingwauk, ultimately made an influential finding on the Indigeneity of Dighton Rock in 1854, winning over even Thomas H. Webb, this did not resolve the Mound Builder controversy (as much as Schoolcraft argued that those relics too belonged to ancestors of Native Americans). Nor did it end the insidious utility of the multiple-migration displacement scenario in deciding to whom America had once belonged, and now ought to belong. Men like John Russell Bartlett and Ephraim George Squier had wielded the authority of the new disciplines of archaeology and ethnology to portray an American prehistory with two distinct pasts. One past belonged to ancestors of Native Americans: primitive, possibly a different strain of humanity entirely, and responsible for Dighton Rock and similar inscribed stones deemed to be of crude execution. The other past belonged to an advanced people of unknown origin—possibly Asiatic, possibly European—who bore no relation to Native Americans, might have arrived on the continent before them, and after being driven off by ancestral Native American hordes, left behind curiosities like the Grave Creek stone and possibly the entire Mound Builder cultural complex. Dighton Rock's purpose in delineating American antiquity had reversed polarity. Charles Vallancey in 1786 had made the rock's inscription evidence of a superior original culture that had been displaced by a later wave of Tartar brutes from Asia that gave rise to living Native Americans. Now, Dighton Rock was the crude product of those brutes, and Shingwauk unwittingly had been enlisted into providing proof of that interpretation.

At the 1860 meeting of the American Association for the Advancement of Science, the Scottish-Canadian academic Daniel Wilson assigned Dighton Rock to the ancestors of modern Native Americans, derided claims of Old World scripts in American relics, and rejected a transatlantic migrationist origin for the Mound Builders.[93] Wilson was a major figure in archaeology, coining the term *prehistoric* and popularizing the three-age system of Stone, Bronze, and Iron Ages conceived by the Danish archaeologist Jens Jacob Asmussen (J. J. A.) Worsaae.[94] In his efforts to reconcile science with Christian morality, Wilson produced a disparaging view of Native Americans that was grounded in a confidence in the innate superiority of white Anglo-Saxon Protestants like himself and their entitlement to overspread North America, if not the world.[95]

Wilson supported the standard multiple-migration displacement scenario of superior and inferior migrants across the Bering Strait. In his seminal work, *Prehistoric Man* (1862), Wilson looked for the origins of Native Americans to the regions of Central Asia, "which have been for unrecorded ages the great hives of wild pastoral tribes, manifesting apparently no intrusion of civilizing arts or settled social habits on their rude nomade life."[96] The more advanced Mound Builders "were exposed to the aggression of barbarian tribes of the North-west," as "the Mound-Builder differed in culture, in blood, and race from the progenitors of the modern Red Indian."[97] Having brought these wild pastoral tribes from the "hive" of Asia (there was that swarming term again), with a resulting change of manners and new modes of life, Wilson insisted on making them unchanged thereafter, living "just such a type of unprogressive life as the wild nomades of the Asiatic steppe. The Red-Indian of the forest of the North-West exhibits no change from his precursors of the fifteenth century," and showed no capacity for change.[98]

On the essential character of Native Americans and the fate of the Mound Builders, there was little to choose between the ideas of the Christian monogenist Wilson and those of the leading polygenists, Josiah Clark Nott and George R. Gliddon, who had published *Types of Mankind* in 1854 and *Indigenous Races* (in which they coined the terms *polygenic* and *monogenic*) in 1857. As the latter duo stated in *Types of Mankind*, American antiquity had seen "one race, with the larger, though less intellectual brain" (ancestral Native Americans) "subjugating the unwarlike and half-civilized races" (the Mound Builders), "and it seems clear, that the latter were destined to be either swallowed up or exterminated by the former."[99]

An émigré himself, Wilson championed the white Anglo-Saxons of Britain as humanity's greatest achievement and made an explicit Transatlantic Gothicist connection between the mother country and New England, as Native Americans necessarily gave way to colonists in a manner Ezra Stiles would have approved: "the old Englander becomes the New Englander; starts from his matured vantage-ground on a fresh career, and displaces the American red-man by the American white-man, the free product of the great past and the great present." Considering the railroad construction driving America's westward expansion, Wilson further welcomed "the peaceful absorption and extinction of races who accomplish so imperfectly every object of man's being."[100] His convictions would have been equally welcomed in

Canada, as planning for westward colonization beyond the Great Lakes began to unfold in earnest in the 1860s.

In Wilson's worldview, granting Dighton Rock the Indigenous attribution that Schoolcraft's reading by Shingwauk made possible was part of the process of damning its creators (and their descendants) as unprogressive, bereft of science, philosophy, and moral teaching, as members of a race that could not fulfill a single objective of humanity's purpose. If the progress of civilization in America, as conducted by white Anglo-Saxon Protestant colonists, proceeded fairly and justly, the Indians who yet remained could be rendered only a living memory of an imperfect, long night of ignorance. Dighton Rock would endure as proof of that banished ignorance. The makers of Dighton Rock belonged in prehistory, not in history, and not in the future of North America as colonization rolled westward on steel rails.

CHAPTER NINE

Meaningless Scribblings

Edmund Burke Delabarre, Lazy Indians, and the Corte-Real Theory

Edmund Burke Delabarre, a psychology professor at Brown University, was preparing the third and final installment of his articles on the historiography of Dighton Rock for the journal of the Colonial Society of Massachusetts when his five years of research leapt in a radical new direction. Sorting through images for the final article, which would be published in two months, Delabarre paused at the best available photograph, taken by Charles A. Hathaway Jr. in 1907. "It may well be imagined with what astonishment, on examining the Hathaway photograph for the hundredth time on December 2, 1918, I saw in it clearly and unmistakably the date 1511. No one had ever seen it before, on rock or photograph; yet once seen, its genuine presence on the rock cannot be doubted."[1]

Until that moment, Delabarre was on course to provide the provenance resolution that the rock had deserved since the day it was first described by John Danforth in 1680. Through more than 400 combined pages of analysis for the Colonial Society of Massachusetts, Delabarre was tracking toward the unavoidable conclusion that the markings clearly were Indigenous, and that every theory to the contrary was a delusion. In the final installment he was on the verge of publishing, Delabarre even remarked: "It is easy to imagine as present on the rock almost any desired letter of the alphabet, especially of crude or early forms; and that, starting with almost any favored story, he can discover for it, if he looks for them eagerly enough, illustrative images to fit its various features, and initial letters or even entire words or names."[2] With his eleventh-hour revelation and addendum to the concluding article, Delabarre became living proof of these analytical pitfalls. He also proved that the rock's marked surface, like so many contested artifacts of American antiquity, was a mirror that reflected whatever expectations and prejudices the viewer brought to the task of interpretation. His initial three-part investigation of the rock's historiography remains a valuable if not definitive source, but the most informative aspect of his entire body of inquiry, which extended his researches another seventeen years, is what it tells us about the wont of men of letters to succumb to their own imaginations and expose unpleasant opinions of Native Americans. His startling conclusion—that the rock bore a 1511 inscription by the lost expedition of Portugal's Miguel Corte-Real—turned his careful historiographical study into another quest to hammer a square peg of European colonization into the round hole of an Indigenous artifact. In the process, he perpetuated many failings of previous theorists, not the least of which were White Tribist explanations of Indigenous capabilities and a contemptuous assessment of Native Americans.

AFTER HENRY ROWE SCHOOLCRAFT concluded in 1854 that Dighton Rock was entirely the work of Native Americans, the Indigenous provenance became the default scholarly presumption. However, in a last gasp of mainstream Transatlantic Gothicist romance, an attempt was made to enlist the rock in the promotion of Leif Eiriksson as the true discoverer and founding father of America. In addition to the established Gothicism of racialized Anglo-American attachments to a Scandinavian past, Dighton Rock was claimed by a powerful new variant on the issue of belonging, of immigrant place-making. The rock became a source of ethnohistorical pride for Scandinavian Americans, who saw their own arrival and settlement as a fulfillment of the stillborn promise of Norse colonization in the Vinland sagas.

The propagandizing of a Norse past in America by Scandinavian Americans is one of the "home-making myths" described by Orm Øverland, in which immigrant groups claim America as a place they rightfully belong.[3] These myths for ethnic groups of European origin fall into three main Øverland categories: "myths of foundation ('we were here first or at least as early as you were'), myths of blood sacrifice ('we fought and gave our lives for our chosen homeland') and myths of ideological gifts or an ideological relationship ('the ideas we brought with us are American ideas')."[4] The Norse discovery stories reflect all of these. The foundation myth made Scandinavians the original colonizers, as Leif Eiriksson beat Columbus to the New World by 500 years. Blood sacrifice was demonstrated by the Norse losses at the hands of the skraelings in the sagas and the more recent nineteenth-century Scandinavian homesteaders killed in skirmishes with Native Americans. And ideological gifts were found in the republican tradition of the Althing, the assembly that had governed Iceland as a commonwealth from about A.D. 930 to 1262, and that was restored in 1843.[5] Home-making fused with place-making when the myths found a physical anchor in the new lands, through the identification of particular locations with saga accounts—Narragansett Bay was Vinland, Mount Hope was Høp. The identification of the Newport Tower as a Norse church was a kind of place-making within this home-making mythology, as was the Fall River burial miscast as a Norse grave, as both lent a sacred cast to a recovered past. And then there were the purported inscribed stones fixed in the landscape, above all the misappropriated Dighton Rock.

No practitioner of Scandinavian immigrant home-making and place-making was more passionate than the violin impresario Ole Bull, a Norwegian nationalist who established a colony for freedom-loving countrymen, New Norway, in Pennsylvania in 1852.[6] In an address to his colonists in September 1852, Bull aligned New Norway with the Vinland sagas and made clear his belief in the Norse authenticity of Dighton Rock and the Newport Tower. But for the hostile reception of "the cruel and savage Indians," Bull left his colonist to conclude, the original Norse settlers of Thorfinn Karlsefni would have established a permanent presence.[7]

Bull's New Norway colony failed in 1857, albeit less violently than Karlsefni's Høp. Bull returned home disillusioned, but not before expressing a desire to own Dighton Rock. A Norwegian jeweler in Fall River, Niels Arnzen, in July 1857 purchased the rock and a sliver of adjoining shoreline on Bull's behalf for $50, registering the deed in his own name. One account contended Bull could not legally hold the property because he was not an American citizen.[8] On a trip to Scandinavia in 1859, Arnzen visited Bull, hoping to transfer title. Bull could then proceed with his preservation plans: a newspaper had reported in October 1857 that Bull would erect an iron fence around the rock to protect it.[9] Bull instead asked Arnzen to determine the cost of having the rock shipped to Copenhagen, as he wanted to donate it to the RSNA.[10] On the way home that August, Arnzen stopped in Copenhagen and called on Carl Christian Rafn, who was still the society's secretary. Rafn was surprised by, and amenable to, Arnzen's proposal to deed the rock to the RSNA, if Bull did not complete the deed transfer himself by June 14, 1860.[11] Bull did not do so, and on June 23, 1860, Arnzen received a letter from Frederick VII, king of Denmark and patron of the RSNA, thanking him for making a gift of Dighton Rock.[12] While Rafn in accepting the deeded gift had imagined the rock becoming "a truly scientific ornament to the Cabinet of American Antiquary," the king made clear the rock should remain where it was.[13]

The RSNA was now the owner of a boulder that the American scholarly community had largely if not unanimously concluded was not a Norse relic. Samuel Foster Haven in "Archaeology of the United States," published by the Smithsonian in 1856, had reviewed the Norse evidence for Dighton Rock, the Fall River skeleton, and the Newport Tower, and found it all wanting.[14] Haven saw no cause to disagree with Schoolcraft's Indian attribution of 1854 for

Dighton Rock. The *New York Times*, in reporting the transfer of title to the RSNA, observed: "since Mr. Schoolcraft's interpretation no one can doubt that it is simply aboriginal Indian."[15] As noted in chapter 8, Daniel Wilson too endorsed Dighton Rock's Indigeneity. Daniel G. Brinton also firmly attributed the glyphs, "long supposed to be a record of the Northmen of Vinland," to Indians in *The Myths of the New World* (1868).[16]

The New England poet, essayist, and Harvard graduate, James Russell Lowell, satirized antiquarian enthusiasms for runic inscriptions, including Dighton Rock, in the second series of *The Biglow Papers* (1862). Writing in the persona of the Rev. Homer Wilber, AM, he remarked: "Touching Runick inscriptions, I find that they may be classed under three general heads: 1. Those which are understood by the Danish Royal Society of Northern Antiquaries, and Professor Rafn, their Secretary; 2. Those which are comprehensible only by Mr. Rafn; and 3. Those which neither the Society, Mr. Rafn, no anybody else can be said in any definite case to understand, and which accordingly offer pecular temptations to enucleating sagacity."[17] The Rev. Wilbur was in the possession of a runic inscription he was able to translate by the following method: "After a cursory examination, merely sufficing for an approximative estimate of its length, I would write down a hypothetical inscription based upon antecedent probabilities, and then proceed to extract from the characters engraven on the stone a meaning as nearly as possible conformed to this *a priori* product of my own ingenuity."[18] He verified the exactness of his translation by reading it with equal success diagonally and upside-down.

Despite the broad rejection of Dighton Rock as a Norse relic, New England's Gothic fascination with things Scandinavian remained strong in the decades following the appearance of *Antiquitates Americanae*. "Like their English and Scandinavian colleagues, whom they often parroted in this matter," according to Oscar J. Falnes, "New England publicists devoted their highest praises to medieval Iceland. On this distant isle, romanticists liked to think, something of the old Germanic spirit had taken refuge from the debilitating effects of Latin and Mediterranean influences dominant everywhere on the continent."[19] New Englanders also saw a historic precedent for their own republican model of government in the Althing, which became cross-pollinated with the Gothic romance of a shared cultural/ethnic origin and the appeal of heroic adventures of the Vinland sagas to their own shores.

Scandinavian-American home-making found a champion in Rasmus Björn Anderson, who was born in Wisconsin and was a friend of Ole Bull. Anderson promoted the evidence in *Antiquitates Americanae* and propagandized the myth of a Norse ancestry for the American republic through works like *America Not Discovered by Columbus* (1874). Anderson insisted on the Norse authenticity of Dighton Rock and the Fall River skeleton, which he proposed was Thorvald Eiriksson, brother of Leif, who on his own voyage to the new lands was killed by a skraeling arrow and buried at a headland called Krossaness.[20] Elisha Shade, a resident of Bristol County, Massachusetts, provided Anderson in 1875 with a stereoscopic view of Dighton Rock and in 1876 assured him the boulder's markings were Norse: "I cannot believe they were made by the lazy Indian of Schoolcraft."[21]

Contemporary Anglo-Americans who embraced Leif Eiriksson as their ancestor were crafting a Transatlantic Gothicist variant of immigrant home-making. In their case, the myths of foundation, blood sacrifice, and ideological gifts were a fusion of white Anglo-Saxon Protestantism and Nordic root-race romanticism that already had been stirred by *Antiquitates Americanae*. A leading Anglo-American practitioner was Thomas Gold Appleton, a wealthy patron of the arts and a trustee of the Boston Public Library and the Museum of Fine Arts.[22] He was also a brother-in-law of Longfellow (who was a friend of Bull), and Appleton's published writings were charged with racially supremacist Gothicism.[23] "Not without meaning, at the head of that swarm which beats and buzzes upon this new continent, God has placed what we call the Anglo-Saxon race," he wrote in *The Atlantic Monthly* in 1871, before lamenting the fact that the Norse were unable to found a successful colony in America. "The natives were too strong and many for them, and were not providentially thinned by pestilence as for the Puritans before their arrival."[24] In 1875 Appleton espoused an environmental determinism in which the English thrived in the new climate of America where others had failed due to their congenital "ennui, indifference in matters of opinion, a certain torpor and dullness." In contrast, "England is the master-race here. In an Anglo-American head all that has made America what it is has been thought out."[25] At the conclusion of his 1871 article, Appleton proposed a Boston memorial to the Norse discoverers of America. He imagined a fountain, surmounted with "the picturesque figure of Eirik or his son Leif."[26]

Scheming over a suitable memorial arose at a reception on December 8, 1876, in Boston's music hall for Ole Bull, who was on another American tour. In a reception address, Bull was adamant the Fall River skeleton was Thorvald Eiriksson, and he made an imaginative effort to turn George Washington into a descendant of Thorfinn Karlsefni.[27] Leading citizens at the reception, including Massachusetts Governor Alexander H. Rice, banded with Bull to create the Norse Memorial Committee, chaired by Appleton. The committee pledged itself to raising a Boston monument in honor of the Norse explorers, and to taking measures for "the protection of the Dighton Rock, now in the Taunton River."[28] On December 28, 1876, a Dighton Rock subcommittee (also led by Appleton) wrote Arnzen, informing him that "it was most advisable that the Dighton Rock and the land on which it is situated should be assigned to them in person."[29] Meanwhile, the Prince Society of Boston was preparing to republish in 1877 *The Discovery of America by the Northmen in the Tenth Century* of 1841 by Ludlow North Beamish, who had died in 1872. Arnzen contacted the RSNA to see if it would agree to transfer title of the rock to the Boston group, which was considering placing it in the city's new art museum. The Museum of Fine Arts had opened in 1876, and the proposal must have originated with Appleton.[30]

The *New York Times* lampooned the Dighton Rock plans of Appleton's committee.[31] "This alleged inscription is absolutely undecipherable and is hence said to be the work of early Norse explorers, who were deficient in education and consequently wrote very illegibly." Editorial opinions in Boston were no more sympathetic (albeit less mocking). The *Boston Daily Globe* on January 25, 1877, asked "Have We Any Norse Monuments?" and answered its own question in the negative.[32] The *Daily Globe* cited Schoolcraft ("the eminent authority on the aborigines of the country") and the reading of his "Algonquin chief," Shingwauk, as well as the 1856 opinion of Haven in supporting the Indian attribution. The *Daily Globe* endorsed the idea of preserving Dighton Rock, but felt "it should be done in justice to the Indians, rather than to the Norsemen."

Editorial disdain was followed by a dispiriting opinion from the RSNA. The Society informed Arnzen on July 22, 1877, that it had no objection to transferring the deed to the Boston committee "for its future protection and eventual removal, although the Society adheres to their opinion heretofore expressed that the removal of an Antiquarian object from its original place, is generally detrimental."[33] But the Danes opposed the plan to showcase the rock as a Viking relic. Rafn had died in 1864, and any notion of the inscription's Norse origin among the RSNA executive had died with him. "[T]he Society must confess that the inscribed figures on the Rock, have according to the later investigations, no connection with the Northmen's journeys of discovery or sojourn in America, but rather that it is the work of the original races of Indians."[34]

Although a statue of Leif Eiriksson was erected in Boston in 1887, the plan to acquire and relocate Dighton Rock there collapsed. The practice of scouring petroglyphs and other archaeological finds for evidence of Old World visitors and original inhabitants superior to Native Americans already was unbecoming of a serious scholar or scientist. Brinton in *The Myths of the New World* had assured "all those old dreams of the advent of the Ten Lost Tribes, of Buddhist priests, of Welsh princes, or of Phenician merchants on American soil, and there exerting a permanent influence, have been consigned to the dustbin by every unbiased student, and when we see such men as Mr. Schoolcraft and the Abbé E. C. Brasseur [de Bourbourg] essaying to resuscitate them, we regretfully look upon it in the light of a literary anachronism."[35] Schoolcraft evidently had earned Brinton's contempt for his Grave Creek delusions.

As Garrick Mallery observed in 1881:

> Alphabets, Runic, Akkad, Phoenician, and of all other imaginable origins, have been distorted from the Dighton Rock and multitudinous later precious "finds," while other inscriptions are photographed and lectured upon to exhibit the profound knowledge by some race, supposed to have existed some time in North America, in the arbitrary constellations of astronomy, and its familiarity with zodiacal signs now in current use. Our learned associations are invaded by monomaniacs, harmless save for their occupation of valuable time, who declare that every ancient cisatlantic object means something different from what is obvious to common sense; and their researches are gratified by frauds and forgeries, sometimes originating in mischief and sometimes in sordid speculation.[36]

The idea that the Mound Builders were a single mysterious people, distinct from and markedly superior to the ancestors of Native Americans, also was in retreat, thanks to Cyrus Thomas's decisive Smithsonian report to the contrary, published in 1894.[37] By then, of course, living Native Americans had been alternately massacred and moved onto reservations, which were greatly reduced under the General Allotment (aka Dawes) Act of 1887, by which Congress directed the president to negotiate the allotment of reservation lands to Indians and to sell the surpluses to the United States to open for homesteaders.[38] With the westward colonization plan having reached the Pacific, whether or not the Mound Builders were ancestors of Native Americans was a moot point from the perspective of transcontinental manifest destiny.

After the collapse of the Boston memorial plan, the OCHS in Taunton in 1879 initiated its own plan to rescue Dighton Rock from any further threats of physical removal by acquiring the rock itself.[39] The transfer of title from the RSNA to the OCHS was finally accomplished on January 30, 1889.[40] By then, Dighton Rock was being vandalized more than studied. In an 1889 report to the OCHS, Niels Arnzen recommended a sign be erected on the rock, as he was worried about "disfigurement by the thoughtless and the vandalism by evil-disposed persons. . . . There are persons who write their names or cut their initials wherever they think people will see them. The rock has been somewhat defaced in that manner and it is important that means should be taken to put a stop to such mutilations."[41] At an unknown date, Arnzen's advice to erect a sign was heeded.

Arnzen was convinced a sign was needed to protect a Norse artifact, but with Dighton Rock's ownership repatriated and its Indigenous attribution now only challenged by fringe theorists, more than two centuries of study and speculation appeared to draw to a close. The provenance was all but settled: Dighton Rock as private property belonged to the OCHS, but its authorship belonged to Native Americans of antiquity.

Then Edmund Burke Delabarre spied the boulder.

BORN IN 1863 in Dover, Maine, Edmund Burke Delabarre was one of six children of Edward Delabarre, a Belgian immigrant who operated wool mills in Massachusetts, and Maria Hassel, who was born in Dover.[42] Their son received his undergraduate education at Brown University and Amherst College and began studies in a young field, experimental psychology, under its leading international practitioners. After attending the University of Berlin in 1887–88, he received a master's degree in 1889 from Harvard under William James, who had established one of the world's first experimental psychology laboratories at Harvard in 1875.[43] Returning to Europe, Delabarre was awarded his doctorate in psychology in 1891 at Freiburg in Baden, Germany, under Hugo Münsterberg. Delabarre was appointed an associate professor of psychology at Brown in 1891, becoming the university's first professor in the subject, and pursued further studies at the Sorbonne (University of Paris) in 1891–92. He established a psychology laboratory at Brown in 1892 (there were only nine in the country in 1891), was promoted to full professor in 1896, and in 1896–97 spelled off Münsterberg as director of Harvard's laboratory. Leonard Carmichael of Tufts praised Delabarre in an obituary as "a brilliant, meticulous, and studious psychologist."[44]

Delabarre's clinical studies were pioneering. During his Harvard duties in 1896–97, Delabarre devised a set of inkblot tests to study imagination in relation to personality types.[45] His studies were also controversial. His main research for thirty-eight years, from 1893 to 1931, was on the effect of drugs on perception, although he only published one paper, in 1899.[46] He used cannabis, hashish, peyote, and cocaine, self-dosing (although one experiment involved an orangutan named Joe) and recording the effects on visual perception, but also on most every conceivable response: reaction times, pain, memory, detection of high-pitched sounds, direction of sounds, taste, smell, muscular reactions, subjective feelings, and "bodily states."[47] As a Brown faculty memorial remarked of Delabarre in 1945, some of his experiments "seemed to involve personal risk of a sort that invited rather sensational publicity. This annoyed him for he was a sincerely modest man who scorned such notoriety and was prompted only by eager desire to establish the factual basis of his theory and its utmost implications."[48]

The only book-length work Delabarre published, other than *Dighton Rock* in 1928, was an offset print of his report on the Brown-Harvard scientific expedition to northern Labrador in 1900. Delabarre by his own account was "nominally leader" of the Labrador expedition, despite "the absence of material sufficient to occupy him largely in his own specialty."[49] With nothing psychological to concern him, he collected plants.[50]

In 1907, Delabarre married Dorothea Cotton. He was forty-three and she was nineteen, a former "special" or day student at Brown. By 1910 they had two children, Maria and Edmund Jr.; Maria would figure significantly in the Dighton Rock story through her marriage (see chapter 10). That year, Delabarre purchased a twenty-two-acre farm as a summer retreat on Assonet Neck.[51] The farm was about a mile south of Dighton Rock, and he would recall it was around 1913 that the boulder caught his interest.[52]

He was probably alerted to it by ongoing commotion over signage that Arnzen had recommended be installed. A local man, Donald G. Merrill, would recall taking down an iron sign on the rock around 1912 and accompanying a mason who chipped off all the offending initials of vandals, drilled a hole in the rock, and cemented in place a sign that quoted from a local statute regarding the defacement of monuments. The next year the sign had disappeared, presumably carried away by ice. Merrill installed yet another sign on a pipe secured with molten lead. On his first attempt the lead exploded, and we can imagine the 1913 detonation as the shot that attracted the vacationing professor's attention. When Merrill returned in the spring of 1914 the pipe was bent ninety degrees. The sign stayed that way, the pipe too stiff for a man to straighten yet not stiff enough to withstand the river's tidewater ice.[53]

Alerted to Dighton Rock, the focal point of the rest of Delabarre's intellectual life was set. "For several years I entertained no notion that I could contribute anything to its interpretation," he would write in 1932, "but became absorbed in revising the history of investigation and discussion of it, current accounts of which I found exceedingly defective and untrustworthy."[54] Delabarre became the foremost scholar of Dighton Rock's historiography, but his studies were a paradox of obsessive detail and blindness to the fact that the markings had been so interfered with and mutilated that they were likely beyond the point of affording any useful lesson on antiquity or ethnography. In addition to the graffiti that inspired the ice-doomed signage, the markings had been chalked, painted, scrubbed, and more than likely clarified or improved with steel tools by people who wanted to see an inscription that was anything other than Indigenous. As an archaeological resource—perhaps even as an Indigenous cultural resource—it may have been ruined. Garrick Mallery had recognized this unfortunate fact in consigning Dighton Rock to a paragraph in his 1886 study of pictographs, within his discussion of frauds. He briefly recounted the attempts to cast its markings as Scandinavian and Hebrew before noting: "this inscription has been so manipulated that it is difficult now to determine the original details."[55]

Delabarre's efforts to craft a new provenance for Dighton Rock recall the late nineteenth-century efforts of Eben Norbert Horsford to assert Massachusetts Bay as the locus of Viking activity in the New World. Both men were esteemed professors associated with Harvard who wandered outside their fields of expertise and abandoned scholarly rigor. Horsford served for sixteen years as the Rumford Professor of Chemistry at Harvard before securing independent wealth through the Rumford Chemical Works. Horsford had been a member of Appleton's memorial committee, and his eccentric archaeological efforts placed Leifsbúdir on a bend of the Charles River, near Harvard Square.[56] Just as Delabarre would, Horsford resorted to White Tribism, asserting that "there were white people through the territory of New England. . . . It is recorded of the whites that they had blue eyes and red hair, and that they maintained habits eminently characteristic of the Northmen."[57] Horsford was an amateur philologist familiar with Indigenous languages, and paid to have *Vocabularies by Zeisberger* published from manuscripts held by Harvard in 1887. Horsford nevertheless went word hunting, as he alleged that white colonists of pre-Columbian America preserved their traditions in sagas, and were known as saga-men. He asserted the term found its way into Indigenous languages for leaders and orators, who were identified by Lescarbot as *Sagamos* and later by New England historians as *Sagamores*.[58] To Horsford, the Wampanoag of Philip and his father Massasoit were the people of Wampanakka, which was "Indian for 'White-man's land,'—Huítra-manna-land."[59]

As Oscar J. Falnes remarked of Horsford: "It almost takes one's breath away to see with what unbridled imagination and what leaves in the deductive process, he—a one-time Rumford Professor trained in the empirical discipline of chemistry—could take his point of departure in prosaic and ordinary materials and proceed until he was ready to describe in superlative terms the medieval Norse life on the Charles. He visualized nothing less than a flourishing Norse colony."[60] Delabarre's interpretive misadventure as a trained academic is as arresting as the case of Horsford—and of Barry Fell, the Harvard marine biologist who in retirement in the 1970s veered into detecting European Bronze Age standing stones and ogham script in rocks (including Indigenous petroglyphs) throughout North America. Ironies within the Delabarre episode abound, but foremost is the fact that Delabarre was a psychology professor who specialized in studies of human visual perception and was a pioneer in the use of inkblots in clinical research. Dighton Rock was an inkblot in the form of a boulder, an analogy that eluded Delabarre until 1932, in spite of the fact that James Winthrop's rendering published in 1804 was based on an impression pulled from the rock with printer's ink.

Delabarre's misadventure had a compelling corollary in the mania for canals on Mars, which were first detected in 1877 and were championed especially by the American amateur astronomer Percival Lowell.[61] This mania among the world's leading astronomers, which faded from scientific literature after 1907, was perhaps the most celebrated example of observational failure at the time of Delabarre's studies in human visual perception, yet he appears to have paid the phenomenon no attention. He picked up where the discredited Mars mapping efforts had left off, examining and producing photographs of Dighton Rock in which slanting light revealed his own version of canals: Roman numerals and letters.

Delabarre was like his own Cassandra, having repeatedly issued warnings about the perils of interpreting the inscription, which he ultimately failed to heed. As he wrote in 1918: "Its history illustrates almost every variety of scientific error, almost every type of psychological process. . . . As a study in the correct method and common errors in science, and as a subject for illustrating the natural psychology of perception and belief, there is nothing more instructive. . . . Whoever will take each drawing, and, giving free rein to his selective imagination, find it fully justified in the Burgess photograph [made without chalking in 1868], as can be done with practically every one of the originals."[62] Delabarre was describing (without using the term) the phenomenon he studied with inkblot tests, called pareidolia, in which someone viewing an amorphous shape or pattern suddenly discerns something significant, such as an elephant in the clouds or the face of Jesus in a slice of toast.[63] Leonardo da Vinci had advised that a stain-spotted wall could provide a painter with the inspiration to create landscapes, figures in combat, facial expressions, outlandish costumes, and more.[64] Delabarre in 1918 called Gébe-lin, Hill, Magnussén and Rafn, and Dammartin "of the type in whom the possession of a theory, the imagining of the presence of a particular figure, creates a blindness to all other possibilities."[65] Yet despite his own warning in his third and final installment of his Dighton Rock study of how easy it was "to imagine as present on the rock almost any desired letter of the alphabet," Delabarre did precisely that.[66] On February 27, 1919, Delabarre appeared be-fore a meeting of the Colonial Society of Massachusetts, as the final install-ment was published by the society, to announce in person that he had found the inscriber of the 1511 date: "the name Miguel Cortereal could be read upon the rock with a fair degree of plausibility."[67]

ALTHOUGH DELABARRE WAS not a historian, his overall analysis and dedi-cation to verifying sources were of a high caliber, better than in most previous investigations, with the possible exception of Kendall, whose effort he ad-mired, even if Delabarre did not detect Kendall's Masonic subtext. Dela-barre's investigation of Dighton Rock was also an education for him. The process of learning included absorbing the perspectives and prejudices of earlier theorists, if some aspects were not already borne by him and exposed through his own theorizing. By the time he completed his second install-ment, on the "Middle Period" of the rock's interpretation, Delabarre had internalized two important points. The markings were probably Indigenous, and if they were Indigenous, they were of no interest to history, or most any other field of study. Not even the new field of cultural anthropology held out much hope for insights. Brinton's *The Myths of the New World*, repeatedly re-printed and last revised in 1896, had made clear that there was little chance of deciphering such Indigenous glyphs. As the 1905 edition would have in-formed Delabarre of Chippewa song scrolls: "On what principle of mental association a given sign was adopted to express a certain idea . . . is hard to guess. The difficulty grows when we find that to the initiated the same sign calls up quite different ideas, as the subject of the writer varies from war to love, or from the chase to religion. The connection is generally beyond the power of divination, and the key to ideographic writing once lost can never be recovered."[68]

Delabarre was a nineteenth-century New Englander, born and raised in a part of the country where authentic Indians were no longer considered to ex-ist, and when last encountered in their independent state were considered bloodthirsty savages. A paradoxical aspect of Delabarre's extracurricular stud-ies was the parallel interest he took in Indigenous archaeology, with two papers and a research note accepted for publication by *American Anthropologist*. In 1920 he coauthored a paper on "Indian corn-hills" in Massachusetts, the mounds used by Native Americans for mass plantings, which survived as landscape features on Assonet Neck (including on Delabarre's farm) to an extent that impressed Delabarre.[69] In 1925 he published a paper on a "possible Pre-Algonkian culture in southeastern Massachusetts," based on his excavations of a site he thought might be 1,000 years old. The site was on Grassy Island, a rise of land now submerged under seven or eight feet of water at high tide in the widening of the Taunton River, about 1,000 feet from Dighton Rock.[70] He followed up his Grassy Island report with a note published in 1928 on cremated human remains found on the site.[71] If at least some of the glyphs on Dighton Rock were contemporary with the Grassy Island find, when water levels were much lower, it was possible they were made when the rock was only partially submerged by the high tide, or not at all. But Delabarre never considered Grassy Island in conjunction with the famous relic right next to it. Delabarre's active interest in Indigenous archaeology may seem baffling in the face of his indifference in defending Dighton Rock as a purely Indigenous artifact, until one considers the nineteenth-century division between the object-based epistemology of archaeologists digging into mounds and the interest of philologists and semioticians in inscribed rocks. Indigenous corn plantings, bones, and arrowheads intrigued Delabarre; unintelligible markings made by people considered to have lived well shy of the minimal standards of civilization did not.

"Considered simply as a rude scrawl of unknown meaning made by uncultured Indians, Dighton Rock would be worthy of but scanty notice," Delabarre wrote in 1918. This had been Kendall's opinion at the start of the nineteenth century, and by the end of that century, the opinion remained among leading historians that Daniel Wilson's *prehistory* was precisely before recorded history, with nothing to be gained for their field from trying to understand Indigenous oral traditions or relics, with the possible exception of the confounding glyphs of Palenque and other Mesoamerican sites whose temple ruins suggested a semicivilized state. Even if scholars found Native American history worthy of study, the learned opinion was that Native Americans themselves were incapable of having preserved it. As Brinton wrote: "The most distinguished characters, the weightiest events in national history faded into oblivion after a few generations . . . their myths are myths only, and not the reflections of history or heroes."[72] If the "rude scrawl" of Dighton Rock was outside the purview of proper historical study, then Delabarre was left to make a case for why it absorbed so much of his time and energy. He decided that his ongoing study's utility lay in what it could reveal about scientific inquiry and the pitfalls awaiting learned men along the way: "As the center of interest around which has raged a storm of controversy; as the leading motif in a developing symphony that passes through many movements to a final clarity and harmony of many subordinate motifs; as the plot which has involved in an unfolding story a multitude of strange and varied actors; as a mystery which has led through crude and errant stages at last to a sound scientific understanding—Dighton Rock is unsurpassed in its appeal. Its history illustrates almost every variety of scientific error, almost every type of psychological process."[73]

Delabarre's historiographical model for Dighton Rock was one of scientific progressivism: investigative methods gradually improved, as did interpretations, with his own investigation serving as the crowning achievement. But the history of Dighton Rock's interpretation was only progressive in the way Delabarre proposed if he accepted (as scholars by the late nineteenth century had), that its markings were of Indigenous origin. Otherwise, as his own scholarship showed, analysis had moved through different phases of Euro-American enthusiasms, none entirely supplanting another, each one illustrating how educated men could persuade themselves (and others) of baseless interpretations. Nor did Delabarre bring the symphony to a final clarity and harmony as he promised. As a professor specializing in perceptual psychology, he succumbed to the foible he deftly perceived in the efforts of his predecessors: it was possible to stare at the rock's markings and see almost any character or symbol the viewer wished. And in reinvigorating centuries of scholarly misadventure by instigating a new phase of misattribution, Delabarre made one of the most forceful denigrations of Indigenous capability.

Delabarre knew well where his study was bound as he drafted "Middle Period," the second installment of his three-party study. "In spite of the poetic appeal of theories that plausibly ascribe [the rock's markings] to some people or other of long ago and far away, we have had to recognize repeatedly that accumulating evidence is removing more and more completely all objections urged against the Indian hypothesis, and that all competent archaeological authorities now agree that there are no sound reasons for rejecting it."[74] Delabarre, however, may have been nagged by the realization that if his study left the rock's markings in the undecipherable provenance of Native Americans, he would have conducted an exhaustive proxy study of progressive scientific method of limited interest. Surely if he detected an inscription from a more culturally worthy source, that would propel the study into the realm of legitimate history, and his efforts would command interest from a much broader audience, both general and academic. And so there may have been at least a subconscious desire by Delabarre to arrive at a solution more satisfying than "rude scrawls" by "uncultured Indians." He also probably found it impossible to resist the long-standing Western intellectual determination to decipher an inscription (if it might indeed be decipherable) where so many others whose work he had critiqued had failed. When he convinced himself in the course of supposedly concluding his studies that he could see "1511" in a photograph, it was an epiphany that was also a kind of deliverance.

From December 10 to 12, 1918, about a week after he noticed the date 1511 in the Hathaway photo, Delabarre conducted experiments on himself to evaluate the effect of *Cannabis indica* on hyperesthesia, or hypersensitivity, recording reactions to "taps, heat suggestibility, stuttering, colors, sound."[75] If Delabarre ever sought some heightened perception through drugs in examining Dighton Rock, he did not record it, or admit it. Delabarre otherwise was rightly dissatisfied with the way researchers since the mid-nineteenth century had used paint or chalk to highlight the markings for photography. He likely took to heart Edward Augustus Kendall's warnings about the way such highlighting caused the viewer to prejudge what was there. Searching for the inscription that would explain 1511, Delabarre mounted a powerful flashlight on a ladder apparatus to illuminate the rock from an angle that would cast revealing shadows. Delabarre's methodology was in accord with the scientific objective of gathering data untainted by human influence or weakness. In Delabarre's clinical studies, he had designed one of the first long-paper kymographs, an apparatus that made tracings of minute muscular movements over many hours of observation.[76] With his Dighton Rock study, the camera apparatus would only reveal what light and shadow indicated, rather than what the photographer first marked up on the rock with paint or chalk before using a camera to record his handiwork. However, a photograph still had to be interpreted, and in this regard Delabarre was as subjective and as prone to pareidolia as any investigator before him.

"THE DISCOVERY of the date 1511 led me to reflect upon the early explorers who might by any possibility have been in this vicinity at that time," Delabarre recounted at the conclusion of "Recent History," in which he revealed his Corte-Real finding.[77] The Columbus anniversary of 1892 had instigated a fresh wave of archival-based scholarly research into early transatlantic European voyages, resulting in fresh works on the Cabots and the Corte-Reals.[78] Delabarre's research into early explorers, however, was minimal. He noted that the first known (actually, suspected) visit to Narragansett Bay was by

Giovanni di Verrazano in 1524, when he anchored in a place he called Port de Refugio. That was thirteen years after the rock's date of 1511. The brothers Gaspar and Miguel Corte-Real, he avowed, "are the only ones who could possibly have been responsible for our inscription."[79] But Delabarre ignored the candidacy of the second John Cabot voyage, of 1498, whose five ships were considered to have vanished in northeastern North America.[80] Delabarre instead turned to a handful of letters others had thought they could make out, and started shoehorning them into the only candidate that he decided could accommodate them: Miguel Corte-Real. In this regard he acted no differently than Rafn and Magnussén did in forcing the Karlsefni inscription onto the very same area of Dighton Rock.

Little is known about the Corte-Real expeditions.[81] Gaspar Corte-Real sailed from Lisbon in 1500 for northeastern North America, and visited a land of great trees he called Terre Verde, which may have been Newfoundland. After returning to Lisbon in the autumn of 1500, Gaspar departed again in the spring of 1501 with three ships. In the southern part of Terre Verde he abducted about fifty-seven Indians, who may have been Beothuk from Newfoundland. Gaspar had found a new supply of slaves. Seven captives arrived in Lisbon as two of the Corte-Real ships returned, but Gaspar and his crew (along with their captives) were never heard from. In 1502, Gaspar's brother Miguel sailed with two or three ships to the new lands. If the sole, brief (and secondhand) accounts written by chroniclers Antonio Galvam in 1563 and Damiam de Goes in 1566 can be believed, Miguel's flotilla (Galvam said there were three ships, De Goes, two) reached Terra Verde in the summer of 1502. The ships split up to explore the many rivers, and were to rendezvous on August 20. When Miguel did not reappear, the remaining ship(s) returned to Lisbon. Miguel, his crew, and his flagship vanished.[82]

Finding a Corte-Real name on Dighton Rock was not easy. All Delabarre could initially detect was an M, followed by CORTE, and these were some distance to the right of the alleged date of 1511, but by the time he published his final installment, "Recent History," in 1919 he had the confidence to publish a drawing with at least the promise of MIGVELL CORTEREAL DE, two deer below his name, and a suggestion of the white bird, to the right of 1511 (figure 9). With his flashlight photography, Delabarre winnowed away at the problem. By 1923, the presence of the letters MIGV and CORTER "was proven beyond question by our photographs."[83] The remaining letters, in his estimation, were either obscured by overlying Indian glyphs or eroded by ice, but nevertheless to his eyes they were there.[84]

FIGURE 9 Edmund Burke Delabarre's initial depiction of an inscription by Miguel
Corte-Real, including the date 1511, two deer, and a suggestion of the white bird, in "Recent
History of Dighton Rock," *Publications of the Colonial Society of Massachusetts* 20 (1919).

Two months after finding the date 1511, along with the letters M and
CORTE, Delabarre had a scenario, offered in "Recent History," for how
Miguel Corte-Real washed up in the upper reaches of the Taunton River,
nine years after departing Portugal for Newfoundland. Delabarre proposed
that after some misadventure, possibly shipwreck, in Newfoundland, Miguel
attempted to reach the Spanish territories far to the south. His progress would
have been slow, because he had to get past "fierce" and "hostile" tribes in
Nova Scotia and Cape Breton.[85] "It is conceivable that by patience and tact
Miguel Cortereal may have worked his way through these dangers after a long
delay. If we concede that we have reason for suspecting his presence in southern New England in 1511, it would not lack in plausibility on account of the
nine years that had elapsed since his shipwreck."[86] In 1923, Delabarre revealed
more findings—a heraldic symbol of Portugal, and above it a Latin phrase:
V. DEI hIC DVX IND.[87] As Rafn and Magnussén had done with their Norse
inscription, Delabarre resorted to abbreviation to coax a coherent message from
the stone. Expanded, Delabarre's phrase presumably read, "Voluntate Dei hic
Dux Indorum," which provided the following complete inscription: "Miguel
Cortereal. 1511. By the will of God, leader of the natives of India in this place."[88]
    Delabarre incorporated the long-standing story of the fight with the men
in the wooden vessel. After a battle at White Man's Spring, in which the Indians' sachem was killed, "Cortereal escaped, and probably one or two others
who had remained in the boat with him. Undermanned, they could voyage
no farther, and were thus forced to conciliate the natives, who may have been
angered or frightened by some occurrence at the spring, rather than seriously
hostile. With firearms in his possession, sufficient companions to help, and

high qualities of tact and leadership, he may have been able to seize and hold the place of their dead sachem." Corte-Real settled in the area, and wrote his name on the rock in hopes of attracting the attention of some other European explorer, who could carry him home.[89]

Delabarre's Miguel was cut from the same heroic European cloth as the "sturdy Celt" Ephraim Squier had suggested carved the Grave Creek stone and commanded the fealty of the Mound Builders. But where Squier had made a proposal laced with sarcasm, Delabarre was completely serious. His Miguel brings to mind the character Dan (and his accomplice, Peachey) in Rudyard Kipling's novella *The Man Who Would Be King*, published in 1888. Miguel securing the leadership of the Wampanoag was the logical outcome of the appearance of white strangers with firearms and an innate ability to command the respect of lesser peoples. Having turned Miguel into a leader of the Wampanoag, Delabarre took White Tribism into the predictable territory of racial improvement in *Dighton Rock* (1928), attributing to anonymous reviewers of his earlier writings assertions of a beneficial infusion of Portuguese blood:

> "Who can say," says one of them, "that the blood of this Portuguese adventure"—or, we should add, of one of his younger companions—"was not coursing in the veins of King Philip himself some 150 years later?" Another supports the same suggestion in these words: "No trace of European blood was ever noted among the Indians of Assonet Neck. But of course none was ever looked for in the early days when it might have been noted. A trace of Latin blood, a sign of a race marked by black eyes and hair and olive complexion, after a few generations is less easy to find than a Nordic strain that gives a distinct new trend to type." Apart from this possibility of blood descent, a third reviewer has said something that may well be true: "It is not unreasonable to suppose that Cortereal's influence was that which resulted in the Wampanoag's place in history—that of the most intelligent tribe of Indians in America, a tribe that, faced with extermination, preferred to die fighting."[90]

Here was belonging, possession, and dispossession practiced at an unprecedented conjectural level. Where Rafn turned Dighton Rock into a Norse claim-staking and Native Americans into hybridized Gothicist Norse, Delabarre turned the Wampanoag's seventeenth-century rebellion against their Anglo-Saxon colonizers into an act attributable to their earlier biological improvement by Corte-Real and his companions. Indians had succumbed to colonists because of their innate inferiority, but choosing to rally in defiance against colonists must have been because ancestors of colonists had improved them. Delabarre was unconcerned with long-standing convictions in Gothic/ Aryanist theorizing that the Portuguese—southern European and Catholic— were a breed inferior to the preeminent racial stock of northern white Protestant Europeans. He seemed satisfied that *any* European newcomer would have been superior to a Native American. And perhaps there was an implicit assumption that the Wampanoag would have succeeded against English colonists had their ancestors been improved by Englishmen.

Delabarre moved on to word-hunting in *Dighton Rock*. "Suppose that the Indians among whom Cortereal found a home were particularly impressed by two things about their foreign leader and the 'magic' that he had cut into the rock."[91] One "thing" was the first part of his name, *Corte*, which impressed the Indians for reasons Delabarre did not explain. The other "thing" was the heraldic symbol of Portugal. Delabarre had found two small, roughly triangular shapes, one inside the other, with a dot at the center. He argued this was the Portuguese arms, a small shield within a larger shield, with the single dot standing in for the normal five-dot arrangement of the *quina*. He suggested the single dot was a compromise due to a lack of space. Alternatively, there may have once been all five dots, but a person unknown had obscured them with a single, more deeply carved one.[92] Delabarre gave no reason why Corte-Real would have found himself so pressed for space that he reduced the *quina* from five dots to one when he had a blank rock surface eleven feet long for a canvas. In any case, Delabarre thought the *quina* would have symbolized for the Indians the country Corte-Real had come from, and so they learned to call him *Corte-quina*. "Then, according to frequent European custom, this name might have been passed on to later sachems, and have reappeared a hundred years later in the name of Massasoit's brother, Quadequina. White men heard Indian names very inexactly, and spelled them in numerous varying ways; so that the difference in spelling here does not invalidate this derivation."[93] Delabarre presented to William Brooks Cabot, an expert on Indigenous New England place names, his theory that the suffix -*quin* in a number of Indian proper names originated with Corte-Real.[94] That would have made *Algonquin* of Portuguese inspiration, and we should recall that Charles Vallancey had already determined a Phoenician origin, from *al gand gins*. Delabarre admitted that Cabot "can feel nothing but plain Indian in these names," but nevertheless was still arguing in favor of his interpretation in the *Journal of American History* in 1932.[95]

DELABARRE'S THEORY ABOUNDS with so many problems that objections can be raised almost at will, ad infinitum. Delabarre addressed the Corte-Real brothers' slaving only in a footnote in "Recent History," acknowledging that George Patterson thought it "more than likely" that Miguel Corte-Real and his shipmates "should have fallen victims to the vengeance of the friends or clansmen of the kidnapped, or perhaps been overpowered in an attempt to capture more."[96] Delabarre discounted this theory as "no more probable than the one that I make."[97] Delabarre in 1923 incorporated deadly conflict at White Man's Spring, but he gave no cause, including slave raiding. In revisiting his scenario in *Dighton Rock* in 1928, Delabarre asserted that at Narragansett Bay, Miguel "found a race that was kind, gentle, courteous, friendly, according to the testimony of all early voyages. His record seems to indicate he settled among them."[98] Delabarre was unconcerned that "kind, gentle, courteous, friendly" were not terms Indigenous people would have applied to Portuguese slavers. And there was no such "record" for Miguel's doomed voyage, beyond what Delabarre could read with his flashlight on the side of Dighton Rock. Delabarre also did not pause to wonder how Miguel had enough gunpowder and ammunition after nine years in the wilderness to fight first more northern tribes and then the Wampanoag and command the fealty of the latter. He also stretched the limited details of Miguel's voyage in asserting that after splitting up with his other ships in Terra Verde, he sailed south. Galvam (the sole source on this independent surveying and rendezvous plan) said nothing about which direction Miguel had sailed. And why, if the inscription was meant to alert some future explorer to Miguel's presence in his hope of returning home, did Corte-Real choose to inscribe a boulder that spent large parts of every day completely submerged, in the obscure reaches of a tributary of Narragansett Bay, about twenty-five miles inland from the sea? And why would Corte-Real have written the Latin inscription that supposedly instructed Europeans on how to find him in a brain-teasing abbreviated form?

Delabarre also had to explain why the Indians whom Verrazano met in 1524, only thirteen years after the inscription, would make no mention of an amazing white man who had come to lead them.[99] How could the Wampanoag (or neighboring Narragansett) forget the details of Miguel's leadership but remember the initial battle, even while preserving a garbled version of Corte-Real's name? Delabarre did not address why none of the offspring from the infusion of Portuguese blood would have been recognizable to Verrazano through their appearance, remnants of clothing and arms from their fathers (and where were their fathers?), and a creole of Algonquian-Portuguese words. Delabarre knew the silence of Verrazano's account on Miguel's remarkable presence was a significant problem. He ventured: "it is not very surprising that Verrazano tells us nothing about him, for his narrative implies that he explored to a distance of not more than five or six leagues beyond Newport, and if the natives tried to inform him about the strange white man who had recently dwelt and died among them, he would have understood nothing of what they were trying to say. By the time the next white visitors arrived and gained power to converse with the natives, about three-quarters of a century later, the Indians had apparently retained but little memory of the incident." Delabarre insisted a "fragmentary and distorted part of the story did persist" among the Indians in the tale of the wooden ship and the battle at the spring.[100]

WHILE DELABARRE COUNSELED that theorists were wrong to think that "Indians were too lazy and idle to have been capable" of carving Dighton Rock in "Recent History" of 1919, his core attitude toward Native Americans already had begun to surface while writing "Middle Period."[101] For the first time he referred to Indigenous rock markings as "scribblings," in discussing Kendall's researches, a term that recalled Michael Lort's "rude scrawls" of 1786 and Webb's "unmeaning scrawls . . . of the idle Indian, who has spent his time in this lazy manner," in his 1830 letter to Rafn printed in *Antiquitates Americanae*. Calling images that had to be methodically pecked into stone "scribblings" was ridiculous, but it conveyed the lazy, inconsequential haste Delabarre would consistently assign to Indigenous efforts throughout the rest of his writings on Dighton Rock and rock art in general. Delabarre embraced a presumption embedded in the long history of Dighton Rock's interpretation: Native Americans were inferior in moral and intellectual character to whites.

Delabarre's flashlight-assisted photography of the rock had turned up several examples of what he asserted was Anglo-American graffiti. Late in his preparation of his 1923 paper (Delabarre had a penchant for eleventh-hour publishing discoveries), he claimed to have detected an arrow with the word SPRING, presumably a set of colonial directions. He suspected there was an entire phrase: "Injun Path To Spring In Swomp Yds 167 in the direction of the arrow."[102] More sensationally, he then turned up "Thacher 1598," which he ventured was the record of an early English expedition to the New England cod fishery.[103] The supposed 1598 inscription was a significant find, but historians declined to embrace his revelation. Plainly, though, Indians had been inscribing images on Dighton Rock, as the stone was covered in them. Delabarre thought he could detect a second horned quadruped, drawn in the same style, next to the known one, and he believed they were deer.

In "Middle Period," Delabarre had been sympathetic to the idea there might be intellectual substance to Indigenous markings. "If we do not like to believe that the rock presents nothing more than idle and meaningless scribblings" by Indians at various times, he counseled, "then probably we must agree that Kendall was right in saying that without knowing the exact story in advance there is no possibility that the intended meaning can be restored."[104] Delabarre, however, found the reading of the four Mohawk chiefs related by Kendall "too trivial and unappealing for acceptance," and while Shingwauk's reading "is plausible enough . . . it stands exactly on par with nearly a score of rival readings."[105] Delabarre encountered nothing that would persuade him of an Indigenous meaning worthy of anyone's time, and apparently made no effort to learn more about the cultural traditions to which they might have belonged.

Delabarre's explanation of the inscription was the same as that advanced by the Reverend Chapin in 1839, which was borrowed (before being abandoned) by Schoolcraft in 1851. A European visitor made the initial inscription, and the Indians filled in the rock around it—and in the case of Delabarre's interpretation, right over parts of the European handiwork. In "Recent History" in 1919, Delabarre's attitude toward Native Americans, their intellectual capabilities, and culture was one of dismissive contempt:

> On New England rocks, the writer has found Indian carvings that almost beyond question were meaningless haphazard scribblings, the product of an impulse to be active anyhow, as some people slash at shrubbery in passing; further encouraged, no doubt, by finding that their artistic efforts aroused the interest and admiration of watching companions. In some cases, probably, such childish scribblings might be the result of an endeavor to imitate, without knowing how, the white man's marvelous art of writing. In other cases, ornamental and geometrical designs are carved, still without meaning, but satisfying an urge for more pleasing artistic expression and eliciting greater applause from the onlookers. The widespread urge to make crude pictures of familiar objects, men, animals and trees, is also evident, again due to both motives and still having no wider meaning.[106]

Delabarre's opinion recalled Kendall's 1807 suggestion that Indians had been imitating works by a superior people unrelated to them, without understanding what they were depicting. In his 1923 paper, Delabarre made his case in milder yet still contemptuous terms. He thought it "highly improbable" that Indigenous people made markings prior to Corte-Real. "Many of the carvings [on Dighton Rock] are unquestionably later than [Corte-Real's]. Study of the half-dozen other petroglyphs scattered about Narragansett Bay argues for the belief that they, at least, were motivated by the examples of the whites of Colonial days. It seems unquestionable that it was Cortereal's example, reinforced by more intimate acquaintance with white men's writing after 1600, that led to the first attempts of the local Indians to imitate as well as they knew how so wonderful a process."[107] His argument essentially was a repurposing of the one Rafn had made to (and had been accepted by) Webb: the practice of rock inscription spread among Indians from the example of the Norse, or were made by hybridized Norse-Indians.

Delabarre came to the useful conclusion that it was "practically certain that the Indian contributions do not form a connected story, and that they were made by many different individuals and on different occasions extending very probably into Colonial times." But he was adamant that the markings were inspired by whites, and, moreover, that they were not worth studying, as it was "not at all likely that any important meaning or message attaches to any of their glyphs." He wavered in suggesting they were of no less interest than had they been made by Phoenicians or Norsemen, "or by other people whose possible wanderings may intrigue the uncritical imagination." Yet he concluded: "Many of them are probably meaningless scribblings, others merely trivial pictures. Some may possibly have had a more elaborate symbolic purpose, but anything of that sort would have been probably so local and temporary that we are not likely ever to discover what particular objects and ideas their authors had in mind."[108]

EDMUND BURKE DELABARRE's study of Dighton Rock endures as a meta-study of scholarly folly: invaluable in understanding the interpretive errors of the past, yet a major error in its own right. Delabarre deserved to be hoisted with his own intellectual petard. In "Recent History" in 1919, he condemned the "many wiseacres in this country and Europe whose zeal far outstrips their wisdom and who endeavor to make up for want of knowledge in bold assertions and wholesale statements ... in their self-conceit and gross ignorance, they have deemed themselves amply qualified to sit in judgment. ... At one time these 'Know-Everythings' labored most vigorously to break the Dighton Rock to pieces."[109] Delabarre then assured: "To be acceptable, a scientific hypothesis must take into account every single one of the pertinent indubitable facts, fit each into its definite place in a harmonious system, account for all distinctions and variations and conditions. ... There is but one account of the facts which, while it has not solved all problems, is yet inherently capable of accomplishing the task."[110] Delabarre may have thought only his Corte-Real hypothesis met this standard, but it was in truth as satisfactory an example as one can find of a Western inquiry into an Indigenous artifact that failed to meet the minimal requirements of its own methodology. Delabarre likely would have demolished the Corte-Real theory had anyone else authored it.

In 1932, Delabarre admitted: "It may be said with some justice that anyone can read anything he wants to find upon this rock. I have myself made such a claim as a result of a critical historical study of the many drawings and chalkings and translations. An attitude of unrestrained imagination, like that which finds pictures in clouds and in ink-blots, has led men to an almost limitless variety of ill-supported interpretations of these markings. But an attitude of critical and attentive scrutiny can test the validity of such imaginative perceptions. We have adopted that attitude."[111] To the contrary, Delabarre's own published photography leaves a viewer straining to see how he fit particular letters into the rock's markings. Delabarre's greatest failing was his insistence on the triviality and meaninglessness of any rock art attributable to Native Americans, which was inseparable from his presumption of their intellectual inferiority.

Delabarre's Miguel Corte-Real theory was not consigned, as it deserved to be, to the scrap heap of misguided notions that Delabarre had assembled in his investigation for the Colonial Society of Massachusetts. Instead, it inspired the most celebrated and enduring possession of Dighton Rock. The issue of immigrant belonging that had once attracted Scandinavian Americans to claim Dighton Rock for the Norse, through Delabarre became a priority for another immigrant community. Portuguese Americans embraced the rock in an act of place-making within a home-making urge to assert their rightful status as equals in American society, as America's original discoverers.

CHAPTER TEN

American Place-Making
Dighton Rock as a Portuguese Relic

Edmund Burke Delabarre's claim of a Corte-Real inscription on Dighton Rock initially showed as much hope of shifting its provenance as Delabarre would have had of moving the forty-ton boulder with his bare hands. The *Geographical Journal* of Britain's Royal Geographical Society did address his October 1923 article in *Old-Time New England* in its December issue that year. (The speed of the response indicates that someone, possibly Delabarre himself, provided an advance copy.) While praising Delabarre's innovative lighting for photography, the journal advised that his interpretations "call for a good deal of faith for their acceptance."[1] The so-called Portuguese markings "do not stand alone but are picked out from a mass of other lines which are arbitrarily set aside as of later date."[2] The inscription also bore no stylistic resemblance to a known Portuguese rock inscription discovered in 1906, left by Diogo Cão during his exploration of the Congo River in West Africa in 1485.[3]

With Delabarre's theory otherwise raising not a ripple of interest among historians, the Corte-Real chapter in Dighton Rock's annals of misinterpretation might have ended quickly, had there not been a resurgent but shifting interest in America in Viking voyages, as Scandinavian American place-making moved away from the New England relics of *Antiquitates Americanae*. Just as Anglo-American New Englanders allied with Rafn and besotted with Gothicism had drawn historic Vinland toward themselves in the early nineteenth century, so too did Scandinavian Americans in the states of the Old Northwest in the late nineteenth century.[4] The 1898 discovery of an inscribed stone on the farm of Olof Ohman near Kensington in Douglas County, Minnesota, opened fresh terrain for Norse exploits in North America. The Kensington rune stone was declared a fake by scholars in 1899 (and repeatedly thereafter), but it proved to be a hoax that refused to die.[5] Its most ardent proponent was a Norwegian immigrant to Wisconsin, Hjalmar Holand, who studied under Rasmus Anderson at the University of Wisconsin and insisted on the stone's authenticity. Holand decided it was the record of an expedition led by Paul Knutson in 1355 that sailed into Hudson Bay and reached the site of the stone by portages via the Nelson River and Lake Winnipeg. Enduring seven years of hardships only Holand could imagine, Knutson's party left the inscription in 1362 after a bloody battle with Indians. Holand argued his case initially in a pamphlet in 1919 and more elaborately in a self-published book, *The Kensington Stone*, in 1932. While runic experts still thought the stone was a fake, Holand for a time persuaded a few historians and academics that it was authentic, or that at the least he had revived a case otherwise considered closed.[6]

Holand left Vinland on the Atlantic coast and created an additional pre-Columbian Norse presence deep in North America, where Scandinavian immigrants had congregated in the nineteenth century. He did so just as Delabarre was assigning Dighton Rock a Portuguese past, which opened a new chapter in immigrant home-making and place-making in America, at a time America was obsessed with racial fitness. Eugenics was inspiring state and federal laws in defense of biological (white) purity against degeneration.[7] Eugenicists feared (among other things) that less desirable Europeans would dilute the optimal Anglo-Saxon stock that White Tribism theories maintained had improved the inferior Native Americans. The National Origins (aka Johnson-Reed Immigration) Act of 1924 restricted annual immigration from foreign countries to 2 percent of the number of people identified according to national origin in 1890. The new quota system, along with literacy standards, tipped the immigration balance toward northern Europe, and away from southern and eastern Europe, while essentially debarring Asians.[8]

Scandinavian Americans may have struggled against nativist sentiments that considered Norwegian immigrants to be hyphenated Americans who had opposed American participation in the First World War, but they were favored in the immigration restrictions of 1924 and by the racial purity notions of eugenics. Portuguese Americans, however, suffered on both counts, and the area of southern New England near Dighton Rock was one of the most populous Portuguese immigrant communities in the United States. Mass migration of families, which began in the Azores and expanded to include Madeira and mainland Portugal, reached its peak in 1910, when the immigrant community provided 40 percent of mill workers.[9] By 1930, an estimated 80 percent of Portuguese in New England were cotton mill workers.[10] In the mill city of Fall River, only a few miles from Dighton Rock, about one-third of the population was of Portuguese ancestry. Overall Portuguese immigration to the United States reached a decadal peak of 89,732 in the 1910s before crashing to 3,329 in the 1930s under immigration restrictions.[11]

There is no indication that Delabarre had cultivated support in the considerable Portuguese-American community of southeastern New England for his Dighton Rock theory. The fact that his theory was not immediately embraced by the community when first announced in February 1919—evidently because the community was unaware of it—speaks to a considerable cultural divide between the Portuguese mill-worker underclass and establishment New Englanders who held a membership in the OCHS and the Colonial Society of Massachusetts and read Delabarre's initial Dighton Rock articles. (Delabarre's family once may have employed Portuguese immigrants, but his father retired and closed his mills in 1892.)

The Corte-Real theory finally found traction in the Portuguese-American community in 1926. On August 29, Delabarre posed for a photograph on the front page of *The Sunday Standard* of New Bedford, which had a substantial Portuguese-American population. Standing beside Dighton Rock at low tide, he pointed to the alleged 1511 date for the benefit of local author Clara Sharpe Hough, who reclined atop the boulder.[12] Hough had just published a novel, *Leif the Lucky*, dramatizing the purported Norse visits to New England, and the photo directed readers to a full article by Hough in the feature section on Delabarre's Corte-Real ideas.[13] The following day, the feature was noted by a front-page article in *A Alvorada* (*The Dawn*), the Portuguese-language daily newspaper founded in New Bedford in 1919, which by 1926 had expanded operations to Fall River.[14] On September 3, a two-page translation of Hough's article, copiously illustrated, appeared in *A Alvorada*.[15] Dighton Rock became a Portuguese-American sensation. On September 9, *A Alvorada* announced it was organizing a commission to meet with Delabarre and inspect Dighton Rock.[16] About three dozen men and a few boys, most of them Portuguese Americans, visited the rock on Sunday, October 10, to have the inscription explained by Delabarre, and an illustrated article dominated the front page of *A Alvorada* the following day. The article began by stating that Sunday's date ought to be marked in gold letters in the history of the Portuguese colony in New England.[17]

Delabarre's most ardent supporter in the Portuguese-American community was Abilio de Oliveira Águas, the Portuguese consul in Providence. Born in 1890 in mainland Portugal, Águas had served as a Portuguese government official in its colonial territory of Mozambique. He arrived in Providence in January 1924, and was appointed consul in the city in 1925.[18] In November 1926, Águas was busy translating Delabarre's *Old-Time New England* article of 1923 to deliver to the Portuguese government, the Academy of Scientists of Lisbon, the National Geographic Society of Lisbon, and the director the National Library in Lisbon. Delabarre also was being touted as a candidate for one of two Portuguese honors, either the Order of Christ or the Military Order of San Thiago do Espada.[19] Delabarre's article would appear in *Boletim da Agência Geral das Colónias* in 1927, and he would be made an officer of the military order in 1933.[20] Águas became not only a champion of Delabarre's work but his son-in-law as well, marrying his daughter, Maria, in the 1930s.[21] Águas remained devoted to his father-in-law's reputation well after Delabarre's death in 1945, during a heated postwar struggle over the rock's preservation and interpretation.

The Portuguese-American embrace of Dighton Rock was steeped in diaspora politics and culture. In addition to this embrace coming soon after the 1924 changes to U.S. immigration laws that essentially labeled the Portuguese an undesirable class of American citizens, it also coincided with the collapse of Portugal's First Republic and the establishment of the Estada Novo, which ruled Portugal under António de Oliveira Salazar until the democratizing revolution of 1974. Bela Feldman-Bianco has observed that in the 1920s and 1930s Portuguese migrants to the United States were considered second-class citizens in both their new country and their old one, and were confronted with "two conflicting and highly charged ideologies." On the one hand, the pressure of the melting-pot philosophy of the United States stressed "the superiority of American society and ways of life," which encouraged cultural assimilation. On the other hand, Portuguese colonial policies and ideologies of the home country were based on "the superiority and pride of the Luzitan race, which cast aspersions on those who left Portugal, and emphasized the exclusive maintenance of Portuguese culture and language."[22] The shift in Dighton Rock's attribution from Scandinavian to Portuguese, then, involved a precipitous descent from a European culture with most-favored status in America. It was now a place-making tool for an immigrant community searching for ways to assert its pride and its rightful belonging in an adopted country that seemed to regret having admitted them.

The divisions within the Portuguese-American community in events surrounding Dighton Rock would invite a book of its own.[23] Águas was terminated as Portuguese consul in 1929 after criticizing the Salazar regime. He remained in the United States as a businessman and became a leading and well-connected opponent of the Estada Novo, serving as chair of the anti-Salazarist Committee Pro-Democracy in Portugal (CPDP).[24] It is difficult to know if divisions and rivalries that emerged within the Portuguese-American community over Dighton Rock after the Second World War mirrored those in the political realm.[25] Águas, as we will see, despised the greatest postwar champion of Dighton Rock, Manuel Luciano da Silva, but Silva was also an occasional critic of the Estado Novo, to the anger of some fellow Portuguese Americans.[26] Initially at least, Delabarre's theory, coming soon after the shocks of U.S. immigration quotas and the Estada Novo, appears to have been broadly embraced, tapping a complex concept of Portuguese pride, heritage, and belonging called *saudade*. According to Feldman-Bianco, in *saudade*, "collective temporal memory is invariably linked to the discovery era and to the subsequent history of navigation."[27] Dighton Rock became a means by which Portuguese Americans could celebrate a nostalgic reverence for a distant era of daring explorers like the Corte-Reals. Delabarre had also elevated the Portuguese to the role of white improvers of Indians at a time when U.S. immigration policy and eugenics treated the Portuguese as an inferior and undesirable racial stock. As an exercise in place-making, Dighton Rock would become another Plymouth Rock, the means by which Portuguese Americans could assert a new respectability by crafting a home-making myth as the original European founders of their adopted country. In the process, the likely Indigenous significance of Dighton Rock, as a stone that bound living people to human and other-than-human ancestors within the landscape, was again overwritten.

THE NOTORIETY OF DIGHTON Rock as a Portuguese relic grew with Delabarre's publication of his popularizing book-length study, *Dighton Rock* (1928). An unsigned review in the *New York Times* advised: "Professor Delabarre's interpretations, although they appear to be sound and are certainly persuasive, are in part hardly less romantic" than the efforts of Rafn and Court de Gébelin. "There are many Indian drawings, the significance of which he does not pretend to know. He considers them of no great consequence."[28] Undaunted, Delabarre continued to publish on the Corte-Real theory, and on rock art in general. Rock art as a scholarly discipline in North America scarcely existed in the 1920s and 1930s, and would not begin to grow until after the Second World War. Delabarre filled the scholarly and popular void with demeaning ideas about Native Americans.[29] In March 1935, the New Bedford *Standard-Times* published his analysis of a petroglyph at Aptucxet on Cape Cod, known today as the Bourne petroglyph.[30] While fringe theories would propose that the symbols were Norse runes in 1940 and a southern Iberian script in 1975, Delabarre concluded they were a Native American record, made some time after 1658, and were mostly meaningless.[31] The article provided Delabarre the opportunity to disseminate his standard argument that Native Americans did not make markings on rocks before whites arrived, and that even then "a large proportion of their carvings were nothing more than meaningless scribblings or ornamental patterns."[32]

Delabarre's reputation as a petroglyph scholar was abetted by the anthropologist Charles C. Willoughby, director of Harvard's Peabody Museum of American Archaeology and Ethnology. In a kindly review in *American Anthropologist*, Willoughby called *Dighton Rock* "a valuable contribution to New England archaeology, whether or not the reader is able to accept all the author's conclusions, which are presented in a clear and interesting manner."[33] The two men knew each other, as Delabarre acknowledged Willoughby's advice in his 1925 paper on Grassy Island for *American Anthropologist*.[34] Willoughby was a leading expert on Indigenous archaeology and cultural materials of the northeast, and he delivered a kid-gloves treatment appropriate to Delabarre's standing as a major academic figure at Brown (and Harvard). Willoughby gently reproached Delabarre for concluding in his final paragraph (as Willoughby quoted in part): "Their designs were trivial scribblings and pictures, made only for pastime and attendant admiration."[35] Willoughby remarked: "This opinion is hardly in accordance with what is generally accepted by ethnologists. Would the author apply the same reasoning to the many other pictographs in America?"

Where others might have considered Willoughby's question a polite scholarly rebuke, Delabarre took it as a sign to extend his theorizing to the rest of the known rock art in the United States. In the *Journal of American History* in 1932, Delabarre was willing to grant the possibility that Indians elsewhere in America made drawings on rocks of symbolic complexity, but the people of southern New England remained a special case of ignorance, which was curiously at odds with his contention they had been improved by Portuguese blood. Most of the rock inscriptions he had studied "were made by Colonial Indians, between 1620 and 1675, after white men had set them the example. A great majority of their inscriptions are idle scribblings and trivial pictures, with perhaps a few mythological symbols and untranslatable depictions of individual adventure. There is no indication that they approach the complexity of symbolism exhibited in petroglyphs in some other parts of the country." His conviction as to the nature of Dighton Rock had not wavered: "This inscription was carved in 1511, and records in Latin words the fact that Miguel Cortereal, a native of Portugal, had become, 'by the will of God, leader of the natives of India in this place.'"[36]

Delabarre's reputation as a rock-art expert was upheld by Willoughby in *Antiquities of the New England Indians* (1935). Willoughby (now director emeritus of the Peabody Museum) devoted about five pages to examples of petroglyphs, and while he admonished past theories of a non-Indigenous origin for Dighton Rock and pointed out its Indigenous motifs, he ignored

Delabarre's Corte-Real theory and blundered in his historiographical analysis.[37] Willoughby included a version published by Garrick Mallery of the *Antiquitates Americanae* drawing attributed to the RIHS.[38] While Willoughby redated the original RIHS drawing to 1834 as per Delabarre's analysis, his reproduction perpetuated the "Thorfins" inscription Delabarre (and Schoolcraft) had shown was not there. The caption noted: "portions . . . of the group shown near the center are obviously of European derivation." He called Delabarre's *Dighton Rock* "an excellent detailed account of this and other New England petroglyphs. . . . Dr. Delabarre has made an exhaustive study of the many letters and numbers which he attributes to Europeans, and those interested in the subject are referred to this book."[39] Willoughby left unchallenged Delabarre's fundamental contention that New England petroglyphs were meaningless scribblings by Indians inspired by European newcomers. Any reader following Willoughby's recommendation to consult *Dighton Rock*—the only source he recommended on New England petroglyphs—could be forgiven for concluding that the retired director of the Peabody endorsed the ideas Delabarre advanced, not only about Corte-Real and Dighton Rock but about the brutish, imitative, and childish Native American character.

Later that same year in *The Scientific Monthly*, Delabarre continued the speculations he had aired in *Dighton Rock* on why people made inscriptions in rocks. Much of "A Petroglyphic Study of Human Motives" was given over to educated guesses as to why people crafted hoaxes such as the No Man's Land runic inscription he investigated in Massachusetts.[40] Delabarre never turned his analysis back upon the observer to ask why people like himself were wont to see whatever they desired in markings, and why they were so prepared to dismiss an Indigenous provenance. Delabarre continued to allow for an Indigenous origin for some New England inscriptions on the most limited and derogatory terms, repeating nearly verbatim in *The Scientific Monthly* his assertion in the 1919 "Recent History" that rock carvings in New England attributable to Indians were "meaningless haphazard scribblings, the product of an impulse to be active anyhow, as some people slash at shrubbery in passing. In some cases, probably, such childish scribblings might be the result of an endeavor to imitate, without knowing how, the white man's marvelous art of writing."[41]

Delabarre returned a final time to his Corte-Real theory in a paper read before the RIHS in February 1936. Willoughby had concluded in *Antiquities of the New England Indians* that because no breastplates of native copper had been found in Indigenous New England burials such as the ones at Fall River, the masses of copper worn by Native American that were observed by early

European visitors, including Verrazano in 1524, "must have been obtained from still earlier explorers of whom we have no definite account."[42] For Delabarre, Corte-Real was a perfect source for the metals in the Indigenous burials at Fall River and the adornments worn by people encountered by Verrazano.[43] Delabarre did not explain what Corte-Real and his companions were doing with all this copper in the first place, after escaping a shipwreck in Newfoundland.

Delabarre's 1936 paper was mostly dedicated to his White Tribism ideas, as he continued to insist on the Portuguese roots of Native American terminology that he had outright invented, based on his pretzel logic of the linguistic influence of the *quina* symbol on the Portuguese coat of arms. Delabarre defied the objections of anthropologist Frank Speck in insisting that there could have been a term, *Quade-kin,* that meant "great chief," inspired by Corte-Real.[44] Speck, as Delabarre related, had maintained the Indians would not have combined the terms *kehte* (which Delabarre bent into *Quade*) and *kin* in a single word, as they both meant "large." Delabarre countered that the Indians may have followed a practice known to Germans "of piling up successions of superlatives," and so had arrived at a term that meant "heap big chief."[45] Delabarre also continued to portray the Wampanoag as a people improved by interacting and interbreeding with the Portuguese Corte-Real party: "The Wampanoags were a superior race, a fact which might well be accounted for by early white influence and admixture of white blood. It was Wampanoags whom Verrazano found at Newport 'most civilized in customs' and with 'two kings beautiful in form and stature.'... Verrazano was greatly impressed by them and 'formed a great friendship with them;' whereas the nearest other Indians whom he met he speaks of as rude, barbarous and unfriendly."[46]

DELABARRE WAS INITIALLY pleased and even bemused by Portuguese-American interest in his Dighton Rock interpretation. On September 18, 1927, Delabarre informed Frank W. Hutt, secretary of the OCHS, which still held title to the boulder: "My Portuguese friends are rather eager to take some steps for the better protection of Dighton Rock." Delabarre supported the suggestion of the Portuguese-American Civic League (PACL) to move the rock onto higher ground, clear of the ravages of winter ice, and he recounted their plan to purchase a right-of-way so that visitors could reach it. In a follow-up letter on September 23, Delabarre agreed with Hutt that the OCHS should never relinquish title to the rock and that any property acquisitions by the Portuguese Americans should be donated to the OCHS.[47]

As it became clear that the PACL was planning its own land acquisition adjacent to the rock, Delabarre's bemusement turned to concern. He rejected the Civic League's proposal to raise the rock vertically from its tidewater position to build a protective cofferdam around it and establish a "shrine" in Corte-Real's honor, doubtless uneasy about the leading role of Catholic Portuguese-American clergy in the PACL initiative.[48] "Under these circumstances I consider it exceedingly fortunate that our Society owns the rock and a small bit of adjoining beach," Delabarre wrote the OCHS secretary on December 11, 1934. Delabarre vowed he would "seriously oppose any project to make the place a 'shrine' of any sort, whether with a religious cast to it or one which emphasized any foreign nationality. For that reason I hope that the adjacent land might never come into ownership of a Portuguese organization; although over that matter our Society has no control. But I should also vigorously oppose permitting the Portuguese to purchase the Rock, or to do anything at all on the plot owned by our Society, as Portuguese. . . . Whatever is done, the Rock and adjacent land ought to remain forever under ownership and control either of our Society, or of the State, or of the Federal Government."[49]

Delabarre moved to block access to the rock from the shore side. On January 23, 1935, he acquired a small plot of land with 250 feet of frontage on the Taunton River, 125 feet to either side of Dighton Rock, extending back 250 feet.[50] This 1.36-acre lot was exclusive of the waterfront strip owned by the OCHS. Delabarre's purchase included a right of way over adjoining land to Bay View Avenue. On Delabarre's death in 1945, the lot and its right of way became the property by bequest of the OCHS. For a time, the prospect of a Portuguese shrine had been thwarted.

DESPITE DELABARRE'S RECEIPT of a Portuguese knighthood in 1933, Portuguese historians generally rejected his Corte-Real theory. An attempt by Portuguese Americans to persuade the Portuguese government to fund a land purchase adjacent to the rock in the 1930s purportedly led nowhere because, according to the Fall River *Herald-News*, Portugal's "leading archaeologist" dismissed Delabarre's Corte-Real theory. (This authority was probably a Portuguese expert in epigraphy, José Maria Cordeira de Sousa, who in 1934 cast doubt on Delabarre's interpretation based on letterforms.)[51] As well, Portuguese Americans who tried to donate to the city of Lisbon a casting of Dighton Rock (presumably using a mold produced by Delabarre, with Águas's assistance, in 1929) were rebuffed in 1935, due to the lack of historical evidence for Delabarre's claims.[52]

Regardless, Delabarre's Corte-Real theory was largely free of competing claims for any other Old World provenance, as the Norse case for Dighton Rock had all but collapsed. By 1930, as the one thousandth anniversary of

Iceland's Althing was celebrated by international dignitaries, and the American Geographical Society published the Icelandic scholar Matthias Thórdarson's *The Vinland Voyages*, Dighton Rock was reduced to a phantom influence in placing Vinland in southern New England. Thórdarson summarized continuing support for the idea that Mount Hope was Hóp of the Karlsefni voyage, without mentioning Dighton Rock.[53] A fascination with Vinland and pre-Columbian voyages in general endured in eastern North America and remained alive in New England even as the Kensington stone drew the Norse deeper into the American hinterland. But Norse theorists generally no longer had a use for Dighton Rock—in fact, they replaced it with the so-called Northmen's Rock at Mount Hope Bay.[54]

Delabarre, however, was pestered by Olaf Strandwold, a school superintendent in Prosser, Washington, who was convinced of all sorts of runic evidence for Norse visits to America. As Strandwold wrote Hjalmar Holand in 1937, "Had a letter from Delabarre. He is very much against my coming with any claims of runic characters on the Dighton Rock. Does he feel insecure about his MIGUEL CORTEREAL discovery on the rock?" As Strandwold related, Delabarre relied on a pronouncement by the Norwegian philologist Magnus Olsen that no Scandinavian message could be found on the rock. Strandwold had a friend in Massachusetts inspect Dighton Rock for him. "He had a pamphlet with him by Delabarre, showing the Miguel Cortereal inscription. He declared that he could see nothing like that on the rock. . . . Delabarre and Magnus are our greatest opponents."[55] But Holand respected Delabarre's contention that Dighton Rock was the work of Miguel Corte-Real in his ensuing works on pre-Columbian voyages to America. Holand otherwise left the Vinland of southern New England as proposed by Rafn largely intact, including the role of the Newport Tower as a fortified Norse church.[56]

Delabarre seems to have influenced Holand in two important ways. Delabarre's fanciful conjecture of Corte-Real's misadventures, with the nine-year interval between his ship going missing in Newfoundland and the violent clash with the Wampanoag being recorded on Dighton Rock, had a strong echo in Holand's own stirring imaginings in *The Kensington Stone* of how the Knutson expedition managed to end up in northern Minnesota and lose ten men in a violent clash with Indians, seven years after it supposedly set out to find the "lost" Greenland colonists. More striking is Holand's White Tribist contention that (as with Delabarre's Portuguese) these Norse wanderers interbred with and improved the Indians. Holand substituted Norsemen for Welshmen in accounting for the "superior civilization and peaceful disposition" of the Mandan. "The Swedes and Norwegians are of the purest Nordic stock and a relatively small number would therefore have been sufficient to transmit the physical peculiarities for which Mandans were noted than if any other nationality had been represented by these early culture bearers." Only Nordic interbreeding could have made the Mandan "the most intelligent, well-mannered and hospitable of all the tribes of the North."[57] In the case of both Delabarre's Wampanoag and Holand's Mandan, a lost party of European adventurers had left behind genetic and cultural signatures of their presence in the bodies and behavior of Native Americans.

HARVARD'S SAMUEL ELIOT MORISON, a leading historian of transatlantic exploration, recounted in a letter to the *Boston Herald* in May 1954 how Delabarre once gave him a personal tour of the Dighton Rock inscription. Delabarre, he said, "would chalk this alleged inscription when the Rock was dry. That, of course, made it stand out and was quite convincing: but I always felt that with a little work I could just as easily find 'Kilroy Was Here' or 'To Hell With Yale' on the rock."[58] Morison generously granted it was possible that Miguel Corte-Real had visited this coast, and it was "very gratifying to our Portuguese citizens to feel that one of their heroes was here more than a century before the Pilgrim Fathers. But there are a good many arguments against accepting Professor Delabarre's interpretation as authentic. The alleged Portuguese arms on the Rock look to me more like a crude attempt of an Indian to draw a human face, and the '5' of the '1511' is evidently intended for a little man, as it has two legs and a face." Further, Delabarre's interpretation is not "generally accepted by Portuguese scholars."

However, by the time Morison made public his objections to the Corte-Real theory, the state park was a *fait accompli*. The dissensions and legal and political maneuverings that marked the transformation of Dighton Rock into a Portuguese relic in a museum within a dedicated state park after the Second World War are far more complex than can possibly be related here. In brief, the park and its museum came about through the populist will of a politically powerful ethnic community, in defiance of the expertise of leading historians, and without any apparent consultation with the region's displaced Native American communities, as the Wampanoag communities of Gay Head and Mashpee would not be formally recognized as federal tribes until long after the rock had been physically relocated and enclosed in a dedicated museum.

Portuguese Americans may still have been second-class citizens by the measure of persistently restrictive immigration policies and their limited presence in the state power structure, but they represented a considerable bloc of voters in the Portuguese archipelago of southeastern Massachusetts. They also had the support of Portuguese-American legislators such as Congressman Joseph Martin and state Senator Edmund Denis in pursuing the dream of turning Dighton Rock into a public shrine to Corte-Real. Having the rock protected and celebrated within a state park was also agreeable to the OCHS and Abilio Águas, as they had tried and failed in association with the PACL and Martin to secure the rock's status as a national historic site.

The efforts to create a state park nevertheless clashed with the ambitions of the Miguel Corte-Real Memorial Society (MCRMS), which was incorporated in New York City in September 1951 by Joseph Damaso Fragoso, who had emigrated from the Azores in 1920 and was a Portuguese language instructor at the City College of New York.[59] Delabarre was a guest of Fragoso in New York in May 1930 when he addressed the Vasco da Gama Society; in 1931 Fragoso was serving as the society's president.[60] After Delabarre's death in 1945, Fragoso moved into a leading role in asserting the Corte-Real theory for Dighton Rock and arguing for the rock's preservation and veneration. In 1950 Fragoso founded a publication, *The Portuguese World*, through which he could lobby for the creation of a park along with a shrine to enclose the rock, which he argued should be raised from the tidewater and protected by a cofferdam, as the PACL had originally proposed in 1927. Fragoso also claimed in 1950 to have found on the rock at least three fragmentary portions of large renderings of the Portuguese cross of the Order of Christ that Delabarre somehow overlooked.[61] Beside the date 1511, he contended, was a tall version of the cross, surmounted by a five-dot *quina* shield, in perfect accordance with the Portuguese stone *padrões* used in Corte-Real's time to mark territorial claims in Africa and Ceylon; this drawing also coincided with the positioning of the pillar drawing on the left side of the 1485 Cão inscription.

Fragoso alienated the OCHS and various members of the Portuguese-American community (including Delabarre's son-in-law, Abilio Águas) in his fund-raising efforts to purchase about fifty acres of land that Fragoso said "surrounded" the rock, when the holding in fact was adjacent to the lands held by the OCHS.[62] While Fragoso's MCRMS completed the land acquisition in November 1952, in December 1955 the society's land was secured by Massachusetts through eminent domain—over Fragoso's objections— thereby providing most of the land for the state park.[63] Already on January 7, 1955, the OCHS had made a public presentation to the state of its deed to the rock and the associated 1.36 acres bequeathed by Delabarre so that the park could be created. The *Herald News* of Fall River reported the state would develop the rock as a "shrine," and in a few months would move it to higher ground and place it in a cupola in the style of sixteenth-century Portuguese architecture.[64] Although Abilio Águas was on hand for the formal transfer of the deed, his late father-in-law surely would have been mortified that the Portuguese "shrine" he had feared was coming to pass through his bequest to the OCHS.

Fragoso clearly could be vexatious and did not enjoy the confidence of a large part of the Portuguese-American community. Yet in his own peculiar way, Fragoso may have been the relic's best friend in these years. In 1955, the state awarded a low-bid contract to move the rock to higher ground, and the contractor attempted to drag the boulder with chains. In securing a temporary injunction against further attempts to move it, Fragoso presented photographic evidence that the chains had scored and chipped part of the inscribed surface.[65] The legal and legislative battles over the rock's fate dragged on until 1963, when the state finally adopted the option Fragoso had long advised, using a crane to raise the rock eleven feet and place it in its original shoreside position and orientation atop a jetty surrounded by a cofferdam, thus permanently removing it from the river. By then, the case for the Corte-Real provenance had become synonymous with Dr. Manuel Luciano da Silva, whose long association with the rock's celebration as a Portuguese relic dated to his cofounding with Fragoso of the MCRMS.

WHEN MANUEL LUCIANO da Silva arrived in the United States from mainland Portugal as a teenager with his mother in January 1946, he had already heard of Dighton Rock from a high school teacher in Portugal. Silva would recount making his first pilgrimage to Dighton Rock in August 1948, while living and attending school in New York City. As an undergraduate student in biology at New York University, Silva cofounded the MCRMS with Fragoso, serving as its secretary. Returning to Portugal to study medicine in 1952, Silva was absent from the United States for most of the battles in the 1950s over the park's formation and the rock's relocation. While in Portugal, he continued to investigate the rock through photographs and documents, and began to write a book. Silva returned to the United States around 1958 to complete internships in Boston and New Bedford; he would establish a practice in Bristol, Rhode Island, in 1963.[66]

In November 1959, Silva used white paint or chalk to mark up the rock in a manner entirely different from Delabarre's version, and propped atop the rock three interpretive drawings depicting Portuguese national symbols. A resulting photo clearly depicted the name MIGVEL CORTEREAL on the rock, four Portuguese crosses of the Order of Christ, the date 1511, and the tiny shield Delabarre had delineated. Fragoso, as noted, had proposed three of the crosses in 1950, and Silva had surmised a fourth, above Corte-Real's name, from photographs while in Portugal.[67] In addition to tidying up the Corte-Real name and adding four crosses Delabarre had never detected, Silva's rendering erased the entire Latin phrase that Delabarre said indicated Corte-Real had served as the leader of the local Indians. The photo appeared in the *Herald News* of Fall River on November 3, 1959, and would become the new interpretation of the Corte-Real inscription.

Silva practiced the kind of naïve or amateurish history writing Orm Øverland associates with home-making. Called "filiopietistic," as Øverland explains, it "invariably tells of the past excellence or greatness of a particular nation."[68] In September 1960, Silva was able to secure accreditation as one of eight American delegates (the only nonacademic) to the Congresso Internacional de História dos Descobrimentos, a Lisbon symposium organized by the Salazar regime to mark the 400th anniversary of the death of Prince Henry the Navigator.[69] In his presentation, "Prince Henry the Navigator and Dighton Rock," Silva claimed the Portuguese discovered North America in 1424 and asserted the Corte-Real provenance of Dighton Rock. Silva may have eliminated the Latin inscription that Delabarre said indicated Corte-Real had become the leader of the local Indians, but Silva retained the essential White Tribist assertion that the Portuguese had remained in America and improved the Native Americans, biologically and culturally—using much the same evidence Rafn, Holand, and Anderson had for similar assertions about the Norse. Silva informed the assembly that Native Americans "have Portuguese blood," because his investigations showed "the first civilized language that the Wampanoag Indians spoke was Portuguese, before Columbus arrived in America." If not from the Portuguese, Silva posed, from whom did American Indians learn such words as *bacalhau* (codfish), *canada* (narrow passage), *abrigada* and *abrigador* (bay, shelter), *saco* (sac), *curvo* (curve), *akoa* (water), *fogo* (fire), *brigs* (fight), "and so many other words typical of the old Portuguese." As further proof of Portuguese blood in Native Americans, Silva tabled his "original discovery" that they had Portuguese names. Plainly inspired by Delabarre's tortuous efforts to turn the sachem name Quadequina into a remembrance of Corte-Real and the *quina* shield symbol, Silva outlined his own assertions surrounding the presence of *quina* in Algonquian names. Silva would come to argue in his self-published *Portuguese Pilgrims and Dighton Rock* (1971) that *Algonquin* was Portuguese in origin, a combination of the suffix -*quina* and one of two Portuguese terms: *Algarve*, the southern province of Portugal, "where Prince Henry the Navigator developed his school of Navigation at Sagres, and where the Corte Real family origi-nated," or *algo*, "a person who is important or prominent." Saugus, an Algon-quian name for a town north of Boston, was derived from Sagres. "In addition to its phonetic similarity to Sagres, it also meant in Indian 'wet by over-flow,' which is somewhat descriptive of Sagres, where the Promontory is always wet by the splashing of waves."[70]

White Tribism became the essence of Silva's arguments and researches. He devoted a chapter of his book, "White American Indians," to his word-hunting and scouring of atlases for phonetically promising place names in New England, in a manner no different from Rafn. Along with historic accounts of light-skinned natives, Silva included material from Theodosius Dobzhanksy's *Mankind Evolving*, which proposed the Mendelian combinations behind *mestizo* people of Mexico, to account for a similar "mulatto" or "half breed" popu-lation in New England. The Wampanoag, Silva asserted, bore "the imprint of civilized manners and light skin color."[71] Corte-Real's men had "mixed with the natives, imparting their language and physical characteristics."[72]

Silva was no more accepting than Delabarre of Portuguese slaving during the heroic age of exploration, refusing to consider its role in the Corte-Real voyages. In a fund-raising letter issued under his name by the newly formed MCRMS on November 7, 1951, Silva vilified a children's encyclopedia for saying that Gaspar Corte-Real seized a number of Indians on the coast of Labrador and sent them back to Lisbon to be sold as slaves. "The 'Book of Knowledge' does not present the true facts," Silva wrote. "These and other published insults against the Portuguese certainly would not be tolerated if they were printed against any of the other racial groups living here." He sug-gested that Portuguese Americans "who have inherited from their fathers one of the noblest cultures of the World, do not seem to care if their forefathers are maliciously labeled as 'murderers, robbers, rapists and slave-traders.'"[73] Yet Silva's own book quoted without comment Alberto Cantino's 1501 ac-count of Gaspar Corte-Real's abduction of about fifty Indigenous people, as well as the Venetian Pietro Pasqualigo's 1501 letter from Lisbon indicating the Portuguese king was pleased to learn the new land to the west offered (in Sil-va's uncredited translation) "slaves fit for any work."[74] In Silva's rubric, slaving did not exist, as an activity or an objective. America had already been discov-ered by the Portuguese, and the Corte-Real brothers were making voyages of exploration, "in preparation for the third stage: Colonization."[75]

Silva was in conflict with the mainstream historical community before he had even completed his 1960 presentation in Lisbon, as Spanish delegates withdrew from the hall to discuss his pre-Columbian Portuguese contentions.

After the presentation, he clashed on stage with Francis M. Rogers, a Harvard professor of romance languages and literature. Born in New Bedford and descended from Azorean immigrants, Rogers was prominent in celebrations of Portuguese history and heritage.[76] Rogers would write: "the cult of the Portuguese past, when carried to excess, with the same details repeated ad nauseam, became very boring indeed to younger Portuguese, who referred to it as the 'História Bombástica de Portugal' (Bombastic History of Portugal)."[77] Rogers drew the line at Dighton Rock in celebrating the Portuguese past, endorsing Samuel Eliot Morison's dismissal of Delabarre's findings. When Rogers suggested onstage at the Lisbon conference that Silva had overreached in his assertions and asked where he got his proof for the Portuguese origin of Native American names and words, Silva tapped Rogers's shoulder and replied: "I got this information from the old books that exist in the catacombs of the University [Harvard] where you teach Portuguese!" and added: "When we refer to Plato or Aristotle do we ask them if they have the title Professor?"[78] Rogers and Silva clashed again at a state Senate hearing in January 1961 on plans to reposition Dighton Rock atop a cofferdam, which Silva supported and Rogers opposed. "I feel just as strongly as Dr. da Silva does that the rock should be preserved," Rogers said, but added that it should never become the property of a "hyphenated group."[79]

Relations were no happier within the MCRMS. Silva and Fragoso fell out irrevocably after Silva's Lisbon presentation; according to Silva, Fragoso was becoming mentally unstable and thought he should have been the one to make the presentation.[80] Silva assumed the presidency of the society from Fragoso and carried on without him. He was no less controversial than Fragoso had been in championing the Corte-Real interpretation of Dighton Rock. "Silva was a divisive figure in the community, largely because of his outspoken and quirky personality, domineering ways, conceit, and affected erudition," according to historian Gilberto Fernandes. "These attributes underscored his chauvinist ethnic memorializations and also were cause for embarrassment to other Portuguese American public figures."[81] He delighted in his outsider's role, telling the *Boston Globe* in 1966: "I used the bullfight technique. I say, harrooomph, let he go, (he whisks an imaginary cape through the air) ha, ha, until she cools off." Asked to comment on Silva's language ideas, Harvard historian Oscar Handlin told the *Globe*: "I don't take any of that very seriously. We get reports of Croatians settling in Virginia in the 15th century because the Indians there had words similar to Serbo-Croatian. But nobody really has a very good idea of what those Indians spoke like. If you start reaching for little bits of information, you can attempt to prove anything."

Silva replied: "I don't need any big professor to tell me how to do this kind of thing. If I didn't have the scientific method, I couldn't be a doctor."[82] Like other amateur practitioners of fringe history, Silva claimed superior insights rooted in the methodologies of his professional life. "Everyday I had to use the scientific methods of making medical diagnoses," he would say. "I also applied these scientific methods to my historical researches and because of this I was able to discover new things that the so called professional historians missed."[83]

Silva's home-making equated the Corte-Real arrival at Dighton Rock with the American space program. "Dighton Rock was the last stepping stone of the period of discovery," Silva told the *Boston Globe* in August 1966, at the height of the Gemini program's flights. "Five centuries ago, the Portuguese explored the unknown seas with as much courage and dedication as the American astronauts demonstrate today. The Americans are taking up where the Portuguese left off."[84] Just as the Portuguese had been in a race with Spain to reach India in the fifteenth century, he lectured in his 1971 book, so too the United States had become engaged in a race to the moon with Russia.[85] "The courage in face of the unknown is a characteristic of both the Portuguese explorers and the American astronauts," he argued, adding: "Just as long ago the Portuguese planted landmarkers in the lands they discovered, the astronauts will place on the planets, planet-markers with American National Symbols."[86] The Portuguese symbols on Dighton Rock were the first statements of claim in America's reach for the stars.

Abilio Águas loathed Silva. He saved a clipping of the 1966 *Boston Globe* profile, drawing a red box around the photo of Silva and writing beneath it "CHARLATAN."[87] For Águas, Silva's interpretation of Dighton Rock might as well have been another form of vandalism the rock had suffered, with his late father-in-law Delabarre's interpretation overwritten and otherwise erased. Águas wrote to reporter Walter Hackett, objecting to his article in *The Christian Science Monitor* of August 20, 1969, espousing the Bristol doctor's ideas and featuring the 1959 photo of Silva's version of the markings.[88] Águas recounted how on a visit to the rock two years earlier he "unexpectedly came upon Dr. Silva, clad in hip rubber boots, his camera upon a tripod facing the petroglyp[h], busily chalking grooves to which only his imagination gave form. We stopped to watch the embarassed [sic] 'archaeologist' and I told him that the figures he had drawn there were not on the rock." Águas contended "the Bristol physician's unsubstantiable [sic] fallacy may indirectly and adversely affect, if only temporarily, the authentic value of the Portuguese Navigator Miguel Corte Real's message as honestly and scholarly deciphered by Professor Delabarre."[89]

Silva may have been of a particular type drawn to fringe ethnohistorical and home-making causes, but also he may have modeled his advocacy of the Corte-Real provenance on the precedent of another figure in American immigrant home-making, Rasmus B. Anderson. Paul Knaplund has described Anderson as "a compound of many traits strangely mixed," a "born crusader" who was "fearless, pugnacious, and zealous."[90] Anderson's popular writings on the Norse in America were boisterous, polemical rather than scholarly, and peppered with exclamation marks, all of which appeared in abundance in Silva's efforts. Silva adopted the same obstinate attitude as Anderson to contrary evidence and the primacy of his own interpretation. In the preface to a new edition of *America Not Discovered by Columbus* (1877), Anderson declared: "until sufficient proof of some other origin of the Newport Tower and the Dighton Rock inscriptions are given, we shall persist in claiming them as relics of the Norsemen."[91] It cannot be a coincidence that in describing his researches to the *Boston Globe* in 1966, Silva recounted: "I saw the name of the town, 'Saugus,' and I said: This is Portuguese until proven otherwise." The *Globe*'s Sara Davidson called this a "pearl of chauvinistic reasoning." Silva titled the fourth chapter of his book "Discovered by the Portuguese until Proven Otherwise." Until proven otherwise, Silva was going to claim Dighton Rock, the Newport Tower (as well as a colonial-era fort at Ninigret), and an array of Native American place names and personal names as Portuguese, and the genes of the living Wampanoag for good measure.

WHEN SEVERAL HUNDRED New England residents of Portuguese descent gathered at Dighton Rock State Park on September 24, 2011, to celebrate "500 years in southern New England" for the Azorean people, among the attendees watching cultural groups perform traditional folk dances to live music was Manuel Luciano da Silva. Eighty-five years of age, now retired from medical practice, Silva was saluted, along with his wife, Silvia Jorge, for their many years of research into the connection between Dighton Rock and Miguel Corte-Real. The day marked the sixtieth anniversary of the creation of Silva's nonprofit MCRMS. He had outlasted his critics and enemies and remained the leading figure in promoting Dighton Rock as proof of a visit by the lost Corte-Real expedition.

For ten years after Dighton Rock was raised and set on its shoreside berm, it was protected behind a chain-link fence. In 1973 the rock was enclosed within its protective octagonal structure—which, while not quite the sixteenth-century Portuguese cupola envisioned in 1955, was an unmistakable echo of the eight-sided Newport Tower that supporters of the Corte-Real interpreta-

FIGURE 10 Dighton Rock Museum, Dighton Rock State Park. Photograph by the author, July 2013.

tion like Silva insisted was a Portuguese relic. The adjoining octagonal museum structure (figure 10) opened in 1978, and would soon house an interpretive display conceived and constructed by the Friends of Dighton Rock Museum, Inc., a charitable nonprofit organization Silva established in 1963; Silva was the first and only president until 2011, after which he served as a director until his death in October 2012.

A second Portuguese immigration wave after the passage of the Immigration and Nationality Act of 1965, which eliminated the quota system and gave preference to immigrants who could demonstrate family relations in the United States, proved critical in the acceptance and promotion of Dighton Rock as a Portuguese relic.[92] In the 1970s, Portuguese immigration reached a historic decadal peak of 101,710 before entering another sharp decline.[93] A "Portuguese Archipelago" was affirmed in southeastern Massachusetts, centered on the major cities of Attleboro, Fall River, New Bedford, and Taunton. In the 2000 U.S. census, 30.5 percent of residents of this archipelago were of Portuguese heritage, peaking at 49.6 percent in Fall River, where a statue of Prince Henry the Navigator was erected in 1940. In spite of the surge in immigration in the 1970s, Portuguese Americans in that decade were still viewed, according to Feldman-Bianco, as "the invisible minority" and the "case of the disappearing ethnics."[94] Dighton Rock's museum became one answer to reasserting and celebrating an ethnic identity within the American melting pot. When *National Geographic* published a feature article on the Portuguese-American community of southern New England in 1975, it included a photo (captioned "Forty-ton calling card?") of Silva posing with the rock, pointing to the purported date of 1511, which was accompanied by an unquestioning illustration of Silva's interpretation of the Corte-Real inscription.[95]

During the celebration at Dighton Rock State Park in September 2011, Silva complained to visitors that no governor of Massachusetts had ever visited the museum, not even when it was opened in 1978. The museum, he told them, could become a better-known landmark, and needed more support.[96] Silva was never satisfied with the degree of recognition the rock received as a relic of Corte-Real and a symbol of Portuguese greatness. He was still attacking doubters (living and dead) of the Corte-Real connection with trademark abrasiveness through a website dedicated to his Dighton Rock researches when he died after a short illness in October 2012. Nevertheless, Silva had managed, at times almost single-handedly, through books, his website, and hundreds of free public lectures (he delivered by his own count his 511th lecture in late August 2012, which resonated with the 1511 date on the rock, two months before his death) to convince Portuguese Americans, and people in general worldwide, that Dighton Rock and its little museum deserved to be a shrine to Portuguese daring. He brooked no wavering of belief in the Corte-Real attribution. Jane Hennedy, a staff member of the OCHS, in a public lecture at Dighton Rock Museum on the history of the rock's interpretation in May 2012, acknowledged the numerous theories about who carved the rock. Even though Hennedy stated she was inclined to accept the Delabarre theory of the Corte-Real connection, it was not enough for Silva, who charged on his website "she did not have the GUTS to affirm that the Phoenician and Viking theories are two BLUNT FRAUDS."[97] He continued to criticize Delabarre on his website, contending he was so "scared" of fellow academics that he had felt obliged to critically weigh all the other theories in his monumental evaluation of the rock's convoluted historiography.[98]

No one in Silva's judgment ever came close to proving Dighton Rock's provenance belonged to anyone other than his beloved Miguel Corte-Real. And having lived to see Dighton Rock enshrined in a state park museum chock-a-block with Portuguese memorabilia that he had helped to create, there was little reason for him to consider otherwise.

Conclusion

The Stone's Place: Dighton Rock Museum and Narratives of Power

"Celebrations straddle the two sides of historicity," according to Michel-Rolph Trouillot. "They impose a silence upon the events that they ignore, and they fill that silence with narratives of power about the event they celebrate."[1] For more than 300 years, Dighton Rock has attracted an array of explanations through which power has been narrated as well as actively exercised. In its latest expression, this power has distilled the history of its own exercise within a museum display. As an interpretation of interpretations, the museum is a crowning exercise of that power.

As Susan Roy has written, "the history of the loss of cultural objects to anthropological and nationalistic projects is part and parcel of colonialism."[2] Dighton Rock is a reminder that control of any object in a museum environment affords powers of interpretation, and that colonialism in that regard extends beyond a culture's loss of objects to include the messages such objects are made to speak to the world. Where the interpretive presentation of such apprehended objects might deliver ethnological messages about Indigenous peoples that uphold the colonizing culture's superiority, Dighton Rock is exceptional in having been captured by the colonizers and transformed from an Indigenous artifact into the very statement, the very proof, of colonization.

DIGHTON ROCK MUSEUM in Dighton Rock State Park was open by appointment only in July 2013. I was asked to call ahead (forty-eight hours notice was preferred) and leave a request on an answering machine at Freetown State Forest.[3] The park, which occupies eighty-five quiet acres within the town limits of Berkley, Massachusetts, includes frontage on the Taunton River, where I found the museum and the much-disputed boulder housed within it. The museum was constructed as two conjoined, single-story octagonal structures. The octagon nearest the water housed the rock, raised from its original position in the river's tidewater. The octagon I initially entered was devoted to the rock's interpretation.

The interpretation was based on George F. W. Young's *Miguel Corte-Real and the Dighton Writing Rock*, published by the OCHS in 1970. Young was a lecturer in history at the State University of New York at Buffalo in the late 1960s when he undertook the monograph while completing doctoral dissertation research at Harvard.[4] Young's dissertation, for which he would earn his doctorate from the University of Chicago in 1969, was on German immigration and colonization in Chile from 1849 to 1914, but in planning a course on Portuguese exploration at SUNY he wrote Manuel Luciano da Silva in August 1967, expressing his fascination with Silva's research.[5] Young methodically dismantled and dismissed Delabarre's White Tribist arguments and judged his Latin inscription "doubtful," with "very little evidential value," thus providing academic support to Silva's not-unfounded insistence it didn't exist.[6] Young, however, found credible the crosses identified by Fragoso and Silva.[7] He also concluded that "there is very little doubt that the letters M . . . V . . . COR (T) ER . . . and the date 1511 are indeed incised upon the Rock."[8] For Young, the evidence of Miguel Corte-Real's name "ought now to be regarded as a verifiable fact," and he was satisfied the rock's inscription indicated "Miguel Corte-Real, or a part of his 1502 expedition, passed some time at Assonet Neck."[9]

Young organized the investigations of Dighton Rock into four phases: the Puritan period (seventeenth century), the Phoenician period (eighteenth century), the Viking period (nineteenth century) and the Portuguese period (twentieth century). Young cautioned: "Of course it should be remembered that throughout the four 'periods' of Dighton Rock history there has always been a groundswell of opinion that has held that the local Indians, and they alone, were responsible for the Writing on Dighton Rock. Perhaps this, the simplest, is the sanest and most sensible theory of them all. We shall see."[10] Yet the reader never does see. The volume is overwhelmingly devoted to exploring and defending the Corte-Real provenance, albeit while discarding most of Delabarre's arguments.

Young did not consider the Indigeneity of the many glyphs on the rock's surface, the phenomenon of riverside "sacrifice" rocks Kendall addressed, or recognize any of the past arguments supporting an Indigenous provenance by the likes of George Washington, George Catlin, Ephraim Squier and Edwin Davis, Henry Schoolcraft and Shingwauk, and Garrick Mallery.[11] Young went so far as to suggest that the quina shield supposedly atop the cross that was found on the left side of the rock by Fragoso only appeared to be a face made of three dots (eyes and mouth) in the manner of the petroglyphs at Bellows Falls because Indians "retouched" the Portuguese inscription.[12] This purported defacement was the sole Indigenous contribution that Young recognized.

Installed in 1982, the museum's numbered wall panels were composed and created by the directors of the Friends of Dighton Rock Museum: Manuel and Silvia da Silva, Nelson Martins (a clinical psychologist who also edited Silva's book), Roswell Bosworth Jr. (publisher of the *Bristol Phoenix*), and T. Steven Tegu (born in Greece, a professor of romance languages at Rhode Island College). In 1972, Professor Tegu largely dismissed Dighton Rock's utility as an ethnohistorical resource, asking: "what can an isolated rock with a few incoherent petroglyphs tell us about the history of the indigenous people of New England? What can a few figures, scratched on a boulder tell us about the Indians? When the settlers arrived, the Indians were present and it did not require any deciphering of petrographs to learn something about them, all the settlers needed to do was to ask the Indians. I do not advocate abandoning research on the petrographs on the rock. However, regardless of their age, they can tell us very little, because they are the products of a civilization in a primitive state of development."[13]

After display 1 explained how the rock came to be housed within the museum, four more numbered displays guided me through Young's theory periods, with one crucial modification. Display 2, rather than being labeled the Puritan period, was labeled "American Indian, 17th Century." In addition to defying Young's caution that the Indigenous provenance was proposed through all four periods, the interpretation was implicitly progressive. Each display moved from one century to another, from "American Indian" (seventeenth) to "Phoenician" (eighteenth) to "Norse or Viking" (nineteenth) to "Portuguese" (twentieth).

The first two panels in the American Indian, 17th Century display were devoted to the Danforth drawing and description of 1680. The third panel addressed the petroglyphs at Bellows Falls in Vermont. The fourth panel reproduced the 1853 daguerreotype of Seth Eastman sitting on Dighton Rock, and pointed out similarities between glyphs at Bellows Falls and on Dighton Rock, albeit without also presenting Young's suggestion that these similarities indicated that Indians defaced the Portuguese inscription at Dighton Rock. Consistent with Young's monograph, there was no mention of other examples of Indigenous rock art known in southern New England, or indeed in eastern North America.

The Portuguese-theory display featured several plaques devoted to Silva's interpretation, including one showing the rock as marked up by Silva in 1959 and rephotographed in 1971,[14] labeled "The Complete Corte Real Theory." It was almost impossible to resist the conclusion that Dighton Rock is a Portuguese relic—not only because of the implicitly progressive scheme of the interpretive display and the Silva materials therein, but also because the museum had so much Portuguese seafaring content as to qualify as a cabinet of curiosities of historic Lusitanian navigation. In the center of the small museum were two cases containing large ship models: the *São Gabriel*, Vasco da Gama's flagship on his 1497 voyage to India around the Cape of Good Hope (a gift of the prime minister of Portugal, Admiral Pinheiro de Azevedo), and the *Victoria*, the Spanish flagship of the Portuguese navigator Fernão de Magalhães (Fernand Magellan) on the first circumnavigation voyage of 1519–22 (the model a gift of Don Juan Carlos, the king of Spain, with the display case sponsored by the Banco Espírito Santo of Lisbon). Walking toward the adjoining octagon containing the rock, I passed beneath a large wooden carving of a cod, suspended from the ceiling. When this "sacred cod," commissioned by Silva, was installed in August 2011, Silva explained that the cod "is the crown, the motif, the inspiration for why navigators came to these lands."[15] To the left, before I entered the rock's octagon, was a shrine within the shrine, a display case largely devoted to memorabilia related to Dr. Silva. On my visit I gathered a printed handout there in Portuguese, "Musea da Pedra de Dighton," which had the unmistakable style of Silva and which was issued with his website address. The handout pronounced both the Phoenician and the Viking theories a *fraude*. The Portuguese theory, it asserted, was discovered more than ninety-three years ago, and had never been refuted.[16] (In the introduction to Silva's book, T. Steven Tegu wrote: "The history of America is now correct and complete.")

At the right side of the entrance to the rock's octagon was a gift of the Gulbenkian Foundation of Portugal: a tall stone replica of one of the Portuguese *padrões*, of the sort that Fragoso identified on the left side of the rock's face. Entering the octagon, I confronted a four-foot by eight-foot mosaic of natural stone, an "Indian Lithocollage" made of pieces of New England slate. It depicted in the left background the Profile Rock of Freetown, Massachusetts, a stone outcrop that is said to resemble a Native American face and embodies the idea of the noble Vanished Indian. In the foreground, six Native Americans emerged head-and-shoulders from the ground, like petrified stumps.[17] The label said it was "an allegorical portrait of the Indians of North Eastern America." T. Steven Tegu had visited the Wampanoag community in Mashpee with Silva to photograph residents to ensure the ethnic authenticity of the portraits in stone, and Silva would assert that they depicted "real Indian people."[18] There was no indication the non-Indigenous artist was aware of stone's place in the ontology of New England peoples—that stone is not impenetrable and inert, but rather a permeable medium of sacred exchange and transformation, a domain of ancestors who remain available to the living.

FIGURE 11 Dighton Rock, with interpretive panels. Photograph by the author, July 2013.

At last, I reached the long-contested boulder (figure 11). In front of the inscribed face were four plaques, each offering a visual interpretation that reflected a museum panel display: American Indian, Phoenician, Norse or Viking, and Portuguese, with the latter showing Silva's version of the inscription. Two of them, I had been told by the Portuguese-language handout, were frauds, and one of them had not been disproven in ninety-three years.

Dighton Rock—declared the official Explorer's Rock by the state of Massachusetts in 1981—was enclosed in a windowless cinderblock octagon, surrounded by glass and artificially lit from close range.[19] It had been raised eleven feet from the tidewater river that revealed and concealed its markings twice a day. The sun did not rise behind it every morning or set on its face every evening. If its top ever received offerings that bound through stone the living and recently departed to grandmothers and grandfathers, to spirits human and other-than-human, no one could place them there anymore. The horned quadruped was still plainly visible.

Notes

Introduction

1. Quotes and details of the day's events are from Marc Larocque, "Celebrating 500 years of Azores history," *Taunton Daily Gazette*, September 25, 2011.

2. Williams, *Fantastic Archaeology*, 214.

3. Bragdon, in *Native Peoples of Southern New England, 1500–1650*, chooses the Indigenous term Ninnimissinuok, "a variation on the Narragansett word Ninnimissinnûwock, which means roughly 'people,'" for the collective peoples of southern New England (xi). I employ tribal labels as understood within the context of King Philip's War, and in general refer to the local people as the Wampanoag (which is consistent with modern tribal self-identity). As Bragdon notes, *Wampanoag* was probably not their original self-designation, and seems to have derived from *Wampanoos*, a Delaware word meaning "easterner" likely used by Dutch traders and explorers.

4. Williams, *Fantastic Archaeology*, 213.

5. In 1998 Edward J. Lenik corresponded with and later visited a man in New Hampshire who called himself Manitonquat, or Medicine Story. Lenik accepted in good faith his status as "an elder, storyteller, and spiritual leader of the Assonet Band of the Wampanoag Nation." Manitonquat related to Lenik an elaborate story regarding the meaning of Dighton Rock, which he said he had learned from his grandfather. Lenik reported the story in *Picture Rocks*, 133–34. However, Lenik's source has been the subject of intense scrutiny from Native American activists on the Forum of the website NAFPS (New Age Fraud and Plastic Shamans). They contend that Medicine Story is a white man passing himself off as a Wampanoag spiritual authority, who they also charge has been associated with cultish psychotherapy/counseling. See the topic "Francis Talbot AKA Medicine Story AKA Manitonquat," on the Forum at NAFPS (newagefraud.org). The evidence assembled at NAFPS persuades me that the Dighton Rock interpretation Lenik attributes to Medicine Story is not worth repeating.

6. In August 2016 the First Light Resort and Casino project hit a major snag when a U.S. District Court judge sided with an anti-casino group of local residents, who claimed the U.S. Department of the Interior in 2015 had no legal standing in approving the Mashpee Wampanoag request "to place 'in trust' 151 acres in Taunton and 170 acres in Mashpee as sovereign, Indian reservation territory." See Charles Winokoor, "Casino construction in Taunton shifts from building to filling trenches," *Taunton Daily Gazette*, August 5, 2016. In December 2016, the Department of the Interior and the Mashpee Wampanoag filed notices of appeal. See Chris Lindah, "Tribe and feds challenge court decision over Taunton casino lands," *Taunton Daily Gazette*, December 8, 2016.

7. Center for Policy Analysis, University of Massachusetts Dartmouth, "Portuguese-Americans in the Massachusetts Power Structure," 4–5.

8. Marc Larocque, "Wampanoag Tribal Leaders Hold Presentation at Dighton Rock Museum," *Taunton Daily Gazette*, November 11, 2013. Indigenous voices and authority and southeastern New England are greatly complicated by self-identifying Native Americans and tribes not (yet) recognized at the state or federal level. The Pocasset Wampanoag Tribe of Wattupa

242 Notes to Chapter 1

Reservation in Fall River, Massachusetts, is one such group. "The Mashpees don't have any ties to this area," said Pocasset Tribal Council Vice Chairman Daryl Black Eagle Jamieson in opposing Mashpee Wampanoag casino plans in December 2010. "This is a tribe that basically never left the Cape." Jay Pateakos, "Pocasset Wampanoags say casino is behind land deal," *Herald News* (Fall River), February 4, 2010.

9. Bragdon, *Native Peoples of Southern New England, 1500–1650*, 209.

10. Snow, *Archaeology of New England*, 64–65.

11. Black, "Ojibwa Taxonomy," 92.

12. Snow, "Solon Petroglyphs," 285.

13. Rajnovich, *Reading Rock Art*, 20.

14. Ibid., 19.

15. Norder, "Creation and Endurance," 398.

16. Bednarik, "Creating Futile Iconographic Meanings," http://home.vicnet.net.au/~auranet /interpret/web/icono.html.

17. See Aileen Moreton-Robinson for "possession" and the white conceptualization of race, which she ties to the Western conception of property and the construction of inferior races as a means of appropriating lands. Chapter 23, "Race Matters: The 'Aborigine' as a White Possession," in Warrior, ed., *The World of Indigenous North America*.

18. The concept of *terra nullius* in a 1454 papal bull "resides in the right to dispossess all Saracens and other non-Christians of all their goods (mobile and immobile), the right to invade and conquer these peoples' lands, expel them from it and, when necessary, to fight them and subjugate them in a perpetual servitude . . . and expropriate their possessions." Mudimbe, "*Romanus Pontifex*," 60–61.

19. Pearce, *Savages of America*, 160.

20. Trigger discusses diffusionism and migrationism in *History of Archaeological Thought*, 217–23.

21. Trigger, "Alternative Archaeologies," 361.

Chapter One

1. Delabarre, "Early Interest in Dighton Rock," 248. Lewis A. Carter memo, n.d., DRC.

2. Hurd, *History of Bristol County*, 781.

3. See the entry for Rev. John Danforth in May, *Danforth Genealogy*, 30.

4. See Delabarre, "Early Interest," 275–96.

5. Transcription by Delabarre, "Early Interest," 291. For photo reproduction of the original slip, see the plate between 288 and 289.

6. Silverman, *Red Brethren*, 18.

7. McInnes, *Sounding Thunder*, 63.

8. Simmons, *Spirit of the New England Tribes*, 17. For an overview of the conflicts, see Silverman, *Red Brethren*, 11–27.

9. See Hurd, *History of Bristol County*, 729–36.

10. I visited the park on Route 44 containing Anawan Rock on July 18, 2013. A sign erected by the Rehoboth Historical Commission reads: "Site of the capture of the Wampanoag Indian Chief Anawan by Captain Benjamin Church on August 28, 1676, thus ending King Philip's War."

11. For Taunton casualties and Walker's house burning, see Hurd, *History of Bristol County*, 741–45. For the display of Metacom's head, see Lepore, *Name of War*, 174.

12. Simmons, *Spirit of the New England Tribes*, 17–18.

13. DeLucia, The Memory Frontier," 980; Silverman, *Red Brethren*, 23.

14. Hurd, *History of Bristol County*, 745.

15. Bragdon, *Native People of Southern New England, 1500–1650*, 27–28.

16. Simmons, *Spirit of the New England Tribes*, 5. See also Lepore, *Name of War*, 184–85.

17. DeLucia, rso Lepore, and Tribesgland

18. Doughton, "Unseen Neighbors," 208.

19. O'Brien, *Firsting and Lasting*, xii. See also Simmons, *Spirit of the New England Tribes*, 3–4.

20. O'Brien, *Firsting and Lasting*, xiii.

21. Ibid., 107.

22. Ibid.

23. Pearce, *Savages of America*, 160.

24. In Diaz-Granados and Duncan, ed., *Rock-Art of Eastern North America*. "Eastern Woodlands" is given as a phenomenological region (xxv), which overlaps with the anthropological category of "Woodlands" peoples of prehistory.

25. From *A New Dictionary of the Terms Ancient and Modern of the Canting Crew*, reprinted as John Simpson, "Introduction," *First English Dictionary of Slang 1699*, 10.

26. Cotton Mather, *Wonderful Works*, 7–8 (unpaginated).

27. Delabarre, "Early Interest," 256–57. For the first publication of the Danforth drawing, see Lort, hAccount."

28. Cotton Mather, *Wonderful Works*, 121.

29. Lepore, *Name of War*, xiv.

30. Elliott, *Empires of the Atlantic World*, 78.

31. Ibid., 74–75.

32. Silverman, *Red Brethren*, 17.

33. Dechêne, *Le Peuple, l'État et la Guerre au Canada*, 167–70, 183; Faragher, *A Great and Noble Scheme*, 86–93; Eccles, *Canada under Louis XIV 1663–1701*, 193–96.

34. Cotton Mather, *Magnalia Christi Americana*, book 7, 60.

35. Hilmer and Sewall, "The Other Diary of Samuel Sewall," 356. Sewall was the only judge to ever recant and ask the public for forgiveness for his role in the witch trials.

36. Lepore, *Name of War*, 178.

37. Delabarre, "Early Interest," 259.

38. See Thomas Danforth's biography in Paige, *History of Cambridge*, 530.

39. Delabarre, "Early Interest," 259–60.

40. For Las Casas, Acosta, and others addressing Indigenous humanity in the sixteenth century, see Huddleston, *Origins of the American Indians*, 14–76.

41. The Gastaldi world map of 1546 showed Asia and North America as a contiguous continent, and the Forlani world map of 1565 perpetuated this configuration. The Grynaeus world map of 1555 depicted Asia as distinct from a protean North America (*Terra de Cuba*). The Zaltieri map of North America in 1566 was the first printed map to apply the label *Anian* to a speculated narrow strait between Asia and North America. See Cumming, Skelton, and Quinn, *Discovery of North America*, 64–65, 103.

42. See Glyndwr Williams, "Americas: Exploration Voyages, 1539–1794 (Northwest Coast)," in Hattendorf, ed., *Oxford Encyclopedia of Maritime History*, vol. 1, 44.

43. I use the term "Beringia" to address historic Bering land bridge theories, including those predating Vitus Bering's discovery of the strait in 1741.

44. Kidd, *Forging of Races*, 21.

45. Ibid.

46. Ibid.

47. For the chronicle of Annius, see Stephens, *Giants in Those Days*, 101–38.

48. Bruce G. Trigger in 1970 critiqued the "dendritic, or branching, model of cultural development," noting that this model had a long history and correctly suggesting it could be traced to biblical sources. "The influence of these Biblical traditions upon Western thought, even as late as the nineteenth century, should not be under-estimated. They created a strong unconscious bias in favor of the dendritic-migrationary model of human history." Trigger, "Strategy of Iroquoian Prehistory," 7–8.

49. Wesley, *Explanatory Notes*, vol. 1, 44.

50. For a discussion of ambiguity in Genesis and evolving interpretations of the sons of Noah, see Braude, "The Sons of Noah." See also Kidd, *Forging of Race*, 22.

51. John Eliot to Thomas Thorowgood, "The Learned Conjectures of Reverend Mr. John Eliot," in Eliot, *The Eliot Tracts*, 417.

52. Vespucci, *Letters of Amerigo Vespucci*, 6, 7.

53. Dickason, *Myth of the Savage*, 33–34, quoting Martire, *De Orbe Novo*, vol. 1, 161.

54. Cogley, " 'Some Other Kinde of Being and Condition,' " 37.

55. Strabo, *Geography of Strabo*, vol. 1, 121–23.

56. See, for example, Chapter 7, "Great Tartary," in Moll, *Atlas Geographus . . . Vol. 3*.

57. Huddleston, *Origins of the American Indians*, 121.

58. Humphrey Gilbert, *Discourse of a Discoverie for a New Passage to Cataia* (London, 1576), reprinted as "A Discourse Written by Sir Humphrey Gilbert, Knight, to Proue a Passage by the Northwest to Cathaia, and the East Indies," in Hakluyt, *Principal Navigations*, http://ebooks .adelaide.edu.au/h/hakluyt/voyages/v12/chapter15.html.

59. Acosta, *Naturall and Morall Historie*, 67.

60. The key source for the Lost Tribes is the Fourth Book of Esdras in the Apocrypha. See Sayre, "Prehistoric Diasporas," 61–62; Rabinowitz, "Ten Lost Tribes."

61. Lescarbot, *History of New France [Works]*, 43–44, 234.

62. Thorowgood, "Americans Are Jews," in *Iewes in America*, 3.

63. Lescarbot, *History of New France [Works]*, 46–47, 238.

64. See Sayre, *Les Sauvages Américains*, 130.

65. Lescarbot, *History of New France [Works]*, 44, 237. La Roche established a penal colony on Sable Island as part of a French monopoly on the fur trade in New France in 1598. La Roche failed to resupply the Sable Island colony in 1602. When relief arrived in 1603, the inhabitants were found to have revolted and killed their two overseers. Eleven leaders of the uprising were returned to France. Lescarbot had a dozen survivors appear before the king wearing sealskin clothing. They actually presented the king, Henri IV, with animal pelts. Henri rewarded each of them with fifty écus. See Lanctot, "La Roche de Mesgouez, Troilus de."

66. Brerewood, *Enquiries*, 96–97.

67. For an English translation, see Grotius, *On the Origin of the Native Races of America*.

68. Grotii, *De origine*, 39.

69. Ibid., 43.

70. Grotius, *On the Origin*, 11.

71. Ibid., 12.

72. Morton, *New English Canaan*, 18–19.

73. Ibid.

74. Ibid., 20.

75. See Wright, "Origin of American Aborigines," and Huddleston, *Origins*, 118–28.

76. Humboldt in vol. 2 of *Cosmos* (published originally in German as *Kosmos* in 1847) observed how arguments in support of a "race of Celto-Americans" had "disappeared since the establishment of an earnest and scientific ethnology, based not on accidental similarities of sounds, but on grammatical forms and organic structures" (609).

77. Acosta, *Naturall and Morall Historie*, 74–77.

78. Cogley, "Ancestry of the American Indians," 306.

79. Ibid., 306–7.

80. John Eliot, "The Learned Conjectures of Reverend Mr. John Eliot," in Thorowgood, *Jews in America*, 2.

81. For Thorowgood, Menasseh, and Lost Tribes theories for Native Americans circa 1650, see Braude, "Les contes persans"; Cogley, "Ancestry of the American Indians," and " 'Some Other Kinde of Being and Condition.' "

82. Martire, *De Orbe Novo*, vol. 1, 133; see also Dickason, *Myth of the Savage*, 44–45.

83. See Sayre, "Prehistoric Diasporas," 61–62.

84. Menasseh, *Hope of Israel*, sig. 44–45.

85. Ibid., sig. 44.

86. Braude, "Les contes persans," 1118–19.

87. Ibid., 1109.

88. Roth, *Life of Menasseh ben Israel*, 302.

89. Deloria, *Indians in Unexpected Places*, 20.

Chapter Two

1. Kittredge, "Cotton Mather's Election," 85–87. Mather was not actually formally elected until April 11, 1723 (111).

2. Cotton Mather, "Extract of Several Letters."

3. Transcribed by Delabarre in "Early Interest," 261.

4. *Jewish Encyclopedia* (1906), s.v. "Zaphnath-Panneah," http://www.jewishencyclopedia.com/articles/15167-zaphnath-paaneah.

5. For Greenwood's biography, see Leonard, "Harvard's First Science Professor"; entry for July 15, 1724, in Cotton Mather, *Diary of Cotton Mather*, 741.

6. For the endowment of the Hollisian chair and the election of Greenwood, see Quincy, *History of Harvard University*, 14–19. For Greenwood's firsts, see Leonard, "Harvard's First Science Professor," 135, 147.

7. Leonard, "Harvard's First Science Professor," 135.

8. Isaac Greenwood to John Eames, December 8, 1730, DRC.

9. For Mather, Greenwood, and the smallpox inoculation controversy, see Fenn, *Pox Americana*, 31–32; Kittredge, "Cotton Mather's Election," 103; Leonard, "Harvard's First Science Professor," 137–40.

10. Leonard, "Harvard's First Science Professor," 139.

11. Ibid., 140.

12. Delabarre assumed that Greenwood was "induced" by Eames to make a fresh investigation of Dighton Rock, but it is not clear how Delabarre came to this conclusion. See Delabarre, "Middle Period," 58.

13. The Bear, Wolf, and Tortoise were the three clans of the Mohawk and Oneida, and every Iroquois (Haudenosaunee) Confederacy village had segments of at least one of these clans.

Richter, *Ordeal of the Longhouse*, 21, 45. Douglass evidently gleaned his "heraldry" insight from the account of the death of the Jesuit missionary Isaac Jogues in 1646 at the hands of the Mohawk, as described by Charlevoix in *Histoire et description générale de la Nouvelle France*, 428. *Histoire* was published in 1744, three years before Douglass wrote his letter, and was a popular source for eighteenth-century writers on Native Americans. While Douglass's allusion to Charlevoix places the composition of his printed attack on Mather after 1744, I nevertheless believe it likely Douglass was circulating his essential case against Mather at the time of the Greenwood letter of 1730.

14. Delabarre, "Middle Period," 48.

15. West, "John Bartram," 465–66.

16. Isaac Greenwood to John Eames, December 8, 1730, DRC.

17. William Wood, *New England's Prospect* (1635), in Mancall, ed., *Envisioning America*, 151. Berkhofer in *White Man's Indian* notes how white colonists employed "description by deficiency." Colonists stressed "laziness" and set Indians apart from whites through the contrast of "indolence rather than industry" as they "invented the Indian as a conception" (27–29).

18. Said, *Orientalism*, 51.

19. See Murr, "Indianisme et militantisme protestant."

20. Isaac Greenwood to John Eames, December 8, 1730, DRC.

21. Sayre, *Les Sauvages Américains*, 129. See also Pagden's discussion of Lafitau's "antirationalist" defense of Christianity in *Fall of Natural Man*, 198–209.

22. Fenton, preface to Lafitau, *Customs of the American Indians*, xlv.

23. Lafitau, *Moeurs*, vol. 4, 185.

24. Ibid., vol. 1, 31–32.

25. Ibid., vol. 4, 171.

26. Ibid., vol. 4, 179.

27. Ibid., vol. 1, 37–38.

28. Isaac Greenwood to John Eames, December 8, 1730, DRC.

29. Greenwood's first letter to Eames of 1730 went awry, and a replacement copy in 1732 did not lead to anything appearing in *Philosophical Transactions*. See Delabarre on the Danforth materials and Greenwood's letters in "Early Interest," 275–96.

30. Leonard, "Harvard's First Science Professor," 159. Quincy, *History of Harvard University*, 11–13.

31. Lort, "Account," 295.

32. For Winthrop's travels with "Mr. Danforth," see the annotated almanacs in Papers of John and Hannah Winthrop. There is only one annotation in the 1739 almanac, which is not relevant to these travels, and no 1740 almanac survives. Winthrop's September 3, 1741, notation ("Went to Bost wth Mr Danforth & came back") in the 1741 almanac is the first mention of these travels.

33. For Samuel Danforth's biography, see May, *Danforth Genealogy*, 40–41, and Paige, *History of Cambridge*, vol. 3, 532.

34. For Winthrop's weather observations, see Meteorologic Observations at Cambridge in New England, Papers of John and Hannah Winthrop.

35. For Winthrop's travels with Danforth in 1744, see Annotated Almanac, 1744, Papers of John and Hannah Winthrop.

36. Leonard, "Harvard's First Science Professor," 162.

37. The career and ideas of Rudbeks (also known as Olaus Rudbeck, among other variants) are well covered in Ekman, "Gothic Patriotism." For the influence of Cassiodorus and Jordanes, see Vidal-Naquet, "Atlantis and the Nations"; Christensen, *Cassiodorus*, 8; Croke, "Cassiodorus";

and Goffert, "Jordanes's 'Getica.'" For an overview of the European roots of Gothicism and its appeal in nineteenth-century America, see Horsman, *Race and Manifest Destiny*, 25–42.

38. Ekman, "Gothic Patriotism," 54.

39. Ibid., 60, 61.

40. Translated from Montesquieu, *De l'Esprit des loix*, vol. 1, 440–41.

41. Ibid., vol. 1, 433.

42. André Thevet, *Les Singularitez de la France antartique* (1557), in Schlesinger and Stabler, *André Thevet's North America*, 9–10.

43. Montesquieu, *De l'Esprit des loix*, vol. 1, 439–41.

44. See the arguments of Bernard de Las Casas summarized in Todorov, *The Conquest of America*, 162–63. See the chapter "The Theory of Natural Slavery," in Pagden, *The Fall of Natural Man*. See also Chaplin, "Race," 180.

45. Montesquieu, *De l'Esprit des loix*, vol. 1, 443.

46. A map and paper by the French mathematician and cartographer Joseph-Nicolas Delisle based on the second Bering expedition's findings was presented before the French Academy of Sciences in Paris in April 1750, two years after Montesquieu published *De l'Esprit des loix*. "Histoire abregée des nouvelles découvertes au nord de la mer du sud," 11–18, in Delisle, *Nouvelles cartes*.

47. See Lutz, "Relative Influence," 190.

48. Koerner, *Linnaeus*, 28. See also "Georges-Louis Leclerc, Comte de Buffon," http://www.academie-francaise.fr/les-immortels/georges-louis-leclerc-comte-de-buffon.

49. Buffon, *Histoire naturelle*, vol. 3, 528.

50. Translated from Buffon, *Histoire naturelle*, vol. 3, 515.

51. Ibid., vol. 3, 378.

52. Translated from Buffon, *Histoire naturelle*, vol. 3, 490.

53. Ibid., vol. 3, 514.

54. Ibid., vol. 3, 491–92.

55. Sagard, *Le grand voyage*, 145.

56. For Mallet's basic biography, see Senarclens, "Mallet, Paul-Henri."

57. Mallet, *Monumens*, 6. In *Edda*, Mallet dropped the Scythians (9–10).

58. Éric Schnackenbourg has echoed Ernest Tonnelat in calling Mallet's *Monumens* the decisive publication in delivering Icelandic literature true renown in Europe in general and in France in particular in the second half of the eighteenth century. Schnackenbourg, "L'île des confins," 36; Tonnelat, "Romantisme et Scandinaves," 501. Margaret Clunies Ross has credited Mallet with conceiving the "empirically ridiculous but extremely popular theory that the early Scandinavians were the true inventors of concepts of chivalry and the literary genre of the romance." Ross, "Intellectual Complexion," 445. H. Arnold Barton has called Mallet's version of Nordic antiquity "largely mythical" and credited him (along with his translator Percy) with "giving rise to a pre-romantic 'Gothic' cult in European literature." Barton, "Discovery of Norway Abroad," 27–28.

59. Koerner, *Linnaeus*, 24–25. See 36–37 as well for Linnaeus and the Rudbeks family.

60. Thomas, *Skull Wars*, 37.

61. Exhibits at Brown University Library, "The Founding," http://www.brown.edu/Facilities/University_Library/exhibits/education/founding.html; Holmes, *Life of Ezra Stiles*, 106, 109.

62. Holmes, *Life of Ezra Stiles*, 128–30; Morgan, *Gentle Puritan*, 142.

63. Holmes, *Life of Ezra Stiles*, 112.

64. Stiles, *Literary Diary*, vol. 3, 24.

65. Morgan, *Gentle Puritan*, 126–27, 138.

66. Stiles, *Extracts*, 234–35. See also Delabarre, "Middle Period," 150.

67. Trigger, *History of Archaeological Thought*, 70.

68. Delabarre, "Middle Period," 55.

69. Stiles, *Extracts*, 237.

70. Holmes, *Life of Ezra Stiles*, 258.

71. Benjamin Franklin to Ezra Stiles, July 5, 1765, Ezra Stiles Papers.

72. Delabarre, "Middle Period," 60.

73. Ibid.

74. Lort, "Account," 295.

75. Isaac Greenwood to John Eames, December 8, 1730, DRC.

76. Lort, "Account," 296–97.

77. For editions of Kalm, see Benson, "Pehr Kalm's Writings on America."

78. See "Kalm, Pehr," in Sterling, Harmond, Cesavo, and Hammond, eds., *Biographical Dictionary*, 421–23. See also Jarrell, "Kalm, Pehr."

79. Merriam, "Pehr Kalm." See also Koerner, *Linnaeus*, 117–18, for Linnaeus's role in planning Kalm's journey.

80. For Forster's biography, see Hoare, *Tactless Philosopher*.

81. Kalm, *Travels into North America*, vol. 3, 123.

82. For the original published Kalm discussion, see Kalm, *En Rasa til Norra America*, vol. 3, 401–3. Kalm also addressed the enigmatic stone in his unpublished travel journal, on which he drew for *En Rasa til Norra America*. See Kalm, *Voyage de Pehr Kalm*, 185–86, 226. These journal entries did not mention La Vérendrye by name. The journal included an entry for August 20, 1749, omitted from *En Rasa til Norra America*, as well as the Foster translation. In this entry, Kalm recounted a meeting on August 20, 1749, with a Jesuit priest at Baie-Saint-Paul who had traveled greatly in the country and told him of another inscribed stone that supposedly had once been a pillar (*Voyage de Pehr Kalm*, 347–48).

83. Quotes from Kalm, *Travels into North America*, vol. 3, 124–26.

84. Lawrence J. Burpee, editor of the journal and letters of La Vérendrye and his sons, reproduced Kalm's account of his conversation with La Vérendrye and called it "interesting, although he seems to have misunderstood some of the things La Vérendrye or others said to him." La Vérendrye, *Journals and Letters*, 27.

85. Bassin, "Russia between Europe and Asia," 6. Biographical information on Strahlenberg is elusive. Strahlenberg does mention "my thirteen Years Captivity"; *Historico-Geographical Description*, 5. Since he published the original work in High German, it seems clear he was of German origin. He also remarked: "I must own, that when I first was carried Captive into these Countries, I knew just as much of the State of them, as an Ostiac knows of Germany" (5). In 1891, three Russian scholars asserted that Strahlenberg actually was a Swedish prisoner of war named Fabbert, but provided no references. Tolstoi, Kondakov, and Reinach, *Antiquités de la Russie méridionale*, 370. Also, in "L'Exploration de la Siberie" (note 4, p. 199), Benitez gives a variation on this, but provides no source.

86. Strahlenberg's early attempt to link Siberian and Native American languages has been acknowledged by modern scholars. See Jakobson, "The Paleo-Siberian Languages," 603.

87. Forster footnote in Kalm, *Travels into North America*, 125–27.

88. Ibid.

89. Forster, *Observations*, 228.

90. Kidd, *Forging of Races*, 9. For Meiners, see Baum, *Rise and Fall*, 84–88.

91. Baum, *Rise and Fall*, 76–77.

92. Ibid., 84.

93. Ibid., 85.

94. Translation by Baum, *Rise and Fall*, 88.

95. Hoare, *Tactless Philosopher*, v, 41.

96. Baum, *Rise and Fall*, 87. Note, however, that Baum does not link Meiners's terminology to the clear Gothicist/Celtic precedents of Rudbeks and Mallet.

97. For citations of Mallet, see Meiners, *Grundriss der Geschichte der Menschheit* (1793), 65, 185, 222, 224, 260, 275, 298, 299, 309.

98. For the remarks of Meiners in *Grundriss der Geschichte der Menschheit* (1785), see Baum, *Rise and Fall*, 85. For citations of Montesquieu's *De l'Esprit des loix*, see *Grundriss der Geschichte der Menschheit* (1793), 147, 204, 206, 208, 209.

99. Kidd, *Forging of Races*, 23.

100. Baum, *Rise and Fall*, 128–29.

Chapter Three

1. For Voltaire's induction ceremony, see Weisberger, *Speculative Freemasonry*, 84; Amiable, *Une loge maçonnique*, 64–70. Amiable recorded Court de Gébelin presenting the lodge with a new volume of *Monde primitif* and giving a reading from it "concernant les anciens mystères d' Eleusis" (69). The first volume of *Monde primitif* was published in 1777, and he probably based his reading on it. The second volume, of 1778, was concerned with demonstrating a universal grammar and seems a less likely candidate.

2. Weisberger, *Speculative Freemasonry*, 86–87.

3. For Court de Gébelin's biography, see "Antoine Court de Gébelin," http://www.musee protestant.org/notice/antoine-court-de-gebelin-1724-ou-1728-1784.

4. Godwin, *Theosophical Enlightenment*, xii.

5. Jacob, *Radical Enlightenment*, 133.

6. Humanities at Stanford, "Dark Side of the Enlightenment," http://humanexperience .stanford.edu/supere.

7. Court de Gébelin, *Monde primitif*, vol. 8, 499.

8. Lafitau, *Moeurs*, vol. 1, 130–37.

9. Weisberger, *Speculative Freemasonry*, 90.

10. Antoine Court de Gébelin to Stephen Sewall, August 19[?], 1781, Papers of Stephen Sewall.

11. Manuel and Manuel, *James Bowdoin*, 199.

12. Antoine Court de Gébelin to Stephen Sewall, August 19[?], 1781, Papers of Stephen Sewall.

13. For Du Ponceau's life, see the five-part article by Du Ponceau and Whitehead, "Notes and Documents."

14. Du Ponceau and Whitehead, "Notes and Documents, V," 261.

15. Manuel and Manuel, *James Bowdoin*, 197.

16. Ibid., 198. Antoine Court de Gébelin to Stephen Sewall, March 3, 1780; August 19[?], 1781, Papers of Stephen Sewall.

17. Sewall's communications are referenced by Court de Gébelin in his letters to Sewall of March 3, 1780, and August 19[?], 1781, Papers of Stephen Sewall. The Mayhew material was sent by Sewall on October 1, 1780, and, as Court de Gébelin explained in his second letter, arrived too late to be incorporated into vol. 8 of *Monde primitif*.

18. Antoine Court de Gébelin to Stephen Sewall, March 3, 1780, Papers of Stephen Sewall.

19. The date Sewall sent the Dighton Rock drawing is unknown. As Court de Gébelin did not mention having received it in his March 3, 1780, letter (when he acknowledged the Hawley material), it must have been part of a later Sewall missive.

20. For Court de Gébelin's discussion of Dighton Rock, see "Si les Phéniciens ont connu l'Amérique," 57–59, and "Observations sur le monument Américain," 561–68, in *Monde primitif,* vol. 8.

21. Court de Gébelin, *Monde primitif,* vol. 8, 59.

22. Delabarre, "Middle Period," 61–62.

23. Information and translation from Antoine Court de Gébelin to Stephen Sewall, August 19[?], 1781, Papers of Stephen Sewall.

24. Jean de Thévenot was a mid-seventeenth-century Orientalist who wrote about the Middle and Near East. Court de Gébelin must have been thinking of the sixteenth-century French royal geographer André Thevet, who did write about New World peoples.

25. See Coe, *Breaking the Maya Code,* 18–19, for a discussion of semasiography, including its relation to road signs.

26. Court de Gébelin, *Monde primitif,* vol. 8, 563.

27. "Antoine Court de Gébelin," http://www.museeprotestant.org/notice/antoine-court-de -gebelin-1724-ou-1728-1784. "L'Affaire Calas," http://www.museeprotestant.org/notice/laffaire -calas/.

28. Holmes, *Life of Ezra Stiles,* 272.

29. Stiles, *Literary Diary,* vol. 3, 19–20.

30. David McClure to Ezra Stiles, November 11, 1771, in Stiles, *Letters and Papers,* 36–38.

31. Stiles, "United States Elevated to Glory and Honor (1783)." The idea that America was God's chosen land, a New Jerusalem, of course was not new. Increase Mather in 1676 called New England "the English Israel" in *A Brief History of the War with the Indians in New-England* (1676), reprinted in Increase Mather, *History of King Philip's War,* 46.

32. Stiles, "United States Elevated to Glory and Honor (1783)," 7.

33. Annette Kolodny argues that Samuel Mather's pamphlet outlined a "justifying providential history" for revolution on the eve of the American rebellion. *In Search of First Contact,* 26–31.

34. J. Fuller also issued the work in 1743 and 1745.

35. *American Traveller,* 134.

36. Samuel Mather, *Attempt,* 17.

37. Ibid., 19.

38. Stiles, "United States Elevated to Glory and Honor (1783)," 10.

39. Ibid.

40. Ibid., 11.

41. Ibid.

42. Ibid., 10–11.

43. Ibid., 12–13.

44. Samuel Mather, *Attempt,* 6.

45. Ibid., 7.

46. Stiles, "United States Elevated to Glory and Honor (1783)," 12. The printed version of Stiles's sermon gave the date of 1001 for Madoc, but this was likely a misprint.

47. Stiles, *Literary Diary,* vol. 3, 25.

48. Stiles, "United States Elevated to Glory and Honor (1783)," 8–9.

49. Morgan, *Gentle Puritan,* 125.

50. Stiles, "United States Elevated to Glory and Honor (1783)," 14.

51. Stiles, *Literary Diary*, vol. 3, 72.

52. Pickles, "Lort."

53. Lort, "Account," 297.

54. Bray, "Observations."

55. Lort, "Account," 298.

56. Ibid., 299.

57. Jones quoted by Vance, "Vallancey."

58. Moore, "Vallancey."

59. For biographical details, see Nevin, "General Charles Vallancey."

60. Vallancey, *Grammar*, vii.

61. "Father Lafitau has endeavoured to shew, from an affinity, or rather an agreement of customs, that some of the Americans are descended from the Pelasgi, or first planters of Greece, who were probably of Phoenician extraction." *Additions to the Universal History*, 243. Vallancey even mentioned the support for a Phoenician origin by "the *Universal History*" in *Grammar* (vi). *Additions to the Universal History* considered it probable that some Native Americans were descended from Phoenicians or Egyptians and conducted cross-cultural comparisons that appear indebted to *The American Traveller*, which, as I have noted, was largely a translation/paraphrase of Horni's *De originibus Americanis* (*Additions to the Universal History*, 242).

62. Lafitau, *Moeurs*, vol. 2, 483–84.

63. Vallancey, *Grammar*, iv.

64. Thorowgood, *Iewes in America*, 24. Lafitau articulated his main ideas about the peopling of the Americas in *Moeurs*, vol. 1, 27–41.

65. *Additions to the Universal History*, 241. For Comte's dissertation, see Wright, "Origin of American Aborigines," 273, n. 52.

66. Vallancey, *A Grammar*, vii.

67. Nevin, "General Charles Vallancey," 30.

68. Edward Ledwitch to Thomas Percy, August 28, 1802, in Nichols, ed., *Illustrations*, 824.

69. Vallancey, "Observations," 302–3.

70. Ibid., 304.

71. Published in three volumes from 1784 to 1787, *Arctic Zoology*, according to Charles W. J. Withers, "was one of the first major studies of the zoology of the northern hemisphere and was widely acclaimed." Withers, "Pennant."

72. Pennant, *Arctic Zoology*, clxvii.

73. Ibid., clxi.

74. Ibid.

75. James Cook and James King, *A voyage to the Pacific Ocean*, 3 vols. and atlas (London, 1784). Cook (who was killed mid-voyage in the Hawaiian Islands) was credited posthumously with volumes 1 and 2; volume 3 was credited to King.

76. Pennant, *Arctic Zoology*, clxiii.

77. Vallancey, "Observations," 303.

78. Much pseudohistorical ink has been spilled on similarities between Mi'kmaw pictographic writing and Egyptian hieroglyphics. I believe it possible that Jesuit missionaries in the late seventeenth century, familiar with the eccentric published efforts of the contemporary Jesuit scholar Athanasius Kircher to decipher Egyptian hieroglyphs (*Oedipus Aegyptiacus* appeared in three volumes from 1652 to 1654), melded Kircher's examples with existing Mi'kmaw glyphs to create a script for the Mi'kmaw language. For Kircher's deciphering efforts, see Stolzenberg, *Egyptian Oedipus*. David L. Schmidt and Murdena Marshall discuss the origin of the

Mi'kmaw writing system in *Mi'kmaq Hieroglyphic Prayers*. They cite Mi'kmaw oral tradition that the glyph system, *komqwejwi'kasikl*, existed before the arrival of Europeans and was used for inscribing maps and tribal records (4), but they do not address the possibility that Jesuit priests may have drawn on Kircher to add symbols for terms and concepts required for their proselytizing. This to me is a far simpler explanation for quasi-Egyptian glyphs in the Mi'kmaw glyphic system than a visit to Atlantic Canada by ancient Egyptians.

79. Laughton, "King, James."

80. Vallancey, "Observations," 305.

81. See Oppitz, "Drawings," 63.

82. Vallancey, "Observations," 306.

83. Silverberg, *Mound Builders*, 25. Silverberg states that Zeisberger discovered mounds "and mentioned them in his *History of the North American Indians*." As this work was not published (in an English translation from an original German manuscript) until 1910, it seems doubtful to credit Zeisberger with popularizing knowledge of the mounds. See Zeisberger, *David Zeisberger's History of the Northern American Indians*. Zeisberger asserted that the mounds were built as defensive works (31).

84. Silverberg, *Mound Builders*, 3.

85. They include the massive geometric earthworks of Louisiana's Poverty Point (1000–700 B.C.), the numerous sites of the Adena culture (600–200 B.C.) and its successor, the Hopewell (200 B.C.–A.D. 400), whose heartland was in southern Ohio, and the sprawl of Mississippian and related cultures that ranged as far east as Georgia and as far north as Minnesota from about A.D. 500 to 1500, although the Fort Ancient culture of the Ohio River region is considered to have persisted until about 1750. See Chappell, *Cahokia*, 37–48, for a discussion of cultures associated with mounds.

86. Silverberg, *Mound Builders*, 65–67.

87. Ibid., 216.

88. Calloway, *One Vast Winter Count*, 372; "Samuel H. Parsons," http://www.ohiohistorycentral .org/index.php?title=Samuel_H._Parsons&oldid=28394; "Treaty of Fort Finney (1786)," http:// www.ohiohistorycentral.org/index.php?title=Treaty_of_Fort_Finney_(1786)&oldid=32505.

89. Stiles, *Literary Diary*, vol. 3, 215.

90. Samuel Parsons to Ezra Stiles, April 27, 1786, in Stiles, *Extracts*, 549 50.

91. Stiles, *Literary Diary*, vol. 3, 216.

92. About two weeks before Parsons called on him, on April 13, 1786, Stiles was visited by "a young Miss Kennedy of New York," about seventeen years old. Apparently an imposter, she claimed to be the orphaned daughter of one Colonel Kennedy, a member of the British Army who supposedly had joined the American rebels and moved his family from New York to Schoharie, which was all but destroyed by British forces and their Mohawk allies. Stiles wrote: "the Indians beset his Family. He was killed, & the Children captivated & all killed but this Daughter, who was three years with the Mohawk Indians, being seven years old when captived." See April 13, 1786, entry in Stiles, *Literary Diary*, vol. 3, 213. A parenthetic addition by editor Dexter noted: "[An imposter.]" There was, according to Stiles's diary entry, an estate inheritance in question. Dexter provided no further details. Guy Park, the residence of the British Indian superintendent Guy Johnson, was occupied by a man named Henry Kennedy and his family after Johnson abandoned it in 1775. Simms, *History of Schoharie County*, 117. In November 1786, Stiles noted giving his name to an English boy who had been captured by the Seneca at Susquehanna when he was two and a half during the Revolution. "He remembers to have seen his Father shot down by the Indians in the Stoop of his Door, & his Mother after being carried half a mile he saw

killed, & some Children's Brains dashed out." Entry for November 7, 1786, Stiles, *Literary Diary*, vol. 3, 245.

93. Morgan, *Gentle Puritan*, 162.

94. Parsons, "Discoveries," 125.

95. Ibid., 126.

96. Heart, "Account," 425–27.

97. Noah Webster to Ezra Stiles, October 22, 1787, 80; December 15, 1787, 85, in Stiles, *Letters and Papers*.

98. Silverberg, *Mound Builders*, 26–27.

99. Noah Webster to Ezra Stiles, January 20, 1788, 93, in Stiles, *Letters and Papers*.

100. Jefferson, *Notes on the State of Virginia*, 103–5.

101. Noah Webster to Ezra Stiles, January 20, 1788, 93, in Stiles, *Letters and Papers*.

102. For Barton's biographical details, see Pennell, "Benjamin Smith Barton as Naturalist"; Spencer and Barton, "Two Unpublished Essays"; and Jeffries, "Barton's Unpublished Materia Medica."

103. Barton, *Observations*, 53.

104. De Pauw is discussed by Ouellet with Tremblay, "From the Good Savage to the Degenerate Indian," 167.

105. De Pauw, *Recherches philosophiques* (1770), vol. 1, 106–7.

106. Ibid., vol. 1, 35.

107. Buffon, *Histoire naturelle*, vol. 4 (1777), 525.

108. Jefferson, *Notes on the State of Virginia*, 72–73. Greene, "American Science Comes of Age," 35. See also Church, "Corneille de Pauw."

109. Thomas Jefferson to Ezra Stiles, June 10, 1784, Ezra Stiles Papers.

110. Barton, *Observations*, 17.

111. Ibid., 30.

112. Spencer and Barton, "Two Unpublished Essays," 568. Spencer did think it possible Barton met some Native Americans when he accompanied his uncle, David Rittenhouse, on his survey of the western boundary of Pennsylvania. Ibid.

113. Barton's description makes it clear that he had not visited the site himself, and while he allowed that the "annexed plan is a copy" of an original drawing (*Observations*, 34), he did not state who made it.

114. Ibid., 39–40.

115. Ibid., 65.

116. Ibid., 66–67.

117. Ibid., 66.

118. Delabarre, "Middle Period," 74.

119. Pennell, "Benjamin Smith Barton as Naturalist," 110.

120. Stiles, *Extracts*, 330, 402. See also Delabarre, "Middle Period," 73–74.

121. Rev. John Smith to Ezra Stiles, July 25, 1789, quoted by Delabarre, "Middle Period," 86.

122. Quoted by Delabarre, "Middle Period," 87.

123. Webster, "Letter 1—No Title: Note," 11. See also Sayre, "Mound Builders," 229.

124. See Delabarre, "Middle Period," 94–97.

125. Quoted by Delabarre, "Middle Period," 96. See also Manuel and Manuel, *James Bowdoin*, 198.

126. Heart, "Letter," 217.

127. Barton, *New Views*, preliminary discourse, i, xvi.

128. Ibid., dedication, v.

129. Ibid.

130. See Conn, *History's Shadow*, 24–26.

131. Barton, "Observations and Conjectures," 197.

Chapter Four

1. Lathrop, "John Lathrop D.D., to Judge Davis."

2. Blake, "Davis, John, LL.D.," in *Biographical Dictionary*.

3. Biographical details of Samuel Webber in "Webber, Samuel." For the letter to Webber, see Davis, "Attempt to Explain."

4. Davis, "Attempt," 199.

5. For our purposes, "Freemasonry," "Freemasons," "Masonry," and "Masons," capitalized and noncapitalized, all refer to the same fraternal movement and its members.

6. Bullock, *Revolutionary Brotherhood*, 137.

7. Ruffin, *Paradise of Reason*, 125.

8. Bentley, *Diary*, vol. 3, 99. Bentley delivered numerous discourses at other lodges; among those he published was one delivered at Roxbury, Massachusetts, in 1796 before the Grand Lodge of Massachusetts, whose master was "The Most Worshipful Paul Revere." *Diary*, vol. 1, xxxvii.

9. Bullock, *Revolutionary Brotherhood*, 77.

10. See Ibid., 143.

11. Jacob, *Living the Enlightenment*, 54.

12. Clarke, *Secrets of Masonry*, 7–8.

13. Josiah Bartlett, *Discourse*, 9–10.

14. In *An Argument*, Kendall discussed the Dublin Charter (126) and critiqued a letter to the editor in a "Dublin newspaper" (207–8, 231, 253). More pointedly, he published the Irish anti-Catholic tract *Letters to a Friend, on the State of Ireland, the Roman Catholic Question, and the Merits of Constitutional Religious Distinctions* (1826). The only clue to his Canadian years is his entry in Watkins's *Biographical Dictionary* (1816), which states he was "lately employed in a civil capacity in Canada" (187). The dictionary references the "literary calendar" of 1814 for its entries. Guy Arnold asserts that he was employed in Canada prior to his American tour, based on the *Biographical Dictionary* entry. See Arnold, "Kendall." But there is no reason to conclude this, and a spell in the civil service in Canada immediately following the publication of *Travels in New York* in 1809, with a return to England perhaps encouraged by the outbreak of war in 1812, better aligns with the "lately" qualification of Watkins. Kendall likely was employed in Lower Canada (Quebec), as he was familiar with the perpetuation of the custom of Paris there in the civil code (*An Argument*, 249).

15. Notice in *The Literary Chronicle* No. 7, Monday, May 11, 1818.

16. Goodwin, "Kendall, Edward Augustus (1776?–1842)." Arnold's Oxford DNB entry for Kendall gives the initial year of publication for *The Literary Chronicle and Weekly Review* as 1819, but issues from 1818 survive.

17. "Deaths. 1842," *The Gentleman's Magazine: And Historical Review* 12 (July 1856–May 1868): 670–75.

18. Personal communication from David DeBono Schafer, Senior Collections Manager and Interim Director of Collections, Peabody Museum of Archaeology and Ethnology, Harvard University, February 12, 2014.

19. Jacob, *Living the Enlightenment*, 56.

20. Denon's *Voyage dans le Basse et la Haute Égypte, pendant les campagnes du Général Bonaparte* (1802) immediately appeared in English translation in a multitude of editions in London and New York; WorldCat lists eighteen editions in 1803 alone. Kendall appears to have contributed his essay at least to Vivant Denon, *Travels in Upper and Lower Egypt*.

21. James Winthrop, "Account of an Inscribed Rock." See also Delabarre, "Middle Period," 77–81.

22. Samuel Johnson pronounced the poems fakes in *A Journey to the Western Islands of Scotland* (London, 1775), 273–74. However, James Mullholland has stated: "It is impossible to confirm the veracity of Macpherson's claim that his Ossian poems originate in Scotland's oral traditions, but there is ample evidence for the continued existence of these traditions during the eighteenth century." Mullholland, "James Macpherson's Ossian Poems," 396.

23. Kendall, "Account," 176.

24. Kendall, *Travels*, vol. 1, 227.

25. Ibid., vol. 1, 223. Fathoms measure ocean depths, and it is not clear if Kendall was playfully exaggerating the depth of excavations or saying the shoreline on both sides of the river had been excavated for a distance of 600 feet.

26. See Taylor, "Early Republic's Supernatural Economy." Delabarre in "Middle Period" ventured that there might have been some historical basis to piracy being associated with the area around Dighton Rock (108). Two of the six lots on Assonet Neck in 1688 were purchased by Henry Tew of Newport, Rhode Island, and John O. Austin presented evidence that Henry was the brother of the pirate Thomas Tew in *The Genealogical Dictionary of Rhode Island*, 395–96. Delabarre made Thomas Tew a resident of Newport as well, but there is no reference to Newport in the profile he cites ("Captain Tew," 67–90) in Johnson's *The History of Pirates*. Delabarre cited (without reference pages) an 1814 edition. Delabarre failed to mention that, according to the 1900 federal census, his next-door neighbor on Arlington Avenue in Providence was Lillie Tew. I suspect Delabarre gathered the family pirate lore from his neighbors. I doubt any connection between Tew and the pirate-treasure stories heard by Kendall, for if there were local lore about Tew, Kendall surely would have heard it, rather than fanciful references to Kidd and Blackbeard.

27. Kendall, *Travels*, vol. 3, 86.

28. Hurd, *History of Bristol County*, 223–24.

29. Kendall, *Travels*, vol. 3, 230.

30. The identification of the men named Baylies in investigations of Dighton Rock is confusing. Kendall mentions both "the Honourable Judge Baylies," who possessed one of the drawings he examined (*Travels*, vol. 2, 226), and "Major Baylies, a gentleman of the most pleasing and polished manners, and to whom I owe no less for his personal attentions, than for his zealous assistance in all my undertakings and enquiries concerning the Writing Rock" (*Travels*, vol. 2, 232). Major Hodijah Baylies would be known as "Judge Baylies" later in life, but did not receive an appointment as judge of probate for Bristol Country until 1810, three years after Kendall met him. His brother, Dr. William Baylies, was named a judge of the county's court of common pleas in 1784. He was presumably the "Judge Baylies" responsible for the drawing Kendall examined, and also would have been the "Dr. Baylies" who was part of the team that had assisted Stephen Sewall in making his 1768 drawing. The Reverend Bentley, in his October 13, 1807, diary entry, noted that Kendall had seen "the figures from the two Baylies, who have been attentive to the Dighton rock & live not far from the spot on which it stands" (Stiles, *Literary Diary*, vol. 3, 322–23). Delabarre for some reason thought these two Baylies were Dr. William Baylies and one of his sons (Delabarre, "Middle Period," 91). Thomas Webb provided a drawing for *Antiquitates*

Americanae that was identified as "Dr. Baylies and Mr. Goodwin's 1790." Presumably, this effort
involved "Judge Baylies" (Dr. William Baylies). To confuse matters, a writer for the *Newburyport
Herald* of May 4, 1819, "recollects about the year 1791 or 2, of seeing two copies of the writing on
the Rock, taken by two gentlemen of Dighton, one by Dr. H. Baylies, the other by Mr. William
Goodwin" (Delabarre, "Middle Period," 90). This writer appears to have fused Hodijah Baylies
and Dr. William Baylies into a single new entity, "Dr. H. Baylies." For Baylies family biographies,
see Hurd, *History of Bristol County*, 233–35.

31. Kendall, *Travels*, vol. 3, 228.

32. Ibid., vol. 3, 230–31.

33. Ibid., vol. 3, 227.

34. Ibid., vol. 3, 227–28.

35. Joseph G. Waters, "A Biographical Sketch of Rev. William Bentley," ix–xxi, in Bentley,
Diary, vol. 1, xviii.

36. Grimes, "Curiosity, Cabinets, and Knowledge," http://www.pem.org/aux/pdf/mission
/Grimes-Cabinets-Curiosity-Knowledge-sm.pdf.

37. The East India Marine Society was a benevolent organization, formed in Salem in 1799,
open to ship captains and supercargoes who had rounded Cape Horn or the Cape of Good
Hope. Members brought home a wealth of material culture from the northwest coast of America, Asia, Africa, Oceania, and India, among other locales. "About PEM," http://pem.org/about
/museum_history.

38. Bentley had known Rich for about twenty years. He is first mentioned in Bentley's diary
on May 13, 1786 (*Diary*, vol. 1, 37). An entry for July 9, 1791 (vol. 1, 274), captures Rich returning
to Salem from Bengal.

39. Entry for October 7, 1803, Bentley, *Diary*, vol. 3, 52.

40. According to *The Boston Directory* of 1807, an engraver named Samuel Harris Jr. lived on
Spring Lane (12), which was two blocks from Turell's museum at 3 Tremont St. (148). http://cdm
.bostonathenaeum.org/cdm/landingpage/collection/p16057coll32.

41. "Notice of Mr. Samuel Harris," *Harvard Lyceum*, July 28, 1810.

42. Entry for September 18, 1805, Bentley, *Diary*, vol. 3, 191.

43. Ibid.

44. Entry for October 5, 1805, Bentley, *Diary*, vol. 3, 194.

45. Preble portrait, *The Polyanthos* (1805–14), January 1, 1806. Winthrop portrait, for "Sketch
of the Life of John Winthrop, Esq.: First Governor of Massachusetts," *The Polyanthos* (1805–14),
June 1, 1806.

46. Raynal, *Histoire philosophique*, 130.

47. Jefferson, *Notes on the State of Virginia*, 97–100. Paine, *Letter A Letter Addressed to the Abbe
Raynal* (London, 1791).

48. Rich's death is noted in Rich, "Richard Rich of Eastham."

49. The society wrote Turell on August 25, 1807, demanding the return of the loaned items,
without result; it expelled him from membership in 1811. Malloy, *Souvenirs of the Fur Trade*, 91.

50. The quote is from the *Harvard Lyceum* article "Notice of Mr. Samuel Harris," July 28, 1810,
which states that Harris was admitted to Harvard "after only about one year's application."
Delabarre, who had access to registry records, indicated he prepared for thirteen months.
Delabarre, "Middle Period," 99.

51. Entry for October 13, 1807, Bentley, *Diary*, vol. 3, 322–23.

52. Kendall, *Travels*, vol. 3, 224–25.

53. Entry for October 13, 1807, Bentley, *Diary*, vol. 3, 322–23.

54. Kendall, "Account," 184.

55. Ibid., 189.

56. Sheola, "The Harris Family," http://www.bostonathenaeum.org/node/861.

57. "The Journal of a Tour into the Territory North-West of the Allegany Mountains. Rev Thaddeus M Harris," *The Polyanthos* (1805–14), December 1, 1805.

58. Entry for October 13, 1807, Bentley, *Diary*, vol. 3, 322–23.

59. Hoare, *Tactless Philosopher*, 39.

60. "The Coins of Colonial and Early America," http://www.coins.nd.edu/ColCoin/index.html.

61. Harris, "Account of Copper Coins," 196.

62. Kendall, "Account," 166.

63. Ibid., 168.

64. See description, 29–31, illustration, 31, in Amiable, *Une loge maçonnique.*

65. Kendall, "Account," 169.

66. Ibid., 174.

67. Ibid., 173.

68. Ibid., 171.

69. Ibid., 172.

70. Ibid., 181.

71. Ibid., 182.

72. Ibid., 183.

73. Delabarre, *Dighton Rock*, 166.

74. Ibid., 70.

75. Hinderaker, *Two Hendricks*, 161.

76. Lort, "Account," 296.

77. Hinderaker, *Two Hendricks*, 164.

78. Delabarre, "Middle Period," 110.

79. Kendall, "Account," 183.

80. Conway, *Spirits on Stone*, 36–37. See McInnes, *Sounding Thunder*, 67, for alternate Ojibwa spellings. McInnes gives *mshi-gnebigook* as the plural form for the serpents. Note that different orthographic systems and dialects account for varying spellings.

81. Rajnovich, *Reading Rock Art*, 36.

82. F. Kent Reilly III, "The Great Serpent in the Lower Mississippi Valley," in Lankford, Reilly, and Garber, eds., *Visualizing the Sacred*, 119. See Pomedli, *Living with Animals*, 168–92, for a discussion of "water creatures" in Ojibwa cosmology. While I have preserved the past tense in quotes, the reader should be aware the cosmology endures in Indigenous communities, sometimes observed alongside Christian practices.

83. I inspected the rock in July 2013. While its presentation and the state of its markings made it impossible for me to be confident about much of what was on its surface, the horned quadruped was clearly visible.

84. Pomedli, *Living with Animals*, 186.

85. Tanner, *Narrative*, 378.

86. See Carol Diaz-Granados, "Early Manifestations of Mississippian Iconography in Middle Mississippi Valley Rock-Art," in Diaz-Granados and Duncan, ed., *Rock-Art of Eastern North America*, 90–91.

87. Hamell, "Iroquois and the World's Rim," 452.

88. Cath Oberholtzer, "The Living Landscape," 156–57.

89. Hamell, "Long-Tail," 258.

90. Bohaker, citing Phillips in "Indigenous Histories," Kindle location 1846.

91. Kendall, *Travels*, vol. 3, 214.

92. Ibid., vol. 2, 49–50. Kendall likely learned about these rocks between Sandwich and Plymouth from the papers of Ezra Stiles, to which John Davis gave him access, as Stiles in *Extracts* discusses them in similar (but not identical) terms. See Stiles, *Extracts*, 160–61. See also Eva L. Butler, "The Brush or Memorial Stone Heaps of Southern New England," *Bulletin of the Archaeological Society of New England* 19 (April 1946): 3–12; and Frank G. Speck, "The Memorial Brush Heap in Delaware and Elsewhere," *Bulletin of the Archaeological Society of Delaware* 4, no. 2 (May 1945): 17–23.

93. Bragdon, *Native People of Southern New England, 1670–1775*, 176. Goddard and Bragdon, *Native Writings in Massachusett*, vol. 1, 5. *Pokanoket* was an early colonial term, possibly Narragansett in origin, for people later collectivized as the Wampanoag.

94. Goddard and Bragdon, *Native Writings in Massachusett*, vol. 1, 5.

95. Kendall, *Travels*, vol. 2, 47.

96. Kendall's walking companion replied: "She frankly answered, that for herself, when she wanted to be sober and fit for work, she did not dare to taste any liquor whatever; a very small quantity overpowering either her strength or her prudence." *Travels*, vol. 2, 48.

97. For Hawley's career, see Freeman, *History of Cape Cod*, 682–97. Entries in Gideon Hawley's journal and letter book end in 1806, and so can provide no insight into Kendall's encounter with him in 1807, shortly before his death. See "Hawley, Gideon. Journal and Letterbook," http://www.congregationallibrary.org/nehh/series2/HawleyGideon1237.

98. Kendall, *Travels*, vol. 2, 50.

99. Ibid., vol. 2, 50–51.

100. Cipolla, "Being and Becoming Stone."

101. Kohl, *Kitchi-Gami*, 59.

102. Mackenzie, *Voyages*, xcix.

103. For the development and governance of these Christian communities, see Goddard and Bragdon, *Native Writings in Massachusett*, vol. 1, 5–6. Silverman addresses the Brothertown and Stockbridge communities in *Red Brethren*.

104. Freeman, *History of Cape Cod*, 689–90.

105. Quoted by Freeman, *History of Cape Cod*, 684.

106. For the recent history of tribal recognition in the United States, and in particular the Mashpee Wampanoag, see Amy E. Den Ouden and Jean M. O'Brien, chapter 11, "Recognition and Rebuilding," in Warrior, ed., *World of Indigenous North America*.

107. "The spirit of Loda was not acknowledged as a deity by Fingal; he did not worship at the stone of his power" (vol. 1, 147); "Their words are not in vain, by Loda's stone of power" (vol. 1, 228). Macpherson, *Poems of Ossian*.

108. Kendall, *Travels*, vol. 2, 58.

109. On Masons and Druids, see Jacob, *Radical Enlightenment*, 153–54, and Godwin on Godfrey Higgins and his landmark work of masonic esotericism, *The Celtic Druids* (1829), in *Theosophical Enlightenment*, 76–91.

110. Kendall, *Travels*, vol. 2, 103.

111. Ibid., vol. 3, 240.

112. Bellows Falls Island Multiple Resource Area, http://www.crjc.org/heritage/V06-62.htm.

113. Kendall *Travels*, vol. 3, 205.

114. Ibid., vol. 3, 205–6.

115. Ibid., vol. 3, 206.

116. Kendall, "Account," 173.

117. Kendall, *Travels*, vol. 2, 221.

118. Ibid., vol. 2, 224–25.

119. Basso, *Wisdom Sits in Places*, 5–7.

120. Kendall, "Account," 190–91.

121. Megill, *Historical Knowledge*, 189.

Chapter Five

1. Delabarre, "Middle Period," 99.

2. Bentley, *Diary*, vol. 3, 530.

3. Ibid., vol. 3, 530.

4. Ibid., vol. 3, 530–31.

5. Ibid., vol. 3, 532.

6. "Notice of Mr. Samuel Harris," *Harvard Lyceum*, July 28, 1810.

7. Ibid.

8. Ibid.

9. Bentley, *Diary*, vol. 3, 532.

10. Delabarre, "Middle Period," 100. For Delabarre's account of Samuel Harris, see "Middle Period," 97–104. Harris's worksheet is plate 27.

11. For the founding of the AAS and its place in American letters, see Shipton, "American Antiquarian Society."

12. American Antiquarian Society, *Archaeologia Americana*, vol. 1, 2–3.

13. *Le printemps* is so obscure that I could not find a record for it in any library. Delabarre was similarly stymied in attempting to locate a copy. Its contents with respect to Dighton Rock are known only through the transcription of the original French and an English translation provided by "ART. 3. *Le Printemps*," in *American Monthly Magazine and Critical Review*, August 1817, 257. Samuel Latham Mitchill is the presumed author and translator. Mitchill and his friend De Witt Clinton were prominent contributors to this short-lived New York magazine, and as Mitchill included this unsigned item in a collection of his writings he forwarded for inclusion in *Archaeologia Americana*, vol. 1, it is as good as certain that he wrote it. For the magazine, see Mott, *History of American Magazines*, 297–98. Mitchill noted the publication of *Le printemps* at Nancy, by Haener, and its length as twenty-eight pages. Durrieu in "Miniatures" assigned it a publication date of 1816.

14. "Mitchill, Samuel Latham," http://bioguide.congress.gov/scripts/biodisplay.pl?index=m 000831.

15. "Biography," Samuel Latham Mitchill Papers, http://quod.lib.umich.edu/c/clementsmss /umich-wcl-M-2015mit?view=text.

16. One Charles-Léopold Mathieu wrote an article on a quarry for strontium sulfate (a raw ingredient for nitrates used in pyrotechnics), "Description de la carrière de sulfate de strontiane," *Journal de physique, de chimie, d'histoire naturelles et des arts*, Nivose, an 6 [January 1798]: 199–202. He was identified as a resident of Nancy and a former adjunct commissioner of "poudres & salpêtres de la république," in the departments of Vosges, La Meurthe, La Moselle, and La Meuse, as well as a correspondent of the French republic's mining journal.

17. See Durrieu, "Miniatures," for the career of the presumably younger Mathieu of *Le printemps*.

18. Translation from Durrieu, "Miniatures," 6. As Durrieu noted, these other brochures included *Ruines de l'ancien château de ludre et du camp romain* (1829) and *Ruines de Scarpone, l'antique Serpanc, et histoire de cette ville etc.* (1834).

19. Mitchill, "ART. 3. Le Printemps."

20. Ibid.

21. Conn, citing Warren K. Moorehead in 1901, *History's Shadow*, 118.

22. Trigger, "Alternative Archaeologies," 357.

23. Williams, *Fantastic Archaeology*, 31.

24. American Antiquarian Society, *Archaeologia Americana*, vol. 1, 3–4.

25. Cornog, *Birth of Empire*, 9. For biographical sketches of Clinton, see "De Witt Clinton," http://www.newnetherlandinstitute.org/history-and-heritage/dutch_americans/dewitt-clinton/; "Clinton, De Witt," http://bioguide.congress.gov/scripts/biodisplay.pl?index=C000525. See also the Introduction to Hanyan with Hanyan, *De Witt Clinton*, and the Introduction to Cornog, *Birth of Empire*.

26. Bullock, *Revolutionary Brotherhood*, 145, 153.

27. Ibid., 145.

28. Cornog, *Birth of Empire*, 5.

29. Ibid., 5–6.

30. New-York Historical Society, "Historical Sketch," in *Collections*, 458–59.

31. Madison, "A Letter."

32. Clinton, "Address," 222–23.

33. Ibid., 260.

34. Ibid., 260.

35. Ibid., 261.

36. Ibid., 264.

37. Ibid., 264–65.

38. Ekman, "Gothic Patriotism," 54.

39. Translated from Montesquieu, *De l'Esprit des loix*, vol. 1, 441.

40. Pennant, *Arctic Zoology*, clx.

41. Clinton, "Address," 264.

42. Clinton, *Memoir*, 8–9.

43. Robert Silverberg has stated that Clinton appeared before the NYHS in 1811 to "speak on behalf of the theory that [the mounds'] builders were Scandinavian in origin" and that Clinton amplified his ideas in his 1817 paper and 1820 *Memoir*, "again affirming his belief that the mounds had been erected by errant Vikings" (*Mound Builders*, 53–54). Clinton never mentioned Scandinavians in his 1811 address, and as I point out, Clinton never said Danes (or Vikings) actually visited America and built the mounds. Bruce Trigger relied on Silverberg in repeating the error that Clinton attributed the mounds to Vikings (*History of Archaeological Thought*, 159).

44. Cornog, *Birth of Empire*, 62.

45. Barton, "Hints," 145.

46. Conn, *History's Shadow*, 9–10. See also Conn's discussion of the object-based epistemology of American museums in *Museums and American Intellectual Life*, 22–24.

47. Conn, *History's Shadow*, 116.

48. Ibid., 9–10.

49. Mitchill, "Heads," 339–40.

50. See digitized examples from Stiles's *Itineraries* at Beinecke Rare Book and Manuscript Library, http://brbl-dl.library.yale.edu.

51. Mitchill, "Heads," 341.

52. Ibid.

53. Zoltvany, "Gaultier de Varennes et de la Vérendrye, Pierre."

54. Stiles, *Literary Diary*, vol. 3, 216.

55. Barton, *Observations*, 45.

56. Williams cited a letter published in *Gentleman's Magazine* in 1740, allegedly written in 1685 by a Welshman, John Jones, living in New York, who recounted being taken captive by the Tuscarora while he was a soldier in the Virginia colony in 1660. Jones claimed his life was spared when he was heard to speak Welsh, as it turned out his Tuscarora captors were fluent in it. Williams, *Enquiry*, 21–24.

57. Dinisi, "Evans, John Thomas (1770–1799)."

58. Southey, *Madoc*, vol. 1, viii.

59. Clinton, "Address," 259–60.

60. Fiske, "Conjectures," 305.

61. Daniel Wilson would attribute notions of a Madoc colonization to confusion arising from an early nineteenth-century Welsh colony in Ohio. Wilson, *Lost Atlantis*, 38–39.

62. Mitchill, "Heads," 341.

63. Ibid., 342.

64. Barton, *Observations*, 46–47.

65. Mitchill, "Original Inhabitants of America Shown," 332.

66. Jefferson, *Notes on the State of Virginia*, 163. Mitchill's racial concept is also discussed by Stanton in *Leopard's Spots*, 9.

67. Mitchill, "Original Inhabitants of America Consisted," 323.

68. Ibid., 324–35.

69. Mitchill, "Original Inhabitants of America Shown," 327.

70. Ibid. Melli Melli arrived in Washington in November 1805, and was fascinated by Native American delegations in the capital. See Wilson, "Dealings with Mellimelli," 3. Having foreign visitors remark on the similarity between Native Americans and Tartars was not a new experience for Americans. In 1792 Ezra Stiles would sit for a portrait in Newport by the Scottish artist John Smibert. Stiles had explained in his "Election Sermon" that Smibert had previously been employed "by the grand Duke of Tuscany, while at Florence, to paint two or three Siberian Tartars, presented to the Duke by the Czar of Russia." When Smibert arrived in Newport, he "instantly recognized the Indians here to be the same people as the Siberian Tartars whose pictures he had taken." Stiles, "United States Elevated to Glory and Honor (1783)," 11–12. Benjamin Smith Barton also related this Smibert story in *New Views*, xvi–xvii.

71. Mitchill, "Heads," 342.

72. Ibid., 343.

73. See Mitchill biographical sources above.

74. The 9,000-year-old skull of Kennewick Man, discovered in Washington State in 1996, was touted as a Caucasian, based on a preliminary (erroneous) determination that the skull was "caucasoid," as Thomas explores in *Skull Wars*.

75. Weisenburger, "Caleb Atwater," 19.

76. Ibid., 19–20.

77. Ibid., 21.

78. Atwater, "Description," 209.

79. Trigger, *History of Archaeological Thought*, 114.

80. Godwin, *Theosophical Enlightenment*, 15–18; Said, *Orientalism*, 77–79.

81. Atwater, "Description," 210.

82. Ibid., 209.

83. Kidd, *Forging of Races*, 228–29.

84. "Primary Documents in American History: Indian Removal Act," http://www.loc.gov/rr/program/bib/ourdocs/Indian.html.

85. "Andrew Jackson," http://www.presidency.ucsb.edu/ws/?pid=29472.

86. Dippie, *Vanishing American*, 60–61. In critiquing the American removal program (57–78), Dippie does not recognize the role of Mound Builder theorizing in official justification.

87. Monroe, quoted by Dippie, *Vanishing American*, 61.

88. "Andrew Jackson."

89. Thomas, *Skull Wars*, 21.

Chapter Six

1. Yates and Moulton, *History*, vol. 1, 85.

2. Hill, *Antiquities*, 42.

3. Ibid., 44.

4. Ibid., 75–76.

5. Ibid., 76.

6. Ibid., 83.

7. Ibid., 33.

8. All quotations from Finch, "Antiquities."

9. Finch, *Travels*, 173.

10. "Discovery of America. *From the National Gazette*," *Niles' Weekly Register* 35, no. 895 (November 8, 1828): 165.

11. Washington Irving, *A History of the Life and Voyages of Christopher Columbus* (New York: G. & C. Carvill, 1828). For Irving's biography and the coincident enthusiasm for locating Vinland, see Kolodny, *In Search of First Contact*, 114.

12. Lowenthal, "G. P. Marsh," 46.

13. Wilson, *Lost Atlantis*, 41–42.

14. McManis, "Traditions of Vinland," 797–98. McManis acknowledges that Fridtjof Nansen argued that Norse voyages from Greenland to America were a certainty but had nevertheless felt the Vinland sagas were "historical romances" that could not be relied upon for facts (McManis, 798). "I look upon the narratives somewhat in the light of historical romances, founded upon legend and more or less uncertain traditions," Nansen wrote in *In Northern Mists* (314). He argued the sagas' description of Vinland was based on the medieval legend of Insulae Fortunatae, or the Fortunate Isles (352). George Bancroft dismissed the historicity of the sagas in the first edition of *A History of the United States* (1834)—"The geographical details are so vague, that they cannot even sustain a conjecture"—and considered Vinland "but another and more southern portion" of Greenland (6). As McManis notes, Bancroft's skepticism disappeared from subsequent editions (798). See also Kolodny, *In Search of First Contact*, 117, on Bancroft's reversal.

15. McManis, "Traditions of Vinland," 797.

16. Trigger, "Alternative Archaeologies," 358.

17. Mallet asserted that in volume 2 of *En Resa til Norra America*, Kalm stated that Vinland "was in the island of Newfoundland, which is only separated from the continent of Labrador by a narrow streight of a few leagues called BELLE-ISLE. This he has undertaken to prove in a part of his work not yet published" (translated as Mallet, *Northern Antiquities*, vol. 1, 303). This was a curious assertion on two counts. Kalm's cited second volume was not officially published until 1756, the year after Mallet's assertion appeared, and Mallet's paraphrase went far beyond what Kalm actually wrote about Vinland on the cited page. While Kalm in volume 2 of *En Resa til Norra America* did

promise he would return to the subject of Vinland's location, Kalm only ventured in the third volume that "vine land" actually referred to fields of wild wheat or grass (translated as Kalm, *Travels*, vol. 3, 210–11). For the discovery of the L'Anse Aux Meadows site, see Ingstad, *Westward to Vineland*.

18. Pennant, *Arctic Zoology*, vol. 1, clxv.

19. Mallet, *Northern Antiquities*, vol. 1, 305. Kolodny notes the influence of Mallet on speculations about Vinland in *In Search of First Contact*, 113–14.

20. McManis in "Traditions of Vinland" reviews the scholarly debates over the sagas' reliability. The introduction to Magnusson and Pálsson's *Vinland Sagas* also reviews the history of the sagas as oral traditions, documents, and works of literature. Chapter 2, "Contact and Conflict," of Kolodny's *In Search of First Contact* is an interpretive reading of the sagas that applies literary criticism to their structure and seeks historicity in the accounts of meetings with Indigenous peoples. For additional overviews of the sagas and related Icelandic sources, see Seaver, *Frozen Echo*, 14–43; Cumming et al., *Discovery of North America*, 45–51; Macpherson, "Pre-Columbian Discoveries," 24–61; and Gisli Sigurdsson, "Introduction to the Vinland Sagas," 218–21, in Fitzhugh and Ward, ed., *Vikings*. Magnusson and Pálsson include a chronological table of saga events in *Vinland Sagas*, 119. I have relied on Magnusson and Pálsson for orthography of names of individuals and places and their English equivalents. For a discussion of *skroellings* or *skraelings*, see Seaver, " 'Pygmies' of the Far North."

21. See Seaver, *Frozen Echo*, 15, for the name Thorfinn Thordsson *karlsefni*.

22. See Jones, "Historical Evidence;" McManis, "Traditions of Vinland."

23. Lowenthal, "G. P. Marsh," 44–45. Kolodny addresses Wheaton in *In Search of First Contact*, 114–16.

24. For Wheaton's career, see William Beach Lawrence, "Introductory Remarks by the Editor," in Wheaton, *Elements of International Law*. For his writings, see Benson, "Henry Wheaton's Writings on Scandinavia."

25. MHS, *Proceedings*, vol. 1, 418.

26. Wheaton was born in Providence in 1785, graduated there from Brown in 1802, and practiced law in the city from 1806 to 1813. Rafn's letter to the RIHS was "mislaid" by its secretary, Thomas H. Webb, but it is referenced in the response by Webb reproduced in Rafn, ed., *Antiquitates Americanae*, 356–61. For Webb's recollection, see Webb, "February Meeting," 189.

27. Wheaton, "Art. VIII," 481.

28. Rafn, *Report*, vi–viii.

29. Wheaton, *History of the Northmen*, 22–31.

30. For the missteps and hoaxes in efforts to prove a Norse presence in North America, beginning with *Antiquitates Americanae*, see Birgitta Linderoth Wallace and William W. Fitzhugh, "Stumbles and Pitfalls in the Search for Viking America," 374–84, in Fitzhugh and Ward, ed., *Vikings*. See also chapter 3, "Anglo-America's Viking Heritage," in Kolodny, *In Search of First Contact*, as well as Krueger, *Myths of the Rune Stone*, passim.

31. John Russell Bartlett would recall for the RIHS that he and Webb initiated contact with Rafn after they saw a circular letter by Rafn in newspapers in 1829. Webb wrote Rafn and told him about Dighton Rock. Rafn made a "prompt" reply, and an RIHS committee consisting of Webb, Bartlett, and Greene then took up the matter. Bartlett's recollection is flawed and compressed, as this chapter makes clear. Delabarre's use of RIHS correspondence indicates that Rafn initiated contact with the society in 1829, and the RIHS committee was not formed until 1833. As stated, I believe Rafn may have been directed toward the RIHS for assistance by Wheaton in Copenhagen. See RIHS, *Proceedings 1872–73*, 70–76, for the society's dealings with Rafn, including Bartlett's recollection.

32. Rafn, ed., *Antiquitates Americanae* (356–72) transcribes four letters from Webb to Rafn between September 22, 1830, and October 31, 1835. The Rafn letters to Webb, nineteen in all (counting the ones written at different dates within the same letter), range from May 30, 1833, to April 6, 1843, and are in the Carl C. Rafn Papers.

33. Quincy, "Memoir," 337–38.

34. For the Franklin Society, see *Encyclopedia Brunonia*, http://www.brown.edu/Administration /News_Bureau/Databases/Encyclopedia/search.php?serial=F0260. Webb's contributions to the *American Journal of Science and Arts* included "Notice of Fluor Spar" and "New Localities of Tourmalines and Tale," 7 (1824): 54–55, and "Notices of Miscellaneous Localities of Minerals," coauthored in part with Steuben Taylor, 8, no. 2 (August 1824): 225–29. For Webb's essential biography, see Quincy, "Memoir."

35. A lawyer who served as attorney general of Rhode Island, Greene was also a poet and a leading figure in local literary circles. Greene, like Webb, was a graduate of Brown. See "Leaves of an Hour: The Harris Collection: The Original Collectors: Albert Gorton Greene," http://www .brown.edu/Facilities/University_Library/exhibits/leaves/harrearly.html.

36. For Bartlett's biography, see "Historical Note," http://www.rihs.org/mssinv/Mss286.htm, and "About John Russell Bartlett," http://www.brown.edu/Facilities/John_Carter_Brown _Library/jrb/about.html. See also "John Russell Bartlett," in Bartlett, *Genealogy*, 128–33. Note that no descent is noted from Josiah Bartlett, grand warden of the Massachusetts Grand Lodge mentioned in chapter 4. The bulk of the John Russell Bartlett Papers is devoted to materials after 1848. None of the correspondence addresses events relating to *Antiquitates Americanae.*

37. Thomas H. Webb to John Ordronaux, May 27, 1854, DRC.

38. Thomas H. Webb to Carl C. Rafn, September 22, 1830, quoted in Rafn, ed., *Antiquitates Americanae*, 356.

39. Ibid.

40. Ibid.

41. Ibid., 358.

42. Ibid., 356.

43. Thomas H. Webb to Carl C. Rafn, September 22, 1830, in ibid., 361.

44. Wheaton, *History*, 24.

45. The idea dated back to Thormoder Thorfaeus's proposal in *Historia Winlandiae Antique* (1705) that the day mentioned was eight hours long, which led Thorfaeus to argue that Vinland aligned with Newfoundland. Wheaton's observation at least in part reflected the nine-hour day determined by Gerhard Schöning in *Historia Regum Norvegicorum* (1777), which indicated a more southern location for Vinland. See Bancroft, *History of the United States*, vol. 1, 5–6.

46. The astronomical evidence would be discussed in Rafn, ed., *Antiquitates Americanae*, 435–38, and explained by Finn Magnussén in "On the Ancient Scandinavians' Division of the Times of Day." Rafn revisited the issue in "Astronomical Evidence."

47. Delabarre, "Recent History," 292.

48. Rafn's May 1834 letter is referenced by Webb in his response of November 30, 1834, which includes Rafn's questions. See Rafn, ed., *Antiquitates Americanae*, 361–72. Delabarre adds Rafn's assertion of confidence that he could decipher the rock's inscription in "Recent History," 292.

49. The Webb letter drafted November 30, 1834, was sent (along with the new drawings) to Rafn on or soon after January 19, 1835. That package included copies of the drawings by Kendall of 1807, Winthrop of 1788, Sewall of 1768, and Danforth of 1680. See Delabarre, "Recent History," 292–93.

50. Rafn, ed., *Antiquitates Americanae*, 372.

51. Edward Everett, in his review of *Antiquitates Americanae*, observed: "We have seen no proof that there is any such Indian word as Mountaup; and if there be, it lies a wide way off from Hop." Everett, "Art. IX." No such evidence seems to exist. I wonder if this *haup* was a corruption of the German *haupt*, whose meanings include head, or leader, and peak, all of which would have been consistent with Metacom's main residence on a prominent rise of land. For the Ethiopian inscription, see Morse, *American Universal Geography*, 332.

52. Thomas H. Webb to Carl C. Rafn, September 22, 1830, quoted in Rafn, ed., *Antiquitates Americanae*, 356.

53. For Kendall's investigation, see *Travels*, vol. 3, 229–35.

54. Carl C. Rafn to Thomas H. Webb, April 16, 1835, Carl C. Rafn Papers.

55. Morse, *American Universal Geography*, 344.

56. Rafn, *America Discovered*, 19. Helge Ingstad would concur: "*Hop* means a bay or lake, with a narrow channel or river through which the tide rises and falls." *Westward to Vinland*, 55.

57. Rafn, ed., *Antiquitates Americanae*, 370.

58. Rafn, *America Discovered*, 19–20.

59. Birgitta Linderoth Wallace addresses the three settlement sites in "An Archaeologist's Interpretation of the *Vinland Sagas*," 225–31, in Fitzhugh and Ward, ed., *Vikings*.

60. Magnusson and Pálsson concluded from their translation of the passage ("on the shortest day of the year, the sun was already up by 9 a.m., and did not set until after 3 p.m.") that Vinland could have been located anywhere between latitudes 40 and 50 north, or between the Gulf of St. Lawrence and New Jersey (*Vinland Sagas*, 56). Helge Ingstad recounted nine different efforts to locate Vinland using this phrase. The results ranged from 31 north (southern Georgia) to 55 north (the Labrador coast above Hamilton Inlet). Ingstad, *Westward to Vinland*, 77–78.

61. Rafn, ed., *Antiquitates Americanae*, 378–96.

62. Wahlgren, *The Kensington Stone*, 158.

63. Delabarre reviews Magnussén's decipherment in "Recent History," 305–12.

64. See Rafn, ed., *Antiquitates Americanae*, 396–405, and Delabarre, "Recent History," 310.

65. Dammartin based his analysis on the Gébelin drawing. Delabarre addressed Dammartin's theory in "Middle Period," 131–46. Quotation from Dammartin translated by Delabarre, 132.

66. Thomas H. Webb to John Ordronaux, May 27, 1854, DRC.

67. Delabarre, "Recent History," 312.

68. Beamish, *Discovery of America*, 122.

69. Chichester, "Beamish."

70. Magnusson and Pálsson, *Vinland Sagas*, 103.

71. Ibid.

72. See Macpherson, "Pre-Columbian Discoveries," 52, for the Mársson voyage tale.

73. Rafn summarized the evidence for Hvítramannaland in *America Discovered*, 23–24; quotation, 24.

74. Johnston, "Account," 273.

75. John Witthoft and William A. Hunter paid no regard to Johnston or to an oral tradition of a recent arrival from Florida in "Seventeenth-Century Origins of the Shawnee." They concluded, based on eighteenth-century sources, "the Shawnee were indigenes of the Ohio and are to be equated with at least a part of the Fort Ancient archaeological culture" (42). Fort Ancient was a late expression of the mound-building cultures that may have persisted in the Ohio Valley until about 1750. Stephen Warren in *World the Shawnees Made* presents similar evidence that the Shawnee emerged from the Fort Ancient culture of the Ohio Valley.

76. See De Costa, *Pre-Columbian Discovery*, 86–88, for an early skeptical view of Hvítraman-naland in *Antiquitates Americanae*. Ingstad in *Westward to Vinland* stated the late nineteenth-century Norwegian historian Gustav Storm "has decisively shown that this is a purely legendary account that has nothing to do with Vinland" (29). Nansen asserted that Hvítramannaland was "an Irish mythical country," but complicated the case against its historicity by arguing that Vin-land was mythical as well (*In Northern Mists*, vol. 1, 354). Magnusson and Pálsson in their transla-tion of Eirik the Red's Saga note: "The concept of a country of White men (Albania-land) occurs in Icelandic versions of medieval European works of learning and was associated with Asia, somewhere to the north of India" (*Vinland Sagas*, 103). They suggest a connection between the story of Hvítramannaland and the *Tír na bhFear bhFionn* (Land of the White Men) of Irish legend (ibid.). Seaver in *Maps, Myths, and Men* advises that Hvítramannaland "probably has more in common with Irish tales than with actual Norse peregrinations at any time in history" (43). "White Men's Land" in an Irish tradition also could have been Iceland, which is believed to have been visited by Irish hermits prior to Norse colonization. See Orri Vesteinsson, "The Ar-chaeology of Landnám," 164–65, in Fitzhugh and Ward, ed., *Vikings*.

77. See, for example, William Brownell Goodwin, *The Ruins of Great Ireland in New England* (Boston: Meador, 1946). Seaver in *Maps, Myths, and Men* notes that Luka Jelic (who she consid-ered a candidate for the forgery of Yale's Vinland map) believed Hvítramannaland was part of a medieval Greenland Norse colonization of North America that stretched from Labrador to Florida (263). Frederick Pohl was adamant that the Hvítramannaland stories proved the Norse "reached North America, and when they got there they found that Irishmen had arrived there before them." Pohl, *Atlantic Crossings before Columbus*, 44. See also Kolodny, *In Search of First Contact*, 121–31, for William Gilmore Simms's efforts in 1841 to leverage *Antiquitates Americanae* and Hvítramannaland to assert an a priori white claim to the southern United States.

78. Carl C. Rafn to Thomas H. Webb, April 16, 1835, Carl C. Rafn Papers.

79. Carl C. Rafn to Thomas H. Webb, June 20, 1835, Carl C. Rafn Papers.

80. Webb, "February Meeting," 190.

81. Ibid., 198–99.

82. Carl C. Rafn to Thomas H. Webb, April 26, 1839, Carl C. Rafn Papers.

83. Carl C. Rafn to Thomas H. Webb, April 21, 1840, Carl C. Rafn Papers.

84. Carl C. Rafn to Thomas H. Webb, April 26, 1839, Carl C. Rafn Papers.

85. See Simmons, *Spirit of the New England Tribes*, 172–234, for variations on the Maushop and Squant tradition, including the Freeman account (178).

86. See Kolodny for an explanation of this episode in Eirik the Red's Saga, *In Search of First Contact*, 84–85.

87. Carl C. Rafn to Thomas H. Webb, April 21, 1840, Carl C. Rafn Papers.

88. Carl C. Rafn to Thomas H. Webb, October 22, 1841, Carl C. Rafn Papers.

89. Wallace, "Literature," 10.

90. See Carl C. Rafn to Thomas H. Webb, April 21, 1840; May 4, 1840; January 1, 1841; and October 22, 1841, Carl C. Rafn Papers.

91. Webb, "February Meeting," 199.

92. Ibid., 193–98.

93. Webb, in Webb and Rafn, "Account of an Ancient Structure," 361.

94. Brooks, *Controversy Touching the Old Stone Mill*.

95. For debunkings of Newport mill misinterpretations, see William S. Godfrey, "The Archaeology of the Old Stone Mill in Newport, Rhode Island," *American Antiquity* 17, no. 2 (Oc-tober 1951): 120–29; and "Vikings in America: Theory and Evidence," *American Anthropologist*

n.s. 57, no. 1, pt. 1 (February 1955): 35–43. In its latest pseudohistorical incarnations, the tower is either a Chinese pagoda lighthouse, as per Gavin Menzies in *1421: The Year the Chinese Discovered the World* (London: Bantam, 2002)—a book that also turns Dighton Rock into a Chinese inscription—or a relic of Knights Templar, as argued by Scott F. Wolter in *The Hooked X: Key to the Secret History of North America* (St. Cloud, MN: North Star Press, 2009) and *Akhenaten to the Founding Fathers: The Mysteries of the Hooked X* (St. Cloud, MN: North Star Press, 2013). Friends of Dighton Rock Museum has hosted public talks by Templar enthusiast David S. Brody, for example, "Knights Templar and the Exploration of America Before Columbus," April 10, 2016. See https://www.facebook.com/FriendsOfDightonRockMuseum/.

96. Sparks, "Antiquities of North America."

97. See Mayer, *Memoir of Jared Sparks*, for essential biographical details, as well as Cappon, "Jared Sparks," and Story, "Harvard and the Boston Brahmins," 104.

98. Kolodny remarks on the relationship between American enthusiasms for *Antiquitates Americanae* and forced removals of the Seminole and Cherokee, *In Search of First Contact*, 128–29. See also her discussion of Gothic race politics in antebellum America, 131–50.

99. See Seeman, *Death in the New World*, 170–71, for such burials.

100. Sparks, "Antiquities of North America."

101. Ibid.

102. Ibid.

103. Ibid.

104. These items would enter the collection of the Ethnographiske Museum in Copenhagen; two brass-covered wood tubes were then acquired by Dr. Samuel Kneeland in Copenhagen and presented to Harvard's Peabody Museum in 1886. See Willoughby, *Antiquities of the New England Indians*, 232–44, for the Fall River artifacts and similar finds.

105. Rafn, in Webb and Rafn, "Accounts of a Discovery," 110.

106. Calloway, *One Vast Winter Count*, 141; Winship, *Coronado Expedition*, 509.

107. See Gabriel Archer's "Account of Captain Bartholomew Gosnold's Voyage to 'North Virginia' in 1602," in Quinn and Quinn, *English New England Voyages*, 122. John Brereton's *A Briefe and True Relation* (1602) on the Gosnold voyage offered an extensive inventory of Indigenous copper items, including arrowheads and chains that sound precisely like the one recovered from the Fall River burial. In Quinn and Quinn, *The English New England Voyages*, 155–56.

108. "Portrait of an Indian Chief (Possibly Wingina)," in Sloan, *New World*, 138–39.

109. Sparks, "Antiquities of North America."

110. Rafn, in Webb and Rafn, "Accounts of a Discovery," 116.

111. Ibid.

112. Henry W. Longfellow to Samuel Ward, December 1, 1840, quoted by White, "Longfellow's Interest," 75.

113. Longfellow, "The Skeleton in Armor," in *Ballads and Other Poems*, 29–41.

114. For the 1671 document, see Hurd, *History of Bristol County*, 740.

Chapter Seven

1. According to A. Irving Hallowell, Schoolcraft's reputation "as an authority on American Indian myths, legends, and tales was established" by *Algic Researches*. Hallowell and Schoolcraft, "Concordance of Ojibwa Narratives," 139.

2. Shingwauk is sometimes referred to as Shingwaukonse (The Little White Pine). Schoolcraft in volume 1 of *Historical and Statistical Information* called him both Chinguak and

Shingwaukönse. Shingwauk's descendants, Fred Pine and Dan Pine, explained to Thor Conway that he had a personal shamanic name, Sah-Kah-Odjew-Wahg-Sah, meaning "Sun Rising over the Mountain," that conveyed to him the power of the moment of sunrise. He would be called Shingwauk from noon to early evening, and then the diminutive Shingwaukonse from early evening to sunset to indicate the sun's waning power. Conway, *Spirits on Stone*, 91–94; Chute, *Legacy of Shingwaukonse*, 22–24.

3. For Schoolcraft's full discussion of Dighton Rock and Shingwauk's interpretation, see *Historical and Statistical Information*, vol. 1, 108–20. For the life of Shingwauk(onse) up to his interpretation of Dighton Rock, see Chute, *Legacy of Shingwaukonse*, 1–90.

4. For Schoolcraft's early life in upstate New York, see Bremer, *Indian Agent and Wilderness Scholar*, 4–15.

5. Wilcox and Fowler, "Beginnings of Anthropological Archaeology," 129.

6. Cass, "Art. III," 94. The unsigned article is attributed to Cass by Bieder in *Science Encounters the Indian*, 154. See Dippie, *Vanishing American*, 35–36, for Cass's early career.

7. Cass, "Art. III," 107.

8. Bremer, *Indian Agent and Wilderness Scholar*, 190.

9. Schoolcraft, *Narrative Journal*, 92.

10. Ibid., 186.

11. Ibid., 211–12.

12. Ibid., 166.

13. Ibid., 212–13.

14. Ibid., 282.

15. Examples of pictographs had been published as early as 1724 by Lafitau, who included an illustration of dendroglyphs in *Moeurs*, vol. 3, 38. Bray's "Observations" appeared in *Archaeologia* in 1782. Fred E. Coy Jr. shows that dendroglyphs were well known in eighteenth-century America, in "Dendroglyphs of the Eastern Woodlands," 3–16, in Diaz-Granados and Duncan, ed., *Rock-Art of Eastern North America*. As noted in chapter 4, George Washington was familiar with them. See also Bohaker, "Indigenous Histories," for a discussion of "non-alphabetic semiotic systems."

16. Bremer, *Indian Agent and Wilderness Scholar*, 96–97.

17. Jameson, *Winter Studies and Summer Rambles in Canada*, 394.

18. For Schoolcraft's indebtedness to his wife Jane and her family, see Mumford, "Mixed-Race Identity," 12–13. Bieder notes that linguist Peter Stephen Du Ponceau was impressed with Schoolcraft's apparent expertise in Chippewa in his *Narrative* of 1834, assuming he had been fluent for a long time. But as an Indian agent and superintendent he always employed interpreters, and relied on his wife Jane and brother-in-law, George Johnston, for vocabulary (Bieder, *Science Encounters the Indian*, 158).

19. Bremer, *Indian Agent and Wilderness Scholar*, 101.

20. Mumford, "Mixed-Race Identity," 19.

21. Ibid., 19–20.

22. Schoolcraft may be a textbook example of the "overwhelming majority of Whites who remained orthodox Christians," for whom Enlightenment and post-Enlightenment ideas about humanity "had to be grafted onto or reconciled with the traditional scriptural history or be rejected," according to Berkhofer. "Degeneration therefore remained a powerful analytical tool in White discussion of the Indian well into the nineteenth century for the orthodox, scholar and non-scholar alike, even for those persons called the founders of modern American ethnography." Berkhofer, *White Man's Indian*, 37–38.

23. Schoolcraft, "Art. II. *Archaeologia Americana*." Although unsigned, the style is unmistakably Schoolcraft's, and the reviewer's use of the term "Algic" can only point to Schoolcraft.

24. Schoolcraft, "Art. II. *Archaeologia Americana*," 35.

25. Schoolcraft, "*La Découverte des Sources du Mississippi*," 104.

26. For Du Ponceau, see "Report of the Historical and Literary Committee to the American Philosophical Society. Read, 9th January, 1818," quoted by Haas, "Grammar or Lexicon?" 239–40.

27. Peter Stephen Du Ponceau to Edwin James, November 10, 1834, quoted in Bremer, *Indian Agent and Wilderness Scholar*, 237–38.

28. Schoolcraft, "Art. II. *Archaeologia Americana*," 39.

29. Ibid., 44.

30. Schoolcraft, *Algic Researches*, vol. 1, 12–13.

31. Ibid., vol. 1, 13.

32. Ibid.

33. Rafinesque, *American Nations*, 24.

34. Schoolcraft, *Narrative Journal*, 309–10.

35. The first edition of the standard Javanese-Dutch dictionary in 1847 defined *abang* as "red." (Ricklefs, "The Birth of the Abangan," 36–37). An 1858 missionary report mentioned the " 'red population' (*bangsa abangan*)" (40).

36. Brinton, *Myths of the New World*, 27.

37. Vallancey, *Grammar*, iv.

38. Buffon, *Histoire naturelle*, vol. 3, 378–79. Strahlenberg, *Historico-Geographical Description*, 4.

39. Schoolcraft, *Algic Researches*, vol. 1, 16–17.

40. Ibid., vol. 1, 25.

41. Kohl, *Kitchi-Gami*, 134.

42. Schoolcraft, *Algic Researches*, vol. 1, 25–26.

43. Ibid., vol. 1, 21.

44. Ibid., vol. 1, 21–22.

45. Ibid., vol. 1, 22.

46. Mott, *History of American Magazines*, vol. 1, 372.

47. Edward Everett, "Art. IX. *Antiquitates Americanae*." Alexander H. Everett, "The Discovery of America by the Northmen" and "The Discovery of America by the Northmen, Article Second." Folsom, "Article IV. *Antiquitates Americanae*."

48. Thomas H. Webb to John Ordronaux, May 27, 1854, DRC.

49. Schoolcraft, "Article IX," 435.

50. Ibid., 440–41.

51. Ibid., 441.

52. Everett, "Art. IX. *Antiquitates Americanae*," 197–98.

53. "[Article 2—No Title], A Theory Knocked in the Head," *New-York Mirror*, December 1, 1838, 183.

54. All quotes from George Catlin, "Letters from Correspondents. The Dighton Rock," *New-York Mirror*, December 29, 1838, 213.

55. Catlin did not report on the method used to make the markings in the especially hard quartzite at the pipestone quarries, but archaeologists in the 1970s determined the makers of glyphs at Jeffers Petroglyphs, seventy miles west, used the common strategy of pecking or percussion with another hard stone. Clouse, "Pattern and Function," 112. At the Peterborough Petroglyphs, Joan and Romas Vastokas recovered a number of gneiss hammerstones and abraders used to peck and grind the images into the crystalline limestone. Vastokas and Vastokas, *Sacred*

Art of the Algonkians, 17–18. I am not aware of any study on the methodology at Dighton Rock, but the same strategy would have been used.

56. My initial suspicion was that Catlin, while referring to the sacred quarries, was also describing the nearby Jeffers Petroglyphs, as he described far more glyphs than are known today (104) at Pipestone National Monument. Catlin described seeing thousands of carved as well as painted images in his exhibition catalog material. See the text in Thomas Donaldson's report on the George Catlin Indian Gallery, which formed part 5 of the *Annual Report of the Board of Regents of the Smithsonian Institution . . . to July, 1885, Part 2* (Washington: Government Printing Office, 1886), 248–53. However, Tom Sanders, site manager at Jeffers Petroglyphs, informed me: "I believe that Catlin was talking about the petroglyphs at the monument not those at Jeffers" (personal communication, July 21, 2016). For the Jeffers Petroglyphs, see Clouse, "Pattern and Function," and Sanders, "Jeffers Petroglyphs," http://sites.mnhs.org/historic-sites/sites/sites .mnhs.org.historic-sites/files/docs_pdfs/Jeffers-Petroglyphs- history.pdf.

57. Thomas H. Webb recalled Smith in "February Meeting," 188.

58. Smith, *Northmen in New England*, 311–12.

59. Ibid., 311–12, footnote.

60. Ibid., 311–12.

61. Schoolcraft, "Article IX," 442–43.

62. Ibid., 444.

63. Ibid.

64. Ibid., 444–45.

65. Ibid., 445.

66. Ibid., 446.

67. Ibid., 447.

68. Ibid., 446–47.

69. I am uncertain of Schoolcraft's "Shingaba." He may have misunderstood *masinibiigan* (picture) or *masinitchigan* (image). See Baraga, *Dictionary of the Otchipwe language*, 525, 570. Schoolcraft may have been transposing to the Lac Travers anecdote the name of Shin-ga-ba-was-sin, the Ojibwa leader at the Sault Ste. Marie rapids until 1828, whose name Schoolcraft translated as "The Image Stone." See Schoolcraft, *Historical and Statistical Information*, vol. 1, 357. See also Chute's description of "Shingabaw'osin" in *Legacy of Shingwaukonse*, 13.

70. Schoolcraft, *Narrative of an Expedition*, 46.

71. See the translation of stone as *assin* by Baraga, *Dictionary of the Otchipwe language*, 619. Cuoq in *Lexique de la langue algonquine* translated stone as *asin*, and further noted *asin* in *Asinib-wan* (Assiniboine), the name given the Stone Sioux, with *Bwan* denoting the Sioux (62, 77).

72. Schoolcraft, "Article IX," 441.

73. Chute, *Legacy of Shingwaukonse*, 20. Shingwauk had an unknown European father—his descendant, Fred Pine Sr., would assert that Shingwauk's father was no less than the son of Napoleon Bonaparte, with another tradition recorded by Kohl making him a British military officer of Scottish birth. Chute, *Legacy of Shingwaukonse*, 21; Kohl, *Kitchi-Gami*, 374.

74. Chute, *Legacy of Shingwaukonse*, 11. See also Schoolcraft's description of him in *Historical and Statistical Description*, vol. 1, 112.

75. Chute, *Legacy of Shingwaukonse*, 9.

76. Ruggle, "McMurray, William."

77. Chute, *Legacy of Shingwaukonse*, 75–79.

78. Schoolcraft, *Historical and Statistical Information*, vol. 1, 112.

79. Ibid.

80. Ibid., vol. 1, 113.

81. Ibid., vol. 1, 114–17.

82. Ibid., vol. 1, 115.

83. Ibid., vol. 1, 339.

84. Woodcock, "Tanner, John."

85. Schoolcraft, *Historical and Statistical Information*, vol. 1, 304.

86. Ibid., vol. 1, 118.

87. Ibid., vol. 1, 406–8.

88. For the "authenticity" of Schoolcraft's legends, and scholarly tensions between ethnography and literature, see Hallowell and Schoolcraft, "Concordance of Ojibwa Narratives"; Hegeman, "Native American 'Texts' and the Problem of Authenticity"; Bauman, "Nationalization and Internationalization of Folklore"; and Clements, "Schoolcraft as Textmaker."

Chapter Eight

1. Born in Stockbridge, Massachusetts, in 1799, Marshall Spring Bidwell was raised in Upper Canada, and as a lawyer and a member of the Reformers was embroiled in the controversies of representative government. He fled to the United States in 1837 after William Lyon Mackenzie's attempted insurrection. He became a leading lawyer in New York, lectured at Columbia's law school, and received a doctorate of laws from Yale in 1858. Craig, "Bidwell, Marshall Spring."

2. See "Message of the President of the United States," in Schoolcraft, *Historical and Statistical Information*, vol. 1, iii.

3. "Due to his own declining health, his lack of system, and the rapid publication schedule mandated by Congress, he produced a study that was too disorganized to be of much use to either scholars or administrators. It won him fame but little respect." Mumford, "Mixed-Race Identity," 21. Dippie notes the volumes cost the federal government about $100,000 and "were untidy compilations of Indian miscellanea flawed by Schoolcraft's own enthusiastically eclectic approach to ethnology." Dippie, *Vanishing American*, 74.

4. For Schoolcraft's marriage to Howard, see Bremer, *Indian Agent and Wilderness Scholar*, 284–91.

5. For Schoolcraft's declining health, see ibid., 297–98. His second wife, Mary Howard, in her dedication to *Black Gauntlet* (1860), wrote: "For twelve years that you have been imprisoned at home by a stroke of paralysis" (ix).

6. Bremer, *Indian Agent and Wilderness Scholar*, 249.

7. Ibid., 253–56.

8. "Historical Note," John Russell Bartlett Papers, http://www.rihs.org/mssinv/Mss286.htm. Wilcox and Fowler, "Beginnings of Anthropological Archaeology," 134. Bieder, *Science Encounters the Indian*, 43–44. For Schoolcraft's role in founding the AES, see Osborn and Osborn, "Schoolcraft and the American Ethnological Society."

9. For officers of the NYHS, see Kelby, *New-York Historical Society*, 83–91.

10. Carl C. Rafn to Thomas H. Webb, October 22, 1841, Carl C. Rafn Papers.

11. John Russell Bartlett, "Observations," 160.

12. Everett, "Art. IX. *Antiquitates Americanae*," 197–98.

13. RIHS, *Proceedings, 1872–3*, 75.

14. Schoolcraft is among the members listed at the front of volume 2 of *Mémoires*, covering 1840 to 1844, with Detroit given as his location. He thus joined around the time he wrote the 1839 review.

15. Fellows of the society's American section, listed in the *Mémoires* of 1844, included Peter Stephen Du Ponceau, president of the American Philosophical Society; John Howland, president of RIHS; Henry W. Longfellow of Harvard; philologist John Pickering; Peter G. Stuyvesant, president of NYHS; and Henry Wheaton, then the U.S. "minister plenipotentiary" in Berlin.

16. Chapin, "Article XI," 191.

17. For Schoolcraft's initial interpretation and Chapin's rejoinder, see also Kolodny in *In Search of First Contact*, 121–25.

18. Chapin, "Article XI," 191.

19. Carl C. Rafn to Thomas H. Webb, October 22, 1841, Carl C. Rafn Papers.

20. For an overview of the Grave Creek fraud, see Williams, *Fantastic Archaeology*, 80–87.

21. Schoolcraft and Rafn, "Brief Notices," 127.

22. Schoolcraft, "Observations," 370.

23. Ibid., 418.

24. Ibid., 415.

25. Ibid., 416.

26. Ibid.

27. For Schoolcraft's honorary membership, see Bremer, *Indian Agent and Wilderness Scholar*, 253.

28. Schoolcraft, "Observations," 418.

29. Schoolcraft, *Historical and Statistical Information*, vol. 1, 62.

30. Ibid.

31. Schoolcraft, *Historical and Statistical Information*, vol. 1, 105.

32. Barnhart, "Iroquois as Mound Builders," 127.

33. Ibid., 128.

34. Conn, *History's Shadow*, 124.

35. Squier and Davis, *Ancient Monuments*, 298.

36. Ibid., 300.

37. Ibid., 242.

38. Ibid., 301.

39. See, for example, Morton, *An Inquiry*. See Fabian, *The Skull Collectors*, passim, for Morton and his fellow skull measurers. Redman summarizes and contextualizes Morton in *Bone Rooms*, 23–26.

40. Bartlett, *Progress of Ethnology*, 15.

41. Ibid., 13–14. Bartlett cited Eugene Vail, *Notice sur les Indiens de l'Amérique du Nord* (Paris, 1840), stating that Vail asked the French traveler Edme-François Jomard for his opinion on the Grave Creek stone in 1839, and he replied "they were of the same character with the inscriptions found by Major Denham in the interior of Africa, as well as in Algiers and Tunis" (*Progress of Ethnology*, 14). Bartlett also cited a paper forwarded to him by Jomard (cited by Bartlett as "Second Note sur une pierre gravée dans un ancien tumulus Américaine, et a cette occasion, sur l'idiome Libyen"), delivered before the Académie royale des inscriptions et belles-lettres in Paris in 1845, in which Jomard "hints at their Phenician origin" (*Progress of Ethnology*, 14).

42. Bartlett, "On the Historical Evidence."

43. Bartlett, *Progress of Ethnology*, 15–17.

44. Henry S. Patterson, a professor of materia medica at the University of Pennsylvania and an ardent polygenist, wrote in 1854: "The men who, in the middle of the nineteenth century, can still find the ancestors of Mongolians and Americans among the sons of Japhet, or who talk about the curse of Canaan in connexion with Negroes, are plainly without the pale of contro-

versy, as they were beyond the reach of criticism." Henry S. Patterson, "Notice of the Life and Scientific Labors of the Late Samuel Geo. Morton, M.D.," in Nott and Gliddon, *Types of Mankind*, xliii.

45. Bieder, *Science Encounters the Indian*, 126, 137.

46. Ibid., 137.

47. Quoted by Bremer, *Indian Agent and Wilderness Scholar*, 218–19.

48. Schoolcraft, *Incentives*, 8.

49. NYHS, *Proceedings 1846*, 28.

50. Schoolcraft, *Historical and Statistical Information*, vol. 1, 129.

51. Ibid., vol. 1, 109.

52. Ibid., vol. 1, 120–24.

53. Ibid., vol. 1, 109.

54. Ibid., vol. 1, 108.

55. Ibid., vol. 1, 109.

56. Ibid., vol. 1, 109.

57. Ibid., vol. 1, 118.

58. Squier and Davis, *Ancient Monuments*, 274.

59. Squier, "Observations," 202.

60. Henry Rowe Schoolcraft to John Russell Bartlett, January 14, 1848, quoted by Bremer, *Indian Agent, Wilderness Scholar*, 315.

61. Bieder, *Science Encounters the Indian*, 139–40.

62. Ephraim George Squier, "Observations on the Memoir of Dr. Zestermann," in Zestermann, *Memoir*, 20–21. Squier mentions the recent publication of *The Serpent Symbol* on 23.

63. Schoolcraft, *Historical and Statistical Information*, vol. 4, 116.

64. Ibid., vol. 1, 334; vol. 2, vii, 86–88.

65. See Chute, *Legacy of Shingwaukonse*, 152–59.

66. Schoolcraft, *Historical and Statistical Information*, vol. 2, 88.

67. Ibid.

68. Ibid., vol. 3, 85.

69. Ibid.

70. Ibid., vol. 3, 86.

71. Bieder, *Science Encounters the Indian*, 206–7.

72. Schoolcraft, *Historical and Statistical Information*, vol. 3, 85–86.

73. Ibid., vol. 1, 343.

74. Kohl *Kitchi-Gami*, 87, 285.

75. Mallery, "Pictographs," 248–50.

76. See "Elements of the Pictorial System," in Schoolcraft, *Historical and Statistical Information*, vol. 1, 350–66.

77. Isaac Day, in "Rock Paintings," states that rock paintings are called "mzinabiginigan in our language" (86). Day does not include *kekeewin* or *kekeenowin* in his glossary (101).

78. I have quoted from the paper as published by Mallery as "Spurious Symbolism" in *The International Review*, January 1882.

79. Mallery, "Spurious Symbolism." Mallery was overly harsh, as "power," associated with medicine, remains a valid concept in interpretations of shamanic glyphs.

80. Mallery, "Pictographs," 20.

81. Ordronaux's letter does not survive, only Webb's responses, dated May 9 and May 27, 1854, DRC.

82. Emery, *History of Taunton*, 695–96. For Ordronaux and the founding of the OCHS, see also Emery, "Historical Sketch."

83. All quotations herein are from Thomas H. Webb to John Ordronaux, May 27, 1854, DRC.

84. Quincy, "Memoir," 337.

85. Ibid. Quincy further noted that Webb had married Lydia Athearn of Nantucket, and that he died in 1866 without leaving any children (337).

86. Bartlett, *Personal Narrative*, vol. 1, viii–ix.

87. See Sutherland, *Rock Paintings at Hueco Tanks State Historic Site*.

88. Bartlett, *Personal Narrative*, vol. 2, 195–96.

89. The art described is attributed to Mescalero Apache warriors and dated to A.D. 1500–1879. Sutherland, *Rock Paintings at Hueco Tanks State Historic Site*, 23.

90. Webb must have arranged a daguerreotype with one of the earliest practitioners in the United States, as the daguerreotype process had only been introduced in France in 1839. Possibly he used Albert Sands Southward and Joseph Pennell, who opened a studio in Cabotville (now Chicopee), Massachusetts, adjacent to Springfield, no later than May 1840, then moved their studio to Boston in April 1841. Newhall, *Daguerreotype in America*, 41–42.

91. Schoolcraft, *Historical and Statistical Information*, vol. 4, 119–20.

92. Ibid., vol. 4, 117, 118.

93. "Third Day," *New York Times*, August 6, 1860, 5.

94. For Wilson's popularizing of Worsaae's three-ages system, see Conn, *History's Shadow*, 137–38. Trigger notes that Wilson applied the three-age system in *The Archaeology and Prehistoric Annals of Scotland* (1851), the "first scientific synthesis of prehistoric times in the English language" (*History of Archaeological Thought*, 133).

95. For Wilson's struggles to reconcile science with religion, see Cook, *The Regenerators*, 14.

96. Wilson, *Prehistoric Man*, vol. 1, 9.

97. Ibid., vol. 1, 458.

98. Ibid., vol. 1, 11.

99. Nott and Gliddon, *Types of Mankind*, 279.

100. Wilson, *Prehistoric Man*, vol. 1, 4.

Chapter Nine

1. Delabarre, "Recent History," 411.

2. Ibid., 311.

3. Øverland, *Immigrant Minds*, 8.

4. Ibid., 19.

5. Oslund, *Iceland Imagined*, 56. For the history of the Althing, see Helgi Thorláksson, "The Icelandic Commonwealth Period," 175–85, in Fitzhugh and Ward, ed., *Vikings*.

6. For Bull's Norwegian colony, see Wilkinson, " 'New Norway,' " and Wilkinson, Currin, and Kennedy, "Ole Bull's New Norway."

7. Ole Bull, quoted in the Lock Haven *Democrat*, November 2, 1852. Transcribed by Wilkinson, "New Norway," 127–28.

8. Hall, "Dighton Writing Rock."

9. A damaged newspaper clipping from *The Republican* in October 1857 asserts this plan. DRC.

10. George M. Young address, October 1890, DRC.

11. According to Arnzen, the rock's shipment to Denmark was arranged with the frigate *Shielland*. "But in consequence of war breaking out between Denmark and Germany, it was found

necessary, as Prof. Rafn wrote, 'to countermand the orders, as we need our whole war strength at home.'" Arnzen, "Report," 94. Arnzen's recollections, however, are not credible. If any such arrangement and countermand occurred, Arnzen did not preserve the correspondence. Moreover, war did not break out between Denmark and Germany until 1864.

12. Carl C. Rafn to Niels Arnzen, August 16, 1859, and March 7, 1860; Frederick VII to Niels Arnzen, June 23, 1860. DRC.

13. Carl C. Rafn to Niels Arnzen, August 16, 1859; Frederick VII to Niels Arnzen, June 23, 1860, DRC.

14. Haven, "Archaeology of the United States," 107.

15. "Final Disposal of the Famous Dighton Rock," *New York Times*, August 3, 1861, 4.

16. Brinton, *Myths of the New World*, 10.

17. Lowell, *The Biglow Papers*, 2nd ser., 92

18. Ibid., 93.

19. Falnes, "New England Interest," 217–18.

20. Anderson, *America Not Discovered*, 4th ed., 20–23. See Kolodny, *In Search of First Contact*, 225–31, for a discussion of Anderson.

21. Elisha Shade to Rasmus B. Anderson, March 13, 1876, in Anderson, *America Not Discovered*, 4th ed., 23.

22. The best (indeed the only) scholarly biography of Thomas Gold Appleton is Hughes, "Thomas Appleton," http://uudb.org/articles/thomasappleton.html. See also his short biography, "Appleton, Thomas Gold," in Wilson and Fiske, ed., *Appleton's Cyclopaedia of American Biography*, 85.

23. Appleton's spouse was Fanny Longfellow. Henry Longfellow was a close friend of Bull, and wrote him into "The Tales of the Wayside Inn." Falnes, "New England Interest," 223.

24. Appleton, "Flowering of a Nation," 318.

25. Appleton, *Sheaf of Papers*, 263.

26. Appleton, "Flowering of a Nation," 318.

27. From a report on Ole Bull's address in the *Daily Advertiser*, quoted by his spouse Sara C. Bull in *Ole Bull*, 274.

28. "Norsemen Memorial" card, dated Boston, January 12, 1877, DRC. Anderson recounted details of the December 8, 1876, and January 12, 1877, meetings, in *America Not Discovered*, 2nd ed., 29–34. See also Bull, *Ole Bull*, 271–76, for an account of the December 8, 1876, concert, as reported in the *Daily Advertiser*.

29. Francis L. Hills to Niels Arnzen, December 28, 1876, DRC. The subcommittee under Hills consisted of Thomas G. Appleton, William Emerson Baker, E. N. Horsford, Edward E. Hale, Percival L. Everett, and Curtis Gillis.

30. Arnzen's recollections tend to be unreliable, although he quoted from an undated letter from Thomas G. Appleton, chair of the Boston memorial society, to the RSNA: "We shall protect it and see that it receives no injury and perhaps have it placed in our new Art Museum in Boston." Arnzen, "Report," 95–96. Arnzen also asserted that the Boston committee secured title to the rock from the RSNA in February 1877, but correspondence Arnzen left to the OCHS makes it clear no such thing happened.

31. "The Boston Archaeologists," *New York Times*, January 17, 1877, 4.

32. "Have We Any Norse Monuments?" *Boston Daily Globe*, January 25, 1877, 4.

33. RSNA to Niels Arnzen, July 22, 1877, DRC.

34. Ibid.

35. Brinton, *Myths of the New World*, 20. The observation remained intact in his 1896 revision.

36. Mallery, "Spurious Symbolism," 45.

37. Thomas, "Report," 17.

38. Deloria and Lytle, *Nations Within*, 25.

39. Lucien Blake to Niels Arnzen, March 19, 1879, DRC.

40. Hall, "Dighton Writing Rock," 99–100.

41. Arnzen, "Report," 97.

42. *Amherst College Biographical Record*, "2979. Delabarre, Edmund Burke," http://acbiorecord .yanco.com/1886.html#delabarre-eb. See also "Delabarre, Edmund B." in *Encyclopedia Brunoniana*. For the Delabarre mills, see Van Slyck, *New England Manufacturers and Manufactories*, 392–93; and Pease, *History of Conway*, 114.

43. See Harper, "First Psychological Laboratory," Table 1.

44. Carmichael, "Edmund Burke Delabarre," 406.

45. Ibid., 407.

46. See Delabarre and Popplestone, "Cross Cultural Contribution," in which Popplestone reconstructs some of Delabarre's findings from the Delabarre Papers at the Archives of the History of American Psychology, University of Akron.

47. See "Folder (AHAP): Notebooks," in Finding Aid, Delabarre Papers.

48. Quoted in "Delabarre, Edmund B.," in *Encyclopedia Brunoniana*.

49. Delabarre, "Report of the Brown-Harvard Expedition," 70.

50. The expedition in hindsight was noteworthy for the fact that it encountered Ramah chert deposits. Only in the 1970s would these deposits (including a source at the locale the expedition named Delabarre Bay) be identified as a quarry that through long-distance trade provided the raw material for lithic (stone) tools found in Maine, New York, Delaware, and even Florida. See M. E. Colleen Lazenby, "Prehistoric Sources of Chert in Northern Labrador: Field Work and Preliminary Analyses," *Arctic* 33, no. 3 (September 1980): 628–45.

51. Manuel Luciano da Silva dated the farm's purchase to July 16, 1910. "Dighton Rock, What Will Happen to You after I Die?" http://www.dightonrock.com/dightorockwhatwillhappentoyou .htm (accessed December 4, 2012).

52. Delabarre, "Rock-Inscriptions of New England," 81.

53. Donald G. Merrill, West Hartford, CT, to Walter A. Merrill, Taunton, MA, [n.d.] with an invoice September 25, 1913, from monument maker John B. Sullivan & Son of Taunton to OCHS for "cutting hole and setting sign on Dighton Rock." DRC

54. Delabarre, "Rock-Inscriptions of New England," 81.

55. Mallery, "Pictographs," 250.

56. For Horsford's Norse enthusiasms, see Kolodny, *In Search of First Contact*, 231–41.

57. Horsford, *Landfall of Leif Erikson*, 108.

58. Ibid., 109–10.

59. Ibid., 108.

60. Falnes, "New England Interest," 236.

61. See Lane, "Mapping the Mars Canal Mania."

62. Delabarre, "Middle Period," 70–71.

63. Archaeologist Kenneth Feder has called the approach to evidence of Erich von Däniken (*Chariots of the Gods?*) the "Inkblot Hypothesis." As he notes, "the picture seen in an inkblot is entirely dependent on the mind of the viewer. The images themselves are not necessarily anything in particular. They are whatever you make them out to be, whatever you want them to be." *Frauds, Myths, and Mysteries*, 221–22.

64. Da Vinci, *Leonardo Da Vinci's Notebooks*, 172–73.

65. Delabarre, "Middle Period," 71.

66. Delabarre, "Recent History," 311.

67. Delabarre, "Rock-Inscriptions of New England," 81.

68. Brinton, *Myths of the New World* (1905), 22.

69. Delabarre and Wilder, "Indian Corn-Hills in Massachusetts."

70. Delabarre, "Possible Pre-Algonkian Culture."

71. Delabarre, "Prehistoric Skeleton."

72. Brinton, *Myths of the New World* (1905), 17.

73. Delabarre, "Middle Period," 70.

74. Ibid., 118.

75. "Folder (AHAP): Notebooks. Can. Ind. (III) = IV, V, VI, Record Book 2, c Hyperaesthesia, Subject—Delabarre and Recorder—Manly, Kymograph, 12/10/—12/18/—, seven tables of reactions, tabs, heat suggestibility, stuttering, colors, sound." Finding Aid, Delabarre Papers.

76. Carmichael, "Edmund Burke Delabarre," 407.

77. Delabarre, "Recent History," 169.

78. Henry Harrisse produced important works on John and Sebastian Cabot and the brothers Gaspar and Miguel Corte-Real. *Les Corte-Real et leurs Voyages au Nouveau Monde* (Paris: Ernest Leroux, 1885) was followed by *Jean et Sébastien Cabot* (1882), published in translation as *John Cabot, the Discoverer of North America, and Sebastian His Son* (London: Benjamin Franklin Stevens, 1896). Samuel Edward Dawson published *The Discovery of America by John Cabot in 1497* (Ottawa: Royal Society of Canada, 1896). Charles Raymond Beazley published *John and Sebastian Cabot: The Discovery of North America* (London: T. Fisher Unwin, 1898). The Canadian government archivist Henry Percival Biggar published *The Precursors of Jacques Cartier 1497–1534: A Collection of Documents Relating to the Early History of the Dominion of Canada* (Publications of the Canadian Archives, No. 5. Ottawa: Government Printing Bureau, 1911).

79. Delabarre, "Recent History," 169.

80. At least some ships of Cabot's 1498 flotilla are now thought to have returned. See Douglas Hunter, "Rewriting History," *Canada's History* 90, no. 2 (April/May 2010): 19–25, 26. See also Evan Jones, "Alwyn Ruddock: 'John Cabot and the Discovery of America,'" *Historical Research* 81, no. 212 (May 2008): 224–54; and Evan T. Jones and Margaret M. Condon, *Cabot and Bristol's Age of Discovery* (Bristol: University of Bristol, 2016), chapter 6.

81. I have written about the Corte-Reals in Hunter, *Race to the New World*, 114–15. For documents related to the Corte-Real family and their voyages, see Harrisse, *Les Corte-Real*.

82. Harrisse, *Les Corte-Real*, 167. For transcriptions of Galvam and de Goes in the original Portuguese, see Appendices 34 and 35, 232–35.

83. Delabarre, "Dighton Rock," 63.

84. Delabarre, *Dighton Rock*, 170–71.

85. Delabarre, "Recent History," 415.

86. Ibid.

87. Delabarre, "Dighton Rock," plate 14.

88. Delabarre, *Dighton Rock*, 173, 181.

89. Delabarre, "Dighton Rock," 69. Delabarre offered a more elaborate version in 1928 in *Dighton Rock*, 177–78.

90. Delabarre, *Dighton Rock*, 179.

91. Ibid., 179–80.

92. Ibid., 173–74.

93. Ibid., 180.

94. See "Cabot, William B. (William Brooks)," http://socialarchive.iath.virginia.edu/ark:/99166/w6p27h3x.

95. Delabarre, *Dighton Rock*, 180; "Rock-Inscriptions of New England," 92.

96. Patterson, "Portuguese on the North-East Coast of America," 133.

97. Delabarre, "Recent History," 415.

98. Delabarre, *Dighton Rock*, 175.

99. See Verrazano, "Cellère Codex."

100. Delabarre, *Dighton Rock*, 175–76.

101. Delabarre, "Recent History," 418.

102. Delabarre, "Dighton Rock," 69–71.

103. Delabarre, *Dighton Rock*, 181.

104. Delabarre, "Middle Period," 118.

105. Ibid.

106. Delabarre, "Recent History," 428.

107. Delabarre, "Dighton Rock," 72.

108. Ibid. Delabarre summarized in similar terms in *Dighton Rock*, 185.

109. Delabarre, "Recent History," 426.

110. Ibid., 427.

111. Delabarre, "Rock-Inscriptions of New England," 89.

Chapter Ten

1. "A New Interpretation," 470.

2. Ibid., 471.

3. Ibid. The *Geographical Journal* had published a paper that included a photo of the Cão inscription, which had been discovered in 1906. See Thomas Lewis, "The Old Kingdom of Kongo," *Geographical Journal* 31, no. 6 (June 1908): 590–91. Harry J. Johnston determined it was made on Cão's second voyage to the Congo, in 1485, in *A History of the Colonization of Africa by Alien Races*, 2nd ed. (1913; repr. New York: Cambridge University Press, 2011), 80.

4. See Kolodny, *In Search of First Contact*, 329.

5. Notwithstanding Alice Beck Kehoe's radical proposal of its authenticity in *The Kensington Runestone: Approaching a Research Question Holistically* (Long Grove, IL: Waveland Press, 2005), runic experts and archaeologists have consistently declared it a fake. See Krueger, *Myths of the Rune Stone*.

6. For Holand's basic biography, see Hjalmar and Harold Holand Papers, "Biography/History," http://digital.library.wisc.edu/1711.dl/wiarchives.uw-whs-gb0060. Hjalmar Rued Holand, *The Kensington Runestone* (Menasha, WI, 1919); *The Kensington Stone: A Study in Pre-Columbian American History* (Menasha, WI, 1932). For Holand and related rune stone fascinations, see Krueger, *Myths of the Rune Stone*. "No impartial person will deny, at least, that this book reopens to debate a question which been generally regarded as a *res judicata*," James S. Cawley, a New Jersey historian, concluded an otherwise critical review of *The Kensington Stone* in *New England Quarterly* 6, no. 1 (March 1933): 217. Supporters of Holand included the Canadian arctic explorer and author Vilhjalmur Stefansson and Geoffrey Malcolm Gathorne-Hardy, librarian of the House of Lords in London. Gathorne-Hardy wrote supportive reviews in the *Geographical Journal*, *Antiquity*, *English Historical Review*, and *Scandinavian Review* and provided Holand a letter endorsing the stone's authenticity for *Westward to Vinland*.

7. For an overview of the American eugenics movement in the early twentieth century, see Stern, *Eugenic Nation*, 10–23.

8. Ibid., 67–68.

9. Feldman-Bianco, "Multiple Layers of Time and Space," 58.

10. Ibid.

11. Center for Policy Analysis, "Portuguese Americans," 2–3.

12. "A Savant Points the Way," *Sunday Standard* (New Bedford), August 29, 1926.

13. Clara Sharpe Hough, *Leif the Lucky: A Romantic Saga of the Sons of Erik the Red* (New York: The Century Co., c. 1926).

14. "Corte Real, um Portuguez, Foi o Primeiro Europeu que Se Estabeleceu na America do Norte" [Corte Real, a Portuguese, Was the First European to Settle in North America], *A Alvorada*, August 30, 1926. The newspaper's name was changed to *Diário de Notícias* in 1927.

15. Clara Sharpe Hough, "Estará' Gravado na Pedra de Dighton o Nome dum Navegador Portuguez?" [Is the Name of a Portuguese Navigator Engraved in Dighton Rock?], *A Alvorada*, September 3, 1926.

16. "Pregerinação a' Pedra Dighton," *A Alvorada*, September 9, 1926. "Pregerinação a' Pedra Dighton," *A Alvorada*, September 20, 1926.

17. "O dia de hontem Domingo, deve ficar assignalado, em letras de ouro, na Historia da Colónia Portugueza da Nova Inglaterra, pelo seu alto e grandioso significado." "A Peregrinação a Dighton Rock," *A Alvorada*, October 11, 1926.

18. Passenger Lists of Vessels Arriving at Providence, RI, 1911–43; Series: T1188; Roll: 24. Social Security Death Index; Number: 050-09-0239; Issue State: New York; Issue Date: Before 1951. Fernandes, "Of Outcasts and Ambassadors," 304.

19. "Lisbon May Honor Brown Professor," *Providence Journal*, November 19, 1926.

20. Delabarre, "A Rocha de Dighton e Miguel Côrte Real."

21. I have not been able to secure a marriage license to verify the date, and I presume the ceremony was outside the United States. A private listing for Abilio D. Águas on Ancestry.com lists his marriage to Maria Elizabeth Delabarre on November 28, 1936, but provides no supporting information.

22. Feldman-Bianco, "Multiple Layers of Time and Space," 52.

23. For more on the postwar struggle within the Portuguese-American community to commemorate Dighton Rock, see Fernandes, "Oh Famous Race!"

24. See Fernandes, "Of Outcasts and Ambassadors," 303–10, for Águas's political activities in opposition to Salazar. He would receive the Order of Freedom from the Portuguese government in 1980 (304).

25. For the role of *A Alvorada/Diário de Notícias* in Portuguese-American politics and culture, see Rui Correia, "Salazar in New Bedford: Political Readings of *Diário de Noticias*, the Only Portuguese Daily Newspaper in the United States" in *Community, Culture and the Makings of Identity: Portuguese Americans Along the Eastern Seaboard*, ed. Kimberly DaCosta Holton and Andrea Klimt (North Dartmouth: University of Massachusetts Dartmouth, 2009), 227–46.

26. Fernandes, "Oh Famous Race!," 34.

27. Feldman-Bianco, "Multiple Layers of Time and Space," 51.

28. "Dighton Rock," *New York Times*, December 23, 1928.

29. See Wellman, "Trends in North American Rock Research." Eastern Woodland sites were addressed by twenty-five works before 1930 and just fourteen works between 1930 and 1949. Table 6, 537.

30. Edmund B. Delabarre, "Moonlight Pact with White Man Seen Recorded on Ancient Indian Rock Preserved at Aptucxet," New Bedford *Standard-Times*, March 17, 1935.

31. See Lenik, *Picture Rocks*, 138–39, for Bourne petroglyph theories.

32. Delabarre, "Moonlight Pact."

33. Willoughby, review of *Dighton Rock*, 521.

34. Delabarre, "Possible Pre-Algonkian Culture," 365.

35. Willoughby, review of *Dighton Rock*, 521. Delabarre's statement, *Dighton Rock*, 312.

36. Delabarre, "Rock-Inscriptions of New England," 110.

37. Willoughby, *Antiquities of the New England Indians*, 166–70.

38. Ibid., figure 93, "The Dighton Rock Inscription," 168.

39. Ibid., 166–67, 168.

40. See Delabarre and Brown, "Runic Rock," 365–77.

41. Delabarre, "Petroglyphic Study," 428.

42. Willoughby, *Antiquities of the New England Indians*, 230.

43. Delabarre, "Miguel Cortereal," 2–3.

44. Ibid., 13.

45. Ibid.

46. Ibid., 7.

47. Edmund Burke Delabarre to Frank W. Hutt, September 18, 1927, DRC.

48. See, for example, "Pastor Believes Dighton Rock Should Be Preserved as Shrine," New Bedford *Standard-Times*, June 19, 1927, transcribed in Fragoso, *Historical Report*, 6–7. Fragoso's pamphlet, in the DRC, contains transcriptions of newspapers articles dating back to the 1920s that are punctuated with arch commentary by Fragoso.

49. Edmund Burke Delabarre to Secretary, OCHS, December 11, 1934, DRC.

50. Quitclaim deed, Elizabeth Wentworth Patterson to Edmund B. Delabarre, January 23, 1935, DRC.

51. "Portuguese American Civic League Plans for Preservation of Famed Dighton Rock," *Herald-News* (Fall River), November 22, 1934, in Fragoso, *A Historical Report*, 15–16. See Young, *Miguel Corte-Real*, 76, for Corderio de Sousa's article, "A inscrição da pedra de Dighton," *Arquivo histórico de marinha* (Lisbon, 1934), 111–15.

52. "Lisbon Officials Question Value of Dighton Rock," *Providence Journal*, July 28, 1935, in Fragoso, *A Historical Report*, 33–34.

53. For Thórdarson's discussion of Hóp, see *Vinland Voyages*, 38–45. William H. Babcock in *Early Norse Visits to North America* favored an Indigenous interpretation for Dighton Rock (44), yet supported Rafn's contention that Mount Hope Bay was Hóp (136).

54. The rock was considered to bear a runic inscription and the image of a ship. According to Delabarre, in a June 1919 ceremony overseen by the RIHS, the rock was "christened in the ancient manner with corn, wine and oil, receiving the name 'Lief's Rock'" (Delabarre, *Dighton Rock*, 191). Delabarre seemed unaware that this was a standard Masonic anointing ceremony. Delabarre argued it actually was a nineteenth-century inscription in a syllabic writing system invented by a Cherokee, George Guess, in 1821. Jill Lepore discusses Northmen's Rock in *The Name of War* and found Delabarre's translation effort credible (230). Lenik in *Picture Rocks* rejects both the Norse and the Delabarre scenarios. He argues an unknown Wampanoag made the glyphs during the 1600s (153). I would be remiss were I not to note that Barry Fell thought the inscription was "Tartessian" (a Phoenician script from Iberia) and read "Mariners of Tarshish this rock proclaims" (*America B.C.*, 99–100).

55. Olaf Strandwold to Hjalmar Holand, June 22, 1937, Hjalmar Holand Papers.

56. Holand would support Frederick J. Pohl's contention that Leifsbúdir was at Follin's Pond on the south shore of Cape Cod. Pohl steered clear of Dighton Rock in his popular speculative histories on pre-Columbian voyages. See Holand, *Explorations*, 42–43; Pohl, *Lost Discovery*, passim.

57. Holand, *Westward to Vinland*, 264, 278, 264. See also Krueger, *Myths of the Rune Stone*, 35.

58. Samuel Eliot Morison, "'Kilroy Was Here' on Dighton Rock?" Letter to the editor, *Boston Herald*, May 24, 1954. See also "No One Agrees on Meaning of Dighton Rock Markings," *Boston Globe*, October 14, 1956, for a revisit of Morison's "Kilroy Was Here" quip.

59. Silva reproduced the document of incorporation, dated September 25, 1951, in "Dighton Rock, What Will Happen to You after I Die?" http://www.dightonrock.com/dightorock whatwillhappentoyou.htm.

60. Joseph D. Fragoso, "O Club Vasco da Gama de New York promove uma importante sessão a 23 do corronte," *Diário de Notícias*, August 15, 1931.

61. See Fragoso *Historical Report*, 7. Silva outlined Fragoso's theory of the crosses in *Portuguese Pilgrims*, 57–58.

62. See Fundraising letter, MCRMS, November 7, 1951, DRC. "O Concerto Musical de Ontem na High School de N. Bedf.," *Diario de Notícias*, February 25, 1952. W. Wallace Austin to João R. Rocha, March 10, 1952, DRC. W. Wallace Austin to *Standard-Times* (New Bedford), March 12, 1952, DRC. "O que se passa de verdade com a famosa e célebre 'Pedra de Dighton'?" *Diario de Notícias*, March 12, 1952. Harry Neyer to OCHS, March 17, 1952, DRC. OCHS to Harry Neyer, March 21, 1952, DRC.

63. Acts, 1955. Chapter 538. An Act Authorizing the Department of Natural Resources to Acquire Certain Land in the Town of Berkley. Approved July 13, 1955.

64. "State Given Dighton Rock for Development as Shrine," *Herald–News* (Fall River), January 8, 1955.

65. "Dighton Rock Controversy Rages as New Court Hearing Looms," *Taunton Daily Gazette*, March 24, 1956.

66. Early biographical information from Silva, "Manuel Luciano da Silva, M.D. Biography," http://www.dightonrock.com/biografia_luciano.htm (accessed July 22, 2013).

67. Silva, "My Dates with Dighton Rock!" http://www.dightonrock.com/mydateswithdighton rock.htm (accessed July 22, 2013).

68. Øverland, *Immigrant Minds*, 8.

69. Silva recounted the events at the congress on his website, employing in part his own English translation of an account in *Diário de Notícias* of Portugal, September 9, 1960. "My Historical Communication to the First Internacional Congress of the History of Discoveries in 1960," http://www.dightonrock.com/myhistorialcommunicationtothefir.htm (accessed July 28, 2013).

70. Silva, *Portuguese Pilgrims*, 72–73.

71. Ibid., 68–69.

72. Ibid., 67.

73. MCRMS fundraising letter, November 7, 1951, DRC. It is not clear what if any publication Silva was quoting when he quoted references to the Portuguese as "murderers, robbers, rapists and slave-traders."

74. Silva, *Portuguese Pilgrims*, 30–31.

75. Ibid., 82.

76. See "Várias conferências integradas nas Comemorações Henriquinas," *Diário de Notícias*, February 11, 1960; "Discoveries under Prince Henry Commemorated by 600 Here," *Boston Globe*, October 9, 1960. For Rogers's ancestry, see Rogers, *Atlantic Islanders*, 17–19.

77. Rogers, *Atlantic Islanders*, 293–94.

78. Silva, "My Historical Communication."

79. Earl Banner, "The Doctors Still Disagree: Dighton Rock Row Up Again," *Boston Globe*, January 15, 1961.

80. Silva, "My 'Impossibles' with Dighton Rock!" http://www.dightonrock.com/myimpossible swithdightonrock.htm (accessed July 28, 2013).

81. Fernandes, "Oh Famous Race!" 34.

82. Sara Davidson, "Battle at Dighton Rock: Who Came First[:] Pilgrims or Portuguese," *Boston Globe*, August 14, 1966.

83. Silva, "My 'Impossibles' with Dighton Rock!"

84. Silva, quoted by Sara Davidson, "Battle at Dighton Rock."

85. Silva, *Portuguese Pilgrims*, 92.

86. Ibid.

87. Águas-Delabarre Collection, OCHS.

88. Walter Hackett, "Were Portuguese the First White Settlers in New England?" *Christian Science Monitor*, August 20, 1969.

89. Abilio de Oliveira Águas to Walter Hackett, August 26, 1969, Águas-Delabarre Collection, OCHS.

90. Knaplund, "Rasmus B. Anderson," 23.

91. Anderson, *America Not Discovered*, 2nd ed., 21.

92. Center for Policy Analysis, "Portuguese Americans in the Massachusetts Power Structure," 3.

93. Ibid.

94. Feldman-Bianco, "Multiple Layers of Time and Space," 72.

95. O. Louis Mazzatenta, "New England's 'Little Portugal,'" *National Geographic* 147 (January 1975): 98.

96. Marc Larocque, "Celebrating 500 Years of Azores History," *Taunton Daily Gazette*, September 25, 2011.

97. Silva, "'Old Colony Historical Society of Taunton' Visited Dighton Rock!" http://www .dightonrock.com/oldcolonyhistoricalsocietyoftaun.htm (accessed December 10, 2014).

98. Silva, "Professor Delabarre Was Afraid of Being Criticized!" http://www.dightonrock .com/professordelabarrewasafraid.htm (accessed December 4, 2012).

Conclusion

1. Trouillot, *Silencing the Past*, 118.

2. Roy, *These Mysterious People*, 5.

3. "Dighton Rock State Park," http://www.mass.gov/eea/agencies/dcr/massparks/region -south/dighton-rock-state-park.html.

4. Young would become a professor of history at St. Mary's University. See "Biographical Note," George F. W. Young Papers, http://www.oac.cdlib.org/findaid/ark:/13030/c8w37xsr /admin/#ref2. Nothing in his papers relates to his Dighton Rock monograph. Young's dissertation was published as *The Germans in Chile: Immigration and Colonization, 1849–1914* (New York: Center for Migration Studies, 1974).

5. Young's letter of August 23, 1967, to Silva apparently was forwarded by Silva to Portuguese authorities in the course of soliciting support for a museum at Dighton Rock and was filed in Pedra de Dighton (PEA M333). Transcription provided by Gilberto Fernandes.

6. Young, *Miguel Corte-Real*, 99.

7. Ibid., 96.

8. Ibid., 100.

9. Ibid., 102.

10. Ibid., 13.

11. Young only acknowledged Schoolcraft and Shingwauk in a footnote (p. 73) to make the point that Shingwauk did not think two "central alphabetical characters" belonged with the rest of the glyphs the Anishinabe leader interpreted as Indigenous. Schoolcraft and Shingwauk thus served to advance Young's case that there was alphabetic writing attributable to Corte-Real.

12. Young, *Miguel Corte-Real*, 95.

13. T. Stephen [*sic*] Tegu, "The Talking Rock[:] What Does It Say?" *Taunton Daily Gazette*, June 2, 1972.

14. Silva, "Casting Light on Dighton Rock," http://www.dightonrock.com/pilgrim_credits .htm (accessed July 22, 2013).

15. Casey Nilsson, "Cod Almighty," *Taunton Daily Gazette*, August 14, 2011.

16. "A Teoria Portuguesa foi descobeta há mais de 93 anos e até à data ainda ninguém a refutou."

17. In addition to the display label information, see William K. Gale, "Dighton Rock Slates Tribute," *Providence Sunday Journal*, June 27, 1976.

18. Silva, "Dighton Rock, What Will Happen to You after I Die?" http://www.dightonrock .com/dightorockwhatwillhappentoyou.htm.

19. The building was constructed with small windows, over the objections of Silva, who was concerned that "humidity from the river would increase the oxidation" of the rock's face. "It took twenty more years for the State to close those small windows!" (Silva, "Dighton Rock, What Will Happen to You after I Die?") They were boarded up at the time of my 2013 visit. At the time of my visit, the glyphs were lit harshly from below. An improved lighting system was installed in 2016 that illuminated the glyphs, still at close range, from the front.

Bibliography

Archival Collections

Boston, MA
  Harvard University Archives
    Papers of John and Hannah Winthrop, 1728–89
    Papers of Stephen Sewall, 1764–97
  Massachusetts Historical Society
    Carl C. Rafn Papers, N-767
Cambridge, MA
  Beinecke Rare Book and Manuscript Library, Yale University
    Ezra Stiles Papers
Green Bay, WI
  Archives and Area Research Center, University of Wisconsin
    Hjalmar Holand Papers
Lisbon, Portugal
  Arquivo Histórico-Diplomático do Ministro dos Negócios Estrangeiros
    Miguel Corte-Real Memorial Society, 1951–59 (Pedra Dighton) (PEA M181)
    Pedra de Dighton (PEA M333)
Taunton, MA
  Old Colony Historical Society
    Agua–Delabarre Collection
    Dighton Rock Collection

Published Sources

Acosta, Ioseph [José de]. *The Naturall and Morall Historie of the East and West Indies*, translated by E.G. [Edward Grimeston]. London: 1604.

Adair, James. *The History of the American Indians*. London: 1775.

Additions to the Universal History, in seven volumes, in folio. London: 1750.

American Antiquarian Society. *Archaeologia Americana*, vol. 1. Worcester, MA: American Antiquarian Society, 1820.

The American Traveller. London: 1741.

Amiable, Louis. *Une loge maçonnique d'avant 1789, la R.—L.—Les neuf soeurs*. Paris: Ancienne Librairie Germer Baillière & Co., 1897.

Anderson, Rasmus Björn. *America Not Discovered by Columbus: An Historical Sketch of the Discovery of America by the Norsemen in the Tenth Century*. Chicago: S. C. Griggs & Co.; London: Trübner & Co., 1874; 2nd edition 1877; 4th edition, 1891.

Appleton, Thomas G. *A Sheaf of Papers*. Boston: Roberts Brothers, 1875.

Appleton, Thomas Gold [T. G.]. "The Flowering of a Nation." *Atlantic Monthly* 28, no. 167 (September 1871): 316–19.

Arnold, Guy. "Kendall, Edward Augustus (1775/6–1842)." *Oxford Dictionary of National Biography.* Oxford: Oxford University Press, 2004. http://www.oxforddnb.com.ezproxy .library.yorku.ca/view/article/15344 (accessed February 1, 2014).

Arnold, Samuel Greene. *History of the State of Rhode Island and Providence Plantations,* 2 vols. New York: D. Appleton, 1859–60.

Arnzen, Niels. "Report of Committee on Dighton Rock." In *Collections of the Old Colony Historical Society, No. 5,* 94–97. Taunton: Old Colony Historical Society, 1895.

Atwater, Caleb. "Description of the Antiquities Discovered in the State of Ohio and Other Western States." In *Archaeologia Americana,* vol. 1, 105–268. Worcester MA: American Antiquarian Society, 1820.

Austin, John O. *The Genealogical Dictionary of Rhode Island.* Albany, NY: Joel Munsell's Sons, 1887.

Babcock, William H. *Early Norse Visits to North America.* (Washington, DC, 1913).

Bancroft, George. *A History of the United States,* vol. 1. Boston: Charles Bowen, 1834.

Baraga, Frederic. *A Dictionary of the Otchipwe Language Explained in English.* Cincinnati: Jos. A. Hemann, 1853.

Barnhart, Terry A. "The Iroquois as Mound Builders: Ephraim George Squier and the Archaeology of Western New York." *New York History* 77, no. 2 (April 1996): 125–50.

Bartlett, John Russell. *Genealogy of That Branch of the Russell Family, which Comprises the Descendants of John Russell of Woburn, Massachusetts, 1640–1878.* Providence, RI: private printing, 1879.

———. "Observations on the Progress of Geography and Ethnology, with the historical facts deduced therefrom. Read at the meetings in November and December, 1846." In *Proceedings of the New York Historical Society for the year 1846,* 149–210. New York: Press of the Historical Society, 1847.

———. "On the Historical Evidence Adduced by the Welsh in Favor of the Discovery of America by Madoc ap Owen Gwinedd, in the XII Century. By John R. Bartlett." In "Papers Read before the American Ethnological Society." *Transactions of the American Ethnological Society* 1 [unnumbered].

———. *Personal Narrative of Explorations and Incidents in Texas, New Mexico, California, Sonora, and Chihuaha,* 2 vols. New York: D. Appleton & Co., 1854.

———. *The Progress of Ethnology, an Account of Recent Archaeological, Philological and Geographical Researches in Various Parts of the Globe.* New York: American Ethnological Society, 1847.

Bartlett, Josiah. *A Discourse on the Origin, Progress and Design of Free Masonry.* Boston: Thomas and John Fleet, 1793.

Barton, Benjamin Smith. "Hints on the Etymology of Certain English Words, and on Their Affinity to Words in the Languages of Different European, Asiatic, and American (Indian) Nations." In *Transactions of the American Philosophical Society* 6 (1809): 145–58.

———. *New Views of the Origins of the Tribes and Nations of America.* Philadelphia: John Bioren, 1797.

———. "Observations and Conjectures Concerning Certain Articles which Were Taken Out of an Ancient Tumulus, or Grave, at Cincinnati." In *Transactions of the American Philosophical Society* 4 (1799): 181–215.

———. *Observations on Some Parts of Natural History: To Which Is Prefixed an Account of Several Remarkable Vestiges of an Ancient Date, Which Have Been Discovered in Different Parts of North America: Part I.* London: C. Dilly, c. 1787.

Barton, H. Arnold. "The Discovery of Norway Abroad." *Scandinavian Studies* 7, no. 1 (Spring 2007): 25–40.

Bassin, Mark. "Russia between Europe and Asia: The Ideological Construction of Geographical Space." *Slavic Review* 50, no. 1 (Spring 1991): 1–17.

Basso, Keith. *Wisdom Sits in Places*. Albuquerque: University of New Mexico Press, 1996.

Baum, Bruce. *The Rise and Fall of the Caucasian Race: A Political History of Racial Identity*. New York: New York University Press, 2006.

Bauman, Richard. "The Nationalization and Internationalization of Folklore: The Case of Schoolcraft's 'Gitshee Gauzinee,'" *Western Folklore* 52, no. 2/4 (April–October 1993): 247–69.

Beamish, Ludlow North. *The Discovery of America by the Northmen in the Tenth Century*. London: T. and W. Boone, 1841.

Benitez, Miguel. "L'Exploration de la Siberie." *Dix-huitième siècle* 18 (1986): 191–200.

Benson, Adolph B. "Henry Wheaton's Writings on Scandinavia." *Journal of English and German Philology* 29, no. 4 (October 1930): 546–61.

———. "Pehr Kalm's Writings on America: A Bibliographic Review." *Scandinavian Studies and Notes* 12, no. 6 (May 1933): 89–98.

Bentley, William. *The Diary of William Bentley*, 4 vols. Salem, MA: Essex Institute, 1905–14.

Berkhofer, Robert E., Jr. *The White Man's Indian: Images of the American Indian from Columbus to Present*. New York: Vintage Books, 1979.

Bieder, Robert E. *Science Encounters the Indian, 1820–1880: The Early Years of American Ethnology*. 1986; repr. Norman: University of Oklahoma Press, 1989.

Black, Mary B. "Ojibwa Taxonomy and Percept Ambiguity," *Ethos* 5, no. 1 (Spring 1977): 90–118.

Blake, John Lauris. *A Biographical Dictionary*, 13th ed. Philadelphia: H. Cowperthwait & Co., 1856.

Bohaker, Heidi. "Indigenous Histories and Archival Media in the Early Modern Great Lakes." In *Colonial Mediascapes: Sensory Worlds of the Early Americas*, edited by Matt Cohen and Jeffrey Glover. Lincoln: University of Nebraska Press, 2014. Kindle e-book.

Booth, G. *The Historical Library of Diodorus the Sicilian, in 15 Books*. London: Edw. Jones, 1700.

Bragdon, Kathleen J. *Native People of Southern New England, 1500–1650*. Norman: University of Oklahoma Press, 1996.

———. *Native People of Southern New England, 1650–1775*. Norman: University of Oklahoma Press, 2009.

Braude, Benjamin. "Les contes persans de Menasseh Ben Israel: Polémique, apologétique et dissimulation à Amsterdam au xviie siècle." *Annales: Histoire, Sciences Sociales* 49 (September–October 1994): 1107–38.

———. "The Sons of Noah and the Construction of Ethnic and Geographical Identities in the Medieval and Early Modern Periods." *William and Mary Quarterly*, ser. 3, 54, no. 1 (January 1997): 103–42.

Bray, William. "Observations on the Indian Method of Picture-Writing." In *Archaeologia*, vol. 6, 159–62. London: Society of Antiquaries of London, 1782.

Bremer, Richard G. *Indian Agent and Wilderness Scholar: The Life of Henry Rowe Schoolcraft*. Mt. Pleasant, MI: Clarke Historical Library, Central Michigan University, 1987.

Brerewood, Edward. *Enquiries Touching the diversity of Languages, and Religions, through the Chiefe Parts of the World*. 1614; repr. London: John Norton, 1635.

Brinton, Daniel G. *The Myths of the New World: A Treatise on the Symbolism and Mythology of the Red Races of America*. New York: Leypoldt and Holt, 1868.

Brooks, Charles Timothy. *The Controversy Touching the Old Stone Mill, in the Town of Newport, Rhode Island*. Newport, RI: Charles E. Hammett Jr., 1851.

Buffon, Georges-Louis Leclerc, Comte de. *Histoire naturelle, générale et particulière*, vol. 3. Paris: Impremerie royale, 1749.

———. *Histoire naturelle, générale et particulière, Supplement*, vol. 4. Paris, 1777.

Bull, Sara C. *Ole Bull: A Memoir*. Boston: Houghton, Mifflin and Co., 1883.

Bullock, Steven C. *Revolutionary Brotherhood: Freemasonry and the Transformation of the American Social Order, 1730–1840*. Chapel Hill: University of North Carolina Press, 1996.

Calloway, Colin G. *One Vast Winter Count: The Native American West before Lewis and Clark*. Lincoln: University of Nebraska Press, 2003.

Cappon, Lester J. "Jared Sparks: The Preparation of an Editor." In *Proceedings of the Massachusetts Historical Society*, 3rd ser., 90 (1978): 3–21.

Carmichael, Leonard. "Edmund Burke Delabarre, 1863–1945." *American Journal of Psychology* 58, no. 3 (July 1945): 406–9.

Cass, Lewis. "Art. III. Documents and Proceedings Relating to the Formation and Progress of a Board in the City of New York, for the Emigration, Preservation, and Improvement of the Aborigines of America. July 22, 1829." *North American Review* 30, no. 66 (January 1830): 62–121.

Center for Policy Analysis, University of Massachusetts–Dartmouth. "Portuguese-Americans in the Massachusetts Power Structure: A Positional Analysis," September 2005.

Chapin, Rev. A. B. "Article XI. Ante-Columbian History of America. Dighton Rock. Language of Skroellings, etc." *American Biblical Repository*, July 1, 1839, 191.

Chaplin, Joyce E. "Race." In *The British Atlantic World, 1500–1800*, 2nd ed., edited by David Armitage and Michael J. Braddick. New York: Palgrave Macmillan, 2009.

Chappell, Sally A. Kitt. *Cahokia: Mirror of the Cosmos*. Chicago: University of Chicago Press, 2002.

Charlevoix, Pierre-François-Xavier de. *Histoire et description générale de la Nouvelle France*, vol. 1. Paris: 1744.

Chichester, Henry Manns. "Beamish, North Ludlow (1797–1872)." *Dictionary of National Biography, 1885–1900*, vol. 4. London: Smith, Elder, and Co., 1885.

Christensen, Arne Søby. *Cassiodorus, Jordanes and the History of the Goths*, translated by Heidi Flegal. Copenhagen: Museum Tusculanum Press, 2002.

Church, Henry Ward. "Corneille De Pauw, and the Controversy over His *Recherches Philosophiques Sur Les Américains*." *PMLA* 51, no. 1 (March 1936): 178–206.

Chute, Janet E. *The Legacy of Shingwaukonse: A Century of Native Leadership*. Toronto: University of Toronto Press, 1998.

Cipolla, Craig N. "Being and Becoming Stone: Material Semiotics in Indian Religion and Spirituality." *Semiotic Review 4: Im/Materialities*. Posted September 10, 2016; updated November 14, 2016. http://www.semioticreview.com/index.php/thematic-issues/issue-immaterialities/36-being-and-becoming-stone-material-semiotics-in-indian-religion-and-spirituality.html.

Clarke, Abraham Lynsen. *The Secrets of Masonry Illustrated and Explained*. Providence, RI [1799].

Clements, William M. "Schoolcraft as Textmaker." *Journal of American Folklore* 103, no. 408 (April–June 1990): 177–92.

Clinton, De Witt. "Address before the New York Historical Society on the Iroquois or Six Nations." In *The Life and Writings of De Witt Clinton*, edited by William W. Campbell, 205–64. New York: Baker and Scribner, 1849.

———. *Memoir on the Antiquities of the Western Parts of the State of New-York*. Albany, NY: E. & E. Hosford, 1820.

Clouse, Robert Alan. "Pattern and Function at the Jeffers Petroglyphs, Minnesota." In *The Rock-Art of Eastern North America: Capturing the Images and Insight*, edited by Carol Diaz-Granados and James R. Duncan, 110–25. Tuscaloosa: University of Alabama Press, 2004.

Coe, Michael D. *Breaking the Maya Code*. New York: Thames and Hudson, 1992.

Cogley, Richard, W. "The Ancestry of the American Indians: Thomas Thorowgood's *Iewes in America* (1650) and *Jews in America* (1660)." *English Literary Renaissance* 35, no. 2 (April 2005): 304–30.

———. "'Some Other Kinde of Being and Condition': The Controversy in Mid-Seventeenth-Century England over the Peopling of Ancient America." *Journal of the History of Ideas* 68, no. 1 (January 2007): 35–56.

Conn, Steven. *History's Shadow: Native Americans and Historical Consciousness in the Nineteenth Century*. 2004; repr. Chicago: University of Chicago Press, 2006.

———. *Museums and American Intellectual Life, 1876–1926*. Chicago: University of Chicago Press, 1998.

Conway, Thor. *Spirits on Stone: Lake Superior Ojibwa History, Legends and the Agawa Pictographs*. Sault Ste. Marie, ON: Heritage Discoveries, 2010.

Cook, Ramsay. *The Regenerators: Social Criticism in Late Victorian English Canada*. Toronto: University of Toronto Press, 1985.

Cornog, Evan. *The Birth of Empire: DeWitt Clinton and the American Experience, 1769–1828*. New York: Oxford University Press, 1998.

Court de Gébelin, Antoine. *Monde primitif*, vol. 8. Paris, 1781.

Coy, Fred E., Jr. "Dendroglyphs of the Eastern Woodlands." In *The Rock-Art of Eastern North America: Capturing the Images and Insight*, edited by Carol Diaz-Granados and James R. Duncan, 3–16. Tuscaloosa: University of Alabama Press, 2004.

Craig, G. M. "Bidwell, Marshall Spring." In *Dictionary of Canadian Biography*, vol. 10. Toronto: University of Toronto/Université Laval, 2003–. http://www.biographi.ca/en/bio/bidwell_marshall_spring_10E.html (accessed September 25, 2014).

Croke, Brian. "Cassiodorus and the *Getica* of Jordanes." *Classical Philology* 82, no. 2 (April 1987): 117–34.

Cumming, W. P., R. A. Skelton, and D. B. Quinn. *The Discovery of North America*. New York: American Heritage Press, 1972.

Cuoq, J. A. *Lexique de la langue algonquine*. Montréal: J. Chapleau, 1886.

Da Vinci, Leonardo. *Leonardo Da Vinci's Notebooks, Arranged and Rendered into English with Introductions*, translated by Edward McMurdy. New York: Empire State Book Co., 1923.

Davis, John. "An Attempt to Explain the Inscription on the Dighton Rock." In *Memoirs of the American Academy of Arts and Sciences*, vol. 3, pt. 1, 197–205. Cambridge MA: Hilliard and Metcalf, 1809.

Day, Isaac. "Rock Paintings: The Quest for Medicine and Knowledge." In *Anishinaabewin Niswi*, edited by Alan Corbiere, Deborah McGregor, and Crystal Migwans, 85–101. M'Chigeeng, ON: Ojibwe Cultural Foundation, 2012.

Dechêne, Louise. *Le Peuple, l'État et la Guerre au Canada sous le Régime français*. Montréal: Boréal, 2008.

De Costa, B. F. *The Pre-Columbian Discovery of America by the Northmen*. Albany: Joel Munsell, 1868.

Delabarre, Edmund Burke. *Dighton Rock: A Study of the Written Rocks of New England.* New York: Walter Neale, 1928.

———. "Dighton Rock: The Earliest and Most Puzzling of New England Antiquities." *Old-Time New England* 14, no. 2 (October 1923): 51–72.

———. "Early Interest in Dighton Rock." In *Publications of the Colonial Society of Massachusetts,* vol. 18, transactions 1915–16, 235–98. Boston: Colonial Society of Massachusetts, 1917.

———. "Middle Period of Dighton Rock History." In *Publications of the Colonial Society of Massachusetts,* vol. 19, transactions 1916–17, 46–158. Boston: Colonial Society of Massachusetts, 1918.

———. "Miguel Cortereal: The First European to Enter Narragansett Bay." *Rhode Island Historical Society Collections* 29 (October 1936), reprint.

———. "A Petroglyphic Study of Human Motives." *Scientific Monthly* 41, no. 5 (November 1935): 421–29.

———. "A Possible Pre-Algonkian Culture in Southeastern Massachusetts." *American Anthropologist* n.s. 27, no. 3 (July 1925): 359–69.

———. "A Prehistoric Skeleton from Grassy Island." *American Anthropologist* n.s. 30, no. 3 (July–September 1928): 476–80.

———. "Recent History of Dighton Rock." Reprinted from the *Publications of the Colonial Society of Massachusetts,* vol. 20, transactions 1918–19. Cambridge: John Wilson & Son for the University Press, 1919.

———. "Report of the Brown-Harvard Expedition to Nachvak, Labrador, in the Year 1900." *Bulletin of the Geographical Society of Philadelphia* 3, no. 4 (April 1902): 65–212. Offset print, *Report of the Brown-Harvard Expedition to Nachvak, Labrador.* Providence, RI: Preston & Rounds Co., 1902.

———. "A Rocha de Dighton e Miguel Côrte Real." *Boletim Da Agência Geral das Colónias* 3, no. 20 (February 1927): 143–66; 3, no. 30 (December 1927): 44–58.

———. "The Rock-Inscriptions of New England—Miguel Cortereal in Massachusetts, 1511." *Journal of American History* 26, no. 2 (1932): 69–110.

Delabarre, Edmund Burke, and Charles W. Brown. "The Runic Rock on No Man's Land[,] Massachusetts." *New England Quarterly* 8, no. 3 (September 1935): 365–77.

Delabarre, Edmund Burke, and John A. Popplestone. "A Cross Cultural Contribution to the Cannabis Experience." *Psychological Record* 24 (Winter 1974): 67–73.

Delabarre, Edmund Burke, and Harris H. Wilder. "Indian Corn-Hills in Massachusetts." *American Anthropologist* n.s. 22, no. 3 (July–September 1920): 203–25.

Delisle, Joseph-Nicolas. *Nouvelles cartes des decouvertes de l'amiral de Fonte.* Paris, 1753.

Deloria, Philip J. *Indians in Unexpected Places.* Lawrence: University Press of Kansas, 2004.

Deloria, Vine, Jr., and Clifford Lytle. *The Nations Within: The Past and Future of American Indian Sovereignty.* New York: Pantheon, 1984.

DeLucia, Christine. "The Memory Frontier: Uncommon Pursuits of Past and Place in the Northeast after King Philip's War." *Journal of American History* 98, no. 4 (March 2012): 975–97.

Denon, Vivant. *Travels in Upper and Lower Egypt: During the Campaigns of General Bonaparte, Translated by Arthur Aikin, with an Historical Account of the Invasion by the French, by E. A. Kendal[l],* 2 vols. London: B. Crosby, 1802, and Cundee, 1803; New York: Heard and Forman, 1803.

de Pauw, Cornelius. *Recherches philosophiques sur les Américains,* 3 vols. Berlin, 1770.

Diaz-Granados, Carol, and James R. Duncan, eds. *The Rock-Art of Eastern North America: Capturing the Images and Insight.* Tuscaloosa: University of Alabama Press, 2004.

Dickason, Oliva Patricia. *The Myth of the Savage: And the Beginnings of French Colonialism in the Americas.* Edmonton: University of Alberta Press, 1984.

Dinisi, Thomas. "Evans, John Thomas (1770–1799)." In *Dictionary of Missouri Biography*, edited by Lawrence O. Christensen, William E. Foley, and Gary Kremer, 286–87. Columbia: University of Missouri Press, 1999.

Dippie, Brian W. *The Vanishing American: White Attitudes and U.S. Indian Policy.* Lawrence: University Press of Kansas, 1982.

Doughton, Thomas L. "Unseen Neighbors: Native Americans of Central Massachusetts, A People Who Had 'Vanished.'" In *After King Philip's War: Presence and Persistence in Indian New England*, edited by Colin Gordon Calloway, 207–30. Hanover, NH: University Press of New England, 1997.

Dunglison, Robley. *A Public Discourse in Commemoration of Peter S. Du Ponceau, LL.D.: Late President of the American Philosophical Society.* Philadelphia: American Philosophical Society, 1844.

Du Ponceau, Peter Stephen, and James L. Whitehead. "Notes and Documents: The Autobiography of Peter Stephen Du Ponceau" (in five parts). *Pennsylvania Magazine of History and Biography* 63, no. 2 (April 1939): 189–227; 63, no. 3 (July 1939): 311–43; 63, no. 4 (October 1939): 432–61; 64, no. 1 (January 1940): 97–120; 64, no. 2 (April 1940): 243–69.

Durrieu, le Comte Paul. "Miniatures pour l'illustration d'une oeuvre du roi René retrouvée à Metz." *Comptes rendus des séances de l'Académie des Inscriptions et Belles-Lettres* 64ᵉ année, no. 1 (1920): 3–9.

Eccles, W. J. *Canada under Louis XIV 1663–1701.* Toronto: McClelland and Stewart, 1964.

Ekman, Ernst. "Gothic Patriotism and Olof Rudbeck." *Journal of Modern History* 34, no. 1 (March 1962): 52–63.

Eliot, John. *The Eliot Tracts: With Letters from John Eliot to Thomas Thorowgood and Richard Baxter*, edited by Michael P. Clark. Contributions in American History No. 199. Westport, CT: Praeger, 2003.

Elliott, J. H. *Empires of the Atlantic World: Britain and Spain in America 1492–1830.* New Haven, CT: Yale University Press, 2007.

Emery, Samuel Hopkins. "Historical Sketch of the Old Colony Historical Society." In *Collections of the Old Colony Historical Society: Papers Read before the Society during the Year 1878*, 5–11. Taunton, MA: Old Colony Historical Society, 1879.

———. *History of Taunton, from Its Settlement to the Present Time.* Syracuse, NY: D. Mason & Co., 1893.

Everett, Alexander H. "The Discovery of America by the Northmen." *United States Magazine and Democratic Review* (April 1838). In *The United States Magazine and Democratic Review*, vol. 2, 85–96. Washington: Langtree and O'Sullivan, 1838.

———. "The Discovery of America by the Northmen, Article Second." *United States Magazine and Democratic Review* (May 1838). In *The United States Magazine and Democratic Review*, vol. 2, 143–58.

Everett, Edward. "Art. IX. *Antiquitates Americanae.*" *North American Review* 46, no. 98 (January 1838): 181.

Fabian, Ann. *The Skull Collectors: Race, Science, and America's Unburied Dead.* Chicago: University of Chicago Press, 2010.

Falnes, Oscar J. "New England Interest in Scandinavian Culture and the Norsemen." *New England Quarterly* 10, no. 2 (June 1937): 211–42.

Faragher, John Mack. *A Great and Noble Scheme: The Tragic Story of the Expulsion of the French Acadians from Their American Homeland.* New York: W. W. Norton, 2005.

Feder, Kenneth. *Frauds, Myths, and Mysteries: Science and Pseudoscience in Archaeology*, 8th ed. New York: McGraw-Hill, 2014.

Feldman-Bianco, Bela. "Multiple Layers of Time and Space: The Construction of Class, Ethnicity, and Nationalism among Portuguese Immigrants." In *Community, Culture and the Makings of Identity: Portuguese-Americans along the Eastern Seaboard*, edited by Kimberly DaCosta Holton and Andrea Klimt, 51–94. North Dartmouth: University of Massachusetts Dartmouth, 2009.

Fell, Barry. *America B.C.: Ancient Settlers in the New World.* New York: Simon & Schuster, 1978.

Fenn, Elizabeth A. *Pox Americana.* New York: Hill and Wang, 2001.

Fernandes, Gilberto. "Of Outcasts and Ambassadors: the Making of Portuguese Diaspora in Postwar North." PhD dissertation, York University, September 2014.

———. "Oh Famous Race! Imperial Heritage and Diasporic Memory in the Portuguese American Narrative of North America." *Public Historian* 38(1) (February 2016): 18–47.

Finch, John. "Antiquities: Art. XX. On the Celtic Antiquities of America." *American Journal of Science and Arts* 7, no. 1 (January 1, 1824).

———. *Travels into the United States and Canada.* London: Longman, Rees, Orme, Browne, Green, and Longman, 1833.

Fiske, Moses. "Conjectures Respecting the Ancient Inhabitants of North America." In *Archaeologia Americana*, vol. 1, 300–7. Worcester, MA: American Antiquarian Society, 1820.

Fitzhugh, William W., and Elizabeth I. Ward, eds. *Vikings: The North Atlantic Saga.* Washington: Smithsonian Institution Press, 2000.

Folsom, George. "Article IV. *Antiquitates Americanae.*" *New York Review* 2, no. 4 (April 1838), in *The New York Review*, vol. 2 (1837–42), 352.

Forster, Johann Reinhold. *Observations Made during a Voyage round the World, on Physical Geography, Natural History, and Ethic Philosophy.* London: G. Robinson, 1778.

Fragoso, Joseph D. *A Historical Report of Twenty-Eight Years of Patriotic and Dramatic Efforts to Save Dighton Rock.* New Bedford MA: Joseph D. Fragoso/Miguel Corte-Real Memorial Society, 1954.

Freeman, Frederick. *The History of Cape Cod*, vol. 1: *The Annals of Barnstable County, including the District of Mashpee.* Boston: Author, 1858.

Frost, Alan. "Pacific Ocean: Explorations in the Eighteenth Century." In *The Oxford Encyclopedia of Maritime History*, edited by John B. Hattendorf, vol. 3, 225–30. Oxford: Oxford University Press, 2007.

Gallatin, Albert. "A Synopsis of the Indian Tribes of North America." In *Archaeologia Americana*, vol. 2, 1–421. Cambridge: Printed for the Society at the University Press, 1836.

Goddard, Ives, and Kathleen J. Bragdon. *Native Writings in Massachusett*, 2 vols. Philadelphia: American Philosophical Society, c. 1988.

Godwin, Joscelyn. *The Theosophical Enlightenment.* Albany: State University of New York Press, 1994.

Goffert, Walter. "Jordanes' 'Getica' and the Disputed Authenticity of Gothic Origins from Scandinavia." *Speculum* 80, no. 2 (April 2005): 379–98.

Goodwin, Gordon. "Kendall, Edward Augustus (1776?–1842)." *Dictionary of National Biography*, vol. 30. New York: Macmillan and Co., 1892.

Greene, John C. "American Science Comes of Age." *Journal of American History* 55, no. 1 (June 1968): 22–41.

Grotii, Hugonis [Hugo Grotius]. *De origine gentium Americanarum dissertatio.* Paris, 1642.

Grotius, Hugo. *On the Origin of the Native Races of America: A Dissertation,* translated by Edmund Goldsmid. Edinburgh, 1884.

Haas, Mary R. "Grammar or Lexicon? The American Indian Side of the Question from Duponceau to Powell." *International Journal of American Linguistics* 35, no. 3 (July 1969): 239–55.

Hakluyt, Richard. *The Principal Navigations, Voyages, Traffiques and Discoveries of the English Nation,* edited by Edmund Goldsmid, 16 vols. Edinburgh: E. & G. Goldsmid, 1885–90. http://ebooks.adelaide.edu.au/h/hakluyt/voyages/v13/ (accessed June 25, 2014).

Hall, Capt. J. W. D. "Dighton Writing Rock." In *Collections of the Old Colony Historical Society,* No. 4, 97–100. Taunton: Old Colony Historical Society, 1889.

Hallowell, A. Irving. "Bear Ceremonialism in the Northern Hemisphere." *American Anthropologist* n.s. 28, no. 1 (January–March 1926): 1–175.

Hallowell, A. Irving, and Henry R. Schoolcraft. "Concordance of Ojibwa Narratives in the Published Works of Henry R. Schoolcraft." *Journal of American Folklore* 59, no. 232 (April–June 1946): 136–53.

Hamell, George R. "The Iroquois and the World's Rim: Speculations on Color, Culture, and Contact." *American Indian Quarterly* 16, no. 4 (Autumn 1992): 451–69.

———. "Long-Tail: The Panther in Huron-Wyandot and Seneca Myth, Ritual, and Material Culture." In *Icons of Power: Feline Symbolism in the Americas,* edited by Nicholas J. Saunders, 258–91. New York: Routledge, 1998.

Hanyan, Craig, with Mary L. Hanyan. *De Witt Clinton and the Rise of the People's Men.* Montreal: McGill-Queen's, 1996.

Harper, Robert S. "The First Psychological Laboratory." *Isis* 41, no. 2 (July 1950): 158–61.

Harris, Thaddeus Mason. "Account of Copper Coins, Found in Medford, Massachusetts." In *Memoirs of the American Academy of Arts and Sciences,* vol. 3, pt. 1, 195–96. Cambridge, MA: Hilliard and Metcalf, 1809.

———. *The Journal of a Tour into the Territory Northwest of the Alleghany Mountains; Made in the Spring of the Year 1803.* Boston: Manning & Loring, 1805.

Harrisse, Henry. *Les Corte-Real et leur Voyages au Nouveau Monde.* Paris: Ernest Leroux, 1885.

Hattendorf, John B., ed. *The Oxford Encyclopedia of Maritime History,* 4 vols. Oxford: Oxford University Press, 2007.

Haven, Samuel Foster. "The Archaeology of the United States." In *Smithsonian Contributions to Knowledge,* vol. 8, article 2. Washington: Smithsonian Institution, 1856.

Hayne, David M. "Lom d'Arce de Lahontan, Louis-Armand de, Baron de Lahontan." In *Dictionary of Canadian Biography,* vol. 2. Toronto: University of Toronto/Université Laval, 2003–. http://www.biographi.ca/en/bio/lom_d_arce_de_lahontan_louis_armand_de_2E.html (accessed January 20, 2014).

Heart, Jonathan. "Account of the Remains of Ancient Works, on the Muskingham, with a Plan of these Works." *Columbian Magazine* 1 (May 1787): 425–27.

———. "A Letter from Major Jonathan Heart, to Benjamin Smith Barton, M.D. Containing Observations on the Ancient Works of Art, the Native Inhabitants, &c. of the Western Country." *Transactions of the American Philosophical Society* 3 (1793): 214–22.

Heart, Jonathan, and Consul Winshield Butterfield. *Journal of Capt. Jonathan Heart.* Albany: Joel Munsell's Sons, 1885.

Hegeman, Susan. "Native American 'Texts' and the Problem of Authenticity." *American Quarterly* 41, no. 2 (June 1989): 265–83.

Hill, Ira. *Antiquities of America Explained.* Hagerstown, MD, 1831.

Hilmer, Mary Adams, and Samuel Sewall. "The Other Diary of Samuel Sewall." *New England Quarterly* 55, no. 3 (September 1982): 354–67.

Hinderaker, Eric. *The Two Hendricks: Unraveling a Mohawk Mystery.* Cambridge, MA: Harvard University Press, 2010.

Hoare, Michael E. *The Tactless Philosopher: Johann Reinhold Forster 1729–98.* Melbourne: Hawthorne Press, 1976.

Holand, Hjalmar Rued. *Explorations in America before Columbus.* New York: Twayne Publishers, 1956.

———. *Westward to Vinland: An Account of Norse Discoveries and Explorations in America, 982–1362.* New York: Duell, Sloan & Pearce, 1940.

Holmes, Abiel. *The Life of Ezra Stiles.* Boston: Thomas & Andrews, 1798.

Horsford, Eben Norbert. *The Landfall of Leif Erikson A.D. 1000 and the Site of His Houses in Vineland.* Boston: Damrell and Upham, 1892.

Horsman, Reginald. *Race and Manifest Destiny: The Origins of American Racial Anglo-Saxonism.* Cambridge, MA: Harvard University Press, 1981.

Howard, Mary. *The Black Gauntlet: A Tale of Plantation Life in South Carolina.* Philadelphia: J. B. Lippincott & Co., 1860.

Huddleston, Lee E. *Origins of the American Indians: European Concepts, 1492–1729.* 1967; Austin: University of Texas Press, 2015.

Hultkrantz, Åke. *The Religions of the American Indians,* translated by Monica Setterwall. 1967; Berkeley: University of California Press, 1979.

Humboldt, Alexander von. *Cosmos: A Sketch of a Physical Description of the Universe,* vol. 2, translated by E. C. Otté. London: George Bell and Sons, 1900.

Hunter, Douglas. *The Race to the New World: Christopher Columbus, John Cabot, and a Lost History of Discovery.* New York: Palgrave Macmillan, 2011.

Hurd, Duane Hamilton. *History of Bristol County, Massachusetts, with Biographical Sketches of Many of Its Pioneers and Prominent Men.* Philadelphia: J. W. Lewis & Co., 1883.

Ingstad, Helge. *Westward to Vineland.* London: Jonathan Cape, 1969.

Jacob, Margaret C. *Living the Enlightenment: Freemasonry and Politics in Eighteenth-Century Europe.* New York: Oxford University Press, 1991.

———. *The Radical Enlightenment: Pantheists, Freemasons and Republicans.* London: George Allen & Unwin, 1981.

Jakobson, Roman. "The Paleo-Siberian Languages." *American Anthropologist* n.s. 44, no. 4, (October–December 1942): 602–20.

Jameson, Anna Brownell. *Winter Studies and Summer Rambles in Canada.* 1838; Toronto: McClelland & Stewart/New Canadian Library, 1990.

Jarrell, Richard A. "Kalm, Pehr." In *Dictionary of Canadian Biography,* vol. 4. Toronto: University of Toronto/Université Laval, 2003–. http://www.biographi.ca/en/bio/kalm _pehr_4E.html (accessed June 30, 2014).

Jefferson, Thomas. *Notes on the State of Virginia,* 2nd English ed. London: 1787.

Johnson, Charles. *The History of Pirates.* Haverhill, MA: Thomas Carey, 1825.

Johnston, John. "Account of the Present State of the Indian Tribes Inhabiting Ohio." In *Archaeologia Americana,* vol. 1, 269–77. Worcester, MA: American Antiquarian Society, 1820.

Jones, Gwyn. "Historical Evidence for Viking Voyages in the New World." In *Vikings in the West,* edited by Eleanor Guralnick, 1–12. Chicago: Archaeological Institute of America, 1982.

Kalm, Pehr. *En Resa til Norra America,* 3 vols. Stockholm, 1753–61.

————. *Voyage de Pehr Kalm au Canada en 1749*, translated by Jacques Rousseau, Guy Béthune, and Pierre Morisset. Montréal: Pierre Tisseyre, 1977.

Kalm, Peter [Pehr]. *Travels into North America*, translated by John Reinhold Foster, 3 vols. Warrington, UK: William Eyres, 1770.

Kelby, Robert Hendre. *The New York Historical Society 1804–1904*. New York: New York Historical Society, 1905.

Kendall, Edward Augustus. "Account of the Writing-Rock in Taunton River." In *Memoirs of the American Academy of Arts and Sciences*, vol. 3, pt. 1, 165–91. Cambridge, MA: Hilliard and Metcalf, 1809.

————. *An Argument for Construing Largely the Right of an Appellee of Murder, to Insist on Trial by Battle*. 1817; London: Baldwin, Cradock, and Joy and Clarke and Sons, 1818.

————. *Travels through the Northern Parts of the United States, in the Years 1807 and 1808*, 3 vols. New York: I. Riley, 1809.

Kidd, Colin. *The Forging of Races: Race and Scripture in the Protestant Atlantic World, 1600–2000*. New York: Cambridge University Press, 2006.

Kittredge, George Lyman. "Cotton Mather's Election into the Royal Society." In *Publications of the Colonial Society of Massachusetts*, vol. 14, 81–113. Boston: Colonial Society of Massachusetts, 1912.

Knaplund, Paul. "Rasmus B. Anderson, Pioneer and Crusader." *Norwegian-American Studies* 18 (January 1, 1954): 23–43.

Koerner, Lisbet. *Linnaeus: Nature and Nation*. Cambridge, MA: Harvard University Press, 1999.

Kohl, Johann Georg. *Kitchi-Gami: Wanderings around Lake Superior*. London: Chapman and Hall, 1860.

Kolodny, Annette. *In Search of First Contact: The Vikings of Vinland, the Peoples of the Dawnland, and the Anglo-American Anxiety of Discovery*. Durham, NC: Duke University Press, 2012.

Krueger, David M. *Myths of the Rune Stone: Viking Martyrs and the Birthplace of America*. Minneapolis: University of Minnesota Press, 2015.

Lafitau, Joseph-François. *Customs of the American Indians Compared with Customs of Primitive Times*, vol. 1, edited and translated by William Nelson Fenton. Toronto: Champlain Society, 1974.

————. *Moeurs des sauvages Ameriquains, comparées aux moeurs des premiers temps*, 4 vols. Paris, 1724.

Lanctot, Gustave. "La Roche de Mesgouez, Troilus de, Marquis de La Roche-Mesgouez." In *Dictionary of Canadian Biography*, vol. 1, Toronto: University of Toronto/Université Laval, 2003–. http://www.biographi.ca/en/bio/la_roche_de_mesgouez_troilus_de_1E.html (accessed April 28, 2015).

Lane, K. Maria D. "Mapping the Mars Canal Mania: Cartographic Projection and the Creation of a Popular Icon." *Imago Mundi* 58, no. 2 (2006): 198–211.

Lankford, George E., F. Kent Reilly III, and James F. Garber, eds. *Visualizing the Sacred: Cosmic Visions, Regionalism, and the Art of the Mississippian World*. Austin: University of Texas Press, 2011.

Lathrop, John. "John Lathrop D.D., to Judge Davis." In *Proceedings of the Massachusetts Historical Society, 1867–1869*, 114–16. Cambridge: John Wilson and Son, 1869.

Laughton, J. K. "King, James (*bap.* 1750, *d.* 1784)," rev. Andrew C. F. David. *Oxford Dictionary of National Biography*. Oxford: Oxford University Press, 2004. http://www.oxforddnb.com.ezproxy.library.yorku.ca/view/article/15567 (accessed July 6, 2014).

La Vérendrye, Pierre Gaultier de Varennes et de. *Journals and Letters of Pierre Gaultier de Varennes et de La Vérendrye and His Sons,* edited by Lawrence J. Burpee. Toronto: Champlain Society, 1927.

Lenik, Edward J. *Picture Rocks: American Indian Rock Art in the Northeast Woodlands.* Hanover, NH: University Press of New England, 2002.

Leonard, David C. "Harvard's First Science Professor: A Sketch of Isaac Greenwood's Life and Work." *Harvard Library Bulletin* 29, no. 2 (April 1981): 135–68.

Lepore, Jill. *The Name of War: King Philip's War and the Origins of American Identity.* New York: Alfred E. Knopf, 1998.

Lescarbot, Marc. *Histoire de La Nouvelle-France.* Paris: Adrian Perier, 1617.

———. *History of New France [Works],* vol. 1, edited by W. L. Grant. Toronto: Champlain Society, 1907.

Longfellow, Henry Wadsworth. *Ballads and Other Poems.* Cambridge, MA: John Owen, 1842.

Lort, Rev. Michael. "Account of an Antient Inscription in North America." In *Archaeologia,* vol. 8, 290–301. London: Society of Antiquaries of London, 1787.

Lowell, James Russell. *The Biglow Papers,* 2nd series, part 1. London: Trübner & Co., 1862.

Lowenthal, David. "G. P. Marsh and Scandinavian Studies." *Scandinavian Studies* 29, no. 2 (May 1957): 41–52.

Lutz, Donald S. "The Relative Influence of European Writers on Late Eighteenth-Century American Political Thought." *American Political Science Review* 78, no. 1 (March 1984): 189–97.

Mackenzie, Alexander. *Voyages from Montreal through the Continent of North America to the Frozen and Pacific Oceans in 1789 and 1793,* vol. 1. New York: Barnes and Co., 1903.

Macpherson, Alan G. "Pre-Columbian Discoveries and Exploration." In *North American Exploration,* vol. 1: *A New World Exposed,* edited by John Logan Allen, 13–70. Lincoln: University of Nebraska Press, 1997.

Macpherson, James, translator. *The Poems of Ossian,* 2 vols. London: Cadell and Davies, 1807.

Madison, James. "A Letter on the Supposed Fortifications of the Western Country, from Bishop Madison of Virginia to Dr. Barton." *Transactions of the American Philosophical Society* 6 (1809): 132–42.

Magnussén, Finn. "On the Ancient Scandinavians' Division of the Times of Day." In *Mémoire de la Societé Royale des Antiquitaires du Nord, 1836–1839,* 165–92. Copenhagen: Royal Society of Northern Antiquaries, 1839.

Magnusson, Magnus, and Hermann Pálsson. *The Vinland Sagas.* Harmondsworth, UK: Penguin, 1965.

Mallery, Garrick. "Pictographs of the North American Indians." In J. W. Powell, *Fourth Annual Report of the Bureau of Ethnology to the Secretary of the Smithsonian Institution, 1882–83.* Washington: Government Printing Office, 1886.

———. "Spurious Symbolism." *International Review* (January 1882): 45.

Mallet, Paul Henri. *Edda, ou Monumens de la mythologie & de la poésie des anciens peuples du nord.* Geneva and Paris, 1787.

———. *Monumens de la mythologie et de la poésie des Celtes, et particulièrement des anciens Scandinaves.* Copenhagen: Claude Philibert, 1756.

———. *Northern Antiquities: Or, a Description of the Manners, Customs, Religion and Laws of the Ancient Danes, and Other Northern Nations; Including Those of Our Own Saxon Ancestors. With a Translation of the Edda, or System of Runic Mythology, and Other Pieces, from the Ancient Islandic Tongue,* translated by Thomas Percy, 2 vols. London: T. Carnan, 1770.

Malloy, Mary. *Souvenirs of the Fur Trade: Northwest Coast Indian Art and Artifacts Collected by American Mariners, 1788–1844*. Cambridge, MA: Harvard University Press, 2000.

Mancall, Peter C., ed. *Envisioning America: English Plans for the Colonization of North America, 1580–1610*. Boston: Bedford/St. Martin's, 1995.

Manuel, Frank E., and Fritzie Manuel. *James Bowdoin and the Patriot Philosophers*. Memoir No. 247. Philadelphia: American Philosophical Society, 2004.

Martire D'Anghiera, Pietro. *De Orbe Novo: The Eight Decades of Peter Martyr D'Anghera* [*sic*], translated by Francis Augustus MacNutt, vol. 1. New York: G. Putnam's Sons, 1912.

Massachusetts Historical Society. *Proceedings of the Massachusetts Historical Society*, vol. 1 (1791–1835); vol. 2 (1835–38).

Mather, Cotton. "An Extract of Several Letters from Cotton Mather, D.D. to John Woodward, M.D. and Richard Waller, Esq." *Philosophical Transactions* 29 (1714–16): 62–71.

———. *Diary of Cotton Mather 1709–1724*. Massachusetts Historical Society Collections, ser. 7, vol. 8. Boston: Massachusetts Historical Society, 1912.

———. *Magnalia Christi Americana, or Ecclesiastical History of New-England*. London: Thomas Parkhurst, 1702.

———. *The Wonderful Works of God Commemorated*. Boston: S. Green, 1690.

Mather, Increase. *A Brief History of the Warr with the Indians in New-England*. Boston, 1676. Reprinted in Mather, Increase. *The History of King Philip's War*. Boston: Samuel G. Drake, 1862.

Mather, Samuel. *An Attempt to Shew, That America Must Be Known to the Ancients*. Boston, 1773.

May, John Joseph. *Danforth Genealogy*. Boston: Charles H. Pope, 1902.

Mayer, Brantz. *Memoir of Jared Sparks, LL.D*. Baltimore: Author, 1867.

McInnes, Brian D. *Sounding Thunder: The Stories of Francis Pegahmagabow*. Winnipeg: University of Manitoba Press, 2016.

McManis, Douglas R. "The Traditions of Vinland." *Annals of the Association of American Geographers* 59, no. 4 (December 1969): 797–814.

Megill, Allan. *Historical Knowledge, Historical Error: A Contemporary Guide to Practice*. Chicago: University of Chicago Press, 2007.

Meiners, Christoph. *Grundriss der Geschichte der Menschheit*. Frankfurt, 1785; 2nd ed., Lemgo, 1793.

Menasseh Ben Israël. *The Hope of Israel*. London, 1652.

Merriam, Daniel F. "Pehr Kalm: A Swedish Naturalist's Geological Observations in North America, 1748–1751." Abstract. *Earth Sciences History* 25, no. 1 (2006).

Mitchill, Samuel Latham. "ART. 3. Le Printemps, premier chant du Poeme Chinois, Des Saisons." *American Monthly Magazine and Critical Review* (1817–19) (August 1817): 257.

———. "Heads of That Part of the Introductory Discourse." In *Archaeologia Americana*, vol. 1, 338–44. Worcester, MA: American Antiquarian Society, 1820.

———. "The Original Inhabitants of America Consisted of the Same Races with the Malays of Australasia, and the Tatars of the North." *The Medical Repository*, February 1, 1817, 187. Reprinted in *Archaeologia Americana*, vol. 1, 321–25. Worcester, MA: American Antiquarian Society, 1820.

———. "The Original Inhabitants of America Shown to Be of the Same Family and Lineage with Those of Asia." New York, March 31, 1816. In *Archaeologia Americana*, vol. 1, 325–32. Worcester, MA: American Antiquarian Society, 1820.

Moll, Herman. *Atlas Geographus . . . Vol. 3, Asia is One Volume*. London: John Nutt, 1712.

Montesquieu, Charles-Louis de Secondat, Baron de. *De l'Esprit des loix*, 2 vols. Geneva, 1748.

Moore, Norman. "Vallancey, Charles (1721–1812)." *Dictionary of National Biography, 1885–1990*, vol. 58.

Morgan, Edmund S. *The Gentle Puritan: A Life of Ezra Stiles 1727–1795*. 1962; repr. Chapel Hill: University of North Carolina Press, 2011.

Morse, Jedidiah. *The American Universal Geography*, 6th ed. Boston: Thomas & Andrews, 1812.

Morton, Samuel George. *Crania Aegyptica*. Philadelphia: American Philosophical Society, 1844.

———. *An Inquiry into the Distinctive Characteristics of the Aboriginal Race of America*. Boston: Tuttle & Bennett, 1842.

Morton, Thomas. *New English Canaan, or, New Canaan: Containing an Abstract of New England*. Amsterdam, 1637.

Mott, Frank Luther. *A History of American Magazines, 1741–1930*, 5 vols. Cambridge, MA: Belknap Press of Harvard University Press, 1958.

Mudimbe, Valentin Y. "*Romanus Pontifex* (1454) and the Expansion of Europe." In *Race, Discourse, and the Origin of the Americas: A New World View*, edited by Vera Lawrence Hyatt and Rex Nettleford, 58–65. Washington, DC: Smithsonian Institution Press, 1995.

Müller, Gerhard. *Voyages from Asia to America*, translated by Thomas Jefferys. London, 1761.

Mullholland, James. "James Macpherson's Ossian Poems, Oral Traditions, and the Invention of Voice." *Oral Tradition* 24, no. 2 (October 2009): 393–414.

Mumford, Jeremy. "Mixed-Race Identity in a Nineteenth-Century Family: The Schoolcrafts of Sault. Ste. Marie, 1824–27." *Michigan Historical Review* 25, no. 1 (Spring 1999): 1–23.

Murr, Sylvia. "Indianisme et militantisme protestant: Veyssière de la Croze et son *Histoire du christianisme des Indes*." *Dix-Huitième Siècle* 18 (1986): 303–24.

Nansen, Fridtjof. *In Northern Mists: Arctic Exploration in Early Times*, 2 vols. London: William Heinemann, 1911.

Needall, Jeffrey D. "Identity, Race, Gender, and Modernity in the Origins of Gilberto Freyre's Ouevre." *American Historical Review* 100, no. 1 (February 1995): 51–77.

Nevin, Monica. "General Charles Vallancey 1725–1812." *Journal of the Royal Society of Antiquaries of Ireland* 123 (1993): 19–58.

Newhall, Beaumont. *The Daguerreotype in America*. New York: Dover Publications, 1976.

"A New Interpretation of the Dighton Rock Inscription, Massachusetts," in "The Monthly Record." *Geographical Journal* 62, no. 6 (December 1923): 470–71.

New-York Historical Society. *Collections of the New-York Historical Society*, ser. 2, vol. 1. New York: H. Ludwig, 1841.

———. *Proceedings of the New-York Historical Society, 1846*.

Nichols, John Bowyer, ed. *Illustrations of the Literary History of the Eighteenth Century*, vol. 7. London: J. B. Nichols and Son, 1848.

Norder, John. "The Creation and Endurance of Memory and Place among First Nations of Northwestern Ontario, Canada." *International Journal of Historical Archaeology* 16 (2012): 385–400.

Nott, Josiah Clark, and George R. Gliddon. *Types of Mankind*. Philadelphia: Lippincott, Grambo, 1854.

Oberholzter, Cath. "The Living Landscape." In *Before Ontario: The Archaeology of a Province*, edited by Marit K. Munson and Susan M. Jamieson, 153–64. Montreal: McGill-Queens University Press, 2013.

O'Brien, Jean M. *Firsting and Lasting: Writing Indians Out of Existence in New England*. Minneapolis: University of Minnesota Press, 2010.

Oppitz, Michael. "Drawings on Shamanic Drums." *RES: Anthropology and Aesthetics* 22 (Autumn 1992): 62–81.

Osborn, Chase S., and Stellanova Osborn. "Schoolcraft and the American Ethnological Society." *Science* n.s. 97, no. 2511 (February 12, 1943): 161–62.

Oslund, Karen. *Iceland Imagined: Nature, Culture, and Storytelling in the North Atlantic*. Seattle: University of Washington Press, 2013.

Ouellet, Réal, with Mylene Tremblay. "From the Good Savage to the Degenerate Indian: The Amerindian in the Accounts of Travel to America." In *Decentring the Renaissance: Canada and Europe in Multidisciplinary Perspective*, edited by Germaine Warkentin and Carolyn Podruchny, 159–70. Toronto: University of Toronto Press, 2001.

Øverland, Orm. *Immigrant Minds, American Identities: Making the United States Home, 1870–1930*. Urbana: University of Illinois Press, 2000.

Pagden, Anthony. *The Fall of Natural Man: The American Indian and the Origins of Comparative Ethnology*. 1982; Cambridge: Cambridge University Press, 1986.

Paige, Lucius R. *History of Cambridge, Massachusetts, 1630–1877*, vol. 3. Boston: H. O. Houghton, 1877.

Parsons, General [Samuel Holden]. "Discoveries Made in the Western Country." In *Memoirs of the American Academy of Arts and Sciences*, vol. 2, pt. 1, 119–27. Boston, 1793.

Patterson, George. "The Portuguese on the North-East Coast of America, and the First European Attempt at Colonization There. A Lost Chapter in American History." In *Proceedings and Transactions of the Royal Society of Canada*, ser. 1, vol. 8 (1890).

Pearce, Roy Harvey. *The Savages of America: A Study of the Indian and the Idea of Civilization*, rev. ed. Baltimore: John Hopkins Press, 1965.

Pease, Charles Stanley. *History of Conway (Massachusetts) 1796–1917*. Springfield, MA: Springfield Printing and Binding Co., 1917.

Pennant, Thomas. *Arctic Zoology*, vol. 1. London: Henry Hughs, 1784.

Pennell, Francis W. "Benjamin Smith Barton as Naturalist." *Proceedings of the American Philosophical Society* 86, no. 1 (September 25, 1942): 108–22.

Pickles, John D. "Lort, Michael (1724/5–1790)." *Oxford Dictionary of National Biography*. Oxford: Oxford University Press, 2004. http://www.oxforddnb.com.ezproxy.library.yorku.ca /view/article/17022 (accessed July 2, 2014).

Pohl, Frederick J. *Atlantic Crossings before Columbus*. New York: W. W. Norton, 1961.

———. *The Lost Discovery: Uncovering the Track of the Vikings in America*. New York: W. W. Norton, 1952.

Pomedli, Michael. *Living with Animals: Ojibwe Spirit Powers*. Toronto: University of Toronto Press, 2014.

Quincy, J. P. "Memoir of Thomas Hopkins Webb, MD." *Proceedings of the Massachusetts Historical Society* 19 (1881–82): 337–38.

Quincy, Josiah. *The History of Harvard University*, vol. 2. Cambridge: John Owen, 1840.

Quinn, David B., and Alison Quinn. *The English New England Voyages 1602–1608*. London: Hakluyt Society, 1983.

Rabinowitz, Louis Isaac. "Ten Lost Tribes." In *Encyclopaedia Judaica*, 2nd ed., edited by Michael Berenbaum and Fred Skolnik, vol. 19, 639–40. Detroit: Macmillan Reference USA, 2007.

Rafinesque, C. S. *The American Nations; Or, Outlines of Their General History, Ancient and Modern: Including the Whole History of the Earth and Mankind in the Western Hemisphere*. Philadelphia: Author, 1836.

Rafn, Carl [Charles] Christian. *America Discovered in the Tenth Century*. New York: William Jackson, 1838.

———, ed. *Antiquitates Americanae sive scriptores septentrionales rerum ante-columbianarum in America*. Hafniae [Copenhagen]: Royal Society of Northern Antiquaries, 1837.

———. "Astronomical Evidence for the Site of the Chief Settlement of the Ancient Scandinavians in North America." In *Mémoires de la société royal des antiquaries du nord, 1840–1844*, 128–30. Copenhagen: Royal Society of Northern Antiquaries, 1844.

———. *Report Addressed by the Royal Society of Northern Antiquaries to Its British and American Members*. Copenhagen: Royal Society of Northern Antiquaries, 1836.

Rajnovich, Grace. *Reading Rock Art: Interpreting the Indian Rock Paintings of the Canadian Shield*. Toronto: Natural Heritage/Natural History, 1994.

Raynal, Guillaume-Thomas. *Histoire philosophique et politique des établissemens & du commerce des Européens dans les deux Indes*, vol. 7. La Haye: Gosse Fils, 1774.

Redman, Samuel J. *Bone Rooms: From Scientific Racism to Human Prehistory in Museums*. Cambridge, MA: Harvard University Press, 2016.

Rhode Island Historical Society. *Proceedings of the Rhode Island Historical Society 1782–3*. Providence: Rhode Island Historical Society, 1873.

Rich, Evelyn. "Richard Rich of Eastham on Cape Cod and Some of His Descendants" (in five parts). *New England Historical and Genealogical Register* 83 (1929): 261–78, 394–414; 84 (1930): 34–62, 117–34, 294–304.

Richter, Daniel. *The Ordeal of the Longhouse*. Chapel Hill: University of North Carolina Press, 1992.

Ricklefs, M. C. "The Birth of the Abangan." *Bijdragen tot de Taal-, Land- en Volkenkunde* 162, no. 1 (2006): 35–55.

Rogers, Francis M. *Atlantic Islanders of the Azores and Madeiras*. North Quincy, MA: Christopher Publishing House, 1979.

Ross, Margaret Clunies. "The Intellectual Complexion of the Icelandic Middle Ages: Toward a New Profile of Old Icelandic Saga Literature." *Scandinavian Studies* 69, no. 4 (Fall 1997): 443–53.

Roth, Cecil. *A Life of Menasseh ben Israel: Rabbi, Printer and Diplomat*. Philadelphia: Jewish Publication Society of America, 1934.

Roy, Susan. *These Mysterious People: Shaping History and Archaeology in a Northwest Coast Community*. Montreal: McGill-Queen's University Press, 2010.

Ruffin, J. Rixey. *A Paradise of Reason: William Bentley and the Struggle for an Enlightened and Christian Republic in America, 1783–1805*. New York: Oxford University Press, 2007.

Ruggle, Richard E. "McMurray, William." In *Dictionary of Canadian Biography*, vol. 12, Toronto: University of Toronto/Université Laval, 2003. http://www.biographi.ca/en/bio/mcmurray_william_12E.html (accessed April 20, 2016).

Sagard, Gabriel. *Le grand voyage du pays des Hurons*, edited by Réal Ouellet. Québec: Bibliothèque québecoise, 2007.

Said, Edward W. *Orientalism*. New York: Vintage Books, 1979.

Sayre, Gordon M. *Les Sauvages Américains: Representations of Native Americans in French and English Colonial Literature*. Chapel Hill: University of North Carolina Press, 1997.

———. "The Mound Builders and the Imagination of American Antiquity in Jefferson, Bartram, and Chateaubriand." *Early American Literature* 33 (1998): 225–49.

———. "Prehistoric Diasporas: Colonial Theories of the Origins of Native American Peoples." In *Writing Race across the Atlantic World: Medieval to Modern*, edited by Philip D. Beidler and Gary Taylor. New York: Palgrave Macmillan, 2005.

Schlesinger, Roger, and Arthur P. Stabler. *André Thevet's North America: A Sixteenth-Century View*. Montréal: McGill-Queen's University Press, 1986.

Schmidt, David L., and Murdena Marshall. *Mi'kmaq Hieroglyphic Prayers: Readings in North America's First Indigenous Script*. Halifax: Nimbus Publishing, 2006.

Schnackenbourg, Éric. "L'île des confins: Les représentations de l'Islande et des Islandais dans la France moderne (XVIIᵉ–XVIIIᵉ siècles)." *Histoire, Économie et Societé* 29, no. 1 (March 2010): 24–38.

Schoolcraft, Henry Rowe. *Algic Researches, Comprising Inquiries Respecting the Mental Characteristics of the North American Indians*, 2 vols. New York: Harper & Brothers, 1839.

———. "Art. II. *Archaeologia Americana*." *North American Review* 45, no. 96 (July 1837): 34–59, 258.

———. "Article IX. The Ante-Columbian History of America." *American Biblical Repository* (April 1839). In *The American Biblical Repository*, ser. 2, vol. 1, 430–49. New York: Gould, Newman and Saxton, 1839.

———. *Historical and Statistical Information Respecting the History, Condition and Prospects of the Indian Tribes of the United States*, 6 vols. Philadelphia: Lippincott, Grambo & Company, 1851–57.

———. *Incentives to the Study of the Ancient Period of American History: An address, delivered before the New York Historical Society, at its forty-second anniversary, 17th November, 1846*. New York: Press of the Historical Society, 1847.

———. "*La Découverte des Sources du Mississippi*." *North American Review* 27, no. 60 (July 1828): 89–114.

———. *Narrative Journal of Travels through the Northwestern Regions of the United States Extending from Detroit through the Great Chain of American Lakes, to the Sources of the Mississippi River*. Albany: E. & E. Hosford, 1821.

———. *Narrative of an Expedition through the Upper Mississippi to Itasca Lake, the Actual Source of This River*. New York: Harper & Brothers, 1834.

———. "Observations Respecting the Grave Creek Mound." In *Transactions of the American Ethnological Society*, vol. 1, 369–420. New York: Bartlett and Welford, 1845.

Schoolcraft, Henry Rowe, and Carl Christian Rafn. "Brief Notices of a Runic Inscription Found in North America, communicated by Henry R. Schoolcraft in Letters to Charles C. Rafn, Secretary, with Remarks annexed by the latter." In *Mémoires de la société royal des antiquaires du nord*, vol. 2, 1840–1844, 119–127. Copenhagen: RSNA, 1844.

Seaver, Kirsten A. *The Frozen Echo: Greenland and the Exploration of North America ca A.D. 1000–1500*. Stanford, CA: Stanford University Press, 1996.

———. *Maps, Myths, and Men: The Story of the Vinland Map*. Stanford, CA: Stanford University Press, 2004.

———. "'Pygmies' of the Far North." *Journal of World History* 19, no. 1 (2008): 63–87.

Seed, Patricia. *Ceremonies of Possession in Europe's Conquest of the New World, 1492–1640*. Cambridge: Cambridge University Press, 1995.

Seeman, Eric R. *Death in the New World: Cross-Cultural Encounters, 1492–1800*. Philadelphia: University of Pennsylvania Press, 2011.

Senarclens, Jean de. "Mallet, Paul-Henri." *Dictionnaire historique de la Suisse*. http://www.hls-dhs-dss.ch/textes/f/F25673.php (accessed August 8, 2014).

Shipton, Clifford K. "The American Antiquarian Society." *William and Mary Quarterly*, ser. 3, 2, no. 2 (April 1945): 164–72.

Shoemaker, Nancy. *A Strange Likeness: Becoming Red and White in Eighteenth-Century North America*. New York: Oxford University Press, 2004.

Silva, Manuel Luciano da. *Portuguese Pilgrims and Dighton Rock: The First Chapter in American History*. Bristol, RI, 1971.

Silverberg, Robert. *Mound Builders of Ancient America: The Archaeology of a Myth*. Greenwich, CT: New York Graphic Society, 1968.

Silverman, David. *Red Brethren: The Brothertown and Stockbridge Indians and the Problem of Race in Early America*. Ithaca, NY: Cornell University Press, 2010.

Simmons, William Scranton. *Spirit of the New England Tribes: Indian History and Folklore, 1620–1984*. Hanover, NH: University Press of New England, 1986.

Simms, Jeptha Root. *History of Schoharie County, and Border Wars of New York*, vol. 3. Albany, NY: Munsell and Tanner, 1845.

Simpson, John. *The First English Dictionary of Slang 1699*. Oxford: Bodleian Library, 2010.

Sloan, Kim. *A New World: England's First View of America*. Chapel Hill: University of North Carolina Press, 2007.

Smith, Joshua Toulmin. *The Northmen in New England, or, America in the Tenth Century*. Boston: Hilliard, Gray, and Co., 1839.

Snow, Dean R. *The Archaeology of New England*. New York: Academic Press, 1980.

———. "The Solon Petroglyphs and Eastern Abenaki Shamanism." In *Papers of the Seventh Algonquian Conference*, edited by William Cowan, 281–88. Ottawa: Carleton University, 1976.

Southey, Robert. *Madoc*, 2 vols. London: Longman Rees and Orme, 1805.

Sparks, Jared. "Antiquities of North America." *American Monthly Magazine* (January 1836): 67

Spencer, Frank, and Benjamin Smith Barton. "Two Unpublished Essays on the Anthropology of North America by Benjamin Smith Barton." *Isis* 68, no. 244 (December 1977): 567–73.

Squier, Ephraim George. "Observations on the Original Monuments of the Mississippi Valley." *Transactions of the American Ethnological Society* 2 (1848): 131–207.

Squier, Ephriam George, and Edwin Hamilton Davis. *Ancient Monuments of the Mississippi Valley, from the Smithsonian Contributions to Knowledge*. New York: Bartlett & Welford, 1848.

Stafford, Fiona. "Dr. Johnson and the Ruffian: New Evidence in the Dispute between Samuel Johnson and James Macpherson." *Notes and Queries* 36, no. 1 (March 1989): 70–77.

Stanton, William. *The Leopard's Spots: Scientific Attitudes toward Race in America 1815–59*. Chicago: University of Chicago Press, 1960.

Stephens, Walter. *Giants in Those Days: Folklore, Ancient History, and Nationalism*. Lincoln: University of Nebraska Press, 1989.

Sterling, Keir B., Richard P. Harmond, George A. Cevaso, and Lorne F. Hammond, eds. *Biographical Dictionary of American and Canadian Naturalists and Environmentalists*. Westport, CT: Greenwood Publishing Group, 1997.

Stern, Alexandra Minna. *Eugenic Nation: Faults and Frontiers of Better Breeding in Modern America*. Berkeley: University of California Press, 2005.

Stiles, Ezra. *Extracts from the Itineraries and Other Miscellanies of Ezra Stiles, D.D., LL.D., 1755-1794 with a Selection from His Correspondence*, edited by Franklin Bowditch Dexter. New Haven, CT: Yale University Press, 1916.

———. *Letters and Papers of Ezra Stiles, President of Yale College, 1778–1795*, edited by Mark Harkness and Isabel M. Calder. New Haven, CT: Yale University Library, 1933.

———. *The Literary Diary of Ezra Stiles*, edited by Franklin Bowditch Dexter, vol. 3. New York: C. Scribner's Sons, 1901.

———. "The United States Elevated to Glory and Honor (1783)," edited by Reiner Smolinski. Electronic Texts in American Studies, Libraries at the University of Nebraska–Lincoln, Paper 41. http://digitalcommons.unl.edu/etas/41 (accessed July 1, 2014).

Stolzenberg, Daniel. *Egyptian Oedipus: Athanasius Kircher and the Secrets of Antiquity*. Chicago: University of Chicago Press, 2013.

Story, Ronald. "Harvard and the Boston Brahmins: A Study in Institutional and Class Development, 1800–1865." *Journal of Social History* 8, no. 3 (Spring 1975): 94–121.

Strabo. *The Geography of Strabo*, translated by H. R. Jones and J. R. S. Sterrett, 8 vols. London, 1917.

Strahlenberg, Philip John [Philipp-Johann] von. *An Historico-Geographical Description of the North and Eastern Parts of Europe and Asia*. London: W. Innys and R. Manby, 1738.

Sutherland, Kathy. *Rock Paintings at Hueco Tanks State Historic Site*. Texas Parks and Wildlife, 2006.

Tanner, John. *A Narrative of the Captivity and Adventures of John Tanner, (U.S. Interpreter at the Saut de Ste. Marie,) During Thirty Years Residence among the Indians in the Interior of North America*. New York: G. & C. & H. Carvill, 1830.

Taylor, Alan. "The Early Republic's Supernatural Economy: Treasure Seeking in the American Northeast, 1780–1830." *American Quarterly* 38, no. 1 (Spring 1986): 6–34.

Thomas, Cyrus. "Report on the Mound Explorations of the Bureau of Ethnology." In *Twelfth Annual Report of the Bureau of Ethnology to the Secretary of the Smithsonian Institution, 1890–91*, by J. W. Powell, 17–722. Washington, DC: Government Printing Office, 1894.

Thomas, David Hurst. *Skull Wars: Kennewick Man, Archaeology, and the Battle for Native American Identity*. New York: Basic Books, 2000.

Thórdarson, Matthias. *The Vinland Voyages*. New York: American Geographical Society, 1930.

Thorowgood, Thomas. *Iewes in America*. London, 1650.

———. *Jews in America*. London, 1660.

Thwaites, Rueben Gold, ed. *The Jesuit Relations and Allied Documents: Travels and Explorations of the Jesuit Missionaries in New Frances 1610-1791*, 4 vols. Cleveland: Burrows Brothers, 1898. http://puffin.creighton.edu/jesuit/relations/ (accessed June 25, 2014).

Todorov, Tzevetan. *The Conquest of America: The Question of the Other*, translated by Richard Howard. New York: Harper & Row, 1984.

Tolstoi, I. [Ivan], N. P. [Nikodim Pavlovich] Kondakov, and Salomon Reinach. *Antiquités de la Russie méridionale*. Paris: E. Leroux, 1891.

Tonnelat, E[rnest]. "Romantisme et Scandinaves." *Annales d'histoire économique et sociale* 7, no. 35 (September 30, 1935): 501–2.

Trigger, Bruce G. "Alternative Archaeologies: Nationalist, Colonialist, Imperialist." *Man* n.s. 19, no. 3 (September 1984): 355–70.

———. *A History of Archaeological Thought*, 2nd ed. Cambridge: Cambridge University Press, 2006.

———. *Natives and Newcomers: Canada's "Heroic Age" Reconsidered*. Montreal: McGill-Queen's University Press, 1985.

———. "The Strategy of Iroquoian Prehistory." *Ontario Archaeology* 14 (1970): 3–48.

Trouillot, Michel-Rolph. *Silencing the Past: Power and the Production of History*. Boston: Beacon Press, 1995.

Vallancey, Charles. *An Essay on the Antiquity of the Irish Language*. Dublin: S. Powell, 1772.

———. *A Grammar of the Iberno-Celtic, or Irish Language*. Dublin: R. Marchbank, 1773.

————. "Observations on the American Inscription." In *Archaeologia*, vol. 8, 302–6. London: Society of Antiquaries of London, 1787.

Vance, Norman. "Vallancey, Charles (c.1726–1812)." *Oxford Dictionary of National Biography*. Oxford: Oxford University Press, 2004. http://www.oxforddnb.com.ezproxy.library.yorku.ca /view/article/28051 (accessed July 2, 2014).

Van Slyck, J. D. *New England Manufacturers and Manufactories*, vol. 1. Boston: Van Slyck and Co., 1879.

Vastokas, Joan. "The Peterborough Petroglyphs: Native or Norse?" In *The Rock-Art of Eastern North America: Capturing the Images and Insight*, edited by Carol Diaz-Granados and James R. Duncan, 277–89. Tuscaloosa: University of Alabama Press, 2004.

Vastokas, Joan, and Romas Vastokas. *Sacred Art of the Algonkians: A Study of the Peterborough Petroglyphs*. Peterborough, ON: Mansard Press, 1973.

Verrazano, Giovanni da. "Cellère Codex." Translated by Susan Tarrow. In *The Voyages of Giovanni da Verrazzano, 1524–28*, by Lawrence C. Wroth. New Haven, CT: Yale University Press for the Pierpont Morgan Library, 1970.

Vespucci, Amerigo. *The Letters of Amerigo Vespucci and Other Documents Illustrative of His Life*, edited by Clements R. Markham. London: Hakluyt Society, 1894.

Vidal-Naquet, Pierre. "Atlantis and the Nations [translated by Janet Lloyd]" *Critical Inquiry* 18, no. 2 (Winter 1992): 300–26.

Wahlgren, Eric. *The Kensington Stone, a Mystery Solved*. Madison: University of Wisconsin Press, 1958.

Wallace, Birgitta Linderoth, and William W. Fitzhugh. "Stumbles and Pitfalls in the Search for Viking America." In *Vikings: The North Atlantic Saga*, edited by William W. Fitzhugh and Elizabeth I. Ward, 374–84. Washington, DC: Smithsonian Institution Press, 2000.

Wallace, W. S. "The Literature Relating to the Norse Voyages to America." *Canadian Historical Review* 20, no. 1 (March 1939): 8–16.

Warren, Stephen. *The World the Shawnees Made*, Chapel Hill: University of North Carolina Press, 2014.

Warrior, Robert, ed. *The World of Indigenous North America*. New York: Routledge, 2015.

Watkins, John. *A Biographical Dictionary of the Living Authors of Great Britain and Ireland*. London: Henry Colburn, 1816.

Webb, Thomas H. "February Meeting. Letter of James Sullivan; Professor Rafn," *Proceedings of the Massachusetts Historical Society* 8 (1864–65): 171–201.

Webb, Thomas H., and Carl C. Rafn. "Account of an Ancient Structure in Newport, Rhode-Island, the Vinland of the Scandinavians, Communicated by Thomas H. Webb, M.D., in Letters to Professor Charles C. Rafn; with Remarks Annexed by the Latter." In *Mémoires de la Societé Royale des Antiquaries du Nord, 1836–1839*, 361–85.

————. "Accounts of a Discovery of Antiquities Made at Fall River, Massachusetts, Communicated by Thomas H. Webb, M.D., in Letters to Charles C. Rafn, Secretary, with Remarks by the Latter." In *Mémoires de la Société royale des antiquaries du Nord, 1840–1844*, 104–19.

Webster, Noah. "Letter 1—No Title: Note," *American Museum* 8 (1790): 11.

Weisberger, R. William. *Speculative Freemasonry and the Enlightenment*. New York: Columbia University Press, 1993.

Weisenburger, Francis P. "Caleb Atwater: Pioneer Politician and Historian." *Ohio History Quarterly* 68, no. 1 (January 1959): 18–37.

Wellman, Klaus F. "Trends in North American Rock Research: A Quantitative Evaluation of the Literature." *American Antiquity* 45, no. 3 (July 1980): 531–40.

Wesley, John, *Explanatory Notes upon the Old Testament*, vol. 1. Bristol, UK: William Pine, 1765.

West, Francis D. "John Bartram and the American Philosophical Society." *Pennsylvania History* 23, no. 4 (October 1956): 463–66.

Wheaton, Henry "Art. VIII. Scandinavian Literature," *American Quarterly Review* 3 (June 1, 1828): 481.

———. *Elements of International Law*, edited by William Beach Lawrence, 6th ed. Boston: Little, Brown and Co., 1855.

———. *History of the Northmen, or Danes and Normans, from the Earliest Times to the Conquest of England by William of Normandy*. Philadelphia: Carey and Lea, 1831.

White, George L., Jr. "Longfellow's Interest in Scandinavia During the Years 1835–1847." *Scandinavian Studies* 17, no. 2 (May 1942): 70–82.

Wilcox, David R., and Don D. Fowler. "The Beginnings of Anthropological Archaeology in the North American Southwest: From Thomas Jefferson to the Pecos Conference." *Journal of the Southwest* 44, no. 2 (Summer 2002): 121–234.

Wilkinson, Norman B. " 'New Norway'—A Contemporary Account." *Pennsylvania History* 15, no. 2 (April 1948): 120–32.

Wilkinson, Norman B., Robert K. Currin, and Patrick A. Kennedy. "Ole Bull's New Norway." *Historic Pennsylvania Leaflet* No. 14. Harrisburg: Pennsylvania Historical and Museum Commission, 1995. http://www.portal.state.pa.us/portal/server.pt/community/places/4278/ole_bull's_new_norway/472266 (accessed September 18, 2014).

Williams, John. *An Enquiry into the Truth of the Tradition Concerning the Discovery of America, by Prince Madog ab Owen Gwyned about the Year, 1170*. London: J. Brown, 1791.

Williams, Stephen. *Fantastic Archaeology: The Wild Side of North American Prehistory*. Philadelphia: University of Pennsylvania Press, 1991.

Willoughby, Charles Clark. *Antiquities of the New England Indians*. Cambridge, MA: Peabody Museum, 1935.

———. Review of *Dighton Rock: A Study of the Written Rocks of New England*, by Edmund Burke Delabarre. *American Anthropologist* n.s. 31, no. 3 (July–September 1929): 518–21.

Wilson, Daniel. *The Lost Atlantis: And Other Ethnographic Studies*. New York: Macmillan and Co., 1892.

———. *Prehistoric Man: Researches into the Origin of Civilization in the Old and New World*, 2 vols. London: Macmillan and Co., 1862.

Wilson, Gaye. "Dealings with Mellimelli, Colorful Envoy from Tunis." *Monticello Newsletter* 14, no. 2 (Winter 2003): 1–3.

Wilson, James Grant, and John Fiske, eds. *Appleton's Cyclopaedia of American Biography*, vol. 1. New York: D. Appleton and Co., 1887.

Winship, George Parker. *The Coronado Expedition 1540–1542*. Washington, DC: Government Printing Office, 1896.

Winthrop, James. "Account of an Inscribed Rock, at Dighton, in the Commonwealth of Massachusetts, Accompanied with a Copy of the Inscription." Cambridge, November 10, 1788. In *Memoirs of the American Academy of Arts and Sciences*, vol. 2, no. 2, 126–29. Charlestown: Samuel Etheridge, 1804.

Withers, Charles W. J. "Pennant, Thomas (1726–1798)." *Oxford Dictionary of National Biography*. Oxford: Oxford University Press, 2004. http://www.oxforddnb.com.ezproxy.library.yorku.ca/view/article/21860 (accessed July 9, 2014).

Witthoft, John, and William A. Hunter. "The Seventeenth-Century Origins of the Shawnee." *Ethnohistory* 2, no. 1 (Winter 1955): 42–57.

Woodcock, George. "Tanner, John." In *Dictionary of Canadian Biography*, vol. 7. Toronto: University of Toronto/Université Laval, 2003–. http://www.biographi.ca/en/bio/tanner _john_7E.html (accessed September 24, 2014).

Wright, Herbert F. "Origin of American Aborigines: A Famous Controversy." *Catholic Historical Review* 3, no. 3 (October 1917): 257–75.

Yates, John V. N., and Joseph W. Moulton. *History of the State of New-York*, vol. 1, pt. 1. New York: A. T. Goodrich, 1824.

Young, George F. W. *Miguel Corte-Real and the Dighton Writing Rock*. Taunton, MA: Old Colony Historical Society, 1970.

Zeisberger, David. *David Zeisberger's History of the Northern American Indians*, edited by Archer Butler Hulbert and William Nathaniel Schwarze. Columbus: F. J. Heer for Ohio State Archaeological and Historical Society, 1910.

———. *Grammar of the Language of the Lenni Lenape or Delaware Indians*, translated by Peter Stephen Du Ponceau. Philadelphia: American Philosophical Society, 1827.

Zestermann, Christian Augustus Adolph. *Memoir on the European Colonization of America in Ante-Historic Times, by Dr., of Leipsic, with Critical Observations Thereon, by E. G. Squier, Esq., from the Proceedings of the American Ethnological Society, April 1851.* S.l.: s.n., 1851.

Zoltvany, Yves F. "Gaultier de Varennes et de la Vérendrye, Pierre." In *Dictionary of Canadian Biography*, vol. 3. Toronto: University of Toronto/Université Laval, 2003–. http://www.bio graphi.ca/en/bio/gaultier_de_varennes_et_de_la_verendrye_pierre_3E.html (accessed September 28, 2016).

Web Resources

"About John Russell Bartlett." John Russell Bartlett Society of Brown University. http://www .brown.edu/Facilities/John_Carter_Brown_Library/jrb/about.html (accessed August 18, 2014).

"About PEM." Peabody Essex Museum. http://pem.org/about/museum_history (accessed August 14, 2014).

"L'Affaire Calas." Musée virtuel du Protestantisme. http://www.museeprotestant.org/notice /laffaire-calas/ (accessed July 1, 2014).

Amherst College Biographical Record, Centennial Edition (1821–1921). http://acbiorecord.yanco .com/index.html (accessed September 24, 2014).

"Andrew Jackson, VII President of the United States: 1829–1837, Second Annual Message, December 6, 1830." American Presidency Project. http://www.presidency.ucsb.edu/ws/?pid =29472 (accessed August 9, 2014).

"Antoine Court de Gébelin (1724 ou 1728–1784)." Musée virtuel du Protestantisme. http://www .museeprotestant.org/notice/antoine-court-de-gebelin-1724-ou-1728-1784 (accessed July 1, 2014).

Archives of the History of American Psychology, University of Akron. Finding Aid, Delabarre Papers (M260). http://cdm15960.contentdm.oclc.org/cdm/ref/collection/p15960coll10/id /682 (accessed June 4, 2016).

Bedarik, Robert G. "Creating Futile Iconographic Meanings." http://home.vicnet.net.au /~auranet/interpret/web/icono.html (accessed December 13, 2013).

Beinecke Rare Book and Manuscript Library, Yale University. http://brbl-dl.library.yale.edu (accessed December 10, 2014).

Bellows Falls Island Multiple Resource Area. http://www.crjc.org/heritage/V06-62.htm (accessed December 10, 2014).

"Biographical Note." George F. Young Papers. Online Archive of California. http://www.oac .cdlib.org/findaid/ark:/13030/c8w37xsr/admin/#ref2 (accessed June 4, 2016).

"Biography." Samuel Latham Mitchell Papers, 1802–15, William L. Clements Library, University of Michigan. http://quod.lib.umich.edu/c/clementsmss/umich-wcl-M-2015mit?view=text (accessed August 9, 2014).

Boston Athenaeum. http://cdm.bostonathenaeum.org (accessed December 10, 2014).

"Cabot, William B. (William Brooks)." Social Networks and Archival Context (SNAC), University of Virginia. http://socialarchive.iath.virginia.edu/ark:/99166/w6p27h3x (accessed October 3, 2014).

"Clinton, De Witt, (1769–1828)." Biographical Directory of the United States Congress. http://bio guide.congress.gov/scripts/biodisplay.pl?index=C000525 (accessed August 9, 2014).

"The Coins of Colonial and Early America." Department of Special Collections, University of Notre Dame. http://www.coins.nd.edu/ColCoin/index.html (accessed September 12, 2014).

"De Witt Clinton (1769–1828)." New Netherland Institute. http://www.newnetherlandinstitute .org/history-and-heritage/dutch_americans/dewitt-clinton/ (accessed August 9, 2014).

"Dighton Rock State Park." Energy and Environmental Affairs, Government of Massachusetts. http://www.mass.gov/eea/agencies/dcr/massparks/region-south/dighton-rock-state-park .html (accessed December 10, 2014).

Encyclopedia Brunonia. Brown University. http://www.brown.edu/Administration/News _Bureau/Databases/Encyclopedia/ (accessed August 13, 2014).

"The Founding." Exhibits at Brown University Library, Brown University. http://www.brown .edu/Facilities/University_Library/exhibits/education/founding.html (accessed June 29, 2014).

Friends of Dighton Rock Museum. https://www.facebook.com /FriendsOfDightonRockMuseum/ (accessed June 4, 2016).

"Georges-Louis Leclerc, Comte de Buffon." Académie française. http://www.academie -francaise.fr/les-immortels/georges-louis-leclerc-comte-de-buffon (accessed June 30, 2014).

Grimes, John R. "Curiosity, Cabinets, and Knowledge." In *A Perspective on the Native American Collection of the Peabody Essex Museum*. http://www.pem.org/aux/pdf/mission/Grimes -Cabinets-Curiosity-Knowledge-sm.pdf (accessed August 14, 2014).

"Hawley, Gideon. Journal and Letterbook." Congregational Library and Archives. http://www .congregationallibrary.org/nehh/series2/HawleyGideon1237 (accessed June 11, 2014).

"Historical Note." John Russell Bartlett Papers (MSS 286). Rhode Island Historical Society. http://www.rihs.org/mssinv/Mss286.htm (accessed August 18, 2014).

Hjalmar and Harold Holand Papers, 1922–72. Wisconsin Historical Society. http://digital .library.wisc.edu/1711.dl/wiarchives.uw-whs-gb0060 (accessed October 19, 2014).

Hughes, Lynn Gordon. "Thomas Appleton." Dictionary of Unitarian and Universalist Biography. http://uudb.org/articles/thomasappleton.html (accessed September 14, 2014).

Humanities at Stanford. "Dark Side of the Enlightenment." Stanford Humanities Center. http: //humanexperience.stanford.edu/supere (accessed July 1, 2014).

Jewish Encyclopedia (1906). http://www.jewishencyclopedia.com/ (accessed June 25, 2014).

"Leaves of an Hour: The Harris Collection: The Original Collectors: Albert Gorton Greene."
Brown University Library. http://www.brown.edu/Facilities/University_Library/exhibits
/leaves/harrearly.html (accessed August 19, 2014).

"Mitchill, Samuel Latham," Biographical Directory of the United States Congress. http://bio
guide.congress.gov/scripts/biodisplay.pl?index=m000831 (accessed August 9, 2014).

Musée virtuel du Protestantisme. http://www.museeprotestant.org.

"Papers of Stephen Sewall, 1764–1797: An Inventory." Harvard University Archives. http://oasis
.lib.harvard.edu/oasis/deliver/~hua57010 (accessed July 1, 2014).

Portuguese-American Digital Newspaper Collections at the University of Massachusetts
Dartmouth. http://www.lib.umassd.edu/PAA/portuguese-american-digital-newspaper
-collections (accessed December 10, 2014).

"Primary Documents in American History: Indian Removal Act." Library of Congress. http:
//www.loc.gov/rr/program/bib/ourdocs/Indian.html (accessed August 9, 2014).

"Samuel H. Parsons." Ohio Historical Society. http://www.ohiohistorycentral.org/index.php
?title=Samuel_H._Parsons&oldid=28394 (accessed July 9, 2014).

Sanders, Tom. "Jeffers Petroglyphs: A Recording of 7000 Years of North American History."
http://sites.mnhs.org/historic-sites/sites/sites.mnhs.org.historic-sites/files/docs_pdfs
/Jeffers-Petroglyphs- history.pdf (accessed October 22, 2015).

Sheola, Noah. "The Harris Family." Boston Athenaeum. http://www.bostonathenaeum.org
/node/861 (accessed September 12, 2014).

Silva, Manuel Luciano da. www.dightonrock.com. No longer extant. Archived by the author.

"Treaty of Fort Finney (1786)." Ohio Historical Society. http://www.ohiohistorycentral.org
/index.php?title=Treaty_of_Fort_Finney_(1786)&oldid=32505 (accessed July 9, 2014).

"Webber, Samuel, 1759–1810. Papers of Samuel Webber: An Inventory." Harvard University
Archives. http://oasis.lib.harvard.edu//oasis/deliver/deepLink?_collection=oasis&uniqueId
=hua06005 (accessed July 9, 2014).

Index

References to figures appear in bold

Norder, John W., 8

Norse: in Anglo–American Gothicism, 58, 136–37, 152–53, 194–95, 200, 223–24; in Danish "nationalist" archaeology, 134; and Dighton Rock, 2, 3, 9, 15–18, 113, 132–53, 161–62, 164, 172, 173, 177–80, 185, 186, 194–98, 200, 202, 206, 223–24, 236–39; in Grotius, 32; misunderstood in Clinton, 119; and Northmen's Rock, 224, 280n54; in Scandinavian-American place-making, 192–93, 214, 215–16; in Stiles, 69. *See also* Vinland

Northwest Ordinance (1787), 77

Nott, Josiah Clark, and George R. Gliddon, *Types of Mankind*, 189

O'Brien, Jean, 23–24, 37

Ohio mounds. *See* Mounds: American, and Mound Builders theory

Ojibwa people and language, 6, 7–8, 21, 55, 102–3, 106, 154–57, 164, 166–68, 182. *See also* Anishinabe; Chippewa

Old Colony Historical Society (OCHS): founding, 183; Hennedy lecture at Dighton Rock Museum, 234; ownership of Dighton Rock, 16, 197–98, 222–23; presentation of Dighton Rock deed for state park, 226–27; and rock's transformation into Portuguese relic, 16, 217, 226–27; and Young, 235

Oneida, 66, 125; clans, 245n13

Onondaga, 106, 122, 125; Ononhaghwage, 106

Ontology. *See* Indigenous cosmology

Ordronaux, John, 183–87

Orientalism, incl. Indo-European studies, 43, 58, 70, 112, 126–27

Osage, 125

Øverland, Orm: and "filiopietistic" history, 228; and immigrant "home-making," 10, 192–93

Pacific, European exploration of, 61, 73–74

Paddack, Elisha, 52

Paine, Thomas, 40, 97

Parsons, Samuel Holden, 77–79, 81–83, **82**, 121, 252n92

Peabody Essex Museum, 96

Peabody Museum, Harvard, 92, 220–21, 267n104

Pearce, Roy Harvey, 10, 24

Pennant, Thomas: and Barton, 83, 86, 122, 123; Beringia and multiple-migration displacement scenario, 12, 73–75, 79, 80, 83, 118, 251n71; and Clinton, 117–19; and Forster, 54–55, 73; and Jefferson, 80; on location of Vinland, 134–35; on Madoc, 122, 123; and Mitchill, 122; and Schoolcraft, 182–83; and Vallancey, 73–74, 87

Pequot, 21, 106

Percept ambiguity, in Indigenous glyphs, 7–8, 202

Percy, Bishop Thomas, 72, 247n58

Petroglyphs. *See* Rock art

Philip. *See* Metacom (Metacomem, Philip, Pumetacom)

Phillips, Ruth B., 103

Philology, antiquarian, 120–21; defined, 113; versus archaeology, 120

Philosophical Transactions. See Royal Society of London

Phoenicians: and Algonquian language, 71, 159, 209; and Celtic/Irish language, 71, 123, 159, 209; and Dighton Rock, 2, 14, 17, 51–54, 60–75, 85, 87, 89, 90, 94, 98, 108–9, 113, 114, 115, 117, 130–31, 149–50, 197, 213, 236–39; and Grave Creek stone, 272n41; and Northmen's Rock, 280n54; as transatlantic migrants, 119, 213

Pickering, John, 32, 146, 148, 272n15

Pictographic writing (Indigenous), 75, 89, 156, 172, 179, 182–83, 268n15

74–75; "Tartarian" coins in Massachu-
setts, 99, 139; "Tartarian" inscription in
Strahlenberg, **76**; Tartary, 29–30
Tegu, T. Steven, 237–38
Ten Lost Tribes. *See* Lost Tribes of Israel
Terra nullius, 10, 242n18
Thevet, André, 48, 64
Theyanoguin, Hendrick Peters, 101–2
Thomas, Cyrus, 77, 197
Thorhall the Hunter, 143, 147
Thorowgood, Thomas, 30, 33, 34, 38, 40
Trail of Tears, 13, 129, 149, 267n98
Transatlantic Gothicism: in antebellum
America's race politics, 267n98; in
Appleton, 195; arising from European
Gothicism, 12, 14, 58, 66, 87; in Barton,
15, 83, 122; in Clinton, 117–19; in Finch,
131–33, 137; and Grave Creek stone,
174–75, 182; Kendall's rejection, 90,
109; in Longfellow, 15, 152; in Marsh,
136; in Mitchill, 15, 122–27, 174–75, 182;
mocked by Squier, 179–80, 208; New
England enthusiasm, 16, 136, 194–96,
215; Pennant's rejection, 74, 128; in
Rafn, *Antiquitates Americanae*, and
RSNA Mémoires, 2, 15, 135–37, 145–48,
152–53, 208; in Scandinavian-
American place-making, 192, 194–95,
215–16; in Schoolcraft, 182; in Stiles,
14–15, 69–70, 74, 78, 87, 119; in
Webster, 80, 84–85; in Wheaton,
136–37; in Wilson, 189–90
Treasure hunting, 3, 94, 110, 116, 255n26
Trigger, Bruce G., 13–14, 115, 126–27, 134,
244n48, 260n43, 274n94
Trouillot, Michel-Rolph, 235
Turell, Samuel, 96–97, 256n40, 256n49
Tuscarora, 74, 123, 158, 261n56
Tyre, 52; Tyrians, 130

Vallancey, Charles: on Algonquian and
Phoenician languages, 71–75, 159, 209;
on Dighton Rock and multiple-

migration displacement scenario, 13,
16, 70–88, 93, 113, 116, 118, 119, 121,
124–25, 127, 128, 188
Verrazano, Giovanni di, 1524 voyage,
205–6, 210–11, 222
Vespucci, Amerigo, 29, 67
Veyssière de La Croze, Mathurin, 43
Vinland: location, 15, 58, 69, 132–53, 161,
172, 192, 224, 262n14, 262n17, 264n45,
265n60; sagas, 2, 15, 50, 58, 134–47, 153,
161, 172, 192, 262n14, 262n17, 262n20,
266n76; Thórdarson's *Vinland
Voyages*, 224
Voltaire (François-Marie Arouet), 60–61,
65, 109

Walker, James, 19, 21
Wampanoag: Assonet group, 6; in
Delabarre's Dighton Rock theory,
208–14, 219, 222; Dighton Rock
relationship, 3, 141, 165; Gay Head
community, 5, 22, 63, 107, 225; and
King Philip's War, 9, 19–24, 109, 141;
Mashpee community, 5–6, 22, 63,
105–6, 107, 225, 238; and Mashpee
Wampanoag's Taunton casino plan,
5–6, 241n6, 241n8; Massasoit's land
sale to Williams, 33; missionaries to,
63, 105; and Northmen's Rock,
280n54; Pocasset Wampanoag, 241n8;
Rev. Hawley's grammar, 63, 106; in
Silva's Dighton Rock theory, 17,
228–29; terminology, 241n1; and
White Man's Land, 200; and "wooden
house" story, 43. *See also* Pokanoket
(Wampanoag)
Washington, George, 89–92, 95, 195
Webb, Thomas H., 15; Dighton Rock
daguerreotype, 185–86, 274n90; early
life, 138; marriage, 274n85; and RSNA's
Antiquitates Americanae, *Mémoires*,
and Rafn, 137–43, 161, 183–84, 211, 213,
255n30; and Schoolcraft, 138–39,